FORT LEE: THE FILM TOWN

Richard Koszarski is a member of the Fort Lee Film Commission and Associate Professor of English and Cinema Studies at Rutgers University. His books include An Evening's Entertainment: The Age of the Silent Feature Film *and* Von: The Life and Films of Erich von Stroheim. *He is the 1991 recipient of the Prix Jean Mitry for his contributions to silent film scholarship.*

Dedicated to Tom Hanlon and Ted Huff.
Who knew that where Fort Lee is concerned, local history and film history are pretty much the same thing.

FORT LEE: THE FILM TOWN

Richard Koszarski

British Library Cataloguing in Publication Data

Fort Lee: The Film Town

   1. Motion picture industry – New Jersey – Fort Lee – History   2. Motion pictures – Production and direction –
   New Jersey – Fort Lee – History   3. Fort Lee (NJ) – History

   I. Title

   384.8'0974921

ISBN: 978 0 86196 652 3 (Paperback)

ISBN: 978 0 86196 942 5 (ebook)

Published by
John Libbey Publishing Ltd, 205 Crescent Road, East Barnet, Herts EN4 8SB,
United Kingdom   e-mail: john.libbey@orange.fr; web site: www.johnlibbey.com

Distributed Worldwide by
Indiana University Press, Herman B Wells Library—350, 1320 E. 10th St., Bloomington,
IN 47405, USA. www.iupress.indiana.edu

Reprinted 2017 without images in colour.

Printed and bound in the United States of America..

Contents

BOROUGH OF FORT LEE

Office of the Mayor

309 Main Street
Fort Lee, New Jersey 07024-4799

Telephone (201) 592-3546 • Facsimile (201) 592-1657
E-mail: mayor@fortleenj.com

JACK ALTER
Mayor

Fort Lee celebrates one hundred years of life as a Borough in 2004. The history of Fort Lee predates our Centennial. General George Washington named our community in the fateful year of 1776. During this Centennial Celebration, we commemorate the important dates, events and people who make this American community historically important. The story of our great nation contains many chapters and Fort Lee's role in American History is being written anew in this Year of 2004.

Film Scholar and Fort Lee Film Commission Member Richard Koszarski has produced the first comprehensive book to detail Fort Lee's role as the "Birthplace of the American Film Industry". The citizens of Fort Lee could ask for no greater gift in our Centennial Year than to have this book released and read by scholars and the general public alike.

Our story is America's story.

Jack Alter
Mayor

Acknowledgements

This book, *Fort Lee: The Film Town*, has been published in conjunction with the film retrospective 'Fort Lee: The Film Town, 1904–2004' which was seen at the Giornate del Cinema Muto, Sacile, Italy from 9–16 October 2004, and the American Museum of the Moving Image, Astoria, New York, 20 November – 12 December 2004.

The publication of this book has been facilitated by the cooperation of the Giornate del Cinema Muto, and the Fort Lee Film Commission.

Fort Lee: The Film Town was not quite one hundred years in the making, but it may have felt that way for those who contributed so much of their time and energy to various pieces of this project. Special thanks to our very patient publisher, John Libbey, and to:

Alison Abalsamo, Richard Allen, Jack Alter, Rita Altomara, Mary Lea Bandy, Jennifer Bean, Jim Beckerman, Lucille Bertram, Stephen Bottomore, Robert and Mary Boylan, Ben Brewster, Kevin Brownlow, Elaine Burrows, Bruce Calvert, Anne Carré, Jared Case, Kevin Cerragno, Maryann Chach, Pierre Courtet-Cohl, James Cozart, Stacy D'Arc, Al Dettlaff, Dennis Doros, Karen Latham Everson, Andrew Farkas, Barbara Hall, Patrick Hammer, Stephen Higgins, Len Iannaccone, Diane Koszarski, Anthony L'Abbate, Pei-Hua Lee, Kevin Lewis, Joseph Licata, Patrick Loughney, Ron Magliozzi, Karl and Rick Malkames, Cindy Mamary, Scott Manginelli, Mike Mashon, Madeline Matz, Alison McMahon, Linda Mehr, Russell Merritt, Eric Nelson, Dana Nemeth, David Pierce, David Reese, Herbert Reynolds, David Schwartz, David Shepard, Charles Silver, Anthony Slide, Paul Spehr, Casey Stumm, Catherine Surowiec, Paul Spehr, Julie Tibbott, Edward Wirth, Caroline Yeager, Joe Yranski.

And fellow members of the Fort Lee Film Commission, 2000–2004:

Louis Azzollini, Donna Brennan, Thomas Meyers, Steve Monetti, Kay Nest, Nelson Page, Marc Perez, Armand Pohan and Loretta Weinberg.

Richard Koszarski

Introduction.
City of Intrigue and Mystery

Paul Spehr

ort Lee, New Jersey is the town with the bridge and it is not just any bridge. It is The George Washington Bridge and it is large, impressive, important and busy – very busy. When jammed with traffic, as it often is, commuters curse and revile it, but it has its admirers. Le Corbusier called it the most beautiful bridge in the world. It connects northern New Jersey to Manhattan Island, providing access to the city for thousands of Jerseyites, and access to New Jersey and points beyond for people from New York. More than that it carries Interstate 95, the main artery connecting Maine to Florida and one of America's busiest thoroughfares. Each day thousands and thousands and thousands of cars, truck and busses carry a seemingly endless stream of people and goods through Fort Lee. The opening of the bridge in 1931 changed the small town forever. It was removed from the margins of suburban New York and put squarely into the mainstream. Easy access to the city brought commuters and gave birth to high-rise apartment buildings in which the most fortunate (and prosperous) have an unequaled view down the majestic expanse of the Hudson River to the skyline of Manhattan.

Today, as it celebrates its centennial, Fort Lee is a crossroads for many, a bedroom for a few and, for some, a place of employment. The once predominantly blue collar town has grown to a small city of more than 30,000 people, a heterogeneous community with diverse backgrounds and occupations. Recent emigrants from Europe, Asia and Latin America live near the descendants of families who were in Fort Lee when it was incorporated in 1904. Sushi and croissants co-exist with that great New Jersey tradition, the Diner (and Fort Lee has one of the best!). The newcomers are attracted not only by the convenient commute, but by the mix of urban amenities, small town convenience and near-by green spaces, particularly the large park that borders the Palisades north of the city.

Although it is an attractive residential and business community, not many of the thousands passing through it would call Fort Lee a place of mystery and intrigue, of fantasy and illusion. Most of them have little idea that drama and comedy were the town's major commodity during its first two decades, or that the bridge and the network of highways connected to it slice through an area that was once the location of a dozen or so busy movie studios. Comedy, tragedy, suspense and melodrama were the daily business of those studios and fulfilling the appetites of a growing audience of movie enthusiasts was their particular concern. Although not all the studio names are familiar today, several of Hollywood's major companies trace at least part of their beginnings to Fort Lee. Readers of this book will find chapters on Fox, Universal, Goldwyn, and Selznick. Productions made for Metro and Famous Players-Lasky (distributed through Paramount) were also made here. Many legends of the pioneer years, people who shaped American cinema, worked there: Griffith, Pickford, Bitzer, the Gish sisters, Blaché, Loos, Marion, Tourneur, Fairbanks, Walsh, Dwan, Sennett, Arbuckle, Bara, Brenon, the Talmadge sisters, the Barrymores and many, many others. They were the names and faces that made the movies the movies.

The era when the studios were busy on a daily basis ended during the 1920s but movies continued to be a part of the town's commerce. As the character of the town changed, the memory of its former eminence faded, remembered only as a legacy of the past. This was particularly true in the years after World War II when the town's character changed dramatically.

Restoring a forgotten history

The communities of Northern New Jersey have an identity problem. The millions of tourists visiting New York City stay in Manhattan, and except for the sports facilities in East Rutherford, there is little to lure them – or residents of New York – across the river. Outsiders have only vague, often misleading notions of what the communities in Jersey are like and certain negative images have persisted beyond their time – a curious, difficult to understand accent; mobsters burying their dead in the trash and garbage mounds of the "meadowlands" or the rioting that scarred Newark in the 1960s. And, in truth, many of the towns that commuting outsiders see are hard to tell apart because they run together in confusing succession. They line an elevated peninsula of rock bordering the Hudson River and continue on the other side of the large marshland (the "Meadowlands") that separates the ridge from New Jersey proper. The communities often appear so much alike that it is no wonder that strangers have a hard time telling which is Hoboken, Union City, or Weehawken; Kearney, North Arlington or Lyndhurst; or Fort Lee, Ridgefield and Palisades Park.

But if the communities of suburban and ex-urban New Jersey seem to lack glamor, the movies have it to spare and Fort Lee once had movies to spare. Politicians and civic leaders hoping to lure tourist dollars and shore-up the local image periodically rediscover Fort Lee, the Hollywood that once was; their revived interest is often stimulated by nostalgic newspaper articles, a number of which are reproduced here.

While the interest of local leaders has fluctuated, there have been a number of resident devotees whose genuine interest in the area's role as a center of film production have contributed to preserving New Jersey's film history.

- In 1935, Englewood film historian Theodore Huff produced *Ghost Town: The Story of Fort Lee*, a documentary account of the surviving Fort Lee studios. He later wrote an influential article about Fort Lee for the February 1951 issue of *Films in Review*. Huff's work was probably influenced by a series of articles by Edmund J. McCormick which appeared in the *Bergen Evening Record* in July, 1935 (reprinted here for the first time) but Huff had cultivated contacts with a number of prominent film veterans who worked in Fort Lee, among them D.W. Griffith, Lillian Gish and Josef von Sternberg. These interviews and his knowledge of film history enhanced his work. A volatile, sometimes controversial figure, Huff is perhaps best remembered for his efforts to preserve classic cinema by making it available on screen.

- John Allen was a photographic specialist from Rochester, New York who settled in New Jersey about 1950. He was also a lover of classic cinema and in Rochester he began collecting and showing films in association with his friend James Card. There is an unconfirmed story that Allen learned that film and related material from the Triangle Company was found in a studio building in Fort Lee. He is supposed to have acquired it and shared the find with Card and the legendary French cineaste Henri Langlois. Unfortunately, according to John Allen, Jr., much of his father's film collection was destroyed in the early 1960s by an arsonist who set fire to the building where it was stored. However, Allen continued to collect and show film at his home in Park Ridge, New Jersey. He built a thriving business supplying stock footage to television producers and documentary film makers, a business continued by his son who expanded it and created a highly respected laboratory specializing in quality film reproduction.

- Although he was not a New Jersey resident, Donald Malkames deserves special recognition. He was one of the New York area's leading cinematographers and his long professional career made him aware of the changes taking place as the years went by. His efforts to preserve the industry's history, particularly its technical history, were unique. Malkames collected cameras, printing machines and related equipment such as Mutoscopes – most maintained in working condition. He also collected films and showed them in a theater in his home. He was cameraman on a number of films made in Fort Lee studios and in the 1930s he produced several short films in Fort Lee.

- Fort Lee resident Tom Hanlon was a diligent and skilled amateur historian who documented the local studios. He was employed for many years at the US Army Pictorial Center in Astoria, Long Island, so he knew and understood film production. Hanlon knew Fort Lee well and he loved to share his knowledge and enthusiasm for the city's film heritage with others.

- Another collector who enjoyed showing his films to fellow enthusiasts was Nutley, NJ resident Bob Lee. Like John Allen, he had a small theater in his home. He was an associate of Tom Hanlon at the US Army Pictorial Center in Astoria, Long Island.

The interest of civic leaders, boosters and politicians has ebbed and flowed. In the late 1960s the Mayor of Fort Lee encouraged residents to sport a red and white bumper sticker emblazoned with the motto: "Fort Lee, New Jersey, Birthplace of the Movies". It was embellished with a picture of the bridge and a movie camera. A local real estate and insurance firm put out a map with points of interest and a brief historical note which proclaimed that the town "...was Hollywood when Hollywood was a cow pasture". The mayor also commissioned Tom Hanlon to make the documentary film *Before Hollywood There Was Fort Lee, NJ*. The film incorporated portions of Huff's *Ghost Town*, and was also influenced by his article in *Films in Review*. Now available on DVD from Image Entertainment, it remains one of the best records of the industry in Fort Lee.

In the early 1970s the Newark Museum asked me to curate an exhibit on New Jersey's early film history. It was presented in 1976 as the Museum's major event for the Bi-Centennial celebration of American independence. Although Fort Lee's glory days were an important aspect, the exhibit covered movie activities in the entire area: the development of the Kinetograph/Kinetoscope and film making at Edison's laboratory in West Orange, New Jersey; filming at various locations in the state, and studios in other communities such as the Pathé Studio in Jersey City and the Horsley-Centaur-Nestor Studio in Bayonne. As I began exploring Fort Lee's past I found that the enthusiasm of the 1960s had faded, but Tom Hanlon's had not. He was immensely helpful. He showed me his film and took me on a memorable tour of the city which included a stop at Rambo's, the legendary bar-hotel which was a favorite watering hole and occasional film location in the one-reel film days. In the 1970s it was still a working tavern and the man who served us a beer, Gus Becker, claimed to have served D.W. Griffith (see page 21). I believed him because he was still vigorous even though he was in his 90s. I also received help from Don Malkames, Bob Lee and John Allen. The exhibit was well received and stimulated interest again. The state of New Jersey's Film Commission became interested in their history but, since the Commission's purpose was/is to attract film production to the state they used it more for promotional purposes than for support of activities to preserve the state's movie history. In Fort Lee, the Public Library which had only a small collection of movie material began to collect more actively and continues to add to its collection.

Once again interest waned, only to revive again in the 1980s when Mayor Nicholas Corbiscello announced plans to establish a film museum. But according to the *Bergen Record* ("Remembering Fort Lee's Place on the Silver Screen" by Dennis Bloshuk, 16 September 1987), the Mayor's proposal ran into opposition. He was accused of using it for political purposes and was apparently unable to raise funds to restore the stable he hoped to use for the project.

In recent years there has been another, more promising revival of interest. With the support of the current mayor, Jack Alter, the Fort Lee Historical Society established a permanent museum in the landmark Judge Moore house on Palisade Avenue, a portion of which is dedicated to local film history. The Fort Lee Film Commission is also exploring ways to make their filmic past more tangible. They have placed historic markers at many local studio sites and in 2004 began organized tours of the old "film town". They have a useful website (FortLeeFilm.org) and have launched a series of film showings at an auditorium at the Fort Lee National Historic Park. It is a promising beginning!

Before Hollywood?

It is not really true that Fort Lee was Hollywood before Hollywood was .... Actually, both production centers developed about the same time and for much the same reasons: scenery, light and security. As story films became the dominant movie format and the number of production companies increased, producers found that audiences preferred outdoor scenes that were actually filmed outdoors rather than in front of crudely painted scenery. Since there was more flexibility in the open air and it was not much more expensive to film outside the studio, producers began to roam the countryside in search of suitable and attractive locales. Companies based in New York had a variety of locations nearby: the Catskill and Adirondack Mountains, beaches in Jersey and Long Island; pleasant farm country in Connecticut, New York and New Jersey; marshland along the coast and just beyond the Palisades in Northern New Jersey. The sheer cliffs of the Palisades near Fort Lee were particularly attractive. Chicago was the second film center and the companies based there had fewer choices. There was plentiful farmland and the waters of Lake Michigan, but it was particularly difficult to find a mountain. So it is not surprising to find Chicago's Selig company filming in Colorado as early as 1904. The Essanay Company, founded in Chicago in 1907, was in Colorado in 1908. By 1909 Selig was in Hollywood and had set-up a studio facility. The following year Essanay opened a studio in Niles, east of San Francisco. Both companies specialized in Westerns and the attractive scenery around both California studios improved their authenticity – and quickly made westerns filmed in New Jersey look spurious.

But scenery was not the only motive. Harsh weather and lack of natural sunlight during the winter months slowed production in northern cities and by 1910 production crews began wintering in Florida, Texas and California.

One of the most frequently cited reasons for filming outside the cities was the need to evade the detectives and goon squads hired by Edison and the Motion Picture Patents Company. While this was a factor for the new independent companies, it was not the reason that Kalem, Selig, Essanay and Biograph, all members of the Patents organization, headed for New Jersey, California and Florida. Historians have tended to emphasize the impact of harassment because it is more dramatic than prosaic factors like sunlight, scenery and warmth.

Although Fort Lee has the reputation as the film center, the studios were actually scattered about town and several neighboring communities. This is a characteristic it shared with Hollywood where many of the best known studios were and are in nearby communities like Burbank, Studio City, Universal City and Culver City. As readers of this text will discover, Fort Lee shared film making with Edgewater, Grantwood, Cliffside, Hudson Heights and Coytesville. The studio in Coytesville, Champion, is the only building that survives and it is tucked inconveniently away from the center of Fort Lee. It is ironic that it still exists because it was the first built, and it survives because it was made to look like a factory in order to deceive snoops from the Patents Company. After the cameras were shut down it was converted into a real factory. It survived because it could be used, whereas others perished because they were only suitable for film production.

No, except as an occasional shooting location, Fort Lee did not really exist "before Hollywood". In reality, the main difference between the two early production centers is that Hollywood was a long way from the home offices, while Fort Lee was (and is) inescapably linked to New York City – and by more than the bridge.

Always a film town

By all accounts, Fort Lee was a very busy place in the mid-teens. Studios humming; people bustling about in costume and make-up; film crews at various locations about the area; townspeople offering their houses and open spaces for rent; hopefuls standing in line at casting room doors and here and there a recognizable face. But it ended almost as quickly as it had begun. Following the First World War one studio after another closed. The town was a quieter place during the twenties and thirties, but the movie industry never left Fort Lee. A few stages survived and they were used occasionally. The former Paragon Studio was used for several feature film productions in the 1920s and in the 1930s the former Peerless Studio was operated as Metropolitan Sound Studios. But a hoped for revival of the town's glory days never occurred.

The former Universal lot survived longer than any of the others, though it was primarily used as a film laboratory and storage vault. Indeed, by the 1920s there were a half dozen film laboratories in Fort Lee and nearby communities. One of particular interest was the Kelley Color Laboratory, home of a significant, but unsuccessful attempt to bring color to the screen. These labs gradually closed, but one of the industry's largest, Consolidated Film Industries, remained in Fort Lee for many years. Along with the company's lab in Hollywood, Consolidated developed and printed many of the industry's best known films. Consolidated was headed by Herbert J. Yates who also established and ran Republic Pictures.

Film storage may seem one of the least romantic facets of the industry, but control of access to film properties was and is the foundation of the studio system. Concerns about piracy and illegal duping go back to the beginning of cinema. From the earliest days producers took strong measures to ensure that their films did not fall into the wrong hands, and this particularly applied to their pre-print elements (negatives and printing masters). Because the New York-based home offices frequently mis-trusted production folks on the other coast, negatives were often shipped East as soon as films were ready for release. Over the years Fort Lee became a major depository for several studios, among them Warners and RKO. The largest of the storage companies, Bonded Film Storage, operated facilities in Fort Lee well into the 1970s.

In the years before World War II, the largest supplier of professional film stock was Jules Brulatour, who used Fort Lee as one of his major distribution centers. He began selling film in the late 1900s and when the Patents Company enticed Eastman to join them, Brulatour began selling Lumière stock to the rival independent companies (and may have sold them Eastman's film surreptitiously). Eastman grew unhappy with his tie to the Patents Company and in 1911 Brulatour persuaded Eastman to sell to the independents. It was the beginning of a long and fruitful association. Brulatour and George Eastman developed a close working relationship which gave Brulatour special access to Kodak's production. It proved a highly successful business – for many years motion picture film was Kodak's most profitable product.

If Fort Lee ever erects a statue to a someone who personified their film experience, Jules Brulatour would be an interesting candidate! He had a unique role in bringing the film industry to Fort Lee. As new companies began organizing, Brulatour was available to advise them – after all, new companies were new customers. He helped Eclair build their studio in Fort Lee; he was involved in the organization of Universal and he facilitated the opening of the Peerless studio. A Creole from Louisiana, Brulatour spoke French and Spanish which doubtless helped him establish a special relationship with the sizable community of French film makers who worked in Fort Lee. He was especially close to the legendary director Maurice Tourneur. Although Brulatour had offices in New York and a branch in Los Angeles, he maintained the facility in Fort Lee until his death in 1946.

Fort Lee also had a connection with the movie's sister, television. The *New York Times* reported on 13 August 1928 that Hugo Gernsback had begun "the first regular broadcasting of images by television over the radio from New York" through WRNY's transmitter at the Villa Richard in Coytesville. Decades later the National Broadcasting Company also operated a television transmitter on nearby Sylvan Avenue (and stored their film and tape in Fort Lee, as well).

Traces of the past

The efforts to recover Fort Lee's film heritage have faltered in the past because, despite well meaning champions, they confronted serious problems. Sadly, there are few traces of the industry left. A visitor walking down Main Street or Lemoine Avenue in Fort Lee would have a difficult time locating where the studios were. In 1975, when Tom Hanlon took me through the area, most of the studio structures were gone or in ruins. In contrast to the industry's reputation for glamour, films are made in unglamorous factory buildings. The studios in Fort Lee and surrounding communities sprang-up rapidly. Most were constructed between 1913 and 1917 and they were fragile buildings put up in haste. Because daylight was crucial to proper exposure of the available film, walls and roofs of glass were their common characteristic. Touring Fort Lee in 1915, Channing Pollock compared them to the Crystal Palace or a section of a World's Fair. But from a less romantic point of view, what they most resembled was a collection of green houses, and once they fell into disuse they became the victims of time, weather and small boys with rocks.

The situation with the films produced in Fort Lee is almost as discouraging. Most are gone; lost to neglect, chemical deterioration, fire and, most unfortunately, deliberate destruction. No one has done an accurate count, but it is probable that eighty to ninety per cent survive only in the form of still photographs, descriptions and reviews. The elements of production – scenery, costumes, scripts, stills, posters and other advertising materials – have long since been destroyed or scattered about the country – and the world. For example, of the forty or so features that Theda Bara made – most, but not all, made in Ft. Lee – only two survive in complete form. There are fragments of only one or two others. And she was one of the most popular and sensational stars of the era. A list of the missing Fort Lee productions would be tragically long.

Having said that, is should be stated that the story of Fort Lee and its movie industry is colorful and fascinating. Jersey residents have good reason to take pride in it because Fort Lee was an integral part of a significant transition period for the American movie industry during which it changed scope, style and format. In the decade or so that Fort Lee was a busy film center the length of productions changed from a short, single reel to multiple reels; studios grew from crude shooting stages to industrial plants with several stages, dressing rooms, shops for wardrobe and scen-ery and laboratories to process the productions; store-front nickelodeons were replaced by purpose made theaters and the size and make-up of the audience changed; the star system was born, abetted by the ever-more important publicity office; the cost of productions increased as the pioneer companies that started the industry faded and were replaced by large production firms that would dominate the industry for the rest of the Century. During this period America became the dominant producer of filmed entertainment that was popular world wide. Fort Lee provides a microcosm of this vital period.

Today Fort Lee's cinema heritage survives primarily in the form of paper documents, microfilm, still pictures and a few surviving films. These have been scattered about in libraries, museums, archives and private collections in the US and abroad. Fortunately, largely thanks to the growing interest in silent films stimulated by showcases like Le Giornate del Cinema Muto, it is now possible to see more of the films that were made there. The images, both still and moving, are particularly impressive – Gloria Swanson was right, they did have faces then! To give substance to the images, this book brings together the words of participants and first hand observers who tell the city's story as it evolved – and quite a story it is!

Happy One Hundredth Birthday, Fort Lee, city of mystery, intrigue, fantasy, illusion – and memories worth recapturing.

May 2004

Paul Spehr *is a film historian, archival consultant and retired Assistant Chief, Motion Picture, Broadcasting and Recorded Sound, Library of Congress.*

1.

Fort Lee: Legend and Reality

STUDIO TOWN 1:
Fort Lee, Movies' Battleground, and its Glamorous First Days

Sleepy Borough Here Became Scene of Producers' War

1st Wild West
Its 'Prairies' Long In Use Before The Studios Went Up

By Edmund J. McCormick

(from *Bergen Evening Record*, July 8–12, 1935)

Sprawled out on the top of the majestic Palisades that wall the Hudson on the West, under the shadow of the George Washington Bridge from New York City is the little town of Fort Lee.

Here in the shadows of New York skyscrapers are fertile fields that give to the town its principal industry, farming. Serving as a severe contrast to its rural life is a giant stretch of steel, the George Washington Bridge that joins the cliff town to New York City, pouring into the small town thousands of cars a day.

At Fort Lee years ago when the colonies were fighting England in the war for independence was located one of the most formidable forts in the East, Fort Constitution.

Battleground again

Protected by the natural rock wall hundreds of feet high, the fort was one of the colonists' strongholds. It was here that General Nathaniel Greene, greatly outnumbered, put up a gallant fight, finally going down to defeat before England's Lord Cornwallis and where General Anthony Wayne was turned back in his attempt to capture the cliff fort.

Years later the town was again to become a battleground. Quite a different struggle, the conflict was waged between shrewd businessmen fighting with film and camera for the life of a new born industry, motion pictures.

In 1907 Sid Olcott, right hand man at Kalem's New York motion picture studio, discovered a new Wild West lying in the shadow of New York City. Around Fort Lee were acres of delicious scenery, dense woods, steep slopes, distant mountains, open plain marsh, sheer hundreds of feet of solid rock rising high above the Hudson, and to put the icing on the cake was the town itself: dirt roads, dirt sidewalks, and old fashioned houses could be found in plenty. When Olcott saw the cliff town he knew it was the spot for Kalem's western pictures, so the Kalem Company, with horses and tepees, came across the Hudson.

Griffith came in 1908

In the trail of Kalem in 1908 came D.W. Griffith with the Biograph Company, bringing with him Lillian and Dorothy Gish, Mary Pickford and Mack Senett.

The center of gathering for the companies on location was at Rambo's

The Palisades, looking south to where the George Washington Bridge now stands.

Hotel, situated on an ill kept dirt road called Rambo's Lane. On the upper floor of the small hotel were the rooms where the actors dressed. In the rear yard tables were set up for the companies to eat; here knights and ladies sat with Indians under the shade of apple trees that sided the tables. In the background could be seen a three-story frame house, the home of Maurice Barrymore.

An old property man who worked with Griffith and Kalem, and who still lives in a small house in back of Rambo's, prepared the stage for the first picture Griffith directed.

It was a Biograph picture called *The Adventures of Dolly*.

"Griffith wasn't the least bit nervous", the old property man said. "We put everything in place up on Hammett's Hill and were wondering what would happen. But the minute he walked on the scene we knew we were working for a real master. He gave orders clear and direct and had the whole thing done in a couple of days. [N.B. This may actually be a recollection of the filming of *The Battle*; see the account in *The Palisadian* reprinted on page 66.] Griffith liked soldier pictures. I've seen the time when he had seven hundred soldiers fighting at once – and that was a big crowd for those days. Kalem's specialty was Indians. It got so after a while that if the day was clear I'd know Kalem would call from New York and say 'Teepees' – then I'd rush over with the wagon and fetch a couple of dozen, set them up here and there and we would be ready to go in no time. They weren't particular then."

Alice Joyce made her debut in motion pictures riding a horse for the Kalem Company in 1909. Another Kalem horseman was Robert Vignola who later directed Marion Davies in *When Knighthood Was In Flower*.

Fort Lee tolerated this violent disturbance of its former peaceful dignified

The rise and fall of Fort Lee, the film town, is a legend which has been told and retold for generations. As early as September 1921, *Filmplay Journal* published a photo essay on "Fort Lee, the Deserted Village", highlighting the sudden abandonment of several large studio facilities (the obituary was a bit premature). The *New York Times Magazine* reported on "Ghosts in the Cradle of the Movies" on May 31, 1931, a piece which contrasted the beginnings of the motion picture industry with the "ghastly cemetery … of scaling concrete, crumbling brick, warped steel and shattered glass" now to be found there. Irving Browning's account of his visit to "A Crumbled Movie Empire" appeared in the August 1945 issue of *American Cinematographer*. Browning, a veteran cinematographer, walked through the ruins of the studios with his friend Francis Doublier. Depressing photos of burned-out industrial buildings and weed-ridden vacant lots illustrated the piece. In February of 1951 film historian Theodore Huff, an Englewood native, published "Hollywood's Predecessor" in *Films in Review*; Huff had already made a brief documentary film on the same theme, *Ghost Town: The Story of Fort Lee*, in 1935. Both were clearly influenced by "Studio Town", a series of articles which appeared in Huff's local paper, *The Bergen Evening Record*, between July 8 and 12, 1935, and which are reprinted here for the first time.

This remarkably astute survey of Fort Lee film history was written by one of the *Record's* staff writers, Edmund J. McCormick. He appears to have interviewed local residents, trawled through clipping files, and tapped at least one industry insider, publicist Paul Gulick, whose name appears on illustration credits. McCormick does introduce one significant error when he claims that D.W. Griffith's first film as a director, *The Adventures of Dolly*, was shot in Fort Lee (it was actually Sound Beach, Connecticut). Perhaps he misunderstood what his informant meant by "Griffith's first picture." We have slightly reorganized the text at one point, where the original editorial work garbled the correct order of several paragraphs, and deleted one irrelevant aside.

life with a patient indifference. It would end in a short while, the town reasoned, so let them be. But the disturbance didn't end – it became increasingly violent as the movie makers found that people would pay to see their pictures whether they were good or bad.

Studios go up in 1908

Rough wooden shacks had been erected at Fort Lee, but nothing that resembled a studio until Mark H. Dintenfass promised the Edison Company in 1908 that he wouldn't make any more motion pictures.

In 1903 Mark Dintenfass was a salt

(Above). Scaffolding, complete with mattresses, intended to safeguard actors during stunt action on the Palisades (c. 1918).

(Left). A page of advertising from the program of the Patrolmen's Benevolent Association of Bergen County's Second Annual Picnic and Games, Cella's Park and Casino, 4 October 1911. Rambo's and the Champion Studio take space along with other local businesses.

herring salesman working for his father. A few [years] later he was a proprietor of Philadelphia's second movie house, a small store with little over a hundred seats. Holding title to a camera after an experiment with talking pictures in his playhouse had failed, Dintenfass decided to sell his theater and become a producer. He opened up the Actophone Studios in New York.

His movements were carefully watched by a powerful group of movie makers who had pooled their patents, among which was the patent for the Latham Loop, heart of the motion picture camera.

The movie trust squeezed out independents by virtue of its practical control of all motion picture cameras. Bold independent producers had to resort to all [manner of] tricks to hide from the rubber sneakered patent trust investigators. Some hid in cellars, others concealed cameras in scenery or under cloth hoods.

He couldn't quit

Dintenfass botched the job of hiding his camera and was caught one day by an Edison man. After loud arguments in which the Edison Company always won, Dintenfass, in return for a promise from the trust that he wouldn't be prosecuted in court, said he would forget that he ever wanted to be a producer.

But it was in his heart. He couldn't give up his ambition so easily. A short while later, well hidden in a shanty at Fort Lee, he continued to grind out pictures. In 1909 [actually 1910 - ed.] he built the first studio at Fort Lee, called his company Champion, and started production.

Fort Lee's first studio wasn't an impressive structure when compared with the giant studios of today. But its 150 feet of shingled building with small glass studio was significant then for it marked the beginning of a pe-

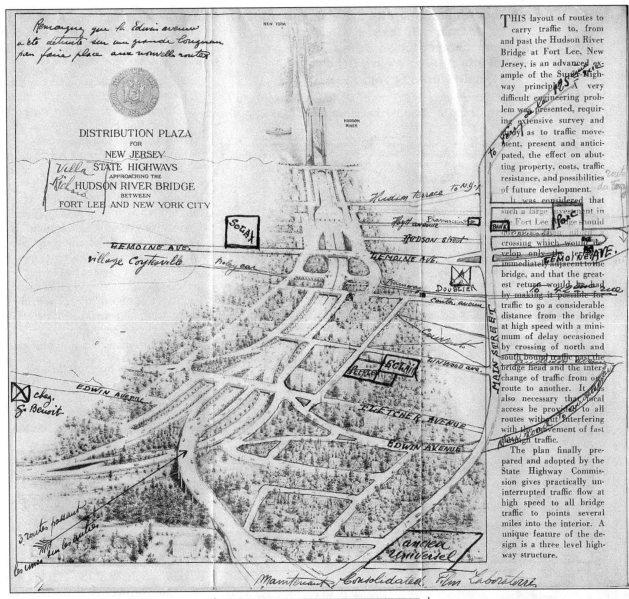

THIS layout of routes to carry traffic to, from and past the Hudson River Bridge at Fort Lee, New Jersey, is an advanced example of the Super-Highway principle. A very difficult engineering problem was presented, requiring extensive survey and study as to traffic movement, present and anticipated, the effect on abutting property, costs, traffic resistance, and possibilities of future development.

It was considered that such a large investment in a Fort Lee bridge should be a general utility crossing which would develop only the area immediately adjacent to the bridge, and that the greatest return would be had by making it possible for traffic to go a considerable distance from the bridge at high speed with a minimum of delay occasioned by crossing of north and south bound traffic past the bridge head and the interchange of traffic from one route to another. It was also necessary that local access be provided to all routes without interfering with the movement of fast through traffic.

The plan finally prepared and adopted by the State Highway Commission gives practically uninterrupted traffic flow at high speed to all bridge traffic to points several miles into the interior. A unique feature of the design is a three level highway structure.

A map of the approaches to the proposed Hudson River (George Washington) Bridge, annotated in the late 1920s by Eclair animator Emile Cohl, indicating the locations of various studios and the homes of other members of the French filmmaking community. Cohl's own house on Hoyt Avenue, not shown, would have been directly under the main bridge approach.

riod when producing companies were about to band together in settlements.

In 1909 there were several minor centers of the industry, but no large groupings as were later to form at Fort Lee and Hollywood. Largest number of companies was found in New York City where Vitagraph, Edison, Kalem, Biograph and Carl Laemmle's Imp roosted. Chicago and Philadelphia ranked as secondary centers.

California already had several companies on location. The movement to the West was headed by the Selig Company in 1907. Essanay followed with its Wild West Company in 1908.

Baumann and Kessel deserted their Florida and Fort Lee locations for the West in 1909. D.W. Griffith went west with Biograph a year later.

The pictures taken at the period when Champion started were simple affairs consisting of one or two reels. The subjects were mainly thrillers involving the cowboy and Indian theme. Few pictures cost over $10,000 to produce.

STUDIO TOWN 2: The Public Becomes Critical; Fire, Movies' Menace, Strikes.
Stupid Plots, Monotonous Stories Bore Audiences As Novelty Of Film Wears Off
Éclair Studio Leveled

The procedure that evolved as a movie maker's formula for success in terms of dollars was many pictures at lost cost. Plots were seldom considered seriously.

They grew as the pictures went along. The use of a story prepared in detail before the picture was taken was not to come for several years.

A typical story of the period is *Caprices of Fortune* starring Barbara Tennant and Alec Francis. The picture was produced by the Eclair Company, the second company to locate at Fort Lee. It was a story of a poor young man madly in love with a wealthy second cousin. He asked her mother for her daughter's hand but she, reminding him of his low station in life, refused. He was considerably shaken but mustered up enough strength to ask, "Auntie, if I make my fortune, may I hope to marry Bertha?" He left to make his fortune in Homestead, Pennsylvania. From there he drifted to the West and then to Mexico. Finally he won money in a lottery and went back to marry his aunt's maid.

Eclair, the producer of this bit of drama, came to Fort Lee in 1911. It was the American branch of the mildly profitable Cinema Éclair in Paris, a company headed by Charles Jourjon. Foreseeing the golden harvest to be reaped in America, Charles Jourjon capitalized a company for $1,250,000, set aside $200,000 for buildings and equipment, and set the carpenters to work at Fort Lee.

Francis was star

The late veteran of the screen, Alec Francis, was the mainstay of the company. Supporting him in his pictures was leading lady Barbara Tennant.

Éclair's pictures were usually only a reel long. One spectacle called *The Land of Darkness or Through the Bowels of the Earth* set a high-mark in the company's history. It was advertised as staged "at a cost of $50,000 – 200 people in its mighty cast" – but cutting both figures twice would give a more

The Éclair Bulletin *for March, 1913. Many studios would publish their own promotional house papers.*

accurate picture of the spectacle's proportions. If the story ran short, as it usually did, Éclair would tack on enough footage of a nature study to even up the reel.

The year that brought Éclair on the scene at Fort Lee also brought Herbert Blanche [i.e. Blaché] who erected a series of buildings in the cliff town and opened up a producing company called Solax. But Solax was to be a dull star in the constellation of youngsters who sprang up during this period. Hanging on for years, finally passing out of the scene entirely in the early twenties after a serious fire, the company reached only mild success pushing Olga Petrova to stardom during the vampire period.

Champion, Éclair and Solax were all members of the independent group who were battling with the Edison patent trust. As a result of their persistence the independents were enjoying more freedom. By 1911 they were coming into the open emerging from dark cellars, taking the hoods off their cameras. Carl Laemmle of Imp was the leader of the independents. His violent attacks on the trust finally achieved victory when a court order declared the Latham Loop patent no longer existent.

As the fear of opposition from the patent trust become less pretentious [sic], Fort Lee's three studios began to prosper, until one crisp clear day brought disaster cloaked in the form of the film industry's ugliest enemy, fire.

The scene was set for *The Gentleman From Mississippi*. The place, inside the Éclair studio. Alec Francis stood on the sideline waiting to be called by the director for his part. The studio door opened with a bang, a breathless employee rushed on the set. "Clear out! The whole place is on fire", he yelled. Pandemonium reigned. Employees scrambled for the exits. Next to the studio was the film laboratory housing thousands of dollars worth of in-flammable film. The fire caught the laboratory in a wave of flame and it burned as if drenched with oil. Heavy yellow smoke rose lazily into the air blotting out the sky. A few fire engines rush up. Rubber coated firemen set hose in position. The pressure was turned on. A small trickle of water spouted from the fire hose. Film executives collected on the sidewalk wailed in dismay. "Sorry, no water pressure", was the firemen's answer. And thus Éclair departed from the list of producing companies in America. Insurance money collected was sent to the company headquarters in Paris. War broke out. The money never came back. Éclair struggled valiantly for a few months but gave up.

This great calamity happened in the year 1914, a year that brought to Fort Lee much good fortune, to make up for the loss of one of its three companies.

First in the list of events was the arrival of Kessel and Baumann's New York Motion Picture Corporation, which erected a large studio next to the Éclair lot. The Willat studio, named for C. A. Willatowski, who was for years one of the leaders in Carl Laemmle's old Imp Company, was not to be occupied by the New York Motion Picture Corporation, for a former shoe polish salesman, William Fox, who turned producer after a successful career as exhibitor, leased it almost upon completion. Fort Lee became the center for the William Fox Company.

The entrance of William Fox upon the scene at Fort Lee marked an era of great prosperity. During this era, which was to last for five years, Samuel Goldwyn was to embark upon his career as producer, World Film Company was to be launched and Lewis Selznick was to form his Select Picture Company.

The cliff town was to become the seat for the formation of fabulous fortunes made overnight. It was to enjoy the period; share in the fortunes being made. School children, fathers, mothers were to be drafted as extras. The Fort Lee Fire Company was to be as indispensable to the picture makers as their most valuable star. The acres around Fort Lee were to forget their normal scenery and become a rapidly changing panorama of the World. Thousands of stars and extras were to parade through the street of this eastern movie center.

This period also marked the establishment of the feature picture of several reels, which supplanted the one reelers of the years previous. Movie makers were spending more money on their products. "The time has come", said J.J. Kennedy of Biograph to D.W. Griffith a year previous, "for the production of big fifty thousand dollar pictures".

Audiences were becoming critical. The idea that the public enjoyed a picture because it was a picture, whether it was good or bad, no longer held true. The novelty of the picture idea having worn off, audiences were beginning to analyse each offering, picking out the flaws ....

STUDIO TOWN 3:
Enter Theda Bara, and the Whole Nation Picks Up The Vamp Fad
Star A Gold Mine For Fox, Who Found Her
The War Starts
And With It, Fort Lee Begins To Feel Decline

William Fox, after taking over the Éclair as well as the Willat studios at Fort Lee, was to become not only interested in realism in his pictures, but was to delve into the super-natural. An attractive girl christened Theodosia Goodman cast for the Fox picture *The Stain* [actually, a Pathé film-ed.] made such an impression upon Fox Director Frank Powell that she was slated for the leading role in a Fox picture called *A Fool There Was*.

The Peerless-World studio gleaming in the sun, around the time of its construction in 1914.

ning of Lucretia Borgia, till now held up as the world's wickedest woman, her mouth is the mouth of the sinister, scheming Delilah, and her hands are those of the blood bathing Elizabeth Bathrog [sic], who slaughtered young girls that she might bathe in their life blood and so retain her beauty.

To William Fox, Miss Bara was a gold mine. Despite his sidetracks into colossal features into which he packed all the stars he could get, Miss Bara's pictures were his only consistent big money makers during his days in the East. Other stars that played at Fort Lee for Fox were Frank Morgan, June Caprice, Valeska Suratt, William Farnum, Warner Oland, George Walsh, William Courtleigh, Virginia Pearson, Noah Berry, Milton Sills and Virginia Corbin.

The second incident that more than balanced the loss of Éclair was the erection of the Peerless Studio next to the old Éclair Laboratory. Builder of the studio was Jules Brulatour, contact man for the film trade to George Eastman. The Peerless Studio was to be the headquarters for the World Film Corporation, the only producing company to spend its entire life at Fort Lee.

In 1914, having previously served as a distributing agency for the producers, the World Film Corporation, formed as the World Special Film Company to produce motion pictures, bought the Peerless Studio and proceeded to hire stars.

The leading figure in World during its youth was colorful Lewis J. Selznick who had made his entrance into the motion picture world when he sold his jewelry store and moved into Carl Laemmle's Imp Company. Selznick had the title of vice-president and general manager of the World. President was Arthur Spiegel of mail order house Spiegel, May, Stern & Company. Financial backer was Laddenberg Thalman and Company, one of

She became a star overnight. Dubbed Theda Bara, she immediately was wrapped in a veil of mystery, classified as a vampire. The movie audiences, newspapers, grubbed for every grain of information they could get about her every movement. A national craze developed. Hats, dresses, new drinks, were named after the vampire. Women acquired a slinking walk, darkened their eyes. The word "vamp" came into common parlance. Absurd publicity stunts were staged. Writers wrote words of nonsense that were shoved to an eager public. One mumble jumble writer, a New York phrenologist and physiognomist, wrote, "I write this with a photograph of Theda Bara the William Fox 'Vampire', before me. Never in all my experience have I gazed into a face portraying such wickedness and evil – such characteristics of the vampire and sorceress."

She's a gold mine

Louella Parsons, then writing for the Chicago *Herald*, found it necessary to dip into history to give full flavor to a description of Miss Bara. She wrote, "Her hair is like the serpent locks of Medusa, her eyes have the cruel cun-

the first financial houses to back a motion picture company.

Miss Young is star

The master stroke that put World on the right track from the start was a contract that brought Clara Kimball Young from Vitagraph to World. The contract was Selznick's victory. Much like their neighbor across the fence, William Fox, World was to depend upon a single leading lady to put its pictures across. During the first year with World, Miss Young was starred in *Camille, The Yellow Passport, The Feast of Life.*

With Selznick at the helm World prospered. Because of a contract signed with Shubert it had an unlimited supply of stories to draw from. It was well financed, for Selznick had furnished the directors' board with a hand-picked group of bankers. All looked rosy, until Selznick decided early in 1916 that his hand-picked bankers were entirely too bossy. He packed his bag and resigned from the World, taking with him the corner stone of the plant, Clara Kimball Young. The company felt the shock of the blow. William A. Brady, veteran Broadway showman who took over the wheel was outraged, for he realized that without Miss Young's pictures as a premium, World would be handicapped in peddling its productions.

During the year of Selznick's exit from World another studio located at Fort Lee. It was to be the final link in the chain of studios that were erected in the Cliff Town. Designed by Francis Doublier who had distinguished himself as an aide to Lumiere in Paris, and who was the hero of the old Éclair fire, where he rushed into the flames and saved thousands of dollars worth of valuable film, the Paragon studio was the most modern in the world at that period

The studio property covered five acres on the crest of a small valley. Costing almost a million dollars to build, the studio was equipped with a two hundred foot stage and a film laboratory capable of developing 2,000,000 feet of film a year. Financial backers of the project were William A. Brady, head of World; Jules Brulatour, builder of Peerless and George Eastman's contact man; and Maurice Tourneur, a director for World. Upon completion Paragon became a part of World Studios supplementing Peerless.

Becomes main firm

World, now re-enforced with Paragon, became one of the leading producers in the country. In its Peerless Studios were filmed *The Pit, The Deep Purple, Alias Jimmy Valentine, Hearts in Exile, The Wishing Ring* [*The Wishing Ring* was made at the Peerless]. The latter picture by accident brought Vivian Martin stardom, and Maurice Tourneur fame as a director. Selznick had arranged an elaborate preview for a Canadian production titled *The Seats of the Mighty.* When his guests arrived Selznick was in a turmoil, for his spectacle had not arrived. To satisfy his guests he brought out the only picture available, *The Wishing Ring.* The picture was proclaimed an immediate success.

Stars who padded through the gates at Peerless were Alice Brady, Wilton Lackaye, Milton Sills, Doris Kenyon, Holbrook Blinn, Warner Oland, Dorothy Dalton, Priscilla Dean and Madge Evans.

At Paragon *Little Women* was first produced for the screen. During the studio's checkered career, first with World and then with Famous Players-Lasky, many of the leading stars in the country appeared at Paragon: Mary Pickford, Norma Talmadge, Hope Hampton, Douglas MacLean, Noah Beery, Thomas Meighan, made pictures on the 200 foot Paragon stage.

On a hilltop across the valley from Paragon, majestically overlooking the Fort Lee scene stood the largest studio in the world, Universal.

When in 1912 the independent producing companies were enjoying their new found independence from the Edison trust as a result of Carl Laemmle's persistent attacks, there formed among the independents internal dissension.

With internal dissension came the founding of separate groups of independents.

Early in 1912 Harry R. Aitken and John R. Freuler of Majestic Pictures challenged the whip hand Carl Laemmle held over the independent producers by forming one wing of the independents into the Mutual Film Company. Laemmle took the blow and came back to grab the other wing which he quickly molded into a large producing company, the Universal Film Manufacturing Company.

For three years Laemmle conducted the business of Universal at his New York Imp Studio. But expanding too rapidly for his small quarters, he decided in 1915 to erect a tremendous studio.

Laemmle selected for the site of his studio a property on which was standing a huge empty house called "Marks [i.e. Marx] Mansion". When the problem of tearing down the house presented itself, Laemmle quickly decided the job should pay its own way. Cameras were set up, actors called on the scene and the torch was applied. At least four two reelers released in 1915 contained the fire as their smashing climax.

Determined to have the finest studio in the country, Laemmle selected his architect – Ernest Flagg who had previously designed the Singer Building in New York and the Naval Academy at Annapolis. Flagg designed a series of buildings that covered several acres. Built in the main studio was the second largest stage in the world, a mammoth stretch 150 feet by 85 feet. To accommodate the stars he built 100 dressing rooms. For the laboratory men Flagg designed a huge building behind the main studio.

The Fort Lee studio was opened in the fall of 1915 a few months after Laemmle had built Universal City in California. With the two studios in operation the old Imp studio in New York City was closed.

Universal remained at Fort Lee until 1917 when Laemmle, deciding that operating an East and West studio was a little too much for the firm's pocketbook, closed down his Fort Lee plant.

In 1918 Fox erased from his list of stars Theda Bara and added Evelyn Nesbit, former wife of Harry K. Thaw. Evelyn Nesbit had made her debut to the screen several years earlier reenacting the murder of Sanford White in a picture called *The Great Thaw Trial.* Her name can still be found on a scarred door hidden among the ruins of the Éclair Studio.

The big works start

As great as were Fox's activities they were over-shadowed by a gentleman who had moved into the Universal Studio in 1917, a few months after Carl Laemmle had left for California. He brought to Fort Lee the first taste of the stupendous production.

In 1916 Samuel Goldfish, chairman of the board of directors of the Lasky studios in California, decided that the time was ripe for his venture as an independent producer. He sold his interest in the Lasky Company for a reputed $1,000,000, gathered together Edgar Selwyn of the dramatic firm of Selwyn and Company, author Margaret Mayo, and formed the Goldwyn Pictures Corporation.

In April 1917, Goldfish leased the Universal Studio and began production under a schedule that called for a limited number of releases a year. Goldfish was determined to follow the famous stories and famous actor idea that Famous Players had used to advantage and with this in mind hired his staff.

His first star was Mae Marsh; in rapid succession he hired Jane Cowl, Maxine Elliott, Allan Dwan, Madge Kennedy, Mary Garden and Director [Ralph] Ince. For authors he had Margaret Mayo, Irving Cobb, and Basil King.

Under his production schedule Goldfish was to devote months to each picture, a radical change from the short schedules directors had previously been working under. A famous author and famous star were inked together in each of his pictures. Announcement of the pictures was withheld until a complete series had been produced. First to be released was Margaret Mayo's *Polly of the Circus* starring Mae Marsh. The production of this picture was awesome even to the veterans of Fort Lee. At times 3,000 people were working on one

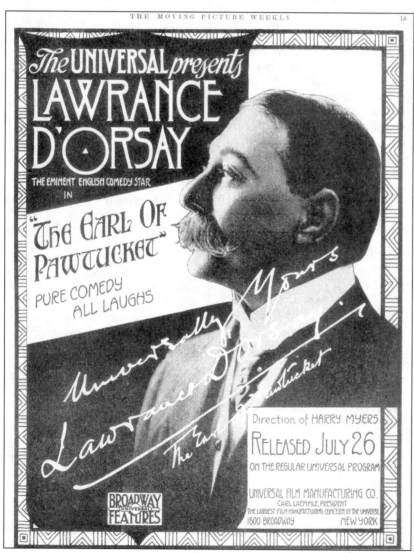

Full page ad for The Earl of Pawtucket, *produced by Universal at the Champion studio in Coytesville. From* Moving Picture Weekly, *3 July 1915.*

set. To make the picture Goldfish had hired an entire circus including all employees from stake men to concessions and sideshows. Almost every available citizen in Fort Lee were [sic] drafted as extras. An entire village was erected. To Goldfish's delight thousands of people came across the Hudson to view the making of the spectacle.

Following the release of *Polly of the Circus*, Goldfish released in rapid succession the rest of his gunfire.

STUDIO TOWN 4:
A Faithful Few Stick, But Fort Lee Begins To Lose Movie Hold
Fox Moves To New York, But Some Encouragement Is Given When Selznick Imports Big Stars

For Fort Lee the War meant the loss of its largest producing company. Goldfish felt the scarcity of fuel, the conservation of light, the scarcity of labor, for it made it almost impossible to operate his Fort Lee studio. At times he had to use four studios to complete a day's production. California with its extra hours of winter daylight, its warm climate that made fuel almost unnecessary, looked mighty inviting to Goldfish as he surveyed production costs that were increasing at an alarming rate. He decided to desert Fort Lee in the summer of 1918.

During its stay, the company produced many pictures [including Maxine] Elliott in *Fighting Odds* and Jane Cowl in *The Spreading Dawn*. But the release of the pictures was poorly timed. The United States had just entered the World War. As a result the country's interest centered in Europe, transportation was tied up. The first handicap had cut seriously the theater attendance; the second had made it difficult to distribute the pictures to the theaters.

Despite Samuel Goldfish's departure, Fort Lee in 1918 had enough busy producers to still be considered a studio town of importance. At Willat and Éclair, Fox was prospering. World, although losing ground as a major motion picture company, continued to produce important pictures at Peerless. A branch of Famous Players-Lasky, who occupied the Universal studio, and Solax completed the list of active companies.

Stage stars aid

Meanwhile, Champion, Fort Lee's pioneer studio, had done well by itself in the period from 1912 to 1917. Becoming a part of Universal when Laemmle consolidated the wing of independents in 1912, Champion gained by the move a great many stars and a full production schedule.

When the wave that swept Broadway stars into the movies was at its crest in 1915, a goodly number trooped to Champion. One of the first glass roofed exterior scenes was introduced on the Champion lot when the stage star, Lawrence D'Orsay, appeared in *The Earl of Pawtucket*. Other pictures taken at Champion were *The Sphinx*, leading roll held by Wilton Lackaye, and *Under Southern Skies*, directed by Lucius Henderson, starring Mary Fuller.

When Laemmle left his large Fort Lee studio in 1917, Champion was closed.

The citizens of Fort Lee were measuring the growth of the movies by the size of the sets the moviemakers were erecting in their town. During the days of cowboy and Indian pictures the producers were satisfied with the erection of a few shanties, the setting up of a few teepees. Then a few of the townsfolk made extra money riding on horses. As the years went on more were called from their homes to play in the pictures. The architects, builders and carpenters got fatter contracts for studio sets.

When William Fox erected his sets for

The Town That Forgot God, Fort Lee stood in amazement and reasoned that indeed the picture men were spending beyond reason.

Fox built a wooden trough three city blocks long. On each side of the trough he built three city blocks of houses complete from rear windows to front door. To the scene he brought thousands of gallons of water packed in large cans, supplemented this with the entire equipment of the local fire company. At the director's signal the deluge of water was released into the trough, and in a few minutes the three blocks of homes that had taken weeks to build were swept away.

The profits from his pictures piling up, he made over $2,000,000 in 1919. Fox was casting his eyes about for a suitable place to erect a modern studio of his own. For his location, he chose New York City and early in 1919 work was started on a $2,500,000 plant. With the erection of his New York studio, Fox began to leave the scene at Fort Lee. He continued to produce minor pictures in the Éclair Studio for a few years, but never again on the scale of the days from 1915–19. By 1921 he had completely left the cliff town. Éclair and Willat were to remain deserted until they were finally torn down.

By 1919 World was ready to give up producing pictures. Ever since the date Selznick left, the company had not been in the best of health. For awhile Brady gave it the breath of life, but he left in1918. After Clara Kimball Young had left World, Brady had managed contracts with a few box office stars such as Carlyle Blackwell, Milton Sills, Warner Oland, Douglas MacLean, Alice Brady and Madge Evans, but one by one these stars were tempted away by offers from other companies. By 1919 World's principal assets were a contract with Carlyle Blackwell, rights to distribute Charles Chaplin reissues, and a storehouse of screen plays. The company was definitely on its last stretch.

The swift decline of the town's motion picture industry was increased in pace when Solax was almost totally destroyed by a raging fire.

It was indeed a gloomy picture for the studio town. The town tax assessor added many a furrow to his brow as he visualized the future. But the black clouds were not to remain for long. Lewis J. Selznick was restless. His Select Pictures Corporation had grown at a tremendous rate and he needed a new studio. Deeply etched in his memory was his episode in the cliff town. It would be a major triumph to return to the cliff town as a producer of importance. The Universal Studio was vacant, so Selznick moved in.

Selznick had prospered since he left World in 1916. His venture with Clara Kimball Young brought huge profits. One after another famous stars were drawn under his banner. In succession he hired the Talmadge sisters and Alla Nazimova. The success of the Lewis J. Selznick Enterprises attracted Adolph Zukor of Famous Players who bought a half interest in the company. With Zukor, Selznick formed the Select Picture Corporation which he brought to Fort Lee in 1919.

STUDIO TOWN 5:
Lack of Quick Transportation Blamed For Fort Lee's Decline
That And California's Scenery Factors In Shift
Labs Held On
Last To Surrender Fight To Stay In Bergen

To Fort Lee Selznick brought Elaine Hammerstein, Elise Janis, Eugene O'Brien, Olive Thomas, Owen Moore, Zena Keefe and Director Ralph Ince. Although fabulous salaries were announced in the press, Selznick never paid his stars huge figures. Olive Thomas, reputed to be receiving $1,000 a week, was paid $500. Elaine Hammerstein, Eugene O'Brien and Owen Moore each received $300 a week. In comparison to the thousands Pickford, Chaplin, and other stars in rival companies were receiving, Selznick's payments were modest. Just as he was a strict accountant with salaries so he was with the production of his pictures.

Fort Lee had never known before such order and planned production as Selznick brought. He set up charts for every series of operations, took all his shots on one set in immediate succession and not as the story progressed. As a result, his company prospered.

When World studios were put up for sale in November 1919, Selznick bought them. With that purchase he became the largest producer in the East.

Leaves in 1922

Selznick maintained his brisk business at Fort Lee for three years. Notable additions to his list of stars during this period were Conway Tearle, Martha Mansfield, Vera Gordon and William Faversham. In 1922 Selznick left Fort Lee entirely.

Behind him was left a scene of desolation. Peerless and Universal were empty. Paragon was being rented on short term lease to Emile Chautard, formerly a director with Fox. Willat and Champion were long deserted. Éclair, still held by Fox was idle. Solax

The Peerless-World studio photographed by Alan Brock in 1939. Compare with page 14.

had resorted to the production of animated cartoons to keep its studio open.

After Selznick's departure Fort Lee lost the right to the title of Studio Town but could very well have been named Laboratory Village, for although the producing companies had left, many of their laboratories continued to run at top production. In addition to Paragon's large laboratory capable of developing 2,000,000 feet of film a year, there were the laboratories of Universal, Kessel, Hirlagraph, Film Service Corporation and NYMP which were turning out millions of feet of film a year.

The largest laboratory at Fort Lee, a huge four-story brick plant called the Sen Jacq, was built during the period of George Eastman's bitter fight with the independent laboratory men.

After the War a flow of inexpensive raw stock, unprinted film, from Europe, mainly from Agfa in Berlin, threatened to flood the country and ruin Eastman Kodak's profitable business with the film trade. Because the raw stock was good, and a great deal cheaper than Eastman's domestic stock, the laboratory men responded to the German inflow with enthusiasm. The matter was serious to Eastman and in 1921 he uttered loud protests. He demanded huge protective tariffs on the imported stock and was bitterly disappointed when the House of Representatives, in response to his protests, only recommended a 15 per cent raw stock tax.

Determined to continue his monopoly he decided to hit the laboratory men in their weakest spot by erecting developing laboratories of his own. The laboratory men suspecting his intentions wailed in opposition. Jules E. Brulatour, Eastman's representative to the film trade, said that the charges of the laboratory men were "silly drivel". But in spite of the vigorous denials, Eastman in August 1921 entered the laboratory business with the purchase of three large plants. It was in this period that the Sen Jacq laboratory was erected by Jules Brulatour.

Expensive, not used

When he erected the Sen Jacq, Brulatour was determined to spare no expense. He outfitted the building with quantities of expensive equipment, even bought coal for the huge furnaces. The complete building represented an investment of several hundred thousand dollars.

The Laboratory was never used. Not a single foot of film for resale ever went through the expensive machines. Floors have been kept dusted, equipment oiled, windows cleaned, for fourteen years the plant has been kept in condition ever ready to be used. Its value as a threat has long passed, for seeing that Eastman meant business the laboratory men quickly came to terms.

The laboratory men continued to prosper at Fort Lee until 1925 when a serious explosion wiped out the Evans Laboratory killing several people, blowing a next-door neighbor suffering with pneumonia out of his window. After 1925, one by one, the remaining laboratories closed up and added their skeletons to the graveyard that was quickly forming in the Cliff Town.

Today the only hangovers from the film trade are the Consolidated Film, which occupies the old Universal Studio, and a branch of Jules Brulatour's system of laboratories. No other laboratories, no other film studios are in operation.

Scattered over the town are the remains of the once prosperous companies. Paragon Studio where William Brady and Jules Brulatour invested their money stands deserted, used only for scenery storage where Brady keeps odds and ends for Broadway plays. The film block where Willat's fence touched Éclair's, and Éclair sided Peerless, would be a source of delight for ruin pokers. Bare concrete blocks that once served as foundations are the only evidence of Doc Willat's studio. Huge concrete blocks in curious position and twisted steel mark the Evans Laboratory. A neat one storied building, behind which stand half buildings and bare foundations strewn with thousands of film reels, are the remains of Éclair where Alec Francis starred and where Evelyn Nesbit later performed for William Fox.

A two storied brick building looking remarkably well preserved from the outside, but behind whose steel doors are concrete floors with huge holes, broken iron staircases, smashed glass, is all that remains of the Fox Laboratory. Peerless, long boarded up, remains as a large building with two huge cracked additions housing studio and scenery storage room. Near the George Washington Bridge, a half building and nearly empty foundations are the only evidence that Solax once produced pictures. Mark Dintenfass's Champion Studio is now a cheaply tar shingled one story, frame structure where greeting cards are printed.

Why had one company after another deserted Fort Lee? There were two number one reasons in the minds of the movie men. One was Fort Lee's poor transportation system. The other was California's scenery.

To get to the studios from company headquarters in New York, the troops would sometimes spend hours. The reason was the Fort Lee Ferry where on busy days lines of cars, blocks long, would be waiting to cross the Hudson. On the Jersey side of the river those on foot in order to reach the cliff top had to take a trolley. If the troop was large, this meant another long wait. By the time actors arrived on the set many precious hours had been lost in a day's work Producers felt this situation acutely during a Jersey trolley strike in 1919.

California's ideal scenery was a losing

argument for Fort Lee. Scenery that delighted the movie pioneers when they first visited Fort Lee seemed shallow in comparison to California's variety. To make snow in summer and sun in winter is expensive. Another pet thorn in the movie men's sides was the trouble they had with the electric company to get enough current to light their studios. Goldwyn complained of this during the war. Other producers found it difficult to work at night. One day during 1919 the producers were completely cut off from all supply and had to hold up production.

Today the town remains as a scene of ruin and desolation. Empty broken

(Below): Unidentified western produced at Rambo's, c. 1911.

buildings remain like the cast off shells of giant turtles. In the breasts of hundreds of young men trained in the movie studios from childhood remains the hope that some day the producers will return.

While the facts in McCormick's article were remarkably accurate, as was his analysis of the reason for the rise and fall of local filmmaking, over the next few decades the legend developed a life of its own. Historians of Hollywood had little interest in digging up the truth regarding what had happened in Fort Lee. Local memories did strange things: some achievements were forgotten, others inappropriately transplanted. Even those old timers who knew the story first hand had reduced it to a series of favorite anecdotes, blending their own memories with facts and fantasies suggested by others. Gus Becker, interviewed here in 1974, may have been on the spot when D.W. Griffith filmed *The Battle* on the open land just behind Rambo's. But by this time, the name of one of Griffith's Civil War epics was about as good as another. Becker remembered the filming of *Les Miserables*, but not who directed it. He knew that Theda Bara made many films in Fort Lee, although the title he suggested was not one of them. And William S. Hart? Fort Lee had a councilman by that name, but the cowboy actor never made pictures here. That would have been Broncho Billy Anderson.

ON LOCATION IN FORT LEE

By Lawrence Vianello
(from *The Dispatch,* 18 April 1974)

Next time you are in Coytesville, stop in the old saloon on First St., the one that looks more like a private home than a bar. This bar was the social center when Fort Lee was the movie capital of the world.

Rambo's Hotel served ham and eggs, and steak, and pie with coffee, to a long line of movie stars, to name a few, Mack Sennett, Donald Mackenzie, Pearl White, Mary Pickford, and Cecil B. DeMille.

Gus Becker, the present owner, remembers most of these people. Becker bought the building in 1933 after working there since 1912.

"Movie crews would come across the Hudson by ferry, and then come up the Palisades by trolley or motorcar. Then they'd shoot their scenes and have a meal at our saloon", said Becker.

"And they used this store, inside and outside, in many of their movies."

Many a pair of cowboys stepped out the front door of Rambo's saloon and squared off on the dusty road for a shoot-out. It was also the place where the stage coach picked up passengers and reported the hold up to the sheriff. Within a stone's throw stood a tree where each day at least one bad man finished hanging from a rope.

At the back of the saloon was a cistern with a pump where the "Indians" washed the red war paint from their bodies. The livery stable rented out horses, saddles, cowboys chaps, etc., to the movie companies.

Under the grape arbor extras would eat their sandwiches, while the "principals" ate inside with the saloon keepers.

Never drank

"But the principals never drank. They couldn't, or they couldn't act", said Becker.

Becker fondly remembers Mary Pickford and Pearl White. Miss White starred in *The Perils of Pauline* filmed on location at the cliffs of the Palisades.

But she was only one of the many who began their screen careers in Fort Lee. The list is endless, but to name a few:

– Cowboy favorite William S. Hart starred in the film *Tumbleweeds* on location in Fort Lee.

– Theda Bara, called the screen's first vamp, starred in *Cleopatra*, filmed in Fox Studios of Fort Lee.

– *Birth of a Nation* filmed in Fort Lee by D. W. Griffith, and the Paris scenes of *Les Miserables* by Cecil B. DeMille.

Becker, 89 as of 3 April, said, "They worked by the weather. When it was fine, there would be three companies here. When they needed to, they would create their own rain storms, with machines right in front of the store."

After owning a store in New York City, Becker came to Coytesville because of his poor health. He regained his health in two years, after recovering from walking pneumonia.

Rambo's sign no longer hangs out front, but his name for the place still remains, in spite of the fact that Becker has called it his tavern since 1933.

The two-story frame building is much the same as it always was. The nine-foot ceilings and the woodwork around the bar are the originals. Upstairs, once the dressing room of the stars, lives Becker's great grandson, Fort Lee Patrolman Daniel McGuirl with his wife.

"When was this place built? Oh, way before my time", said Becker.

2.

Into the Woods

Thomas Edison's first films were produced at his West Orange laboratory in the 1890s, but by 1901 he had opened a primitive motion picture studio in Manhattan. The competition was already there. Yet within only a few years, with the demand for longer and more dramatically complex films increasingly rapidly, all these producers began looking to the suburbs for fresh scenery and increased studio space. Edison preferred the Bronx, while Vitagraph relocated to Brooklyn. Biograph stayed in Manhattan, but like Kalem, Pathé, NYMPCo and various others, began to see Bergen County, New Jersey, as a very attractive location. Gene Gauntier, a pioneer film actress, screen writer, and (apparently) location scout, was one of the first to recognize the Fort Lee area as more than just another wooded backdrop. Although mainly associated in this period with Kalem, she also worked for Biograph long enough to also infect them with her enthusiasm for Coytesville and Shadyside.

BLAZING THE TRAIL

By Gene Gauntier
(excerpted from *Woman's Home Companion*, October and November 1928)

The summer of 1907 saw a general improvement in pictures all along the line and the Kalem Company settled down to a regular release of a one-reel picture weekly. Mr. Olcott, the director, gathered about him a score of actors who were his personal friends and threw himself whole-heartedly into the work. The Chief requisite of the actor who would work for Sid was a telephone number, so those whose lodgings had no telephones must arrange for calls at the corner delicatessen or at some friend's home, dropping in every evening to see whether their services were required for the morning. Another necessity for Kalem actors was "rough stuff". How often over the phone did listening ears catch the voice of the director:

"Hello! That you, Jim? We're going to do a picture tomorrow. Shadyside. Be at the Forty-second Street ferry at seven-forty-five. Bring your rough stuff."

And in suitcases or paper bundles the "rough stuff" would appear with Jim – and Joe and Bill and Harry; an old flannel shirt, bandanna handkerchief, rough trousers and shoes, and a cap or wide-brimmed shabby hat. Bob Vignola had a particularly good character shirt, a dark red flannel with plaid marking of dingy

white. Again and again that shirt appeared in Kalem pictures, worn either by Bob or some friend to whom he had loaned it, for they seemed to think that on a different person it would not be recognized. Finally one day after watching the shirt get in its deviltry for the tenth time in as many pictures, Mr. Marion remarked to Sid:

"I think you had better give that shirt of Bob's a rest. It'll soon be known as the Kalem trademark."

Compare this with the elaborate wardrobes of today!

The general procedure for taking a picture was always the same. There was never a scenario on hand and Sid, after finishing up the previous week's work, would hang about the lean-to office waiting for something to turn up. About Wednesday, Mr. Marion would come down from his home in Connecticut, a black scowl on his face and an unfriendly attitude toward everyone. And Sid would whisper, "Either his liver is bad or he has a story to get off his chest". Sid would then "beat it" till after lunch, returning to face a smiling buoyant Marion looking up expectantly over his desk.

"That you, Sid? The report is for good weather earlier tomorrow. You'd better get your people together and run out to Shadyside and take this picture. It's about a horse thief and there's a dandy climax. The last scene shows him after the vigilance committee has lynched him, hanging over the Palisades by his neck. Here's the dope. You'll better get busy on the 'phone right away." And he would hand Sid a used business envelope on the back of which, in his minute handwriting, was sketched the outline of six scenes, supposed to run one hundred and fifty feet to the scene – as much as our little camera would hold. A half dozen words described each scene; I believe to this day Mr. Marion holds the championship for the shortest working scenario.

So the next morning at quarter of eight a bunch of sleepy actors would be grouped before the ferry gate as the boat clanged in, with Sid running excitedly back and forth scanning the entrance for some late comer, and marching him forward scolding volubly just before the gates closed. Or if the delinquent did not appear:

"Frank, Bill isn't here. If he doesn't come on the next boat, you'll have to double one of the posse. We need him in the first scene and the sun is only on that barn early in the morning. Better make it smooth face, you'll wear whiskers as the father."

Shadyside, lying at the foot of the Palisades, furnished the background for practically every picture we made that first summer. It was a crude ugly little settlement with miserable shacks clinging to the side of the hill, but we had discovered it and had tested its possibilities, so we guarded it jealously from other picture companies.

We carried our suitcases and props up and down the steep road on each trip, and we made our headquarters in a boarding house run for laborers. We made up in hot cell-like rooms, uncarpeted and furnished with lumpy beds which we eyed with distrust. Rickety washstands from which we removed chipped bowls and pitchers served as our dressing tables, all in striking contrast to the cool inviting dressing-rooms of today's wonderful studios.

The food served by the German couple who ran the house consisted largely of muscle-making dishes like stewed beef with noodles, corned beef and cabbage or sauerkraut, boiled potatoes, cabbage slaw, rye bread, huge mugs of beer or coffee; but after a grueling day on location we did not find it distasteful.

It was Olcott's ambition to finish each one-reel picture in a single day, so he held a stop watch on the final rehearsal. If during the actual training he heard the cameraman say quietly,

"Speed up, Sid; film's running out", he would dance up and down shouting, "Hurry up, folks; film's going. Grab her, Jim; kiss her; not too long; quick! Don't wait to put her coat on – out of the scene – hurry now! Out, Max? Good lord! Why didn't you hurry? You should have cut across the side-lines."

For the first pictures, technique did not permit of the action's being stopped midway. If the actors were headed for an exit outside the carefully marked lines they must be at the end of the scene.

This early technique, which like Topsy "just growed", requires some explanation. The marvelous photographic effects of today were far beyond the possibilities of the pioneer moving picture cameras and film. Klieg lights were unknown and interior or studio pictures were not successful. Producers demanded outdoor background

It served as a New England tavern, for many a western saloon, for Civil War recruiting stations, and dozens of other sets. Banisters and railings could hastily be added, old-fashioned chairs, tables and flowering pots dragged out and, with the camera shooting the opposite direction, the old place could be, and has been, used for two different sets in the same picture. At the side was a wide old double wooden gate leading to a typical barnyard, with latticed pump, barns, haystacks, chicken yard, cowshed, wagons, horses, and all the other paraphernalia necessary to add color to a scene. And the prices were so reasonable. A dollar apiece for dressing-rooms, fifty cents each for the smoking hot dinner and nothing at all for the use of the exteriors and props. A year or so later, when Mr. Griffith, with his (for then) luxurious ideas, discovered this place which we had considered wholly our own, he started what to us was a riot of extravagance. Everything was paid for! Twenty five dollars for the use of the exterior of the house! Two dollars each for rooms! And more elaborate dinners were ordered, at two dollars a plate.

Here we made The *Days of '61*, the first picture of the Civil War ever produced. The battle scenes were taken up at St. John's Military Academy at Manlius, New York, near Syracuse. The costumes came from Gus Elliott's, an old German down in St. Mark's Place, and everyone went to select his own. It was a queer old shop such as Dickens might have written about. Costumes were rented for one dollar each, if not elaborate or of extra fine materials. Wigs also could be had.

The Thompson Seton place supplied the background for our first Indian pictures. An unforgettable lake was encircled by a primeval forest and tangled underbrush, all reflected on the

for all scenarios. There were no close-ups, no subtle pauses. There could be no action directly across the foreground because this meant a blurred picture. If Mary and John were strolling through the woods they must be seen entering the path at an angle from the sidelines and they must exit the same way. A stare had to be held, a start had to be violent. If the director wished certain spoken words to register, they were enunciated with exaggerated slowness, leaving no doubt in the mind of the spectator ... .

That summer of 1907 introduced us to two wonderful new locations. Rambo's in Coytesville, New Jersey, and Windy Goal, the Ernest Thompson Seton place at Cos Cob, Connecticut.

Coytesville was the same sleepy little village it had been for a hundred years, with winding dirt roads and clapboard houses nestling among rose and lilac bushes, an ideal background for pictures. Rambo's, since pictured in hundreds of films, was our discovery. It was merely a barroom where light lunches were available at all hours. Substantial home-cooked hot meals were ordered in advance. Above were small bare sleeping-rooms where we made up. It was run by Mr. and Mrs. Rambo and Mrs. Rambo's sister, kindly interested folks who did everything in their power to aid us.

A narrow porch supported by uprights ran across the front of the house, which was plain, even to ugliness, but typical of almost any part of the United States.

mirror-like surface of the water, on which floated birch-bark Indian canoes. The owner was a nature lover, so wild birds and small animals lived unafraid in the grounds.

With this environment, plus costumes and props, we turned out pictures which were things of beauty even in those crude days. Here also the next summer we took *Hiawatha*, *Evan-geline* and *As You Like It*. For by that time, you see, we had begun to reach for higher things.

Some of the best accounts of early film production in Fort Lee can be found in the reports of detective agencies hired by the Edison Manufacturing Co. to collect evidence for legal proceedings. Because Edison's main patent claims were based on the method for moving film through the camera, his agents were always trying to convince gullible independent operators to let them see how motion picture film was threaded up. In the following reports, detectives Buckbee and McCoy are shadowing members of the Carson Company, an obscure independent producer quite active during 1909. Correspondence was generally addressed to George F. Scull, an Edison attorney and secretary of the Patents Company.

Report of C.A. Buckbee –

New York, June 21st 1909.

According to instructions I proceeded to the Red Gate, on the road to Fort Lee, NJ, and found some people had engaged a shack in the woods to take pictures today. As no one had arrived as yet I waited half an hour when the company arrived and proceeded to make a western scene. Pictures were taken by the Carson Co., and in the party were Mr Carson, Pierce Kingsley, the stage manager, and "Lew" Johnston, the operator; also a number of actors.

Mr. Johnson [Buckbee spells the name three different ways in this report] is the same man I shadowed from the Knickerbocker Building to # 527 Sixth Avenue some two weeks ago.

Mr. Carson told me that his place is in Philadelphia, and that he has a first class operator there, also said that he does not think much of Johnston as he is very slow, and always about two hours late. The film they used was not correctly perforated and it took them all day to take the one drama. They used a Pathé camera, the same kind I saw used at 155th St & 8th Ave some days ago, and Johnson said it was made in France. The Pathé name plate was on the front of camera.

About 5.15 P.M. Mr. McCoy and I went down to Edgewater and waited for Johnston to come down to the ferry which he did about 6 P.M., and we went over on boat with him. I offered to carry his film case for him and did so right to his door, 527 Sixth Ave. When I left him he told me his name is Johston, and said he is over in the Fort Lee district about twice a week taking pictures. I informed him that I often went over there on hot days, and left him so that if I run on him again he would not think anything of it.

Edgewater, NJ June 21st 09

Mr. George F. Scull

Dear Sir:

I arrived at Red Gate about 11.45 A.M. Mr. Carson, Kingsley, and all others who were to take part in the moving pictures were on hand except Mr. Johnston who came about 12.10.

After Johnston had his camera in position I called him over and said that I was informed that they were going to take pictures today, and that I would like for to see the operation in full. Johnston said you will have an opportunity for to see how they take moving pictures today, as he said that he expected to be working until late in the afternoon.

Johnston said that he was taken [sic]

pictures today for the Carson Co. of Philadelphia, Pa. and that he has been doing considerable work for them both in New York and in Philadelphia. He said this spot here is the best there is in the country for taking moving picture scenes, and that moving picture camera men come from Chicago, Ill. and from other portions of the country for to take scenes in and around this section.

Pierce Kingsley was the manager and directed the players in regards to the parts they were to take and the positions they were to be in during the scene, as he had the play typewritten and called out from the paper what each was to do during each scene.

George Carson had considerable for to say during the day, as he was telling me that he had to pay the bills, and if anything went wrong he had to stand the loss.

> Scene 1st. Hero receiving mail from the Postmistress.
>
> 2. Indian & Mexican playing cards.
>
> 3. Stealing girl and robbing post office.
>
> 4. Taking girl to Cabin.
>
> 5. The chase –
>
> 6. Thief captured
>
> 7. At the stockade.

8. Grand finale all hand in the picture.

Johnston said that he had run 1670 feet of film during the day, as he marked down the amount of film that was used during each scene –

During the first, second, third and fourth scenes he was using stock film that was not perforated accurately and the film was running off the pawls quite often. Johnston said that it was stock film and made by a firm in England.

At the fifth scene they put in Lumiere film that they perforated themselves, he said, and they would have no more trouble in regards to the film running off the pawls, as he called them.

I was interested in the workings of the Camera and had Johnston to explain the operations of the film at times when he was not engaged and waiting for Kingsley to get the people in shape.

The films, he said, comes in rolls of 50 meters or about 166 feet. He then has the film perforated as he has a machine for that purpose. The film from the upper box is carried over a small hook to a sprocket wheel and then run over the lens by means of the two metal panels that draw down a section about one inch before the camera. The shut-

ter is automatically opened, allowing film to receive the light, drawn over another sprocket wheel and into the lower box which is light proof.

When turning the crank, he said that 16 pictures a second is taken, and that is why he has a stop watch on his camera. Also his indicator registers the amount of films used during each scene taken, and in that way he always knows how much films he has for any scene wanted. Johnston was using a Pathé camera today, as it had a name plate on the front of the Camera –

> Cinematographe
> Pathé Frères
> Paris

Mr. Buckbee was at Edgewater before I arrived there and he was there during all the time Johnston was operating the camera.

Buckbee and I came down together and we waited at the Hotel at Edgewater until Johnston came down to the ferry with his camera and films.

Johnston was telling me coming in the subway that he was glad I was up there today, and if I want a picture taken I will know about what to do in regards to getting the people in shape. But he has had over twelve years experience with the moving picture camera, and he can help out in a great many cases. Buckbee continued down in the subway with Johnston.

McCoy

2 June 21st 09
Mr. George F. Scull

Dear Sir:

I called at Johnston's #527 Sixth Ave Saturday morning and found that he had started for Fort Lee for to take a picture, and was not expected back until about 1 P.M.

I called again at 1:30 P.M. Johnston said that he was up at Fort Lee all morning, but they did not take a picture as there was only six people in their party which was not enough, and

Film companies arriving from New York would take the ferry to the Fort Lee terminal, and either drive to the top of the Palisades, or take a trolley.

they were unable for to get the required number of people that they wanted for their canoe race.

Johnston said that the canoe race was postponed until Sunday, June 27th as on that date there is to be a regatta and a larger crowd of people are expected to be there and they will run their canoe race and take a picture of it at that time. Johnston said that he was up to Fort Lee on Friday and that he run off 2675 feet of film. They were taken a comedy picture and he said that all of their work is taken out doors. I called to see Johnston in regards to a picture that I wanted him to take and wanted to know what days during the coming week that he was not engaged by other people. He said that I could have any day this week that I might select.

I will call and see him about Tuesday and tell him that I am unable for to get my people together again to take part in the games on account of the warm weather.

McCoy

The canoe race and the regatta is to take place just above Fort Lee at the next Station. He said it was to be quite an event up there on Sunday June 27th 09.

Suddenly, cameraman Johnston is gone. The Carson-Kingsley films are now being photographed by a Mr. Standish, who appears to be secretly in league with McCoy and the detectives.

Edgewater, NJ June 24th 09
Mr. George F. Scull

Dear Sir:

I arrived at the old saw mill at Undercliff on the Hudson in time to see the Carson people take nine scenes from the story of Robinson Cruso [sic].

Standish gave me all the chance that I wanted to see the workings of the Schneider Camera which he was operating for the Carson people.

Pierce Kingsley was directing the actors and instructing them in regards to their parts, how they were to perform them in the different scenes, as he had a typewritten sketch of the story which he referred to from time to time.

George Carson was with Standish most of the day, helping him with the camera, also locating for Standish assistance and space that was required for taken [sic] the picture in.

I did not speak to Standish any time during the day.

Mr. Carson was all right he said good morning to me when I arrived but after they had things in shape for taken the pictures they were pretty well occupied until they finished what [balance of report missing].

[McCoy]

One of the most persistent of the early independent producers, Carl Laemmle, had been an exhibitor and exchange operator working out of Chicago. In battling the motion Picture Patents Company he had first tried to guarantee himself a source of supply by importing films from European producers not already aligned with Edison. When this proved impractical he formed his own production company, the Independent Motion Picture Company (IMP), which in 1909 made its first film, *Hiawatha*, in Fort Lee. The following is an excerpt from an unpublished autobiographical manuscript prepared around 1927.

THIS BUSINESS OF MOTION PICTURES

By Carl Laemmle (excerpt)

When pictures appeared on the scene, the early producers, realizing that thrills and excitement form the integral part of a photoplay, fell back upon the red man for assistance. The result found a preponderance of these Indian pictures for which there was always a ready market. This fact influenced us to use [ ] to our advantage, but we also decided to avoid the stereotyped theme of scalping, massacres and treachery. In history's pages, we found the character of Pocahontas, but alas, Biograph had made use of her previously. We next turned to our native literature and presto, it yielded the saga of that one Indian "Hiawatha", known to every American schoolboy and girl. The reason, I surmise, that others passed it up, lay in the fact that no white person appears in the poem and no manufacturer would dare take liberties with a story known to every American. Nor would he risk making a picture containing all Indians.

The mere mention of "Hiawatha" struck me and I knew that our first story for American consumption was discovered at last. The English have their St. George and Beowulf, the French their D'Artagnan, the Germans, Siegfried, the Americans, Hiawatha and so we began transplanting upon the screen that famous Indian brave conceived by Longfellow, minus any of the morbid characteristics as construed by palefaces. Not only would we defer following the footsteps of the eight or nine producers then making pictures, but we would not tamper with the original story to suit the conventional requirements of the screen. Our next step was to assemble a production unit to make this picture.

It was hinted among renters and exhibitors that the production cost of pictures approximated one dollar per

Carl Laemmle, around the time he entered the nickelodeon business.

THE TRUST CONTROLLED PATENTS

In order not to bring down the wrath of the Film Trust, we purchased a Schneider camera, not controlled by the monopoly. We were certain that we would be unmolested but subsequent events conclusively proved the contrary, for we were shadowed, harassed, threatened and assaulted without regard to our legal rights. Let me repeat that the members of the Patents Company had each pooled their so-called patents into a joint combination. These patents concerned the projecting machines in use at theatres and the cameras, the life's blood of pictures. Lawyers will tell you that mere grant of a patent is insufficient to establish a claim for infringement, but the validity of the said patent must be established in court before a judge will decide for the plaintiff.

No one had dared to challenge the Patents Company at the time, for the powerful reason that it possessed unlimited resources. My own attorney, in fact it was whispered about by everyone, had informed me that the several patents alleged to be controlled by the Trust could never be substantiated in any legal proceeding, but the expense of disproving these claims would be costly. I determined not to risk litigation and for that reason I invested in a motion picture camera that was not controlled by the Trust.

THE BIRTH OF "HIAWATHA"

To return to our first producing venture, we had already engaged the unit for making *Hiawatha*. Ranous made the scenario from the book and he used couplets from the poem for subtitles. A fund of fifteen hundred dollars was put at his disposal. We had already made arrangements to photograph the few interior scenes, chiefly of the wigwam variety, in an old warehouse in New York City facing the Hudson River and we would "shoot"

linear foot. We also knew that before a picture was completed, some fifteen hundred to eighteen hundred feet of film had been exposed and then invariably cut down to fill the required reel. Beyond that our knowledge was limited and our production experience being *nil*, we sought experienced personnel. The first to apply was one William V. Ranous, who had forsaken the Vitagraph organization due to a disagreement. He had directed many pictures for that company and even acted on several occasions. That qualified him for our purposes and we promptly engaged him at a weekly salary of one hundred dollars. We hired an ingenue at a nominal stipend which today would cause snickering among our Hollywood friends.

the exterior shots in Coytesville, a small village on the Jersey side of the river. In the meantime, I invaded New York City where I opened a branch office at 111 East 14th St., next door to the old Steinway Building.

Having laid the foundation for our initial production, I made a trip to Europe during June, 1909, where I visited England, France, and Germany for purposes of making a film survey of these countries. American producers had not, as yet, established their offices in these regions, preferring to dispose of their foreign rights to the highest bidder.

When I returned four months later, I learned that *Hiawatha* was almost completed at nearly five times the estimated cost. Of course, due allowances must be made that it was our first effort and we had to grope our way, which is ever the case with film makers, who must deal with the whims of the public. Reference had been made from time to time in the trade publications as to our progress with *Hiawatha* and this stimulated the interest of exhibitors and renters, who wrote us for the release date. We were forced to postpone this notification owing to the fact that we desired a steady supply of weekly material on hand, so that there would be no waiting for further pictures once we launched our first subject.

Finally *Hiawatha* was finished and it recorded some nineteen hundred feet of film, but the judicious application of the shears brought it down to nine hundred and eighty-four feet. I had not, as yet, seen any of the action screened and my associates sought to surprise me. When they finally informed me that it would be shown on a certain date, I proudly invited a number of exhibitors to be in attendance in our Chicago office. We had constructed a small projection room in the basement, where we ran off film for inspection purposes. There, some fifty or sixty exhibitors crowded one

day during October of 1909 and together with them I saw our first product, *Hiawatha,* screened. It would be idle for me to deny that I suppressed my enthusiasm as I saw the first scene flashed before my eyes. The lusty cheers from our guests caused a leaping of joy and pride within me. Gold type can never convey my feelings upon that occasion, as their "aha" and "Huzzas" and "O you Biograph" rang in the cellar where we were assembled.

The reference to Biograph was made by way of comparison in photography, for the story, acting and direction were less important in the eyes of theatre proprietors. Pictures were measured by photographic standards and all had accorded the laurels to the Biograph organization. But now I witnessed a gallant ovation accorded to our first subject by men who really knew the difference and I must confess that it thrilled me with pride to hear their favorable comments. Vanity is a trait of human nature that is in all of us and I admit to its coming to the surface in me on that occasion.

The story had been followed faithfully and it pleased many to see the couplets from the poem, used as subtitles. We were the first to do this. A few months later a fellow competitor made *Maude Muller*, Whittier's pastoral poem, and likewise used couplets for subtitles.

Everyone in the trade agreed that *Hiawatha* possessed national interest and now that I return to the period of its film birth, I can visualize how adroitly our director had handled the story. He split up the poem into a number of scenes, so that a connected narrative was maintained from the first appearance of "Hiawatha" to the poetical moment when he leads his bride away. I was surprised to witness some magnificent snatches of scenic effects in the picture and when I had occasion to interrogate Bob Cochrane, he told me that they were actual scenes of the famous Minnehaha Falls in Minnesota, which had

inspired Longfellow. These scenes had been purchased from an outside source and in the parlance of the trade were known as "stock shots". A producer, for instance, desires to make a picture in which a passing reference is made to either Monte Carlo, London, Berlin, Niagara Falls, marching troops, general scenes of a racetrack or boxing contest, etc., he is spared both the expense and time by purchasing any of such scenes from organizations which specialize in that branch.

Judged by present day standards, *Hiawatha,* with its white cast smeared with bronze paint and crude photography, would only serve, after these seventeen years, as a target for ridicule; but the old picture, nevertheless, with the famous Falls as its background, made a popular appeal for its time.

THE EARLY SCENARIOS

Those were the stirring days when anything served as an idea for a scenario. Each day we were serenaded with the chorus of "waddle we do?" Someone would think of a title and then we would promptly proceed to weave a story around it. Our players would appear before the footlights in the evenings and the following morning report at the movie studio to make a picture. It was not unusual for one set of players to penetrate the wilds of New Jersey in the morning and telephone in about noon that their assignment had been finished. We'd call a hurried consultation and cast about for another idea, until a plausible item, either out of fancy or fact, would come into view and the next day the director was prepared to transpose this idea upon a thousand feet of celluloid. A good many of these pictures were so short that we often inserted a scenic in order to make one complete reel.

Then started a rampage that would dwarf all the romantic battles I have heard of being waged between gigantic monopolies in Wall Street. Wher-

Hiawatha (IMP, 1909), the first film produced by Carl Laemmle, later the founder of Universal.

of the van. The Trust had two detectives constantly employed, whose duty it was to detect and seize or smash any 'outlaw' cameras in use by me.

These two private detectives were known by every 'pirate' then operating and their presence would be promptly reported by scouts, enabling the camouflaged express wagon to retreat hastily, only to later meet the director and company at another appointed rendezvous. There the filming was continued until the "bulls" again hove in sight and the process of evading them was repeated. It was a dangerous procedure for any Trust detective or any suspicious looking stranger to be found in a studio without credentials.

Dummy cameras were a frequent occurrence. More than once I used an 'extra man' to turn the crank of a fake camera to distract attention from the real machine, secreted on some other portion of the set.

To continue our schedule we were forced to practice these wiles notwithstanding that cameras patented by others than the Trust were used. The latter soon claimed every make of camera as an infringement. On another occasion, R.H. Cochrane and myself were forced to hide in a Fort Lee, NJ cellar all night with the company's cameras, while sleuths from the Patents Company scoured the neighborhood. As a matter of fact, cameramen were selected in the early days not for their artistic ability, but for their fistic prowess.

Pitched battles between rival factions were frequent and the ultimate release of a picture usually depended on the fleetness of the cameraman in escaping his pursuers, generally recruited from unsavory neighborhoods to interfere with the opposition's production activities. In fact, some of the best skirmishes of the period took place over the possession of the motion picture cameras.

ever we went, the Trust sent its paid spies and plug-uglies to dog our footsteps. The Patents Company's spies were employed to guard against any violation of the various court orders issued against us, thereby arrogating upon itself a sort of police power. Once we eluded them by concealing ourselves in back of a Brooklyn beer garden. We were soon discovered and had to move on and each day we would concoct some new ruse whereby the enemy could be outwitted. Exteriors were photographed by a camera artfully concealed in a closed express wagon. Certain patent points controlled by the opposition necessitated taking pictures with these "bootleg" cameras.

In the studio, the players never saw a camera, as the machine was hidden, together with its operator, in a huge ice chest. This was done so that in the event of a law suit, the actors, if called to the witness stand, could truthfully testify they had seen no camera in any way resembling that protected by the now famous Latham Loop patent.

Outside the studio, which was then located at Columbus Ave. and 100th Street in New York City, the camera was always concealed in a closed express wagon, its shutter projecting through a small aperture in the back

"SHOOT" MEANT SOMETHING

When the present day director instructs his cameraman to "shoot" he probably does not realize that a similar order a couple of decades ago might have been taken literally. A six-shooter was part of a cameraman's equipment in the early days. Cameras were nailed up in camouflaged boxes to prevent spies of the powerful Motion Picture Patents Company detecting their presence, as all the machines were supposed to violate certain patent rights controlled by the monopolistic Trust. These sleuths were always lurking around the Imp and other independent studies, seeking to prevent the "pirates" (as we were known) from using the contraband machines.

Immediately the studio hands managed to sneak into their plant, shades were drawn and every precaution taken to prevent the spies viewing the taking of scenes from adjacent roofs. The Trust's hirelings were sometimes sufficiently enterprising to gain entrance by devious methods into the studio. Their presence detected, production halted, while the entire staff joyously and strenuously ousted them ....

Laemmle and his operation were indeed prime targets of the Motion Picture Patents Company. But reports from the Buckbee Detective Agency suggest that Edison was more interested in gathering evidence concerning the inner workings of their cameras than in breaking up their location work. The mysterious Mr. Standish, no longer working for Carson, again appears to be functioning as a double agent.

Date: April 11, 1910

Subject: Indept. M.P. Co. of AM.

Opr. No. 50

Report on Case Number 222 –

I began covering the 14th St office of above firm at 7:40 A.M. and did not see any of the operators either enter or come out, and no camera left place up to 9:50 A.M. when Mr. Buckbee arrived and told me to accompany him to the 128th St ferry. When we arrived there the boat was waiting and we found the operator of above company on boat with his camera. Upon arriving on the other side we were joined by Opr. #2 who had followed the actors over ferry and he said the whole company was in a hotel near ferry, and the operator joined them there. They had two carriages and also a wagon they had brought from Doyle's Livery Stable #510 West 56th St. After some delay they started off in the direction of Grantwood, but continued on down the shore road and drove to a place called Shadyside where they took pictures in front of a shanty. The camera they used did not look anything like a Pathé, nor like any I have ever seen. I saw the operator open the camera and it did not look like a Pathé inside (see report of C.A.B.)

We remained until they took all the pictures and until the whole company left on way back to Edgewater."

Date: April 11th 1910

Subject: Indept. M.P. Co of Am.

Opr. No. 1

Report on Case Number 222 –

"I reported at 128th St ferry at 9 A.M., and met Mr. Standish, who informed me that the Independent Co were in the ferry house, and that he could not go over with them as there was some one in party who knew him.

The company took the boat to Edgewater and at 11 A.M. they left a small hotel near ferry in carriages. They drove to Shadyside where they took pictures at a shanty. The camera was about the size of the one used by Thanhouser & Co, only it was made of wood. It was about 12in high, 6in thick, 8inches wide, and opened different from any other camera; it opened in back as if it was cut in half. The film was perforated, and inside the camera it ran over a spool on top of lens and a gate pushed film close to lens, then another larger spool received the film after passing lens. Mr Salter was manager and a Mr Johnson was operator. At 2 P.M. they stopped taking pictures and drove back to Edgewater. I heard one of the party says [sic] they would be over there again tomorrow."

Date: April 11th 1910

Subject: Indpt. M/P. Co of AM

Opr. No. C.A.B.

Report on Case Number 222 –

"I received a 'phone message from Mr Standish that the actors for above company were at the 128th St ferry, and Opr. #2 had followed them to Edgewater. I then stopped at 14th St where I picked up Opr. #50 and took ferry to Edgewater. On the boat going over we found the camera man with his camera. Upon arriving at Edgewater we were joined by Opr. #2, and he said the company were in a hotel near ferry. The camera man went to this hotel and after some little delay they all came out and got into two carriages and a wagon from Doyle's Livery Stable, #510 West 56th St.

Mr Standish had informed me that they were bound for the Romboe [sic] place, but they went in the opposite direction, and drove to Shadyside where they took some pictures in front of a shanty. The camera was similar to one used by the Powers Co, and I saw it opened three times by operator. It had a small gate, and camera was about 1 foot high, 5 inches thick, and about 8 inches wide. It had a box for unexposed films on top and another box for exposed films on the

Charles Buckbee made this sketch of the camera he saw being used at Shadyside on 11 April 1910. Judging from photos provided by Rick Malkames, curator of the Malkames collection of early cinema apparatus, it appears to be a 1902 model Lubin.

back of camera. These boxes were removed to be filled, and the film used was "Lumiere Film", and it was perforated. Enclosed please find a piece of same.

Mr Salter was the manager, one of the actors was named King, and I believe the operator was a Mr Johnson. He was about 5ft 8in tall, weight 150lbs, 35 years of age, dark brown curly hair, and wore glasses. He had a small brown mustache. We discontinued when the company finished and drove back to Edgewater.

The Buckbee Detective Service
21 Park Row
New York

April 12th 1910.

Mr. George F. Scull
Orange, NJ

Dear Sir: –

Enclosed please find a drawing of the interior [sic; sketch was actually of exterior] of camera used by the Laemmle people at Shadyside yesterday. This will give you some slight idea of the appearance of camera.

When film was run into place the operator inserted it from the right hand side of camera after opening the gate which seemed to me to be made of very dark red glass, or possibly a dark metal, but it seemed to be one solid piece, with no openings like the gate on a Pathé camera.

When this camera was ready to operate the broad side was toward the subject. The finder stuck out from the side just above the crank used to operate the machine.

Respectfully yours,

The Buckbee Detective Service
Charles A. Buckbee, Principal

Date: April 15th 1910

Subject: Laemmle Co.

Opr. No. C.A.B.
Report on Case Number 222 –

This morning at 9:15 o'clock Mr Standish telephoned this office that the Laemmle Co had crossed at 139th St., and I then went to 42nd St ferry to get Opr. #2 who was covering for them there, but he was not at the ferry so I went to Edgewater myself and joined Mr Standish. We then took car to Coytesville where Mr Standish said the company had gone, but upon arriving there we found it was the Pathé company. I then telephoned the office and learned that Opr. #2 had caught the Laemmle company crossing at 42nd St and had followed them to Dumont NJ, and was two miles out of Dumont in the woods. We then returned to New York.

The Buckbee Detective Service
21 Park Row
New York

April 16th 1910

Mr George F. Scull
Orange, NJ

Dear Sir: –

As I have every opportunity to observe how your present plan of operation works out I would suggest that another plan be adopted because the present plan only adds to confusion. The reasons for this are numerous, and I would suggest any one of the following plans:

1st. We know that the Laemmle people are going to Long Island, as well as Jersey, and I would suggest that we shadow Mr Johnson from his house each morning until we get him located with his camera, then my men can telephone Mr Standish who must remain in one spot until called.

2nd. Another plan would be to have one man live at Coytesville and another man at the 130th St ferry each morning to get those crossing there. This would catch not only the Laemmle crowd but all those going to Jersey, and there are many of them.

3rd plan. Let Lowenkamp and Mr Standish have an automobile and make the rounds beginning at the Red Gate, Old Mill, Coytesville, Shadyside, etc. If they made this trip three times between 9 and 1 o'clock each day they would know what was going on over in Jersey. The distances are great, the hills so numerous, that a rig of some kind is always necessary, but we are afraid to take a rig from the Ferry at Edgewater as a rule because the cabmen all know these picture people and stand in with them.

Another plan would be to shadow both the 14th St office of the Laemmle Co and the factory. By this plan we could get any of their people leaving the plant. I urge any of the above plans as great improvements on the present way of working.

Respectfully yours,

The Buckbee Detective Service
Charles A. Buckbee, Principal

Fred Balshofer, another of the pioneer independent producers, hired a teenager named Arthur Miller to help out in his Brooklyn film lab in 1908. Before long they were traveling to Fort Lee almost every day, learning to make westerns while dodging spies from the Motion Picture Patents Company. The first part of this excerpt from their joint memoir was written by Balshofer, the second by Miller, who would later become one of Hollywood's most accomplished cinematographers.

"The Early Film Companies" and "Making *The True Heart of an Indian*"

By Fred Balshofer and Arthur C. Miller

From *One Reel a Week* (Berkeley: University of California Press, 1967) pp. 24–37

In December, 1908, American Mutoscope & Biograph Company (generally called the Biograph) had gone in with those who already were paying royalties for the use of the Edison patents. The other companies, as mentioned earlier, were Edison, Vitagraph, Selig, Kalem, Lubin, Essanay, Pathé, and George Kleine. All of these companies now officially announced the formation of a new organization called the Motion Picture Patents Company in January, 1909. Their plan was to stop anyone outside of their trust from making moving pictures in the United States. However, they didn't take into account an old saying to the effect that the best laid plans of mice and men often go astray. The announcement of the Patents Company was tantamount to a declaration of war on the independents. The Patents Company's next move was to contract with the Eastman company to buy Eastman's entire United States output of perforated film as a move to protect their monopoly.

Adam Kessel took this to be the first shot fired in their declared war and reacted as I expected he would. We had a session at Mouquin's French Restaurant on Sixth Avenue and 28th Street. Seated around the table were Charles and Addie Kessel, Charles Baumann, and me . The minute the talk started, I could tell I had not misjudged my partners, for, as I had figured, Addie Kessel was full of fight. To counteract the Eastman deal with the trust, it was decided that the next day I would see Jules Brulatour, the New York importer of Lumiere film manufactured in France, to make ar-

rangements for our supply of film, as well as to make inquiries about having the film perforated. After our plans were set, we had our dinner, and somehow it seemed as if we were celebrating a victory. When the waiter brought the check on a small plate, Charlie Kessel placed a ten-dollar bill on it. As he did so, his eye caught the picture of a buffalo on the bill. With a smile he pushed the plate toward the center of the table and said, "Here's a good trademark for your company. It will fit right in with your western pictures." Addie thought it looked pretty good, but didn't think Buffalo Pictures sounded quite right. The waiter standing by spoke up and said, "They call those animals bison, too". So Bison became the name and trademark of our company.

The next day I went to see Eberhard Schneider who had an optical store on East 12th Street where he sold movie equipment that he had designed and built himself. Fortunately, he could let me have one of his perforators immediately, and he agreed to deliver a second one as soon as possible. We placed the first perforator on the bench in the printing room and arranged to run it slower than the recommended speed as a precaution against static. As well as being my camera boy, it became young Miller's job to carefully perforate the supply of negative film on days when there was no photographing to be done.

It was now about the middle of March and, although the weather was still a bit cold, we decided to make our first picture. From the beginning I had wanted to make westerns, which meant that our locations would be across the Hudson River in and around Fort Lee and Coytesville, New Jersey. Most of the trust and independent companies worked there and it was ideal for westerns. I knew, though, that it meant trouble as the trust had their spies on the job.

Both Kessel and Baumann thought it

When the first filmmakers arrived in Fort Lee they found the town filled with hotels, saloons and livery stables, businesses which had been developed to serve the summer tourist trade, but also very useful for their own purposes.

wise to make a few pictures as far away from the Patents Company's spotters as possible. They felt that this would give us a chance to assemble a small company as well as time to make certain that when we were set we would have people we could rely upon for our entry into the lion's den in Jersey. Some of the independents already were working over there, despite the continued harassment by the Patents Company. I agreed with my partners that this was the only solution.

Two or three weeks prior to our decision to make a few pictures quietly, a young fellow dropped in at the Brooklyn laboratory. He was a good-looking chap,

Young Deer, Red Wing and Evelyn Graham in an unidentified western made by Fred Balshofer and Arthur Miller in Fort Lee, c. 1909.

about thirty years of age. He had written a story called *Disinherited Son's Loyalty*, and he said that if I gave him the leading role in the movie, the story would be mine for nothing. The young man claimed to have had experience playing small parts in a stock company in a downtown Brooklyn theater. The day we started the picture, however, I could tell at once that he had never put on greasepaint makeup in his life. This was part of the actor's profession, as makeup men were unheard of at that time. As an actor, he turned out to be as phony as one historian's tale to the effect that Adam Kessel and Charlie Baumann appeared as actors in this picture.

This incident decided us that from now on we would make use of experienced actors wherever possible. I was acquainted with a young actor, Charles French, who had worked for the Biograph on and off. For our second picture, I made a deal with him to play the leading male role as well as to help direct. For our leading lady, we selected Evelyn Graham, a stage actress. We made the picture around the waterfront at Sheepshead Bay in Brooklyn and called it *A Fisherman's Romance*. It was while making this picture that I began to take staging and directing seriously. I had been watching young Miller's progress with the camera as I had become fond of the youngster. I had taught him to grind at the correct speed, and he could thread a camera without any trouble. His one problem was that he was small for his age, and I realized that when the time came for him to grind the camera, he'd have to stand on a box to reach it.

A Fisherman's Romance was a great improvement over our first picture; they both ran a little over eight hundred feet. The next story I bought from Charlie French for ten dollars was called *Davy Crockett in Hearts United*. Here again the same historian made an actor of Adam Kessel, for he reports Kessel took the part of Davy Crockett. Actually, Charlie French was Davy with Evelyn Graham as his leading lady. What the historian didn't report was that Charlie Baumann, who had never before acted, played the girl's father. It was Baumann's first and last appearance as motion picture actor.

The Davy Crockett picture called for wild, virgin countryside so the company crossed the Hudson on the 42nd Street Ferry, hired a horse-drawn rig called a stage to drive us to the location in the woods between the towns of Palisades and Fort Lee, New Jersey. Here we found a picturesque road through the woods that paralleled what is now Anderson Avenue. The first day we drove over to Pete Cella's hotel for lunch. Cella's hotel was about a quarter of a mile from Main Street in Fort Lee, at that time a small, rural town with a dusty, unpaved dirt street. A horse-drawn water wagon with two sprinklers at the rear laid the dust twice a day. In the middle of the road was a single trolley track with a siding at intervals to allow a trolley going in one direction to switch off and let a trolley headed in the opposite direction pass. On either side of the street were large telegraph poles with dozens of wires stretched from one to the other.

After lunch, not far from the hotel, I found just the mansion we had in mind as the residence of the girl and her wealthy father. The people in Fort Lee were accustomed to the movie companies using their homes (for a small fee, of course), so we made arrangements to work around the house the next day. We shot some more scenes in the woods the following morning and, after lunch, moved to shoot the last scene at the mansion. This scene required Baumann, as the father, to walk from the background to join his daughter and a dressed-up eastern dude who was waiting with the parson for Baumann to give his

daughter's hand in marriage. The daughter, according to the script, did not love the dude. She loved Davy Crockett who came charging by on horseback in the nick of time to sweep the girl off her feet and ride away. Ladies were a little more plump in those days and Charlie French had one hard time trying to accomplish this bit of heroism. The scene ended with Davy riding his horse holding the heroine's hand as she ran alongside until they were out of camera range. The next and last scene was played in front of Davy's cabin in the woods, where the minister performed the wedding ceremony while Davy delivered his spoken title, "Mother, I have brought you a daughter".

Davy Crockett was the type of picture we had decided we would make when we formed the Bison Company, and the sale of prints proved how right our judgment was. Our next film was *A Squaw's Revenge*, followed by a split-reel with one picture a comedy and the other a drama. The number of prints sold of the split-reel decreased substantially and forced us to the conclusion that if we were going to succeed as film-makers, we would have to take the final step in defiance of the trust and make only westerns, which meant we would have to work exclusively around Fort Lee and Coytesville, New Jersey. Both Kessel and Baumann agreed that now was the time to sink or swim.

We had acquired a story with the unlikely name of *The True Heart of An Indian* and had hired an actor, who also had done some work with the Biograph, to play the Indian character lead. The actor was to help in directing the picture, too. Our favorite historian says the actor in question was Charles French, but this is incorrect, for it was Charles Inslee, who wore a black wig parted in the center with two braids that reached below his shoulders. He was costumed in a breechcloth, giving him an excellent

opportunity to display his fine physique. Again we used Evelyn Graham as the leading lady, and for realism and color, we added two authentic Indians to the cast, Young Deer and his wife Red Wing.

We followed the practice of the other independents and employed a tough-looking fellow named Al Richard whom Kessel found for us through some old bookmaker friends. Richard weighed close to 225 pounds, stood over six feet tall, and at first glance looked very much like a prizefighter. His job was to stand by the camera to discourage anyone from getting too close.

The day before we were to start the new picture, I went to the laboratory in Brooklyn, told young Miller to meet me at the New York side of the Fort Lee Ferry at 125th Street early the next morning, and told him to bring four loaded camera magazines with him. The hiding place of the camera itself was always my secret and responsibility.

Making *The True Heart of an Indian*

At the laboratory the next morning I loaded the four camera magazines as instructed and took one extra roll in a can to be on the safe side. We had a stock of Lumiere film that came in 60-meter rolls (about 180 feet). It was early and nobody had yet arrived at the lab so I left a note for George Lane, the accountant, to let him know I had gone. The trip to the 125th Street ferry house took a little over an hour.

The New York Motion Picture Company had prospered. Fred was waiting and waved me into an auto he was driving. Beside him was a pretty tough-looking character, and I presumed he was the fellow who was going to stand by the camera in case we had trouble with the trust's detectives. He looked like he was well-qualified for the job. The tripod was

St. Stephen's Church in Coytesville, walking distance from Rambo's, was one of the locations used in The New York Hat *during the autumn of 1912. D.W. Griffith directed Mary Pickford.*

The grape arbor behind Rambo's, where rival film crews would gather to swap stories about new camera tricks and Patents Company detectives. This photo, dated 16 September 1900, was discovered by the present owner of the Rambo building, Gloria Limone, during renovations in 2002.

lying on the floor in the back of the auto, and the camera was up front, well covered. Fred drove on the ferry boat in line with the other cars and when we landed at Edgewater, on the Jersey side, it looked like another world to me. Separated from the busy city of New York by the Hudson River, we were at the foot of the high cliffs of the Palisades. We drove along the river road, well shaded by trees, for about three miles. Then began the steep climb up the Palisades and, as the road neared the top, the grade was so steep the car barely made it. As we leveled off, at the crest, we looked straight down Main Street, Fort Lee.

It certainly never occurred to any of us that this small rural town would soon become the movie capital of the world, years before Hollywood, California, gained that title. The trolley tracks from the ferry joined Main Street, a little beyond the top of the hill, and about four blocks farther we turned onto Fourth Street, now called Lemoyne Avenue [sic], and drove through the woods to Coytesville, a little over a mile up the river, and two

miles west from the cliffs of the Palisades. Coytesville was sparsely popu-
lated, but there were tree-lined dirt
roads, and steep, wooded hills and
forests. First Street was perhaps a mile
long, and about halfway was Rambo's
roadhouse and saloon. Rambo's is a
landmark and a historic spot of the
early moviemaking days. The saloon
then was a two-story frame building
with a wooden front porch topped by
a steep, slanted roof. There were no
poles or wires to spoil photographing
from any direction, and the dirt road
Rambo's faced had a typical western
appearance. Many a pair of ugly cowboys stepped out the front door of
Rambo's Saloon and squared off on
the dusty road for a shoot out. This
was also the place where the stagecoach picked up passengers and reported the holdup to the sheriff who
immediately formed a posse and
started the chase of the bandits.
Within a stone's throw was a tree
where each day at least one bad man
finished his life dangling from the end
of a rope.

The second floor of this now historic
place was used as dressing rooms for
most of those who became the early
stars of the motion picture business.
At the back of the saloon was a cistern
with a pump where the "Indians"
washed the Bole Armenia or reddish
water paint from their bodies after a
hard day's work. Any morning the sun
shone there would be extras waiting at
Rambo's hoping to be chosen by one
of the different companies that came
to Coytesville.

On the street in back of the saloon was
Capt. Anderson's livery stable where
the companies rented their horses,
western saddles, cowboy chaps, and
whatever else it took to make a cowboy. When we arrived, Charlie Inslee
was waiting for us in front of the
stable, and the rest of the company,
including a couple of extras all done
up as cowboys and mounted on
rented horses, ready to go. Our two

cars drove slowly, the extras following
on horses, and a short distance down
the road we shot the first scene. Since
it was our first day, things didn't go as
smoothly as Fred would have liked
them to. Having Charlie Inslee play
the character lead as well as help direct
naturally slowed things down a bit.
The transition from stage technique to
broad pantomime that Inslee insisted
upon was difficult for Miss Graham.
Fred Balshofer, always conscious of
the final effect, was anxious to select
pleasing compositions, so he insisted
that western pictures, to be successful,
must consist of a series of beautiful
pictures combined with fast-moving
action to tell a story, with as few subtitles as possible. He felt that at the
end of the picture the villain should
get the worst of it while the hero got
the girl. Inslee, as an actor first and a
director second, took a lot of convincing, but finally agreed.

The camera never moved during the
taking of a scene. The actors played
their scenes within a predetermined
area that was marked off by stretching
sash cord from wooden pegs that were
driven in the ground. It was the director's job to see that the actors played
within the confines of the marked
area. The mild friction at the start
wasn't helped by the ever-present
worry of having the Patents Company's snooper appear on the scene.
We had moved to three or four locations to shoot scenes by the time the
lunch hour came around. After pack-
ing up, we drove back to the livery
stable, where Fred stashed away the
camera, and we all walked over to
Rambo's for lunch.

At one side of the hotel was a grape
arbor, at least one hundred feet long.
Underneath it was a planked table
which ran the full length, with
benches on both sides. Several other
companies were already seated along
the table having lunch, and several
people greeted Fred Balshofer and
Charlie Inslee. The only food ever

served at Rambo's was ham and eggs,
bread and butter, coffee and home-
made apple pie. The experience of sitting under the grape arbor with
actors, directors, and cameramen and
hearing them swap stories, gossip and
ideas was delightful, and was something I enjoyed for the next few years.
Both trust and independent companies met there on the most friendly
terms. It seemed to me that the only
ones who wanted to cause trouble
were the detectives hired by the trust
and, particularly, their head man, Al
"Slim" McCoy.

I don't think I'll ever forget when Fred
introduced Billy Bitzer, then with the
Biograph, to me as "the best cameraman in the business". I listened but I
couldn't believe that anyone was a
better cameraman than Fred Balshofer. But, years later, when I saw
Birth of A Nation, *Way Down East*, and
Broken Blossoms, I at last realized how
great Bitzer was. I remember that
once he showed Fred a special magnifying glass he had placed in the long
focusing tube of his camera. Bitzer
told Fred the name of the shop where
he could have his camera altered. Fred
took his advice and claimed that the
new magnifying tube helped to make
the pictures he photographed much
sharper in focus.

We finished our lunch and went back
to work until midafternoon when it
started to cloud over. While we were
working, I don't think I ever took my
eyes off the camera and what Fred was
doing. During waiting periods there
was time enough for me to ask questions. Sometimes Fred moved the
camera a few inches one way and then
moved it again before he decided just
where the camera should be placed to
shoot the scene. When I asked him for
an explanation, he told me to remember always that there was a particular
spot that would produce the best composition. He would expound at length
as to how the clearness of the sky and
whether the background was light or

dark determined the exposure, and the direction of the sun was best when it came from three-quarters front. This, he said, gave perspective to photography.

As I look back on those formative years, I realize how extremely fortunate I was to have had such an instructor. After waiting awhile that afternoon for the sun, Fred gave up, and we quit for the day. Fred, Al Richard, and I drove to the laboratory in Brooklyn. During the return ride I began to like Richard, for he didn't seem like such a tough customer after all. Actually, he turned out to be a gentle sort of man, and when I learned he lived in Brooklyn not far from the lab, I liked him even more. He stayed at the laboratory and watched while Fred developed the negative and soon was hooked by photography. Fred was pleased with the result of the developed negative. The use of exposure meters, machine developing, and the perfection of film processing today, all make it hard to understand the satisfaction and pleasure experienced in those days when you were sure that what you had spent the day photographing had turned out satisfactorily.

On the second and last day of the picture, we had no sooner arrived to pick up the horses at the livery stable than Fred was tipped off that McCoy of the Patents Company was in town. We had built a small, slab log cabin deep in the woods in a clearing, on the theory that this was too far away to be easily detected. We worked around it all morning. After lunch the picture was finished except for one scene where the cabin was to catch fire and Red Wing was to run in and rescue Miss Graham, who was supposed to be overcome by smoke. All day each of us had his attention diverted by trying to be on the lookout for McCoy. As a consequence, when the prop man prepared the cabin for the fire, no one paid much attention to what he was doing. When everything was in readiness, it somehow seemed a better idea not to put Miss Graham inside the cabin before starting the fire. Instead it was decided to have her wait outside until the right

Horses were important to Fort Lee's economy from its days as a farming community, and continued to serve later waves of summer tourists and visiting filmmakers.

amount of fire was burning, then run in and close the door. Fred was to start turning the camera; Red Wing was to dash into the burning cabin, open the door, and help Miss Graham to safety. Both girls took their places on the sidelines close to the corner of the cabin. Inslee, who stood beside the camera some distance away, gave the prop man the signal to toss in the lighted piece of paper. As soon as the burning paper reached the cabin there was a tremendous explosion as the whole cabin burst into flames. The heat was unbearable. Both Fred and Inslee ran to the aid of the girls under the impression that both must have been injured. Luckily, both Red Wing and Miss Graham had had enough presence of mind to cover their faces and back off from the fire. I thought the camera was lost as the intense heat stopped anyone from approaching it. Al Richard, blanket in front of him like a shield, moved in and carried off the camera to safety. Nobody was aware that the prop man had literally soaked the slabs of the cabin with kerosene. Needless to say, that was the end of the day as well as of that prop man.

The girls were rushed by automobile to Rambo's, where first aid was administered at once. The news traveled fast. Some of the people around Rambo's were talking about what happened when, of all things, Fred Balshofer and Slim McCoy met face to face. Not a word was spoken. They just hesitated a moment, then passed one another. This was the first encounter since that day at the Crescent Film Company in the summer garden in Brooklyn. I pointed out McCoy to Al Richard, who was not impressed.

Fred had the front of the cabin rebuilt and shot the fire scene again with much more precaution. That finished the picture. Al Richard now worked in the lab any time we weren't out photographing. Fred cut the first print. It was then decided what scenes should be dye-toned or tinted.

Balshofer and Miller were right to be concerned about spies from the Motion Picture Patents Company. The following report is from the "New York Motion Picture" file at the Edison Historic Site in West Orange. Note that the filmmakers are traveling from Brooklyn to Fort Lee via public transportation.

J.J.D. reports:

Brooklyn, NY, Wednesday, November 3, 1909.

I arrived in the vicinity of #1535 72d St. at 7:00 A.M. At 10:00 A.M. Mr. Balshofer came out and proceeded to factory at #466 17th St., where he remained until 1:10 P.M., when he went to lunch in the Greenwood Restaurant, returning to factory at 1:50 P.M., and remained there until 6:10 P.M., when he left in company with man #1 and #2, and walked to 7th Ave., boarded car to 15th St. and 5th Ave., took train for Bath Beach at 6:20 P.M., and, as lights were all left burning in the factory, and Mr. Balshofer was on his way home, I returned to factory, and, at 6:30 P.M., a machine and stand [i.e., camera and tripod] left the factory in the care of two men, whose names, I later learned, are Maxwell Smith and Wm. Hedwig. They boarded a car for 15th St., and, on the way, I got into conversation with them about the machine, and invited them to have a drink when they got off at 3d Ave. and 15th St. During the course of the conversation one of the men, Smith, told me that they were going to Edgewater, NJ, to take some motion pictures; that he was to meet Fred Balshofer at 130th St. station at 8:30 A.M., and go over the Fort Lee Ferry at W. 130th St., and take exterior pictures; that they will stop at the Buena Vista Hotel in Edgewater, NJ, where they will eat

dinner. I received an invitation to meet them at Edgewater, NJ, and see them take the pictures.

I discontinued at 7:40 P.M.

Reported,

New York, 11/4/1909. N.

This news report, one of the earliest accounts of location filming in a major daily, suggests just how quickly the Fort Lee area seemed to have filled up with motion picture activity. It also indicates how problems with crowd control endemic to such hit-and-run filmmaking would soon lead to more formalized production procedures and the acquisition of permanent studio facilities with the privacy of their own walled back lots.

WOES OF THE MOVING PICTURE MAN
SCENES THAT NEVER COME BEFORE THE PUBLIC
–
AN OPEN AIR PERFORMANCE

(from the *New York Times,* December 19,1909, p. SM 11)

The fields and woods about historic Fort Lee, just across the Hudson, are the scene nowadays of a continuous performance of extremely animated, open-air theatricals. On almost any fine day one many enjoy historic pageants, sham battles, tragedies, comedies, and the bill is changed daily. A few motorists are attracted to this region and they, with the native population, form the only audience.

The manager of all these one-night,

or, rather, one-day, stands is the moving picture man. Here one may see the premier performance of scores of dramas which later will be repeated in thousands of darkened halls all over the country. The delights of a first night at the theatre are nothing, however, to those of a real, living, moving picture show.

To watch the staging and rehearsals of one of these open-air dramas is to go behind the scenes with a vengeance. A wide assortment of properties is kept on hand in a near-by barn. The stage is shifted from place to place to take advantage of the natural setting. The actors and actresses dress and make up in tents which are pitched near the stage selected for the day's performance.

The native population has become accustomed to bands of Indians yelling and dashing about the roads and by-paths, to troops landing on the river bank, to dancing villagers, and every variety of battle, murder, and sudden death at their very doors. It sometimes happens, however, that a stranger chances upon the shows, to his unbounded astonishment, and complications follow.

The moving picture impresario has not alone all the troubles of this craft to encounter, but he must guard against interference as well. The performances rarely go off smoothly despite every precaution.

Within a few days an animated scene from the French Revolution was enacted, for instance, beside the River Road. A guillotine had been erected and a howling mob assembled about it. The "execution" was going forward in the most lifelike manner. The long film was speeding smoothly through the camera. The dramatic moment arrived. The condemned man, with the priest beside him, ascended the scaffold. The chorus waved their arms, swaying to and fro.

Just at this most inopportune moment

an automobile swept around the curve of the road, and several ladies it carried suddenly found themselves face to face with this exceedingly realistic picture. They broke into wild, piercing screams. The automobile stopped. The excitement was too much for the chorus. It stopped its performance then and there, and turned, even to the condemned man and the priest, to look at the automobile. The motorists saw their mistake in a moment and sped away. But the film was ruined.

Another day the entire company met at the picturesque stone church which crowns the Palisades for an old-fashioned wedding ceremony. Some one connected with the church had agreed to allow the procession to form in the church and leave it, in full costume to the rattle of the moving-picture machine.

After many rehearsals the final performance was commenced. Everything was moving finely. The bride in all the loveliness of her property bridal veil and paper orange blossoms was walking with becoming timidity down the steps.

Suddenly, without an instant's warning, several excited figures rushed into the picture. A wild scene of confusion followed. The groomsmen tried to eject the strangers. An unseeming [sic] struggle ensued. All this was recorded with pitiless exactness by the moving-picture machine. Another film was ruined past hope.

When the confused crowd of bride and groom, bridesmaids and groomsmen, in eighteenth century costume was separated from the strangers, it was found that they were Trustees of the church who had their own ideas of moving-picture shows. Arguments were useless. They pointed out that the stage clergyman, for all his white wig and sanctimonious expression, was of no sect permitted in their church.

Many remarkable films are made from time to time by these chance interruptions which, needless to say, the public is not allowed to enjoy.

Two Little Rangers, *filmed by Solax in the summer of 1912. Note the activity on the Hudson River shoreline in the distance.*

By the end of 1907, the French film giant Pathé-Frères was selling twice as much film in the United States as all of George Eastman's domestic customers put together, and that year opened a large factory in Bound Brook, New Jersey in order to better manage this business. Pathé established an American production unit in 1910 with the intention of making films in the American style for the local market. Before the opening of its Jersey City studio two years later many of these were westerns, civil war pictures and comedies, often shot in Fort Lee, including *White Fawn's Devotion, The Girl from Arizona,* and *Under Both Flags.* The "girl from Arizona" who rode to the rescue in Pathé's first American production is generally thought to have been Pearl White in one of her first screen roles. Kalem, which also made films in the open in Fort Lee before building its own studio in the area, agreed that New Jersey was a perfectly appropriate western locale. Note the fascination with cliffs and "precipices", uncommon in Hollywood westerns, but not in those shot in Fort Lee.

"THE GIRL FROM ARIZONA" (PATHÉ)

(from *Moving Picture World*, May 28, 1910, p. 889)

A thrilling story of Arizona life, with considerable love, a good many Indians, some cowboys and a man about to be burned at the stake when he is rescued. The most thrilling scene, and one of the most thrilling ever put into a motion picture, is the illustration of a fall down a steep cliff. It is so natural that one holds one's breath, quite as one would to see an actual fall of that sort. The entire picture is alive with human interest, and the audience is ready to applaud the girl whose bravery saves her lover from death by alarming the cowboys who go to his rescue. The pictorial features are of the same high quality that are characteristic of the Pathé's mechanical department. It is unnecessary to say more, except that Pathé's American company of producers have scored a headliner in their first picture.

KALEM INDIAN STORIES POPULAR

(from *Moving Picture World*, June 25, 1910, p. 1099)

Just what was the special attraction in the Kalem Indian stories puzzled us for some time. Now the secret is out. They are as historically correct as they can possibly make them and the scenes are carefully selected with a view to realism. Before a Kalem director puts on a play he is provided with a correct description of the costumes and an understanding of the customs of the particular tribe of Indians gathered from the most authoritative sources. What matters it if the actors disport themselves in the mountains of New Jersey instead of the wilds of Arizona or New Mexico. Rocks and trees are rocks and trees anywhere and our impression of a Kalem picture was convincing – at least as to the details of setting. And it ended with a weird scene of a band of Indian marauders committing themselves to the Great Spirit and leaping to death over a great precipice rather than fall into the hands of the enemy. Yes, the precipice was real, and the leap was real, and because the life-net far below is out of range of the camera the thrills that are dear to the heart of the exhibitor will make *The Cheyenne Raiders* as popular as other Kalem stories.

PATHÉ'S AMERICAN COMPANY MAKING GOOD

(from *Moving Picture World*, July 30, 1910, p. 246)

When Pathé Frères first proposed to make pictures in this country, exchangemen and exhibitors awaited their first American release with interest, for they knew that if Pathé Frères could produce good American subjects with the same photography and finish that they placed in their French films, they would have some great features for their audiences. They were not disappointed. The first release of an American production by Pathé Frères was *The Girl from Arizona* on May 16, just two months ago. This was followed by some fine features, the best of which have probably been *The Flag of Company H, The Great Train Holdup*, and *White Faun's Devotion*. But Pathé Frères with their well-known energy and push are never satisfied, and are always striving for something better. They are now announcing for early release some American productions that they state far excel those mentioned above. The most pretentious is *Under Both Flags*, announced for release on Wednesday, August 3. This is a tale of the civil war portrayed in the most realistic manner and staged regardless of expense. The story is a good, interesting one and the battle scenes are most vividly shown. They will release on Friday, July 22, a Western drama, *The Cowboy's Sweetheart and the Bandit*, which is full of snap and go, and which is as good a Western picture as was ever projected on the screen. Two full reel comedies are also slated for release. *Tommy Gets His Sister Married* will appear on Friday, July 29, and *Her Photograph* on Saturday, August 5. Both of these are crackerjacks and full of original situations that are sure to please. This last film is especially good and has won great praise from some of the film men who have seen the sample.

Although Edison's spies continued to haunt the area around Fort Lee in the winter of 1910, most filmmakers had already taken off for warmer climes. D.W. Griffith's Biograph company, for example, had left for California on 19 January. Nevertheless, the detective agencies continued to file their daily reports.

Date: Jan 22nd 1910
Subject: Fort Lee
Opr. No. 2
Report on Case Number 222 –

"I went to the Buenevista Hotel, Fort Lee, and engaged a room. The proprietor informed me that there has not been any party over there taking pictures since Christmas, and that these people always stop at his hotel on their way over. He also told me that the Indian woman Gwanda Mohawk and family are away on the road, and he does not know of any other people living there that pose for pictures. He said the parties take pictures at the Old Mill, The Red Gate, and Coytesville, about three miles from his place. I then found out how to get to these places, and in the P.M. remained around the hotel to see if I could pick up more information, but there was only two or three men came in and they did not know anything about pictures."

Date: Jan 23rd 1910
Subject: Fort Lee
Opr. No. 2
Report on Case Number 222.

"I covered the Fort Lee ferry from 8:30 A.M., and at 1:30 P.M. went in café near the ferry where the parties sometimes stop. I talked with some people in there, and was told there had been no one taking pictures over there for some time and they thought the picture people are waiting for clear weather. They spoke of two men who posed and who live in Fort Lee, but these two have not been seen around lately. I was further informed that the companies that come over now to take pictures are the Edison Co., the New York [Motion Picture Co.] and a firm from Philadelphia, and they bring their own actors with them from New York.

I then went to the Old Mill, Red Gate, and Coytesville, and talked with people I met around and they said they had not seen any pictures taken for some time. I then returned to hotel and remained around the place trying to pick up something more. Will visit the cafe near ferry again and have a talk with the proprietor [sic]."

Pat Powers, another independent producer, had established a studio at 241st Street and Richardson Avenue, once a training headquarters for New York's Mounted Police. Joseph A. Golden was his "stage director", and Ludwig G.B. Erb the technical manager. The "Italian camera" they are said to be using may have been the Bianchi, not an import, but an American model designed to avoid Edison's key patents. Although Powers could film both inside his studio and up on the roof, he still traveled to Fort Lee when the need arose; Pearl White would be his new star that year. Mr. Standish continues to provide inside information.

Date: Jan. 24th 1910
Subject: Powers Co.
Opr. No. 2
Report on Case Number 222.

"As per instructions I went to the Power's Co and covered the place to pick up Mr Erb if he went out to take pictures.

At 1.45 P.M. I received word from Mr. Standish that they would not take pictures on the outside today as they were taking them inside the building.

I then returned to Fort Lee where I learned there had been no party over there today taking any pictures.

Date: Jan 26th 1910
Subject: Powers Co
Opr. No. 2
Report on Case Number 222

"I arrived at the Powers Co at 9 A.M., and covered said place until 11.30 A.M. when I was informed by Mr. Standish that they would be ready to take a picture very soon. At 11.45 A.M. I found them taking pictures on the roof of the building. They were taking two acts of a play with two different cameras. Mr. Erb ran one camera and some other man ran the other.

About 1.10 P.M. they finished and went inside. They took a western picture, Mr Goulden [sic] acting as stage manager. Shortly afterwards Mr Standish informed me that they would not take any more pictures today so I went to our office. The camera Mr Erb ran looked to me like the Italian camera. I climbed to top of a private house near the factory and took several snap shots of the Powers Co plant and the company on the roof. From our office I returned to Fort Lee where I found there had been no one taking pictures today."

The 2 February report contains a curious error: the Buckbee Detective Service identifies Harry Salter as managing a Biograph company in Fort Lee. In fact, Biograph had already left for California, and Salter and his wife, Florence Lawrence, were no longer working for them, but for Laemmle. Did Buckbee simply assume this was the Biograph company because he had seen Salter with them previously? Or did the crew purposely misinform him, recognizing him as a spy, by claiming that they were Biograph – a Patents Company member?

Date: Feb 2nd 1910
Subject: Power's Co.
Opr. No. 2
Report on Case Number 222

"I went to Edgewater, NJ, and had a talk with the hackman at the ferry who takes the picture parties to the grounds they use. This man told me that he had taken a party this morning to Coytesville, that he has lived in Edgewater for twenty five years and never heard of any place called the "spring". I then took a carriage to Coytesville where I found the Kalem Co taking a picture with a Warwick camera. Mr Worten was the manager.

"I then returned to Fort Lee where I found another company taking a picture on the street. I got into a conversation with this crowd and found they were the Biograph Co, Mr Salter, manager. I then went to Old Mill, Red Gate, and the pond but saw nothing of a third party, and no one in the neighborhood of the Old Mill ever heard of any spring near there. I also asked in café and the trolley starter but they all said there is no such place. All these people said the two above companies were the only two that came over from New York today. I then covered the boats until 4 P.M., but saw nothing of any other company.

It seems to me that the different companies are starting out again in Fort Lee, and it might be a good idea for me to go over there again for a few days and board."

On 16 March Edison received more bad news when the Buckbee Detective Service reported that someone was about to open "a factory", in Fort Lee. The term generally meant a laboratory, but might also refer to a studio. Where was this place? Could they have meant Mark Dintenfass's Champion Studio in Coytesville? Or perhaps the Dramagraph Company, run by a pair of exhibitors named Shaw and Sherwin, whose first two films, *Beyond Endurance* and *Only a Jew*, were screened for the trade in July? *Moving Picture World* reported on July 31 that Dramagraph "has adapted premises in a convenient section of New Jersey at Fort Lee, where, amongst agreeable surroundings, they have every opportunity for making good studio and out-of-door pictures." But a few months later Dramagraph was out of business and this same paper noted on November 26 that their "plant on the Palisades" was for sale. And how did Pierce Kingsley, late of the Carson Company, fit into all this?

Date: March 16th 1910
Subject: Fort Lee
Opr. No. 2
Report on Case Number 222

"Reporting at the Fort Lee ferry at 9 A.M. I watched same until 10.30 A.M., then went across to Fort Lee, the Red Gate, Old Mill and then to Coytesville where I found the Kalem Co taking pictures. This was the only company that took pictures over here today.

I also learned that a company is getting ready to open a factory at Fort Lee, and the man who has charge of it is known as Percy [i.e., Pierce] Kingsley. The hotel people at Coytesville told me that there were five different companies over there last week making pictures."

By the summer of 1910 filmmakers were swarming all over the Fort Lee area, and nickelodeon audiences had begun to recognize most of the area's familiar landmarks. So much so, in fact, that "Jersey scenery … became a synonym for mediocrity." Here are two examples from an ongoing critical debate regarding the use or misuse of New Jersey locations, well before there was any sustained production in places like Hollywood.

"SPECTATOR'S" COMMENTS

(from *The New York Dramatic Mirror*, July 16, 1910, p. 18)

An anonymous writer in *The Film Index* reports that a party of motion picture men fell to discussing the film reviewer of *The Mirror* the other day, somebody evidently having a grievance. Neither *The Mirror* nor the reviewer is mentioned by name, but the coat, though a bad fit, can be put on, so here goes. According to the anonymous writer the picture men preferred to accuse *The Mirror* film critic of having a grudge against New Jersey.

"It is the failing of the critic in question", says the writer, "when there is nothing in the picture itself deserving of condemnation or of damnation by faint praise, to say: 'We recognize the familiar Jersey scenery.'" *The Film Index* writer then goes on to argue that "a train robber or an Indian desperado can be hunted as successfully in the Orange Mountains as in the Rockies", providing the "simulation" be good, or in other words providing the scenes chosen for backgrounds bear a reasonable resemblance to scenes where the events are alleged to have taken place. "To hold a picture up to scorn because of its Jersey affiliations is not criticism", concludes this critic of the critic, "neither is it worthy of the critic to thusly sneer at an otherwise satisfactory effort".

Wonder who it is that feels that his corns have been stepped upon? But no matter, whoever it is he can get no argument here on the proposition that if the scene alleged in the picture story

(Above): Trolley lines were carved out of the Palisades at the turn of the century, stone blasted from the cliffs later being used to construct massive embankments to support the roadways.

These embankments often doubled as prison or fortress walls for imaginative filmmakers. Barney Gilmore in Brennan of the Moor (Solax, 1913).

story. Therefore, hurrah for New Jersey! Likewise hurrah for every other State in the American Union. But hurrah for New Jersey in particular because its peculiarities are distinctive. There are many special things to the credit or discredit of New Jersey – some of them good and some of them bad, but all of them distinctive. There are Jersey "skeeters", referred to by the *Film Index* writer, which are said to be the worst on earth; there is Jersey justice which used to be called the surest and swiftest in the whole broad land, and there is "Jersey lightning" which is good or bad according to one's individual view. So many excep-

be properly "simulated" it makes no difference where the photograph be taken. New Jersey is just as good a State as any other in which to make motion pictures, always providing the appropriate scenery and atmosphere be found to fit the

tional things, therefore, have come from New Jersey that we on this side of the river without having any particular grudge against the State have come to use the word Jersey as meaning something distinctive. Probably we have abused the privilege, but that is another story.

In the matter of motion pictures, in which the *Index* writer claims New Jersey leads the world, it has been unfortunate that nine-tenths of them have been photographed over practically the same ground – not often the Orange Mountains as he mentions, but the familiar Palisades and the country round about, so that the peculiarities of the landscape are recognizable by picture spectators the world over. When *The Mirror* reviewer has seen these backgrounds peopled with cowboys or Mexicans or some other inconsistent class of characters he has referred to them as Jersey scenery. From this he has come to apply the term sometimes in a general way to obvious Eastern scenery when used in picturing a story requiring scenery of another sort, but never when in his best judgment he considered that the scenes even measurably "simulated" the backgrounds intended. Correct "simulation" has been his one guide. If his judgment has been bad that is again another story.

It is quite natural in the continued discussion of a subject, such as the criticism of motion pictures that a writer should coin new terms to indicate certain things that might otherwise require a number of words to explain. *The Mirror* reviewer has unconsciously invented or adopted a number of expressions of this class and Jersey scenery is one of them, the Jersey, as shown above having a special distinctive significance of its own. Therefore when the complaining film maker sees these words in the review of one of his films purporting to tell a story alleged to be located in some remote part of the country or the

world, he may consider that in the reviewer's opinion the maker has failed to "simulate" the desired scene. Nor will the reviewer go bail that the scene he so designates is really located in New Jersey. It will be enough that it looks like some other part of the world. This may be bad literary practice, but is it criticism that is "unworthy of the critic?" Hardly, although it may seem a bit unfair to New Jersey whose complaint should be against the picture makers who have made so many films in familiar Jersey scenes that the word has become a by-word. And this leads to the thought: If, as our friend of the *Index* alleges, "it is a matter of statistics that New Jersey raises a larger crop of pictures to the acre per annum than any other State in the Union or any country in the world, for that matter", is it not about time the picture makers commenced breaking new soil? Isn't New Jersey about worked out or at least that part of it which they have been cultivating?

MOTION PICTURE BACKGROUNDS

By H.F. Hoffman

(from *Moving Picture World,* July 30, 1910, p. 287)

An article by "Spectator" appeared in the *Dramatic Mirror* of July 16 in which he feels called upon to defend himself against certain objections that had been raised by some of his previous remarks about "Jersey Scenery". The "Spectator's" previous remarks were inspired by his being obliged to witness many so called "Western pictures", in most of which he was able to recognize the old familiar Palisades in the background.

He perceived in this constant repetition a monotonous lack of versatility, and made bold to say so on several occasions. In fact, it bored him so that he began to use the term "Jersey Scenery" in a sarcastic sense, and, later on, as a matter of evolution, he fell into

the very unjust habit of applying the term "Jersey Scenery" to everything in the way of bad backgrounds, regardless of whether the subject was photographed in Staten Island, Long Island, New York or Connecticut. He made the term general, and with him "Jersey Scenery" became a synonym for mediocrity, in much the same sense that we speak of Connecticut tobacco, or Michigan watermelons, or American Swiss cheese.

When the vials of wrath were opened and poured upon his head, the "Spectator" came to the front with as much grace as possible and made public confession of his sinful habit. Moreover, he did a penance by stating that New Jersey abounds with some of the finest natural scenery on God's footstool, and by so doing he and I are still friends, for I live in Jersey and had he not made this retraction I would never speak to him again. He said at last what he should have said at first: that the scenery is there all right, if the film makers would only go after it, but they found it so convenient to skip just across the river from New York to the dear old Palisades for anything and everything that required an outdoor background, that the interior stood neglected and unexplored; which is true to a great extent.

The scenery is there, surely enough, and it is only begging for some man to come along and find it. The same is true of the localities north, south and east of Manhattan. But the man never comes. The idea of keeping a man out scouting for pretty scenes strikes the average manufacturer as scandalous waste of money. He is willing to pay a scenic artist and stage carpenter their union scale from sheer force of circumstances, but with regards to natural scenery, the usual way is to pack the whole troupe into a motor bus and send them off to select their own backgrounds, and the result is usually much wasted time and indifferent or accidental success.

(Left): In Oscar Micheaux's Symbol of the Unconquered *(1920), the heroine's log cabin in the wild west is represented by a Fort Lee tourist cabin.*

(Above): Undated snapshot of a visitor enjoying one of the tourist cabins built near the shore for summer residents.

Mack Sennett's claim that Keystone shot its first films in Fort Lee has recently been discounted by historians, who note that the initial Keystone releases were obviously shot in California. But as this early recollection makes clear, those first Keystone films were so poor they were never released, leading Sennett and his players to decamp for California, where they started again from scratch. Mabel Normand's recollections (see page 161) support Sennett's claims. Historians reviewing Sennett's 1934 "as told to" autobiography, *Father Goose*, cringe at the faulty memories and wholesale fabrications which litter the manuscript. But Sennett's recollections only four years after the fact have more claim to reliability, despite his later distortions of many of the same stories. In this version, for example, his cameraman merely "looked like a Russian grand duke." By 1934 it seemed more interesting to describe him as an actual Russian named "Sergei Androv." Twenty years later, in a subsequent autobiography, Sennett decided that the name "Ishnuff" was even funnier. He never changed the part about Fort Lee, however.

SLIM DAYS IN KEYSTONE BEGINNINGS
Starting A New Company Not So Easy As It Seemed – Coupons Very Soon Displaced Pawnbroker's Slips, However.

By Mack Sennett

(from *Moving Picture World*, March 10, 1917, p. 1535)

The motion picture has been galloping ahead at such a gait that to be ten years old is to be almost archaic. Five years ago we were just beginning work at the little shanty on the vacant lot where the Keystone studio finally grew and thrived.

Mr. Kessel, Mr. Baumann and myself had started the company on a shoestring. I had been acting in and directing comedies with another company. It looked very easy to start a new company. All you had to do was to hire some actors and put them up in front of the camera and take the picture and – well, there you were. We found out afterward that it wasn't so easy.

All the money we had between us went up with one puff and whoof. Then we had to start in pawning the family jewels. And sometimes it looked as though there wouldn't be enough family jewels to last.

The first pictures we took were at Fort Lee. We didn't have any studio and

panies which regularly work under the Keystone banner.

Carl Laemmle's IMP Company continued to film in the Fort Lee area even after the creation of Universal and the establishment of studios on the west coast. King Baggott and Herbert Brenon were two of IMP's most significant east coast employees during this period. The account of Baggott's unfortunate experience in a minor cave-in reveals that Laemmle's people had been filming in the same part of "Leonia Heights" for four years, long before their August 1914 purchase of land here for a great new studio. Fort Lee's significant Italian population occupied the lowest rung in terms of local ethnic status (the 1915 census counted only two "negro" inhabitants, for example). Where blacks or Asians are all but invisible, Italians appear in many Fort Lee films in a variety of stereotyped roles, ranging from "Black Hand" gangsters to religious fanatics. Note how these two "news" stories characterize the local Italian population as superstitious and "resentful" (for reasons not specified), unreliable workers who occasionally need to be replaced by Irishmen.

there was one scene where we just had to have an interior; so we borrowed the house of some worthy and kind hearted Christian, and moved the furniture out on the front lawn and used that for an interior.

We had a cameraman who looked like a Russian grand duke and talked as though he had invented the art of photography. We didn't have money enough to hire automobiles, so we went out in the street cars or walked. We pinned our faith to this photographer with the grand air. When his first pictures were developed we found that he had spoiled the whole thing and that all our watches and our sacrifices had gone for nothing.

We braced up our flagging courage and moved the company out to Los Angeles and started the Keystone studio. In those days I was author of all the scenarios, actor, director, film cutter and telephone girl.

Oddly enough the first pictures we made at the new studios were also failures.

Just when things looked to be so bad they couldn't get much worse they turned and began to improve. Finally the grand day came when our first dividends were paid.

The Keystone now has one of the largest studios in the world. We have a big electric light studio where eight or ten companies can work at once. There are two big outdoor stages, a wild west town, a swimming tank and all manner of equipment for the accommodation of the twenty-one com-

BAGGOT BURIED ALIVE WHEN BANK CAVES IN

(from *The Universal Weekly,* December 1, 1913, p. 17)

King Baggot, leading man and director, and Frank Smith, his assistant, were partially buried when several tons of dirt from a bank, under which they were working during the taking of a scene in *King, the Detective*, a detective drama soon to be released, caved in upon them. The accident, which occurred at Leonia Heights, NJ, Wednesday, November 19, resulted in Mr. Smith having to undergo treatment for a sprained back and Mr. Baggot to nurse a lacerated hip. It took the combined efforts of a score of Italian workmen, employed previously to dig a tunnel under the embankment, nearly half an hour to shovel the gravel and wet clay away sufficiently to extract the two men.

The cave-in was attributed to a heavy rain which fell during the night before. The ground of clay and gravel, had absorbed the water to a depth of several feet, loosening it to such an extent that, when the men's bodies jarred it from below, the earth came down. It is likely that had the tunnel run several feet deeper into the embankment, the accident would have proven fatal for both Mr. Baggot and Mr. Smith.

The scene in which the accident occurred is one of the important and unique features of Mr. Baggot's detective drama, directed and acted by himself. There had to be a tunnel leading from an old recluse's house to a neighboring clump of bushes. Instead of faking this scene in the studio, as is wont with many directors, Mr. Baggot conceived and carried into execution the idea of shaving off an embankment and digging a tunnel along its side. A gang of workmen were sent out to Leonia Heights last week and spent several days in completing the task. Owing to the mishap, the taking of the picture was delayed for several more days.

A peculiar incident connected with the affair was the finding of a coffin by the workmen buried in the ground on the day previous. Mr. Baggot not having arrived on the scene, the local authorities were called in and made an examination of the find. Inside the box was found a rotted dummy of a man. When this was brought to the attention of Mr. Baggot he recalled the burying of the same coffin four years ago by Bob Daly and Tom Ince during the making of an Imp comedy, *Uncle Pete's Ruse*. Director Daly also recalled the incident. However, the Italians insisted that the find was a bad omen and Mr. Baggot experienced trouble in forcing them to finish the work. On the following day, when the accident happened, the Italians threw down their shovels and refused to continue. A crowd of Irishmen had to be secured to dig away the earth and reconstruct the tunnel.

RELIGIOUS PROCESSION STAGED FOR BAIRD-SHAY FEATURE
Priests, Prelates, Acolytes And Devotees Parade For "The Price Of Sacrilege".

(from *The Universal Weekly,* February 14, 1914, p. 16)

Fort Lee hasn't got over talking about it yet; and this is remarkable, because Fort Lee is supposed to be "picture-broke". But then *The Price of Sacrilege* is a remarkable film drama, and its taking, last November, involved some stunts that no combination other than Director Herbert Brenon and the Imp-Universal Company would dare to attempt.

One of these was the staging of a scene depicting an Italian religious procession, with priests and prelates, acolytes and flower-girls, censor-swingers and devotees, and a great palanquin whereon rested a gorgeous jeweled figure of the Madonna, under a canopy of embroidered silk. The devotees comprised some two hundred denizens of Little Italy in the picturesque garb of their father-land. The whole procession was headed by an Italian band of twenty pieces, playing appropriate music.

A representative of the *Universal Weekly* at the invitation of Mr. Julius Stern, superintendent of the Imp studios, witnessed the taking of this great scene and was wonderfully impressed with the reverence with which the subject was approached, and the skill with which the atmosphere of devotion was maintained.

The Price of Sacrilege is the first of the new features that Herbert Brenon has attempted since his return from Europe, and it is certain to add materially to his fame. It gives unusual opportunities to those excellent stars – William Shay, Leah Baird and William Welch. Even in *Absinthe* Miss Baird does no finer work than her portrayal of the heartless Italian coquette. Real tears well up in her eyes and flow down her cheeks as she seeks repentance for her sins at the shrine of the Madonna, and the mad scene in which she is the center of a vicious mob is realism rampant.

This latter scene was taken in the heart of Fort Lee's Italian quarter, and additional realism was secured by the commingling of the resentful inhabitants.

William Shay and William Welch enact some of the best work of their careers in contrasting types of Italian manhood, both victims of the wiles of the coquette.

You should see *The Price of Sacrilege*. It will thrill you.

Once a student at Seton Hall, Raoul Walsh had already worked as a sailor and a cowboy when his skill with a rope earned him an offer from Pathé. After a stint with D.W. Griffith, he would return to Fort Lee as one of William Fox's most valuable directors. Walsh maintained a larger-than-life aura throughout his career, and, as may be the case here, was not the sort of person to let the truth get in the way of a good story. It is not clear, for example, who 'Emile Couteau' actually might have been.

Magnifique!

By Raoul Walsh

(from *Each Man in His Time* (New York: Farrar, Straus & Giroux, 1974) pp. 64–69

I expected to be given a horse when I showed up at the Union Hill [Jersey City] studio bright and early next morning but I did not see one. I was still wearing my handmade boots, and a gardenia I had picked up on my way to the ferry. I also brought two of my ropes, just in case. I was a hybrid, somewhere between a bum and a banker.

They shoved a contract at me calling for three pictures, and I signed it. The director, a Frenchman named Emile Couteau, told me to get some makeup on. I had no idea what he was talking about until one of the actors took me in tow and showed me what to do. I got my baptism of grease paint and felt half Indian, half idiot.

There was not even a Shetland pony in that first picture. It was called *The Banker's Daughter,* and I played the part of a bank clerk in love with the president's only female offspring. The daughter was played by Dolly Larkin, an ex-burlesque queen who liked her kisses long and tonguey. The plot would have sickened a third-grader. One Sid Carter, a teller, also in love with the heroine, embezzled a tidy sum and – you guessed it – laid the blame on me. My light-o'-love was in the bank when the law arrived to arrest me, and she did a routine job of sobbing and wringing her hands while her father delivered a telling tirade on the wages of sin. The janitor saved me; he had seen the teller taking the loot. Clinch. Handcuffs on the villain. The heroine came to me, threw her arms around me, kissed me, and ran her tongue down my throat.

After the day's work, Dolly Larkin complimented me on my debut in the motion-picture business, and invited me to come to her apartment, which was just around the corner from the studio, boasting that she was a great cook.

Her apartment, small but cozy, included a living room, kitchen, and bath. My hostess had told me she would cook one of the best spaghetti dinners I had ever had. While preparing the meal, Dolly helped herself to a couple of good slugs of bourbon. When she finally placed a huge dish of spaghetti in front of me, she opened a can of tomatoes and poured it over the delicacy. She was still nipping the bottle when we sat down to talk.

Dolly related that she had been in burlesque for three years, from which she had derived her "dramatic experience". Then she joined the circus and for her it was really rough going. "I had to frig everyone in the outfit to become the leading acrobat", she confessed. "I closed the show by doing cartwheels all around the arena while the band played 'Dixie'. I insisted on that number because I was born in Atlanta. I got top billing as the 'star acrobat'." She was an acrobat all right, which I discovered later in her bedroom ….

After we made *A Mother's Love* over in Brooklyn, we returned to the Fort Lee Meadows on the Jersey side where we had shot *The Banker's Daughter*. It was an inspiring location, full of history, sprinkled with farmhouses and stone fences dating from the 1700's. Biograph and other motion-picture companies often filmed alongside us. The 125th Street ferry provided cheap and handy transportation.

My third picture, besides putting me in the saddle again, freed me from the threat of Dolly Larkin's trained tongue. During the filming of *A Mother's Love*, I had been almost frightened to eat when she played opposite me in the love scenes. *Paul Revere's Ride* was scheduled after I had complained that, although I had been hired to ride, so far I had only seen horses in the pasture. Couteau got hold of the French scriptwriter, who said, "*Alors*, I will write you a horse story. I will put childrens in wagon. Horses will run away and you will leap" – he jumped about a foot off the ground – "on your own horse, take your rope, and catch the runaways before childrens fall over cliff".

"Bullshit!" I interrupted him. You don't have a horse fast enough to catch a one-legged whore on crutches and you know it."

"Then I will do another story about a famous American – how you say – jockey named Paul Revere."

He did, and I galloped all over hell shouting, "The British are coming!" interspersed with a few cowboy whoops and Indian yells to make it more realistic. Before I got the part, Couteau made sure that I could handle a horse. When I took a running lope at him and stopped short about a yard away, he shook the dirt off his jacket and nodded. He may have been getting some of his own back when he made me gallop between the car

Raoul Walsh.

tracks. The steel was slick and we skidded a couple of times. I took occasion to remind him that streetcars were not running in 1775 and he pulled rank on me. "Who direct these pictures, you or me?" he shouted. "You", I told him, "but I'm riding in it". The thought suddenly struck me that if this man could please the public with his bumbling, perhaps I might direct a picture myself one day.

He had me riding across country, jumping ditches and stone walls, to rouse the outlying farmers. The last sequence included galloping through a cemetery. My horse was a good jumper but, when I put him at the tombstones, he clipped a few and knocked them over. The sheriff showed up while Benjamin Franklin and John Adams were patting my back and calling me a brave patriot. The sheriff arrested everybody and Pathé was fined twenty-five dollars for malicious mischief and had to replace the fallen tombstones. There was the final love clinch at the end of the picture, which audiences of that day demanded. My film sweetheart, miffed because my ride had kept her from attending a dance, now forgave me, melting into my arms and calling me her hero.

Pathé's next production was a picture that was never made. It was to have been a one-reeler and the plot was simple. It called for the villain to throw the heroine out of a boat on a lake and for the hero (me) to dive in and rescue her. The sun was fighting a bank of cloud and it looked like rain, but Couteau was in a hurry. The cameraman set up at the edge of the water and the villain rowed himself and the heroine about fifty yards out. Then he shipped the oars and they began to

'I have never met a director who did not hate clouds.' Cartoon by Thornton Fischer in the Moving Picture World, 23 June 1917, p. 1929.

quarrel. My cue came when he grabbed her. As soon as she hit the water, I dived in, clothes and all, and rescued her with the approved flounderings and gaspings because she was supposed to be half drowned. When I towed her to shore, there was a lot of shouting going on in excited French around the camera. I finally managed to understand that the film magazines had been left behind and the scene had been shot on an empty camera. On top of that it began to pour, our transportation broke down, and we had to walk home in the rain.

Near Fort Lee there was an inn called Oliver's that claimed to have been founded before the Revolution. It was popular with the picture people not only for the cheap food and good service but because it was a handy place to rest while waiting for the sun to shine. At the time, sunlight was the only illumination available. No sun, no picture. I never met a director who did not hate clouds.

Christy Cabanne (pronounced Cabannay) was a good man in every way. He had been a good actor, worked up to be a good director, and became my good friend. He was directing for Biograph when I met him.

Our meeting took place while I was working with a rope in front of Oliver's after an overcast had interrupted shooting. A few people were watching me and I had not noticed the sharp-eyed man in the cap and tweed jacket until he spoke. "That's the best rope-handling I ever saw". His tone seemed to hold genuine interest. "Where did you learn how?"

I was good and I knew it, but something about the way he said it pleased me. I stopped long enough to tell him a little about my friend Ramirez and my experience as a cowboy in Texas. When he introduced himself and suggested lunch, we went inside and he mentioned that he had seen the cemetery action. "You sure know how to handle a horse. Too bad about the nosy sheriff."

The upshot of our meeting was that he offered me a job. "I can use a man like you. How do you stand with Pathé?"

"*Revere* was my last picture." I did not think it was necessary to mention the one that was never filmed. "They may have another one in mind. I don't know."

"Good. Don't sign a new contract. And consider yourself hired. All right?"

I had seen a couple of Biograph pictures. They were not as God-awful as the stuff Pathé was making. Both the directing and the acting seemed superior to anything I had so far experienced.

When he left, after telling me to report to the Biograph studio on Fourteenth Street the next day, I took stock of myself, feeling a bit chesty and pleased with the way things were shaping. Not many weeks earlier, I had been riding that treadmill [in a stage production of *The Clansman*] and feeling more foolish each night. Now I was a full-fledged actor and had played the lead in three motion pictures, terrible as they were. When I got home that evening and Father asked me what I had done with my day, I mumbled something inane because my head was full of dreams.

Even when established in their own studio, as this unnamed "Fort Lee" company appears to have been, location shoots in and around Bergen County were still highly entertaining for the locals. It was as if the circus had come to town – unannounced – and every nearby porch (or tree) offered the best seat in the house.

$50,000 MOVIE MADE IN PALISADE ON SATURDAY CALLED "RENEGADE" WITH INDIANS, COWBOYS AND GIRL

Big Film Concern Gets Use of The Playgrounds For a New Thriller Soon To Be Out – The Director Gets On a "High Horse", But Doesn't Ride – Hot Day Made Horses Slow in Stampede, and Ample Fun For Small Boy Audience

Troubles Of Director Test All His Patience

(from *The Palisadian*, July 24, 1915, p. 2)

A film company was making movies in Palisade last Saturday morning down by the Playground. One of the scenes was enacted on the outfield of the baseball diamond. The movie is to be called *The Renegade* and required some eighty odd horses and men and women and Indians galore. The particular scene on the Playground represented a large company of cowboys at the noon hour when they had turned their horses out to graze while they partook of their typical meal amid the nowhere-to-be-found shadows of the prairie grass all around where the horses grazed. The stunt was to get one of the cowboys killed, or so badly knocked in the head that he could be tied with ropes where he would be out of the running on the fight thing. While the horses were all turned loose in center and left fields, a man with a

In the Great Big West, *shot in Fort Lee by Champion, 1911.*

red bandana around his head like a roman gladiator, a regular delight as a horseman, went out and rounded up the horses preparatory to a stampede, the stampede to be pulled by the Indians as soon as others of their number were satisfied that the poor cowboy was all dolled up with ropes and was bleeding from the devilish tommyhawk he had been nailed over the head with by two Indians who crawled up and hit him kerplunk behind the left ear while he was standing beside his roan pony thinking of his gal at the brook down in old Kentucky. It did look awful cruel to see the chap get that blow and keel over, but just at that moment the stampede was to be commenced. The director, who had a fog-horn voice, stood just north of the grand stand, and was giving orders in stentorian tones that could be heard clean to Fort Lee.

"Start 'em! Start 'em!" he cried to the man supposed to give the cue to the Indians when to lope in on their mustangs, and stampede the horses. The day was so tarnation dadburned hot that the horses ridden by the Indians just about crawled across the foul line of left field, and then the director let out a ripping "hellfire there!" meaning that the speed was execrable. Then he recalled them and the thing had to be done over again.

"Say", the director added, as the Indians, painted white riders from the Hippodrome, one of the attendants told *The Palisadian* man, "who hired those men? If you half-naked idiots don't do better than that this time I'll send you back through the streets of New York without your clothes." They were dandy riders and, like all good Indians, were riding the datratted ponies without saddle or bridle, and it was no cinch on a hot day that would melt the stirrups off the saddles the other riders used, to make the ponies get-up-and-git in the soft earth and tall grass.

"Maybe a couple of six shooters would make them move faster", suggested the man with the red bandana on his forehead.

"Yes, that's it – that's it!" answered the director. "Get a dozen guns – get a dozen, I say. And then if the damned things don't move, shoot 'em."

At the next rally the Indians got away with more speed and the camera man said it was good, so the thing was not done again. "You tell that rider with the big belly", said the manager, "he's too d – -d fat for an Indian. Don't let him in the pictures any more."

Before the Playgrounds scene was put on, there had been several other pictures made of cowboys and Indians defiling down paths through the forests of Montana near Palisade just west of the Playgrounds. There had been run off one of the swellest things ever done in a movie. A company of U.S. Soldiers had been rung in on the scenario, and were supposed to rescue the cowboys and a beauty of a girl from the Indians. The long line of soldiers got started just as Charles Logan, who is a Justice of the Peace, had heard a gun shot near the ball field, and he started out to catch the perpetrator of the deed, for pistol shooting is not allowed in the woods of Palisade.

"Heh, there! heh, there!" called out an Italian assistant to the movie man, "Fo' godamightysaka gitabackadere meesta, and don't spoila deesa fillum – gitaback! gitabacka – oh, pleasa, meesta, gita backa!"

When the local judge saw that only blanks were being fired, he stood back out of line with the camera and at that moment one of the most beautiful young girls in the world, about eighteen, rode down the hill on a naying steed at breakneck speed. She was a radiant beam of sunshine and if she comes out in the pictures as beautiful as she looked that morning in Palisade, the fame of that film is accomplished. The director had been watching the flying squadron from the side lines, and when he saw a rickety old horse with ribs that looked like slats, ridden by a man made up for a yankee farmer, a regular downeaster, and who was so wobbly in the saddle that he almost fell out, the director almost had a spasm. "Take that man out of the picture", he roared "and never let him ride again – never let him in again! D'ye hear? Take him out!"

The beautiful girl who had made such a conquest of the picture, and who heard only the end of the sentence, rode up to the director, and with almost tears in her eyes said, "Please, I rode the very best I could. Indeed, I did. I'll do better next time, I am sure I shall."

The director went up to her horse and patted her on the arm. "It wasn't you. You're all right, I never saw anything done better. It was the jumping jack out yonder." The girl turned in her saddle and asked, "Which way is Fort Lee? I'll go back to the studio. Do I come back Monday?"

"Yes, Monday, if it's a fair day. Come right here again", said the director very admirably.

"If that fellow had sworn at that girl as he did the others", said the reporter, "I believe I would have turned on him. My! but she is a beauty."

So you, Mr. Bailey Millard, and other movie fiends, when you see the *Renegade* advertised, go to it and watch for the stampede and the pretty girl. And you can tell that it was made on the Palisade Playgrounds because one of the horses in the stampede concluded he'd take a wallow just when the Indians started shooting, and the director swore like a Chinese sailor.

Rudolph Valentino, Norma Shearer, Ronald Colman and Mary Astor all worked in the Fort Lee studios as extras or bit players before establishing themselves in Hollywood (as had Raoul Walsh). For Ben Lyon, later the star of *Hell's Angels* (1930), the economics of extra work simply did not add up. Adolphe Menjou, who like Walsh started out on a horse, did better for himself in Hollywood as the sophisticated "man of the world" in films like *A Woman of Paris* (1923) and *Morocco* (1930).

LIFE WITH THE LYONS

By Ben Lyon and Bebe Daniels
(London: Odhams Press, 1953), pp. 56–59.

I found film work at Fort Lee, then the Hollywood of the east where some rather primitive studios had been set up, and I made the journey to New Jersey with just enough money in my pocket for the bus fare, and little else.

In this crazy aura I worked in a Pearl White picture, in some of the saloon mob and dance scenes. A generation has arisen since those days who do not even know what the name Pearl White, and the film serial, stood for. "*To Be Continued Next Week*" now falls on deaf ears.

Audiences went to the cinema week by week to follow the installments, to watch the same hero, the same heroine and the same gang of villains fighting it out amid raging torrents, on cliff tops or in blazing buildings. Always each episode would end on a note of terror, maybe with the heroine bound hand and foot to the railway track, and

an express train approaching. Then the screen would black out, and the legend appeared: *To Be Continued Next Week*. Little wonder the audiences came faithfully, week by week. The suspense was terrific and the very titles bring back these days to every man and woman over forty who will recall the weekly cinema-going habits to see what would happen next week to poor Pearl in *The Exploits of Elaine*, *The Laughing Mask* or *By Force or Trickery*.... Other stars took part in these serials, too. I recall Ruth Roland in *The Red Circle* and *The Sacred Tiger*, Leon Bary in *Ravengar*, and yes, even Houdini in *The Master Mystery*.

When people today talk of "Hollywood", as though it is synonymous with motion pictures, it is worth remembering that it was New York (strictly speaking, Fort Lee, New Jersey) which gave birth to heroics such as *The Perils of Pauline*, wherein heroines and villains brought the public to the cinemas far more regularly, alas, than is the habit today.

The genius of the French director, Louis Gasnier, allied to American

crime fiction and production methods, gave the public the first screen death rays, mad scientists, international criminals, bandit hunts, and some of the best trick photography in the movie world.

My little contribution to the Pearl White serials was all too brief, and when my mob scenes were over and paid for the cashiers' office did not hang out the sign for me "*To Be Continued Next Week*". I began to make the rounds of agents, looking for work. When you are just seventeen, unknown and at the start of your career, that has its heartbreaking moments. My father's reluctantly given permission to tolerate one ham in the family (and Mother's practical expression of this by giving me fifty cents a day while I went the rounds of the agents) gave me a boyish but determined notion that I would get work, and I would keep myself.

It did not take long to discover that the two things were quite incompatible. If I did not succeed in getting work then I was out of pocket each day by precisely the fifty cents Mother had given me. If I did get work I was still fifty cents in the red. How? Let me explain.

The maximum pay for extras at Fort Lee was two and a half dollars a day, and for the dancing scenes I had to wear a dress-suit. As most movie actors then did not have one of their own, this item had to be hired. It cost me two dollars a day.

The bus-fare to and from Fort Lee was thirty cents. My lunch (even at most economic standards) could not easily be less than twenty cents, and my dinner at night fifty cents. Even at those prices, in those days, I did not eat so well! And, as you can see, I was exactly fifty cents in the red for each day I worked.

It was hard work, too. We started on the set at eight in the morning, so, of course, had to be there some time before that to get dressed and made-up. At nights I would be making the rounds of the agents again, or getting ready for the following day's work – maybe.

Like all exciting jobs, it had its compensations. Norma Shearer, later to become so great a star, and the wife of the late Irving Thalberg, production head of the entire M.G.M. organization, was one of my earliest buddies. We made the rounds of the agents many time together. She was a scrawny kid in those days, but she made her mark in the film world sooner than I did, and I looked up to her as an angel and a genius.

The day came when this angel and genius accepted my invitation to lunch. Norma, will you ever forgive me? I can remember that day now as clearly as yesterday. I can remember how lovely you looked. I can't remember what you wore, but I remember what you ate.

Oh, the shame and embarrassment of it all!

I had for so long been pestering you

to come out to lunch, and when at last you accepted I had the grand sum of four dollars in my pocket. Trying to impress you, I suggested we should lunch at Claridge's, one of New York's swankiest restaurants.

In a glamorous dream I escorted you to the table, and the waiter produced the menu. While you were busy reading the long list of luscious things to eat, I was busy reading the prices.

You thought: hors d'oeuvre, lamb chop, peas, ice-cream.

I though: ninety cents, one dollar fifty, forty cents, fifty cents....

All the while I was figuring out if I had enough money, and if there would be sufficient margin out of the four dollars for me to order anything. Not that I cared about going hungry, for I was in my seventh heaven just to be in your company; but I didn't want to look like a silly ass sitting there with only a glass of water.

You called it a day after the ice-cream. I ordered a cheese sandwich....

I'm certain that waiter hasn't forgotten me, as not doubt it was the only lunch he ever served at Claridge's without getting a tip.

THE CRUCIAL TEST

By Adolphe Menjou and M.M. Musselman

(from *It Took Nine Tailors,* New York: Whittlesey House, 1948, pp. 51–54)

Back in those days, when you applied for work, you always left a few photographs with the casting director and filled out a blank telling all about yourself. You gave your name, address, telephone number, height, weight, age, color of eyes and hair, etc. Then there was a check list of outdoor and indoor accomplishments. It went something like this:

WHICH OF THE FOLLOWING
CAN YOU DO? PLEASE CHECK.

Swim
Dive
Play Tennis
Row a Boat
Ride Horseback
Play Ping-pong
Drive a Car
High-jump
Pole-vault
Box
Wrestle
Dance
Play Golf
Turn Handsprings

And there was always a blank space for special accomplishments such as wiggling one's ears or taming lions. An actor in search of a job always checked the whole list. He never could tell when he might get a job because he had said he could row a boat, dance, and turn handsprings.

That was how I got an important part in *The Crucial Test* [1916]. I had said I could ride horseback when actually I'd never been on a horse in my life. But when they hired me, nobody mentioned that I would have to ride a horse. The casting director only explained the best features. He said it was a wonderful part – I was to be a Russian aristocrat, a colonel of the Czar's Hussars, aide to His Excellency the Grand Duke Boris. Naturally no actor could resist a part like that.

The producer of the picture was William Brady, Broadway entrepreneur and prize-fight manager, and the star was Kitty Gordon, a well-known Broadway actress. The scenario was written by Frances Marion, who is still a prominent screen writer.

After I had landed this prize part of the aide to Grand Duke Boris, they fixed me up with a uniform and a karakul hat and told me to report to Fort Lee for outdoor scenes. I knew it would be cold on location, so I borrowed a raccoon coat from a well-

heeled friend. Everyone admired the coat so much that I wore it in all the outdoor scenes, thus lending a bizarre note, to say the least, to the general Russian atmosphere of the picture.

I should have guessed, when we were ordered to Fort Lee, that there was riding to be done, for that was where most of the western pictures were made. Tom Cameron had a stable of horses there that he rented to the various picture companies. Tom was known as "The Captain of the Fort Lee Cossacks", and any actor who got on one of his horses and stayed on for the shooting of one complete scene automatically became a member of the outfit. It didn't matter whether you lost your stirrups and had to put a full nelson on the horse in order to stay in the saddle; as long as you stayed on top you were a Cossack.

When we got to Fort Lee, John Ince, the director and a brother of Thomas Ince, one of Hollywood's greatest producers, explained the script to me; it was then that I discovered that I was supposed to actually ride a horse.

"Do I have to?" I asked. "I'm not feeling very well today."

"What's the matter?" demanded Ince. "Don't you know how to ride a horse?"

He had a look in his eye that made me think that perhaps he had a cousin who did know how to ride a horse, so I lied glibly, "Of course I can ride a horse. I was a member of the Black Horse Troop at Culver."

I was stuck then. And when they introduced me to my horse, he immediately took a kick at me. I guessed at once that he didn't like me and I knew I didn't like him. He was one of the imitation cow ponies they used in westerns. The aide to the Grand Duke should have had a more distinguished-looking animal, but here were no distinguished-looking animals available.

Finally Cameron and a couple of other fellows helped me get on the horse and I rode over to the head of my detachment of hussars. It was wintertime and I was cold; so was the horse. He was anxious to get going and

Adolphe Menjou in A Hungry Heart *(World-Peerless, 1917), one of his many unbilled "dress extra" appearances. Director Emile Chautard is trying to make Piermont, NY, stand in for Venice.*

warm up. We waited around for fifteen minutes for the cameraman to get ready to shoot, and each minute the horse grew more and more restless and I grew more and more uncomfortable. The saddle on which I was sitting was made of wood, and it practically cut me in half. The picture had to be authentic so the saddle was strictly Cossack; but the horse was from Brooklyn.

Finally we got the signal to charge. We stood up in our stirrups and galloped toward the camera shouting and yelling. I was in the lead, trying to look like a man who had been born in the saddle. But suddenly a gust of wind blew a newspaper in front of the horse. He shied and tossed me right over his head into a snowbank.

Director Ince had quite a time getting me to climb back on that horse, but I finally did and we shot the scene. As I was climbing off, the horse took one more kick at me and caught me right in the place he was aiming for. That was too much. I sneaked up behind him and kicked him back in the same spot.

The Crucial Test turned out to be a horrible picture, but I had a good part. I could hardly wait for it to be released so that I could see the reviews. Finally the big day came. I rushed out and bought all the papers. But only one reviewer said anything about me, and he got my name wrong:

> "J. Herbert Frank, in the role of the pursuing Grand Duke, gave a very forceful performance and was ably assisted by Adolph Merjou as his companion ...."

> When *The House of Fear* was shot, Universal was not quite ready to shift production from Manhattan to their new Fort Lee studio. In this case, that meant a night time location expedition in early winter. But the transportation problems described here would only increase when the studio opened, as entire studio populations were forced to make the journey across the Hudson and up and down the Palisades every day.

IN SEARCH OF "THE HOUSE OF FEAR"
Universal Company Leads A Midnight Expedition To The Wilds Of Jersey

By Hanford C. Judson

(from *Moving Picture World,* December 5, 1914, pp. 1388–1389)

This is no account of a motion picture, but a true story of an adventure and it will relate how Julius Stern, Eastern Studio Manager, and Paul Gulick, manager of the Universal's publicity, took a band of scribes across the Hudson in a horseless hill-climber to see a motion picture made. If the motion picture in question had been any ordinary affair, or even the best work of art that the greatest producer ever conceived, it is more than probable that not one of the scribes would have ventured to such a lonely place at the dim hour of midnight. It wasn't art that drew the reviewers, but mechanics. The picture that we saw is going to be a good one, the Imp Company had Stewart Peyton [i.e. Stuart Paton] on the job – he's a genius for wild tales – and Peyton had with him a cast of strong players – four of 'em looked like "cops". But the reason of our going was that the picture was going to be taken out of doors in the darkness,

against the brightly lighted windows of a dwelling – a thing not tried successfully before – and was to make clear not merely the outlining of the figures, but their faces – the story depends on the spectator's recognizing the individual faces and seeing the emotions and characters of them.

We met at the Mecca Building [Universal's offices at 1600 Broadway]. The chauffeur was entrusted with a piece of paper with 50 Edgewater Road written on it and warned by Mr. Stern not to lose it; he didn't. We crossed the river and climbed the hill and went some along the road. Soon there were branches overhead. Dickinson opened the window of the limousine to let the smoke out and the cold night come in. Denig, out in front with his fur collar turned up, saw a light in the distance. The machine came as near as possible to it and it was proposed that Dickinson ask the way; but he wanted a guarantee against the dog. Someone held up a lamp at the window and we learned that we had passed our objective and had to go back. Back a bit there was a road with possibilities both ways. We turned to the left and soon passed three who said they were strangers, but assured us that there wasn't no numbers around there. A bit further at another house we learned that we should have turned to the right. After covering a good bit of the State in the other direction we were told again that our way was straight back with no turning, so back we went and came to a stop between two buildings – one looked like a castle and stood on the left, and toward this Denig and Condon made their way. They hadn't gone far before Julius Stern, looking to the right, noticed a bright light in the distance and recognized the haunted house.

As we drew near the building – it is a little innocent home by day, but lives a double life – was blinking at us with all its eyes. Some natives had crept up and half hidden in the trees were wondering; for the house seemed half-stupid with some fiery liquor that it had been imbibing and would wink a lot of bright light out through one of its windows for a moment and then blinking this would open another. Perhaps something excited it for all at once it sent a smash of light through all its eyes at once, stood fairly pouring out brightness. We went inside where it was like day – the people outside saw our black outlines as we melted into what was like a furnace.

The place was fitted out with plenty of sets of the new Panchrome Twin Arcs, each with its reflector and two bright arc lights which can be used on either direct or alternating current and need only fifteen amperes on a 110-volt circuit. The great value of this outfit is that as many of them as a director needs can be carried along and used, as in this case, in any home where current is to be had. Each set with its rheostat weighs nineteen pounds and can be lifted about – in one scene the electrician took one up a tree to play the role of a full moon. The light they give is very clear and bright. They are made by Allison & Hadoway, 235 Fifth avenue, New York City. John W. Allison soon arrived to see whether his new arc-set was doing all that he hoped.

Stewart Peyton, the director, had a pretty young lady there named Francis Nilson, whom he assured us was an heiress with heart disease and that she had been brought by her villainous uncle, Howard Crampton, to the House of Fear solely to be scared to death. He had the ugliest old hag you ever saw in or out of pictures to keep her and a queer creature with boar's tusks among his teeth was to be seen prowling about the premises. This

was a lunatic we were told named Allen Holubar. Paul Gulick says he was loaned to the Imp Company by the warden of Sing Sing for the evening; but we suspect that some one up in 1600 Broadway has a pull with the devil and that the creature didn't come from Sing Sing at all. Mr. Gulick is a strictly truthful man; but – at this point Director Peyton ordered us all outside.

We stood across the road where Eugene Gaudio, the Imp camera man, had placed his instrument. After the director had looked over his house and disposed of one or two of his electricians who wanted to look out of the windows, he shouted, "Come out". The door slowly opened, a flood of light behind it silhouetting the outline of the girl, her piteously disheveled hair falling in long curls around her shoulders, and as quickly closed. The moon, that the electrician had taken up the tree, its light hidden from us by its tin hood, now beamed effulgently on the girl's frightened face. She was fright to her finger tips and greatly appealing as she crept softly across the piazza and darted away to the left; but she wasn't to escape. Now the bright door opened again, and what issued from it will be seen later by spectators on the film and they will also see how the hero (Hobart Henley) of the tale came in time to see the girl taken back through the door, the hag holding it open for them to bring her in, and how he caught Boar's Tusks looking through the window and how he brought the cops.

These scenes were taken and taken again. Twelve solemn notes, by distance mellowed, came from a church tower in the Valley. The newspaper men stood in the frozen grass. One found a grape vine and we all skipped

rope waiting for the "spread" that had been promised. One remarked, "What the New Jersey are we here so long for" and then Gulick talked turkey. We piled into the limousine of John Allison, the head of Allison & Hadaway, makers of the bright portable lights, and motored to a lager beer saloon about a mile away. It was a joyfully dirty looking place and there were some thoroughly delightful neighborhood characters lounging at the bar or seated at the little tables, half finished beer glasses, cards and blue and white chips around them. The pool table had a rent in it a foot long and the cues lacked tips. The Ladies' Epiphany Circle has an advertisement of a fair on the wall and there is to be a barn dance given by some other charitable association. Under a table lay a St. Bernard dog weighing about 250 pounds, and Mr. Gulick said that it was to be used to help frighten the heroine; but didn't say that it was to be used in *The House of Fear* picture.

There was a big empty dance hall back of the barroom and a table in it set for dinner – fricassee of chicken, fried potatoes, beets, peas, coffee and other things, all very good. Some one put five cents into a sideboard like contraption at one end of the room and it began to bellow a tune. We don't know what the tune was, but the scribe sang "Tipperary" to it. The machine didn't like the song; for it whined and howled all through the next nickel's worth and the host came in and asked if we didn't like the dinner. It ended like the famed party of Hans Brightman and the automobile took us all back to the city. The scribe thinks the pictures will be good, but knows that Paul Gulick is a good entertainer.

3.
Biograph

The American Mutoscope and Biograph Company (by 1909 simply Biograph) was already filming exteriors in the Fort Lee area when D.W. Griffith began directing for them in 1908. The following list, based on Biograph production records, is adapted from *Film Beginnings, 1893–1910* (American Film Institute, 1993) and *The Griffith Project, 1911* (British Film Institute, 2001). Although their records no longer listed locations after 1911 (and even the existing records are obviously incomplete), Biograph continued working in the Fort Lee area, shooting exteriors here for such landmark films as *The Lonely Villa, The New York Hat*, and even *The Musketeers of Pig Alley*.

The amount of location footage could vary widely in such films, and even a one-reeler might have been filmed in several different communities (for example, *The Son's Return* [1909] was shot in both Coytesville and Leonia). Interiors would normally have been shot in the Biograph studio at 11 East 14th Street, but there is some evidence that open-air stages were constructed on location when the need arose.

THE BIOGRAPH COMPANY IN FORT LEE, 1898–1911

FORT LEE
1898

An Overloaded Donkey; A Ride on a Switchback; "Rushing the Growler;" "Teeter Tauter;" The Wheelbarrow Race; When the Girls Got Frisky; The Last Round Ended in a Free Fight.

1905

The Gentlemen Highwaymen; The Fire-Bug.

1908

The King of the Cannibal Islands; The Man and the Woman; The Fatal Hour; Balked at the Altar; The Girl and the Outlaw.

1909

The Welcome Burglar; The Cord of Life; The Girls and Daddy; Tragic Love; The Curtain Pole; The Hindoo Dagger; The Salvation Army Lass; The Lure of the Gown; A Sound Sleeper; A Troublesome Satchel; The Drive for a Life; 'Tis an Ill Wind That Blows No Good; One Busy Hour; The Cricket on the Hearth; What Drink Did; Eradicating Aunty; The Lonely Villa; The Peach Basket Hat; Tender Hearts; Jealousy and the Man; A Convict's Sacrifice; What's Your Hurry?; Two Women and a Man; In the Window Recess; A Trap for Santa Claus; In Little Italy; To Save Her Soul.

1910

Her Terrible Ordeal; All on Account of the Milk; The Call; The Course of True Love; The Final Settlement; The Affair of an Egg; In Life's Cycle; The Proposal; Simple Charity; Love in Quarantine; Not So Bad As It Seemed; Happy Jack, a Hero; Turning the Tables; The Lesson; White Roses.

1911

Bobby, the Coward; The Sorrowful Example; Dan, the Dandy; The Revenue Man and the Girl; The Old Confectioner's Mistake; The Making of a Man; Her Awakening; The Adventures of Billy; The Long Road; The Trail of Books; Through Darkened Vales; A Woman Scorned; The Miser's Heart; Sunshine Through the Dark; A Terrible Discovery; The Voice of the Child; For His Son.

COYTESVILLE
1908

A Night of Terror; The Outlaw; The Kentuckian; The Call of the Wild; Taming of the Shrew; The Guerrilla; A Woman's Way.

1909

A Rural Elopement; The French Duel; The Son's Return; Jones' Burglar; The Better Way; The Open Gate; The Death Disc: A Story of the Cromwellian Period; The Test.

1910

The Honor of His Family; His Last Burglary; The Final Settlement; A Midnight Cupid; Her Father's Pride; The House With the Closed Shutters; An Old Story with a New Ending; When We Were in Our Teens; Mugsy Becomes a Hero; The Masher; The Broken Doll.

1911

Conscience; The Rose of Kentucky; Swords and Hearts; The Eternal Mother; Italian Blood; The Battle; A Tale of the Wilderness; Billy's Strategem.

EDGEWATER
1904

Personal.

1909

At the Altar; His Duty; A New Trick; The Children's Friend; Getting Even; The Broken Locket; The Awakening; Pippa Passes; In the Watches of the Night; Through the Breakers; In a Hempen Bag.

1910

The Rocky Road; The Dancing Girl of Butte; The Passing of a Grouch.

SHADYSIDE
1908

The Stage Rustler; The Fight for Freedom; The Black Viper; The Greaser's Gauntlet; The Feud and the Turkey.

1909

The Renunciation; The Heart of an Outlaw.

PALISADES
1907

The Fencing Master

PALISADES PARK
1905

The Barnstormers.

1906

The Lone Highwayman.

1909

Trying to Get Arrested.

CLIFFSIDE
1908

The Zulu's Heart.

ENGLEWOOD
1909

Was Justice Served?; Nursing a Viper.

1911

The Failure.

GRANTWOOD
1905

The Nihilists.

1908

The Invisible Fluid.

LEONIA
1905

The Summer Boarders.

1908

Her First Adventure.

1909

The Son's Return; The Little Teacher.

1910

His Wife's Sweethearts

FAIR HAVEN
1902

The Accomodating Cow; Alphonse and Gaston; Belles of the Beach; Biograph's Improved Incubator; The Lovers' Knot; Milking Time on the Farm; The Polite Frenchman; A Seashore Gymkana; A Spill; "A Sweet Little Home in the Country", Will He Marry the Girl?

GUTENBERG
1900

Little Sister; Love in the Suburbs; A Water Duel.

LITTLE FALLS
1908

Farmer Greene's Summer Boarders; Fun in the Hay; The Romance of an Egg; The Redman and the Child; The Red Girl; The Planter's Wife; A Woman's Way.

1909

They Would Elope; The Heart of an Outlaw; Pranks; The Restoration.

Linda Arvidson, who was married to D.W. Griffith throughout his years at Biograph, published the first extensive memoir of filmmaking in Fort Lee in 1925. Like the other actresses who worked for him, she never lost the habit of referring to her director as "Mr. Griffith".

WHEN THE MOVIES WERE YOUNG

By Linda Arvidson Griffith
(New York: Dutton, 1925, pp. 82–89, 77–80)

Before the first winter drove us indoors there had been screened a number of Mexican and Indian pictures. There was one thriller, *The Greaser's Gauntlet* [1908], in which Wilfred Lucas, recruited from Kirke La Shelle's "Heir to the Hoorah" played the daring, handsome, and righteous Jose. And Wilfred Lucas, by the way, was the first real g-r-a-n-d actor, democratic enough to work in our movies. That had happened though friendship for Mr. Griffith.

They had been in a production together.

For a mountain fastness of arid Mexico, we journeyed not far from Edgewater, New Jersey. No need to go further. Up the Hudson along the Palisades was sufficiently Mexico-ish for our needs. There were many choice boulders for abductors to hide behind and lonely roads for hold-ups. New Jersey near by was a fruitful land for movie landscape; it didn't take long to get there, and transportation was cheap. Small wonder Fort Lee shortly grew to be the popular studio town it did.

In those days, movie conveyance for both actors and cargo was a bit crude. We had no automobiles. When Jersey-bound, we'd dash from wherever we lived to the nearest subway, never dreaming of spending fifty cents on a taxi. We left our subway at the 125th Street station. Down the escalator, three steps at a bound, we flew, and took up another hike to the ferry building. And while we hiked this stretch we wondered – for so far we had come breakfastless – if we would have time for some nourishment before the 8:45 boat.

A block this side of the ferry building was "Murphy's", a nice clean saloon with a family restaurant in the back, where members of the company often gathered for an early morning bite. We stuffed ourselves until the clock told us to be getting to our little ferry-boat. Who knew when or where we might eat again that day?

"Ham", Mr. Murphy's best waiter, took care of us. As the hungry break-fasters grew in number and regularity Mr. Murphy became inquisitive. Mr. Murphy was right, we didn't work on the railroad and we didn't drive trucks. So, who, inquired Mr. Murphy of Ham, might these strange people be who ate so much and were so jolly in the early morning?

And Ham answered, "Them is moving picture people".

And Mr. Murphy replied, "Well, give them the best and lots of it".

We needed "the best and lots of it". We needed regular longshoremen's meals. Outdoor picture work with its long hours meant physical endurance in equal measure with artistic out-pourings.

Traffic lining up at the 125th Street ferry terminal in New York, late 1920s. The elevated train station Arvidson refers to was quite a few blocks inland.

George Gebhardt going for a walk on the Palisades in Biograph's The Cord of Life, *shot in January 1909.*

Mabel Normand and Harry Hyde playing a scene on the ferry in Biograph's Her Awakening, *shot in August 1911.*

Ham is still in Mr. Murphy's service, but his job has grown rather dull with the years. No more picture people to start the day off bright and snappy. Now he only turns on the tap to draw a glass of Mr. Volstead's less than half of one per cent.

"But I want to ask you something", said Ham as I started to leave."

"Yes?"

"Would you tell me" – hushed and awed the tone – "did Mary Pickford ever come in here?"

"Oh, yes, Ham, she came sometimes."

"I told the boss so, I told him Mary Pickford had come here with them picture people."

Whether Mary had or hadn't, I didn't remember, but I couldn't deny Ham that little bit of romance to cheer along his colorless to-days.

Ham's breakfast disposed of, we would rush to the ferry, seek our nook in the boat, and enjoy a short laze before reaching the Jersey side. At one of the little inns along the Hudson we rented a couple of rooms where we made up and dressed. Soon would appear old man Brown and his son, each driving a two-seated buggy. And according to what scenes we were slated for, we would be told to pile in, and off we would be driven to "location".

"Old Man Brown" was a garrulous, good-natured Irishman who regaled us with tales of prominent persons who, in his younger days, had been his patrons. How proud he was to tell of Lillian Russell's weekly visit to her daughter Dorothy who was attending a convent school up the Hudson!

Speaking of "Old Man Brown" brings to mind "Hughie". Hughie's job was to drive the express wagon which

transported costumes, properties, cameras, and tripods. In the studio, on the night preceding a day in the country, each actor packed his costume and make-up box and got it ready for Hughie. For sometimes in the early morning darkness of 4 a.m. Hughie would have to whip up his horses in front of 11 East Fourteenth Street so as to be on the spot in Jersey when the actors arrived via their speedier locomotion.

Arrived on location, Johnny Mahr and Bobbie Harron would climb the wagon, get out the costumes, and bring them to the actor. And if your particular bundle did not arrive in double-quick time and you were in the first or second scene, out you dashed and did a mad scramble on to the wagon where you frantically searched. Suppose it had been left behind!

Hughie had a tough time of it trucking by two horsepower when winter came along. So I was very happy some few years later, when calling on Mr. Hugh Ford at the Famous Players' old studio in West Fifty-sixth Street, NY,

Other filmmakers took advantage of Fort Lee's scenery as well, even if they did have to shoot intimate scenes like this one in public parks. The Marked Card *(Champion, 1913).*

Griffith had favorite locations in Fort Lee to which he returned again and again. The Miser's Heart, *shot in October 1911, made use of a favorite storefront on Main Street.*

now torn down, to find Hughie there with a comfortable job "on the door".

David Griffith was always overly fastidious about "location". His feeling for charming landscapes and his use of them in the movies was a significant factor in the success of his early pictures. So we had a "location" woman, Gene Gauntier, who dug up "locations" and wrote scenarios for the princely wage of twenty-five dollars weekly. Miss Gauntier will be eternally remembered as the discoverer of Shadyside. Shades of Shadyside! with never a tree, a spot of green grass, or a clinging vine; only sand, rocks, and quarries from which the baked heat oozed unmercifully.

Miss Gauntier's aptitude along the location line, however, did not satisfy her soaring ambition, so she left Biograph for Kalem. Under Sidney Olcott's direction, she played "Mary" in his important production *From the Manger to the Cross* [1912], and was the heroine of some charming Irish stories he produced in Ireland.

The Redman and the Child [1908] was the second picture Biograph's new director produced, and his first Indian picture. Charles Inslee was the big-hearted Indian chief in the story and little Johnny Tansy played the child. The picture made little Johnny famous. He had as much honor as the movies of those days could give a child. Jackie Coogan was the lucky kid to arrive in the world when he did.

When the New Theatre (now the Century), sponsoring high-class uncommercial drama opened, Johnny Tansy was the child wonder of the company. Here he fell under the observant eye of George Foster Platt and became his protégé. And so our Johnny was lost to the movies.

We went to Little Falls, New Jersey, for *The Redman and the Child*, which, at the time, was claimed to be "the very acme of photographic art". I'll say we worked over that Passaic River.

Same angle on the same storefront as in The Miser's Heart. *Mary Pickford in* The Narrow Road, *shot in June 1912.*

The Cord of Life, shot in January 1909, used the same storefront, this time without the awning.

Mr. Griffith made it yield its utmost. As there was so little money for anything pretentious in the way of a studio set, we became a bit intoxicated with the rivers, flowers, fields, and rocks that a munificent nature spread before us, asking no price.

My memories of working outdoors that first summer are not so pleasant. We thought we were going to get cool, fresh air in the country, but the muggy atmosphere that hung over the Hudson on humid August days didn't thrill us much. I could have survived the day better in the studio with the breeze from our one electric fan.

On Jersey days, work finished, back to our little Inn in a mad rush to remove make-up, dress, and catch the next ferry. Our toilet was often no more than a lick and a promise with finishing touches added as we journeyed ferry-wards along the river road in old man Brown's buggy.

Were we ever going anywhere but Fort Lee and Edgewater and Shadyside? I do believe that first summer I was made love to on every rock and boulder for twenty miles up and down the Hudson ... .

Before the summer was over we went to Seagate and Atlantic Highlands. It wasn't very pleasant at Atlantic Highlands, for here we encountered the summer boarder. As they had nothing better to do, they would see what we were going to do. We were generally being lovers, of course, and strolling in pairs beneath a sunshade until we reached the foreground, where we were to make a graceful flop onto the sandy beach and play our parts beneath the flirtatious parasol. Before we were ready to take the scene we had to put ropes up to keep back the uninvited audience which giggled and tee-heed and commented loudly throughout. We felt like monkeys in a zoo – as if we'd gone back to the day when the populace jeered the old strolling players of Stratford town.

Mr. Griffith got badly annoyed when

we had such experiences. His job worried him, the nasty publicity of doing our work in the street, like ditch diggers. So he had to pick on some one and I was handy. How could *I* stand for it? Why was *I* willing to endure it? He *had* to, of course. So thinking to frighten me and make me a good girl who'd stay home, he said: "Something has occurred to me; it's probable the business might get kind of public – someday, you know, you may get in the subway and have all the people stare at you while they whisper to each other, 'That's that girl we saw in the movie the other night.' *And how would you like that?*"

One saving grace the Highlands had for us. We could get a swim sometimes. And we discovered Galilee, a fishing village about twenty miles down the coast, the locale of that first version of Enoch Arden – *After Many Years* [1910].

But when winter came, though we lost the spectators we acquired other discomforts. Our make-up would be frozen, and the dreary, cold, damp rooms in the country hotels made us shivery and miserable. We'd hurriedly climb into our costumes, drag on our coats, and then light our little alcohol stove or candle to get the make-up sufficiently smeary. When made up, out into the cold, crisp day. One of the men would have a campfire going where we'd huddle between scenes and keep limber enough to act. Then when ready for the scene Billy Bitzer would have to light the little lamp that he attached to the camera on cold days to warm the film so it wouldn't be streaked with "lightning". While that was going on we stood at attention, ready to do our bit when the film was.

We weren't so keen on playing leads on such days as those, for when you are half frozen it isn't so easy to look as if you were calmly dying of joy, for which emotional state the script might be asking. What we liked best in the winter was to follow Mack Sennett in the chases which he always led, and which he made so much of, later, when he became the big man in Keystone films. The chase warmed us up, for Mack Sennett led us on some merry jaunts, over stone walls, down gulleys, a-top of fences – whatever looked good and hard to do.

Somehow we found it difficult to be always working with the weather. Though we watched carefully it seemed there always were "summer" stories to be finished, almost up to snow time; and "winter" stories in the works when June roses were in bud. Pink swiss on a bleak November day 'neath the leafless maple didn't feel so good; nor did velvet and fur and heavy wool in the studio in humid August.

But such were the things that happened. We accepted them with a good grace ….

One of our regular "extra" people was Mack Sennett. He quietly dubbed along like the rest, only he grouched. He never approved whole-heartedly of anything we did, nor how we did

For many years historians believed that The Musketeers of Pig Alley, *shot in September 1912, had been filmed on New York's lower east side. In fact, Griffith preferred to shoot his 'urban' locations away from the congestion (and shadows) of the big city. This is the same Fort Lee storefront seen in many other Biographs. Lillian Gish at left.*

Mack Sennett and Mary Pickford in The Italian Barber, *shot in November 1910, using the same storefront as in* The Musketeers of Pig Alley.

it, nor who did it. There was something wrong about all of us – even Mary Pickford! Said the coming King of Comedy productions: "I don't see what they're all so crazy about her for – I think she's affected." Florence Lawrence didn't suit him either – "she talks baby-talk". And to Sennett "baby-talk" was the limit! Of myself he said: "Sometimes she talks to you and sometimes she doesn't". Good-looking Frank Grandin he called "Inflated Grandin".

But beneath all this discontent was the feeling that he wasn't being given a fair chance; which, along with a smoldering ambition, was the reason for the grouch.

When work was over, Sennett would hang around the studio watching for the opportune moment when his director would leave. Mr. Griffith often walked home wanting to get a bit of fresh air. This Sennett had discovered. So in front of the studio or at the corner of Broadway and Fourteenth

Street he'd pull off the "accidental" meeting. Then for twenty-three blocks he would have the boss all to himself and wholly at his mercy. Twenty-three blocks of uninterrupted conversation. "Well now, what do you really think about these moving pictures? What do you think there is in them? Do you think they are going to last? What's in them for the actor? What do you think of my chances?"

To all of which Mr. Griffith would reply: "Well, not much for the actor, if you're thinking of staying. The only thing is to become a director. I can't see that there's anything much for the actor as far as the future is concerned."

Mr. Sennett had come to the movies via the chorus of musical comedy. It also was understood he had had a previous career as a trainer for lightweight boxers. If there was one person in the studio that never would be heard from –well, we figured that person would be Mack Sennett. He played policemen mostly – and what future for a movie policeman? His other supernumerary part was a French dude. But he was very serious about his policeman and his French dude. From persistent study of Max Linder – the popular Pathé comique of this day – and adoption of his style of boulevardier dressing, spats, boutonniere, and cane, Mr. Sennett evolved a French type that for an Irishman wasn't so bad. But even so, to all of us, it seemed hopeless. Why did he take so much pains?

He got by pretty well when any social flair was unnecessary; when Mary Pickford and I played peasants, tenement ladies, and washwomen, Mack occasionally loved, honored, and cherished us in the guise of a laborer or peddler. He had a muscle-bound way about him in these serious roles – perhaps he was made self-conscious by the sudden prominence. But Mary and I never minded. The extra girls, however, made an awful fuss when they had to work in a comedy with

Sennett, for he clowned so. They would rather not work than work with Sennett. How peeved they'd get! "Oh, dear", they'd howl, "do I have to work with Sennett?"

Now 'tis said he is worth five millions!

In *Father Gets in the Game* [1908], an early release, Sennett is seen as the gay Parisian papa, the Linder influence plainly in evidence.

Mr. Griffith was more than willing, if he could find a good story with a leading comedy part suitable to Mr. Sennett,, to let him have his fling. Finally, one such came along – quite legitimate, with plenty of action, called *The Curtain Pole* – venturesome for a comedy, for it was apparent it would exceed the five-hundred-foot limit. It took seven hundred and sixty-five feet of film to put the story over.

Released in February, 1909, it created quite a sensation.

The natives of Fort Lee, where *The Curtain Pole* was taken, were all worked up over it. Carpenters had been sent over a few days in advance, to erect, in a clearing in the wooded part of Fort Lee, stalls for fruits, vegetables, and other foodstuffs. The wreckage of these booths by M. Sennett in the guise of *M. Dupont* was to be the big climax of the picture. The "set" when finished was of such ambitious proportions – and for a comedy, mind you – that we were all terribly excited, and we concluded that while it had taken Mr. Sennett a long time and much coaxing to get himself "starred", it was no slouch of a part he had eventually obtained for himself.

I know I was all stirred up, for I was a market woman giving the green cabbages the thrifty stare, when the cab with the curtain pole sticking out four or five feet either side, entered the market-place. M. Dupont, fortified with a couple of absinthe frappes, was trying to manipulate the pole with sufficient abandon to effect the general destruction of booths. He suc-

Griffith and Bitzer also took advantage of Fort Lee's more rural aspects, as in this scene of Wilfred Lucas in The Failure, *filmed on Catherine Street in October 1911, just two blocks from the "lower east side" setting of* The Musketeers of Pig Alley.

ceeded very well, for before I had paid for my cabbage something hit me and I was knocked not only flat but considerably out, and left genuinely unconscious in the center of the stage. While I was satisfied he should have them, I wasn't so keen just then about Mack Sennett's starring ventures. But he gave a classic and noble performance, albeit a hard-working one.

On 8 and 9 September 1911, citizens of Fort Lee and surrounding areas turned out en masse to watch D.W. Griffith direct *The Battle*. Regardless of their familiarity with hundreds of other film productions, this event was so memorable that for decades residents would claim they had been present at the filming of *The Birth of a Nation*. Of course, the reporter from *The Palisadian* didn't recognize the director, but he did spot Charles West, a Biograph regular already well known to the locals. This article in the local Cliffside Park newspaper is the earliest known account of D.W. Griffith at work.

MAKING MOVING PICTURES
Palisadians See War Pictures Made To Order At Coytesville

(from *The Palisadian,* October 1911, p. 21)

When Palisadians want to take a peep at an imitation war game, all they have to do is to take a run up to Coytesville, and see the moving picture people engaged at the real thing. It looks even to a bystander as nearly like a genuine battle as one would care to see, the only difference being that real bullets do not sing "ping!" through the air, and there is no dodging of shells from the cannon. In all of the essentials, however, it looks like war, and it doesn't require a vivid imagination to see it that way, either. There are real soldiers in uniform, with phalanxes officered in regulation civil war garb, cannons belching forth smoke from imitation bombs, while commands are spoken aloud as soldiers lead a real charge over breastworks or through real woods. These scenes are thoroughly realistic, and are put on with as much realism and vividness as a genuine battle could show between opposing armies.

To the onlooker, however, there comes into the scene a touch of humor at times irresistible. The director of the moving picture forces has to occupy some point of vantage, and the other day when a party of Palisadians were on the side lines, as they say in football, the director was perched standing on an old stump giving orders with as much speed as a gattling gun.

"Here!" he shouted as about seventy-five men stood under a tree in a disordered bunch. "The same fellows who 'died' yesterday must 'die' today, and d – n it! you must put more life in it, too."

One of the best known characters seen in moving pictures is a young fellow named Charlie West. West plays young officer parts, the young lover and other good characters. He was walking over the battle field the other day right through the trenches, with fallen "deads" all around him. He was looking at the "deads" this way and that, turning his head and peering into their faces as though looking for those he knew. As he went over a little hillock the director called out, "Here, Charlie West! You're walking like an old woman! Get out of that, will you!"

Some of the remarks of the visitors are, also, interesting. A young lady from Palisade was watching a civil war battle scene put on. At a point where the Federals routed the Confederates by rushing a barricade, she shouted.

"Go it, boys! We whipped 'em once before – do it again!" And she spoke as she meant every word of it.

Catherine Street in 2004, looking east from the intersection of John Street. Most of the buildings seen in The Failure *are still present, although high rises loom in the background.*

BILLY BITZER, HIS STORY

By G. W. Bitzer

(New York: Farrar, Straus & Giroux, 1973, pp. 69–70, 83 –85)

The eastern sky is a sharp color in the morning, a new color in the afternoon, and each season has different light. Fort Lee, New Jersey, was an ideal place for movies, for it encompassed everything we needed, such as overnight lodging and proximity to the New York studio, and most of all, hearty breakfasts at Murphy's. We got the best photographic results in early morning, without shadows. It is then the light sharpens the distant hills and accentuates the blackness of objects in the foreground....

I will say that the motion-picture world did me a lot of good (unknowingly). I have heard many things about my work which are flattering, but which I was unaware of until I read them in print. When they said of my early photography, "Bitzer was an artist, he followed no accepted school of lighting, neither the German nor French, yet his effects were remarkable", or something along that line, I

America's first great cinematographer, G.W. "Billy" Bitzer had been filming around the Fort Lee area for years before teaming up with D.W. Griffith. Sensitive to the quality of New Jersey sunshine, Bitzer drew on natural lighting effects for his development of backlighting and other pictorial innovations (whose inspiration often came from visits to the Metropolitan Museum of Art). Within a few years he would photograph *The Birth of a Nation, Intolerance,* and other masterworks for Griffith in California. Both men returned to New York in 1919, Bitzer staying to become president of Cinematographers Local 644.

Back at the studio, Bitzer and Griffith examine some film against the light of a Cooper-Hewitt lamp.

hied myself to the Metropolitan Museum and asked one of the doormen to direct me to the French school. He finally understood me, even if I didn't know much about art. Of course I did know that the paintings with the faces coming out of deep shadows were Rembrandts. I also recognized in the Museum a picture that hung in my parlor in my childhood days, "The Angelus", which I thought was painted by Millet and never did learn until later that it was Millay. [Jean Francois Millet painted "The Angelus", "The Gleaners", and other works in the Barbizon tradition. Bitzer may mean that he was originally pronouncing the artist's name Mill-et.] Perhaps all this is irrelevant, but in my Biograph days I did, however, study closely the lights and shadows of reverse-light pictures, like "The Gleaners", with the foreshadows on the field of stubble. Even with the slow orthochromatic film, which did not permit taking faces with the light behind them (as they would come out pretty black), we succeeded at Biograph, with the aid of a huge bedsheet as a light reflector, in lightening up the faces on the screen in a reverse-lighting effect. And we even heard exclamations from the front office, "Ah, just like a Millay painting!" Their reaction was all that seemed to matter to us in those days. Let me tell you how I actually discovered this effect.

Owen Moore and Mary Pickford were seated on a bench having their lunch. I was similarly employed, close to my camera. We were over in Fort Lee on location and it was noon. Looking over at the lovers I noticed the beautiful illumination on their faces and finally figured out that it came from the reflection of the white gravel beneath their feet. I became aware of the total absence of ugly shadows that usually made hollow masks of faces on the screen. Out of curiosity I aimed my camera at them and looked into the ground glass. It sent back a misty rainbow effect, with a haze around the figures. This was caused by the sun shining into the lens. I shaded the lens with my hat and shot a few feet of film experimentally. Mary and Owen were so engrossed in their conversation they had not noticed me. Then came the call, "Back to places, everyone".

I was pleased with the test I had taken, and when I showed it to Mr. Griffith, he was delighted. The reverse-lighting effect was new and splendid. We made several scenes later and again shot into the sun, with my hat to shade the lens. In all we made three scenes without notifying the front office. The first two were great and our hopes soared, but the third was a catastrophe. We had to take the cast back to Fort Lee for another day's retakes and were advised once more to cut out the monkey business. Encouraged by Mr. Griffith, I went ahead with the experiments anyway.

To avoid another accident, I first attached a LePage glue can, which happened to be handy in my workroom, over the small lens of the camera. By cutting out the bottom, it seemed to shade the lens from all sides, solidly, and would not have a tendency to move as my hat apparently had done the third time. I adjusted the glue-can mask, using an incandescent bulb with the lens wide open, of course, to see what I was doing. Next day the conditions were different out in the sunlight. Stopping the lens down had caused the corners of the glue can to darken the corners of the square film.

The laboratory phoned me on location next day, suggesting I examine my camera. Something had got mixed up in the aperture plate, as all four edges of the print were fuzzy cut-offs. I talked the situation over with Mr. Griffith and he wasn't too upset.

"Wait until we get back to the studio", he said. "First things come first. Forget it for now."

By the time we returned to Fourteenth Street, the bosses had seen it and we were credited with an innovation. Their pleasure knew no bounds, but it became company merit, company achievement, and company property. They thought the shaded corners took away the hard edges and added class to the picture. I found with repeated tests that I had to use various sized openings to work with the different lens stops, so by getting a larger can and adding an old iris diaphragm from an old eight-by-ten camera, I could control this corner shading. The present day iris-in and iris-out originated here.

'The Curtain Pole'

4.

THE CURTAIN POLE: D.W. Griffith's Fort Lee Travelogue

The Biograph Company filmed *The Curtain Pole* in Fort Lee on Friday, October 16 and Thursday, October 22, 1908 (on Monday and Tuesday they stayed home at the studio and made *The Song of the Shirt* instead). While the storyline of the film, such as it is, recalls an earlier Pathé comedy called *Le Cheval emballé*, this is no simple remake. Instead, director D.W. Griffith uses the excuse of a chase through the streets to present a Cook's tour of Fort Lee, especially the hotels and saloons which were the familiar haunts of all visiting filmmakers.

In order to shoot this film in two days he picked location changes which could be achieved simply by pointing the camera in another direction, adding variety and saving time by not having to reassemble his cast and crew in some other part of the town.

Shot 1

Shot 2A

Shot 2B

Shot 3

Shot 10

Shot 11

Shot 12

Shot 13

Shot 14

Shot 15

Among the landmarks identifiable here are the Convent of the Holy Angels, with a view west down Main Street (shots 2A, 2B and 23); Peter Diehl's saloon on Main Street (shot 3; also visible to the right in shot 13); a poster-covered fence on Main Street at the intersection of Eichoff Street (now Gerome), which ran between Ferrando's Flats on the left and McNally Bros. Funeral Home on the right (shots 5 and 16); the intersection of Main Street and Hudson – compare with page 34 in this book (shot 13); the view up Parker Street looking towards Richter's Pharmacy on Main Street (shot 14); row of homes on the east side of Centre Avenue, north of Guntzer Street (shot 20); and Jane Street looking north towards the chimney of the Holy An-gels heating plant (shot 21, a different angle on the chimney than in shot 2). All these locations are within a few blocks of one another, and I suspect that those still unidentified are also in the same neighborhood.

The two interior settings were probably shot at the Biograph studio at 11 East 14th Street, but there is no reason they could not have been taken on an open-air stage on location, apparently a more common practice in Fort Lee than previously thought.

The *Biograph Bulletin* described the film as "a veritable seething, whirling cataclysm of comedy", and went so far as to claim that Griffith had been arrested by a Fort Lee policeman for "endangering human lives" during its production, although "trespassing" might have been a more likely charge.

Thanks to Patrick Loughney for providing frame enlargements directly from the Library of Congress paper print materials, which allowed me to read the theatrical posters on that fence, advertising everything from "Vitagraph" to "The Keatons".

Cast: Mack Sennett (M. Dupont), Harry Solter (Mr. Edwards), Florence Lawrence (Mrs. Edwards), Linda Arvidson, Jeannie MacPherson (party planners), Linda Arvidson (woman on street), Arthur Johnson (man in bar), George Gebhardt (man in top hat), Jeannie MacPherson (nurse with buggy), Arthur Johnson (vegetable vendor), Arthur Johnson (party guest).

Summary of the plot

The portières are the finishing touch in preparation for the Edwards' house party. Monsieur Dupont, a Frenchman eager to please his hosts, offers to hang the drapes but manages instead to break the curtain pole [shot 1]. Insisting on righting the wrong, he sets off in search of a replacement rod only to be easily detoured by a friend's invitation to drink [2–3]. Finally arriving at the store, M. Dupont buys a twenty foot long pole since he is uncertain of the door's exact width [4]. By now, the determined party guest is riding high on the vapors of absinthe frappés. First on foot then in the small carriage of an equally intoxicated driver, the pole in the Frenchman's unsteady hands cuts a humorous swath of destruction [5–21]. After all this valiant effort, M. Dupont returns to the Edwards' home and, completely ignored, is infuriated to learn a makeshift pole is already in place [22–24]. Reeling at this ingratitude, he bites the pole in half [25–26].

[This synopsis, as well as the credits, are from *The Griffith Project Volume I* (BFI, 1999), pp. 152–153.]

5.
Champion

(Upper): *The Champion studio at the end of Fifth Street, as seen in* Moving Picture World, *November 18, 1911.*

(Lower): *The Champion studio in 2004, the only surviving studio building in the Fort Lee area.*

ABERNATHY BOYS IN PICTURES

(from *New York Dramatic Mirror*, July 9, 1910, p. 23)

The Champion Film Company has recently been organized as a successor to the Actophone, and has opened an office at 27 Lexington Avenue, New York. The factory and studio is located at Coytesville, NJ Mark M. Dintenfass is the general manager of the concern.

Mark M. Dintenfass abandoned his career as a salted herring salesman in Philadelphia in order to open Fairyland, one of that city's first nickelodeons. By 1910 he was in New York, producing Actophone "talking pictures" in a loft studio on the west side of Manhattan. Forced out of business by the Motion Picture Patents Company, he formed the Champion Film Company and moved across the river to Coytesville. Here he built a studio on Fifth Street, just above the Fort Lee line in Englewood Cliffs, although accessible only from the Fort Lee side.

The first subject to be released is *The Abernathy Kids to the Rescue*, Wednesday, July 18. The film is said to be a thrilling Western drama introducing the famous Abernathy boys, Louis, nine years of age, and Temple, six. It will be recalled that newspapers made much of their famous ride from Oklahoma City to New York, a distance of about 2,500 miles, all alone. These children are the sons of the well-known "Eat-'em-Alive Jack" of Oklahoma City, the friend of ex-President Theodore Roosevelt. The father was known to catch the elusive wolf barehanded, and the children evidently take after the father.

THE CHAMPION ENTERPRISE

A Monument to Perseverance and Hard Work – Dintenfass, A Successful Fighter

(from *Moving Picture World*, November 18, 1911, p. 542)

There are larger and finer plants for the manufacture of motion pictures than the one owned by the Champion Film Company at Fort Lee, NJ., but there are few more effective, or which represent more hard work and perseverance than that which flies the banner of Champion. At the same time it represents the fighting qualities of the president of the company, Mr. Mark M. Dintenfass, one of the pioneers in the independent movement.

While the buildings shown in the accompanying engravings are not pretentious, it must be remembered that they were built at a time when it was extra hazardous for anyone not working under a license from the Edison Company to own anything tangible. It was built when such structures were called upon to serve not only the purposes of manufacture, but to preserve secrecy and afford defense as well against the prying eyes of a score of detectives and United States marshals looking for violations of the patent laws and when the owner was not certain how long he would be permitted to continue in business.

It was against these uncertainties that Mr. Dintenfass undertook to lay the foundation of the Champion fortunes, investing no inconsiderable sum in the plant that has grown and prospered under his direction.

Though unattractive as the building may appear, it houses a very complete equipment for the production of motion pictures and is capable of turning out a surprising quantity of film. The photographic quality of the product is well known and highly commended by picture men, who realize that Mr. Dintenfass has solved the problem of producing good photographic work.

Lack of space is the first thing that impresses the casual visitor at the Champion plant. A representative of the *Moving Picture World* spent a few pleasant hours in company with Mr. Dintenfass a few days ago, inspecting the Champion facilities, and could not but wonder how, in the apparent confusion, such good work could come out of the Champion plant. But, when one has been over the ground, it will be readily seen that the supposed confusion is only orderly profusion and that what is really lacking is more space to spread things out in. In other words, there is a wealth of equipment crowded into the factory building, everything that could possibly be required for picture making is to be found ready at hand and in its place. There are uniforms and accoutrements for a hundred soldiers, as many cowboys, a platoon of police, in the property wardrobe. In the scenic department, flat after flat is stacked up ready for use at a moment's notice. In the machine and repair shop the equipment is there and the tools are there – the need will bring them forth.

In the dark rooms may be seen, if you have cat's eyes, printing and perforating devices of the latest design, installed at a cost that runs into big money, but which are absolutely necessary if good photographs and steady pictures are to be made.

That Mr. Dintenfass realizes the needs of his plant is shown in the work of development now going on. On the occasion of our visit the steel skeleton of a new glass studio was being erected. This is but a beginning of a series of improvements which will increase the effectiveness of the Champion plant and put it in line with the best of them. Though Mr. Dintenfass is well known to most picture men, we present a likeness of him here. He has been associated with amusement interests for years and has been successful in many such ventures. Personally he is a most likable man and enjoys good living. One of his diversions is a high-power Kissel-Kar, which he takes particular pleasure in driving himself, with a standing dare to his friends to accompany him in it. Mr. Dintenfass will further enhance his pleasure in life by taking up his future residence on Palisades Avenue, near the Champion plant, in a delightfully located and handsomely appointed home which he recently purchased.

The *World* representative wishes to add a few words of appreciation of the courteous treatment accorded by Mr. Dintenfass and to thank him for an enjoyable day spent in his company.

STUDIO SAUNTERINGS

By Louis Reeves Harrison

(*Moving Picture World*, May 11, 1912, p. 507)

During the early struggles of the Champion Film Company, Mark M. Dintenfass was as severely [tried] as any producer has ever been, but he must have been made of the right sort of material – criticism only took off the rough edges and left him sound at the core. He was originally a Philadelphia exhibitor, built Fairyland on Market Street, but he was a born rebel and so venturesome that he struck out boldly in the Independent ranks, first as a renter and then as producer, inaugurating the Champion Company about two years ago. My own acquaintance with him dates from the time of his desperate struggles to keep up with the procession, but I never really knew him until recently, when I found him to be a decided and interesting character.

The weak spot of nearly all producers is at the outset a source of strength. The commercial end of the business must be looked after first, then follow a lot of difficulties to be overcome which are largely mechanical, but only

(Left): In 1911 Dintenfass added a
glass-enclosed stage to the Champion studio,
seen here during construction.
(Below, this column): A portrait of
Dintenfass.

a grasp of the artistic requirements of moving pictures can lead to a large and permanent reward in the end. The tremendous and almost instantaneous success of the silent drama has been both blinding and misleading to many who are today doing so well that they might well be excused for thinking that they have nothing more to learn, but it is becoming more and more apparent to those who closely observe the trend of events that the intricate and beautiful New Art is only in process of development.

The big play is looming up like a huge steam roller; it may scatter some of the little ones and lay others out flat, but there will be a vast amount of reorganization and change of method before it comes to its own. The present attempts are merely cautious feelers in the right direction, most of them being revitalizations of old novels and stage plays, and their greatest value lies in the fact that they are preparing and training all concerned in their production for what is

inevitable. At present, there are few directors who could put on a play of any magnitude or importance, and the chances are that it will only reach high success when it becomes as composite as a regular stage presentation.

It appears to me that Mr. Dintenfass has secured the services of a director who is capable of handling large productions in the person of Lawrence B. McGill. I was instantly impressed on meeting Mr. McGill at the 45th Street office of the Champion Company that he was a man of broad grasp, and this was confirmed when I saw the still pictures of his coming release *Camille*. The big scenes, the ensembles, showed me clearly that he can so arrange his settings within the limited scope of a studio as to create impressive pictures. I had an opportunity later on to observe him closely during an actual rehearsal at the studio, and realize now that success with big photoplays so far as he is concerned is a question of opportunity.

Circle C's New Boss, *produced by*
Champion in Fort Lee, 1911.

The big photoplay will need *stage* direction from men of McGill's calibre – they must be tolerant, open to suggestion, patient and fair enough to co-operate with other factors. The playwright may contribute beneficial criticism and art director may add valuable material, and I should not be surprised if a musical director and a composer will eventually be found among those measuring up to the new ideals in production. When the hour comes, the men will not be lacking in this part of the world, and the hour will come before this year goes to join the long and silent procession.

When a commercial man of pluck and clear vision finds out his own limitations, as many a producer of moving pictures has done, and when he perceives that popularity follows close on the heels of artistic presentation, he proceeds to gather about him men and women who can respond to the public demand and becomes a live wire instead of a dead one. I can honestly say that Mark Dintenfass seems to be working on exactly the right lines, and will deserve to win out on that account. He is gathering together a company of superior quality and aiming to turn out photoplays creditable to any firm in the business.

I came upon him by mere accident while on the way to his studio in Coytesville, NJ – this is north of Fort Lee, near which the Eclair studio is located and where that of the Solax Company is in process of construction. I was crossing the Fort Lee ferry and talking to a man in the forward part of the boat when I heard my name called. I answered the hail and found Mark Dintenfass in his auto with a lot of valuable props on the back seat. I piled in among the props and we were soon bowling along the river road in hair-raising style – flying by all other cars on the route, scooting up a stiff hill to the top of the palisades, then north through wild country of clean air to where the directors and actors of the Champion Company work.

I might as well have said "play", because of the delightful absence of formality in the place. Larry McGill was in the midst of rehearsing a scene, with pretty Mary Hall in rigorous training, and he continued with the ease of a veteran while greeting me on the side. I like his style. It is forceful without being irritating to members of the company. His insistence on the interpretation of thought and emotion by the means of facial and gestural expression is quietly determined and none the less effective because it is kindly and humanizing. Nearly all actors are as conservative as lawyers, they are governed by tradition and precedent, allow the rules of the dead to govern the living and their portrayals tend to ultra individualism instead of being responsive to laws of action and reaction, hence we are disturbed by discordant notes of personality instead of being pleased with a delightful harmony of effect.

The appalling self-consciousness of "Stars", whether from the legit or vaud, is destructive to human interest in the screen story. While these people are traveling about the country they become affected by hand-claps of the unthinking and easily pleased – audiences of discrimination are not given to applause – and fail to realize that the same people approve of other acts just as good or bad every night in the week, or raise a storm when the band plays Dixie. Making a noise in the auditorium becomes a matter of habit among those who do the same for the Governor of Arkansas or the Mayor of Oshkosh on the Fourth of July. If stars do not go up in the air on this account, there is always the press agent to inflate them beyond human toleration. Really important individuals do not have to *thrust* their merits upon common recognition.

Thus it is that men and women who have done fairly well on the stage, where their acts are intensified by music or made popular by the sentiments they utter, often become commonplace in moving pictures and have their vanity boxes sadly jarred. It is quite natural for them to think that they are lowering themselves to appear in the moving picture plays and they become as fussy as a prima donna with a sore throat when not permitted to continue, in the picture, their preconceived ideals of stage acting. Among them are to be found very few women who could equal Miss Turner's marvelous portrayal of jealousy in the role of a discarded favorite, when she fills the scene alone for the entire thousand feet of a twenty-minute presentation or the masterly performance of Miss Lawrence in making visible the fading light of human reason in a part where mother-love completely dominated all other sentiments immediately after the death of a newly-christened child.

There is a great deal for the most accomplished actress or actor to learn from the silent picturing of emotion in photodramas. The human voice is a wondrous factor in every phase of life, especially at intense moments. I recently attended the burial of a very dear friend, and found myself only dully affected by the ceremonials, but one faint cry from a true mother's disconsolate heart sent a shock of keen sympathy thrilling through me, and I was unable to repress a smarting outburst of tears. That voice did most to remind me that suffering is not that of the dead, but of the warm and throbbing heart of life. That tiny sound was more deeply moving than the imposing spectacle.

It may be thought that I lay too much stress on the play, but it has always seemed to me that there must be a story, affecting or amusing as the case may be, to admit of artistic interpretation before the performers can show what they can do. Personality counts, there is no doubt about that, but that personality must be typical and not distracting in a play of genuine merit. It is merely a contributor to the general effect. With no vocal appeal and a painful lack of intensifying music during presentation, the play is bound to suffer unless the acting is most carefully adjusted to the sentiment and the situation. Because they can not subordinate individuality to the common good, theatrical stars are not always desirable additions to moving picture companies.

I have reason to think that Mr. McGill will be able to produce successfully, with or without stars, if he is given the right kind of plays to put on as he has a way of calling out the best there is in a performer, but he will need stronger scenic accessories. Each scene in a photoplay must be made a veritable picture,

appropriate and harmonizing, but of sufficient individuality to get away from the wearisome stage effects. Outdoor scenes of beauty lend infinite charm and variety to the effect when they are chosen, but property rooms are usually too meager in resource for the proper arrangement of interiors.

The right kind of plays are going to be scarce for some time to come because of the meager encouragement afforded authors to give their time and energy to this sort of work. All the resources of capitalists, directors and actors have been devoted to the art of expressing something when there was mighty little to express. A scenario without a spark of genius behind it can not be converted into something that stirs the emotions by all the artistic dressing in the world any more than a dead man can be made to act like a live one – the spirit is not there. The attitude of the average producer towards the playwright has been that of a man with a surfeit of plays on hand and an endless stream of them pouring in with promise of an unfailing source of supply.

What is the truth?

From scenario editors, directors and producers themselves there is an average statement that nineteen out of twenty plays submitted to them are not even worth examination, to say nothing of serious consideration. The truth is, then, that not enough scenarios worth producing are received by any big house to keep it going, a large force is engaged in making adaptations, or the directors put on made-'em-on-the-spot variations of what has already been done to death, and this condition has been brought about by a treatment of authors such as would not be tolerated by men of

Florence Lawrence, seen here in her dressing room, made her Victor brand releases at Universal's Champion studio, among them Flo's Discipline *(1912).*

intelligence in any other branch of business.

I believe that Mr. Dintenfass wants the best plays procurable, they constitute the essential starting point of production, but I can only advise him as I have others that the price paid is out of all proportion to the general cost of a reel and not worth a skilled author's while. Twenty-five dollars should be the minimum price paid for a scenario worth converting into a complete photoplay. If it makes a hit, send another check for the same sum. This is often done by publishers to successful writers of short stories even when the first sum is five or ten times that named for the scenario. If an author's work is steadily successful, hang on to him like grim death. Playwrights who have the divine gift are almost as rare as hens' teeth.

Two good releases of the Champion Company are *An Italian Romance*, already reviewed in these columns, and *Brothers*, to which I intended to give particular notice. *Brothers* illustrates powerfully the verifying results of environment, is effective in displaying the quality of mercy and admirable in attention to fine details. While *An Italian Romance* was in process, one of the actors – I think it was Irving Cummings – went out in his make-up and became an object of suspicion. Little Coytesville has long been the headquarters of a gang of Italians who were regarded until recently as the most dangerous counterfeiters in the United States. The gang was broken up last year, but only part of the plant discovered, hence newcomers from "Sunny It" are still under scrutiny. Two Dagos mistook Cummings for one of their countrymen and proceeded to "put him wise to the game", only discovering their error through his inability to understand a word they said. It is the nature of things for men to excel in make-up, such a large portion of the face can be covered with a beard, whereas really pretty women find it difficult to improve on nature and can not be induced to do other than accentuate what charms they have, so that we can't see what we are getting.

The Champion Company's feature play, *Camille, should* be a decided success – I expect to write a criticism of it at a later date – because the great drama lends itself to pictural presentation, Director McGill knows it by heart, and the title role is assumed by Miss Gertrude Shipman, who is considered to be one of our foremost leading women in stock, starring in *The Lion and the Mouse, The Third Degree, The Witching Hour, Seven Days, Camille, La Tosca, Magda, Du Barry,* and others, possibly two hundred stage productions. While her record on the stage is one of high merit, I will reserve opinion of her work in pictures, but there is little doubt that her role will be exquisitely presented.

Of course the auto had to break down on the way home and in the worst possible place, but what care I? The mile walk which ensued was all too short – I was in the company of Evelyn Francis, *the* Champion ingenue of naturally innocent candor that so well suits the character she usually assumes, so I had a full course experience ending with the sweetest of the sweets.

SPLENDID AGGREGATION OF ARTISTS AT COYTESVILLE STUDIOS PROMISES GREAT THINGS

(*The Universal Weekly*, March 28, 1914, p. 9)

At the Universal's Coytesville, NJ studio is an aggregation of artists which promises much for the Victor dramas. Among the more important of these are Irene Wallace, leading woman, Harris Gordon, leading man, and Edward Warren, director. Mark M. Dintenfass, a pioneer promoter and producer in the film industry, is managing the studio and guiding the fate

On 8 June 1912, Champion became part of the new Universal Film Manufacturing Company, with Dintenfass, a minority shareholder, often holding the balance of power in the struggles of his larger partners. The Champion brand was dropped and the Victor Company, created by Laemmle to produce Florence Lawrence's films, replaced it. After Lawrence and her director/husband, Harry Salter, left Universal, Rosemary Theby, Harry Myers and an array of lesser Universal talent kept the Coytesville studio busy until Laemmle opened the great Universal studio on "Leonia Heights" in 1915.

of the various stock members. *The Power of Prayer*, recently released, was the first drama produced. It was a gripping, heart-interest story of the reformation of two men through faith, sacrifice and the good sense of a

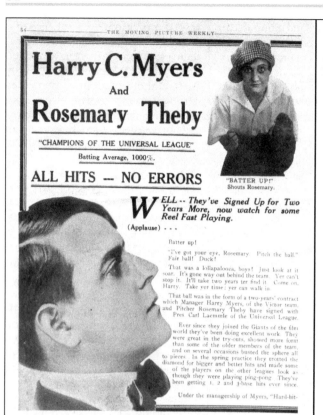

young girl, raised in wealth but reduced to poverty over night. What with the new improvements that have been made at the studio in the way of fresh scenery, lights and an enlargement of the property department, the plant is one of the busiest now being operated by the Universal.

Miss Irene Wallace, for several years a favorite with Messrs. Sam and Lee Shubert, has had an interesting career since her childhood, when she played the Automatic Doll with May Ward in vaudeville. She was born in New York, not so long ago; she is one of the youngest stars in filmdom today. Her love for amateur theatricals increased to such an extent that she adopted a stage career and went with the Shuberts to play with Sam Bernard in Milwaukee.

It was with the old Reliance company that Miss Wallace commenced her screen career. Then she came to the Imp company and played, with wonderful success, the leads in a series of Jewish pictures. Later she was assigned to the Victor company. The little leading lady is a lover of outdoor sports, horses, swimming and automobiling.

Miss Wallace is an American by birth, of Scottish extraction, and her vogue with photoplay lovers was more than lived up to by her excellent work in *Traffic in Souls*, the sensational melodrama, in which she played Trubus' daughter.

Harris Gordon, leading man, was born in Glenside, Pa., in 1884. At an early age he found his way on the stage and won recognition. For one season he played with Louis Mann. For two seasons he played under the management of John Cort; for three seasons he played "The Wife" in vaudeville. His first experience in pictures was with the Reliance company. He played with the Eclair

Two page ad for the Harry Myers-Rosemary Theby films being made by Universal at the Champion studio in Coytesville. From The Moving Picture Weekly, *July 17, 1915.*

and again with Famous Players. He is a splendid artist with a fine physique and a handsome face.

Edward Warren, producer at the Coytesville studio, enjoys an envious reputation as a director of long standing in the motion picture game. An actor for fifteen years, with such stars as Robert Mantell, Viola Allen, Annie Russell, Lillian Russell, and he appeared under the management of both the Frohmans. For ten years he was the director of legitimate productions.

It was with the Solax company that Mr. Warren first gained prominence as a screen producer, making big four and six reel features.

Mr. Warren is a college graduate, speaks five languages and has traveled much.

The following is an excerpt from an internal memorandum summarizing the history and capabilities of Universal's various studios and laboratories, and was probably written around August of 1915. While laboratory capacity was usually measured according to the amount of release print a facility could generate every week, the figure given here for negative footage refers to a capacity for filming: even in 1915 the Coytesville studio was capable of producing a new five or six reel feature every week.

COYTESVILLE STUDIO

The Coytesville studio is under the immediate supervision of the management of Julius Stern, and the management of the Imp and Victor Studios of New York. This studio is located in the heart of the Jersey hills and very recently extensive alterations were made so that at this studio there is a stage which rivals the famous mammoth stage at Universal City.

The Coytesville Studio is equipped with all of the modern conveniences for the making of perfect pictures including its own scene painting docks, carpenter shop, wardrobe and equipment appliances.

One of the most sumptuous sets ever produced in any moving picture, i.e. the lobby and famous peacock alley of the Waldorf-Astoria was made here. This was used in the big scene of *The Earl of Pawtucket* under the direction of Harry Myers, and when it was shown to the management of the Waldorf-Astoria they were astounded that such a true picture of their magnificent lobby and peacock alley could have been duplicated. It was so true to life that the management of the Waldorf-Astoria actually believed that lights had been put into their establishment and the scenes taken in the hotel. At present the following companies are operating at the Coytesville studio:

William Garwood directing Violet Mersereau

Jack Adolphi directing Edwin Stevens

Harry C. Myers and Rosemary Theby have just completed directing Wilton Lackaye

This plant is capable of producing about 5000 to 6000 feet of negative per week.

The Coytesville studio proper which was originally occupied by the Champion part of the consolidation is considered to be one of the most perfectly constructed studios in the east from the lighting standpoint. The most perfect photography has always been received from the Coytesville studio when taken on the stage or the studio proper, or the new big stage which has been constructed just to the rear of the whole studio. This studio and the organization will later be removed to the largest producing plant at Leonia Heights.

Dintenfass sold out his shares in Universal in 1916. In collaboration with the Warner brothers he produced *My Four Years in Germany,* a highly successful screen version of Ambassador James W. Gerard's best selling memoir, filmed in the Biograph studio in 1918. He became one of Bergen County's major real estate developers, and ran unsuccessfully for governor in 1919 as the Single Tax Party candidate. He died at his home on 770 Anderson Avenue, Cliffside Park, in 1933.

6.

Edgewater, Cliffside, Grantwood, Ridgefield ...

MOVING PICTURES SECURE NEW FIRE EQUIPMENT FOR EDGEWATER

(from *Moving Picture World*, May 15, 1915, p. 1054)

The Mayor and Board of Councilmen of Edgewater, NJ, have been trying for some time past to secure new equipment for their fire fighters, but met with much opposition from the citizens. After much thought Mayor Henry Wissel and Mr. Thomas Trolson, chairman of the Finance Committee, called on the Momus Producing Company, who have a studio in Edgewater, to help them out. The Momus Co. took a picture showing Edgewater's present fire fighting apparatus, then showed the territory that had to be protected, and wound up the film by showing a modern automobile fire engine in action.

When the citizens actually SAW, the result at the polls proved conclusively that the Mayor was right. He said: "We have the pictures to thank for the Victory".

Neff Now a Producer
The Battle of the Ballots Will Be the First Release of the Good Luck Film Company – Players Working at Edgewater Studio

(from *Moving Picture World*, June 19, 1915, p. 1916)

M. A. Neff, former national president of the Exhibitors' League of America, has entered the ranks of producers as general manager of the Good Luck Film Company, now making its first picture at the Century studio in Edgewater, NJ Mr. Neff wrote the scenario and copyrighted it under the name of *The Battle of Ballots*, the idea being to show in a picture, of four or five reels, the dramatic and essentially human qualities of the struggle being waged at so many city and state elections between the "wet" and the "dry" factions. Mr. Neff is careful to avoid taking sides; his picture is in no sense to be a part of a propaganda; rather, it will portray with as much exactness as dramatic action permits the intense feeling that may be engendered among the normally peaceful citizens of a small city.

In selecting his company for *The Battle of Ballots*, the general manager did not follow the popular habit of engaging stage stars with a reputation of advertising value. Instead, he sought people whose records had proven their worth in

The Fort Lee Ferry docked in Edgewater, and filmmakers outward bound from New York passed through it every day on their way to the studios. A few of the earliest producers set up their cameras as soon as they got off the boat, but the scenic resources available in Edgewater were limited (unless the filmmakers were looking for oil refineries, chemical works, or freight yards, which they sometimes were). By the time feature films arrived no one was filming in Edgewater anymore, except for M.A. Neff. In 1915 he joined the growing ranks of independent producers and made *The Battle of Ballots* which, despite the claims of the *Moving Picture World*, was straightforward anti-saloon agit prop. After the film's saloon keeper dies in a fit of delirium tremens, a younger generation tears down his saloon and erects a movie theater, a gesture that Neff, himself a theater owner, must have appreciated. Nothing further was heard of the Century studio, Good Luck Films, or M.A. Neff himself. As for the Momus company, exactly what they were doing in Edgewater is still unknown, although they certainly had a knack for playing local politics.

Unidentified crew filming a car wreck at Edgewater, c. 1918.

pictures. Several weeks were spent in interviewing directors, actors and cameramen before the cast was filled, and judging from the sum total of the past achievements of those chosen, the final accomplishment in this instance should be more than ordinarily high.

The director, Frank B. Coigne, is an actor, director and playwright of many years' standing. His experience in pictures started with Mark Dintenfass as a producer of the old Champion brand. Among the productions to his credit are *The Tyranny of the Mad Czar, The Vampire, Hounds of the Underworld* and *Protectors*. Besides directing pictures, Mr. Coigne has written more than one hundred and fifty scenarios.

For the leading feminine role in *The Battle of Ballots* Mr. Neff selected Mayre Hall, a strikingly beautiful young woman, who made a very favorable impression in Bison, Imp and Thanhouser pictures, notably in the Princess brand. Miss Hall, under the name of Dearest St. Clair, is well known on the vaudeville stage, having toured in the Keith and Proctor circuits for a number of years. More recently she originated the Fountain dance at Murray's restaurant.

William Wells, the leading man, was a prominent stock actor before his advent in pictures. He has played important roles with many companies, among them Universal and Lubin, in the latter under the direction of Romaine Fielding. Recently he did excellent work in *The Plunderer* and *The Woman's Resurrection*.

Baroness Dorothy Van Raven – Dorothy Kingdon before her marriage – is another valuable asset to Mr. Neff's forces. On the stage she was credited with being able to play all types of character, and during the past three years she has borne out the reputation in pictures, first under the direction of Lawrence B. McGill, and later with Edgar Lewis, Oscar C. Apfel, Fred Wright, Frank Powell and many other producers.

Robert Web Lawrence has directed stage productions for [Henry?] Savage and is at the present time under contract with the Henry B. Harris Estate. He has produced for the Imp and I.S.P. companies, and scored a marked success in Edison talking pictures. Playing in *The Governor's Pardon* he suffered an accident that nearly cost him his life.

Laura Mackin, the character woman

in the new aggregation, has acted in photoplays since the days when the Cinematograph Company [sic] used the roof of the building at Thirteenth Street and Broadway for a studio. She followed a long stage experience with an equally successful career in photoplays. While in Mexico, Mrs. Mackin directed seventeen pictures for the Universal Company.

Mary Navorro also is thoroughly well qualified by past experience with the Vitagraph Company, Pathé and O. A. C. Lund of the World Film Corporation. One of her most effective parts was that of the Queen in *The Three Musketeers*.

G. Charles Bryant started with Vitagraph, working under Wilfred North and George Baker, and then played juvenile leads in Ethel Grandin films. Wilfred Jessop has appeared in many photoplays both here and in England. He played leads at the Warwick studio in England and, coming to this country, was at different times associated with the Flying A Beauty and Peerless films.

Frank Whitson is a comparatively new recruit in the picture field, but he has ample experience in stock and vaudeville, where he directed his own sketches. Others in the company are John Ellis, Harry Harford and Creston Clark.

Mr. Neff chose an expert cameraman in Eugene Cugnet, who is said to have photographed the first Pathé picture made in this country. Universal and Éclair were among his other affiliations.

"THE BATTLE OF THE BALLOTS" (Good Luck).

(from *Moving Picture World*, July 10, 1915, p. 327)

The Battle of the Ballots will be complete by Saturday, July 4th. This picture is not made along the old lines, but is liberal, entertaining and convincing. It does not appeal to passion,

An original member of the Motion Picture Patents Company, Kalem was famous for its use of itinerant production companies which it sent as far afield as Ireland and Palestine. Early in 1913 it had outgrown the small studio it operated in Manhattan, and built an open air studio at 199 Palisade Avenue (according to current numbering), the site of the old Laird estate in Cliffside Park. By 1915 Kalem built a proper studio here, but continued to maintain other studios in New York, Jacksonville, Hollywood and Glendale, California. Although they had produced a number of important films, including *The Vampire* (1913) and *The Cabaret Dancer* (1914), very little was written about Kalem's Cliffside Park operation until the construction of their permanent studio.

but to reason. The picture is full of action and strong dramatic effect. It shows a large town under the administration of the Wet Forces and then shows the town under the Dry Forces. It vividly depicts the methods employed to carry elections and the hard work done by both sides. There are new and original features in the picture that were never produced before, that will undoubtedly appeal to the public. A romance runs through the story, but at all times the main point of showing the evil of drink is never forgotten and is constantly kept before the audience.

Alice Eis and Bert French perform their famous "Vampire Dance" in Kalem's The Vampire, *shot at Cliffside Park in September 1913. The photograph is taken at a right-angle to the open-air stage, showing another building on the property.*

An exhibition will be given on Saturday. State rights will be sold for *The Battle of the Ballots*. M. A. Neff, who is the author and producer, has copyrighted the picture and will place it on sale in the near future.

KALEM OFFERS NEW IDEA

Proposes to Issue Series of Three-Part features for release on Regular General Film Program

(from *Moving Picture World*, March 6, 1915, p. 1422)

"Broadway Favorites" is the name under which the Kalem Company will presently issue a series of three-reel features to be released on the regular program of the General Film Company. The idea as outlined by Frank J. Marion, of the Kalem Company, is a distinct departure from the policy of that concern as followed since its organization and is, also, somewhat of an innovation in motion picture production.

"It is our intention", said Mr. Marion, "to feature some prominent Broadway star in each of the 'Broadway Favorites' productions. A play especially suited to the peculiarities of each star engaged will be selected and every effort will be made to present the leading player to the best advantage. There will be but one star in each production and he or she will be supported by the best players now in the Kalem stock. Kenean Buell will direct all these productions. In case the star is a woman Guy Coombs will play opposite; if a man, Miss Anna Nilsson will be the principal support.

"This is the first time the Kalem has departed from the stock company plan which it originated when it started business, some years ago", continued Mr. Marion. "But we realize that there is a strong demand for stars – individual players, who have a reputation on Broadway. It is generally known that there are many legitimate players who never leave New York; it is this class that we expect to draw from ...."

Regarding the general activities of the Kalem Company Mr. Marion said that work would be commenced this week on a new studio structure at Cliffside, NJ, after original designs prepared by Storm V. Boyd, Jr. In many respects this studio will be a departure from the usual plan of studio-construction. In the first place there will be no glass sides or top. "This is not surprising", said Mr. Marion, "when one takes into consideration the great improvement in artificial lighting that has been made in the past year or so. With these improvements the glass studio has become obsolete; in fact, I have seen interiors of glass studios completely blanketed with black cloth shades. Methods of lighting have changed completely. We must have the lights and shades where we want them; the new lighting devices have enabled us to do this. Solar light is not so easily controlled, hence the abandoning of the glass studio.

"There are some other original ideas in studio-construction which we have tried out at Jacksonville and while [sic] will be incorporated in the new Cliffside studio; but as these ideas are peculiarly our own we prefer to withhold them from publication at this time."

KALEM FOLK BUSY AT LAIRD ESTATE WITH RENEWED LEASE

(from *The Palisadian*, March 27, 1915, p. 1)

There are scenes of great activity going on this week at the Laird Estate on lower Palisade Avenue. The Kalem Moving Picture Company has renewed its lease on the property for another three years and it has already begun construction of a modern studio that will cost several thousand dollars when completed. New dressing rooms and an office building are also being built. The company will return to Cliffside on May 20 and expects to work on a more extended scale through the season.

SIXTY CHORUS GIRLS AT CLIFFSIDE
How the Kalem Company Is Reproducing "Maxim's at Midnight" – Everything Real, Even to the Waiters

By Lynde Denig
(from *Moving Picture World*, May 22, 1915, p. 1267)

The Cliffside studio of the Kalem Co. is just across the river from Harlem, New York. When one passes through this section of New Jersey it is natural to wonder how land so near to New York can be so vacant. Apparently no one ever goes there from anywhere else unless the call is urgent and then it is not customary to remain long. Nearly all of the houses are marked "to let;" but there are a few exceptions and for the occupants of these exceptions

the past week has been distinguished from all preceding weeks. There have been two free shows, Uncle Sam's grey men-of-war riding at anchor in the river and sixty chorus girls dancing in the Kalem open-air, swept-by-river-breezes studio. Cliffside favored the more alluring of the two spectacles.

William Wright, of Kalem, does not pose as a connoisseur of feminine fascinations; but – well, he has not let the years in New York slip by without acquiring a discriminating judgment, and at a little luncheon party in the Astor he spoke as one having authority on an engrossing subject – the beauty of women, no less. And the very women to whom he referred were soon to be seen pirouetting merrily in the sunlight of Cliffside. The Kalem Company, it appeared, was prepared "to perpetuate for future generations" the American dancing girl at her best. When historians want to know how the husbands of 1915 spent their evenings they may turn to the picture *Maxim's at Midnight* and see the whole performance from soup to nuts, and even imagine the popping of corks. Maxim's can be transported to small hamlets; it can be screened at Sing Sing to remind favored inmates of the way they once spent money; it can be – but why go on? The girls are waiting across the river.

You have seen musical comedies in which the characters are shifted in a jiffy from civilization to a desert island. Well that was the first impression of the Kalem part of Cliffside on Tuesday afternoon, except this time the people had taken a slice of their building with them. On a platform covered with a canvas top stood a three-cornered section of Maxim's. There was no mistaking it and the night birds, in their electric light plumage, were seated at the round tables, sipping wine and smoking cigarettes, just as though it were midnight in New York, instead of a warm

(Top and centre): Two views showing the Kalem company at work on its open-air stage in Cliffside Park, c. 1913.

afternoon with the sun beating down on the canvas and the smell of spring in the breeze.

Carpenters pounded on Kalem's new studio right next to Cliffside's Maxim's; a circle of spectators kept pushing closer to the platform and sixty chorus girls, not to mention a half dozen principals – the combined entertainment forces of Maxim's, Bustanoby's, Rector's and a selected number from other restaurants – either danced or waited their turn. Every stepladder, every over-turned table, every board that could be placed on supporting barrels, held its quota of bare-shouldered, powdered, short-skirted fairness, being kept out in the open air and not appreciating, apparently, the joys of a day in the country. Maxim's orchestra was there, too, and even the waiters were the very ones that look for tips of an evening. Can photoplay realism go further?

Director George Sargeant had been set the task of reproducing the entire performance exactly as it is given at Maxim's, with a few additions. Sans coat and collar, with shirt sleeves rolled up to his elbows, he worked with the energy of a Billy Sunday, exhorting the pajama girls to keep within the lines, calling the property boys from the shade of nearby trees, beseeching the carpenters to rest a moment while the orchestra played, urging the waiters to behave just as though they expected the usual reward and crying for enthusiasm among the midnight birds at the round tables. "Picture", he shouted and presto! it was midnight at Maxim's.

Diagonally south from the platform stood an old house that once, no

(Bottom): Tom Moore and Alice Joyce in Nina of the Theatre (Kalem, 1913).

doubt, was called a mansion. It had become the prison of fairies. Every now and again, the door opened and a new species, ten or a dozen strong, wandered across the grass and looked for a place to rest until Director Sargeant called. The pajama girls were there, the girl's from Rector's and many, many more, but best of all the bon-bon girls in the oddest and most fetching costumes that ever stirred the men of Cliffside to thoughts of a trip to Broadway.

But they were not fairies after all and they were very tired, and there were casualties to ruffle the temper. When the afternoon was over, the smooth expanse of one unprotected white stocking was marred by a smudge of green paint; one of the girls from Rector's regarded sorrowfully a scratch on her arm made by a rusty nail, and a bon-bon girl regretted the broken toe of a silk slipper. You see *Maxim's at Midnight* is human as well as gay, and the beauty of it is, you will be able to enjoy it without staying up late.

"MIDNIGHT AT MAXIM'S"
New York Night Life Is Brought to the Screen in Kalem Picture, Enlivened by Many Chorus Girls

Reviewed by Lynde Denig
(from *Moving Picture World,* June 26, 1915, p. 2111)

For the inauguration of its new policy, whereby multiple-reel productions are to be given to exhibitors on the regular program, the Kalem Company conceived something heretofore unknown to picturedom, a screen portrayal of gayest spots in gay New York in the wee small hours of the morning. In the short space of four reels – it seems short when one is looking at the picture – the revues at Rector's, Bustanoby's and Maxim's are presented precisely as they occur nightly. We have the same girls, the same costumes, the same dances, and if the orchestra leader regards the instructions given by the Kalem Company, we will have the same music. If ever a picture were adapted to carry the glitter of Broadway into the dullness of a village evening this is it.

George L. Sargeant directed the production and to him belongs the credit of catching the spirit of Maxim's when the tables are filled, when the orchestra plays and the dancing girls, in colorful costumes, occupy the floor. The setting for this scene is an exact imitation of Maxim's, and the guests used to provide a background for the performers are true to type – the trio of men out for a good time, all readily susceptible to the blonde beauty of Tottie Twinkletoes; the after-theater supper party with the conservative dowager for chaperone, the westerner and his over-dressed wife, who have come to New York to see the sights, the smoothly groomed youth, described by George Ade as being all right from the collar down – we meet these and many more during the course of the evening and they are as much a part of *Midnight at Maxim's* as the dancers themselves.

Supplementing the many ensembles in this unusual picture are several dances of classic pretentions, two of them given by Baroness Irmgard von Rottenthal, others by the Cameron girls and still others by Bert Weston and Dorothy Ozuman . Clearly photographed and performed in perfect time, these numbers are a distinct asset to the production. First interest, however, undoubtedly will center in the splendid array of chorus girls. It is safe to assume that such an assortment of beauty has never, in the past, been offered in any one picture, and the camera man was kind enough to allow the audience close views of the faces of his most alluring subjects. Every now and again, just by way of a change, the dance is interrupted that one smiling face may monopolize the screen and then, as likely as not, the camera will be lowered for a foreground giving a comprehensive view of the complicated dancing steps in execution. Four reels of a dancing picture may seem a lot, and so it would be, had not the director succeeded in injecting considerable variety.

Of course, there is no real story, but there is a connecting thread in the adventures of the three men who select Maxim's for a gay little party and become rashly extravagant in their efforts to meet Tottie Twinkletoes. Having paid for the privilege, they are, in turn, taken to the chorus girls' dressing room and introduced, and thereafter their enthusiasm for the performers and for Tottie, in particular, knows no bounds. Incidents of this kind provide occasional bits of comedy in a production that is unique and extremely well handled in every respect.

KALEM ARMS NEW JERSEY HOME GUARD
Rutherford Patriots Abandon Canes and Broom Handles for Kalem Rifles.

(from *Moving Picture World,* July 14, 1917, p. 251)

Rutherford, NJ, like many other communities which have organized home guards, found it impossible to secure rifles with which to drill. The local patriots, young and old, began to chafe at shouldering sticks, canes and broom handles while learning the manual of arms and the city fathers doubled their efforts to secure honest-to-goodness guns.

Learning that the Kalem Company has a large arsenal – acquired for their military productions – Rutherford appealed to the Kalem officials, who immediately instructed their Glendale (Cal.) studio to ship two hundred rifles to Rutherford. Major Phil Lang selected rifles practical for firing, equipped them with bayonets and shipped them to Rutherford ....

Leah Baird, who took over the Kalem studio and operated it under her own name.

The Kalem studio, almost brand new, was the first large studio in the Fort Lee area to be abandoned by its builders and thrown on to the rental market. A number of marginal producers worked here over the next few years including Leah Baird, a Vitagraph star now fronting her own company, and Johnny Hines, who made some of his early "Torchy" comedies here, including *A Knight for a Night.* On 8 December 1921 a fire that was visible from Riverside Drive in Manhattan destroyed five of the seven buildings on the property. The last film known to have been shot there, *For His Mother's Sake,* a race movie starring heavyweight champion Jack Johnson, was released only a few weeks later. Despite the destruction, *Film Daily Yearbook* continues to provide an address and telephone number (Cliffside 789) for the Kalem Studio until 1925.

JESTER TO ENLARGE CLIFFSIDE, NJ STUDIO

(from *Exhibitors Herald,* March 9, 1918, p. 34)

William Steiner of the Jester Comedy Company, has just placed his O.K. to plans for extensive alterations to his studio at Cliffside, NJ and also for the building of an additional wing in order to increase the floor space of the interior studio.

At the present time the combined outdoor and indoor studio measures seven thousand, five hundred square

The construction of the permanent studio on Palisade Avenue was too little, too late. Kalem ceased production in 1916, although they continued to maintain their lease through 1921. Alice Joyce, the most important star working at the Cliffside Park studio, had already fled to Vitagraph, and the Broadway favorites featured in films like *Midnight at Maxim's* failed to connect with movie audiences. But with America's entry into the World War Kalem did, at least, find a good use for the armaments they had stockpiled on the west coast.

feet and with the new addition it will raise these figures to twelve thousand, five hundred square feet. The laboratory also will be greatly enlarged, which will give him a capacity of two hundred thousand square feet of film per week, or double what it is at present.

CREATION COMPANY BUYS KALEM CLIFFSIDE STUDIOS

(from *Moving Picture World*, July 12, 1919, p. 205)

One of the most important announcements of the week is that Creation Films, Inc., a new producing company, capitalized at $500,000, purchased the Kalem studios at Cliffside, NJ over a month ago. The amount paid for the property was not made public.

The officers are K. Hoddy Milligan, president; B.D. Biggerstaff, vice-president; and C.C. Shively, secretary and treasurer.

One of Mr. Milligan's first acts was to clean house at the Kalem plant. This was accomplished to the tune of $25,000 worth of repairs, alterations and improvements.

An item of particular interest is the fact that the company will maintain its own releasing organization. Arrangements have been perfected for opening offices and branches in all of the large film centers throughout the United States.

The policy will be to produce high class serials which will be released three reels at a time instead of the customary two. Two reel comedies are also included in the program.

Roy Sheldon, formerly of the Fox Film Corporation, has signed a long term contract to take charge of the production department.

KENYON VEHICLE HAS BIG SETS
Background of Gorgeous Character Is Said to Feature "The Harvest Moon"

(from *Motion Picture News,* February 7, 1920, p. 1486)

"An eye-feast of scenic splendor as a background for the most engrossing and convincing story that has yet come from the pen of Augustus Thomas" is the promise held out to picture fandom by Deitrich Beck, Inc., in *The Harvest Moon*, starring Doris Kenyon, a forthcoming W. W. Hodkinson release, which is rapidly nearing completion at the Leah Baird Studios, Cliffside, NJ, under the direction of J. Searle Dawley.

In describing some of the details of the settings to be found in *The Harvest Moon*, the W.W. Hodkinson Corporation states that during last week "the stage running the entire length and breadth of the studio was transformed into a home of wealth, seven rooms and a gorgeous ballroom with a heavily carpeted staircase, that for realism and beauty far outshines anything of its kind ever done for the screen. A striking feature of the well-appointed dining-room was the presence of two rare andirons and a bronze fern centre-dish, valued at $30,000 which for years graced the dining-room of the George J. Gould palace at Lakewood, NJ.

"The gorgeous ballroom set won admiration from the company, George A. Lessey declaring it the finest bit of workmanship he had ever seen in picture-making, and Marie Shotwell pronouncing it worthy of an Augustine Daly."

Supporting Miss Kenyon in *The Harvest Moon,* besides George Lessey and Marie Shotwell, are Wilfred Lytell, Stuart Robson, Earl Schenck, Peter Lang and Grace Barton.

MOVIE ACTORS IN FIRE TRAP
Exit Was Blocked and Two Men Were in Dire Peril

(from the *New York Times,* April 22, 1914, p. 12)

Kalem was not the only producer interested in this area. The Whitman Features Company produced *Lena Rivers* and *The Toll of Love* at a studio in Cliffside Park, as well as *Jane Eyre*. The account of the fire at their studio suggests an open air stage associated with an enclosed "factory" building. Ramo Films had been renting space in one of Universal's buildings at 102 West 101st Street, but was forced out when the fire department evicted all film manufacturers from the property. They restaged the World War on open acreage in Grantwood, the northern portion of Cliffside Park just south of Fort Lee. Edward M. Roskam's Life Photo Film Corporation also had to leave New York after the 101st Street fire, but already owned property in Grantwood, where their laboratory was located. They built themselves a studio adjacent to the lab and shot as many as ten features there. The account of near-disaster during an unidentified company's production of *The Fire King* suggests the rough-and-ready approach to filmmaking characteristic of the era. No wonder New York's fire commissioner wanted these people out of the city.

Two actors for a moving picture concern, Charles Davenport, of 308 West 139th Street, Manhattan, and Arthur Robinson of the Longacre Hotel in West Forty-Seventh Street, near Broadway, Manhattan, were trapped in a burning building at Cliffside this evening, and for a time were in grave peril. The building had been constructed for moving picture purposes and Davenport, who appeared in the role of the "villain" in a drama entitled *The Fire King,* set it on fire. Robinson was to throw an asbestos bag over Davenport's head and drop through to the cellar and escape. Davenport, who wore an asbestos suit, was to remain in the burning building as long as he could and then beat a retreat.

Robinson found the exit blocked, however, and called to Davenport to aid him. Walter King, who was directing the work of taking the photographs, realized that something had gone wrong, went to the rescue and got both men out. The actors were taken to the North Hudson Hospital, and it was said there that Robinson's condition was serious. Davenport's asbestos suit saved him from serious burns. A crowd of fully 1,000 persons witnessed the rescues.

To The Editor of the *New York Times*:
(from the *New York Times*, April 24, 1914, p. 12)

Could not a law be enacted making it punishable for moving-picture companies to permit or expose their actors unduly to risk their lives in the fulfillment of their duties?

I happened to witness the fire scene at Cliffside, NJ, exclusively reported in the *New York Times* this morning. While the cause of the accident is given as the blocking of an exit, it looked more as if it were a premeditated attempt to see by just how narrow a margin a terrible death could be cheated. The ghastliest part of it was the steady grind of the apparatus even as this poor mortal was dragged, terribly disfigured and writhing in agony, away from the ruins.

And all this for a civilized audience, presumably made up in good part of women and children! To me it looked like something only a little short of murder.

HUMANITARIAN,
Grantwood, NJ, April 22, 1914

FIRE AT WHITMAN'S STUDIO

(from *Moving Picture World*, July 4, 1914, p. 84)

Fire came within an ace of putting the Whitman studio, Cliffside, New Jersey, out of business recently, and only because of rapid action by the studio employees and cast were the flames confined to the exterior settings.

During the garret scene of *Jane Eyre*, a five reel feature written by John William Kellette and directed by Martin J. Faust, wherein the maniac, portrayed by Alberta Roy, is supposed to destroy herself in a fire she creates, too much realism almost added Miss Roy's name to the list of photoplayers sacrificed upon the altar of daring. During the beginning of the scene Miss Roy's kimono caught fire, and she fortunately stepped upon the spot where flames were beginning to make inroads, and tossed herself upon a bed already smoking, and which later burst into flames. Hand grenades [i.e., glass balls containing fire extinguishing chemicals], chemical tanks and the

The south end of Cella's Hotel, photographed in 1939. In 1914 there was enough vacant land to the south to restage the opening battles of the first World War.

factory hose, were put into play and the fire confined to the garret set. About $300 worth of property was destroyed.

The Whitman cast now includes Misses Lisbeth Blackstone, Mary Frye Clements, Alberta Roy, Viola Allen Frayne, Mary Moore, Valerie Sheahan, Mesdames Frayne and Middleton; Harrish Ingraham, Edwin Brandt, John Charles, F.E. Nevin and Emile LaCroix.

FILM FIRM DISPOSESSED

Fire Commissioner Adamson Says They Have No Permits

(from the *New York Times,* June 20, 1914, p. 4)

Fire Commissioner Adamson has started a crusade against manufacturers of moving picture films who do not comply with the fire laws. On Thursday night the Commissioner found three concerns which, he said, were doing business without a permit from the Bureau of Fire Prevention, and he dispossessed them.

The concerns, all on the second floor of 102 West 101st Street, were the Remo [sic] Film Company, the Commercial Nature Picture Company, and the Life Photo Film Company.

The actors of the Remo Film Company were at Fort Lee, NJ, enacting a play called *The Conquerors*. Dressed in costumes of gladiators they returned to the company's offices and were met by inspector Healy and assistants. For a time it looked as if the gladiators would not be able to get their street clothes.

"Have a heart and give me my street costume", implored one warrior."

Inspector Healy relented and the warriors obtained their clothes ....

FIRE DEPARTMENT EVICTS

Ramo, Life Photo Film, and Commercial Motion Picture People Were Inconvenienced But Little, However

(from *Moving Picture World,* July 4, 1914, p. 78)

As a direct result of the recent fire that destroyed Universal Film Manufacturing Corporation property in the building at No. 102 West 101st Street on May 13, three well-known moving picture manufacturing concerns were evicted from the quarters which they had been occupying in the same building Thursday and Friday, June 18th and 19th. Those affected were the Ramo Films, Inc. the Photo Life Film Corporation [sic], and the Commercial Motion Picture Co., Inc. The evictions were the result of drastic rulings by the New York Fire Department after inspections had been made.

While the descent of the Fire department people upon the film men was attended with considerable excitement, it now appears that everything accomplished was for the best – and all those interested seem happy and satisfied.

At the Fire Commissioner's office it was said evictions made had resulted from the fact that the companies had failed to secure the required permits for the conduct of their business in the building uptown and that this fact had been forcibly called to the attention of the department by the recent Universal fire. It was found, the Fire Department's officials declare, that the building occupied by the film concerns was not the kind in which it would be safe to manufacture and store films and that the pursuit of the film industry there was endangering the lives of hundreds of people in the building. It was also announced by the Fire Department officials that, while there had been no sweeping movement against similarly operated places in the city at the time the three evictions were ordered, a careful inspection of the film manufacturing plants in Greater New York was to be made and laws governing the film business in its relation to the Fire Department were to be rigorously enforced, no matter what its effect upon the business might be.

When summary notice to "get out" was served upon the Ramo people, they came back with the statement that before moving into the building at 101st Street they had commissioned an attorney to investigate the requirements of the law in order that they might be complied with and that this attorney had later assured them that everything had been satisfactorily arranged with the city departments. When informed of this Commissioner Adamson very considerately granted an extension of time for the removal of the business, prohibiting, however, the manufacture and storage of films in the building. As a consequence, the Ramo headquarters are still maintained in the building although none of the company's work is being done there. The Ramo people are just now engaged in making a big picture called *The Conquerors* and had been making a lot of exterior scenes at Fort Lee on a piece of property just back of Cella's Hotel which they had engaged for the purpose. With their place in New York closed, the company at once set about rigging up a big outdoor studio on the Fort Lee plot and will soon have it in shape for use throughout the summer for the staging of both interior and exterior scenes. Arrangements have been made with the Eclair Film Company some weeks ago to develop all of the negative on *The Conquerors,* and there was no need of the New York factory for this part of the business. Following the Fire Department's action, arrangements were made with the Standard Film Print Company, of Yonkers, for the removal of the Ramo printing and assembling force to a part of that big plant, and this arrangement solved the problem which the eviction had brought up, at least for the present. At the Ramo offices some days ago it was announced that permanent studios would be erected within the next few weeks, probably in Mt. Vernon.

The Life Photo Film Corporation and the Commercial Motion Picture Co., Inc., allied concerns, were in such shape when the evictions came that they have not been inconvenienced to any great extent. A deal had been on for some time whereby the film concerns were to purchase a studio and factory site in Grantwood, NJ, and had progressed to such an extent that it was possible to close it the day following the descent of the Fire Department. The new headquarters were ready for occupancy in the little Jersey town. The property which they have purchased consists of twelve city lots improved with a fine stone structure formerly the home of Blake Brothers' Animal Training School. The building has been found to be admirably adapted for use as a moving picture factory and but few alterations have been necessary. There was plenty of room on the plot for a glass studio, and construction work on this new building will be completed within a week or two. The Life Photo Company's players left for Canada the day following the Fire Department's action for the purpose of filming *Northern Lights* and, by the time they return, everything will be in readiness at Grantwood. Such a good bargain did the Life Photo concern make in arranging for their new home, it is said, that the day after the deal had been closed another film manufacturing company offered to take over the property at an advance of $8,000 over the purchase price.

Ramo Films Inc., which had been shooting *The Conquerors* in back of Cella's Hotel in July, put the film back into production after war really broke out in Europe the following month. They renamed it *The War of Wars, or the Franco-German Invasion,* and created their version of a World War I battlefield, the first in an American film, in Grantwood. Will S. Davis was the director.

"A FIERCE INFANTRY CHARGE," CAMERA IN LEFT FOREGROUND; DIRECTOR IN MIDDLE DISTANCE IN WHITE SHIRT

THE EUROPEAN WAR – IN GRANTWOOD, NJ

By Robert J. Shores
(from *Motion Picture Magazine*, January 1915, pp. 68–74)

Across the Hudson River from the tomb of General Ulysses S. Grant there came the rattle of musketry and the boom of artillery. It was the first sound of Europe's war to reach the ears of Manhattanites. The Germans and Allies were in deadly conflict!

The scene of this fighting was in a sparsely wooded hollow back of the little suburb of Grantwood, NJ, high up on the Palisades. Two hundred and fifty men were busily engaged in chasing each other up and down the slopes, making wonderful cavalry charges and rushing up with their artillery. First a wing of the "Allies" would be driven back; then they would rally and advance ruthlessly across the positions formerly held by the "Germans".

Even a German village was sacked and the houses burned. Dead heroes lay all about, and the smoke of battle floated up thru the oak-trees and across the little slopes covered with half-withered goldenrod, in clouds far more dense than are seen today in actual warfare, because black powder instead of the smokeless variety was used solely that this should be so.

Some day, doubtless before this writing gets into print, hundreds and even thousands of people will have sat in a darkened "movie" theater and gazed tensely and excitedly at these very scenes enacted so far from Belgium and the French and German frontier.

"Gee!" you can almost hear some deeply impressed young man exclaim to his companion, "I wouldn't wanter be a 'movie' camera man. It must be

---

The filming of The War of Wars *in Grantwood in 1914, as seen in* Motion Picture Magazine, *January 1915.*

dangerous work. I betcher hundreds of them photographers get shot trying to get pictures like these."

This will be the very highest form of praise, not so much for the author of the war scenario as for the director. For two weeks he worked with his men in the open country just outside of Grantwood, NJ, with but one object in view, and that was to make people in the Moving Picture audience thrill as did the young man just mentioned, and believe as implicitly as did he in the perfect genuineness of the "war pictures".

As I visited these New Jersey "battle-fields" during some of the operations, I was told, with a genial wink, that these pictures were being made "for a story", and as I was told this by one of the members of the Moving Picture concern, the director, standing but a few feet from us, shouted: "Here, you, French aide, come over this way, or you won't be in the picture". Then he turned to another man and said: "Get your Germans ready to go down in that hollow. We will begin on the infantry stuff in the second reel!"

As I strolled about, I came upon an "entire German village". It consisted of three "stone" houses on a blind street, an inn on one side, a large house on the other, and a small cottage at the foot of the street. When I got closer, I found they were made of canvas and other scenic materials, and that they were but the front shells of houses. I must say, however, they were good imitations.

It is not the pleasantest thing in the world to come suddenly upon seven or eight dead heroes piled in a grue-some heap, some with livid sabre cuts across their heads. This was the experience I had as I was nosing about with my camera. At first I jumped back in horror, and then I stood and grinned. These "soldiers" had always been dead – they were only dummies and piled in such natural confusion that I am sure many a Moving Picture patron

will gaze on this scene and shed a tear for the thousands of real heroes piled up in the trenches in the cockpit of Europe. These same people will believe they have seen photographs of the soldier dead, nor would you blame them. I believed in them myself when I saw them with the naked eye, while the camera softens them and makes them appear even more natural.

There is reason for all this. War scenes are in demand. The people must have them, and the Moving Picture concerns are in business to give the people what they want. Moving Picture men are not allowed to go to the front; but even if they were, they could get no pictures reproducible on a screen from a distance that would place them out of the danger zone. Were they to go close enough to get clear pictures, it would take an army of camera men, one to relieve the other, until the pictures were made, inasmuch as it would mean certain and instant death, for they would be shot down ten times as rapidly as the men in the trenches.

The reason for all this started when the first shot was fired upon the Belgian border. The sound of it was, to quote a well-worn phrase, "heard round the world". Especially was it heard by the Moving Picture producers. Men in every part of the civilized globe were struck with horror at the significance of it. Business was at a standstill. Throngs gathered before the bulletin boards to spend hours in watching for the latest news from the front. Clerks fussed nervously over their ledgers, impatient to get out and read the latest extra. Staid bankers were seen eagerly discussing the latest development with elevator men. For a moment all considerations of business and of class were laid aside or forgotten while every man talked with the man nearest him, were he friend or stranger, upon the one all-important topic of the hour.

But in the midst of all this excitement there were certain men who did not

lose their heads; men who saw a business opportunity in what others considered a catastrophe – and those men were the Moving Picture manufacturers. Before the first of the Belgian forts had fallen, the Moving Picture companies had their emissaries upon the spot, doing their utmost to obtain the permission of the military authorities upon either side to permit them to take battle scenes. In every capital in Europe the cameras were busily clicking as the soldiers marched thru the streets on their way to entrain for the front. In the studios in America, scenario writers were hammering away at their typewriters, composing war dramas to meet the great demand which the far-sighted "movie magnate" knew was certain to arise in the near future. Office men were fumbling thru the card index, hunting for war plays which had been submitted and rejected months before. Property men were rushing about giving orders for uniforms and peasant costumes. Playwrights were besieged with offers for the Moving Picture rights of every play that had a military feature. Nothing that smacked at all of war was overlooked by the Moving Picture man, and it was not long before advertisements began to appear in the papers. This, with the exception of the address, is an actual copy of one:

FIVE HUNDRED MEN WANTED at once, for Moving Pictures; ex-soldiers or members of military organizations having discharge papers. Apply to R.T., 1128 West 1126th Street.

And this meant that the time had come to recruit the movie army and set about making battle scenes which should equal in interest any that might be taken upon the actual field of battle, and which would, in many respects, be much more artistic.

When war first broke out, the Moving Picture men were filled with a hope that their greatest opportunity had arrived and that they would be able to

The Shooting of Hamilton and Burr
By
R. L. Lambdin

Our artist sees the movie man reproduce the historical duel—but this time the camera does the shooting.

Charlie Grant, as Aaron Burr, assembles his sneer for a close-up.

Ho! For the stagecoach! On the way to scene of the duel.

A native's dog takes sides in the quarrel and almost breaks up a scene.

Director Jack Noble spots a stranger sneaking into the picture and scares him away.

"Is that just part of the play?"

The rendezvous in the Fort Lee woods where comfort and appearances are more important than the dueling weapons.

Illustrator's impression of the restaging of the Hamilton-Burr duel for My Own United States *(Frohman Amusement Corp., 1918), supposedly on the original site, although the 'Fort Lee woods' are not especially close to the notorious Weehawken dueling ground.*

place before their audiences the real battles as taken at the scene of action, but it was not long before they were undeceived. They learnt that the military authorities would not permit pictures to be taken, for strategic reasons, and even if such permission had been obtained, it would have been quite impossible for an operator to get a picture which would in any way answer his purpose. Even if, when near enough, the camera man could escape death, it would frequently happen that the constant cannonading would make it impossible for him to balance his camera upon the shaking ground. But the most insurmountable obstacle of all was the fact that the carnage was so frightful that the pictures could never be shown in public. Moving Picture audiences are fond of a little killing now and then, but they are not fond of wholesale butchery, and had such pictures been brought to America, they would never have been allowed to run for more than a night or two, and the expenditure would have been a sheer waste.

The movie man, knowing little enough about war as it is now conducted, had

not anticipated this, but he was not daunted by such difficulties when a money-making opportunity loomed large before him. If he could not get pictures of the war in Europe, he would "start a war" of his own in America, and that is exactly what he did. It was such a "home-made" war that I visited over in New Jersey. Other Moving Picture concerns were conducting them on Long Island and other battlefronts.

The "volunteers" were paid $2.25 a day to come to the "front" and play the hero. The response was immediate, and the supply was even greater than the demand. Men of every nationality came "flocking to the flag", prepared to "die" as often as twenty times a day, if such a sacrifice of life were demanded by the director.

Some of these men were used in taking pictures which were afterward shown as real scenes from the front; others were employed in the battle scenes of war dramas written especially for the occasion. The chief, and practically the only, requirement was that they should be able to ride, to handle a gun or a sword and be intelligent enough to obey orders quickly and correctly. There were all sorts and kinds of men among them, some short and some tall, some stout and some lean, some old and some young, but every one of them, without exception, had enjoyed some sort of military training, and every one of them knew how to execute the manual of arms, how to march, how to take aim and how to fire a blank cartridge with the most telling effect. In most instances, a day or two of preliminary drilling was all that was necessary to get them ready for the taking of the pictures. They were then costumed in various uniforms and led to the spot selected for the opening scene. Arrived there, they were allowed to stand at ease while the director and the operator discussed the important matters of light and shade, measured the ground and estimated the slope of the land.

The range of the Moving Picture camera at close quarters is not great. If an actor moves a few feet to either side of the lens, he is out of the picture. Only a limited number of men, therefore, could be used in scenes, which would show the actors life-size, though many more could be employed in cavalry charges or assaults upon supposedly fortified positions, where the fighting is seen some distance away.

For two weeks after the "beginning of the war" in Grantwood, NJ, the country roads were full of "soldiers" – French, German, English and Belgian troopers were to be met walking down the roadway, arm in arm, in the greatest good humor, showing no evidence whatsoever of national prejudice. They were to be seen drinking milk at the roadside while the driver of the milk-wagon plied a rushing business with all of those not engaged at the moment in simulating battle. They were to be found in informal picnic parties at noonday, combining business with pleasure by eating their luncheon while the camera man turned his crank and took a picture which would afterward be shown under the title, "Getting their rations while on the march", or something similar. Never before was there such excitement among the schoolboys who happened to live along the Palisades. They came from every direction, from miles around, to stand in open-mouthed awe and admiration as the "movie" soldiers strutted about upon the edge of the mimic battleground.

The busiest man of all was the director of the war pictures. Clad in a peasant costume, in which he appeared for a moment in one of the scenes, he stood in the center of the field, calling out his orders: "Hi! send that French general down there!" or "Spread out, boys, spread out, and when you see the Germans coming, run like the devil – but be sure to run past the camera". Sometimes things did not suit him, and then it would all have to be done over again, but the soldiers were enjoying the game almost as much as the small boys in the audience, and they made no complaint, even when they had to charge up a hill for the fourth or fifth time. In the course of a day's work these soldiers got plenty of exercise, especially those who had to "fall dead" in a charge. One of the cavalrymen engaged in a battle some distance south of Grantwood made a specialty of falling off his horse with his drawn sword and rolling down to the foot of the hill. This scene was tried many times before it was done to please the director, and apparently the cavalryman suffered no ill effects from his numerous and spectacular deaths.

The pictures are not taken in the order that they are to be shown on the screen, but in such a way as to bring all scenes with the same setting together. This makes it quite impossible for a mere spectator to understand the progress of the battle, or to learn which side is the victorious army and which is the vanquished. It is easy to see, however, that the pictures, when shown, will be very effective, and that it must be exceedingly easy to convince an audience that they are "the real thing".

When any particular action is to be taken, as, for example, the storming of a fort, the director and the camera man first visit the ground which is to be the scene of the assault and select the spot on which the camera is to stand. The action is then mapped out with a view to having all the exciting events occur at just the proper distance from the operator and at just the right angle. It is no easy matter for a director to carry so much detail in his head, or to bear in mind that one body of men must run in a particular direction at a certain moment, yet these directors often go out on the battlefield without any script or notes in their hands and direct the action all day without once forgetting an essential detail.

Such care is taken with every detail that in the instance of the "German village" there were even vines growing upon the lattice above the benches which stood before the door of the inn, and the stone well with a long pole for lifting the bucket added a realistic touch to the cottage at the end of the street. The taking of the village and the subsequent looting of it was enacted with a great deal of vim and enthusiasm, the whole performance concluding with an explosion which blew part of the roof from one of the houses and set it on fire. It took them over an hour to extinguish the flames.

The series of pictures in which the sack of the village figured were completed in about two weeks of steady work, with the camera going from early morning until dusk, yet when the finished film is shown, the whole performance will not occupy more than half or three-quarters of an hour. The cost of taking this picture exceeded two thousand dollars. The big cost is in the soldiers employed in it and the consequent expense in costumes and ammunition.

Some of these war dramas are already being shown, but many more will be announced within the next few weeks, and they will continue to be made so long as the good weather lasts. When winter weather comes on and all pictures must be taken indoors, there will be a lull in all such "European wars" as that which was "fought" near the quiet little New Jersey suburb of Grantwood.

LIFE PHOTO FILM CORPORATION COMPLETES ITS NEW STUDIO

(from *Moving Picture World*, March 27, 1915, p. 1945)

The glass-enclosed studio, in addition to the studio heretofore operated by the Life Photo Film Corporation, of Grantwood, NJ, has been completed. Radical innovations devised by Mr. John Arnold, the head camera man of the Life Photo Company, have been installed in this new studio, such innovations being ballbearing trolleys running east west, north and south, for the manipulation of the Cooper-Hewitt lights installed in such addition.

The length of the studio is 110 feet by 68 feet wide, and an unusual method of construction has been inaugurated so as to eliminate entirely all posts and obstructions, the roof of the studio being supported upon the same theory as the cantilever bridge.

The Commercial Motion Pictures Co., Inc. an allied corporation of the Life Photo Film Corporation, are rapidly progressing with their work in enlarging their laboratories.

Within a few months of this announcement Life Photo Film had gone out of business and Edward Roksam was managing the laboratory part of the operation for Eclipse Film Laboratories, which had taken over the premises. The sudden influx of film studios and laboratories was not lost on local businessmen. George Stabel, a Palisade Avenue shopkeeper, built a laboratory of his own in an attempt to siphon off some of this business, which was shifting to New Jersey as New York fire marshals forced many smaller operations out of the city.

ENTERPRISE FILM CO.'S NEW PALISADE HOME

(from *The Palisadian*, March 27, 1915, p. 1)

The building which Geo. F. Stabel is erecting adjoining his store on Palisade Avenue, is to be used as a studio for the developing of moving picture films. Mr. Stabel is president of the company which intends to operate on the premises under the name of the Enterprise Film Co. Mr. Stabel is enthusiastic over his new venture, and says that if business comes in as he expects it to, within a month he will add another story to the building. The building will be a stucco affair and should prove to be an asset to the village from an architectural standpoint.

The new E.K. Lincoln studio in Grantwood, 1915.

E.K. Lincoln, a well-to-do actor who had starred for Vitagraph, Lubin and World, built himself a studio and laboratory at what is now 735 Bergen Boulevard. Although he originally announced that he would produce his own films there, Lincoln found the property more valuable as an investment. In 1916–17 Fox rented the studio, and in 1920 the United States Photoplay Corporation spent many months on an elaborate and unreleased serial called *Determination*. Peter Jones produced a two-reel movie here in 1923, *How High Is Up?*, with Moss and Fry. The *Film Daily* reported in June 1926 that the first episodes of Reginald Denny's *Leather Pushers* series were made here, but the facility was always more valuable as a lab. Originally considered part of the Grantwood neighborhood, the Lincoln studio was technically just across the border in Ridgefield, although such distinctions were often regarded quite casually at the time.

LINCOLN STUDIO AT GRANTWOOD

(from *Moving Picture World*, June 19, 1915, p. 1922)

Ed. Lincoln, the well-known star of *The Littlest Rebel* and many Vitagraph features, is planning to do some big things as an independent producer. A big force of men are working on his own studios and factory in Grantwood, NJ. The plant, which is costing $100,000 to build and equip, promises to be perfect for all-around efficiency and service.

Jack Pratt, as director, will continue the policy of adapting popular novels for the screen features. Mr. Lincoln will be starred in the stories. At present Director Pratt is busy on Robert Chambers' great success *The Fighting Chance*, in which Mr. Lincoln has one of the greatest parts of his career.

DOBBS TAKING OVER LABORATORY
General Manager of Palisade Laboratories Company Ready to Begin Work in Ridgefield Plant.

(from *Moving Picture World*, July 20, 1918, p. 383)

George C. Dobbs, vice-president and general manager of the Palisade Film Laboratories, Inc., announces that the working forces have taken possession of the new steel and concrete building situated at Lafayette Avenue and Bergen Boulevard, Ridgefield, NJ, a short distance from the 130th Street ferry, on the Jersey side.

"Our new home is the largest building in the country devoted exclusively to a laboratory", says Mr. Dobbs, "and consists of three floors, totaling 12,000 square feet of space. The departments are laid out in sequence so that the film progresses in its various stages of development and takes no backward movement.

"Everything in the plant is the most modern and up to date, and elaborate arrangements have been taken to take care of the comfort of our employees and outside directors and cameramen who may desire to project and cut film. The building is strictly fireproof, and large vaults, complying with fire insurance regulations, will protect the film.

"The capacity of the plant is two million feet a week, though I do not propose to handle more than half that amount, which will enable me to give my personal attention to all work in the same manner I did at the Triangle laboratories.

"I will turn out at least as good film as I have in the past, for, while it is a new plant, with new equipment and everything spick and span, I have a lot of my old employees, some of whom have been with me for four or five years.

"The location is an ideal one for a laboratory – on top of the Palisades, several hundred feet higher than New York, where there is very little humidity in the atmosphere."

John Arnold, head cameraman of the Life Photo Film Corp., demonstrates his British Moy camera. Arnold was later head of MGM's camera department.

7.
Éclair

The Société Francaise des Films et Cinématographs Éclair was a French manufacturer of films and film apparatus. In a move to increase their share of the lucrative American market, then dominated by Pathé, they began construction of a studio and laboratory in Fort Lee in February 1911. The original property ran along the west side of Linwood Avenue for 175 feet, to a depth of 250 feet, the current site of Constitution Park. Jules Brulatour controlled the sale of George Eastman's motion picture stock and was one of the most powerful men in the industry. Although Eastman insisted that Brulatour avoid any financial entanglement with the production end of the business, Brulatour found many ingenious ways to get around this, beginning with his silent backing of Éclair's American operation.

AMERICAN ÉCLAIR STUDIO

Branch Of Famous French Picture Makers Established At Fort Lee, NJ – Model Plant Installed

(from *Moving Picture World,* October 7, 1911, pp. 24–25)

Since the manufacture of motion pictures became a serious business in America, no concern, with that avowed purpose, has made a more auspicious beginning than that which marks the entrance of the Éclair Company upon the field of

American manufacture. There are in this country, to-day, several splendidly equipped plants for picture making, but they are the result of several years of development from beginnings of the most humble nature, made without previous knowledge of the craft, which makes them all the more wonderful to contemplate. But under the present condition of things it would be hopeless for anyone to embark in the business of making pictures on similar lines; one must begin practically upon a footing equal to that of the most progressive manufacturer to merit attention. It is this necessity that has been fully recognized by the promoters of the Éclair enterprise in America and through that recognition, or by reason of it, is explained the adequate preparations now being made at the new factory at Fort Lee, NJ.

It was the privilege and pleasure of a representative of the *Motion Picture World* to pay a visit recently to that factory and studio and to meet there the president of the Éclair Company, Mr. Charles Jourjon, of Paris, and his corps of able associates in the building of the new plant. It will not be our purpose in this story to annoy our readers with a technical description of that plant for the reason that it is not easy for those not expert photographers to comprehend the intricacies of that highly specialized and scientific occupation. We will, instead, put ourselves in the places of our several thousand readers who are unable to visit the Éclair plant, and try to see things for them as they would see them if they had an opportunity.

Fort Lee, NJ, is an indefinite place. There are plenty of New Yorkers who never heard of it and have not the least idea where it is. Having received directions and made the trip you will, if you ever should, find it a delightful

Exterior of the original Éclair studio on Linwood Avenue, c. 1913.

little jaunt into the country and to a region that might as easily be a thousand miles from New York as it is within a 45-minute ride. There you will find all the delights of a quiet country village, with plenty of pure air and sunlight and repose, so utterly different from the atmosphere of the city you have left behind you but a few minutes before. You say at once that the choice of location has been a most happy one.

At the time of our visit the work of building was still going on. The factory, which includes the administrative offices and the photographic laboratories and workshop, was the only finished structure. It is of concrete, iron and hollow tile construction – all fireproof material and as complete and compact as one might imagine such a place could be. A guide will take you through and show you where the film goes in and where it comes out the completed product, but we would not advise you to attempt the journey alone. It is a veritable labyrinth of rooms and passageways. In their proper places will be seen perforators for punching sprocket holes in the film; printers for printing the pictures on the positive film; then baths of developers and fixers and tints through which the film must pass before it reaches the big revolving drying drums turned by high-speed motors. To the uninitiated all this is a maze, but through this maze it is possible to pass to completion 40,000 feet of motion pictures in a single working day.

This is the photographic branch of the business and was designed by and built under the direction of the French experts employed at the parent plant of the Éclair Company in Paris – and no one questions the superior skill of the French photographer, so we must accept this specimen of his designing as just about the last word in factory construction.

There are a few features of note. A ventilating system, extending to every nook and corner in the building, distributes filtered air and a heating plant regulates the temperature. All the chemicals used in developing and fixing are mixed in vats and distributed through pipes to the several tanks in the developing and fixing rooms. There is also a refining plant in the basement for the recovery of such constituent parts of the solutions used as may be thus saved.

Adjoining the factory will be two independent studio buildings. One is about completed. It is of similar construction to the factory, with the addition of glass for the roof and sides. Ample accommodations for directors and players have been provided. Private and general dressing rooms, lavatories and showers are provided for the comfort of the players. There is a spacious wardrobe room and quarters for the cameramen, carpenters and scene painters. Every requirement that convenience and approved methods suggest has been provided for in the plan and scope of the enterprise. The capacity of the studio is four sets or scenes. The second studio building will be constructed from the same plans and work will be commenced soon. It is the intention of the Éclair Company to build several of these studio buildings, believing that better results can be obtained by that method than if they were to build one large studio.

When considering this enterprise as a factor in the making of American pictures, the fact should be remembered that it is not an American company bearing the Éclair name, but an American installation or branch of the French Company Éclair, built from plans prepared in France, and will, in as far as is practical, be manned by French experts of long experience from the home plant. The importance of this was explained to *The World*'s representative by President Jourjon, who has been here for the past month inspecting the completed work and directing future construction.

"Our reason for establishing an American plant is based upon a desire to give the trade an American picture made the Éclair way", said Mr. Jourjon. "We feel that there is no doubt about our ability to make good pictures, but we realize that the American market demands a picture produced agreeable to American conventions. We could not do that in Paris with French actors and French producers, so we have decided upon the ideal combination of American producers and players with French photographers and technicians".

"Then you must have a very hopeful view of the American market, Mr. Jourjon?"

"I have", was the quick response. "I am convinced that there is a lot in the future for pictures in America. Your public is demanding better pictures and more of them and there is plenty of room here for those of the highest quality and character. It is to that demand that we will appeal, as you will discover from our first American release. I am so deeply interested in this project that I should like to remain in America for some time to come and be more closely identified with its development. As it is, I am compelled to return to Paris shortly, though I do so with regret, you may be sure. The branch will be in good hands, however, so I am not fearful for the result. My friend, Mr. [Jules] Brulatour, is well known to the trade and has consented to act as our political and financial adviser, so we feel that our interests will be well protected".

Mr. Brulatour, who was present at the interview, smilingly admitted his acceptance of the commission and explained that, while he would like nothing better than to cast his fortunes with the American branch of Éclair, his relations with the trade precluded his taking anything like an active direction of its affairs. To have a finger in the pie to the extent designated by Mr. Jourjon was quite to his

Some of the French technicians acquired by Charles Jourjon pose in front of the Villa Richard, a popular restaurant and hotel at the edge of the Palisades. Lab technician Francis Doublier in the front seat, his eldest son George on the running board. Cameramen Georges Benoit and Lucien Andriot in the back. The man behind the flag is Lucien Bessenay, Doublier's brother-in-law. Photo dated 20 August 1912.

liking and all the glory he could reasonably wish for.

Both President Jourjon and Mr. Brulatour were pleased with equipment and the selection of departmental heads, upon whom the active management of the enterprise will rest. Mr. M. Maire, chief cameraman and photographer, is a young man of wide experience in motion photography, having traveled extensively for photographic purposes. In the mechanical department Mr. C. De-Moos, an expert from the Paris plant, is in charge. Lawrence McGill, George LeSoir and Mr. [Joseph] Smiley at present compose the staff of directors, with Will S. Rising in charge of the scenario department. Ray [i.e., Wray] Physioc, a scenic artist of ability, will have charge of the scenic department and George Rice is stage carpenter.

Important will be the announcement, made to the World representative, of the selection of Mr. Harry Raver for the position of business manager. Mr. Raver has been acting in the capacity of manager of publicity and sales for the Éclair for some time. His knowledge of the amusement business in its relation to motion pictures has impressed the principals of the Éclair Company to the extent that they have decided to extend his field of usefulness. Mr. Raver's early training in the amusement field began in a circus press department, in which he developed the showman's instinct to a remarkable degree. Later he became associated with the Parker enterprises, of Abilene, Kan., out of which association grew the firm of Darnaby & Raver, proprietors of one of the highest class of carnival companies ever organized.

When the craze for carnivals passed, Mr. Raver became interested in motion pictures, in which line his early training has been of great assistance. His knowledge of amusements and of the requirements of the public will enable him to render an uncommon service to the Éclair Company.

President Jourjon will probably remain here for two weeks longer before returning to Paris. He says that he is having the time of his life and there is no doubt that he speaks the truth. That he approves the location and the homelike aspects of the Fort Lee plant is proved by the fact that he spends most of his time there, taking a deep interest in the work of the players. Accompanying him on this trip is M. Maurice, the chief technical expert of the Éclair Company, of

Paris, who seems to be just as happy about the new plant as Mr. Jourjon. He will return to Paris with President Jourjon, having rejected a very flattering proposal to remain here.

We are advised that the first American Éclair will probably be released within the next few weeks and that it will be a two-reel production in recognition of the strong demand for subjects of that scope. Its appearance will be awaited with interest and more will be said about it in next week's *World*.

ÉCLAIR ENLARGES BIG FORT LEE PLANT

(from *Moving Picture World*, December 9, 1911, p.807)

General Manager Raver, of the American Éclair Company, announces the enlargement of its present buildings. Additional property has been added to the space already acquired and the work of erecting another large studio, an office building and a modern garage will be started at once. When asked why this step was found necessary, Mr. Raver said:

"When the Éclair Company, of Paris, decided to invade America, plans were drawn up for a studio equal only to the production of one reel weekly. The intention was to complete the plant some time in advance of the initial release date so as to allow for an ample accumulation of reserve negatives, but building delays made this impossible and it was necessary to engage three directors and a large stock company to meet the emergency. Then came insistent demands for more than one American release and we found studio, dressing rooms, property and scenic departments and the studio offices entirely too small. Mr. Jourjon, head of the Éclair interests in Europe and America, lost no time in deciding to increase the American investment, as he is determined to stop at nothing that Éclair films may attain leadership.

"We are frank in saying that our first release [*Hands Across the* Sea] was not satisfactory to the Éclair Company, although we are in receipt of many complimentary letters and telegrams extolling its quality, and, fully realizing the need of ample working space and adequate facilities to handle large and important productions, we are wisely making additions at time when they are most needed".

Éclair emphasized the French origins of its American company even more than its rivals Pathé and Gaumont. News articles and interviews stressed the French technology behind its cameras and laboratory equipment at a time when similar American apparatus was relatively inferior. But French dramatic skills, lavishly praised here by Louis Reeves Harrison, were beginning to seem inappropriate to a medium whose particular requirements appeared better suited to an American approach. Note Harrison's interest in Éclair's proposed educational film programs, which would later be exhibited non-theatrically on their portable Kineclair film projector.

STUDIO SAUNTERINGS

By Louis Reeves Harrison

(from *Moving Picture World,* March 2, 1912, p. 758)

I crossed the uppermost ferry on the Hudson side of New York City, zig-zagged up the Palisades, scooted across the wilds of New Jersey, where shivering motion-picture companies were doing snow scenes in Alaskan dramas, caromed to the West at historic Fort Lee and finally came in view of the neat-looking structures of the Éclair studio and factory. *Parlez vous Français? J'te crois!* I learned it on the *Boule Miche*, and I was glad that I knew enough to get at the ideas of the Éclair Company's officers, though they were kind-hearted and polite, as Frenchmen of the better class always are.

Another well-known French company established an American factory about a year and a half ago, and I happened to learn about the first picture turned out for this market. It concerned the assassination of Lincoln, on the same general principle that an American company would open up in France by telling the people all about Napoleon. It is hardly fair to relate how they had Booth pass the *liveried flunkies* at the entrance of Lincoln's box and make a speech on the stage after assassinating the President, but they turned one of the nation's greatest tragedies into farce-comedy. The Éclair Company has a new director fresh from Paris, M. [Etienne] Arnaud, long associated with Gaumont, of whom superior work is expected, and I was given an opportunity to criticize his first picture. I was prepared for the inevitable false estimate a man entertains of anything that is strange to him. The Irishman was afraid that God could not understand the Pope because he prayed in a *foreign* language. France is rich in tradition, and for three hundred years French dramatists have been writing plays that are much alike in purpose, the theaters retain ancient forms, the French have done more for the drama than other people, and it is to be expected that a director hailing from the home of the drama would fail to grasp the fact that he is dealing with an entirely new audience.

The plain truth is that French stage plays are not nearly so popular with our people as they were a few years ago, and the American photodramas are more successful outside of this country than those of any other nation. Any man who comes here from abroad is setting foot on the home soil of the photoplay, where the art is in process of rapid evolution, though this class of production is still very primitive in all countries. He is coming to *learn*, and New York City is a poor place to study the Native American audience. I did not expect much of the foreign director's first effort for the Éclair Company, but I was agreeably disappointed.

The theme of his first production, *The Guardian Angel*, was simple and not new, but it was *universal* and especially well adapted to American picture exhibitions attended very largely by women and children who are quick to appreciate and enjoy whatever reaches out for the heart tendrils. *The Aching Void* (Vitagraph Company) was on exactly the same lines and received widespread commendation. There is nothing in this first presentation to show what the new director *can* do with a really great play, but he has used extraordinary judgment in selecting a clean and wholesome motif with a strong social purpose. He has apparently started with the right idea.

In order to present a purely American drama it will always be necessary to reflect in action and characterization our life and people as we recognize them, with the purposes of our thinking men and women embodied or suggested. The settings of the playlet

William Haddock, one of Éclair's American directors, examines a script at the studio while the actors look on. Georges Benoit leans on Haddock, Lucien Andriot leans on the camera.

I saw were appropriate and the types well chosen, so it is to be hoped that the Éclair Company has scored a "find" who will contribute materially to the popularity of moving pictures as a form of entertainment as well as to their value as a fine art.

I was most deeply interested in what President Jourjon had to say concerning educational films in preparation by the Éclair Company, as this line of work is bound to constitute a distinct advance over the great majority of reels now being turned out for temporary, purely commercial and not-at-all entertaining purposes. The wearisome screen-stories with the unfailing and easily foreseen embrace at the end are beginning to get on people's nerves; they are to the ideal photoplay what the hand organ is to grand opera, suited only to monkeys with or without tails. A large percentage of our photoplays are not even fit for American children.

The educational value of stage dramas is just beginning to be understood, while that of presentations on the screen, with their wider opportunity and influence is only appreciated by the enlightened few who realize that superior character in the next generation is bound to be developed by combining the acquirement of knowledge with what appeals to live human interest. The intelligent direction of the dramatic instinct, so common as to be universal among children, is being given consideration by our most advanced teachers, is bound to replace present methods and systems so far as representing important phases of human history is concerned, and may lead to more active interest in the natural sciences. The Éclair Company has in preparation reels demonstrating many of the beauties of chemistry and physics which, if they do not actually instruct, will arouse interest in branches of study, ordinarily regarded as dry, to the tremendous advantage of all who see them. There are millions of grown children who will enjoy these educational reels, not only among those who like to refresh their memories during intervals of leisure, but humbler people in eager search of what may better their condition.

An interesting tragedy exhibited during my visit at the Éclair studio was *Rizzio*, a photodrama showing the conspiracy organized by Darnley, the husband of Mary Queen of Scots, against her favorite and private secretary, Rizzio. The latter exercised such a tremendous power over the Scottish Queen, even after he had promoted her marriage with Darnley, that the

The laboratory business remained a significant part of the Fort Lee economy for decades. This view of the printing room at the Éclair lab was taken in 1912.

husband gathered a number of nobles and wounded the Queen's favorite before her eyes, finally dispatching him outside of her chamber door. The tragedy was vividly correct in unexpected details, and a clear picture of life in those troublous times.

Another interesting and altogether curious drama was *The Glass Coffin* in three reels of a thousand feet each, depicting the restoration to life after apparent death of an Indian Princess who had been long buried in a glass coffin. The story appeared to unravel the snarl of human reality and define the proprietorship of the soul, showing that its perfect existence was impossible without its being shared by another of the opposite sex in which it was merged. The personality of the Princess was attractive, but it was an intrusion of modern social organization, so it was returned to its imprisonment in the sleeping body for a future awakening under more congenial circumstances.

The insistent artistic form of these presentations formed their greatest charm and offered strong testimony in favor of scenic beauty in productions for the screen. Therein lies the only expression suited to lofty success.

As Ben Carré notes in the excerpt from his memoir reprinted below, Éclair did not have a very sophisticated scenario department. Scripts might be little more than "a score of words in French" scribbled on the back of an old engraving. Éclair's *The Raven* followed a similar D.W. Griffith production by three years, although they had their account of the sinking of the *Titanic* in theaters within weeks of the disaster. Dorothy Gibson, a model turned actress who was the current protégé of Jules Brulatour, played herself in this early docu-drama.

POE IN PICTURES

Éclair Company Produces A Two-reel Subject Based On "The Raven".

(from *Moving Picture World*, April 27, 1912, p. 313)

Chalk up another credit for Éclair. In producing a subject like *The Raven*, any picture company is entitled to commendation for doing its share in bringing the business into higher repute. The mention of *The Raven* as a moving picture subject suggests difficulties from the very start. Its production requires that a producer evolve his results from thin air. The problem is – given the poem of Edgar Allen [sic] Poe, with some historical facts; let them be presented before the world at large in the form of two interesting reels of motion pictures. This has been done by the Éclair people in the most praiseworthy manner.

The part of Edgar Allen Poe is played by Mr. Guy Oliver, who seems to have a comprehensive idea of the character and personality of Poe. The first reel has to do principally with events that led up to the writing of the celebrated poem, "The Raven". It is shown how Poe was struggling in poverty as a scrivener in the endeavor to provide sustenance for himself and invalid wife, "Lenore", who required medical attention that further increased their burdens. The great love of Poe and his wife for each other is illustrated, to show the source of inspiration whence sprang the immortal "Raven".

The despair of Edgar Allen Poe, as he began the work upon "The Raven", is well depicted. He began it apparently without inspiration and merely intended no doubt to produce a "pot boiler", something he could turn into ready cash for the immediate needs of his wife. Approaching his task in dejection the muse would not commune with him. At last he fell asleep at his table and dreamed of the children of his brain that had started on before through the ages, but would never return to help him. There is a succession of visions following here illustrative of the successful stories from the pen of Poe. This double exposure work is handled in a manner that will carry the thread of the story along well, and from a technical point of view it is about as perfect as is possible to turn out. These successive scenes from the various stories bring back fond remembrances of his works to those who are familiar with them, and they will surely awaken an interest in Poe among those who have never read him. These visions include scenes from the "Gold Bug", "The Black Cat", "The Murders in the Rue Morgue", "The Descent into the Maelstrom", "Buried Alive", "The Pit and the Pendulum", etc.

The second part of the picture deals with the actual writing of "The Raven". Poe, sitting at his desk, is suddenly transformed, by a mental process, to lovely surroundings. He imagines himself to be in a home of affluence, where all his worldly desires are fulfilled, except for the presence of Lenore. In those delightful surroundings he hears the tapping of "The Raven", and presently the bird appears standing on the bust of Pallas. The hand of the author is shown from time to time, large upon the screen, and as the pen writes, the words of the poem are quite visible the instant they are made. After each phrase of the poem there is a flash back to the Raven and Poe, and so on until the poem is completed.

When the poem is completed we see

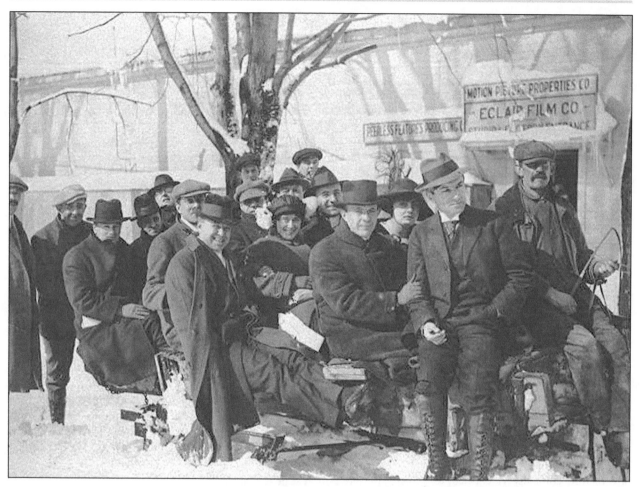

*Arriving for work at Éclair by sled, early 1914. Notice the signs for Éclair, Peerless, and the
Motion Picture Properties Company, all on the same building.*

Poe leaving his home to go to the publisher's to get money for the work that
has occupied him all night. He is shown leaving his homestead in the Fordham
section of New York City. The real Poe homestead was used as the setting for
the picture, just as it stands at the present time near Bronx Park, New York City.
The poet is shown beginning the long walk to New York proper, and then his
arrival at the publisher's office. He is offered there a niggardly $10 for his
masterpiece. Had he been more independent he would have refused, but being
pinched by poverty he was obliged to pawn it like one pawns a beautiful jewel.
His return with flowers and provisions to Lenore makes an artistic ending to a
picture that is well done throughout, and can be called a feature by virtue of its
literary value.

"SAVED FROM THE TITANIC"

(from *Moving Picture World,* May 11, 1912, p. 539)

Miss Dorothy Gibson, one of the survivors of the great disaster, as told in a
previous issue of the *Moving Picture World*, has performed a unique piece of
acting in the sensational new film-play of the Éclair Company, produced last

week and dated for release on May 14.
It is the story of the wreck, founded
upon Miss Gibson's own experiences,
and with a lot of the mechanical and
vision pictures which have made fame
for Éclair's American directors, the
film is creating a great activity in the
market, for the universal interest in
the catastrophe has made a national
demand.

Miss Gibson had hardly recovered
from her terrible strain in the wreck,
when she was called upon to take part
in this new piece, which she constructed as well. It was a nerveracking
task, but like actresses before the footlights, this beautiful young cinematic
star valiantly conquered her own feelings and went through the work. A
surprising and artistically perfect reel
has resulted.

ÉCLAIR NOTES

(from *Moving Picture World*, August 17, 1912, p. 643)

Éclair has completed a new wing to their studio which now makes it possible for three directors to work at the same time. Also their factory is completed to handle outside work such as developing and printing. In view of Éclair's consistently perfect photography, this new department should prove a boon to the small or free lance producer most especially if he is inclined to be finicky as to quality.

Saw their Mr. E. Arnaud, he who directed *Holy City* and *Robin Hood*, directing a forth coming release. He was working without a scenario. He had found an engraving in a New York Art store and it furnished an inspiration. On the back of it were a score of words in French. This was a working scenario – hard on the poor scenario writer who has scripts to sell.

We marveled at this, where upon Mr. Grisel, his right hand man, told us Mr. Arnaud had done all of *Daddy*, an August 13th release, without a working script or a single word of notes. The idea or synopsis was read to him and that was sufficient.

> The arrival in Fort Lee of Ben Carré, a scenic artist sent from Paris to replace Wray Physioc, was seen as another example of the beneficial influence of French theater and film design on local production. Carré eventually moved to Hollywood, where his films included the original version of *The Phantom of the Opera* (1925).

NEW ÉCLAIR ARTIST

(from *Moving Picture World*, November 30, 1912, p. 883)

The Éclair Film Company has been most fortunate in securing the services of the well-known French artist, Benjamin Carré, a student of the celebrated painter, Adelur.

M. Carré hails from the Studio Amable, where the principal scenes for the Grand Opera and Comedie Francaise of Paris, and the Century Theater, of New York, were devised and executed. He has also been the designer and artist in all the large cinematograph studios of Paris, arranging such productions as *Robert le Diable, Christian Martyrs, The Huguenots, Death of Mozart, Chopin, Thais,* and *Belshazzar's Feast*, and his advent, therefore, means a valuable acquisition to the already extensive production department of the Éclair, and will thus enable the company to present even greater and more finished productions than have heretofore been put out.

M. Carré arrived on Saturday, the 9th inst., accompanied by Etienne Arnaud, the Éclair head director, who has just returned from a brief visit to Paris.

> In the 1960s Ben Carré wrote a very evocative autobiographical manuscript, never published, which included considerable material on his work in Fort Lee. The portion reprinted here, courtesy of the late Anne Carré, retains his original Gallicized syntax. Carré's account of the self-contained French community then working in Fort Lee is unsurpassed (a studio with a resident translator!). His imagery is equally remarkable, although it appears that Carré had a better eye for winter light and sunset effects than the political machinations going on all around him.

MY FIRST TRIP TO THE ÉCLAIR STUDIO

By Ben Carré

The daily trip to the Studio was a thrill to me. From Broadway to the Ferry Station, it was a short distance on 127th Street. Passing under Riverside Drive the atmosphere was very much the Water Front type; it was used many times by motion pictures. The Ferry Boat was entirely a new type of transportation for me; my attention was very attracted by it. I did stand outside on both of the exteriors watching forward or backward so not to miss what was to be seen on crossing the Hudson and also to keep away from the interiors of the boat and the smell of the smoke and the cuspidors of which I had a horror. It was enough to have to walk from one end to the other to reach the front or to leave the boat; I could have walked on the driveways where the carriages did park during the crossing by squeezing myself between them and the island of the engine room, but the space was very tight and not too clean either. I just tried to be one of the first at the gates and rushed through holding a handkerchief in front of my nose when I walked the whole length of the ferry boat to reach the forward section.

It was always beautiful and interesting to watch the view on either side of the Hudson, rain or shine, winter or summer; the fog brought thrills also. I, many times, like the ferry boat men, stood as far forward as I could although they were there to signal the pilot if we were going to hit or slide in the sides of the pier. Ice on the Hudson did amuse me: sometimes it was going down to the ocean, sometimes pushed back with the tide, it was going the opposite way toward Albany. I enjoyed the ferry boat going through immense cakes of ice and when going over the top of them when too resisting it finally crushed them and settled on the water. The fleet did and still does anchor on the Hudson. At times…some morning it came as a surprise to see the boats showing their bows toward the bay, which when we went to the Studio were at night showing their sterns or vice-versa, according to the tide that was carrying them around their anchorage. A beautiful effect was a sunset in winter when the apartment houses of Riverside Drive having put up the extra storm-windows and it was a clear day, the setting red sun was reflecting in the hundreds of windows facing the Hudson. It made you believe the entire rows of them were ablaze.

On the way to my first visit to Éclair Studio, I was accompanied by Georges Benoit and Lucien Andriot. I met them at the Ferry boat house where [Henri] Menessier had made the rendezvous. We crossed the Hudson and on the New Jersey side we took the street car that climbed the Palisades. Talking with them did not stop me to register the scenery on the way. The view of the Hudson River and New York behind it enthused me and when we went through the woods I knew that I would like my stay in this country.

At the end of the woods was Fort Lee; a long street block and we were on Main Street, the street car had to turn on the left as the street did not run through. We went three blocks and there was the Éclair Studio behind trees a couple of hundred yards from Main Street. It was the country, a dirt road boarded of trees here and there and going way in the distance, opposite to the studio, an estate which I learned later on was a Seminary.

The entrance of the Éclair lot had an office on the street I could have taken for a Pullman car remodeled as it was standing so high above ground. On the other side a "lab" in retreat from the front and away to the right to let

a full view of the glass stage and its dependence; at the sight of it I did not feel too interested. Inside I felt better; the glass of the three sides and the roof were diffusing like in Gaumont's in Paris. The stage was small to me, even if it was 60 x 30 feet. I was shown the place after having been introduced to the interpreter Mr. [Louis] Grisel, first the Scenic Shop, then the Prop Room, the Wardrobe Lady's sewing room, then we went through a passage almost blocked by windows and doors and pieces of scenery and got to a hall where was the only office big enough for [Etienne] Arnaud's desk and Grisel's table; on the hall [were] four dressing rooms so small that I prefer not to say. All those dependences were the total of the stage area.

I met Mr. Grisel the interpreter, before anyone else in the studio. He spoke perfect French and I was assured by Benoit and Andriot of his friendship. He was in his early 50s, born in Switzerland and he had lots of experience under his paternal aspect. I was introduced to the Scenic artist next. This was a shock, I did not know there was one. The idea of taking somebody's place, me, a stranger, did not seem right but Irving Martin knew I was coming and had been assured of his job. Irving Martin and I became very friendly. Then I met the prop man, Nagel. They told me he was Indian. He did look to me like anybody else at that time. Later the head on the nickel piece reminded me of him. I met also the boss carpenter, Mr. [George] Rice, who showed me right away his friendship. He was an old man. We lost him a year later and I was very sad when it did happen; I cried. The balance of the people I was going to work with were the electrician, a couple of grips, three carpenters, a painter and the wardrobe lady.

I met the stock company Éclair was carrying. I will name the ones I do remember for sure: [Pearl] Cook, [Fred] Truesdell, [Charles] Jackson,

[Bob] Frazer, Mrs. [Julia] Stuart, and Barbara Tennant. There were two girls and a young child of seven or eight, Clara Horton: She was the daughter of the wardrobe lady. She was always dressed with lace and ribbons by her mother. Some of the actors spoke some French and were anxious to speak with the French people of the company. Then I met the still pictures man. In France, I never saw one around the stage. I believe the reason Éclair had one was for protection against the copyists; in this country, not like in France where the advertising is by posters, they need photographs for supplying the lobbies of the theaters. The still picture man was Robert [sic; should be Arthur?] Edeson and naturally wanted a picture of me for a booklet the company was publishing.

My first experience of the difficulty created by a hard winter, was a few weeks after I came to America. When the ferry put me on the New Jersey side, I found some members of the Éclair Studio who had taken the ferry boat before mine, they were waiting for information of what to do as the street cars did not run; the power lines were down; the snow that had started the day before had fallen all night. The freezing wind forced the ones who were waiting and me into the ferry boat building. We got word finally that the studio was sending transportation; it came almost an hour later. It was a flat-top truck mounted on sleds, with benches, that was pulled by two horses. It was almost eleven a.m. when we got inside the studio and we were all freezing. Arnaud was very concerned; he told me he had been called at home and not having gone outside did not know of the difficulties till he walked from his home which was not far from the studio. Grisel, the interpreter, seeing the displeasure on the other's faces explained in English what Arnaud told me in French.

We did not do a thing. The glass roof was loaded with snow which made the stage dark. Once in a while one pane was getting warm enough and the snow started to slide down with increased speed and the load would hit the ground with a deep sound. When we all left around 3 in the afternoon, the blizzard had diminished considerably and everybody was saying it would be nice tomorrow. It was better going down than coming up; at places, in the morning, we had some of us to unload the sleigh and walk behind it as the road was not evenly graded and was like a roller-coaster in places.

The next day was sunny but as the lines were still down the sleigh was waiting at the Ferry to take us up; there was a neighbor of our studio, Lucien Tainguy, the cameraman of the Solax (Studio) who did not know the cars were not running. Solax was not busy. The reason he was there was to take snapshots of snowy landscapes; we gave him a lift. In the night the snow had stopped and it did freeze; we walked a lot in keeping with the sleigh all the way. Tainguy taking pictures, I looking at what was new to me. The snow on the branches had melted and the wind had frozen the water in encircling the branches as in a tube of crystal. This made the trees white and sparkling. Tainguy in taking pictures, watching in the ground glass, did receive something on his head like a piece of ice; he had a good scalp under his cap but he was slightly hurt by the blow. We could not find out what it was, it was buried in the snow. We saw more pieces of ice falling, it turned out that the trees were reacting under the sunlight and the ice around the branches melted, running down the branches that were drooping down, the water frozen by the air and at the ends, it accumulated as a pear-shape and finally fell.

During the day the running of the street cars was reestablished; I walked out of the studio to go home. To let a car pass I stepped on what I thought was the sidewalk, I went down three feet, the snow had frozen and the top was like a soufflé – puffed up – the snow was there but it was a ditch and the vacuum had leveled the whole surface as well as the surrounding surfaces in one.

The streets of Fort Lee for days, did remind me of the battlements of a fortress. The snow on the streets and the sidewalks got packed on the curb by the people who lived there; as the snow settled they cut entrances in the wall of snow which separated then the street and the sidewalk. I saw that wall reach over six feet; at spring the melting snow went directly in the gutter when there was one. Main Street, Fort Lee, was very clean but the side streets were awful. Living in New York I had to wear rubbers on a dry day to face the slush of New Jersey.

All those sights and experiences for me were very amusing and the following winters when I wrote to my friends and family I included snapshots of snow scenes; the most successful were the roofs and the windowsills packed high, also 8 inches of snow resting on 7/8 iron railing and then my hand holding a branch encircled by ice. I did not want them to believe I was living in an imaginary world.

Before quitting the Studio, one afternoon Benoit came to me and said he would like to quit early because he had an appointment downtown before dinner and he would like me to travel with him. When Georges Benoit and I were in the street car, he told me that he was tired also of the trouble in the company and that he had been approached by somebody of D.W. Griffith's staff and was going to 23rd Street to see what they wanted him for. He told me that the only thing that was in the way was his obligation to Arnaud. I told him I could not advise him for or against, but to be certain of the word of the one he was going to see.

We did travel together all the way to 24th Street and 5th Avenue. At the corner I went to our French restaurant, he went down to 23rd where his appointment was. Alone, as Mennesier did not show up and Andriot was on location, I took a small table. I felt it was the end of our group. I was thinking to go back to France again when George Benoit came to face me. I saw that he had good news and I heard that he was going to photograph Mae Marsh.

When we spoke of money he told me he did not know what he would be paid. He started the following Monday, released by Arnaud with mysterious gladness. On his first paycheck we were dining alone, us two. He produced a fifty dollar bill, then a ten, another ten and a five. "That is my salary", he said.

MAURICE TOURNEUR

In my second winter in America I reacted badly to the little work I had to do. Etienne Arnaud and Oscar Lund were the only directors there; the company had opened a studio in Dallas, Texas – a new director had been engaged and put in charge of the western pictures which were going to be made there [actually, Tucson, Arizona – ed.].

My colleague Irving Martin, having contracted a chest ailment, had asked me to use my influence to have him sent there by the studio. I succeeded and I saw him five years later, in Los Angeles during a visit at the Douglas Fairbanks Studio where he made the paintings for the double-exposures for *Robin Hood*. He was feeling fine; he was married and was a father.

Georges Benoit, having joined D.W. Griffith, was by that time with Raoul Walsh in California. Henri Menessier was still going to the French restaurant. I saw him at night and he too was complaining of inactivities at the Solax Studio. Lucien Andriot even when not on location was in and out of us

but I was perhaps the most absentee, the Kit Kat Klub getting more interesting to me – the Sunday morning classes permitted us to use the daylight which was a change from the artificial light we had during the weekday evenings.

When spring came I felt more cheerful. Fort Lee woods were getting green and the atmosphere was not so dull in the studio. I noticed that Jules Brulatour was showing up more often around the place. Rumors were circulating about his successes with Eastman Kodak and how rich he was getting; I did not care about the gossip I was only wishing he did find a way to procure better things around the company. I was getting tired of the last minute stories thought up during the night or the evening before.

Once in a while Brulatour came with visitors; this made me believe that he was a silent partner of Éclair. I was never introduced to visitors, if any of those people was going to be of interest to me it was hard for me to remember his face. When, one day, a man was roaming around the stage Arnaud came to talk to him. They walked and passing by me Arnaud made the introduction. The man was a French director – I heard that his name was Maurice Tourneur – then they went away. I thought it was bizarre, the way things were going on; first I was surprised that Arnaud did not speak of the new comer before I met him, then Grisel refusing to offer any information. Outside of the Studio, I had something more important to worry about, the tension in Europe. In New York the French people did not believe the war was so imminent. I was reassured but it came and I went to report to the Consulate there. I was told that I was not wanted after they saw my military papers.

The next morning coming back from the French Consulate to the studio, I saw seated at a wood table (the type we used for kitchen or saloon), reading a play – the new French director. I said hello to him and went to see Arnaud to tell him about the day before; he was not in but Grisel was. He told me that Arnaud had left for France. I was so surprised that I left the office shocked and on the stage, seeing Maurice Tourneur, I went to him and asked who was in charge now. He answered: "I am". I had not really been introduced to him and I did not expect that sharp answer, still I asked if he had anything for me. I did not introduce myself, I do not know if he knew who I was; he answered: "I have to go through the script. I will tell you later".

Looking back in my memory I wondered what had clicked in my mind when I saw Maurice Tourneur seated in front of that table; something was familiar and it came back: I saw myself in France when sent to retouch before the "premiere", standing in the wings or in the auditorium waiting for the end of the reading to the cast by the stage manager. I had not seen this for many years but I could not forget when I was working for Amable that I saw Rejane, when sent to the Vaudeville Theater, rehearsing a couple of hours without stopping.

"THE MAN OF THE HOUR"

On the afternoon Jules Brulatour showed up, he told me what I knew already about Arnaud and Maurice Tourneur. I did not ask any questions, I would have liked to have heard from him where he was standing but he kept quiet on that matter; the only news I got from him was that they were building a new studio a stone's throw from Éclair. This surprised me, I never heard about it; the building and the structure of the stage was already up when I went to look for it. It was behind Éclair, behind the trees. I never did look that way and no mention of it from the Fort Lee natives working in the studio had come to me.

When I asked who was in charge to

Maurice Tourneur that morning I had glanced at the script and I had time to read a title, *The Man of the Hour*, that was all I saw. Now I was building up on a play that I never saw and with a new French director. A few days later Tourneur came to see me when I was painting on the scenic shop frame and asked me to come down to meet Sam Mayer, a man in the early sixties; very warm. I felt in his handshake that I was going to make friends with him. I was told by Tourneur, in English, that Sam Mayer would be my guide to the places I would have to see for the picture he was going to shoot. Beside the New York City Hall, we would have to go to Washington, me to document myself and Sam Mayer to introduce me to the many people he knew and help us to get carte blanche and hear some interesting comments [Carré seems to be conflating his work on two different films: *The Man of the Hour* (1914) and *The Velvet Paw* (1915)].

When we got to Washington, the first thing Sam Mayer did was to register for us at a hotel on Pennsylvania Avenue. After registering he told me it was the place to meet the people we were interested to talk to. In the lobby he introduced me to many people, many he addressed "Senator". I was rather embarrassed but pleased to see Sam so much at ease with that crowd filling up the hotel lobby.

At dinner I was told by Sam we were going to the Capitol in the morning, to get ready, to take my sketch book as I would be free to take notes and draw what I wanted. I do not mind to say that I felt out of place as a Frenchman among those political men. When we approached the lobby of the House of Representatives I was expecting to get a pass, a card, something to permit me to go through but I did not. I went between Sam Mayer and his friend and I found myself right on the floor of the House in front of the first row. Beside the full view of

the House and the Tribunes I wanted, which the black and white pictures did not show, so I made my mind quick and figured the plan of the rostrum, the design of the walls and a few other things. The two paintings behind the speaker rostrum [of] George Washington and the Marquis de Lafayette that I would have to paint, the souvenir shop would supply. The boys on the floor going back and forth were curious to see what I was drawing. They did peek discreetly but made me nervous, I was afraid they had some gag to pull on me.

I did not know much about politics. Sam Mayer was aware of it. When we left the House we went through a door near the rostrum and I heard, "It is in this hall that the lobbyists are working", I got a quick definition and made a quick memorandum of it suspecting the need of it for the story. When I was through Sam told me we were going to see a member of the House in the Office Building. We went down by the elevator and there we took the tram car like at the beach and went through the tunnel which reminded me of the subway in Paris. In the office of the Representatives we went up and leaving the elevator we went through a long corridor with doors placed at equal distance. Sam knowing where we were going finally decided to look for a number and when he saw it, knocked at the door. We entered a suite and he introduced me to the man who was a member of the House. I shook hands and I was told to go ahead with my notes and my drawings. There was a secretary; she told me a few things and opened the doors of closets and wardrobe. A characteristic of this office was it did look more like a transformed corridor 10 feet wide, 35 feet long, cut in two with one door at one end and one window at the other.

After lunch (I do not remember where), we went to see the House in Session. We did not stay long as we had to take our train. We rushed out

Interior of the Senate chamber, reconstructed by Ben Carré for Maurice Tourneur's The Velvet Paw *(World-Paragon, 1916).*

"What studio?" Lucien Andriot (left) walks across the lot to look at the new Peerless facility.

after I drew a detail of a corner of the main entrance in the Capitol. This is all I saw from Washington that time and I had been very impressed. On the train in the observation car, Sam dozed while I wrote notes of what I had seen and had not had time to put down before. I had a regret not to have seen the Senate Chamber. I promised myself to go back and see the Corcoran Gallery where there was a picture loved by the French people, "L'Angélus de Millet".

When I got to the studio and looked at the Éclair stage space I got scared of how I was going to put the House in that shell. I did the best I could, I did not lose an inch. I concentrated on the rostrum, I painted the two portraits. There was no criticism from the studio, none from the actors, none from the press.

Still an incident did happen when they were rehearsing. I was painting in the shop, somebody came to ask for a gavel. I told him to ask for one in the prop shop. It took me time to come down from the platform of the paint frame, I went on the stage; the speaker was calling order with a walnut mallet. The assistant director saw it and looked at me. I had to rush to have one made of respectable size by one of my men.

I was glad I saw this incident in time and I must give credit to the assistant director who saw it too. A too-late correction would have spoiled for me the memory of the picture.

The Man of the Hour brought to me a new light on the future. I had not worked on anything of great interest since I left France. The presence of big stars was going to demand better stories, better productions. Robert Warwick, the star of the play, spoke French, his humor was a comfort to the workers at the studio. I had pleasant talks with him – he did enjoy my French especially my Parisian expressions.

The play is very vague to me as the only work I remember well that I did for it was the House of Representatives and a set which represented a reception room in City Hall, New York City. It is in this set that Tourneur, who had come to me, had said: "Let us walk through when the camera is turning". I went beside him when he was directing; toward the end of the scene he took me by the arm and we went in before he did stop it. I was worried. I did not want to be on the screen.

In the early days, about 1907, in Gaumont we did go on the stage and mix with the players when a crowd was needed. In a short film, the title I believe was *Chapeau, Chapeau*, it took place in a theater on the balcony section. A woman well-dressed with a large hat with feathers (as was the mode at that period) sat on the front seat of the balcony. The obstruction of the view of the four or five rows behind her brought a protest and the word chapeau (hat, in English) brought also a cadence not only behind the hat owner but all over the spectators of the balcony. I was with the other boys from the shop; I was on the extreme side. I thought I was out of the picture, looking at the marking ropes on the floor which indicated the limits of the view of the camera; the director asking for more action from everybody, I stood on my seat and as a cheerleader engaged in the tumult. I saw myself on the screen some days later when I went to see a show. I was glad it was dark in the audience, I felt sick seeing myself gesticulating. I had sworn never to be in a picture again.

FIRST FILMS AT THE PEERLESS STUDIO

The Peerless Studio was building up, but the people I knew who were interested did not speak of it. I was wondering if, like Moses, I would know of the Promised Land only from the distance. It was mysterious, like the departure of Arnaud. Who was responsible for the idea of starting a new studio, who was the architect, I never knew who discussed about the plans, the arrangements, the material, the necessities. Finally, one day, I was asked: "Do you like the new studio?" I knew of it but I saw it only once after I heard about it from one of my men and that was months back. I answered: "What studio?" I promised to go and see it when I would have a chance. I am positive that Maurice Tourneur could not have been an advisor, as the work had started too close to his coming to America; Brulatour could have been the one to answer questions but it would have been embarrassing if, in turn, he did ask some.

When I visited the Peerless Studio I saw big improvements over the Éclair. The first ones were the offices and the

dressing rooms, and sanitary conditions; but the architect who drew the plans must have looked at a studio already existing and made it larger; most of the theaters in America do not have a regular Scenic Shop, they use the back wall of the stage to put the paint frame on. This draughtsman, not finding a place on the glass stage, put it up above the carpenter shop. The stage did not have a pit or a trap; when we moved in, it took time to be accustomed to the place. The only good improvement for me was the area of the stage which was over three times that of Éclair Studio.

Every part of the studio was under the same roof, half of it being the stage that did run east and west, the long glass wall was on the south.

When the picture was in editing (we really did use the word "cutting" for that work) I was asked to move to the new place. What happened to Éclair Studio after I left I do not know; I did not care. I moved to Peerless like stepping into another room, taking with me my boss carpenter, Harry Conselman, who had been with the Hippodrome in New York, a man of experience who knew well the stage needs.

> Not a member of the Motion Picture Patents Company, Eclair had always been at a disadvantage in terms of its American distribution. It sold its films on the independent market, an increasingly difficult proposition, and eventually affiliated with Universal. This account of a Universal outing to Palisades Park, the famous amusement center located at the southern end of Fort Lee, suggests how "Americanized" Éclair had become.

UNIVERSAL HAS ITS FIRST INNING WITH AN OUTING
The Great Film Company Starts The Ball Rolling At The Convention

(from *The Universal Weekly,* July 12, 1913, p. 5)

In assigning the Universal to the honor place in the entertaining of the guests to the Third National Convention of the M.P.E.L.A., the committee gave tacit recognition of the leadership of the greatest film manufacturing company in the universe. The big doings took place as previously scheduled on Monday, July 4, and when the extensive program was revealed to the amazed delegates and their friends, all agreed that the Universal had set a pace that the others would have difficulty in approaching.

At 1 p.m. a string of auto-busses, headed by Joe Brandt and Fred Gunning in an open car, with the famous Universal Band following in a sight-seeing bus, lined up the crowd at Grand Central Palace. In parade formation, the procession rolled its way over the asphalted streets of Manhattan to the Weehawken Ferry and thence crossed the Hudson to New Jersey. A delightful ride along the crest of the Palisades unfolded a rare panorama of the lordly Hudson and the upper part of Manhattan to the enraptured beholders.

About 3 o'clock, the Universal Éclair Studio at Fort Lee was reached, and here the visitors stretched their nether limbs in a walk through the grounds of this most complete studio. A motion picture of the assembled company was taken, which was immediately developed and printed, and shown to the party four hours later at Palisades Amusement Park, a record-breaking performance. The 800 guests were conducted through the studios where they met the Éclair stars, including Barbara Tennant, Fred Truesdell, Bob Frazer, Will

Emile Cohl.

Sheerer, Alec Francis, Nancy Averill, William Cavanaugh, O. A. C. Lund, and Mildred Bright.

At six o'clock the caravan headed for Palisades Amusement Park where tickets were given to each person entitling him to free admission to the manifold attractions of this beautiful place.

Entering the grounds, the guests were conducted to Nakoff's Casino where a bounteous supper was spread. When appetites had been satisfied, the party dispersed to the various parts of the park, to seek out the pleasures that most appealed to each. In the great open-air natatorium, a swimming contest in which the publicity men of the film game participated, was pulled off, the winner being awarded a gold medal. Prizes of gold and silver watches for the best dancing were also awarded, and a program of Universal and Éclair features was given. Mr. Carl Laemmle and other officers of the company lent their presence to the festivities in the evening, and held a reception in the pavilion for the hundreds of exhibitors who follow their gallant leadership. At midnight, the crowd clambered into the auto-busses again, and after the pleasant moonlight ride through the Jersey forests, returned to New York accounting Universal Day a most enjoyable experience.

In October 1912 pioneer film animator Emile Cohl arrived from Paris to begin work on the cartoon portion of Éclair's newsreel. The "Newlywed" series referred to here, featuring "Baby Snookums", was the first ever marketed as an "animated cartoon". Cohl's talents also extended to stop-motion animation, a startling technical feat highlighted in this review of *A Vegetarian's Dream*.

ÉCLAIR ECHOES

(from *Moving Picture World*, August 30, 1913, p.966)

The artist who makes the "Newlywed" and other trick pictures over at the Fort Lee studio of Éclair has just finished a comedy subject of five hundred feet which has taken a solid month of hard work to put together. It is entitled *A Vegetarian's Dream*, and shows some very amusing antics of vegetables, lemons, etc. This five hundred feet of film is made from some eighty thousand drawings and by some exceptionally clever trick work. When it comes to the showing of the lemons becoming pigs and playing leap frog, this part is not made from drawings and it will keep the public guessing for many weeks to understand how it has been done.

RELEASED SUNDAY, APRIL 6th, 1913

"He Wants What He Wants When He Wants It"
(THE NEWLYWED SERIES)

Snookums at Sea.

The Story

THIS third of the great laughing success series of the "Newlyweds" is based on "Snookums'" experiences playing in a little sea, created by a bursted water-pipe, under the sink.

When "Snookums" discovered this break in the pipe and the splashing water, he thought it was great fun to sit there and let the water spray over his nice clean clothes. He was having the time of his life when his mother found him, but she promptly got him out of the mess and summoned a plumber. But now the poor dear almost lifted the roof with his explosive "wows." He wanted to go back and play in the nice water and he couldn't see why mother wanted him to be dressed in those clean, stiff, starched clothes.

After a few strenuous hours, "Da-Da" came to the rescue, and going to the pipe, which our friend, Mr. Plumber, had just repaired, Papa Newlywed got busy with a hammer and spike and re-opened the pipe, so that "Snookums" might enjoy himself in the nice little lake.

"Snookums" was shortly shouting "Da-Da" and all seemed well, until the neighbors on the floor below came up to complain about the water, which was damaging their apartment. So "Da-Da" had to pacify them with the assertion that they had just sent for the plumber and he would certainly be there soon. While waiting (?) on the plumber "Snookums" was very happy.

There is a laugh in every foot of this subject, because these animated cartoons are a hundred times more humorous than the pictures could possibly be had an attempt been made to get them out with real people in the characters.

The funny twists of the cartoon characters as they are made to move in their very human-like expressions and antics, are certainly a scream.

It is little wonder that this great series of animated cartoons has been such a success, and they promise to be one of the real features of the year.

Advertising in the shape of one, three and six sheets has been prepared, so that exhibitors can do justice to this great comedy success.

On the same reel with this laughing hit is found one of those remarkable scientific subjects for which the Éclair Company is justly famous.

(ON THE SAME REEL)
CRYSTALLIZATION

THIS beautiful scientific subject is not only remarkable for the presentation of its educational phase, but it is also a very attractive subject, owing to the beauty of the different formations secured by the chemist in the transformation of liquids into crystals. It is certainly a most interesting subject and is sure to be one of the very bright spots on any program.

This, with a "Newlywed" subject makes this reel an offering which will be a positive delight to any audience in any part of the country.

The thing for every exhibitor to do is to see to it immediately that his exchange secures every one of the Newlywed series. A few exchanges may need your request to arouse them to the importance of pleasing you.

Don't neglect to inform your exchange at once that you want this reel. Tell them today, and then tell them tomorrow and keep on telling them until you get it.

"SNOOKUMS" HAS THE NATION LAUGHING.

Under the new Universal contract Éclair began producing more westerns and action pictures, employing American directors like William Haddock to produce them. They even opened a satellite studio in Tucson, Arizona specifically for this purpose, but had no trouble making at least a portion of their westerns in Fort Lee.

HELEN MARTEN
THE "LITTLE INDIAN" OF
THE ÉCLAIR-UNIVERSALS

By F. Marion Brandon

(from *The Universal Weekly,* October 25, 1913, p. 8)

Next time you are looking at one of those famous Éclair-Universals depicting the Great Northwest, watch out for Minnehaha, otherwise Laughing Waters, and see if you can recognize in her that remarkably pretty girl with the dimples and the oodles of "waving, luxuriant tresses", as the Sutherland Sisters would say.

Miss Marten is emphatically not the Rexall Girl, the photo herewith notwithstanding. She doesn't have time to do so now, but at one time she was greatly in demand among the best illustrators of today as a model for ideal American girl types. Her beauty wears well. In fact, it grows on you – not literally, of course. She is of exactly the right height, according to the best authorities – just as high as a man's heart.

Indian girls usually ride pretty well. Helen admitted that she can do a few things with a horse. Over at the Éclair Studios in Fort Lee they say she can hold in check the wildest thing that ever grew on four legs. Then, on the side, she has a penchant for aquatics; swims clean and straight, like a torpedo fish. Isn't afraid to do high dives, either. Has a few purely domestic accomplishments in reserve, for possible future developments. Cooks. Simply great. Pies like mother used to make, and coffee that would put the most ingrained-groucho at peace with the world.

It's hard to get Helen to talk about herself and her work. Her stage name is her real name – that much I discovered and none of her folks had ever, in

The Éclair Bulletin promotes Emile Cohl's latest "Baby Snookums" cartoon. April, 1913.

any capacity whatsoever, been connected with that mysterious precinct, the stage.

Helen breaks precedents as easily as hearts when she wants something. She wanted to act. That was all there was to it. The first manager she tackled welcomed her like a letter from home. Couldn't be otherwise. One look into her liquid, luminous azure – or is it turquoise? – orbs would make any man pliable as putty in Helen's lilylike hands. She has been in pictures a scant three years, and during that time has displayed a creditable versatility in the parts she has taken. Her work in the *Spectre Bridegroom* is still recalled with pleasure by picture fans. She also took part in *The Trail of the Silver Fox, The Great Unknown, Right of Way, Rosary, For Better or Worse,* and more recently divided honors in *Jacques, the Wolf.* Miss Marten plays a straight part – just herself – in *Big-Hearted Jim,* the last Éclair-Universal, which is the first picture that has done her beauty justice.

MISS TENNANT HURT BY RUFFIANS

(from *The Universal Weekly,* November 8, 1913, p. 5)

While playing in an exterior scene over on the Palisades of New Jersey, Barbara Tennant was severely bruised by a large rock dropped down from the top by a gang of ruffians. The Éclair director, with a company consisting of Miss Tennant, Will E. Sheerer and Lindsay Hall, had gone to the place in the morning, and it was while they were in the midst of their work that the ruffians set upon them.

It is an example of the difficulties moving picture companies work under sometimes in taking exterior scenes. The male members of the company and the camera operator charged the gang, and, though greatly outnumbered, succeeded in driving the fellows away, and when reinforced by the local police, completely routed them. Four of the disturbers were arrested and fined.

The 1914 Eclair fire was the first major film fire in Fort Lee. Although it was the laboratory which burned, not the studio, Éclair never did resume production in Fort Lee. In January 1914 Jourjon had transferred the Éclair property to the Motion Picture Properties Company, and in February (again with Jules Brulatour as his silent partner) incorporated the Peerless Feature Producing Company, whose studio was about to go up on the adjacent lot. The actors working in the studio at the time of the fire were not even working for Éclair, but for the Shuberts, who were also involved in the Peerless project.

FILM FACTORY BURNS WITH $300,000 LOSS
Many Valuable Reels Destroyed in Éclair Company's Fort Lee Plant

(from the *New York Times,* March 20, 1914, p. 1)

Hackensack, NJ, March 19 – Fire swept through the plant of the Eclair Moving Picture Company at Fort Lee this afternoon, causing damage of $300,000. The negative department and the storage vaults were destroyed. The damage to machinery alone will be more than $100,000. One lathe valued at $1500 was the only piece of machinery which was saved.

Completed film productions valued at more than $200,000 were in the vaults, and in trying to save these Francis Doublier was over come by smoke and carried out unconscious. Among the productions destroyed was *The Caballero's Way,* just completed in three reels, valued at $20,000 and one recently received from Paris entitled *Protea* in six reels, which cost $60,000 to produce. Mr. Doublier saved several reels before he was overcome.

Much of the damage is attributed to insufficient water supply. Arthur Edeson, one of the photographers employed by the concern, said this afternoon:

"The stream of water from the nozzle would not carry six feet above us. If we had had a half decent pressure we could have put the fire out in a few minutes. We even climbed to the roof of the scenery storage building and tried to throw water across the open space of ten feet to where the flames were, but even this could not be done. Before the firemen came the whole factory was doomed."

The heroine of the day was Irene Whipple, a young woman employee of the company, who hurried through the halls to the different departments and warned a hundred employees to run for safety.

The studio, when the fire started, was filled with actors who were rehearsing *The Gentlemen from Mississippi,* in which Thomas Wise appears. All the actors hurried from the studio, and did what they could to aid in saving property. One person was injured – Robert Klein, a boy, whose hand was crushed by falling timber.

Henry Maire, the factory manager, was disconsolate as he watched the ineffectual efforts to fight the fire. Mayor White of Fort Lee, who arrived while the fire was at its height, criticized the water service bitterly.

"For months", he said, "the people in

Fort Lee. 15 avril 1912

The disastrous 1914 Éclair fire began here in the laboratory building.

the eastern part of Bergen County have been complaining of the lack of water pressure in the pipes of the Hackensack Water Company, but it has resulted in nothing. The Eastern Bergen County Improvement Association has joined hands with Senator Hennessy and will take the matter before the Public Utilities Commission at Trenton. I think the moving pictures taken by the Eclair Company this afternoon of a real fire, showing the ludicrous water service, ought to convince the commission that something is wrong."

The Fort Lee Council adopted resolutions last night attacking the rates of the Hackensack Water Company and the low pressure.

Manager Maire said to-night that the company at once would begin the reconstruction of its factory. The plant of the company covers two blocks of ground and is one of the most extensive moving-picture factories in the country.

JANE [sic] ACKER BACK TO SCREEN IN SUPPORT TO GEO. WALSH

(from *Moving Picture World,* January 4, 1919, p. 107)

As an example of the policy of William Fox of surrounding his stars with casts of players of recognized ability, it was announced this week that Jean Acker, formerly one of the best known feminine leads in the profession, had returned to the films as member of George Walsh's company, which is filming *Tough Luck Jones.* Miss Acker, who has been "out of pictures" for two years or more, formerly played in support of some of the leading stars, and is widely known as an actress of considerable ability.

Although Éclair itself dropped its association with the studio in 1914, the name continued to stick. William Fox soon moved in, and many Fox productions moved back and forth between the Éclair and Willat stages, which had also fallen under Fox control. Jean Acker, who would (briefly) become the first Mrs. Rudolph Valentino later that year, was one of the last Fox stars to work at the Éclair before Fox opened its new Manhattan studio in 1920. Regardless of how "well known" she may have been, the *Moving Picture World* was clearly undecided about her actual name.

It is understood that the William Fox organization is negotiating for another well known actress to play the part of the ingénue lead. Mr. Walsh and his company have been making interior scenes at the Éclair Studio in Fort Lee, NJ, during the past week.

After the holidays they will go to Florida to shoot exteriors. The company is being directed by Edward Dillon, who also directed George Walsh in *Luck and Pluck.*

8.
Solax

Herbert and Alice Guy Blaché arrived in the United States in 1907 to promote the Gaumont Chronophone talking film system. Although Alice had been directing for Gaumont in France since 1896, she made no films in America until 1910, when the couple formed their own production company, Solax; Alice would take charge of Solax while Herbert continued to manage Gaumont's studio in Flushing, New York. At first Solax worked out of the same Flushing studio, but the Blachés (doing business as the New Jersey Studio Company) purchased land for a new Solax studio on Lemoine Avenue as early as 21 November 1911. The studio was almost completed when Hugh Hoffman visited it less than a year later. Although Hoffman suggests that Fort Lee was at this time only a potential competitor to Los Angeles as a film production center, it would be years before anyone in Hollywood built anything as sophisticated as the Solax Fort Lee plant.

NEW SOLAX PLANT AT FORT LEE

A Finely Equipped Studio And Factory Representing An Investment Of $100,000 To Be The Permanent Home Of This Popular Company

By Hugh Hoffman

(from *Moving Picture World,* September 14, 1912, pp. 1061–1062)

Fort Lee, New Jersey, and environs, may in time rival Los Angeles as a motion picture community. It is toward that region, quite close to New York, that Manhattan motion picture directors turn instinctively when they want a good scene without going far from New York City. For a number of years Fort Lee and Coytesville have been a favorite stamping ground. As many as seven and eight motion picture companies have been noticed, all working on the same day, around these two Palisade villages. Only a week ago a humorous incident took place when the Biograph Company was working on one side of a fence while the Reliance Company was using the other side of the same fence, both using the gate. The two directors worked in harmony and with much courtesy, somewhat on the "Gaston and Alphonse" order.

With all their excursions into this particular district, it is rather strange that most of the manufacturing companies located their studios elsewhere, but the reason perhaps was that most of the studios were in rented quarters in the city. However, as the business of manufacturing concerns continues to grow to the point where they feel obliged to erect a studio, it is more than likely that Fort Lee will become the ultimate location of a number of picture making companies. The

Alice Guy Blaché poses with her family at the studio site on Lemoine Avenue, 1912.

THE MOVING PICTURE WORLD 605

FORT LEE, NEW JERSEY
is the new home of the Rising Sun Films.

$100,000.00 New Factory and Studio. The Studio and Factory is the best equipped moving picture plant in the World. Planned by people with years of experience in the industry. The knowledge which experience has taught them has been used to advantage in the planning. Efficiency is the keynote of the new plant. Every film coming from the new plant will be a feature, for the facilities for good and big work are unlimited.

COMING FEATURE RELEASES
"The EQUINE SPY"
TWO REELS
RELEASED, FRIDAY, AUGUST 23rd, 1912

Featuring the most intelligent Horse in the World. The Horse with a Million Dollar reputation.

DON
The Horse that can do everything but talk. The Horse with a $20,000 annual earning capacity.

Advertising matter includes—One sheets—three sheets—special photos—lobby displays and "Magnets"

Released Wednesday, August 28th, 1912
HIS DOUBLE

A Comedy dealing with the disturbance created by a young man who masquerades as a Count—his rival. His pranks put a household in a turmoil and incidentally win him a wife.

Solax Company
FORT LEE, NEW JERSEY

Solax announces its arrival in Fort Lee in a full page ad in the Moving Picture World, *15 October 1912.*

Champion Company was the first to locate on the Palisades, having a studio at Coytesville. Pathé Frères, after operating further down the State of New Jersey at Bound Brook, finally erected a large studio on Jersey City Heights, overlooking the Hudson River. About a year ago the Éclair Company erected the first plant and studio in Fort Lee and now the Solax Company has just moved into its fine new studio and factory, which has recently been completed at an outlay of $100,000. That more companies will follow their example is hardly to be doubted, as an hour's automobile ride in either direction from that location will furnish suitable backgrounds for years to come. While very close to New York City, the vicinity of Fort Lee affords many varieties of natural scenery. Jersey scenery has been de-rided by certain critics and writers who probably could not name an equivalent substitute for the scenery of the Palisades without involving much expense for transportation, and other items.

The new Solax plant is a decidedly complete and permanent institution. It is large and roomy and all departments can be conducted there without being cramped in any way. The building is four stories in height, and it is built of brick, with concrete floors and steel girders. The studio proper is constructed of structural iron and glass. The floor of the studio is large enough to accommodate five ordinary stage settings at once, or three extra deep settings. The glass frames surrounding the studio are so constructed as to be easily removable, allowing a full flood of sunlight to enter the place. This arrangement is valuable also for natural backgrounds to interior settings that have windows. The camera, by this means, can record a studio interior with a genuine landscape as a vista.

The entire studio and factory were planned by Madame Alice Blaché, the presiding genius of the Solax Company. She is a remarkable personality, combining a true artistic temperament with executive ability and business acumen. Every detail of the making of a Solax picture comes directly under her personal supervision. She takes full responsibility for the Solax product, and, when one considers that this model factory is the result of her work during the two years existence of the Solax Company, her judgment is hardly to be questioned.

In company with Madame Blaché the World representative was shown about the various departments of the Solax plant. The itinerary began at the business office, which is a delightful place on the ground floor. Fresh from the workman's hand, it is immaculate with its clean walls and woodwork, the new desks and general office equipment. Everything there sparkled with newness and seemed to breathe out an incentive to good work. About the walls many of the Solax posters were hung in frames. These Solax posters are really posters from an artistic point of view. They are not exactly photographs of scenes from the drama, but are done in broad simple poster fashion, much after the manner of "Harper's Weekly", and other large business firms that are experts in poster advertising. The business office opens directly into the shipping department where the finished product is crated for general distribution. There also the posters are piled in large quantities to be shipped with the films. Over these departments, as all others, the sense of newness spread its crisp charm. Next into the projection room where the finished product must meet its final test, which is the all-seeing eye of Madame Blaché. The laboratories and darkrooms are equipped with machinery that is considered the last word in picture making.

The spacious drying rooms are located directly beneath the main studio offices and have a capacity of drying 6,000 feet at a time on the huge drums. The long joining room is flooded with light and along the window sides are clean sanitary work benches for the girls. The factory superintendent's office and the boiler rooms complete the ground floor itinerary, after which the studio proper on the next floor was visited. Opening just off the main studio floor are various accessory departments. The property room is at one end and next to it is the papier-mache working department. The third room is a property room, containing the more solid and unbreakable articles in great profusion. Fourth along the line is the large scene-room where many, many flats are stacked close together. At the extreme right end the carpenter shop is located, and its connection with the scene painting department just above it is ingenious. To get to the scenic department it is necessary to climb a flight of stairs to a balcony that runs the length of the studio.

Scenic and carpentry shops at the Solax studio. From Moving Picture World, *September 14, 1912.*

The scenic artists work directly above the carpenters and at either side of their room is a wide slot through which a sliding frame raises or lowers the scene, according to the desire of the artists. In this way the carpenters and the scenic artists are separated and kept from being in each other's way and yet they are in close touch. The carpenters below build and cover their frames. They are then placed upon these sliding frames and sent up to the scenic artists direct. Along the balcony various doors lead to other departments. Next to the scenic room is another property room for the storing of the more delicate articles, such as bric-a-brac and crockery. The next door down the corridor is the wardrobe room, well stocked for most every requirement. And next to the wardrobe room is the door leading to the labyrinth of dress rooms. The directors room is a comfortable well furnished office, just off the entrance. This section of the plant more resembles a hotel as the rooms are finished in hotel fashion with running water, furniture, carpets, etc. As the World scout peered into the star's dressing room he beheld Miss Blanche Cornwall, the Solax leading lady, who was industriously engaged in beautifying her comfortable sanctum. It surely did look girlish with all the fussy little feminine frills that she had added to it from time to time.

"This is surely heaven", she said. "When I look back and think of two solid years of one night stands that I did before joining the Solax Company."

The men's dressing room is directly opposite and it needs no label to designate it as such. Well distributed cuspidors and a large pinochle table in the center of the room together with muddy boots here and there, and an aroma of well seasoned pipes told the story in an instant. Contrary to general usage, the masculine members of the Solax stock company, by vote, decided that, rather than occupy the individual rooms that were built from them, they would prefer to share together the large room that was originally intended for the extra people, and it was therefore decreed that the regular members will occupy the big room and that the extra people will dress in the smaller rooms. There is only one explanation for this unusual state of affairs and that explanation can be put into one word – "pinochle".

The entire Solax Company, both artists and artisans, as well as business staff, feel the vast improvement of their new environment over their former cramped quarters at Flushing, Long Island. The change has given them all new energy and a new interest in their work, and there is not one of them who does not sincerely believe that Madame Blaché is a wonderful woman.

The new Solax factory has a capacity for turning out 12,000 feet of finished positive film per day. Besides the factory building, a large tract of land surrounding it is also owned by the Solax Company, and already an expert landscape gardener is at work laying out the grounds after a plan that will make them into a beautiful park when completed. In this large enclosure the Solax Company will enact many large outdoor scenes that call for extensive scenic preparations and large ensembles. Among all the various motion picture factories, the Solax plant stands today as one of the most complete, if not the largest motion picture plant in existence.

THE MEMOIRS OF ALICE GUY BLACHÉ

Translated by Roberta and Simone Blaché; edited by Anthony Slide (Metuchen, NJ: Scarecrow Press, 1986, pp. 63–67)

Alice Guy Blaché was very conscious of the importance of her achievements as a film director, producer, and owner of her own studio. But as she grew older she also felt, with considerable justification, that these accomplishments had been ignored by both French and American historians. In this excerpt from her memoir, first published in France in 1976, eight years after her death, she recalls the creation of Solax and its work in Fort Lee.

Our company prospered, making appreciable profits, and as the Gaumont Studio proved inadequate we decided to build our own studio in Fort Lee, New Jersey, which was just then the center of the cinema.

As my husband was held by his contract with Gaumont, for a fairly long time I had to manage by myself, but I already had good co-workers. There was [Wilbert] Melville whom I have already mentioned and Bauries [Joseph Borries?], a Frenchman from Newfoundland, who was literally faithful until his death.

An electrical engineer, Max Mayer (whose name is unjustly forgotten for he was the voluntary victim of the first X-ray experiments) gave our studio an installation unique at that time: an entirely removable ceiling, real keyboard for lights, spot-lights, etc. Our cameras, projectors, printing, perforation, were by Bell & Howell, whose reputation is well known. Finally, our film supplier was Kodak, which had arrived at an unequalled degree of perfection.

We had no difficulty in finding builders or specialized electricians, the American studios being already, from that point of view, better equipped than our own. However, their ignorance of certain procedures really astonished me. The first time that I asked my cameraman to get a special effect (on that occasion, a man walking on the water) he told me that this was impossible. I had to insist and to guide him, step by step, to obtain a result which filled him with admiration and earned me his respect.

One film where I had used a system of masks that permit printing two different views of the same image, and obtain double exposure effects, so intrigued the cameramen that they begged me to explain by what means I had achieved that result.

The care brought to choosing the most favorable angle in photographing a fine landscape, or obtaining a beautiful light effect, by *contre-jour*, was noticed and brought me critical praise.

The Americans caught up quickly, thanks to their scorn for routine, their love of risk, their ready money and many other qualities. They learned quickly, and the First World War, paralysing European industry, permitted them an advantage they have kept ever since....

An important group of new companies was formed, some in New York, some in New Jersey. Stage actors more and more willingly accepted roles in the new art. Clubs were formed, fairs were organized, among others, there was a great annual ball given at the Waldorf Astoria.

This was the epoch of the melodrama. Films had now attained the length of 3,000 feet. In each of the reels, the

TELEPHONE 166 FORT LEE   CABLE ADDRESS "SOLAXFILM" NEW YORK

Solax Company

MANUFACTURERS OF

MOTION PICTURE FILMS
LEMOINE AVENUE
FORT LEE, NEW JERSEY

     I, Alice Blaché, do hereby appoint Herbert Blaché of Palisade, New Jersey, to vote as my proxy at the meeting of the stockholders of the Film Supply Company of America, on the 13th day of December, and at any adjourned meeting thereof.

     IN WITNESS WHEREOF I have hereunto set my hand and seal this thirteenth day of December, nineteen hundred and twelve.

IN THE PRESENCE OF

                                        (Signature)

Alice Guy Blaché preferred to handle the artistic aspects of the business, and left many of the administrative decisions to her husband Herbert. In this December 13, 1912 release she appoints him as her permanent proxy at meetings of the Film Supply Company, their distributor.

public demanded a "punch" or suspense (remember Pearl White).

The Shadow of the Moulin Rouge, A Terrible Night, The Rogues of Paris [all released in 1913], and many others were all of this genre. The abduction of rich heiresses (always young and pretty), pursuit by a lover or detective, entrapment in boats, flooded dungeons, quicksands, etc. Anything went, if only there was a happy ending.

Art and reality were both lost there, surely, and the critics were not always very tender. Alas! "Advisers are not payers". Also, my best critics were the audiences with whom I mingled incognito. There I heard an impartial judgment, sometimes deceiving also, for the same film, coldly received on 45th Street might arouse enthusiasm on 125th, and vice versa.

This genre of film put me in touch with the daredevils who made a specialty of doubling for the stars in perilous moments. Some of them, themselves, proposed to us that they should leap from a bridge onto a moving express train, to be tied between the rails, or face wild beasts, or pass through a fire, etc.

The men did not always have the monopoly on courage. One of them, having offered to make a jump of twenty metres on horseback over a frozen river, bearing a woman on the saddle behind him, at the critical moment asked for a bucket of whiskey to stimulate the horse who refused to jump. He drank the whiskey and it was the woman who courageously gave the decisive spur to the horse.

Generally journalists attended our filming. It was not the least of my surprises to see how much interest in my modest self was shown by the press and the public. I rarely passed a week without being interviewed. If it was impossible for me to receive the reporter he would write his article anyhow, and thus I learned some absolutely unsuspected details about my beginnings, my family, my ancestors.

After submitting, in France, to concealment "under a bushel", in the "heroic" period, I had the right to be surprised. It is true that I passed for a phenomenon, as for seventeen years I had been the only woman film director in the entire world.

Sometimes the studio resembled a menagerie, as wild animals furnished us with excellent material. The trainer [Paul] Bourgeois brought me, one day, a magnificent tigress weighing six hundred pounds. He assured me she was gentleness itself and begged me to caress her through the bars of her cage, to encourage the actors. I admit that I felt a certain hesitancy, but a director must not be a wet hen; I did the thing, and Princess received my advances very nicely, purring under the caress and rubbing against the bars like a great cat. Vinnie Burns, an eighteen-year-old actress whom I had coached was the first to enter the cage.

But Princess caused me a terrible fright one day. Not far from our studio was an old stone quarry. We decided to do an outdoor scene there with Princess. Fortunately I had placed men armed with pitchforks on top of the wall, even though Bourgeois promised me that the animal would not escape. Hardly was the cage opened when Princess cleared the wall in a few bounds and made for the woods. The grilled windows of a convent (in which my daughter was a student) rose hardly five hundred yards away. I imagined the terror of the children seeing that big wild beast. The fright alone could harm a heart patient. I seized a pike myself, and at last Princess returned toward her starting point and we locked her up again, with relief.

In spite of that experience, we drove her one day, in an auto, up to the Bronx Zoo in New York, where the keepers assured me that her condition was not rare, that Princess was…abnormal. She was killed a few months later by a tiger whose favors she refused. Lions and panthers proved less gentle than Princess and gave us several scares.

In a scene representing the Hindu temple of serpents, I was obliged to set an example again and, despite my revulsion, to roll a serpent about my neck. The snake was perfectly inoffensive, but the actor who played the High Priest would perform only on the condition of my going first. Two days later, the whole studio would do the same.

The Pit and the Pendulum [1913] of Edgar Allan Poe was a hard trial for Darwin Karr, my young leading man. We had imagined, as a way to deliver him by cutting his ropes…while he lies tied to the torture rack, waiting for the fatal sweep of the knife…to confide this mission to gutter rats. The cords were copiously smeared with food to attract the rats. They fulfilled their role marvelously, but a few preferred fresh meat, came sniffing at the nose of the actor and even penetrated the legs of his trousers. When at last the ropes broke he was not slow to jump to his feet, swearing there would be no retake.

We had the greatest difficulty in keeping the rats from invading the studio. We had surrounded the stage with metal plates, on which they would slide and be unable to get away. They had to be destroyed on the spot. First we tossed into their midst an enormous cat who, horrified, jumped the barrier at one bound. Then it was the turn of my little bulldog, an excellent ratter…the unhappy beast was immobilized at once by twenty or so rats who attacked him from every vantage point. We had to rescue him from his miserable situation. Finally, all the personnel took arms, cudgels, clubs, and finally, not without difficulty, we won out. We were happy to be rid of the rats, but forced to admire their courage.

The film had an enormous success. I went incognito to the first showing and had great pleasure in observing the shivers and anguished sighs of the public.

Contrary to general opinion, filming often offers real dangers. Mortal accidents are not rare. Fortunately we never had anything of the sort to deplore, as we judged that the best of films was not worth a man's life.

My husband often preferred to take a personal risk. For my film *Dick Whittington and His Cat* [1913], in order to illustrate the sinking of a pirate ship, we had transformed a big old unused sailboat into a magnificent caravelle. The gunpowder and the fuse to provoke the explosion being ready, my husband, arguing that women lacked the sangfroid for this, insisted on executing the task himself. But when the wind had three times extinguished the fuse, he lost patience and tossed the match directly into the powder. The blast was thunderous. I was on the opposite bank with the cameramen and some journalists amused by my anxiety. I saw my husband regain the bank in the little boat into which he had fallen back, fortunately. Worried, in spite of that, I begged my assistant to go get news of my husband. He had taken refuge in a bar, where he lost consciousness.

Stephen Bush's review of The Pit and the Pendulum *(Solax, 1913) in the* Moving Picture World.

Seriously burned on face and hands. It took weeks for him to mend.

The film offered many new effects that were successful.

Do not think that we neglected the artistic side of cinema. The United States offered sites of incomparable beauty, imposing waterfalls, forests of giant trees, magnificent flora and fauna.

We took the greatest possible advantage of that: the most favorable hour for the best light, the setting sun lengthening the shadows, a reflection in a rippling pond, the wind making waves in a field of wheat; all that was studied and used. One begins to recognize that the talking-pictures, in arresting the very promising, very encouraging development of the silent cinema, have deprived it of a great deal of poetry.

During the studio's first year of operation its publicity focused almost entirely on Alice and her dual function as artist and entrepreneur. There was only nominal attention given to the stars, while the various directors working under her supervision were infrequently credited. Herbert Blaché was never mentioned, although, as Alice recounts in her memoir, he was certainly involved in the Fort Lee operation. This *auteurist* slant was quite unusual at the time, and prefigured similar promotion of Thomas Ince, Mack Sennett and D.W. Griffith not generally launched until 1914–15.

THE MAKING OF A FEATURE

Madame Blaché, Of The Solax Company, Is Producing The Story Of Dick Whittington And His Cat

(from *Moving Picture World,* March 1, 1913, pp. 873–874)

It was our singular good fortune this week to drop in at the Solax studio at Fort Lee. The bright sunny building, its atmosphere of cheerfulness and good fellowship, which even the least important employees seem to feel and take part in, and the courtesy of Madame Blaché herself, leave in the visitor's mind at all times, a pleasant memory. Every one who goes out to Fort Lee comes back enthusiastic and full of admiration. It is not only the agreeableness of the place and of the people one meets there that one notices, but the smoothness and the order with which the work is carried on. There is no litter about and seemingly no hurry; it is the best kind of a place for good work and very clearly shows a strong personality behind it. Just at present, to any eye that can weave a story from small suggestions and foresee a fine picture from one or two perfect scenes, it is full of the romance of long ago. For Madame Blaché is working on a three-reel picture that will tell the grand old story of Dick Whittington and his

cat. We were shown the bells – they are of good size – that will sing out encouragement to the footsore lad, "Turn again Whittington, Lord Mayor of London". And we were also shown other things that made us eager to see the finished picture in all its three reels.

It will be a better offering even, so Madame Blaché says, than the Solax *Fra Diavalo*. If she is not mistaken in this, it will indeed be something very fine. For our part, judging by two scenes that we saw being turned, by a reel of what has already been made and by the absolutely perfect sets and furniture prepared for the other scenes, we are sure that it will make a stir on its artistic merits. It was by no means an easy picture to plan and prepare for, since every one of its important scenes had to be constructed; the times of Dick Whittington have passed away. Madame Blaché is not one who is content, in producing this story, to get backgrounds that are something like those among which this hero of at least every English speaking school boy lived; she has aimed at giving an illusion of reality and it is plain that she has spared no pains or money in her determination to get this illusion. In the reels already taken she has reached it in a most remarkable way. We saw a picture of a big kitchen in the house of an English merchant, where Dick has obtained a job as scullion. He had hoped to find gold and be a great merchant at once. But he has at least found a home though he has to work; blow the fires with the bellows and polish up the brass work and pans and pots, all old style, of which the kitchen is full. The suggestion that this scene gives is helped much by the acting, but all together, it is full of reminiscence of old prints and makes us think that

Mme. Blaché enjoyed traveling around Fort Lee on horseback. On the reverse on this photograph she identifies this building as her home.

we have seen just such a kitchen and know that the scene is what it ought to be.

Some of the scenes will need an old time English galleon, the ship on which the cat makes the voyage that is to prove so profitable to Dick. This is so well done that we took pleasure looking it over and noticing its details; it looks like the real thing and will make a picture worth seeing. Then there is a picture of the gate of the city at the time Dick reaches it and where he is stopped by the "Beef Eater" on guard. This will make one wonder where it was found, for it has been made to seem massive and looks like stone. To make these sets, studying and research were called for. Before she began the production, Madame Blaché spent a good many days looking up old prints and studying the times. Knowing what was needed, she has gone ahead to obtain it without regard to expense in reason. That this is so is not only claimed, but quite apparent. And because of it the offering will be not only entertaining, but valuable for its instruction.

A poor picture in the best setting possible would be like a beautiful cup to a thirsty traveler. He might admire it, but unless it held something to quench his, thirst he would hardly take deep interest in it. This picture will be full of the truest humanity, as clear as sparkling water. Those scenes that we saw being played were acted in a thoroughly sincere and natural way. One comes to realize while watching Madame Blaché at work with her players, what alertness and care for smallest things at every instant of a scene is needed in the making of really good pictures. Standing behind this gifted producer and listening to her quietly given admonitions to her players, one gets a vivid impression of what her mind is drawing in its imagination. It seems magical, the closeness of the understanding between her and the player who happens to be the cen-

ter of the story at any seemingly small part of an instant and it is marvelous that the effect she desires is obtained so easily. It is the power of quiet direction attaining its ends. That one feels this influence while watching Madame Blaché at work shows how sharp and clear-cut is her visualizing power and how thoroughly she knows just what she wants.

While a scene is being turned the studio seems as still as a mill pond at sunset; and yet, if anything humorous happens, Madame Blaché is the first to see its fun and the first to laugh. When things happen that spoil the scene even, and such sometimes bob up anywhere, she is apt to catch the humor of it. Such an attitude toward life saves much nervous strain and wear and tear. There were no signs of nerves in the Solax studio; but we did notice a good deal of modulated fun and laughter which never interfered with the work. The admiration and sincere loyalty of all Madame Blaché's artistic household, is apparent everywhere. Fun is not choked down and orderly work certainly flourishes. In one of the picture's scenes a mule is needed to draw an old English cart. He is just an ordinary mule such as can stand on his front legs alone for the time a steel spring might snap and need no hind support at all. One of the players wanted to make friends with his muleship and made overtures to scratch his back. It looked as though a knife blade had shut and opened and the friendly man got a cue for his exit after a scene in which there was no faking.

No estimate of what the players are going to give us would be fair at this time. There is a large cast and we have seen only a few of them; but those few have our admiration. Vinnie Byrnes [i.e., Burns] is Dick at the time he comes to London and we are sure that she, in those scenes we saw, will score a big success, she deserves it anyway. Mrs. Hurley's work is too well known

to need more than a passing notice that it is equal to the best we have seen from her. That is saying a good deal in the way of high commendation. Every other player whose work we noticed seemed to feel the romantic atmosphere of the story and all filled their parts in perfection or something very near to it.

FEATURE PRODUCTION
Madame Blaché Talks Interestingly Of The Difference Between Three-reel "features" And "subjects"

(from *Moving Picture World*, May 17, 1913, p. 711)

A successful showman, in talking about multiple reels and differentiating the feature from the three-real subject, is quoted as saying: "A three-reel feature differs from the three-reel subject as much as the Broadway attraction differs from the road show. A three-reel subject is a story drawn out to three thousand feet with nothing noteworthy achieved, either in its staging or general atmosphere. A feature, however, is a production which has every element of attraction and popularity. By elements of attraction and popularity, I mean what a salesman terms 'talking points'. The 'talking points' of a real feature are popular titles, well established in the public mind, casts with well-known actors in the leading role, good support, exceptional locations, artistic interiors, correct in every detail, and a story with the 'proverbial punch' – technically, well developed."

While there are not many productions such as described by the showman quoted above, productions like *Les Miserables, Quo Vadis,* and *Dick Whittington and His Cat,* come up very near to the perfect feature of our exacting showmen and meet nearly all of the requirements.

In a talk on this subject with Madame

Blaché, president and manager of production of the Solax Company, and herself the producer of features like *Fra Diavolo, Dick Whittington and His Cat,* and a few others [she] said: "Besides an expenditure of large sums of money, the production of a feature means weeks of tedious preparation and research. Before a single foot of film was taken, *Dick Whittington and His Cat* consumed five weeks of my time and the time of my staff. Our coming feature with the famous Barney Gilmore in the leading role, *Kelly from the Emerald Isle,* was produced after six weeks of preliminary work. There were consultations with the director, with Mr. Gilmore, with the author of the scenario, and with the scenic artists. After the scenario was finally in shape, it was beyond the recognition of the author. Then followed the routine work of sketching costumes for the costumers, of laying out plans and sketches of sets, of going the rounds for props and incidentals, and finishing touches. Mr. Gilmore's friends in the old country were of considerable assistance. They sent over a trunk full of stuff for atmosphere and local color. The sheebeens (country tavern of Ireland), Irish sitting-rooms, and dwellings and furnishings for these sets were secured with considerable difficulty.

"There are several scenes in the production which are genuinely thrilling. In one, Kelly, and his sweetheart clinging to his neck, is seen climbing down a declivity several hundred feet deep. Another scene shows Kelly escaping death by jumping on a cow-catcher of a train going at full speed. There is also a spectacular destruction of a hut by gunpowder and dynamite.

"Throughout the production is preserved an atmosphere characteristically Irish. Humor and pathos mingle. To register the story which teems with human

interest, an all-star cast was needed. Selections for the parts were made with the utmost care. Fraunie Fraunholz, the well-known comedian, who has been a member of some of the best stock companies in Baltimore, Philadelphia, Washington, Buffalo, Chicago, Denver and New York, and Joseph Levering, familiar to Biograph, Pathé and Kalem fans, were the specials in the cast, besides Barney Gilmore and the members of the Solax Stock Company.

"If hard work, careful preparation and the expenditure of large sums of money add to the feature definitions of the showman you have been telling me about, then *Kelly from the Emerald Isle,* with Barney Gilmore, should – well, not to blow my own horn – be awaited with interest. There is a surprise coming."

It would seem that Madame Blaché's enthusiastic expressions regarding features are significant. What will be the future policy of the Solax Company and other companies? It had

The 1915 New Jersey state census lists the occupants of the Blaché household on Palisade Avenue. There are two live-in servants, and Alice's occupation is given as "housewife".

been predicted in *The Moving Picture World* a long time ago that manufacturers, because of the demands of exhibitors and the public, will gradually wean themselves from the single-reel production and produce the multiple-reel. The tendency seems to be in that direction.

MADAME BLACHÉ WORKING AT LAKE HOPATCONG

(from *Moving Picture World,* September 20, 1913, p. 1262)

Madame Blaché, president of the Solax Company, and a company of 50 people, together with property men and numerous assistants and an equipment of three wagon loads of properties and scenery, have left for Lake Hopatcong where numerous scenes in the forthcoming Solax feature, entitled *Rogues of Paris*, will be staged. The transfer of the company and the equipment to this famous lake resort means an expense of more than $2,000. A feature of the work up in the country will be the erection of army pontoon bridges and the use of a castle at the present time owned by the Russell Sage estate. Included in the company are Vinnie Burns, Claire Witney, Mr. Truesdale, Joseph Levering, Fraunie Fraunholz, Wallace Scott, James Johnson, James O'Neil, supers, attendants, etc.

"THE SHADOWS OF THE MOULIN ROUGE" A Solax Feature In Four Paris

Reviewed by W. Stephen Bush
(from *Moving Picture World,* January 24, 1914, p. 417)

This is undoubtedly the best feature that ever came out of the Solax studio. It was directed by Madame Blaché who has made notable progress in the art of staging and directing feature productions. The story is distinctly

French in plot and in flavor. The idea of the play has evidently been taken from one of the best tales of Balzac. Balzac was a master of invention and in proper hands his works ought to be a treasure house for the producer who does not specialize in freak features. The directress has achieved such pronounced success in this instance because she has understood how to condense and how to keep away from the diffuse style of the Balzac narrative. This, however, is by no means the only merit of the play. The plot hinges on the substitution of a dead woman for a living one. A series of thrilling, and at times mystifying, adventures follow, the interest of the spectator is kept at high tension through every change in the situation while every trace of confusions happily and skillfully avoided. In the course of the story, and as necessary parts of its development, many of the famous and some of the notorious resorts of Parisian life are introduced. The arrangement of the groups in these scenes, the settings and the selection of characteristic types entitle the director to great credit.

With all the sensations in the plot, and with all the introductions of scenes from the seamy side of life, there is not the faintest trace of any objectionable feature. The acting in this production is decidedly above the average. Throughout I noticed the sympathetic and intelligent cooperation between directress and artists, without which no good picture is possible and which is doubly important in the production of a feature of some pretensions.

Another point of merit, which must not be passed over, is the absence of lost motion. It would be impossible to cut even fifty feet from this feature without endangering its dramatic development and dulling the edge of its climaxes. The settings are superb all the way through and the highest praise must be bestowed upon the

photography and the camera work generally.

SING SING CONDITIONS SHOCK MADAME BLACHÉ Sits Calmly In The "Death-Chair", But Is Affected by The Cramped Cells

(from *Moving Picture World,* April 11, 1914, p. 193)

Madame Alice Blaché, the president and head producer of the Solax Motion Picture Company, has become an enthusiastic exponent of prison reform following a recent visit to Sing Sing, where she made an exhaustive study of that famous institution.

The preparation of a motion picture story for early production was the cause of Madame Blaché's visit and it was while making notes that would help her perfect the details of her picture drama, that she was made to realize the disgraceful manner in which the prisoners are forced to live.

She was invited to sit in the electric chair where 120 men and one woman met their deaths, but she was so affected by the thought of the horrible little cells with their narrow cots, that have to be folded against the wall to allow the prisoner even room enough to move, that she sat in the electric chair without a quiver and discussed the amazing condition of affairs in a great State like New York that could make such a disgrace as Sing Sing possible.

"I would not think that the electric chair would be dreaded very much by a prisoner who had suffered the tortures of the dark, damp, little cells he is forced to live in here", said Madame Blaché. "It is exactly the opposite in the modern French institution of Fennes, where the large bright cells with rounded corners and ceilings to make dirt and dust impossible and the neat little beds and many conveniences cause the people laughingly to remark that it is a pleasure to be a prisoner in France."

Madame Blaché spent considerable time studying the Bertillion System and made pencil sketches of the different apparatus used in taking the measurements of prisoners.

> By the end of 1913 Herbert Blaché had decided to cut his ties with Gaumont, and formed Blaché Features to produce feature length films in Fort Lee. The one-reelers which Solax had been selling in the independent market were now obsolete, but the Blachés had difficulty in finding the proper distribution for longer films like *Shadows of the Moulin Rouge.* Solax ceased production, and Herbert and Alice alternated in the direction of the Blaché Features. In preparation for this they expanded their facilities by moving the laboratory operation out of the main studio building and into a new structure closer to Lemoine Avenue.

EXPANDING THE SOLAX PLANT

(from *Moving Picture World,* December 27, 1913, p. 1558)

This photo shows the Solax plant in the process of expansion. The building in the background is the old plant, 150x150 feet, three and one half stories high. The studio accommodates five sets in a row. The present factory has an equipment sufficient to turn out 100,000 feet of positive film a week. The frame work to the right is an outdoor stage used for light effect purposes and whenever work in the indoor studio reaches a state of congestion. The new two story building in process of construction is on the left, size 50x100 feet and in it will be housed the factory and laboratory to be removed from the main building. The added facilities will make it possible to turn out about 200,000 feet of positive film a week. The space in the foreground, which is also the property of the Solax and Blaché companies, will be improved and fenced in by ornamented iron railings.

> In contrast to the situation at Solax, publicity for the United States Amusement Corporation, the entity which now controlled the Blaché's film operations, was much more heavily centered on Herbert's work. Note the presence on the Board of Jules Brulatour, the Eastman raw stock agent who had a hand in nearly every film operation in Fort Lee.

BLACHÉ FORMS NEW COMPANY
Will Be Known As United States Amusement Corporation And Will Make Big Features

(from *Moving Picture World,* May 2, 1914, p. 653)

Under the name of the United States Amusement Corporation, Herbert Blaché, president of the Exclusive Supply Corporation, and Blaché Features, Inc., has formed a $500,000 company for the production of large feature photodramas. Besides Mr. Blaché, the directors of the company are Madame Alice Blaché, president of the Solax Company; Joseph M. Shear, Charles D. Lithgow, Joseph Borries, Henri Menessier and Jules E. Brulatour.

The Blaché picture producing plant in Fort Lee, NJ, has recently been enlarged by the addition of a new factory which is said to be one of the most perfectly equipped for the developing and printing of film of any in the United States. The old factory is rapidly being remodeled to furnish space for dressing rooms, offices, etc., and

> *The Blachés built a new laboratory and open-air stage after they decided to expand into feature film production.*

the new features will be produced in the Fort Lee plant under the direct supervision of President Blaché.

The product of the new company will be pretentious photodramas of five or more reels in length, picturized from well-known plays and novels. The first feature, which is already well under-way, will be the well-known English star, Mr. Tom Terriss, and his Charles Dickens' Associate Players in *The Chimes*. Herbert Blaché is staging the picture dramatization of this famous novel in collaboration with Mr. Ter-riss, who is a noted student of Dick-ens' works, and has appeared in his own adaptations of "A Christmas Carol", "Cricket on the Hearth", "Oliver Twist" and "Nicholas Nick-leby", all over the English speaking world.

Mr. Terriss, who is perhaps most widely known for his wonderful char-acterization of "Scrooge" in "A Christmas Carol", is a son of the late William Terriss of Sir Henry Irving's great Lyceum Theater Company.

Realizing the importance of the cor-rectness of character drawings and stage settings for the successful pro-duction of one of Dickens' novels, Mr. Terriss has surrounded himself with a company that is experienced in inter-preting the famous authors' works and is also using his valuable collec-tion of Dickens' relics, which includes watchmen's rattles and truncheons of the period of 1840, Georgian bellows, foot warmers, candle snuffers, chest-nut roasters, warming pans, pewter tankards, candlesticks and a hundred and one interesting articles known to all lovers of the author's stories.

The cast of *The Chimes* is headed by Mr. Tom Terriss, who interprets the character of "Trotty Beck", and is sup-ported by his brother, William Terriss as "Mr. Fish", Alfred Hemming as "Alderman Cute", Robert Harvey as "Fern", Cyril Bidoulph as "Richard", Herbert Vivian as "Sir Joseph", Her-bert Cripps as "Tugby", Eliza Mason

as "Mrs. Tugby", Faye Cusick as "Meg" and the little Solax star, Vinnie Burns, as "Lillian".

President Blaché has closed a number of important contracts for Broadway theatrical successes and well-known stars to be produced in the near future. The Solax Company and Blaché Fea-tures, Inc., will not be affected by the activities of the new concern, but will continue to confine their offerings to one four-reel photodrama released every two weeks as in the past, while the United States Amusement Corpo-ration will present only large special productions at intervals depending upon the length of time that is con-sumed.

I.W.W.'S INVADE FORT LEE

(from *Moving Picture World*, July 4, 1914, p. 1387)

If Tom Terriss hadn't yelled "Three cheers for John D. Rockefeller!" as two hundred I.W.W.'s were storming the gates of the palace in one of the mob scenes of *The Chimes*, being staged by Herbert Blaché at Fort Lee, the results of the battle might not have been so serious. But Mr. Terriss was looking for realism, and if a brick in the back of the neck is realism he got it.

The men, consisting of every type from long-haired, sallow-faced dreamers to fierce raw-boned huskies, were carefully costumed to suit the period in which Charles Dickens' in-teresting story is laid and their thoughts were far removed from the sins of their enemies. Thrice did they attack the gates, led by Mr. Terriss, but in spite of the fact that they were well armed with cudgels, rocks and blunderbusses, they failed to put enough spirit into their work to suit their directors. Finally the camera started to grind and Tom Terriss was seized with a brilliant idea at the same minute. "Three cheers for John D. Rockefeller!" shouted Terriss in a loud voice and with a snarl of hatred

the mob rushed forward. Rocks that had been carelessly tossed but a m-inute before were thrown with a will, while cudgels and wads from guns did terrible execution. The large gates were battered down in record time, and not until doors and windows had been smashed and the house entered did the I.W.W.'s realize that they were merely acting.

Between 1914 and 1917 the Blachés were associated with Popular Plays and Players, whose films were distributed first by Alco, then Metro. Most of these productions starred Olga Petrova, who was not, as advertised, a Russian vamp, but an Englishwoman named Muriel Harding. Petrova was one of the more successful Broadway personalities involved in the first wave of feature filmmaking. Her particular acknowledgement of Alice Guy Blaché, who had been entirely forgotten by 1942, reflects their close personal friendship.

BUTTER WITH MY BREAD

By Olga Petrova (New York: Bobbs-Merrill, 1942), pp. 258–259.

Early in November I started my first moving picture in the Fort Lee Stu-dios. The piece, written by Aron Hoff-man, was called *The Tigress* [1914]. My director was Madame Alice Blaché, a charming and cultured French woman.

The first thing that struck me, and most forcibly, was the extraordinary amount of time apparently wasted. One arrived at the studio somewhere around half past nine in the morning and reported, dressed and made up, on the set by ten. Then it was quite possible to sit and sit and sit until lunchtime, when one was free for an hour. After lunch a little friendly chat, to allow for a very proper and necessary digestion, might well bring one to three o'clock before making any kind of a start on the business of the day. By this time one's make-up was messy and one's verve well below par.

As I was still playing *Panthea* in theatres adjacent to New York, it was always arranged that I should be allowed time to make my matinees and evening performances, without risk of being late. But other players, whose scenes didn't need my presence, were liable to be kept until well on into the night. I made up my mind then that if I should ever enter into another contract for the cinema, I would see that a specified number of working hours should be stated. It wasn't

that I begrudged any necessary time or labor, but the scenes taken after unnecessary, uninteresting and prolonged waits were invariably bad. The camera caught the weariness and boredom and recorded them with devastating exactitude.

There were other days, of course, when things went briskly, so briskly that one hadn't the time to be tired. *The Tigress*, I suppose, pleased the firm and the public, for shortly after its release, *Panthea* having now definitely closed and Mr. Shubert not having found a vehicle to follow it, I was permitted to sign a contract for several more pictures at a salary of fifteen hundred dollars a week.

Of these *The Heart of a Painted Woman* and *My Madonna* [both 1915] were directed by Madame Blaché. Then to my great regret, because of contracts calling her elsewhere, we parted and I passed to other directors.

Olga Petrova.

Alice Guy Blaché continued to be good copy, and as late as 1915 (despite the rise of such rivals as Lois Weber) was still being described as "the foremost woman producer of motion pictures in the world". In these two pieces she addresses the question of the "woman director" head on, insisting that women are temperamentally suited to the aesthetic requirements of filmmaking, but often lack the physical strength and creative ruthlessness needed for professional success, perhaps a reflection of the infirmities which would soon cut short her own career.

WOMAN'S PLACE IN PHOTOPLAY PRODUCTION

By Madame Alice Blaché

(from *Moving Picture World,* July 11, 1914, p. 195)

It has long been a source of wonder to me that many women have not seized upon the wonderful opportunities offered to them by the motion picture art to make their way to fame and fortune as producers of photodramas. Of all the arts there is probably none in which they can make such splendid use of talents so much more natural to a woman than to a man and so necessary to its perfection.

There is no doubt in my mind that a woman's success in many lines of endeavor is still made very difficult by a strong prejudice against one of her sex doing work that has been done only by men for hundreds of years. Of course this prejudice is fast disappearing and there are many vocations in which it has not been present for a long time. In the arts of acting, music, painting and literature, woman has long held her place among the most successful workers, and when it is con-sidered how vitally all of these arts enter into the production of motion pictures one wonders why the names of scores of women are not found among the successful creators of photodrama offerings.

Not only is a woman as well fitted to stage a photodrama as a man, but in many ways she has a distinct advantage over him because of her very nature and because much of the knowledge called for in the telling of the story and the creation of the stage settings is absolutely within her province as a member of the gentler sex. She is an authority on the emotions. For centuries she has given them full play while man has carefully trained himself to control them. She has developed her finer feelings for generations, while being protected from the world by her male companions, and she is naturally religious. In matters of the heart her superiority is acknowledged, and her deep insight and sensitiveness in the affairs of Cupid give her a wonderful advantage in developing the thread of love which plays such an all-important part in almost every story that is prepared for the screen. All of the distinctive qualities which she possesses come into direct play during the guiding of the actors in making their character drawings and interpreting the different emotions called for by the story. For to think and to feel the situation demanded by the play is the secret of successful acting, and sensitiveness to those thoughts and feelings is absolutely essential to the success of a stage director.

The qualities of patience and gentleness possessed to such a high degree by womankind are also of inestimable value in the staging of a photodrama. Artistic temperament is a thing to be reckoned with while directing an actor, in spite of the treatment of the subject in the comic papers, and a gentle, soft-voiced director is much more conducive to good work on the part of the performer than the over-stern, noisy tyrant of the studio.

Not a small part of the motion picture director's work, in addition to the preparation of the story for picture-telling and the casting and directing of the actors, is the choice of suitable locations for the staging of the exterior scenes and supervising of the studio settings, props, costumes, etc. In these matters it seems to me that a woman is especially well qualified to obtain the very best results, for she is dealing with subjects that are almost a second nature to her. She takes the measure of every person, every costume, every house and every piece of furniture that her eye comes into contact with, and the beauty of a stretch of landscape or a single flower impresses her immediately. All of these things are of the greatest value to the creator of a photodrama and the knowledge of them must be extensive and exact. A woman's magic touch is immediately recognized in a real home. Is it not just as recognizable in

Alice Guy Blaché (at right) stands with Olga Petrova on the set of My Madonna *(Metro-Popular Plays and Players, 1915).*

the home of the characters of a photoplay?

That women make the theatre possible from the box-office standpoint is an acknowledged fact. Theatre managers know that their appeal must be to the woman if they would succeed, and all of their efforts are naturally in that direction. This being the case, what a rare opportunity is offered to women to use that inborn knowledge of just what does appeal to them to produce photodramas that will contain that inexplicable something which is necessary to the success of every stage or screen production.

There is nothing connected with the staging of a motion picture that a woman cannot do as easily as a man, and there is no reason why she cannot completely master every technicality of the art. The technique of the drama has been mastered by so many women that it is considered as much her field as a man's and its adaptation to picture work in no way removes it from her sphere. The technique of motion picture photography like the technique of the drama is fitted to a woman's activities.

It is hard for me to imagine how I could have obtained my knowledge of photography, for instance, without the months of study spent in the laboratory of the Gaumont Company, in Paris, at a time when motion picture photography was in the experimental stage, and carefully continued since [in] my own laboratory in the Solax Studios in this country. It is also necessary to study stage direction by actual participation in the work in addition to burning the midnight oil in your library, but both are as suitable, as fascinating and as remunerative to a woman as to a man.

THE WOMAN PICTURE MAKER
Madame Blaché, The Distinguished Producer, tells Townsend Black Of Her Wonder Work

(from *Metro Pictures Magazine*, Vol. I, no. 2 [1915], p. 9)

Though it smacks somewhat of the paradoxical, Mme. Alice Blaché, the foremost woman producer of motion pictures in the world, and one of the ablest directors of the silent drama, insists that women are not fitted to be motion picture directors. The fact that Mme. Blaché is a notable exception to her own rule does not alter it a whit, in her opinion, although many would doubt the assertion once they had seen this energetic little woman at work in the Popular Plays and Players' studios at Fort Lee, NJ, where she has produced many of the finest feature pictures that have been shown on the Metro program.

To meet and talk with Mme. Blaché during one of her brief periods of relaxation it is difficult to realize that this reticent, soft spoken and charming little Frenchwoman has achieved some of the most notable artistic triumphs of the screen. Often she has directed as many as 250 people in a production which called for the introduction of elephants, camels, tigers, horses, and other wild or domestic animals, by the score. Mme. Blaché has met and solved the most intricate problems of the silent art with apparent ease. For the average woman, even though possessed of unusual talents, many of these problems would have proved impossible of solution. Successful and artistic motion picture production calls for a wide and many-sided knowledge of human life, and rarely has a woman the qualities for observation and assimilation of this knowledge in the necessary degree.

Mme. Blaché is the exception, which proves every rule. There is no part in the making of motion picture in which Mme. Blaché is not an expert and an artist to her finger tips. Not only does she write scenarios and direct the production of them, but she personally superintends the making of a picture until it is released a finished product. She directs her camera men, and indeed, has taught them many of the "tricks" that Europeans used long before they were known in this country. Mme. Blaché is at home in either

Alice Guy Blaché working with her Solax crew on the My Madonna *set (1915).*

the studio or laboratory, being able to give expert aid at any stage of a film's manufacture.

She likes to select her own cast, and she superintends the selection of all scenery, furniture and costumes used in a production. If the 'script calls for an exterior scene Mme. Blaché does not entrust the selection to another, but promptly goes in her motor car or on horseback, and rides until she finds the desired location.

"What do you find the most difficult things to accomplish in the making of a motion picture, where you are called upon to overcome obstacles that a man director would not encounter?" Mme. Blaché was asked.

Her face lighted up with interest, and a smile played on her lips as she reflected a moment before replying to the question.

"Offhand, I should say there are three things that bother me because I am a woman", she said, with some hesitation.

"First, I am often called to use my voice to such an extent that it absolutely fails me. In the direction of big scenes, where many people are in the picture I generally use a megaphone while standing on a platform or elevation. Sometimes I am obliged to give my voice a rest then. That is a drawback, but it makes little difference in the end. Then again my heart fails me when I direct any of my people in hazardous undertakings. That, of course, is the feminine instinct. I am always so afraid one of them will be injured. I dislike this sort of thing, but, of course, I must do them [sic] at times.

"Thirdly – and I might say this is the greatest drawback of all – I actually suffer agonies when I am forced to cut down a film, eliminating scenes and incidents to reduce the picture to the requisite number of feet. You know, sometimes we take as much as 15,000 feet of film for a five part picture. This

must be cut down to 5,000 or 6,000 feet. It is then that a sort of motherly instinct comes to the surface in me. I love every scene that I have directed. I have lived through every one of them. They are the children of my brain, and I suffer to see them destroyed. Of course, I know they must be but I assure you it is often quite dreadful.

"Another thing I might add, is that women, as a rule, are not as strong as men, and they cannot well withstand the physical strain of directing the making of a picture. Fortunately, I am very strong, and I do not tire any more quickly than the average man director. I learned long ago to conserve my strength, and I do not allow myself to waste any energy. Nervousness and anger are two things that sap one's strength. I do not allow myself to become angry. I am strict with those under my direction, but not severe. I do not believe in scolding them. Scolding actors and actresses is exactly like scolding children – you cannot get the best results that way.

"When I started in the business I was an extremely nervous girl. My first work as a director was directing myself. I taught myself self-control. It required months of training, but I was victorious over myself in the end. Without that control I would never have been able to accomplish anything."

Although the Blachés continued to make their own films in Fort Lee through 1917, they also found it quite profitable to rent out the studio and laboratory operation. Two stars associated with Lewis J. Selznick, Kitty Gordon and Clara Kimball Young, were working at the Solax studio by the summer of 1916.

KITTY GORDON WORKING ON NEW FEATURE

(from *Moving Picture World,* September 23, 1916, p. 1956)

Kitty Gordon, the famous beauty of the musical comedy stage, began work this week at the Blaché Studio on the first production of the Kitty Gordon Film Corporation. This picture will be a film version of *Vera the Medium*, by Richard Harding Davis.

Miss Gordon's new picture is being filmed under the supervision of G. M. Anderson, the famous "Broncho Billy". The story is exceptionally well suited to the statuesque star, giving her many opportunities to appear in startling costumes and to make the most of her noted beauty and superlative gifts of expression.

The Kitty Gordon Pictures have been added to the Lewis J. Selznick Enterprises and will be released by him on the open booking plan along lines similar to those he has adopted for the Clara Kimball Young and Herbert Brenon pictures.

"CAP", A SWEET TEMPERED DIRECTOR

By Allen Corliss

(from *Photoplay,* January 1917, pp. 88–90)

"All done by kindness", says the animal trainer as he makes his bow after putting his troupe of mixed panthers, guinea-pigs and giraffes through their stunt.

"All done by kindness", cry the trained actors and studio employees of Monsieur Albert Capellani, Director General of the Clara Kimball Young Film Corporation, as the last foot of his latest screen creation is reeled off for their benefit in the studio projection room and they realize that the big genial Frenchman has "put another one across" without the use of one harsh command, or utterance more

Albert Capellani.

decorate the lower half of his head. And it isn't that surface sort of geniality, either. It lies far deeper than his true Parisian politeness and hearty laughter. Its proof is in the devotion of the men and women who have worked for him in almost all of his American productions – and the adoration one reads in the faces of his wife and children.

Capellani, or "Cap" as those who labor with him fondly call him, has only been in America a year – but his record on this side of the Atlantic has already established him as one of the half-dozen masters of the screen-art in this country. He came with a long and enviable record for brilliant achievement in France – where for twelve years, or since the photoplay was in its bib and tucker, he had grown up with his art under the banner of the great Pathé Company of Paris, the true father of the industry.

In America "Cap" made his first important impression as the creative genius of that great photodramatic production, *Les Miserables* [made in France in 1913]. Since then he has produced a number of notable pictures, including several of Miss Clara Kimball Young's most popular offerings, such as *Camille* and *The Dark Silence*. And now comes what he considers his finest achievement of all – again with Miss Young as the star – *The Common Law*.

Capellani's excellence lies more in his exquisite valuation of detail and finesse than in breadth and power such as Griffith's or Brenon's. He is as subtle as his mother-tongue; he gets his effects by a stealthy artistry that sneaks up behind one, as it were, and stabs the heart via the back ribs. His handling of delicate situations – such as the disrobing scene in *The Common Law* – is superbly Gallic; he has the true French perception of the exact boundary line between the risqué and the vulgar. In love passages his staging is beyond comparison and when it

profane than a half-stifled "*Parbleu*" or "*Mon Dieu*".

That this is some test of a man's temper-control even the least initiated in the intricacies of motion picture making may well imagine. Thousands of little things many happen – and do – daily in the course of a director's work that would try the patience of our old friend Job himself, and any director who can finish an eight reel picture of such proportions as *The Common Law* and still be on speaking terms with his players, property man or his wife – is entitled to the crown of Old King Cole.

One's first impression of Capellani is that of geniality. It shines from his big boyish eyes; it oozes from the finger-tips that clasp in a firm, hearty hand-shake; it even peeks out in the smile hidden behind those bushy wind-shields that

comes to dramatic climaxes, well, a climax is Capellani's pet; it just walks up and eats out of his hand.

"Be natural", is "Cap's" slogan, displayed in big letters on sign boards all around his studio at Fort Lee, New Jersey. He doesn't want his actors to act, which sounds like a paradox but isn't. To be natural on the stage is one of the most difficult things an actor has to do, because of the fact that he is addressing an audience and has to fight down self consciousness. But according to Capellani, there is no excuse for a motion picture actor to feel self conscious and become "stagy" in his work. His only audience is the director and assistants and it is or should be easy for him to play his scenes without "acting".

Capellani will not tolerate the exaggeration of facial expression and gesture that was thought essential to motion picture acting in its earlier days – and still is one of the great faults of so many screen players.

"Screen acting should be nature herself", says "Cap". "What your Shakespeare – he call the mirror up to nature. The camera – he does not lie. He tells the truth – always the truth.

If you are beautiful – he says so, on the screen; if you are not – not! If you make the grimace, *voila*! on the screen – the monkey-face."

"My artistes – they must be natural. That is why I am what you say – so gentle with them. If I give the big shout and call them by their bad names – what happens? *Pouf!* They get the nerves – they try. Oh! so hard they try to ACT – an' when they try it is worse. The more they try – the – the worser. *Tiens!* I speak soft, always soft. I try to show them what it is they must register. I coax – that is word – I coax them, to be natural, to walk and talk like the real people."

And so he does. You can see him coaxing them to be natural, but you can't hear him ten feet away. He takes

them over the little enclosure in which the action is to take place, and almost in whispers explains in his delightful English – or machine-gun French in the case of his brother Paul or some other French player – just what he wants. Then he steps back to the camera and has the scene run through without lights.

And one thing more – let it be understood that Capellani has every right in the world to be in America at this time. He spent the whole of the first year of the war with his regiment, first on reserve and then in the thick of the fighting. He contracted a form of rheumatism that rendered him unfit for further service and was given an honorable discharge with special commendation for gallantry on the field of battle. As soon as he was fit for the voyage he brought his family to America, as war conditions have completely halted the motion picture industry in France.

With Capellani at his studio are two or three other ex-French soldiers. There is Marcel Morhange, "Cap's" chief assistant, but four months from the trenches with a shrapnel scar on his hip and a slight but permanent limp; Henri Menessier, scenic artist, still suffering from injuries received at Arras, and Jacques Monteran, camera man, twice wounded during the first winter of the war.

Samuel Goldwyn (then Goldfish), who had just established his own production company, made his first films at the Solax studio early in 1917, including *Fighting Odds* with Maxine Elliott. But he moved to the Universal studio in April in search of better facilities. The Blachés made significant improvements that summer and Pathé became a tenant, filming Irene Castle thrillers and portions of various serials. The last film Alice Guy Blaché directed at the studio, *The Great Adventure* with Bessie Love, was made here for Pathé in the winter of 1918.

U.S. AMUSEMENT STUDIOS ENLARGED

(from *Moving Picture World,* September 8, 1917, p. 1512)

The United States Amusement Studios, at Fort Lee, NJ, are being extensively remodeled and enlarged. Although this studio is known to be one of the most complete and modern in the country, Herbert Blaché is anxious to have it second to none, and plans were just completed by a competent contractor. Work was started as soon as *Behind the Mask* was completed.

The new plans will give almost double the floor space of the present arrangement. New lightings are being installed, extra scene docks are being built, and some large open air stages are to be shortly constructed. The effect will be practically to make the place into an entirely new studio, with every modern improvement.

The Blachés separated and Alice, increasingly debilitated, no longer directed after 1918. The studio was leased by her old friend, Albert Capellani, who made films like *The Virtuous Model*, in which portions of Montmartre were recreated inside the studio by designer Henri Menessier. As the incident with Lucien Tainguy's hand grenade indicates, safety was still a problem at the studios.

CAPELLANI PRODUCTIONS ARE ACTIVE

Casting June Caprice - Creighton Hale Offering Completed While Improvements In Studio Are Underway

(from *Moving Picture World,* March 8, 1919, p. 1345)

Adolphe Osso, general manager of the Albert Capellani Productions, Inc., who recently announced that the Solax Studios had been renamed the Capellani Studio, where the Capellani productions will be made, declares he will make extensive improvements and innovations in studio equipment of every nature.

"We shall spare no effort or expense", said Osso, "in order to add to the quality of our productions. I can recall several instances where faulty equipment and poor facilities handicapped one director to such an extent that a certain production which might have become a sensation turned out to be just an average film because of a lack of proper facilities. The fact that the studio is to be our permanent home for several companies we shall soon have working was responsible for our decision. A good start is half the distance."

Henri Menessier, art director, and Lou Jerkowski, studio manager, will supervise the changes now being made at the studio. The alterations will include the sinking and building of a fifty-foot tank, which will be below the studio floor and which will be controlled by an electrical arrangement; replacing the old floor with adjustable concrete flooring; installing Mr. Capellani's own lighting system, which is said to have been brought from France, and numerous other changes in the buildings surrounding the main studio, such as paint shop, carpentry shop, laboratory and wardrobe rooms.

It is announced that these alterations will only delay the actual commencement of the work on the first of the Capellani production but a few days, for the casting of the support for June Caprice and Creighton Hale, who will play the leads in the first company, has already commenced. The title of the story chosen by Mr. Capellani for the first film has not yet been announced.

Bessie Love in The Great Adventure *(Pathé, 1918), the last film Alice Guy Blaché made in Fort Lee.*

HAND GRENADE WRECKS CAMERA

(from *Moving Picture World,* May 31, 1919, p. 1345)

A motion picture camera was wrecked and several feet of unexposed negative were destroyed recently when a Mills hand grenade accidentally exploded at the Fort Lee studio of the Albert Capellani Productions, Inc. Fortunately, the accident occurred during lunch and the only person to witness the explosion was Lucien Tainguy, a member of the Capellani photographic staff, who narrowly escaped injury from the flying shell fragments. The grenade was the property of Tainguy, who had secured it from Camp Dix, where he served as a photographer for the United States Signal Corps.

> The first of two disastrous fires struck the Solax property on 20 December 1919. Fire destroyed the laboratory, where films by Capellani and other local producers were being processed. Note the discrepancy in these two accounts regarding the presence of Capellani, the amount of the loss, and whether or not a film was being shot there at the time.

ACTORS FIGHT STUDIO FIRE
Flames Damage Building Of Motion-picture Concern At Fort Lee

(from *The New York Times,* December 21, 1919, p. 20)

Fort Lee, NJ, Dec. 20 – Damage estimated at $75,000 was done by fire today to the Solax Studio, occupied by A. Capellani, motion picture producer. For a time it was feared the entire plant would be consumed by flames. A stubborn fight made by fire-

men from Fort Lee and other nearby places saved most of the buildings. A structure containing the laboratory was destroyed.

The fire was confined to the factory building, where it originated. This building is across the street [sic] from the studio proper, which was not affected. The fire was caused either by the electric wires in the laboratory or by spontaneous combustion, according to the management of the studio. Many films were destroyed, but most of the film for *The Fortune Teller,* which is now being made by Marjorie Rambeau at the Solax Studio, was saved. Mr. Capellani lacerated one hand when he broke through a window in order to save a part of the film of this picture, which was in "the bath" in the laboratory.

The studio, which is in the same lot with the laboratory building, about ten feet away, was saved. The "movie" actors and actresses who were working in the studio were the first to fight the flames, still in costume.

Among the players who became volunteer firemen were Raymond McKee, Frederick Burton, Joseph Burke and E. Fernandez.

The fire departments of Fort Lee, Englewood, Edgewater and Leonia all worked on the fire, which was under control by 1:30 p.m.

SOLAX FILM COMPANY DESTROYED BY FIRE; MANY NARROW ESCAPES

(from *The Palisadian,* December 27, 1919, p. 5)

Employees to the number of 50 were in extreme peril on Saturday morning last and barely escaped death when the laboratory connected with the Solax Film Company, on Lemoine Avenue, was rocked by an explosion and entirely destroyed by fire that followed. There was indeed a series of explosions in the laboratory, and the girls who were at work on highly inflam-

mable films had narrow escapes. In addition to that which is being treated, there were thousands of feet of film stored in the buildings, and it is estimated that the fire destroyed more than $250,000 worth of finished film.

Miss Stella Whippet, a negative cutter, who had work planned out on her table for six directors amounting to about $100,000, calmly gathered the continuities and the negatives and carried them to a place of safety at the risk of her life. The four volunteer fire companies constituting the Fort Lee fire department were soon on the scene, but were helpless on account of low water pressure. Calls for help were answered by firemen from Edgewater and Englewood, but by that time the entire laboratory building had been destroyed.

So swiftly had the fire spread that the girl employees and many of the men were forced to rush into the street with [without?] an outer wrap and suffered greatly from the cold. Many of them fled to other buildings in the group, but were warned not to stay in them for fear the fire might spread. The greatest loss, it was announced, was suffered by the Selznick Picture Corporation. It was stated that thousands of feet of completed and incompleted film went up in the blast and that some of the company's biggest releases for the future were destroyed. The studio was under the supervision of Mr. Albert Capellani, a widely known motion picture producer. He was not at the studio at the time the fire started, and there were no pictures being shot at that time in the studio.

The fire is supposed to have been due to defective wiring and sparks dropping on the film being manufactured. This is the second disastrous conflagration to the motion picture laboratories in Fort Lee. About five years ago the old Éclair laboratory on Linwood Avenue was burned to the ground and an immense loss suffered due solely to low water pressure.

The Wonder Man *(Robertson-Cole, 1920), with Georges Carpentier and Faire Binney. Directed by John Adolfi and photographed by Georges Benoit at the Solax studio.*

The Blachés repaired the laboratory and Joseph Borries, their manager, continued to look for clients to rent the stages. Robertson-Cole produced *The Wonder Man* here in May 1920, starring French heavyweight Georges Carpentier. But Capellani ceased production and sublet to Lewis Selznick, who made *The Dangerous Paradise* with Louise Huff that summer. In October it was reported that George Arliss was making his first film, *The Devil,* at Pathé's Fort Lee studio, generally a reference to the Solax. Although production in the east dropped to almost nothing after 1920, the newly revamped laboratory was still an attractive operation, and was turned over to George Hirliman's Hirlagraph Motion Picture Corporation. Hirlagraph revamped the two Solax stages in 1924, advertising 70 x 100 and 50 x 70 foot studios for rent, but it is unknown who may have been working there. Consolidated Film Industries seems to have leased the property soon after, and were the tenants of record when a second major fire destroyed the studio building.

TELEPHONE—FORT LEE 166

U.S. Amusement Corporation

Manufacturers ———— Producers

Motion Pictures

General Offices , Studios and Laboratories
Lemoine Avenue   Fort Lee   N.J.

2 Septembre 1920

LABORATORY DIVISION

Chere Madame Blache.

   Bien que je n'aie pas recu de vos nouvelles
depuis votre depart,excepte toutefois par Charles
que j'ai rencontre dernierement,et qui m'a donne
votre adresse,j'ai su que vous etiez arrivee a bon
port en bonne sante.

   J'espere que vous allez profiter de votre
sejour en France,pour vous distraire,et chasser de
de votre esprit les impressions que ne peut faire
que laisser une situation dont vous etes l'innocente
victime.Je vous engage donc a en profiter le plus
que vous pourrez,et j'attends impatiemment votre
retour pour vous entendre me raconter tout le plaisir
que vous avez pris pendant votre sejour la bas.

   Les reparations de la factorie sont presque
terminees,et comme il ne reste plus a faire que les
fenetres et portes,j'estime que vers le milieu de la
semaine prochaine,elles seront finies.

   Mr Blache a donne la charge a Peter Heft des
reparations,mais pas pour un prix a forfait.Tous les
materiaux et la main d'oeuvre seront payes par nous,
mais avances par Heft qui touchera comme compensation
10 % du cout total,lequel sera entre 6 et 7000 dollar

   Depuis 8 jours,je suis avise que Goldie doit
amener un individu desireux d'acheter un studio,pour
visiter le notre.J'usqu'apresent ils ne sont pas

ADDRESS ALL COMMUNICATIONS TO THE CORPORATION.

TELEPHONE—FORT LEE 166

U.S. Amusement Corporation

Manufacturers ———— Producers

Motion Pictures

General Offices , Studios and Laboratories
Lemoine Avenue   Fort Lee   N.J.

LABORATORY DIVISION

encore venus.

   Mr Blache ayant demande a Klotz $ 700 par
mois pour le loyer de la factory,ce dernier surait
accepte ce prix qu'il ne trouvait pas exagere,mais
comme Mr Blache voulait etre paye de 9 mois d'avance
l'affaire est tombee dans l'eau,Klotz estimant
qu'avec la valeur de 9 mois il pouvait construire
une factorie pour lui meme,avec bien entendu de
l'argent de mortgage,en plus

   Il s'en suit donc,que jusqu'apresent personne
ne s'etant presente pour demander a la louer,j'ai
bien peur que nous soyons prives pour quelque temps
de cette source de revenu.

   Les collections pour le loyer du studio se
sont faites jusqu'apresent sans difficulte,quoique
Selznick soit souvent en retard a payer Capellani.
Je sais que vous allez dire que nous n'avons rien a
voir a cela,et vous aurez raison,mais n'oubliez pas
comment toutes ces compagnies a la manque,profitent
du moindre incident pour gagner du temps.

   Presentez je vous prie mes hommages a Madame
Guy,mes amities aux petits enfants,et vous chere
Madame,agreez l'assurance de mes sentiments les
plus devoues.

                                    J Borries

Parmi la correspondance que je vous envoie inclus,je
remarque une envelope de la Corporation Trust Co qui
sans doute contient un cheque.Si vous avez des difficul
tes a le toucher,endossez le,et je vous le collecterai
ici.

ADDRESS ALL COMMUNICATIONS TO THE CORPORATION.

Translation of letter [by Sandy Flitterman-Lewis]:

2 September 1920

Dear Madame Blaché,

Even though I haven't heard from you since you left, except for Charles who I happened to run into and who gave me your address, I knew that you had arrived safely and in good health.

I hope you'll make good use of your stay in France, that you'll be able to relax and let go of any unpleasantness that can only have the effect of making you an innocent victim. I'm telling you to take advantage all you can, and I impatiently await your return so that you can tell me all about your pleasant stay there.

The factory repairs are practically finished, and since all we have left to do are the windows and the doors, I figure we'll be done by the middle of next week.

Mr. Blaché has put Peter Heft in charge, but not at an outright price. All the materials and labor are to be paid by us, but advanced by Heft, who will get 10% of the total cost as compensation, which should be between 6 and 7 thousand dollars.

About a week ago, I was advised that Goldie would bring around someone who wanted to buy a studio, so that he could take a look at ours. So far they haven't come by.

Mr. Blaché asked Klotz for $700/month to rent the factory, which he was willing to pay because he thought the price reasonable, but since Mr. Blaché wanted nine months in advance, the deal fell through. Klotz felt that with the nine months' sum he could construct his own factory, with the mortgage as supplement.

That said, no one has been interested in renting and I'm afraid we'll be deprived of that source of income for a little while.

Up until now we've had no difficulty collecting rent, even though Selznick is often late in paying Capellani. I know you're going to say that it's none of our business, and you're right, but don't forget how all companies who are behind take advantage of the least little thing to gain time.

Please give my good wishes to Mme Guy, my regards to the grandchildren, and to you, my dear Madame, my most devoted sentiments.

[Signed] J. Borries

Among the letters I've enclosed herein, I note an envelope for the Corporation Trust Company which probably contains a check. If you can't cash it there, endorse it, and I'll cash it for you here.

[In handwriting on the side of the page: Would you be so kind as to return the invoice as soon as you've signed it?]

FORT LEE MOVIE STUDIO IS GUTTED BY $100,000 BLAZE

Glass Studio And Adjacent Brick Warehouse Where Film, Scenery And Wardrobes Were Stored, Suffers Big Loss – Four Companies From Fort Lee Respond. Blaze Started After Watchman Left

(from *The Palisadian,* September 27, 1929, p. 1)

A $100,000 blaze gutted the buildings of the Consolidated Film Corporation, in Fort Lee, last Tuesday night, which are located about 150 feet south of the new Fort Lee High School on Lemoine Avenue. Every pane of glass was broken in the movie studio and valuable scenery was burned. The fire extended into the adjacent building, which was used as a storehouse, and films, stage settings and wardrobes went up in smoke. The loss is reported to be uninsured.

The fire broke out at about 7 p.m., shortly after William Updycke, of Main Street, watchman for the Consolidated Film Corporation, had left the buildings. He told the police that everything seemed to be alright when he left.

No active work has taken place in the studio for the past two years but the recent installation of new machinery was evidence that the new concern had future plans.

Thomas McNally discovered the blaze and said that flames broke out immedi-ately following an explosion. All four companies of the Fort Lee department responded and eight streams of water issued forth from the new fire engine.

William Haley, "trouble man" attached to the Public Service Electric & Gas offices in Hackensack, was instrumental in saving the lives of firemen when he appeared ten minutes after being notified and disconnected switches on four high tension power lines leading into the buildings from poles at the curb. It is believed that if the firemen had come into contact with the machinery while it was still connected with the power lines they would have been electrocuted or seriously burned.

An investigation into the cause of the fire was started immediately.

Councilman Peter Grieb, fire committee chairman, last night said that Cecil Charlton, of West 227th Street, New York, treasurer of the Consolidated Film Corporation, of 1776 Broadway, that city, is being held by borough authorities only to insure speedy repairs to, or removal of, the ruins of the company's buildings on Lemoine Avenue, which were destroyed by fire Tuesday night.

The ruins of the studio were razed in 1930, and Consolidated, which was expanding its operations in Fort Lee, purchased the property on May 22, 1931. Chester M. Ross and Emanuel Kandel, owners of Bonded Film Storage, in turn bought the property from Consolidated in 1949, and over the next three years constructed four new buildings on the site. The remaining structures were demolished to make way for a supermarket parking lot in 1965.

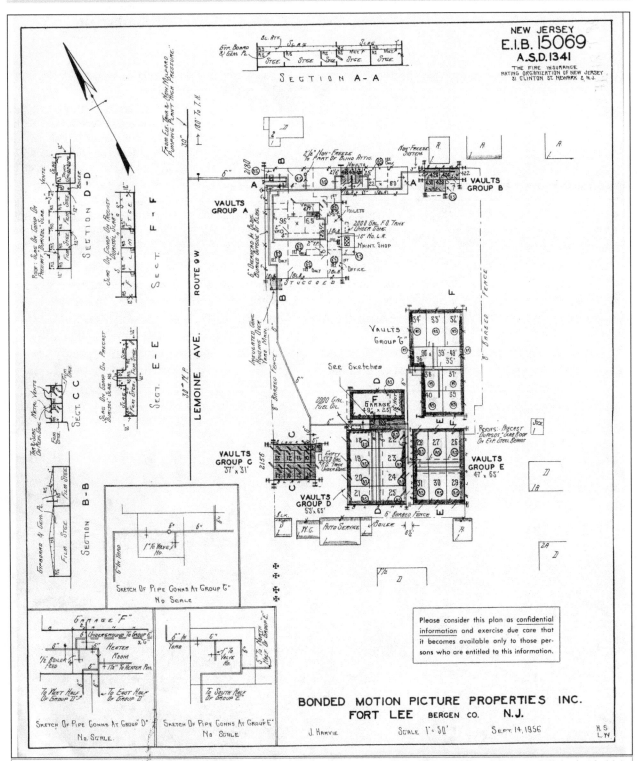

Site plan of Bonded's Fort Lee property prepared prior to 1965 sale and demolition of existing structures. Buildings A-B-C were built by the Blachés in 1913, upgraded by Hirlagraph in 1926–28, and later restored by Bonded, which subsequently constructed additional buildings on the lot. Frame house 'D' (domicile) to north of property stills exists, although heavily reconstructed. It can be seen in the photos on pages 128 and 140.

9.
Pathé

JUST ME

By Pearl White

(New York: Doran, 1919, pp. 156–161)

The idea of serial pictures had just been born over in Jersey, and Pathé offered me the chance to risk my life through a series of episodes called *The Perils of Pauline*. So I dashed over to the studio intending to take the job. I

For the most part, the work of Pathé's Jersey City studio is beyond the scope of this book. But Pathé clearly had a fondness for Fort Lee, dating back to the time when James Young Deer directed their first American films there. For years it remained a favorite location for "cliffhanger" serial endings featuring Pearl White and the rest of the Pathé stock company. Pearl White had arrived in New York in 1910, tired of theatrical life on the road and looking for something more stable and secure. She tried the movie studios, working for Powers, Crystal, and Pathé in one-reel comedies and melodramas. *The Perils of Pauline* [1914] marked her triumphant return to Pathé and director Louis Gasnier (who, she reports, spoke no English when she had worked for him in 1911). By the time this memoir was published William Fox had already signed her for "big dramatic films", but White would never recapture the success she achieved in Pathé's world famous "cliffhangers".

was met by my old director, Mr. [Louis] Gasnier, who was still residing at the head of the firm, and he laid bare the situation. I don't mind telling you that I nearly walked out of the studio without signing the contract that they had prepared. To be sure, they offered me a lot of money and so much advertising that I couldn't escape gaining at least some fame. However, the odds seemed against me. "Hello, girl, how do you like my Paris?" were the words that greeted me from my old boss. "Wonderful", said I. "But what about the job you are tempting me with?" "Well, do you want to become famous?" he asked. "Certainly", I replied, "that's been my lifelong struggle". "Then sign here", he continued, handing me a couple of typewritten pages and casually asking if I carried any life insurance. Now, I had never signed a legal document before, but that speech about life insurance made me hesitate and read the pages before me. The farther into the contract I got the worse things looked for me, and when I got to the clause "the party of the second part, being of age, takes her part in this motion picture play at her own risk, and in case of accident or loss of life she or relations have no claim for damages against the party of the first part", etc., etc., I was all for leaving this offer stand and getting back to New York as fast as the street car would take me. "What do you expect me to do? Lose my life?" I asked. "Accidents do sometimes happen", he volunteered. "Here, read a couple of manuscripts and judge for yourself". Then he handed me some manuscripts and walked out of the office. I read the first three episodes of this hair-breadth escape serial and that was about enough for me. I shouted for help and Mr. Gasnier entered from the next room. "Well, how do you like it?" he asked. "Like it!" I answered. "Here, take a look for yourself", and I began turning over the pages. "You can see for yourself I'm not the person for that part. In the first place, I'm too clumsy, and in the second place I have too much respect for my life." In these first three episodes I had to play tennis, which I could not. I had to take a flight in an aeroplane, which I didn't like much, because it was supposed to crash to the ground in a wreck; then I had to drive a motor car through water, fire

(Facing page): Pearl White rehearsing on the Palisades for The House of Hate *(Pathé, 1918). Arthur Miller at the camera.*

(Below): Director Louis Gasnier "interviewing" Pearl White for his new film.

Pearl White hijacks a car at gunpoint, one of many dangerous automobile stunts in The Perils of Pauline *(Pathé-Eclectic, 1914).*

and sand. This also didn't sound reasonable. Then I had to go out to sea in a yacht, which was all right, only that I was to jump overboard just as the boat was blown up by the villain, and I couldn't swim. Then I was to be in a captive balloon – but ah! The villain was to cut the rope and I was to go sailing about for a while, then drop an anchor, which was to catch in a tree, and I was to descend some two hundred and fifty feet on this, reaching a cliff on the side of a mountain, then I was to be showered with rocks and – but I didn't get any farther than the balloon. I lost my desire for that sport years before. "Well, you see", said I to Mr. Gasnier, these things are not my line. Besides, you want an acrobat for this part. You don't want an actress." "I didn't say I wanted an actress", he very sweetly answered. "Then why did you send for – ". My sense of humor began to gain consciousness and I began to see light. "All right, you win", I had to laugh as I continued. "Give me the papers". And I signed what I thought was probably my death warrant. Now, I had never had time in the days gone by to learn to swim, play golf, tennis, etc., etc. So, as an all-round athlete I wasn't so good. However, as all sports depend more or less on the schooling of one's muscles, and in the old trapeze days I had developed and trained mine until I could control my entire body fairly easy, therefore, it has not been difficult for me to learn to do a lot of different stunts. I started to work in *The Perils of Pauline*, the first serial of thrills that had ever been produced, and have continued in those kind of pictures such as *The Exploits of Elaine, The Iron Claw, Pearl of the Army, The Fatal Ring, The House of Hate, The Lightning Raider* and now *In Secret* [released as *The Black Secret*], which have all been more or less "the always in danger" type of pictures. I would, of course, like to do big dramatic plays and act and all that sort of thing. However, I have been very successful in serials, so I shall just thank my lucky star and continue on until the public tires of me. Then I want to take some promising young girl and try to teach her to be what I would like to have been. But I do want to take one more try on the speaking stage before that time comes. I have worked on these last three and a half years following more or less the same routine. Up early in the morning, work all day long under the strong lights in the studio or in the hot sun or cold winds out of doors. I have remained in New York all the while, wearing furs in the summer and the thinnest kind of clothes in the winter a goodly bit of the time. For it seems that the minds of scenario writers turn toward summer scenes in the winter and toward winter scenes in the summer time; therefore, we poor actors are about half of the time roasting or freezing while we work. The picture business is certainly not one of ease and comfort, and I think I can modestly say that my lot is just a little bit harder than most of the others in the profession, because I'm always doing some new stunt and nursing a lot of cuts, bruises or sprains in consequence; besides – although Pathé Frères have often advertised me as their "Peerless Fearless Pearl" – we can put a very soft pedal on that, because I have been petrified with fear more than once during the filming of pictures. I have actually gotten to like fear, and like the sensation of taking some very dangerous chances that frighten me. My old heart beats a ragtime, and I face the music feeling more thrilled than I would be doing something in which I knew there was no risk.

Arthur Miller had been working for Pathé News as one of the industry's first newsreel cameramen when he was assigned to photograph Pathé's first serial, *The Perils of Pauline.* In later years Miller became something of a historian, and unlike most film industry memoirs, the account he wrote of this film's production is scrupulously detailed, down to the type of lighting units employed, automobiles driven, and roadhouses visited.

THE PERILS OF PAULINE

By Arthur Miller

(from *One Reel a Week* [Berkeley: U. of California Press, 1967], pp. 94–105).

Although I enjoyed making the Pathé news subjects a great deal, it had been my hope ever since I left Porter and the Rex company to return to photographing production, but when I was assigned to shoot *The Perils of Pauline*, I never had the slightest inkling that the serial would be remembered by motion picture historians more than fifty years later. It is for this group that some of the facts are recorded. *Pauline* was made at the Pathé studio located at 1 Congress Street, Jersey City Heights, during 1914. The main entrance to the Pathé studio was on the corner of Congress Street and Webster Avenue. The studio itself consisted of a lower and an upper stage. The upper stage was equipped with a tank about 30' x 30' square and 8' deep. We could lower a fair-sized set inch by inch into the water when shooting such suspense scenes as a dungeon gradually being flooded with water, leaving the heroine helpless, but you could be sure she would be rescued at the beginning of the next episode. The top and sides of both stages were made of small panes of clear glass, much on the order of a garden greenhouse. White and black diffusers inside covered the top and side of each stage and were controlled at will by pulling cords that hung at the sides. Arc lights and Cooper-Hewitt mercury tubes were used to mix with the soft daylight for photographing. Constructed in 1910, the studio was one of the most modern and well-equipped of the time.

The Perils of Pauline was duped and used in showings for many different purposes. Charles Goddard even wrote a novel of the same title in 1914 and used still pictures from the serial as illustrations for it. The original intention of keeping the audience in suspense from week to week was forgotten. In one instance, the entire serial was recut to make each episode a complete story in itself, whereas the original idea had been to leave either the hero or heroine in a rather precarious predicament at the end of each episode, thereby guaranteeing the return of the audience, anxious to know how they were rescued from the clutches of the villain. This "cliffhanger" idea was used for the first ten episodes. It succeeded so well that another ten were added, so that twenty episodes in all of *The Perils of Pauline* were produced.

The man in full charge of *Pauline* as well as of the Pathé studio was Louis J. Gasnier, who directed the first ten episodes but then turned the director's job over to Donald MacKenzie. Donald MacKenzie had played the part of a pirate in one of the early installments. Shooting scripts were written by George B. Seitz and Bertram Millhauser. Seitz always cut the finished episodes. Contrary to many serials produced afterwards, each installment was completed separately. Later, many were made as one picture, shooting every location, from the first to the last episode, in one visit. The interiors were handled in the same manner – serials produced on a sort of production-line basis.

Photographing *The Perils of Pauline* was my assignment, and my second cameraman, as they called them then, was Harry Wood. The very nature of the serial called for peril and dangerous situations, and frequently required extra cameras to shoot several angles of a particular stunt. Cameramen working at the studio who happened to be between assignments operated the extra cameras.

We used negative film manufactured by the Pathé company. Gasnier viewed the developed negative on the screen and chose the desired take of each scene. Aside from the directors, the principal players, and the camera crew, three men deserve special credit for their part in making *Pauline*. One was Frank Redman, Sr., who was the head of the property department. He also played many small parts. Teamed together were two young fellows whose last names, I am ashamed to admit I never knew, but one was called Pitch and the other Cooney. Both played bit parts when necessary and did the work of property men, as well as what would be the work of a grip today – handling camera dollies, reflectors, dolly tracks, and so on. The many times I was perched on a platform or rigged on an automobile in front of the radiator I felt perfectly safe as I had full confidence in their ability and judgment. One of their most important jobs was to figure out and rig stunts that required the use of piano wire – often a life depended on their skill.

Toward the end of the serial, Spencer Bennett, now a director, was made an assistant to Donald MacKenzie and also played parts when called upon. The principals in the cast, of course, were Pearl White, Crane Wilbur, and Paul Panzer, who played the villain. I have had hundreds of inquires about these three personalities, especially Pearl, and can only describe them as they were when we worked together. I have no reason to believe they were any different from other people. Like other movie stars, it was difficult for them to have any privacy. They were mobbed in public just as all the famous stars who followed. It seems to me that there was more cooperation from performers in those days than there is now, and to pile in a car and go on a day's location was like going on a picnic, for all hands worked in harmony. It is true that we didn't have dolly shots to make, no sound equipment to bother about, and everything in general was much less complicated, which could account for much less strain. Most of our locations were around Fort Lee, Coytesville, and

with the Powers Picture Players studio. I have been told that she performed with a circus and she learned then the acrobatics which enabled her to do all her own stunts in *Pauline*. During the time I knew her, Pearl often talked of her days with road shows doing one-night stands in "tank towns" as she called them, but never did I hear her say she had performed with a circus. I am positive that she was neither an acrobat nor a tumbler ….

Crane Wilbur was a handsome young man of the matinee-idol type. He had a full head of dark hair with a natural wave, and his charm on and off the screen left the girls swooning. Paul Panzer, I thought, was perfect in his role of the eager-to-help-type of villain who unsuspectingly laid the plans for the dirty work to enable him to gain the favor of the heroine. Today this kind of broad plotting and planning would be considered the worst kind of corn, but at the time of *The Perils of Pauline* the audience really went for it in a big way. Panzer was a friendly man, one of the very early moving picture actors, and I think that he took his acting career far more seriously than either Pearl White or Crane Wilbur ever did.

Each episode of *Pauline* took about two weeks to make and about the time the eighth episode was out, someone wrote a song called "Poor Pauline". Perhaps this was the start of personal appearances, as Pearl appeared at some of the nicer movie houses. This created a demand for Crane Wilbur, and he gave dramatic recitations at each of his personal appearances. Both were a big hit every time.

I have been asked time and again whether Pearl White performed all the daredevil stunts that occurred in the serial or if doubles were used. Com-

among the rocky cliffs of the Palisades, as well as a little farther up the Hudson River in the town of Englewood, where we made use of the Browning and Morrow estates as "homes" of characters in the cast.

Under Rambo's grape arbor, mentioned earlier in the book, remained the place to eat lunch, and the menu was still ham and eggs, coffee, and apple pie. We rented such automobiles as a Thomas touring car, an Abbot Detroit, a Buick, and a Rambler from Mereo's garage on Hudson Boulevard. The cameraman always rode in the front beside the driver, the most convenient place for him to rest the Pathé camera on the floor between his legs for safety while in transit. The tripod was carried in a fixed bracket attached to the running board of the car.

Pearl White was a trim, attractive girl and her pleasant, unaffected manner made her a joy to work with. She saved all of her acting for in front of the camera and otherwise was never anything but herself. She had begun acting on the stage at the age of four. About 1910 her motion picture career started when she went

mon sense should indicate that if either Pearl or Crane Wilbur had been injured doing these often dangerous stunts, the serial would be out of business, but there were times when both performed hazardous stunts at their own stubborn insistence. I remember a stunt from one of the early episodes that was not considered to be dangerous – just the transfer from running board of one moving automobile to another, also in motion. The cars didn't have to move very fast, as under-cranking the camera created the illusion of high speed for both cars. Pearl struggled free of her captors, got out on the running board of the car, but as she reached for the other automobile traveling alongside that was to rescue her, she somehow lost her footing and fell between the moving cars. Only the quick thinking of the two drivers who turned their cars out and apart prevented a serious accident.

I think Crane Wilbur was more adamant than Pearl about doing his own stunts, especially those that concerned swimming or diving, as he was an expert at both. In my opinion, it was foolhardy for either of them to take chances when they were too far from the camera to be identified.

On one occasion we went to upstate New York on location in order to capture the beauty of Ausable Chasm. Over the centuries, a river had cut high, rugged cliffs that towered straight up on both sides through the chasm, and we played many scenes against this beautiful scenery in the background. Just how the situation arose in the story, I cannot recall, but the hero was called upon to dive from one of the rocks that jutted out from the chasm wall, about forty or fifty feet high, into the water below. I am sure that Wilbur knew the camera was too far away for him to be recognized. Nevertheless, he insisted on making the dive himself and would have it no other way. After we shot the scene, which went off without a hitch, I

wondered if that wasn't the way it was supposed to be. Wilbur knew precisely what he was doing and probably saved some trouble, if not actual injury, for the double, Pitch, who rarely took the time to plan his own stunts carefully.

Another time when both Pitch and Cooney, doubling for Pearl and Wilbur, jumped from a rocky cliff into Lake Saranac below they missed, by only a small margin, bouncing off the sharp rocks they passed on the way down. There was no such person as a professional stunt man in those days. There was an individual named Rodman Law who did crazy things, like jumping off the Brooklyn Bridge. His sister, Ruth, performed similar daring feats, but all they got for it was their names in the newspapers. The present-day professional stunt man makes every effort to plan his stunt so that it will provide the least amount of risk. Even so, every now and then, things fail to work as scheduled.

To sum up, both Pearl White and Crane Wilbur did stunts and sometimes took unnecessary chances. But there were occasions when it would have been absolutely crazy for them to perform the stunts themselves. Of one thing I am certain and that is they both did more dangerous stunts than any performer does today. Using a double is common practice now, and it makes far more sense than the dangerous system that prevailed in the early days.

With all the daredevil thrills and stunts that took place during the course of making the serial, we were indeed fortunate never to experience a serious accident, although there were several narrow escapes. One of these involved a balloon. The so-called airfield was on Staten Island, where a fellow named Leo Stevens kept his biplane. While George Seitz was visiting us at the airfield, he discovered that Stevens also owned a balloon, and by the time we had finished the aeroplane chapter, he had written the next one around

the balloon. The day came when we were working among the rocky cliffs of the Palisades near the town of Coytesville, shooting scenes with the inflated balloon with the square basket hanging from its base. I can't recall the sequence of the scenes but I do remember there were some close-ups of Pearl in the basket to be made. The basket was held fast to the rocks of the Palisades by a one-inch manila rope fastened to it. When we had finished the close shots, Leo Stevens ducked down out of sight of the camera, so we could begin taking shots of the balloon. At the bottom of the picture, Pearl could be seen as she looked over the edge of the basket with the large inflated balloon above against the sky making an imposing composition.

Suddenly some rocks began to tumble, loosening the anchor, and before anyone could do anything except to stand there in amazement, the balloon gained altitude and slowly drifted up and over the Hudson River toward New York with its anchor still dangling from the end of the rope. There were no high buildings in uptown New York at the time. If I remember correctly, the highest building was the Woolworth building and that was near the southern tip of Manhattan.

We had no choice except to pack the equipment and to return to the studio to await information. Since this was an unscheduled balloon flight, those who saw it had no idea who or what was in the balloon. It took off about eleven in the morning and it wasn't until five o'clock in the afternoon that someone called the studio to tell Gasnier that Pearl was safe and on her way back to New York from somewhere in Philadelphia, where they had landed. The next day I asked Pearl if she was frightened during the balloon trip. Her answer was that what upset her most was that the owner of the airship kept repeating that it wasn't equipped to fly, that it didn't have a rip cord, making it impossible to open the valve at the neck of the balloon which would deflate the bag and allow it to descend. Pearl said that when Stevens saw a large patch of open ground below, he climbed up the shrouds, held his nose with one hand to protect himself from the escaping gas and released the valve with the other. As the balloon got closer to the ground, Pearl said, the basket began to swing back and forth, finally hitting the ground rather hard. Pearl averred though, that taking everything into consideration, she wouldn't have missed that trip for anything.

After concluding the foregoing about *The Perils of Pauline*, I came across a book which purports to relate the history of the movie serials. I have read many criticisms of films made in the early days, but for the first time has a would-be historian called the work of someone "crude", when as a matter of fact, he makes it clear in doing so that he hasn't the slightest knowledge of what he is criticizing [Kalton Lahue, *Continued Next Week* (University of Oklahoma Press, 1964), p. 8]. He also states that most of the people who were in the middle of things during what he calls "those glorious days" are gone forever and their memories unrecorded. It may come as a surprise to him that I, who photographed *The Perils of Pauline*, am very much alive and feel compelled to straighten out a few things. Our friend goes on to say that he considers the language used in the subtitles an unforgivable crime for it was so bad even children laughed at it. He apparently believes the reason for this was that the producer, Louis Gasnier, was French. It is amazing to me how anyone who sets out to write a history of the serials wouldn't be aware that the man who made more serials with Pearl White than anyone else was George B. Seitz, a well-educated man. It was Seitz, together with Bertram Millhauser, who wrote each episode of *Pauline*, edited them and wrote the subtitles. After each episode was completed, someone on the staff

of the Hearst newspapers would look at it on the screen so that he could write the story for the Sunday supplement. It seems rather naïve of our author to believe that all of these writers were illiterate. If the reason for ungrammatical subtitles on what must be at the least fourth or fifth duplicate prints, very likely in 16mm, is so obscure, perhaps it is worth the space to explain what actually went on.

In 1916 I tried for personal reasons to obtain a print of one of the episodes of *The Perils of Pauline* and was told by Louis Gasnier that the negative had been shipped to France. Even before that time, the serial had been a big hit in France, and Pearl White became as popular there as she was in America. After the disastrous fire that took the lives of 180 of the cream of French society in the early days of motion pictures, the French government had passed and strictly enforced a law providing that all projection machines must be enclosed in a fireproof booth. In 1912 the Lumiere Brothers placed on the market what was known as "safety" film, and for showing this film a booth was not required. The film, 28mm in width, became known in France as the "educational" film size. *The Perils of Pauline* was in such demand that a duped negative in 28mm size was made. No one knows how many prints were sold that were shown throughout the countryside in tent shows and other places. Of course, the English titles were translated by a French translator and naturally took on a French flavor.

Several years after World War I, American film historians began to be interested in *The Perils of Pauline*, since it was the first American serial. The original negative could no longer be found, and as no 35mm prints were located, it was therefore presumed that they had been destroyed in order to retrieve whatever silver hadn't been removed during the original processing. The French, with their sharp eye for business, gathered some of the 28mm prints and retranslated the French-flavored titles back to what they considered was good English usage. It is true that the results often were funny, but everybody interested knew what had happened. Such prints as found their way back to the United States were again duped to 16mm film. In some instances, the duped negative was blown up to 35mm and reduction 16mm prints made, one of which I have. It is a wonder that anything could be salvaged after the many duping stages *The Perils of Pauline* went through.

We finished photographing *The Perils of Pauline* some time before the end of the year, and my next assignment was to photograph a picture directed by a man named Verno [Henry Vernot?], a Frenchman who had come to the United States to work for the Éclair company in Fort Lee. This was his first picture for the Pathé company. In little more than a week he was replaced by Frank Powell. While we were making the picture, I became intrigued with Powell's brand-new Overland racing model automobile. It was the best-looking sports car imaginable, with two bucket seats and a round gas tank placed crosswise in back of the seats. Chrome plating wasn't the thing then, but the car was trimmed with shiny brass acetylene headlights. The supply tank was fastened on one of the running boards. The car had a large brass horn connected to a flexible brass tube with a rubber bulb at the end that produced a deep-throated honk-honk. The Overland was a shiny blue color with a leather strap over the hood of the engine. The cut-out, which could be opened legally then, made such a racket that the car could be heard a quarter of a mile before it was visible.

When we were on location we usually quit at about three so that our director could take a little spin in his Overland roadster. Even when working in the studio, we would stop at about the same time. Powell and I would pile into his Overland and take off in search of new locations. We always took the same route, up the Hudson Boulevard to Nungesser's roadhouse, onto Anderson Avenue, up to Fort Lee, and finally up Lemoyne Avenue [sic] to the Villa Richard. The Villa Richard was a roadhouse and French restaurant about three miles from Coytesville that was perched on the edge of the Palisades overlooking the Hudson River. There Powell and I had our customary drink as we sat and gazed out the window at the superb view for a little while before driving back to the studio.

DOCTOR FOOLED BY FAKE ACCIDENT

(from *Moving Picture World*, October 10, 1914, p. 199)

Donald Mackenzie, who made such a big hit as the pirate in *The Perils of Pauline* and has for some time been assisting Chief Director Gasnier of Pathé, is directing the 15th, 16th and 17th episodes of *Pauline*. Mr. Gasnier feels that the genial Scotchman is as good a director as he is actor.

Mr. Mackenzie tells a good one that happened while he was working on the 15th episode of *The Perils of Pauline*. He was staging an automobile accident on a country road near Metuchen and had every thing going finely. Crane Wilbur and Pearl White had just run their car into the fence to escape the overturned auto and two "lifeless" men in the road; the cameraman was grinding away from the roadside when into the picture came thundering another car. It stopped, a man hopped out with a little bag in his hand and dashed to the side of the prostrate men. Mackenzie gasped and then howled "Have a heart! Please get out of my picture!" The man's jaw fell. "What" said he, "I'm a physician; isn't this an accident?" Mackenzie explained and then everybody had a good laugh. "Well" said the doctor as he drove away, "this is realism run riot!"

> In a historic essay originally published in 1944, Sergei Eisenstein offered his analysis of the significance of D.W. Griffith and his accomplishments. He praised Griffith for adding "profound emotion" to the American cinema, but what came before was "captivating and attractive" in its own way: the "boundless temperament and tempo" of Douglas Fairbanks in *The Mark of Zorro*, and Pearl White in *two* of her Pathé serials.

DICKENS, GRIFFITH, AND THE FILM TODAY

By Sergei Eisenstein

(From *Film Form*, translated by Jay Leyda [NY: Harcourt, Brace, 1949], pp. 203–204)

There was the role of another film-factor that appeared, dashing along in such films as *The Gray Shadow* [the Russian release title of *The Black Secret*, 1919], *The House of Hate* [1918], *The Mark of Zorro* [1920]. There was in these films a world, stirring and incomprehensible, but neither repulsive nor alien. On the contrary – it was captivating and attractive, in its own way engaging the attention of young and future film-makers, exactly as the young and future engineers of the time were attracted by the specimens of engineering techniques unknown to us, sent from that same unknown distant land across the ocean.

What enthralled us was not only these films, it was also their possibilities. Just as it was the possibilities in a tractor to make collective cultivation of the fields a reality, it was the bound-

Thrills from "The   House of Hate"

Pen points on a Pearl White serial made during the screening at Pathé's Fort Lee Studio.

By R. L. Lambdin

The Malay dashed up the broad staircase. In his wake, a footman sickenly thudded on the first step. Pearl obligingly fainted, according to custom, on the top step.

Pearl having inherited a munition plant, is about to be squashed by part of her inheritance. For her thrilling rescue — See the next episode.

Pulling a dagger the Malay seized Buttons by the throat and — here the artist had to work like mad to catch him in mid-air, for the "faithful servitor" refused to serve another.

Curse their cold hearts! A lady in distress — yet the camera man grinds along the even tenor of his pay, while the artist sketches in ecstasy.

And the actors provide their own clothes! Antonio Moreno carefully surveys the remains of the third derby ruined in the seventh episode.

Just before the explosion the Hooded Terror had lured Pearl into this building!

R. L. Lambdin's impression of the production of The House of Hate *at "Pathé's Fort Lee Studio". From* Picture Play, *May 1918.*

less temperament and tempo of the amazing (and amazingly useless!) works from an unknown country that led us to muse on the possibilities of a profound, intelligent, class-directed use of this wonderful tool.

The most thrilling figure against this background was Griffith, for it was in his works that the cinema made itself felt as more than an entertainment or pastime. The brilliant new methods of the American cinema were united in him with a profound emotion of story, with human acting, with laughter and tears, and all this was done with an astonishing ability to preserve all that gleam of a filmically dynamic holiday, which had been captured in *The Gray Shadow* and *The Mark of Zorro* and *The House of Hate*. That the cinema could be incomparably greater, and that this was to be the basic task of the budding Soviet cinema – these were sketched for us in Griffith's creative work, and found ever new confirmation in his films ....

WORKING FOR GEORGE FITZMAURICE

By Arthur Miller

(from *One Reel a* Week [University of California Press, 1967], pp. 124–125, 132–133).

Returning to the Pathé studio in Jersey City Heights was like coming home. Many of the same people were still there in the same jobs they had when I left. I was happy to sign a one-year contract with the Astra Film Company and was assigned to George Fitzmaurice, the director. "Fitz", as

In late 1917 and early 1918 trade paper accounts frequently refer to work going on in Pathé's "Fort Lee studio". As Arthur Miller reveals here, this was actually the Solax studio, a second home for many local producers in this period. The company he was then working for, Astra, had been formed by Louis Gasnier and George Fitzmaurice to make features for distribution through Pathé. When production overflowed the space available in Jersey City, Astra sent a satellite unit to Fort Lee.

most people called him, had already made his first picture for the Astra company, a film called *Via Wireless* [1915]. He wasn't planning to start another for a month, so I photographed a one-reel comedy, *Toot, the Tailor*, directed by E. Mason Hopper.

The Fitzmaurice company worked as a sort of separate unit and made one picture after another without much time in between. Ouida Bergere, then Mrs. Fitzmaurice, was writing screen adaptations from A. H. Woods' stage successes, and each picture featured some Broadway star. *At Bay* [1915], the first picture I photographed for Fitzmaurice, starred Florence Reed. It was a five- or six-reel feature, and the interiors were photographed with mixed Cooper-Hewitt, arc and daylight, and it often took considerable time to achieve the desired lighting. To my delight, I found that Fitzmaurice was as interested in having quality photography as I, and he was very patient and understanding when problems sometimes arose. He was well educated in art and made many helpful suggestions. He also designed and laid out his own sets. I am sure there must have been art directors even then, but all that I remember are men who came from the carpenter shop. There was a group referred to as "outside" men whose job it was to secure and rent the furniture and dressing for the sets. When the picture was finished, it was my job to wind the scenes on reels, one after another, in sequence and continuity, ready for Fitzmaurice to do the cutting, known as "editing" today … .

In rapid succession, [in 1916–17] we made *Romantic Journey*, *The Iron Heart*, *The Recoil*, *The Mark of Cain*, and *Sylvia of the Secret Service*, which starred Irene Castle and Antonio Moreno. Erich Von Stroheim was a sort of technical director for this picture. Von had considerable knowledge of German militarism, or at least everyone thought he had. The plot of *Sylvia of the Secret Service* had something to do with Germans blowing up an ammunition dump, and Von went to New York to research the names of the different explosives to be painted on cases stored at such a place. I don't believe that anyone ever saw Von Stroheim when he was not dressed other than as a dapper gentleman, with a rather short clipped haircut, Prussian style. These were the war years, and between his appearance and the sort of questions he was asking, it was no time at all before he was in the clink. The studio, of course, immediately went to his rescue and he was released. I am convinced, though, that the clever Von Stroheim pulled the whole thing off for its publicity value.

My contract with the Astra Film Company had expired and, as all the pictures I had photographed for them had been directed by Fitzmaurice, he proposed that I sign a personal contract with him. Gasnier had no objection so we went ahead. On his personal stationery Fitz wrote, "I agree to employ Arthur Miller as a cameraman for a period of one year and to pay him $75 per week as salary", which I signed and dated. Each year for the next eight years this process was repeated. During that period we never had a contract dispute, simply because there was nothing in the contract to dispute. Now when lawyers finish drawing up a cameraman's contract with its thirty pages of whereases and wherefores, there seems to be one continuing argument for its duration.

There were three or four other directors making pictures at this time at the Astra Film Company, but as far as I know Fitz was the only permanent one. All the better directors were striving for recognition and working to reach the heights of D. W. Griffith. Out of this desire, some directors gained further credit by having added to the main title something like "A George Fitzmaurice Production" as well as retaining the usual credit title, the last before the picture started, of "Directed by George Fitzmaurice". I use Fitzmaurice only as an example, not to imply that he began this practice, though he certainly was among the first.

After finishing *Sylvia of the Secret Service*, we moved from the Pathé studio in Jersey City Heights up to the Solax studio in Fort Lee on Lemoyne Avenue, a little bit west of what is now the George Washington Bridge Plaza. The Solax studio was practically the same as the Pathé studio; it had glass sides and top which meant mixing Cooper-Hewitt, arc, and daylight to photograph. Fitzmaurice took a well-deserved rest, while I photographed another picture also starring Irene Castle titled *Vengeance is Mine* [1917]. With Frank Crane as director, most of the picture was made in the Adirondack Mountains around Saranac Lake. We had returned to Fort Lee and were working in the studio when Miss Castle received the news that her husband, Vernon, who had joined the Royal Flying Corps, had been killed in an airplane accident while training in Texas. Both she and her husband had started breeding and training German shepherd dogs for war service. Miss Castle made me a present of one of the puppies which I loved for many years …

10.

Willat-Triangle

The Willat Film Manufacturing Company began assembling property on the northwest corner of Main Street and Linwood Avenue in October of 1913. Eventually they owned an L-shaped plot extending 444 feet west of Linwood Avenue and 648 feet north of Main Street (the Éclair Studio already occupied the land at the center of Linwood Avenue). Carl A. Willatowski, known throughout the industry as "Doc" Willat (for his degree in veterinary medicine), built two vaulted greenhouse studios and a modern laboratory here. He sold his interests to Charles Baumann and Ad Kessel, Jr., who reorganized as Willat Studios and Laboratories in 1914. William Fox rented the stages beginning in 1915, and the following year the Triangle Film Corporation (of which Kessel and Baumann were officers) also moved some of their production into the Willat. After 1917 the studio fell into disrepair, but the laboratory continued to be used by Triangle until being taken over by Nicholas Kessel. It was being operated by the National-Evans Film Laboratories when an explosion and fire destroyed the facility in 1925.

WILLAT WILL MAKE PICTURES

Well-Known Factory Manager Will Build And Equip A Hundred Thousand Dollar Plant In Jersey

(From *Moving Picture World*, December 27, 1913, p. 1553 .)

For several months, or ever since he resigned as factory manager of the New York Motion Picture Company, the trade have been looking anxiously for C. A. "Doc" Willat to announce his future plans as a maker of motion pictures. Those plans are now out and cover the erection of a studio and factory in Fort Lee, NJ, that will cost about $125,000 when fully equipped and ready for business. The new plant will be located on Main Street and Lynwood [sic] Avenue in that village, on a plot just adjoining the plant of the Éclair Company on the south. Excavation work for the foundations was started on December 8, 1913, and it is expected that the plant will be ready for occupancy in May.

The studio building will be 120 feet by 80 feet on the ground and about 53 feet to the peak of the roof. It will be almost entirely enclosed in glass. The front elevation is shown in one of the accompanying engravings. The dressing rooms, property and other departments directly connected with studio work will range along one side of the building. A tank will be constructed in the floor 15 feet by 25 feet, for water and trap scenes. A lighting system of the most approved design will be used, but the novelty will appear in the arrangement and utilization.

The factory building is of the same dimensions as the studio, but will have two floors. Here all the ingenuity of the promoter will be demonstrated.

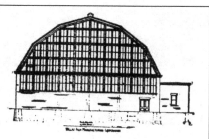

Designs for "Doc" Willat's new Fort Lee studio, showing only a single glass-enclosed studio building. Moving Picture World, 27 December 1913.

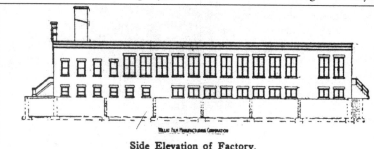

Side Elevation of Factory.   Front Elevation of Studio.

Mr. Willat made a tour of inspection of the principal factories of Europe before he planned his new plant and he has some brand new ideas to work out in its equipment. For example, all air will be washed and cooled or heated to required temperatures before it is distributed through the plant. All film will be washed by spraying and not be dipped as is customary. It will be carried through the various processes on special frames designed by Mr. Willat, and all positive film will be dried on frames. Drums will be provided for drying negative film.

Twelve Bell and Howell perforating machines will be installed and a battery of 36 printers, made after Mr. Willat's own design, will take care of that process. The printers will be automatic, so that one operator can run six machines. Corcoran tanks will be used in the developing and tinting and toning rooms.

In construction the factory is of brick, steel and concrete; fully fireproof.

In explaining his plans to a representative of the *Moving Picture World*, Mr. Willat said that it was his intention to produce features of three or more reels in length and that there would be nothing too large for him to handle. It is his intention to do com-mercial work in his factory for the trade generally. This plan accounted for the large equipment.

"This enterprise is a bona fide business proposition", said Mr. Willat, and not a stock jobbing game. "It is incorporated under the laws of the State of New York for $20,000, and I control all the stock, of which there is none for sale, and am president and treasurer of the corporation – the Willat Film Manufacturing Corporation."

Mr. Willat is known to be one of the best motion picture factory managers in the business. He is a son-in-law of W. T. Rock, of the Vitagraph Company, and received his early training in the making of motion pictures at the Vitagraph plant. When the "Imp" Film Company established a plant at 101st Street and Columbus Avenue, New York, Mr. Willat was engaged to operate it. He remained with that company more than a year, when he resigned to take charge of the New York Motion Picture Company's plant on East 19th Street. He continued to operate that plant successfully until a few months ago, when he resigned to undertake the present enterprise. His work with the "Imp" and the New York companies has been equal in quality with the best.

FILM MEN INSPECT WILLAT STUDIOS
"Doc" Willat and C. O. Baumann Show Friends and Associates Over The Big Plant.

(From *Moving Picture World*, August 15, 1914, p. 967.

On the last day of July a party of film men, friends and associates of "Doc" Willat and Charles O. Baumann, motored from Times Square to Fort Lee to inspect the Willat Studios and Laboratories. What they found on the hill above the Hudson delighted as well as surprised them. While building operations were not finished, at the same time the work had so far progressed that but a few weeks will finish it. The area of the land owned by the company exceeds four acres, sufficient to allow great expansion of studio and factory space. Already completed are two studios, 60 by 120 feet on the ground, and 52 feet in height. They are practically entirely enclosed in glass. The dressing rooms are situated along the side of each structure. The very latest devices for artificial lighting have been installed. In one of the studios there is a tank, 15 by 25 feet, for water trap scenes.

The property is at the corner of Main Street and Linwood Avenue. There is ample room for outdoor staging, and there are a variety of settings for picture work. Among the buildings is a little structure, its walls of uneven-sized brown stone, that has served about every picture company in the neighborhood of New York as an Irish cottage. Arrangements already have been made for the erection of four additional studios, duplicates of two already built. Work on these will be started in a few weeks.

What particularly appealed to the visiting film men was the factory. This structure, as also is the case with the studios, represents the last work in efficiency. It is of two stories and in

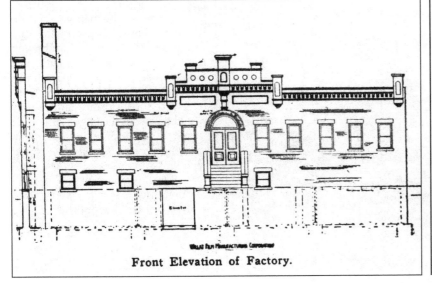

Front Elevation of Factory.

Influential industry figures visit the Willat studio (now boasting a second vaulted-glass stage), on July 31, 1914. Left to right: E.J. Mock, C.O. Baumann, Thomas H. Ince, Mack Sennett, Charles Kessel, Irvin Willat, George Blaisdell, J.V. Ritchie, H.A. Palmer, William Johnston, Worthy Butts, E.J. McGovern, "Doc" Willat, Harry Ennis, Fred Beecroft, Wen Milligan, Adam Kessel, Jr. The building at the far end of the lot is part of the Éclair studio.

dimensions is about 100 by 150 feet. The entire construction is of brick and concrete – absolutely fireproof. In fact, one of the guests was impelled to remark as he passed through the various rooms: "Why, you folks easily may carry your own insurance!"

Many innovations have been installed in the factory. For example, the old tank method of washing will not be used. Instead a large washroom has been built with hundreds of spray nozzles inserted in the ceiling. Water will be forced at high pressure through these nozzles, and the film, which will hang on specially constructed racks immediately below the nozzles, will be thoroughly sprayed. The washroom will accommodate 100 racks of film. The great elevated tank on the grounds has a capacity of 25,000 gallons and will furnish ample water supply.

Another novelty will be the drying room. The air before it enters this compartment is forced through water and "washed" of all dust particles and moisture, thus making the air clean and dry. The machinery for this process was manufactured under "Doc" Willat's supervision, and the air condition of the drying room can be so regulated that all films can be uniformly and quickly dried.

The capacity is 1,500,000 feet per week, and judging by the spacious quarters assigned to the various departments it can be handled with comfort and speed.

In personal command of the entire plant will be C. A. (Doc) Willat, who is known to the entire trade as one of the great technical experts of the motion picture industry. Until a short time ago he was the technical director of the New York Motion Picture Corporation, and for a long time before that he successfully managed and directed the entire output of the Imp Company. The Fort Lee studio and factory represent much thought and long consideration on the part of Mr. Willat. Many months ago he determined to build a plant that not only would be one of the largest, if not the largest commercial establishments in the country, but also one that would represent the composite of the experience of technicians in all picture-making countries. He went abroad last year and visited practically every film

The Willat studio transformed into the Triangle Fort Lee Studios. View looking north up Linwood Avenue from Main Street.

establishment of importance. When he returned to the United States he continued his study of methods. Among the trips he took was one to Rochester, NY, where he spent an entire week in the laboratory of the Eastman Company.

Associated with Mr. Willat is Charles O. Baumann, whose connections with the New York Motion Picture Company and whose progressiveness is thoroughly well known to the trade at large. Mr. Baumann is president of the company, Arthur Butler Graham is vice-president, and Mr. Willat is secretary and treasurer. The executive offices of the company are on the ninth floor of the Longacre Building, Forty-Second Street and Broadway.

On the return from the Studios the party was entertained by Mr. Willat and Mr. Baumann at Reisenweber's, where toasts were drunk to the success of the new enterprise that begins under such favorable auspices.

"FATTY" WORKING IN NEW YORK
Doing Some Big Stunts In "The Bright Lights", A Keystone Comedy Of Life In The Metropolis

(From *Moving Picture World*, March 4, 1916, p. 1456)

Roscoe Arbuckle used Joe Bordeau as a human battering ram at the Keystone studio in Fort Lee the other day and Joe still lives, although he was driven like a wedge through a 12-inch property wall with such force that a gap was opened large enough to admit the bulky "Fatty" to a Bowery dive, where his country sweetheart, Mabel Normand, was held a prisoner. This scene will furnish the big thrill in *The Bright Lights* when that new Keystone comedy is released to Triangle exhibitors. Joe says he'll be at the Knickerbocker [Theater] the first night to see how he survived an experience for which they use 42-centimeter shells in the Champagne.

For more than two weeks Arbuckle has been preparing for this scene. He came from California with a determination to show Mack Sennett that New York was just as fertile a field for the Keystone brand of comedy thrills as the Pacific Coast. He made a good start in *He Did and He Didn't* and then approached *The Bright Lights* with eagerness as he looked over the story and saw that much of the action would take place on the Bowery. Personal representatives began to scour the East Side for types.

BEHIND THE SCENES WITH FATTY AND MABEL

By Wil Rex
(from *Picture Play*, April 1916, p. 46)

One of the most wonderful places you can find anywhere is Fort Lee, that magic New Jersey town across the Hudson from New York City, where murders, robberies, and Indian chases take place while the police force – his name is Pat – leans, yawningly, against

Arbuckle was happy to leave Sennett's supervision, and used the freedom he found in Fort Lee to develop a slightly less frenetic comedy style, where falls and kicks grew naturally out of character and situation (more or less). Tremendously popular during the six months he worked here, Arbuckle was great copy, happy to expound at length on his own theories of comedy, especially insofar as they contradicted those of Mack Sennett (he never did return to Sennett, partnering with Joe Schenck in New York as soon as his Keystone contract expired). Wil Rex's interview, which took place during the production of *He Did and He Didn't*, provides an especially good picture of Arbuckle at work. And although many historians doubt that the first Keystone comedies were made in Fort Lee, Mabel Normand seemed fairly certain about it even at this early date.

a convenient lamp-post. The home of the first Keystone comedy, and now, because of the crowded studios of California, the "fun factory" of Roscoe Arbuckle, Mabel Normand and their gang of devil-may-care comedians.

A better place to spend a day for inspiration, perspiration, and real unvarnished hard work would be impossible to find. So I was commissioned to have my alarm clock in working order.

We met at the ferryhouse early in the morning, and luck was with us. A

The Triangle Film Corporation was organized in 1915 to distribute the films of D.W. Griffith, Mack Sennett, and Thomas Ince. Kessel and Baumann's New York Motion Picture Company controlled the Ince and Sennett pictures, and they became major factors in Triangle, renaming the facility the "Triangle Film Corporation Fort Lee Studios and Laboratories". It was through this connection that "Fatty" Arbuckle and Mabel Normand arrived in Fort Lee to make a series of two-reelers for Mack Sennett's Keystone in 1916.

By the time "Fatty" Arbuckle began working there, the Willat studio had been joined by the Peerless, whose water tower is now visible at the north end of the block.

Mabel just looked at me and laughed.

"Oh, this is nothing", she said lightly. "Only yesterday, my machine backed all the way down, and if it wasn't for the ferryhouse, I would have been doing some 'water stuff' without a camera in sight".

"Cheerful!" I remarked, and stealthily started for the ground, but returned to my seat meekly when I heard Mabel laugh and murmur:

" 'Fraid cat!"

Strange as it may seem, we reached the Keystone-Triangle Studio – one of the largest glass-inclosed film factories in the East – without further excitement. Something was bound to happen, though. Entering the yard, we barely escaped sending Al St. John, "the Bouncing Boy of the Films", into the next county. By a miraculous leap, he jumped on the radiator, and rode away to the garage with us. Keystone should employ one cameraman to do nothing but follow Miss Normand around.

The studio was bristling with activity. Roscoe Arbuckle, the elephantine author-actor-director, was superintending the construction of a set, aided by Ferris Hartmann, his co-worker, and a dozen prop men; Elgin Lessley, the intrepid camera man, who has the reputation of turning out the clearest films of any Keystone crank turner, was loading his magazines. A dozen rough-and ready comedians were practicing falls down a stairway. The heavyweight director turned and saw us.

"Oh, Miss Normand, get ready for the hall scenes, please."

"Very well, Roscoe, and – very good!"

The dainty little comedienne going to her dressing room, I strolled over to the busy throng and exchanged greetings with Arbuckle.

"How are you getting along with your new picture?" I asked.

"Slow, but sure", was the reply. "It's a

racing motor came tearing up, spitting oil and smoke. Almost hidden behind a huge steering wheel was Mabel Normand, the idol of the film fans. Immediately we renewed our acquaintance of years back – who wouldn't? – and the little lady was kind enough to ask us to ride with her.

Reaching the Jersey side of the river, our adventures soon began. Everyone who motors knows that Fort Lee Hill is one of the most dangerous spots in the East. Mabel started up this young mountain at full speed, but the noble car got tired before we reached the top. Slowly, but surely, it was stopping. I looked around nervously, and my heart rose when I saw the water far, far below.

"Maybe I'd better walk?" I suggested nonchalantly. "The car might go easier if I get off".

new theme, and I want to go at it easily. I'm not trying to be a 'highbrow,' or anything like that, but I am going to cut an awful lot of the slapstick out hereafter. If anyone gets kicked, or a pie thrown in his face, there's going to be a reason for it."

"How about that staircase?" I queried. "That looks as though something exciting was going to happen."

"Oh, nothing much", he answered. "St. John and I are going to fall down it, but that's about all. Here, I'll show you", and I snapped the picture as he did.

Oh, it's great to be a comedian – if there's a hospital handy!

As we stood talking, I heard an excited altercation in French and German, with an occasional word in good old U. S. A. I looked frightened, but Arbuckle only laughed.

"Don't get worried", he said. "That noise is only the favorite indoor pastime of Miss Normand's maids. One is a loyal French girl, and the other was imported from the banks of the Rhine. Everything went nicely until the excitement started in Europe. Then things happened. The two maids considered themselves envoys to carry out the fight on this side, and Mabel hasn't yet been able to change their opinions."

As we spoke, a pistol shot rang out.

"Do they shoot, too?" I inquired quickly.

Again Arbuckle laughed. "Oh, that's only St. John shooting apples off Joe Bordeau's head. I'm going to pull that stunt in my next film!"

Miss Normand presently came out, her hair in beautiful curls, crowned with a dainty boudoir cap. The lights were turned on, Lessley got his camera into position, and Mabel and Fatty took their places.

"Now, Mabel", instructed the director, "you start running down the steps, then look over the banister, and start to fall. I'll rush down and catch you before you go over. Let's try it once." Then to Ferris Hartmann: "How does it sound to you – O.K.?" His coworker nodded. "All right", said Arbuckle to Lessley, and the camera turned.

Miss Normand "registered" surprise at the top of the stairs, and then started running down. Suddenly she stopped and looked over the railing. She leaned too far, and started to slide down the banister. At this moment, Arbuckle started after her, and caught her on the way down. The scene was ended, and the players, directors, and camera men got together, and talked it over. Mabel had some suggestions to make – she's quite a director herself, you know. Among other pictures, she produced *Caught in a Cabaret*, with Charlie Chaplin.

Once more the scene was taken, but something went wrong, and Arbuckle slipped all the way down, headfirst. Mabel looked on as though she thought her side partner had broken his neck, but Arbuckle scrambled up, and, grunting, said: "Try it again". Time and again the same scene was filmed until it suited all present. "How many times do you take the same scene?" I asked the director.

"Till I can't do any better", he answered. "Often I use ten or fifteen thousand feet of film for a two-reel production. The average Keystone costs nearly twenty thousand dollars, you know, and we've got to do our best. Generally, I take a month or more to produce a picture that runs less than thirty minutes on the screen. In one of my films, *Fickle Fatty's Fall*, I spent just one week getting the kitchen scenes I was in, alone. I used over ten thousand feet of film just for that. In one part of the play, I had to toss a pancake up and catch it behind my back. I started nine o'clock in the morning, did it on first rehearsal, then started the camera, and didn't get it till four-thirty! I'd hate to tell you how long it took me to catch the plate behind my back in *The Village Scandal*! I seldom rehearse since then."

Arbuckle called to St. John for a scene. He was to hang from a chandelier and kick down a few policemen who were on his trail. Oh, no, no rough stuff in this picture – not at all! The very first time they rehearsed it, a little English chap, playing a cop, got in the way of St. John's feet, and had his jaw damaged more or less. Two minutes later, Lloyd Peddrick, an old friend of Mack Sennett's, broke his nose in a scene in which he was playing a butler.

"Gee, you got your face in the way!" was the only comment from Fatty.

Later, I learned that there is not a member of the Keystone Company who hasn't had bones broken. Some of them retire after one picture.

By this time, luncheon was ready....

Before luncheon was finished, visitors began strolling in from the surrounding studios. Teddy Sampson dropped in from the World, Helen Gardner from Universal, Douglas Fairbanks from the Fine Arts, and dozens of other lesser lights. It was a merry crowd withal, no professional jealousy, but just good-humored jollying one another along. The moving-picture people are certainly a cheerful, devil-may-care aggregation. Doug Fairbanks gave a little, impromptu speech, Teddy Sampson imitated her well-known hubby, Ford Sterling, and Mabel Normand showed us how Theda Bara acts.

After the midday meal, Arbuckle and Lessley decided the sun was right for exterior scenes, and away we all went in motors. Reaching the location, Al St. John practiced a couple of handsprings, and then, when the camera was set up, took half a dozen headfirst dives in a window, and the same number out of it. It's a wonder that energetic youth doesn't break his neck! That was all to be done outside, and we returned to the studio, badly damaging the Fort Lee speed laws.

The next scene was to be St. John coming in the window. Nonchalantly he popped in, turned a somersault over a chair, another over a table, and then took a headlong dive over a sideboard.

"Oh, that's nothing", he yawned, in reply to a question from me. "You ought to see some of the stuff I do out on the coast! I've been doing this kind of stunts all my life. First I was a minstrel man, then a trick bicycle rider, then a clown, then in a musical show with Roscoe, and for the past two years I have played under his direction in Keystones. He's my uncle, you know", he added proudly.

Next, some scenes were taken in a bedroom set. Poor Arbuckle certainly bruised himself up! He and Mabel got on their hands and knees, and crawled around the floor looking for Fatty's collar button. First Arbuckle banged his head on an open bureau drawer. Then, in a rage, he slammed the drawer shut, and got

his finger caught in it. I could see that he really hurt himself. A servant was then sent in the scene, and joined the hunt. Time and again his head and Arbuckle's would come together with a crash, Mabel keeping at a safe distance. Finally, Fatty kicked the servant headfirst into a bureau. The unfortunate fellow hit it so hard that he pushed it against the scenery, nearly knocking it over.

"Retake", said Arbuckle to the camera man.

"Arnica", said the servant to a prop boy.

And thus it went all day long. First one, then another, would work me up to a point where I almost ran for an ambulance. The recruits, who joined the company in the East, resembled nothing more than a trenchful of wounded soldiers. The veterans from California just stood on the side lines and laughed. Getting half killed is second nature to them now. Even little Mabel is not immune from injury. Just before coming to Fort Lee, she was released from the hospital, where she had been confined for over a month. She had brain fever and a few other sicknesses and injuries, which goes to prove that no matter how hard your head may be, a brick wall is harder!

The last scene was a free-for-all pistol fight, in which Fatty and Mabel disposed of Al St. John and Joe Bordeau. Then it was a case of "nothing to do till tomorrow". That is what we thought, but later learned I was wrong.

I went in Arbuckle's dressing room, as he removed his make-up.

"Where do you get your ideas from, anyway?" I asked in wonder.

"Easy!" he laughed. "I get a plot in my head, gather up the company, and start out. As we go along, fresh ideas

"Fatty" Arbuckle and Mabel Normand in He Did and He Didn't *(Triangle-Keystone, 1916).*

pop out, and we all talk it over. I certainly have a clever crowd working with me. Mabel, alone, is good for a dozen new suggestions in every picture. And the others aren't far behind. I take advice from everyone. It's a wise man who realizes that there are others who know as much, if not more, than he does himself. Some of my greatest stuff comes from the supposed dull brains of 'supers'."

Looking through the door, I spied Mabel, all dressed up in velvet and furs. I leaned over to a camera man and told him I wanted an unusual picture of Mabel – one where she looked sad – then I went over to where she stood.

"Want to go for a ride?" she called.

The long, skinny fingers of fear clutched my heart, but bravely I answered: "Sure!"

She sent some one for her car, and I helped her up on a window seat, and asked her to tell me the history of her life while waiting for the buzz wagon.

I saw my camera man come up quietly, but paid no attention to him. Later, I found that he had taken the picture I asked for – while Mabel was talking to me.

"I was born in New York", she said, "and nearly all my life, it seems, has been spent in moving-picture studios. First, I was with the Vitagraph, then played for Mr. Griffith at the Biograph Company, and now I'm with the Keystone. You know, I am one of the original Keystone players. Four years ago, Mack Sennett broke away from the Biograph, and took Ford Sterling, Fred Mace, and myself with him. The four of us organized the Keystone Film Company.

"At first, it was a hard struggle. Money was scarce, and it was a long time before we were sure of our pay check at the end of each week. Our first picture was produced right here in Fort Lee, but we soon went West. This is my first trip back to good old

New York in four years, that is with the exception of a few days a year or two ago, when my mother was very ill.

"For a long time, I directed all the pictures I played in, the best known of which are the Chaplin series. Lately, however, I have given up that end of the game, finding enough to do with acting."

That was all the information this modest little actress would give on her great life. I'll add something that Miss Normand omitted, and say that she is the most popular comedienne in the world, and also the best. She is remarkably pretty, more charming off the screen than on, if that is possible, and as lovely as she is pretty. She is the champion woman swimmer and diver of the Pacific coast, and I look to see her capture many trophies East this coming summer.

She is [an] athlete to a degree, and is fond of all outdoor sports, in many of which she excels her male competitors.

Miss Normand's car was brought to the door, and I hopped in, after bidding "Good by!" to Arbuckle and his various assistants.

"Going to the big city?" I queried, looking for a nice ride all the way home.

"Oh, dear, no!" she said. "I'll take you to the ferry; but I've got to hurry back to the studio to see the scenes we took today run off. You know, Roscoe never leaves the place until he O. K.'s or N. G.'s the day's work, and I always look it over with him. It keeps us busy."

A little more talk, and the ferry was reached. "Too bad you can't come across the river with me", I said, as I was about to leave the pretty little star.

"We might go right over, without the ferry, if this car was a – " Mabel started, but I silenced her in time. This isn't an automobile-joke book.

ARMY OF JERSEY SKEETERS START SPRING DRIVE

Surprise Roscoe Arbuckle And Keystoners Strongly Intrenched At Fort Lee Studio

St. John Sings Song Of Hate

(from *The Triangle,* May 27, 1916)

Add [to the] perils and pains of moving-picture acting – the Jersey mosquito.

And if you don't believe this bird of prey is some notable addition to the horrors of filmdom, ask the members of the eastern Keystone company, who recently journeyed into the wilds of New Jersey to make a new Triangle-Keystone comedy called *The Moonshiner*.

Of course the scenes of *The Moonshiner* are supposedly laid in Kentucky. But why go to Kentucky when New Jersey has the same kind of scenery? No reason at all. So to Jersey the merry Keystoners went, up into the mountains which decorate a considerable portion of the surface of that State.

But never, never again! Never again, for Alice Lake, who played a mountain waif in a ragged knee-length skirt, bare legs and a sleeveless waist. Never again for poor Alice, who tried everything there was in the Jersey drugstores, from penny-royal to formaldehyde, without stopping the onslaught of the Jersey monsters for a moment. Alice's arms and neck won't be fit for polite society for several weeks. Polite society is not concerned with Alice's legs, but Alice is, and if she plays any more Keystones in Jersey she'll play 'em in fishermen's boots, says she.

Hand grenades

Al St. John and Joe Bordeau took a pair of boxing gloves intending to

Mabel Normand on the cover of Photoplay, *August 1915.*

in front of the lenses, because they were present in such thick flocks that they spoiled the pictures if they weren't dispersed.

Those not stung

Worst of all two members of the company emerged from the Jersey wilds thoroughly disliked by everybody else in the party. Nice chaps both of them, and they hadn't done a thing to displease anyone. But nobody would speak to either Horace J. Haine or Mike Eagan, just the same. For why? Because neither Horace nor Mike got a blessed, single, solitary bite throughout all that skeeter siege.

At first the others merely thought Horace and Mike were being accidentally overlooked. "Wait", they said, "your turn will come. They just haven't got around to the tough meat yet." But the days wore on, and the nights wore on, and Horace and Mike worked in peace and slept in peace.

Can you blame the others for hating them? Not a bit. But Al St. John says he'd really like to know, just the same. He'd like to know, he says to Mike and Horace, how a man can soak his system with something a Jersey mosquito won't even nibble at, and still live in good health.

But Horace and Mike just wink and look wise and don't get sore a bit. They should worry.

ROSCOE THE GREAT
His Greatness Can Be Measured With One Eye On His
Accomplishments And The Other On His Waist Line

By W.P. Lecky

(excerpted from *Picture Play,* November 1916, pp. 29–33)

Now it sometimes happens, as all men

have a little exercise. They took turns wearing the gloves at night to keep themselves from scratching. And that led to more trouble. Joe just simply would pull the gloves off when the itching got good and strong. So one night when it was his turn to wear the padded mitts, he got Al to tie them on in such a way that he couldn't get them off without help. And when he wanted them off in the middle of the night Al wouldn't help him. He told Joe he didn't know when he was well off. Joe wanted to fight, but with gloves against bare knuckles, how could he? Oh, it was some merry little camp! Nobody loved anybody else, and everybody wanted to fight about everything. It took a bodyguard of two, for each camera man, when the cranking was being done, to fan the skeeters away. They had to be fanned away from the camera man so the latter would keep on cranking and not stop to fight and scratch, and they had to be fanned away from

know, that in spreading our intellectual nets for the elusive idea, we occasionally capture what is best described as a notion. It is neither fish nor flounder, but rather a sort of bulbous, jellyfish that, because the day's catch is small, we kid ourselves into calling the prize of the whole piscatorial population. It was a nondescript of this kind, a hallucinatory notion, that I drew squirming out of the ether that pervades the editorial sanctum, and conveyed very carefully to the subway, thence across the One Hundred and Thirtieth Street ferry to Fort Lee, New Jersey, by surface car to the Keystone studio, and finally into the sacred dressing room of the hospitable Fatty himself.

"Now, this Arbuckle person", thinks I, feeling the notion tickling me by way of encouragement, "this Arbuckle person is probably one of the few people in the whole world who is glad he is fat. He makes more money than any circus fat man who ever lived. His name is known in every town that has a moving-picture theater. Millions adore him. Indeed, with John Bunny he is spoken of as one of the only two examples, extinct or extant, who proved the exception to the rule that nobody loves a fat man. He is cheerful and healthy, likes his work, and knows he will never have to hide from the rent man for the rest of his natural life. Why shouldn't he be glad he is fat?"

"Certainly", whispered the notion. "Fat is the goose that laid his golden egg". Which curious figure of speech I accepted as further proof of my adviser's genius. I drew out my notebook and the interview began.

"Ever sorry you were fat, Mr. Arbuckle?" I inquired....

Fat, however, is not what got Fatty his job. When he started with Keystone, his salary to begin was three dollars a day – the usual stipend for an extra – and this, too, after he had gained a sizable reputation on the coast as a stage comedian. Mr. Sennett's verdict,

however, was to the effect that a stage reputation, unless extraordinary, was no good in pictures, and it was three dollars for Fatty, or quit. After three weeks of hard work playing the part of a slapstick policeman, he was put in stock at forty dollars a week, and the rest is an old story. Through it all, he has never allowed himself to be tempted away from the farce comedy, his first love.

"I do not think polite comedy will ever amount to much", he confided to me, "certainly not for a long time. The technique is too transparent. The situations are necessarily few, and the majority of the scenes merely build up to them. The audience guesses what is coming, and interest lags."

He confessed that this was largely the fault of the writers, and even admitted that there are people who can write polite comedy that will hold attention and bring the necessary laughs, but he did not believe the time had yet come when the producers were willing to pay such writers their price.

"The companies are waking up now", he said, "but not much. Farce is still 'way in the lead. In the first place, the polite comedy has too much plot. The characters get tied up in it so that it is impossible for them to pick up spontaneous laughs as they go along. They simply *have* to stay with the story, for there are only two or three big laughs to be depended upon in a polite comedy, and if they fail, the picture falls flat.

"Now, my idea of comedy" – he was quite serious now, and I knew that he was expressing an ideal as much as an idea – "my idea of comedy is to fit the picture to women and children; to keep it clean for the women and broad for the children. I think it is well, too, to work in some love interest at times, also for the women. Never mind the men – they bring the women, and have to come, anyway. But all children like things exaggerated, broad, so that they can appreciate them without ef-

fort. This is why the movements and expressions of the farce comedian are so much more unnatural than those of the actor in polite plays. They have to be, if they are to make the children laugh, and I'd rather see the youngsters have a good time, than please every critic under the sun. It isn't as delicate, of course not, but it gets across, and I'm for it."

This was the first time I had met Mr. Arbuckle – I won't call him Fatty anymore – and I was frankly surprised. Fancy ideals in slapstick comedy; yet here they were, and plausible, clean, straightforward ideals at that. It is never easy to accustom oneself to a new point of view, and here was an angle I had never thought of.

"What hurts me most", he went on, "is the idea some people have that I owe my success to being fat. It is the hardest thing I have to overcome. I never play my weight; in fact, I am constantly trying to make the audience forget it. I spend as much time and thought and money on a two-reel comedy as is put into the average five-reel picture, yet you hear people say that my gags would not get over if I were small and thin instead of as I am."

As every picture fan knows, Mr. Arbuckle writes his own plays and, in addition to this, directs, cuts, edits, assembles, and titles the film personally. Many a fat man has applied to Mr. Sennett for a job because of the size of his stomach; Mr. Arbuckle holds his because of the size of his brain. In this direction there is less competition.

And although Fatty's duties might warrant a statement that he is, everything considered, practically an entire motion-picture company, it would be a very hard matter to find him sitting in a corner complaining about too much work. He sits in a corner, yes, and he looks very serious and thoughtful; sometimes he even frowns. But immediately after that you may not see him again for four or five days, and

Roscoe "Fatty" Arbuckle when he started with Mack Sennett.

workmen make a set and rapidly paper two walls with a vivid pink hanging. At the entrance there was bunched an eager group of men and women, hoping against hope that they would have an opportunity to speak to him and get in the cast.

When you see his jolly grin facing you from a picture or the covers of a magazine, you are minded to say, "Hey, there's a Fatty!" Somehow you have no inclination to call him "Fatty" when you came face to face with him in the flesh. True, if he were not fat, he might not be so funny; but there are brains there as well as bulk. And Arbuckle has not been idle all these years that he has been in motion pictures. He has been thinking out his plans and dreaming his dreams, and now he has an opportunity to put them on the screen and see how they pan out. He has passed the acrobatic stage and the business of flapping his hands against his sides, as the symbols of fun.

"Of course, we have to keep up a little of that stuff", he explained. "The public has associated it with the Keystone Comedy, and it would not think it a Keystone without a little rough stuff. Wait a minute, until I call the projection room. I want you to see the first showing of the first picture we did in New York – and you will see what I mean. We have tried to get some fine photographic effects here. I have always thought there was room for beautiful scenic achievements in comedy as well as the kick and the custard pie."

"The motion picture world has turned over several times in the past two or three years", I suggested, while we waited for the man who was to show us the picture. "What is the outlook?"

"Outlook!" repeated the comedy star. "It's as wide as the blue sky. Film

a week later he will have "the funniest comedy ever made" to show you. When Fatty sits in a corner, it is because he wants a story, and stories without plots aren't being made in his studio these days, so he has to think of a plot. Does he work too hard? Ask him, and he'll say: "Complain? Why should I complain? I'm big enough to do a good day's work."

FATTY OFF GUARD

By Elizabeth Sears

(from *Film Flashes: The Wit And Humor of a Nation in Pictures* [New York: Leslie-Judge, 1916])

"Let's go 'round to the office", said Roscoe Arbuckle. "We are not rehearsing today, so there is nothing doing here."

He had been standing in the huge studio, with its roof of glass, watching

standards change so fast and film styles come in so often that the director whose ideas were heralded as the climax of brilliancy six months ago is old-fashioned now. And if he fails to discard his old ideas and keep at least two laps ahead of the procession – you know what's going to happen to him."

The director-author-actor paused long enough to courteously assure a would-be actor that the rehearsals would not begin for a day or two and that there were no good positions open as yet. He bows out his applicants in such a pleasant and friendly fashion that they forget they were turned down and remember only that they have met "Fatty" and found him most delightful in his manner to them.

"I hate to turn 'em down", he apologized, "but I haven't a thing for them just now".

"Just a word about your scenarios", I begged. "Where do you get them, who writes them, and how do you direct from them?"

Mr. Arbuckle paused long enough to bid a courteous good-morning to three or four young women employees who passed through the office and who spoke to him shyly. He held open the door for one of them who wore her black hair low and held fast to her forehead with a blue silk garter.

"Not a scrap of scenario paper in my studio", he admitted. "I wouldn't know what to do with a manuscript in my hand. I plan out the pictures, and we rehearse them – that's all."

Easy enough, isn't it? And Arbuckle has discovered a grand bit of audience psychology that some of the other stars might well copy. He allows a bit of the picture to film along without him once in a while. He gives the rest of the company a chance. He says he'd rather the audience would wish he would come on back than to wish somebody would sweep him out of the picture.

"An actor doesn't lose anything by effacing himself once in a while", he said, as he swung himself comfortably aboard a chair to see the picture in the little projection room. "If he is a favorite, they are all the more certain to welcome him when he gets back in the picture."

We viewed the opening of the picture in silence. Arbuckle, as the doctor in *He Did and He Didn't*, has struck a new note, although the film cutter has cut out a trifle too much footage here and there and leaves the picture a bit minus in continuity once in a while.

"You are breaking away from the slapstick stuff", commented someone from the far gloom of the room. "How'll Mack Sennett like that, huh? Sennett's main idea of humor seems to be one grand slam of kaleidoscopic action that tires the eye and leaves no one strong point in the memory."

Mr. Arbuckle continued to watch himself on the screen diving under the bed for a collar button.

"Well", he said calmly, "Mr. Sennett trusted me to come to New York and put on these plays. He knows what my ideas are along the newer lines of screen comedy."

It may be that Sennett has noted the trend and begun to moderate his inordinate frenzy of acrobatic falls and tumbles and violent and unnecessary smashes through breakfast rooms, with the unvarying accompaniment of broken china and ceiling.

"What's the worst thing that can happen to an actor?" I asked, apropos of the remarkable tumble down the stairs of the doctor in search of the burglar. Mr. Arbuckle handed me the answer slap off the shoulder.

"To arrive", he said promptly.

"I thought that was what they all desired more than anything else", I said, in surprise.

"They do", he replied, "but the trouble is, once they arrive, there isn't much to do but to leave again. When

they are climbing up, the public applauds and says 'That chap is coming right along – doing better everyday.' But once the actor is heralded as an absolute arrival, the public begins to criticize and pick flaws and expect him to better his own standard, and it is a tremendous strain. He simply is forced to keep ahead of the public's opinion and to spring something newer and better every season. The man or woman who can survive an 'arrival' is a star of the greatest magnitude."

There's a bit of thought for you. We mulled it over and watched the picture silently, until Mr. Arbuckle began to chuckle over a scene.

"We had an awful scrap over that", he said. "You see, sometimes some of us disagree on an essential point of the production, and we stop the picture and thrash it out right there. Miss Normand is a very charming little lady, but she has a mind of her own, all the same, and we had some argument over that. My idea was to mystify the audience right there – not let 'em have an inkling of why Mabel gets her visitor into her room there, until they see the burglar hauled out from under the bed."

I noticed that it was his part of the idea that got over, though.

"That's a good bit", commented someone in the group, when the screen flashed the picture of the armchair before the fireplace. Mr. Arbuckle smiled happily.

"That's what I meant when I said that we need not rob the picture of scenic beauty to get humor into it. Clean comedy, with an artistic background, not merely hysterical laughter and situations."

"Think the public wants that kind of comedy?" queried one of the visitors. "I don't believe the public wants to get its laughs mixed up with its thoughts, do you?"

"I'm banking on it", said Arbuckle

confidently, "although older and more experienced men than I am have failed to grasp the way of the public and what it will do at a given period. I believe in the comedy that makes you think, and I believe that the time has come to put it on – and that is what I am going to do."

We stood a moment in the door way, when the picture and the interview were over, and watched the little file of actors and actresses in the yard, who had been informed that there would be no use in waiting.

"I'd like to go out to the car with you", said Mr. Arbuckle, nervously glancing out of the window at the group; "but if I go out there and they see me, they'll all ask me for a job – and I haven't a thing to offer them". His blue eyes looked concerned with a boyish sentiment as he bent them on us. "I – I sort of hate to turn them down", he said deprecatingly.

You see, responsibility takes the laugh out of you sometimes. And although Roscoe Arbuckle loves to see his public laugh, it takes the smile off his own face when he must in any way distress even a small proportion of it.

"Miss Normand has a longing to play drama on the stage", he said, as he bade us good-bye; "but I don't believe there is any finer mission on earth than just to make people laugh, do you?"

Arbuckle and Normand "breaking away from the slapstick stuff" in He Did and he Didn't.

Douglas Fairbanks was also sent East by Triangle, but by the time he arrived there were two Eastern Triangle studios, one in Fort Lee, and another in Riverdale. Because little publicity was issued on this point, it is difficult to discover which studio the Fairbanks unit was occupying at any given moment. It is clear that at least parts of *His Picture in the Papers, The Habit of Happiness* and *American Aristocracy* were made at the Willat-Triangle studio in Fort Lee, although other studios and locations may also have been used. Adolphe Menjou, who was slowly working his way up the extra ranks, counted *The Habit of Happiness* as one of many unbilled early appearances. It was directed by Allan Dwan, who made quite a few silent films in New York and New Jersey (including *Betty of Graystone* with Dorothy Gish, at least part of which was also shot at Triangle's Fort Lee studio).

MONTAGUE OR CAPULET?

By Adolphe Menjou and M.M. Muselman

(from *It Took Nine Tailors* [New York: Whittlesey House, 1948], pp. 60–63).

In 1916 we extras and bit players began to speculate on all the picture making out in Hollywood, but nobody believed that anything important could be happening way out there. After all, the only place to find actors was on Broadway, and no self-respecting actor would be caught any farther from Broadway than the Union Hills Studios in New Jersey, which was considered a distant hinterland, tolerated only because of the peculiarities of motion-picture making.

A few big stars like Pickford and Fairbanks and Chaplin journeyed to Hollywood because the producers tempted them with fantastic salaries; but we were sure that their hearts were really on Broadway and that eventually they would return from the sticks and force the movie companies to follow them back to the rightful center of moviedom. When Doug Fairbanks, after making only one picture in California, returned to New York to complete his contract, we all nodded sagely, then dashed for the Triangle Studios to get jobs.

There were four of us who used to pal around together at that time. We had much in common, for all of us were college men with fathers who disapproved of our ambitions to be movie stars. My roommate was Ned Hay, Jr., from Washington, D.C., whose father was a past grand exalted ruler of the Elks. Then there was John Bennett, a Yale man, whose father owned the Gotham Hotel, and Dudley Hill, who is now a dignified banker.

We organized ourselves into a sort of movie team under the name of "The Gentlemen Riders". This label quickly identified us to casting directors not so much as horsemen but as society types. As a matter of fact the other three were all very capable in the saddle; I couldn't ride, but I could look the part in a rented riding habit. We

Allan Dwan, wearing goggles to avoid "klieg eyes", on the set of Betty of Graystone *(Triangle-Fine Arts, 1916). Actors around the table include Kate Bruce, Owen Moore and George Fawcett.*

all showed to best advantage in dress clothes, sport jackets, riding habits, or cutaways.

One director who always called for "The Gentlemen Riders" when he was casting a picture that needed society types was Allan Dwan. It was through Allan that we landed Doug Fairbanks' second picture, *The Habit of Happiness* [1916], which was shot in two studios that the Triangle Company had just taken over, one in Yonkers and the other in Fort Lee, New Jersey. Both of these studios were of the latest type; they were constructed somewhat on the order of greenhouses, large portions of the walls and roofs being of glass, so that on sunny days it was unnecessary to use artificial light.

Fairbanks played the part of a fellow who believed that laughter was the cure for all of man's ills, both mental and physical. He was the "laugh doctor". One sequence called for him to go down to a flophouse in the Bowery, where he gathered the failures and the misfits together, taught them to laugh, and thus inspired them with new hope and new determination.

Dwan decided that, rather than hire actors to pretend that they were Bowery bums, it would be simpler to go to the Bowery and hire the real thing. One morning he drove down to the Bowery with a big bus and four policemen. They went into a flophouse, rounded up every man in the place, and ordered them all into the bus. At first these Bowery characters thought they were being

pinched and they set up a terrible yammer protesting their innocence. But when they learned that they were to get five dollars for acting in a movie, they went along peaceably.

The whole crowd was ferried across the river and delivered to Fort Lee, where a duplicate of the Bowery flophouse had been built. But about that time most of them began to develop severe cases of the shakes. Director Dwan, realizing that they needed a nerve tonic, sent his assistant for a couple of quarts of whisky. The man came back with bottled-in-bond bour-

Douglas Fairbanks with Allan Dwan's authentic "Bowery bums", brought to Fort Lee for The Habit of Happiness *(Triangle-Fine Arts, 1916).*

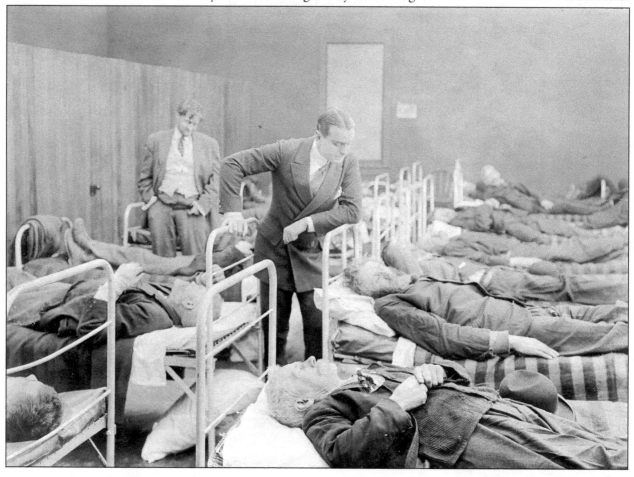

bon. But the Bowery boys viewed the whisky with critical eyes. There was no balm in liquor like that; what they wanted was something with a belt to it. So the good stuff was sent back and exchanged for Old Pickhandle – a headache with every slug.

After that the Bowery actors were ready to perform. Then a more serious problem arose. The scene Dwan was to shoot called for Doug to come bouncing into this flophouse, wake up the inmates, and give them an inspirational speech full of merry quips and cute sayings. But the derelicts from the Bowery were not easily amused. Laughter was something to which they were not accustomed. No matter how much of a pep talk Dwan gave them or how hard Doug worked, they couldn't seem to give out with any hearty laughter.

Finally, in desperation, Doug told them a new off-color joke. For the first time the bums were amused. They gave out with hearty guffaws.

"Keep going", Dwan directed, and he signaled Vic Fleming, the cameraman, to start grinding.

Doug kept making the jokes bluer and bluer. The flophouse gang bellowed louder and louder. Between shots the other actors and the crew racked their brains for more off-color gags. Then, with the camera set for a new shot, Doug continued his supposedly inspirational, cheer-up-and-chuckle speech by giving out with more sizzlers.

Finally the sequence was shot and the Bowery bums were delivered back to their favorite saloon, each with a five-dollar bill clutched in his hand. A few weeks later the picture was finished and released. Immediately letters of protest began to pour into the Triangle offices from deaf people, societies of deaf mutes, and various reform organizations. Anybody who understood lip reading knew that Doug was not making the sort of cute cracks to those booze fighters that the subtitles indicated. The company had to recall all the prints of the picture and get a lip reader to help edit out the ribaldry.

11. Peerless-World

Charles Jourjon, President of the Sociéte Française des Films et Cinématographes Éclair, was eager to expand his operation in Fort Lee, but unhappy with the distribution deal he had entered into with Universal. On January 12, 1914 he incorporated the Peerless Feature Producing Company (he held 48 of the 50 original shares) and began to acquire property adjacent to the existing Éclair studio on Linwood Avenue. This was announced to the trade simply as an expansion of the Éclair operation, but in fact Peerless was a personal holding of Jourjon. Also involved was Jules Brulatour, agent for Eastman Kodak raw film stock and a financial backer of American Eclair, and Brulatour turned to the Shubert theatrical organization for story material. On March 19 a fire destroyed the Éclair laboratory, but only a week later ground was being broken for the new studio next door. The following letter to J.J. Shubert from Joseph L. Rhinock, the head of the Shubert Feature Film Booking Company (courtesy of the Shubert Archives), updates him on the progress of this organization while pushing him to cooperate more fully. Brulatour was unhappy because while he had agreed to pay for the production of films derived from Shubert properties, Shubert had not yet supplied a single manuscript, and Brulatour was forced to draw on other sources for his material. Notice how the fire, which was used as an excuse to stop production of Eclair films in Fort Lee and concentrate activity in their western studios, has not prevented this group from "making our pictures in the Éclair studios" until the new building is completed.

The Shubert Feature Film Booking Co.
223 West 44th Street
New York

April 18, 1914

Mr. J.J. Shubert
Building

Dear Jake:

I received your letter in reference to Mr. Hatfield. He seems to be a bright, capable young man but whether or not he is any good as a director for work in moving pictures, remains to be seen.

Mr. [George B.] Cox and I spent yesterday afternoon looking over the studio at Fort Lee. When it is finished we will have what is said to be the largest studio for the making of moving pictures in the World. Mr. Jourjour [sic – Charles Jourjon], who is the President of the Éclair Company, was over there and is familiar with every plant in the Country, and he made this statement to me. I only mention this because I want you to get busy and give Mr. Brulatour the six or seven manuscripts he has been asking for so that he can have scenarios written and proceed and make pictures. We have now about six pictures under way, being made in various parts of the country through our different connections, but I want to impress you with the fact that unless you furnish him the manuscripts and decide what plays you want made into pictures, the studio will have to look elsewhere for this work.

They are making our pictures in the Éclair Studios during the erection of our building. Now if Mr. Hatfield is a man of merit and as he tells me he has produced several shows for you and directed several productions why wouldn't he be the man to take the manuscripts and get in touch with Mr. Brulatour's scenario writers and in this way keep the studio busy. Brulatour said to me that he has asked you for a week to give him these manuscripts. You are the only one who has possession of them and you must attend to it.

Yours very truly

Joseph L. Rhinock, President

In a May 25 letter to Lee Shubert, Rhinock noted that "This plant will cost about $125,000, and our Company has the right to buy this plant at any time for the original investment plus six per cent on the amount of money invested". He also revealed that Marcus Loew was "very anxious to join us", and was willing to provide both cash and access to his theater chain. But on June 9 Lee and J.J. Shubert came to a formal agreement with Jules Brulatour, and the following day combined their interests with the World Film Corporation, a distributor of feature length pictures backed by Wall Street interests. Within a few months war had broken out in Europe, Charles Jourjon was gone, and Lewis J. Selznick had been appointed General Manager of World, supervising production at the Peerless Studio and riding herd on the various outlying producers with which World was associated.

STUDIO OF THE PEERLESS COMPANY
Located at Fort Lee, NJ, a Model in Point of Construction and Efficiency.

(*Moving Picture World*, September 26, 1914, p. 1781)

Those who appreciate the superiority of well taken daylight interiors over those taken by artificial light for motion pictures, have reason to rejoice at the completion of one of the largest and most practical motion picture studios in America, built adjoining the old Eclair premises, for the Peerless Features Producing Company at Fort Lee, NJ by Edward Barnard Kinsila, architect and technical expert. It is two hundred feet long by one hundred and twenty feet wide.

The Peerless Studio was projected by President Charles Jourjon of the Eclair Film Company to extensively produce photoplays of well-known theater successes. The output will mainly consist of plays and stars made famous on the stage by the Shuberts, Wm. A. Brady and Charles Blaney, and is controlled by the World Film Company.

The immense glass studio enclosure itself is one hundred and twenty feet long with a postless width of eighty feet. All the sides are composed of sash that swing on pivots, and the roof is equipped with a large sprinkler pipe along the outside ridge for flooding and cooling the roof on hot days. The interior contains a thirty-foot water pool for photographic purposes. The ground glass used in this studio was especially imported from France because of its superior merit in freely admitting the actinic rays of light. The roof trusses contain no members over six inches in width, and cast no shadows. No diffusing curtains are necessary, in fact, darkening curtains are employed on bright days to lessen the light, and upon dark days the studio contains fifteen per cent more daylight than exists outside. For emergency an over-head trolley system of Cooper-Hewitt lights are used in combination with Kleig portable side-lights.

The adjoining accessory building annexed to the studio floor contains a triple-decked spacious property room and motor hoist to raise properties to the desired floor level, a scene dock one hundred feet long by forty feet in width, and a postless and roomy carpenter shop equipped with all kinds of modern wood-making machinery for turning out the largest properties. There are no intervening walls between these departments and the studio floor to impede swift setting or striking of scenery. A one-third section of the main floor is taken up with stage directors' and scenario writers' private rooms, a large projection room and administration offices, and the upper floors are occupied with the actors' dressing rooms, toilets, shower baths and a large wardrobe room. Everything appears to have been provided to make the building complete in every particular.

The most important director working in Fort Lee during the early feature film period was Maurice Tourneur. Tourneur had been directing for Éclair in France, and was sent to America by Charles Jourjon to take charge of his new feature film operation. But the studio fire, the start of the European war, and Éclair's decision to stop production in the east changed the course of Tourneur's American career even before it had begun.

MAURICE TOURNEUR

(from *Moving Picture World*, November 28, 1914, p. 1242)

Maurice Tourneur, director of the Peerless studio in Fort Lee, NJ, a newcomer in the American moving picture field, has just shown by his first three pictures that he is one of the best and most finished directors now on the market.

Though still young in years, being only 32, his career from the start has ever been of the most artistic. Having completed his studies as an artist (painter) he worked seven years with Antoine (the French Belasco); then two years at the Odeon Theater in Paris, and for the last two years has devoted his services to directing for the Eclair Company.

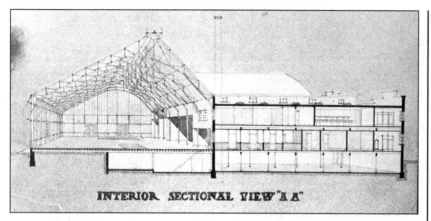

INTERIOR SECTIONAL VIEW "A A"

Plan and elevation for the Peerless studio, designed by Edward Kinsila, who had also designed theaters for the Shuberts.

His films met with the greatest success in Europe, and in America the Leading Players Film Corporation, which marketed them, realized its best sales with *The Sparrow, The Lunatics, Monsieur Lecoq,* and various others.

"Being a great admirer of D.W. Griffith", said Mr. Tourneur, "I had always been possessed with a strong desire to come to America. I felt there was something lacking to our French qualities and this could only be remedied by a personal study in this country. I was only awaiting the opportunity, which was afforded me by Chas. Jourjon, president of the Eclair Film Company, at the time when, in conjunction with Jules Brulatour, he was promoting the Peerless proposition, whose new studio has been placed under my direction. I am glad of the occasion to express my high appreciation of the hearty welcome I have met on all sides and which has in a large degree facilitated my work."

The World Film Corporation has already released three of Mr. Tourneur's prouductions, viz.: *Mother*, with Emma Dunn, *The Man of the Hour* with Robert Warwick, and *The Wishing Ring*, with Vivian Martin. These three films have shown us the talent of this director under three entirely different lights. First, dramatic emotion; secondly, power, strength; and thirdly, high-class comedy.

These various talents expressed in the highest degree by a man who can reproduce with feeling, add to this the minutest care of details, artistic knowledge of settings and costumes, and you have a small idea of the workings of Maurice Tourneur.

Mr. Tourneur is now giving the finishing touches to *The Pit*, with Wilton Lackaye, and if credence can be given to rumor we may look forward to another masterpiece.

His next production will be *Alias Jimmy Valentine*. This is rendered particularly interesting to Mr. Tourneur as he already staged, in Paris, the French version of this celebrated American drama.

We are happy to record the success which is now crowning his first efforts in this country, and together with the three other directors who are collaborating with him, the Peerless productions can be assured beforehand of a glorious future.

TOURNEUR –
Of Paris and Fort Lee, His Methods and His Artistic History

(from *Photoplay*, January 1916, pp. 139–140)

This is a story written, first, for the hundreds of girls who have entered the *Photoplay* Magazine-World Film Corporation "Beauty and Brains" Contest, and second, for the thousands of people from ocean to ocean who are interested in Maurice Tourneur's pictures.

For the former it is an intimate picture of the man who will instruct and direct the eleven successful beauties; for the latter it will give some sidelights on the career and work of a director whose photodramas have furnished enjoyment for them.

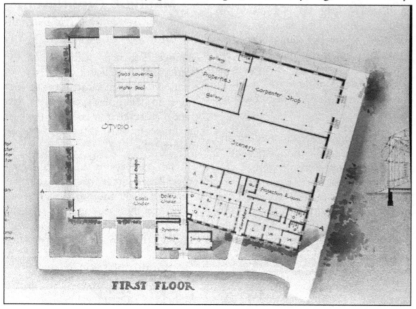

FIRST FLOOR

A sequence of frames from Alias Jimmy Valentine (Peerless-World, 1915).

In the all too short list of great directors that the wonderful new art has produced the name of Maurice Tourneur must be given a distinctive place. Back of the remarkable list of pictures that have come from his camera can be seen the years of training and experience of the French stage.

Yet you will never detect a foreign accent in any picture of American life that he has ever produced. His work is not hyphenated. His American pictures are more American than many Yankee directors can make them; and still he knows Paris so well that he can find true Parisian scenes right in New York City. An instance of this was shown in one of his recent pictures, *Trilby*, in which he took the famous Macdougall Alley, the last trench of Bohemian art in America, and lo – there was Paris.

The first time I saw Tourneur he was perched high on a scaffolding under the hot glass roof of the massive Fort Lee Studio, directing his artillery fire on a scene below. Had he worn a uniform he would have been my idea of a French Artillery officer.

When he is directing a company, he dominates it – because the players bow to his superior knowledge and training. But anyone who gives him a good suggestion is his friend for life.

Tourneur has lived with the stage fifteen years. He was born in Paris 39 years ago. Before he attained note as an actor and student of drama, he was known as a painter of no mean ability. While an actor and producer of the legitimate stage he played leads with Mme. Rejane, in England and South America, and assisted her in the stage direction.

Then came moving pictures. While they were *merely* moving pictures Tourneur was not interested in them, but as the day of the photoplay dawned, Tourneur saw the possibilities in the new art. He writes nearly all his own scripts as he says it is difficult to find anyone who can think photoplays.

Glen White, Lillian Russell and Lionel Barrymore in Wildfire *(World-Shubert).*

Before he starts work he knows just what each player should do and just how each study should be arranged. His capacity for work is great, because of this ability to plan it well before he starts. While it is impossible to at all times produce a photoplay in the order in which the scenes are arranged in the script, he aims to begin with the simpler, easier scenes, and works the actors to a climax as in a stage production. His pictures are comment enough on the success of his practical methods.

Maurice Tourneur believes that the future plays of the screen will be written by men who will devote their lives to this work. He abhors the present so-called scenario writers, and a scenario department that grinds out scripts can get no sympathy from him.

With his intimate knowledge of the mechanism of the stage it is not unnatural that Tourneur prefers artificial sets and the studio to out of door locations.

"Many actors simply won't act in the open", he says. "It is very well to display the beauties of nature, but the story, and the movements and expressions that tell the story in a photoplay are more important. We can get scenery in saddle pictures. Outdoor lights are uncertain and can not be depended upon. The expressions can not be made to register as they should. In a studio with carefully built sets and well regulated lighting, the slightest move and most subtle expression registers accurately. In a studio you may emphasize your story with the slightest glances from one character to another, while the great outdoor locations hurt and artistry would be utterly wasted."

Because early feature length films depended so heavily on theatrical talent, east coast studios were able to take full advantage of their proximity to Broadway. Dramatic stars, opera singers, vaudevillians, and chorus girls found it easy to nip over to Fort Lee for a try at "the movies". California was just too far away for someone like Lillian Russell, who made her only feature film, *Wildfire,* at the Peerless-World studio.

LILLIAN RUSSELL IN "WILDFIRE"

(from *Moving Picture World*, December 12, 1914, p. 1534)

Lillian Russell is one of the best known women before the public today. She holds a unique position in the esteem of the nation. For years she has been a leader of the stage and as a beauty her fame has been of such long duration that men who are now grandfathers can remember the time when they, as college students, eagerly looked forward to seeing Lillian Russell in her wonderful comic opera successes of days past.

At the Fort Lee Studios of the World Film Corporation she is now working on a moving picture version of her greatest stage success, *Wildfire*, the play that was written especially for her by George Broadhurst and George V. Hobart. When the play was originally produced by Joseph Brooks, in Cincinnati, the audience at the opening night were a bit disconcerted because they had come prepared to see a musical play but saw nothing of the sort in *Wildfire*. She was acting a character and she made the audience realize that she was an actress of distinction. They were not disappointed when the final curtain fell. That first performance marked her entrance into the legitimate stage. The packed audience in Cincinnati was the forerunner of a long series of similar audiences that gathered wherever Lillian Russell in *Wildfire* was announced. When her tour was completed Miss Russell decided to retire to private life but she received so many requests from her admirers all over the United States and Canada who were anxious to see her in *Wildfire* that she was receptive to the idea of making a motion picture from the play when that plan was suggested to her by General Manager Lewis J. Selznick of the World Film Corporation. To him is due the credit of placing Miss Russell under contract and her legions of admirers will welcome the opportunity of seeing her again.

Edwin Middleton is in charge of the production which is to be released in the regular World Film Corporation program, January 11th. This is to be one of the trump features in that service and General Manager Selznick is certain that *Wildfire* will set a new record for high grade star features.

> Eugenie Magnus Ingleton was more than just a reference librarian; as E.M. Ingleton, she wrote the scripts for such important World releases as *Trilby* and *The Moonstone*. But until the studio system became more specialized, it was not uncommon to find a single person writing, designing, reading submissions, collecting props, organizing a library, or "anything else I could prove useful in".

NEW WORLD FILM DEPARTMENT
Mrs. Eugenie Ingleton Is Librarian of the Reference Department at Fort Lee Studio

(from *Moving Picture World*, January 30, 1915, p. 662)

When seen recently at the World Film studio at Fort Lee, Mrs. Eugenie Ingleton had the following to say regarding the workings in her new department: "When I first came to the World Film studios I was intensely interested with everything. The beautiful dressing rooms, the shower-baths, the splendid carpenters' workshops, the scenic department, at the head of which is a master of art. All these things, even at a hurried glance, showed possibilities of delightful work for anyone who loved things artistic.

"When I was engaged as reader, writer, designer, and anything else I could prove useful in, I went into the business, heart and soul. Each week has, I think added to my enthusiasm. I have started what I hope will prove a valuable, though never completed, Library of Reference Department. Pictures and sketches of everything under the sun, at all periods, and at all times, I am collecting and classifying, so that directors wanting helpful ideas for scenes, costumes, locations, historic dates or detail, will find several sketches or pictures of whatever they seek. It is amusing to note the unexpected things that are wanted. The first thing I was asked for was a Burne-Jones stained glass window, a plane tree, an angel and a hotel kitchen followed, etc., etc. Everyone is most kind in helping me to add to the collection, bringing all sorts of unexpected little sketches that are bound to come in useful at some unexpected moment. The most of my time is taken up in reading and writing, however. I have just completed a five-reel scenario of Dion Boucicault's play, 'After Dark', which is to be made by the William A. Brady Picture Plays Co., and in which Robert Warwick and Alice Brady are to be starred. I have brought it forward – how many years? Substituted the Spanish-American War for the

Stars and directors of the World Film Corporation, 1915. Left to right, front row, Elaine Hammerstein, Wilton Lackaye and Dorothy Fairchild; second row, Albert Capellani, Frank Crane, Emile Chautard, Holbrook Blinn, Maurice Tourneur, Alice Brady, James Young and Clara Kimball Young.

Crimean, and changed the London of our grandmothers into New York of the present day, and I don't think the good old play, so full of human interest, has suffered one bit by becoming a naturalized American.

"Some years ago I was connected with Mr. Hepworth's fine studios at Walton-on-Thames, England. I wrote scenarios and played the principal parts, but could not decide then to give up theatrical work altogether. Since then I have written the three-act opera, 'Aphrodine,' about which I am in negotiation with Messrs Shubert. My one act opera, 'The Willow Pattern Plate' (originally produced at Terry's Theater, London, seven years ago), was reproduced at Proctor's Fifth Avenue Theater recently, with William Bruette in the leading part. Vernon Dalhart, who sang Ralph in 'Pinafore' at the Hippodrome, was principal tenor. Lately, I have written 'The Little Brown Mouse,' for Miss Charlotte Granville. But every day I work at the World Film studio, the

Maurice Tourneur directing Clara Kimball Young in Trilby *(Equitable-World, 1915).*

managers in America, and during my long engagement with them, I learned to love America. But from Little Eva at ten years old, to an hour spent in New York's wonderful library last night, there is hardly a moment that passes without gaining some knowledge or experience that is helpful to one's work in a big moving picture studio."

"TRILBY" (EQUITABLE)

(from *Moving Picture World*, September 4, 1915, p. 1668)

Almost every street in lower New York was made to contribute its quota to the production of *Trilby*, recently completed by Director Maurice Tourneur for the Equitable Motion Pictures Corporation.

Trilby, the story of which is familiar to almost every reading person, entailed, in the director, the necessity of absolute local color. For several thousand feet "Trilby" and Svengali are made to travel through strange lands. Galicia, Poland, Southern Russia, Italy and Hungary, are shown in the pictorial story and it was absolutely essential to a good production that the atmosphere and detail be perfect. Maurice Tourneur, however, met the authors' obligations by drawing upon the districts of the lower East Side with the result that a most elaborate production is counterbalanced by perfect detail.

As Trilby, Clara Kimball Young does, by far, her very best work. Under the powerful, unseen influence of the dreadful Svengali (Wilton Lackaye is, indeed, a dreadful Svengali) the frail Trilby is given a personality and lovableness that even Phyllis Neilsson

more absorbing and interesting I find it, the more I marvel at the genius of masterful picture direction, the more I strive to write something wonderful and beautiful with full scope for directors, actors, scenic artist and operators. I suppose every scenario department is full of these desires and ambitions, but isn't it very splendid and isn't the competition full of stimulus?

"I played my first part, 'Little Eva', in 'Uncle Tom's Cabin' at the age of ten, and at one time played 104 leading parts in two years at a well-known old London stock theater. I acted with the late Charles Arnold, and was nurse, newspaper correspondent, and did Secret Service work through the South African war, and came to this country first from the Haymarket Theater, London, where I played in 'Bunty Pulls the Strings.' I took Miss Jean Cadell's place when she left the Comedy Theater, New York, and also played the part (Aunt Susie) in Chicago. Messrs Shubert and Brady have been my only

Robert Warwick and Clara Kimball Young in Camille *(World-Shubert, 1915), directed by Albert Capellani.*

Terry failed to instill into the character.

Trilby is in five acts and three hundred and sixty one scenes and required a cast of extreme excellency [sic] to portray: Paul McAllister, recently starred in *The Scales of Justice*, by the Famous Players Film Company; Chester Barnett; and other players of stellar rank, support Miss Young and Mr. Lackaye. *Trilby* will be the initial release of the Equitable Corporation, but before being sent through World Film will be seen at a Broadway house beginning September 6th. September 20th is the Equitable release date for *Trilby*.

> During the winter months, filmmakers from Fort Lee continued to search for warmer climes, working often in Florida, Bermuda, Jamaica and other more temperate spots (unlike its competitors, World never operated a permanent California studio). In 1915 director Barry O'Neil decided to film his adaptation of "McTeague" in Death Valley, predating by several years Erich von Stroheim's use of the same location in *Greed*. Clara Kimball Young, working under Albert Capellani's direction in *Camille,* pursued realism in her own way.

WORKING IN DEATH VALLEY
World Film Players Had Strenuous Time Making "McTeague of San Francisco"

(from *Moving Picture World*, December 11, 1915, p. 2019)

Cooking utensils, provisions, tenting outfits, with the bag and baggage of Holbrook Blinn, Barry O'Neil, Fania Marinoff, and company of over twenty people of the World Film Corporation, landed at a town on the Union Pacific railroad, consisting of a railroad station, combination post office, general store and saloon. They were met there by Death Valley Jim Scott, and the famous twenty-mule team from the Borax mines. Scott, who knows this territory like a book, acted as a guide through the Death Valley, where the World players took scenes for Frank Norris's story, "McTeague of San Francisco".

Before leaving New York, Director O'Neil explained minutely the terrors of the desert and the horrors of camping and the hard work that would befall them, ending this little talk with the remark, "Anyone who is in the least bit afraid shall speak now or forever hold their peace." Instead of any member declining the engagement, they were all most enthusiastic to make the trip and many other people in the studio pleaded to be taken also.

The company arrived on the desert after traveling twenty miles on the backs of mules, accompanied by the twenty-mule team, hauling the supply wagon, in one of the worst sandstorms they had experienced on the desert in many years. The wind blew so hard that they were unable to put up their tents, and at the suggestion of Mr. Blinn, they all set to and unloaded the supply wagon and bunked in it. The next morning they packed their outfit and again started on a tedious journey to the mines. After enjoying a day of getting acquainted, putting up their tents and establishing themselves in their new abode, they started in for real hard work. It was many days before any member of the company saw daylight, for they went into the mines early in the morning and did not return until after dark.

After completing all the inside scenes they then started on the exteriors, traveling many miles each day and erecting their tents in a different locale each night.

Mr. Blinn and Mr. O'Neill are more than pleased with the results of their trip and the company tell many interesting, but harrowing, tales always finishing with "I wouldn't take a million dollars for the experience, but I wouldn't go through it again for ten times the amount."

REALISM IN "CAMILLE"
Clara Kimball Young Made Study of Tuberculosis of World Subject

(from *Moving Picture World*, December 18, 1915, p. 2161)

For the forthcoming production of *Camille* in photoplay form Clara Kimball Young, who is starred in the photodrama, which is from the studios of the World Film Corporation, made an unusually careful, though at first glance not very alluring, study of the inception and progress of consumption. It will be recalled, of course, that the Lady of the Camellias meets an untimely end from this disease and, up to date, in stage presentation her dramatic portrayers have contented themselves with a few hectic coughs, giving rise to the merry quip, "Camille is coughing much better this morning". Miss Young, however, decided that upon the screen a far more minute, and graphic study of the dread disease should be made, and to this end she spent several weeks at Saranac Lake and even braved the wards of hospitals devoted to the treatment of the great white plague in pursuit of her investigations. The result of this minute care is a realistic study of the progress of Camille's affliction which, without being in the least repulsive, is infinitely pathetic in its graphic depiction of the ravages of tuberculosis. It is, in fact, to quote Miss Young:

"A composite page torn from many suffering bedsides and from the lips of

Exterior of the Peerless-World studio, showing the flooring for the open-air stage, 1920.

WATER-COOLED STUDIO IS PLANNED BY WORLD

(from *Exhibitors Herald*, January 1, 1916, p. 18)

If the device to be installed at the World Film Corporation's Peerless studio, in Fort Lee, proves itself up to specifications there will be general rejoicing among the players working in that organization's productions next summer.

The innovation consists of a huge perforated pipe leading along the apex of the great glass roof, so arranged as to send a thin sheet of cold water smoothly down both sides of the roof all day long. The "water sheet" will not interfere with the passage of daylight; in fact, it is believed the power of the light will be magnetized [sic] by passing through the liquid curtain. Experts have passed upon the device and pronounced it sound in every detail.

In order to keep the water at the lowest temperature possible, the pipes leading from the pumping station will be sunk deeply in the ground in coils, with a refrigerating device attached, guaranteed to produce a spray of water almost at the freezing point.

The idea was worked out from a suggestion of Lewis J. Selznick, vice president and general manager of the World Film Corporation, who is determined to combat the great difficulty of summer studio work in this climate. Heretofore it has been impossible for directors and actors to work steadily all day long in the intense heat under the prismatic rays of light passing through the glass studio roof and side. It is hoped this will now be combated.

many brave souls enduring faithfully and without complaint until the end, which they know cannot in the nature of things be far off. I shall never regret my careful study of consumption, undertaken at first merely in the interest of a true characterization of the disease, but latterly in an earnest spirit of horror at the extent to which it has fastened upon the masses of this country. I shall do all that lies in my humble power to aid in stamping it out."

Miss Young did not add that, as a starter, she has forwarded to the largest tuberculosis institution in the United States her check for a large amount to aid in the battle that is being waged against consumption.

> The glass enclosed studios built in Fort Lee not only looked like greenhouses, they generated the same interior temperatures. In an age without air-conditioning, producers tried anything to avoid this heat – even returning to the primitive "open air" settings of a decade earlier, now described as a clever innovation.

Extras waiting for their call at the Peerless studio, c. 1915.

WORLD OPEN-AIR STUDIO POPULAR
Stars of Brady-Made Pictures Are Working in Comfort at Fort Lee

(from *New York Dramatic Mirror*, August 18, 1917, p. 22)

The new outdoors stage for World Pictures Brady-Made is attracting a great deal of attention in the studio colony at Fort Lee, in addition to having drawn the inspection of several automobile loads of visitors from New York.

Curiously, the workers in the extensive plant at Fort Lee were at first averse to making use of the al fresco space provided for them, although the temperature under glass was appalling during the recent record-breaking heat period.

But the reports from members of the first company that tried the open air stage were so enthusiastic that the prejudice disappeared, and now five or six separate picture plays are being made constantly and simultaneously in this added space.

The new stage is rectangular in shape, with dimensions of sixty-five feet by one hundred and twenty-five, giving a floor area of a trifle more than 8,000 square feet. This is the largest outdoor stage in the East, and its equipment is thoroughly modern.

The foundations are a series of heavy concrete piers, which in addition to supporting the general structure sustain a series of large upright columns. From the tops of these, strong bronze wires are strung at various angles, carrying movable overhead sheets and screens which serve as deflectors and diffusers of light.

This system works out perfectly for the elimination of undesirable shadows, enabling the cameramen to secure greatly improved values in lighting effects.

One end of this great stage closely adjoins the side of the Peerless (World) studio, so that it practically becomes a part of that structure. It was built under the supervision of Technical Director William Smart.

At present, picture plays are being completed here by Kitty Gordon, Ethel Clayton, Alice Brady, Carlyle Blackwell and Evelyn Greeley, June Elvidge, Montagu Love and Arthur Ashley and Madge Evans.

"We are making better photoplays than ever, by the use of this stage", said Director General William A. Brady. "This is due not alone to the atmospheric conditions, which are more favorable to photography in the open than inside an enclosure, but also to the fact that everybody naturally does better work in physical comfort than under bodily distress."

LITTLE JOURNEY TO EASTERN STUDIOS – WORLD FILM
Open-Air Studio Is an Important Factor in World Film New Jersey Plant – Mirror Staff Writer Makes Eighth Visit for Little Journey Series

By Alison Smith

(from *New York Dramatic Mirror*, September 1, 1917, p. 13)

The World Film Company has shown an ingenious disregard of geography and climate by combining in their Fort Lee plant the advantages of both the Eastern and Western studios. In addition to its indoor stage, built along the prescribed lines of the Fort Lee studios, there is an outdoor stage of equal size modeled after a typical open air studio in Hollywood. The executives of the company who planned this innovation admit that they were surprised at the number of months through the year in which the outdoor stage could be used without regard for the proverbial rigor of the Eastern climate and believe that much of the hesitancy in adopting this system in the East arises from the bugbear of our snowbound Winters, which really interfere far less than might be imagined with the outdoor work of the moving pictures.

The studio is some distance from the beaten track of the Fort Lee car line and is reached by one of the bypaths that straggle through the thick groves of the Palisades. The first indication that you are approaching the studio is gained from glimpses of a miniature village on the lot whose brilliant Oriental coloring makes a bizarre note in the placid Palisade scenery. The studio itself appears in three sections, the concrete part that houses the administrative departments, the indoor studio arched with glass and the outdoor stage which stretches the entire length of the lot.

The main building

At the entrance to the main building is the office of Robert McIntyre, studio manager, who, in addition to a hundred and one other services, receives visitors in a spirit of genial hospitality which makes the studio tour doubly agreeable. From the business offices, which occupy the front of the building, he conducted us to the indoor studio, which spreads out under its arch of glass to the edge of the lot. It is equipped with every variety of fixed adaptable lights and is cooled by two huge electric fans at each end of the building.

The stage is large enough to accommodate fifteen sets, but on this afternoon only three companies were working inside, since the other directors were making the most of the brilliant sunlight by taking their companies out on locations. June Elvidge, in the fetching disguise of a Breton peasant, was waiting with Carlyle Blackwell for the call of "lights!"

(Above): Production of Vengeance *(World, 1918) at the Peerless studio.*
(Below): Scenic artists at work in the Peerless studio, c. 1918.

on their set, which presented the interior of a European war office. In another corner, a luxurious boudoir awaited Kitty Gordon, while in the center of the stage, Julia Dean was beginning her first World picture, surrounded by all the grandeur of an elaborate screen ball-room.

A novel method of obtaining night effects in broad daylight has been evolved through an arrangement of compote boards, covered with black silk, which frame the set to be snapped as an evening exterior. The scene is lighted by a heavy dome arc and creates the illusion of outer darkness perfectly. This device is constantly in demand by directors who need an extra night scene in a hurry and cannot wait for the actual shadows to fall.

The floor of the stage, which seems perfectly solid, proves on examination to be made up of trap doors which may in a few moments be converted into descending stairways or into tanks filled with water for a swimming pool.

Glass partitions used

Glass partitions open from this inside studio to the outdoor stage, which has been built comparatively recently and is an experiment which has more than justified its existence. It is simply a solid platform, reaching almost to the grove that surrounds the lot. The stage is covered by a light framework on which is stretched the diffusing cloth, serving to cut the direct rays of the sun and spread them into an even and gentle glow.

In addition to the soft effect from above, an unusual radiance is obtained by the use of huge reflectors, which work on exactly the same principle that small boys use in flashing a mirror into the eyes of the person they are tormenting. These reflectors are covered with aluminum leaf, which catch the sun's rays and throw an aureole over the head of the heroine, or give the illusion of sun shining through the windows. An unusually effective picture in which both of these devices have been used has just been completed by Kitty Gordon.

Behind the studio is the large storehouse which is a model of efficiency and order. There are separate compartments for each portion of the set so that one views whole rows of doors, casements, roofs and occasionally whole sets in one piece, all systematically arranged and numbered. Each of the pieces is made of solid wood and fitted together as permanently as in actual building, but they are also so constructed that a given section can be altered and used in several different sets without the repetition being detected. There is an additional advantage in having the storehouse on a direct line with the studio floor where the sets may be put together with the greatest speed and facility.

Efficiency in carpenter shop

Opening off the storeroom is the carpenter shop where the same system of efficiency prevails. The various pieces are turned out in a half finished form in this room and are then raised by a special scenery lift to the paint shop where they are given the finishing touches and then lowered to the stage underneath. One of the most interesting features of the workshop is a young Italian wood carver who turns out exceedingly effective work in wood and plaster. Because of the incessant demand for material from the seven directors of the company, the studio maintains a night as well as a day force of mechanics and carpenters, who are engaged solely in finishing up scenery.

On the floor above are delightfully furnished dressing rooms for the principals and two long lines of make-up rooms for the extra people. The remainder of this space is devoted to the property department which resembles a museum, since nearly all of the properties are of permanent value and kept in glass cases under lock and key.

The technical department has its offices on a small balcony overlooking the stage. William Smart, the technical director, is at the head of a staff of men who are especially qualified to deal with the technical details of every variety of play. A new script is at once turned over to this department and a working sketch is made from the continuity before it reaches the hands of the director. A library is maintained for the use of this department and the members of the staff are in a position to lay their hands on all historical data necessary to the production of plays in every possible period.

Rooms for directors

Each of the seven directors has his individual room in the administrative building with a large general room for conferences. Adjoining this is the director's private projection room where the pictures are reviewed by the staff before being sent over to the New York office. The scenario department under the supervision of Thomas Miranda has a spacious room at the top of the building where a staff of readers and continuity writers is engaged in selecting and reconstructing scripts.

The large lot surrounding the building was covered by a Russian village, which will be the background for a new play dealing with the Revolution and directed by Arthur Ashley. The company has recently bought an additional tract of land adjoining the lot which will extend its limits materially and make room for more elaborate outside productions.

The World Film Company is securely united under the supervision of one man, William A. Brady, who with the title of Director General, personally superintends the constant output of five reel features. He engages the actors, selects the scripts, appoints the heads of the various departments and has been known to take up the work of a temperamental director who left in the midst of an important production. His spirit of coordination has been transfused through the entire plant and is chiefly responsible for the atmosphere of goodwill and efficiency that permeates the World studio.

A TOPSY-TURVY HOUSE

By Jerome Weatherby
(from *Picture Play,* January 1919, pp. 50–56)

"Have you ever seen an out-of-door studio?" asked my Movie Friend the other day. "Nope, never been to California", I answered.

"You don't have to go any farther than Fort Lee, while this warm fall weather keeps up", he replied. And that's how I happened to take a trip over to the Peerless Studio on the New Jersey Palisades the other day, and to see the great big happy family of World players "at home".

I know now what Louise Huff has for lunch, and how well she looks in black lace. I have seen Muriel Ostriche repairing her make-up between scenes. I know what it is like to have to take a scene four times, and that it is worth waiting for to see "Monty" Love's grin when it has finally been shot to the director's satisfaction. My admiration for Carlyle Blackwell has stood the acid test of beholding him at odd intervals one entire afternoon wearing a week's growth of beard. I have attended a picture show in the studio projection room before a foot had been cut, with most of the principals in the audience. It was as entertaining a place as I've ever seen, but instead of calling it a studio I'd call it the "Topsy-turvy House" if it were mine. For nearly everything is just about the way you don't expect it to be.

My first shock was to come in at a prosaic-looking studio door and suddenly to find myself still out of doors, standing on what resembled more than anything else the deck of a gigantic yacht. It was simply a huge platform, covered with white muslin to diffuse the light, and open on three sides. Along the middle of it ran a double row of sets, back to back, facing in opposite directions, much like the deck cabins on an ocean liner.

In a nook sheltered by a pile of scenery sat a young lady whom I recognized as June Elvidge, despite nodding willow plumes in her hair, a snaky evening dress, and the inevitable khaki knitting. Beside her sat a poor, disheveled chap – an extra, no doubt, I thought.

The first set was an English booking office of some sort, decorated with a couple of Union Jacks flanking the Stars and Stripes on the wall, plenty of war posters – English, not American – and a number of extras, including an English officer distinguishable by his Sam Browne belt. The director suddenly stopped fussing around, put his hands to his mouth, and yelled above the din of hammers: "Oh, Blackwell!"

Not until the tramplike person detached himself from Miss Elvidge and came sauntering over did the truth dawn. It was Blackwell himself, camouflaged under a workman's sleeveless blue shirt, a slouch, and an inch of beard. He nodded to a couple of acquaintances, clutched the ungainly bag an attendant thrust into his hand, and walked on.

At a desk in the middle of the two-sided "room" sat a young man clad in the khaki of the U.S.A. He was handsome, and evidently aware of it. His face was a ghastly yellow – the men make up that way, and the women with white. Carlyle walked over, dropped the bag, and held a little conversation with the officer at the desk.

"Hey extra! Don't keep looking at the camera – we're only paying you for your back." The director made this suggestion to the half dozen extras who were writing on the shelf which ran around the room in post-office style. "So if you've got anything to say, let your back say it".

Then came the close-up. The distance between the star and the camera was accurately measured, while the extras looked on as if getting a peep into a seventh heaven which they never expected to attain, and the action for the distance shots was repeated. That's all there was to it – the taking of the picture was as undramatic as the picture itself will probably be dramatic when it is screened. [The film was released in October 1918 as *The Road to France* – ed.]

Half an hour later, when I passed that way, the set was no more. The desk had been pushed to one side, the two walls taken down, and the flags lay like so much bunting on a chair. And Carlyle Blackwell was busily adding another day to the age of his beard in his dressing room.

"Terrible to look like this", he half apologized, glancing up. "I've had to add to my beard systematically every

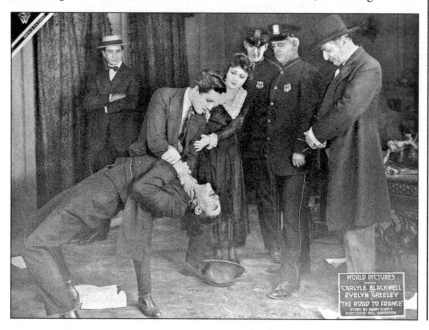

Carlyle Blackwell foils German plans for shipyard sabotage in The Road to France *(World, 1918).*

day since I started to do the picture. The story is about a young man who crosses the water on a cattle ship to get to Europe. And in the story I haven't had a chance to shave yet – one more day and I'll be through with the disguise."

The next scene that I watched was in the business office of some variety of Wall Street king – say, a steel magnate. Montagu Love and a gentleman in a vociferous yellow shirt confronted one another across a rosewood desk. The story, by the way, unless they change the title, was *The Driving Power* [released as *The Steel King* in November 1918].

The door opened, and a little stenographer entered with a paper. She lingered, after the custom of stenographers who hate to make the trip over again in a pair of patent-leather threes with French heels. Mr. Love read the blank sheet, registered amazement, then turned and started to leave the room.

"Do that over!" yelled the director. "Monty – *more* amazement! *Lots* of it! Right, camera! Stenographer, come in!"

This time the lead of the scene fairly grimaced amazement – another foible of the picture art. There must be no mistake about registering an emotion. The only difficulty was that in the elation of registering sufficient amazement, Mr. Love pocketed the paper instead of leaving the incr-r-rimating document – if such it was – on his desk.

Again the camera creaked while the scene was done over – only this time Monty suddenly found himself walking out of the door with his cigar in his mouth and the director shouted: "Throw it away!"

One more retake, and the scene was finished. How Monty did grin! A contagious, generously big smile it was, somewhat reminiscent of a close-up or two in *Rasputin*. Later on, when I

went into the projection room and saw a bit from the same film taken a couple of days before – I found that nearly every scene of Monty's ended with that big-boy grin – the funnier because it contrasted so oddly with the emotional character of the scene he had been acting. Of course, you won't see that grin in the films – for the camera always keeps on grinding a few seconds after a scene is finished, and the film, of course, cut later on.

When the scene was over, Mr. Love threw out both arms with an air of abandon, and threw himself down on a bed in a near-by set, still holding a newly lighted cigar between his teeth.

"Relaxation", he murmured, his eyes still closed, as I came over. "Take it out of me – retakes do".

"Like pictures?"

"Yes, except in hot weather – this place here – great place – only comfortable place in summer."

"Despite the fact that you were born in Calcutta – and raised in India!" He nodded, and spilled cigar ashes on his clothes.

"We dressed for the heat there. Besides, I've lived in England and America since I grew up. Yes, I like pictures", he broke off ruminatively, "when they're real. I really enjoyed doing *Rasputin*. That was because in the first place the Black Monk of Russia was real – an historical person living in our own time – he's history, you know. But for plain humanness, I think I enjoyed *The Cross Bearer* more than any other. These stories of oil kings and copper magnates – ." Mr. Love wrinkled that expressive nose of his in disgust. "Hope I haven't cracked my make-up", he grunted, passing a careful hand over his pale-red hair as he hurried back to pose for a close-up.

"Camera boy", called some one from another set, and June Elvidge, radiant in a gorgeous evening gown, chancing to be near, picked up the black guide card and held it, herself, before the

camera. It seems that, before every scene is shot, they hold up a black card with the working title written on it in white, the name of the director, and of the camera man. Underneath there are two figures, one for the scene, another to designate what shot it is in that scene. That identifies every piece of film, and makes it easy to assemble them in order when the picture is finished.

A tall, good-looking chap in a Norfolk jacket was leaning against the railing of the staircase looking over a bunch of pictures.

"That's rotten – perfectly rotten! I hope they didn't use it! It looks no more like me than – ." Some one stuck a head out of a little door at the foot of the stairs.

"Frank – better come! Show's on." With a whoop the youth in the belted jacket, who proved to be no other than Frank Mayo, crashed headlong into the projection room. The "show" was the first projection of the last scenes of *The Driving Power*, and all the notables of the studio were there – an opportunity not to be missed.

But something had gone wrong with the projecting machine, and so, while we waited, Louise Huff and Johnny Hines volunteered to do an impromptu skit. There was no orchestra, but we didn't mind that, and I thought it was a good deal more amusing and spontaneous than most vaudeville acts I have seen.

At last the machine was fixed, and the showing began.

The picture was – don't gasp – a fight in a wild-West setting. A mountain cabin was attacked, and Mr. Love, who was the only one on the scene, with great presence of mind put up a hasty barricade of tables and chairs behind which he defended himself against the attacks of some eight or nine opponents. Shots rained over Mr. Love's head, hitting everything on the shelf behind him. Only one

(Above): St. Cecilia's Church in Englewood provides a congenial location for The Divine Sacrifice (World, 1918).

(Below): Madge Evans playing herself in The Volunteer (World, 1917). The homes on Palisade Avenue in the background, opposite the Revolutionary War Monument, still stand.

plate, which should have shattered the first time it was hit, received puncture after puncture until it threatened to do service as a colander, and never budged.

"Hang that plate!" breathed some one under his breath in the dark. "Some plate that! Tell me where to get them and I'll take some home", came from the back of the room.

Intermingled with the fight scenes were bits of film in which Miss Castleton, heroine, clung to Mr. Love's hand. Now and then Frank Mayo burst in. Once there was a sudden close-up of the photograph of that young man, at which Frank made a gesture indicating that life was no longer worth living.

"Gee, what's the use", he groaned. "and I had dozens of pictures that I'd rather have had them use".

It was almost impossible to get any idea of the story. There were "repeats" of each – they make two films of the action in nearly every case to guard against accident, and everything was shown. For instance, the fight would be enacted, then done all over again, then the surrender, and again a surrender just as if you had not quite understood the first time. One love scene would be followed by the same thing, just as ardent, all over again. Suddenly the screen went black and the light came on. The showing was over.

Outside the door of the studio several cars were drawn up, though it was still early. There were cries of "Who's coming in my car?" and "Any one going my way?" The "at home" was over and the members of the happy family were through with their part of the day's work.

But from the inside of the studio came the ringing blows of the carpenters and set builders-who were getting things ready for the next day and the next. For the day's work was still going on in the World Studio.

Actors frequently complained that they were forced to film summer scenes in winter, and winter scenes in summer – and had to dress inappropriately for the real weather conditions in both instances. When not sweltering under greenhouse conditions inside the studio, companies often tried to bend conditions on location to suit themselves. Emile Chautard, for example, felt that Venice could be recreated in Piermont, New York, in December for *Frou-Frou* (released as *A Hungry Heart)*.

WORLD BUILDS VENETIAN STREET FOR AN EPISODE IN "FROU FROU"

(from *Exhibitors Herald*, December 9, 1916, p. 31)

A street in Venice with a film of ice along the edges and a flurry of snow-flakes eddying between the house fronts was the scene which greeted

"THE VOLUNTEER" PLAY WITHIN A PLAY STARS MADGE EVANS AND HENRY HULL

(from *Exhibitors Herald*, December 29, 1917, p. 29)

The current World Picture Brady-Made, in which Madge Evans, the World's "kiddie star" and Henry Hull are featured equally, has motion pictures as its topic. It starts in the World's studio at Fort Lee, NJ and follows the picture which supposedly is being taken at that particular time with little Madge as its star and Harley Knowles directing.

The Play Within a Play shows Madge's

Alice Brady and the players in one of the episodes in *Frou Frou* recently in Piermont, NY, as they alighted from their automobiles to make a retake.

Director Emile Chautard, under whose care the motion picture had been prepared for the World Film Corporation, had decided that the Venetian Street built at the Peerless studio was not quite realistic enough and had selected the location at Piermont, where Sparkill Creek empties into the Hudson River, twenty miles above Fort Lee.

About a quarter of a mile back from the mouth of the creek there is a depth of four or five feet of water with stone embankments on both sides, and above these the outer walls of several buildings, including a lyceum hall, the manor house, and the jail of Revolutionary times. This stretch of water, about 200 feet in length, now is lined from end to end with the facades of picturesque Venetian houses and several gondolas float upon the placid surface of the stream.

The entire construction of this street in Venice was accomplished in the carpenter shops of the studio at Fort Lee from drawings supplied by Technical Director T.K. Peters.

father going off to war (which he did in real life) and Madge's mother departing for France as a member of the Red Cross.

This makes it necessary for little Miss Evans – in the story – to abandon her

As Miss Brady removed her heavy furs before the gates to the Barberini palace facing Sparkill Creek, she was shivering in her gossamer garments, for the air was cold and penetrating, although the snow had ceased and the sun for which all had been waiting finally made its appearance.

ABOUT THE TRADE IN NEW YORK

(from *Exhibitors Herald*, December 16, 1916, p. 38)

Over in Piermont, NY, Director Chautard has been picking warm afternoons to film Alice Brady, carrying a rose and playing in a brook. When the brook is coated with ice it is plainly apparent to the camera, and Alice's shivering figure belies the warm atmosphere the picture is supposed to have.

The chilly weather almost stopped work on *Frou Frou*, the World picture in which Alice Brady is starring. A gondola is supposed to float upon the placid waters of a Venetian street and the creek froze up on 'em. Piermont, NY, isn't Venice by a long shot.

Filmmaking, especially as it related to the daily lives of both fans and filmmakers, was a frequent subject of World releases. *A Girl's Folly, The Stolen Voice,* and *The Volunteer* all made use of the studios themselves as backdrops, and involved Fort Lee and the surrounding area as often as possible. This approach traded on the popular notion of "the film town" as an accessible, humanly scaled location, where the stars ate at the same lunch counters as their public. The image of Hollywood as a "magic kingdom of make-believe" was a very different concept, promoted by the film industry in the 1920s.

professional career for the time being and go to live with relatives out West, until her parents return. These relatives are Quakers, and the head of the family is so firmly set against war that he and his son, who is filled with patriotic fervor and desires to enlist, keep the household in perpetual riot.

Little Madge among Quakers

Neither does the iron-clad old Quaker countenance moving pictures or other forms of amusement, so that when little Madge's last photoplay comes along to the small town near which her relatives live, he sternly forbids the others to go near it, and then sneaks off by himself to have a secret look.

His wife, his warlike son and little Madge similarly repair to the movie theater, each by himself and sit in different parts of the house, viewing the play. When the crowd files out the elder members of the Quaker family are at first a very shame-faced lot. But the end justifies the means, for the deep patriotism of the story they have just witnessed has the effect of lighting the fire in the old man's heart and he gladly sends his son to the service of his country.

The Volunteer is the motion picture play in which all the stars of World-Pictures appear personally, each for a moment, as one by one they bid Madge good-bye when she is leaving the studio for her new home. These include Kitty Gordon, Ethel Clayton, Evelyn Greeley, June Elvidge, Carlyle Blackwell, Montagu Love and director-general William A. Brady, together with Madge's own director, Harley Knowles.

The first scene, showing all the World companies working in the studio, was photographed from a platform built sixty feet high just outside the great structure of glass and steel. At this point a section of the glass was removed, and the camera was inserted in the aperture.

There were many hazards involved in film production, not all of which were related to making movies. One significant problem of filming in the Fort Lee area was the poor condition of the local roads. When combined with the reckless driving of many in the film community, and the lack of safety features in early automobiles, this resulted in a startling number of accidents, many of which were reported in local newspapers and industry journals. More exotic accidents and production problems were often leaked to the press in order to gain a few lines of free publicity, but what happened to Harley Knowles during William A. Brady's independent production of *Stolen Orders* was unique. Kitty Gordon's lawsuit, on the other hand, was simply another reminder of the general carelessness regarding the use of fire and explosives.

PICTURE FOLK IN AUTO CRASH

(from *Moving Picture World,* April 17, 1917, p. 246)

In a head-on automobile accident which took place on the Hudson Terrace Road between Fort Lee and Englewood, NJ, on a recent midnight, Joseph Kaufman and his wife, Ethel Clayton, very narrowly escaped fatal injuries, while driving to their apartment in the Englewood Inn, when they were struck by a limousine. Both cars were traveling at a comparatively slow rate of speed on account of the heavy fog, which is the only reason why the accident did not result more seriously [sic]. Mr. Kaufman was thrown forward and crashed through the glass front, receiving such severe cuts about the right eye and ear, chin and chest that he was immediately rushed to the Englewood hospital in another automobile, where many stitches were taken. Miss Clayton, sitting alongside her husband, was resting her knees against a box she was carrying, and

Harley Knowles (wearing hat) directing Julia Stewart and Madge Evans in The Master Hand *(PremoWorld, 1915). Arthur Edeson is using an Eclair Gillon camera, in common use at the Eclair and Peerless studios. Note separate director for Madge Evans.*

escaped with only a slight bruise on her arms and shoulders. Joseph Kaufman and Miss Clayton are well known in motion picture circles. Mr. Kaufman has just directed George M. Cohan in his first motion picture production, now being shown in a Broadway theater, while Miss Clayton is a star working at the Peerless studio for the World Film Corporation.

HARLEY KNOWLES WALKS INTO ACID

Quickly Hauled Out of Vat, However, by Party Led by William A. Brady

(from *Moving Picture World*, March 2, 1918, p. 1213)

Harley Knowles, general director for William A. Brady, had a close call from serious injury and possible death at Longport, NJ, February 17, while inspecting preparations for a film thriller that calls for the explosion of a $15,000 dirigible in a fight with a seaplane in midair over the ocean.

A large vat of acid, which gives off the gas to inflate the dirigible's 100-foot bag, was buried in the ground alongside the temporary hangar. The lid had been removed, and in the darkness Knowles stepped into the vat and went down to his shoulders.

Led by Mr. Brady, other members of the party quickly hauled him out and slashed off his clothes, which prevented serious burns. Knowles was wrapped in a blanket and taken to a hotel in Atlantic City, where a physician dressed his injuries.

WORLD FILM APPEALS KITTY GORDON CASE; ACTRESS WAS INJURED IN BATTLE SCENES

(from *Moving Picture World*, October 30, 1920, p. 1252)

The appellate division of the New York Supreme Court yesterday listened to arguments on the appeal of the World Film Corporation of 130 West Forty-sixth street from a judgment of $1,400 awarded to Kitty Gordon, the motion picture star, last spring by a jury in the supreme court, for medical expenses and a week's salary lost, due to injuries received at the Fort Lee studios of the film corporation, in a battle scene in the picture, *The Beloved Adventures*, in which she played the part of a Red Cross nurse and rescued another nurse in a battlefield scene.

Miss Gordon was engaged at a salary of $1,250 a week, and the scene in which she was injured represented a shack in "no man's land", where a group of refugees were being attacked from afar and Miss Gordon was to rescue the other nurse in the midst of exploding bombs. In effecting the rescue, she stepped in the path of one of these exploding bombs and suffered the injuries complained of.

Charges carelessness

She charged the film company with carelessness and with failure to live up to a promise to use a less effective and harmless way of doing the explosive act. Nathan Burkan, counsel for Miss Gordon, argued that "whether the tools in question were reasonably safe, considering all the circumstances, including the nature of the risk, is primarily a question for the jury", and as

Despite its connection with the Shuberts, after William Brady took charge the World Film Corporation continued to lose money. A 12 November 1917 letter from Board member Ben Heidingsfield to Moritz Rosenthal (Shubert Archives, Correspondence file) noted that the weekly take had recently dropped from $60,000 to $50,000, largely because their competition had moved to the promotion of individual features, while World was still selling exhibitors a seasonal program. And even that figure was below the $75,000 weekly take that management had promised. The fact that World had 22 features completed and unreleased was further evidence of bad management.

The following figures are taken from a weekly summary of receipts prepared for World board members. The original document also included separate breakdowns for World's short comedy productions, as well as features distributed by them but produced by others. All but a few of the following titles were "Brady" or "Shubert" productions made at the Fort Lee studios. Data was also provided on each film's receipts for the previous week and the preceding six month period. While the performance of any film might vary slightly (even spiking on occasion), the numbers indicate that receipts for World's product were strongest for the first ten weeks or so, fell by around 80% during weeks 11–25, and dropped significantly again afterwards – although every film on this list was still making money (*The Dollar Mark*, for example, pulled in $257.19 during its 66th week in release). From Shubert Archives, File 2890, Correspondence August 1916-December 1918.

they decided in favor of the actress he held that their judgment should be affirmed.

Counsel for the World Film argued that as the defendant had furnished her with a place to work, which was reasonably safe, under all the conditions, with ordinarily safe appliance with which to prosecute the work, and with skilled and competent fellow workmen, that as she had voluntarily entered upon the work, she assumed the risk which was incident to the taking of the picture under these conditions.

It was further contended for the film corporation that as the accident was the result of carelessness in the firing of the bombs, it was part of the risk she assumed and a detail for which defendant was not responsible, and that her complaint, therefore, should have been dismissed. The court took the briefs of both sides and reserved decision.

World Film Corporation: Collections, From Release to 25 December 1915

Weeks in Release	Title	Collections to Date	Weeks in Release	Title	Collections to Date
			33	The Butterfly	28,101.82
			32	When It Strikes Home	42,002.06
			31	The Boss	48,550.89
66	Dollar Mark	85,643.83	30	Builder of Bridges	33,167.90
65	Mother	55,985.20	29	Little Miss Brown	32,370.84
64	Gentleman from Mississippi	56,832.55	28	Fine Feathers	31,656.77
63	The Man of the Hour	73,781.22	27	The Moonstone	24,930.16
62	Mystery of Edwin Drood	28,507.90	26	Face in the Moonlight	36,197.16
61	When Broadway Was a Trail	31,843.72	25	Col. Carter of Cartersville	17,397.67
60	Across the Pacific	32,831.31	24	After Dark	28,985.36
59	The Wishing Ring	56,217.28	23	The Cub	27,356.22
58	One of Millions	26,358.89	22	Marrying Money	37, 887.55
57	Lola	62,491.30	21	Sunday	20,454.23
56	Dancer and the King	34,760.23	20	The Stolen Voice	31,506.88
55	Seats of the Mighty	35,431.31	19	The Master Hand	31,417.09
54	The Marked Woman	34,829.35	18	Little Dutch Girl	23,421.07
53	As Ye Sow	59,022.09	17	The Cotton King	20,428.56
52	The Pit	71,085.55	16	The Imposter	19,840.57
51	Mrs. Wiggs of the Cabbage Patch	49,753.54	15	Ivory Snuff Box	27,200.32
50	The Deep Purple	65,986.37	14	Evidence	26,256.12
49	Mignon	44,843.41	13	Little Mademoiselle	13,854.75
48	Wildfire	61,571.81	13	Lure of Woman	6,528.29
47	Money	45,788.35	12	The Flash of an Emerald	24,883.04
46	Old Dutch	59,250.93	11	Family Cupboard	20,907.57
45	Daughter of the People	39,562.75	10	Blue Ridge	22,925.70
44	Alias Jimmy Valentine	72,674.61	9	Salvation Nell	23,628.30
43	The Fairy and the Waif	24,419.38	8	Bought	19,541.53
42	M'Liss	34,922.52	7	Hearts of Men	11,586.92
41	The Fight	32,041.68	6	Butterfly on the Wheel	19,835.13
40	What Happened to Jones?	28,848.06	5	Body and Soul	9,943.29
39	Arrival of Perpetua	28,707.39	4	Sins of Society	10,725.84
38	Man Who Found Himself	49,385.01	3	Gray Mask	7,080.89
37	Hearts in Exile	62,814.41	2	Siren's Song	2,911.85
36	The Fifth Commandment	35,182.81	1	Over Night	967.24
35	Lily of Poverty Flat	28,948.71	0	The Rack	3,287.20
34	The Model	47,713.26	Total		$2,345,773.51

1918 was a crucial year for the World Film Corporation. On January 15 they took out a $450,000 second mortgage, using their film rights, contracts, studio facilities and real estate as collateral. A $150,000 mortgage dating from 1915 was still outstanding. With fewer important stars now working at the studio, publicity was being sent out on such trivia as the number of nails used each year. The War began to cut into studio personnel – lab supervisor Joe Sternberg signed up to work for the Signal Corps at the training school they had established at Columbia University (as Josef von Sternberg he would later win fame directing *The Shanghai Express, The Scarlet Empress*, and other Hollywood classics). And despite the fact that World had stockpiled enough fuel to sit out that winter's coal shortage, even their doors were forced to close under the onslaught of the influenza epidemic.

WHAT GOES INTO MAKING OF PICTURES

World Film Compiles Statistics as to Amount of Material That Goes Into Year's Program

(from *Moving Picture World*, May 4, 1918, p. 707)

An efficiency expert at the World studio at Fort Lee has compiled the following figures of the amount of material required that goes into the making of a year's program: To those who are not familiar with studio activities it may be of interest to know that in the past year, for the sets built for fifty-two pictures, it was necessary to use 1,500,000 feet of lumber, 12,000,000 nails, 100,000 screws, 5,000 locks, hinges and door knobs, 75,000 feet of wallpaper, 1,500 gallons of paint, over 100,000 pieces of furniture and 300,000 props. There was consumed in lighting these sets 1,000,000 amperes of current, also 1,500,000 feet of film and countless number of horses, cows, sheep, goats, birds, goldfish, dogs and oxen were employed. As for bears, snakes, raccoons, lions and elephants, the number of these animals used would equip the Barnum & Bailey Circus several times over.

WORLD PICTURES EMPLOYS 1500 MEN IN BUILDING BIG SET

(from *Moving Picture World*, May 11, 1918, p. 869)

What is claimed to be the largest set ever built in West Fort Lee, NJ was erected there, in record time, in the World Film studios when on Sunday, April 14, working the entire day and until 4 o'clock in the morning, it almost continuously employed 1,500 persons, working with Director Jack Adolfi and a full company for the important forthcoming World production, *The Heart of a Girl*. It is scheduled for release July 1.

The set occupied the entire indoor stage of World's West Fort Lee studios. Seven hundred chairs on the ground floor of the set, these roped in tiers of one hundred each, seated as many persons. The tiered balconies seated a like number. The fluted columns supporting the balconies were each made for this particular set in the World studio carpenter shop, where extra help was employed for the occasion.

Following the new rule of Studio Manager McIntyre, no plaster of Paris was used in the construction of any of the parts or detail of the set. Every piece was of solid wood, hand carved. All the doors were made solid, so that no vibration was registered in opening, closing or slamming. Five hundred flags were used in decorating the balconies and seven thousand pieces of literature in the finale of the court scene.

Working from 9:30 o'clock Sunday morning until 4 o'clock Monday morning, director Jack Adolfi and his cameraman and captains achieved an unparalleled record in the filming of sixty-one scenes so as to turn over the studio to the various working directors at 9:30 o'clock Monday morning.

AMATEUR AFTERNOONS AT WORLD STUDIOS

Directors Try Out Screen Aspirants and Find Some Promising Material

(from *Moving Picture World*, May 25, 1918, p. 1125)

For the purpose of getting new faces and new talent in World Pictures and thereby getting variety in casts, World Pictures has set aside one afternoon a week at the World studio for the purpose of trying out new material and making selections of people for the smaller roles in new productions.

A comprehensive and successful plan for the selection of these has been inaugurated. On the afternoon the aspirants are gathered in the studio and are there tried out by the directors as to their quickness of perception, their ability to grasp the essentials of a scene and their success in depicting emotions. Those who prove capable along these lines are then given screen tests – that is, they are put through their

William Brady indicating the fine print to one of his stars, Kitty Gordon.

paces before the camera by the directors. If they show up well when the tests are developed and printed they are hired for some production in which they will fit well.

Recently at one of these try-outs afternoons thirty-five young women were given a trial. Of the thirty-five, six developed enough ability to warrant screen tests and of the six, two were hired for work in new pictures.

Love and the Woman (1919), was one of the last films produced by World. The slate indicates that Tefft Johnson was directing and Phillip Hatkin was cameraman. June Elvidge appears to be holding Johnson's megaphone.

TO HOLD UP AMERICAN WOMEN TO CHINA
Alice Lee Preparing Film to Show Her Countrymen How Gentler Sex Is Regarded Here

(from *Moving Picture World,* June 15, 1918, pp. 1553–1554)

Asking a million questions a minute and carefully storing away in her keen mind all the information she absorbs for future use in the elevating of womankind in her native country, Alice Lee, a bright young Chinese girl, is the busiest person about the World Pictures studio in West Fort Lee, NJ, these days. Miss Lee realizes that motion pictures are the greatest propaganda force in the world, and it is for that reason that she has chosen the screen as the mode of bringing her countrywomen to higher things.

Miss Lee is appearing as one of the leading characters in a World Picture, *Mandarin's Gold,* in which Kitty Gordon is starred, and she is utilizing every moment she has at the studio in studying the making of motion pictures, from the staging of the plays to the developing of the negatives and the making of the prints.

"Everyone knows", said Miss Lee, "how the Chinese father considers a son a blessing and a daughter a curse. Everyone knows how different things are here – how American women are looked up to and respected and what an important place they take in the daily life, especially in these war times. There is no reason why the Chinese women should not also be looked up to and respected by the Chinese men and with the aid of the knowledge I have gained in this country I hope to be successful in bringing this change about or at least starting the change.

"I am going back to China soon and with me I will take some thousands of feet of film showing the way American men treat American women – with the utmost respect everywhere.

Then, when I am in China, I will take pictures showing the way that Chinese men treat our womenfolk. After this I will show both pictures, one after the other, and in this way forcibly bring home to my countrymen the difference in the standing of women in America and China. It is so that I may be able to have success in taking the pictures back home in China that I am studying so hard here now and asking so many questions which everybody so kindly answers for me."

STERNBERG JOINS ARMY

(from *Exhibitors Herald and Motography,* August 10, 1918, p. 59)

Joe Sternberg of the World laboratory, who has had charge of film for this concern from the time if left the camera until it was shipped to the branches, has joined the photographic division of the Signal Corps. He has been stationed at Columbia University, where he will help in the production of a film to be used in training recruits.

MANY ACTORS STRANDED BY REMOVAL OF STUDIOS

(from *Exhibitors Herald and Motography,* November 2, 1918, p. 40)

A salutary effect of the removal of eastern producing plants to California is already being felt at the World Pictures studio at Fort Lee. One morning last week more than 300 actors called and asked that they be registered with the casting director. Many of them were actors who have played important parts. Some stated that as the railroad fares to California are so high and they had saved no money they were unable to follow their companies.

Actors who have been paid as high as $200 a week are willing to accept jobs at half that money if they can be assured of receiving regular employment in the east. The question with the casting director now is not so much the assembling of a proper cast, but rather that of elimination and the

drafting of virtually an all star cast at salaries that three months ago would have been utterly impossible.

WORLD PICTURES RETAINING EMPLOYEES

(from *Moving Picture World,* November 2, 1918, p. 607)

During the enforced layoff because of the influenza epidemic, World Pictures is keeping its office organization intact and at work in order that a resumption of its activities may not suffer through inability to keep the machine properly geared.

The scenario department shows no let-up. Stories, novels and plays are being read and passed upon. Last week World Pictures purchased from Kobby Kohn an original story, which will be converted into a photoplay for Montagu Love and June Elvidge. Mr. Kohn has just sold to A.H. Woods two plays which will be produced some time during the present season.

The sales force has been retained as the company considers the saving on salaries would not offset the losses growing out of the engaging of new men. By having at least six months' reserve of negatives the hiatus of four weeks at the studio in no way affects the release dates on the pictures supplied exhibitors. This also holds good for the advertising material which has been made months in advance of the required time for its distribution.

While not the first dramatic film completely shot in "natural color" (Kinemacolor had been doing this for years) Prizma's *The Little Match Girl* did have several technical advantages over the earlier process. Popular for travelogues and insert sequences in the post-war years, Prizma Color never succeeded in establishing itself in the feature film market.

MADGE EVANS IN NATURAL COLOR FILM

(from *Moving Picture World*, March 15, 1919, p. 1456)

Madge Evans is the star in a one reel Prizma Natural Color Picture which is now being made by the Prizma Company at the World Studio at Fort Lee. It will be released under the title of *The Little Match Girl*. This will be the first picture ever made in America where the entire photoplay has been photographed in natural colors.

Up-to-date
Rental and Contracting Studio
Controlling a Vast Capacity of Floor Space

REBUILT WITH MODERN EQUIPMENT

FORT LEE STUDIOS, Inc.

FORMERLY THE PEERLESS

LEWIS STREET, FORT LEE, N. J.   Phones Fort Lee 200-1

(Above): Although it was still operating, the World-Peerless studio was becoming quite ramshackle by 1920.

(Left): Fort Lee Studios advertisement, Film Daily Yearbook of Motion Pictures *(1926).*

Famous Players-Lasky, which had earlier been leasing space at the Paragon studio, returned to Fort Lee for a time when their New York studio plans fell behind schedule. Adolph Zukor had decided not to centralize all his production in California, but could no longer put up with the transportation difficulties associated with Fort Lee filmmaking. The new studio he was building in Long Island City (Astoria) was accessible from Manhattan by both bridge and subway.

NEW LASKY STUDIOS NEARING COMPLETION
World Peerless Studio Taken for Temporary Use of Dorothy Dalton

(from *Exhibitors Herald,* November 22, 1919, p. 44)

J.N. Naulty, general manager of the Eastern studios of the Famous Players-Lasky Corporation, has obtained a short lease on the World Peerless studio at Fort Lee, NJ, whereby a part of that studio not now being used may provide room for at least two companies. Dorothy Dalton, now working on *The Dark Mirror*, and Irene Castle, who will begin work shortly on a new picture [released as *The Amateur Wife*], will probably be the first to work there.

A delay was brought about in occupying the Amsterdam Opera House, the lease of which was announced a short time ago. The cables supplying current to the opera house were not large enough to hold the high voltage necessary to supply the Kleigs and Cooper-Hewitts used in the making of pictures. The New York Edison Company, at great expense, tore up 44th Street for a block and laid the necessary cable that would allow production to start on *Dr. Jekyll and Mr. Hyde.*

Work is being rushed on the new studio at Long Island City in an attempt to get the exterior concrete construction completed before the cold weather starts in. The laboratory exterior has been finished, the windows are being put in and everything made ready to receive the interior fittings. It is expected that in a short time the laboratory will be ready to handle all the developing and printing of the films made in the Eastern Studios.

At the beginning of 1920 a Newark exhibitor named Herman Jans leased the Peerless studio for a series of independent features, including *Love Without Question* and *Madonnas and Men,* a low-budget version of *Intolerance* which compared the excesses of ancient Roman with modern debaucheries. Later that year Emile Chautard directed *The Black Panther's Cub* here for William Ziegfeld. A liberal adaptation of Swinburne's "Faustine", it was the younger Ziegfeld's only film. Lewis Selznick was said to have acquired the studio when Ziegfeld left, but was himself forced out of business soon after. The World Film Corporation was adjudicated an involuntary bankrupt on July 26, 1921, when it could no longer maintain payments on two large mortgages, by then totaling more than a million dollars in interest and principal; the property was also in arrears on taxes. In April 1925 four local businessmen organized Fort Lee Studios, Inc. to reopen the Peerless, agreeing to pick up the back taxes, repair the roof, cover up the glass in the studio, and make an additional payment to the Peerless Feature Producing Company of $40,000 (plus interest) over five years. The new regime attracted director Wesley Ruggles, who made two George Walsh features here for Excellent Pictures, *The Kick-Off* and *A Man of Quality* (both 1926), but the studio was still caught in the general slowdown in local film production at the end of the silent period.

12

Cartoon Department

(Left): Picture Play, *August 1917.*

Any Day at Any Movie Studio

Impressions of an amusement
factory as seen from the ceiling.

By Charles Gatchell

During the silent film era, many newspapers and magazines employed cartoonists to supplement the work of their reporting and editorial staffs.

The motion picture fan magazines were no exception, and the most committed of these was *Picture Play*, which featured the work of Charles Gatchell and R.L. Lambdin in nearly every issue during the late 'teens.

Picture Play gave more attention to the east coast studios than any other fan magazine, so they sent their artists to Fort Lee rather than Hollywood, providing a unique impression of the way in which the movies had transformed daily life in an otherwise unexceptional suburban village.

Seen at Movie- Mad Fort Lee

By R. L. Lambdin

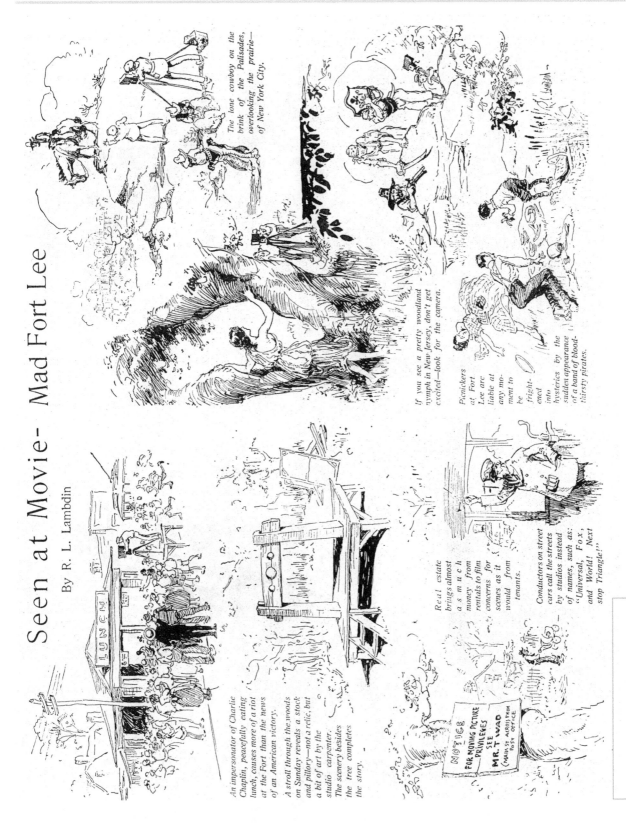

The lone cowboy on the brink of the Palisades, overlooking the prairie— of New York City.

If you see a pretty woodland nymph in New Jersey, don't get excited—look for the camera.

Picnickers at Fort Lee are liable at any moment to be frightened into hysterics by the sudden appearance of a band of bloodthirsty pirates.

An impersonator of Charlie Chaplin, peacefully eating lunch, causes more of a riot at the Fort than the news of an American victory.

A stroll through the woods on Sunday reveals a stock and pillory—not a relic, but a bit of art by the studio carpenter. The scenery besides the tree completes the story.

Real estate brings almost as much money from rentals to film concerns for scenes as it would from tenants.

Conductors on street cars call the streets by studios instead of names, such as: "Universal, Fox, and World! Next stop Triangle!"

NOTICE FOR MOVING PICTURE PRIVILEGES SEE MR. T IWAD (WALK ST. ACROSS FROM POST OFFICE.)

Picture Play, December 1917.

The Noon Hour at Fort Lee

By R. L. Lambdin

Hunger, like politics, makes strange bed fellows—and so does thirst and the tobacco habit.

Remarkable self-control while waiting for the director's dismissal.

More important than lunch.

Nothing doing. It's only scenery.

Trading jokes with the enemy.

In a Fort Lee lunch room.

Not a picnic party—just a few cave men at lunch.

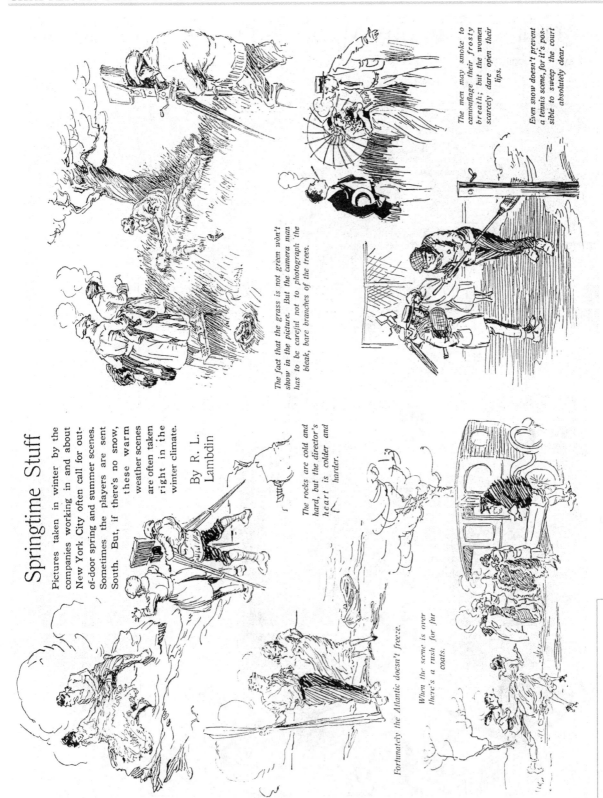

Springtime Stuff

Pictures taken in winter by the companies working in and about New York City often call for out-of-door spring and summer scenes. Sometimes the players are sent South. But, if there's no snow, these warm weather scenes are often taken right in the winter climate.

By R. L. Lambdin

The fact that the grass is not green won't show in the picture. But the camera man has to be careful not to photograph the bleak, bare branches of the trees.

The men may smoke to camouflage their frosty breath; but the women scarcely dare open their lips.

Even snow doesn't prevent a tennis scene, for it's possible to sweep the court absolutely clear.

The rocks are cold and hard, but the director's heart is colder and harder.

Fortunately the Atlantic doesn't freeze.

When the scene is over there's a rush for fur coats.

Making a Famous Movie Actress

In which occupation every one seems to work except the actress.

By Charles Gatchell

(*Left*): Picture Play,
November 1917.

Photoplay,
February 1917.

AT WORK WITH LADY YOUNG: ALL IN FORT LEE

Miss Young and Mr. Tearle talk it over while M. Capellani does a little shooting himself.

Yes, the signature is Clara Kimball's own.

The above isn't a' mob scene; it's the leading lady with some new photographic proofs; at the left, a little incidental music not at all hard on the ears.

59

13.
Fox

William Fox was a local film renter and exhibitor who, like Carl Laemmle, had run afoul of the Motion Picture Patents Company. Backed by John F. Dryden, president of Newark's Prudential Insurance Company, he formed Box Office Attractions in 1914 to distribute feature length films. Within a few months he was also producing them. The first, *Life's Shop Window,* was shot at the Éclair studio in Fort Lee or on a farm in Staten Island (or both), depending on which source one believes. Over the next few years Fox was in and out of many different studios in the New York and New Jersey area, although the Willat and Éclair studios on Linwood Avenue were the center of his east coast operations. Raoul Walsh, who started in Fort Lee in Pathé westerns, later established himself in Los Angeles working for D.W. Griffith. In 1915 he returned to Fort Lee and quickly became one of Fox's most successful directors. His description of the rough-and-ready approach to filmmaking he employed on films like *Regeneration* and *Carmen* is not inconsistent with the style of such later Walsh films as *The Cock-Eyed World* (1929) or *The Bowery* (1933). Walsh would become one of the most active east coast directors of this period, making most of his films in New York or New Jersey before finally settling in Hollywood in 1920.

THE CENSORS WILL HANG US

By Raoul Walsh

(from *Each Man in His Time* (New York: Farrar, Straus & Giroux, 1974), pp. 124–132.

Winter was breathing down our necks when we started building the sets for *The Siren of Seville* across the river at Fort Lee. I liked the script, but I was afraid of the weather. New Jersey is not like southern California, where it seldom freezes except in the mountains. Northerns came whistling down from Canada and dropped the thermometer forty degrees in a matter of hours. Cold would not necessarily hurt production, but cloudy skies could wreck us. When the sun went out, everything came to a standstill. It was that simple.

Fox was more optimistic. "Shoot it", he ordered, "if you have to use candles". He had signed Theda Bara for the female lead. I had met her, but never directed her. She seemed tractable, even humble, rare qualities in a rising star of her magnitude.

They were still looking for a male lead when the snow caught us. The papers labeled it the heaviest fall New Jersey had ever had. I believed them when I saw the drifts piled against the façade of the church, covering the plaza where much of the *Siren* action was scheduled to take place. We were sunk. Instead of sunny Spain, we had Lapland – and more snow was predicted. By the time the sets and the countryside thawed out, the third and last feature picture specified in my contract would be a year overdue.

We held a brain session in Fox's office. There were some people there with that strained look bankers and board chairmen assume when the market drops. Everybody seemed to be looking at me, as though the snow was my fault. "We'll have to scrap *The Siren*", Fox said, and Sheehan backed him up. "No good riding a dead horse any further than we have to".

"We can't do that", one of the money types objected. "The picture has already been sold." He was referring to the current practice of "booking in" a picture before it was made. The studio salesmen signed the theater owners in advance and took a down payment.

One of them got up and headed for the door. Fox barked at him, "Where are you going?"

"To kill myself", the salesman said. "I told Mendel in San Francisco that I had *seen* the goddamn thing."

"Why don't we compromise?" I looked around for support and got only blank stares. Nobody apparently was willing to stick his neck out any farther with the weather against us. "We're not licked yet." I was talking to keep up my nerve. "We'll make a different picture."

Fox scowled at me. "Like what?"

"A – a Russian picture." At least it snowed in Russia.

"Keep talking." Sheehan bit on his cigar. "What sort of Russian picture?"

My mind did handsprings. What indeed? Russia, Rasputin, revolution. I had it. Rasputin, the monk who took over because he could treat the czarevitch's hemophilia. Who would Theda Bara play? Only the best for Bara – one of the grand duchesses. Anastasia, the youngest one. Throw in a love triangle. Grand duke wants to marry her, but she is in love with – who cares? – make him romantic, a boyar colonel of hussars who has been spared by the Bolsheviks because of his war record. I could see it. Booze and balalaikas and Cossacks leaping over the furniture while the lovers, united at last, fade into the steppe. "Call your writers in", I yelled at Fox. "I'll tell you what sort of Russian picture."

We worked all that night, and by daylight we not only had a story but I had written a shooting script. I went out and sent a telegram to my brother George. "Get here. Run all the way." I had cast him to play Anastasia's big beautiful boyar. After working under Cabanne, he should be right for the part. When I went to brief Miss Bara, she laughed. "That's another of your Irish ideas." George arrived in five days.

The day we began shooting *The Serpent* (named for Rasputin, the snake in the Romanov grass) the sun was melting the snow. Soon everyone was walking around up to their ankles in slush. I had to postpone some of the scenes until later, including the end where Theda and George fled in a two-horse droshky to his country dacha. I intended to show Miss Bara, all cuddly in sables, snuggled up to her adoring lover and making a heart-

warming exit. For that I needed another snowstorm.

The script followed the story of Czar Nicholas and the trials and tribulations of the royal family under the malign influence of the rascally monk. In the mob scenes where the rebels stormed the Winter Palace, the mud was natural. It favored the sequences and gave them reality. Scenes like Rasputin seeming to hypnotize the czarina and bend her to his will while Nicholas was away at the front, and bullying Anastasia because she refused to marry the grand duke, I purposely crowded into the early shooting. For the love scenes, I waited for crisper days with plenty of sunlight reflected from the drifts. My shooting schedule was useless and finally I threw it away. The New Jersey weather, not I, was running the show.

After some alterations, the original church façade we had built for *The Siren* looked Orthodox enough to get by. For more atmosphere, we hired a troupe of Russian dancers who were breaking their national tour in New York. They put on a fine act and I wished I could have recorded their voices in the folk songs. Casting sent us some buxom blondes for serving girls in the café scenes. One of them came up and said, "Remember me, Mr. Walsh?" It was Dolly Larkin, about thirty pounds heavier.

When I asked what she had been doing, she shrugged. "You know show biz. Chicken one day and feathers the next." I was safe from her tongue now and I passed the word to keep her on for the entire picture. Fox's moneymen could afford a little charity for old times' sake. And so we put it together: Bara, the vamp of all time; George, dashing in his hussar uniform; a beak-nosed actor whose name escapes me playing Rasputin; peasants, dancers and café wenches – and all that lovely snow. Nicholas and Alexandra were two Broadway stage types, and for the "bleeder" czare-

vitch, casting picked up a juvenile who later became a star. We had the makings and soon we had a property. *The Serpent*, instead of being the dog I was afraid of, got a good press and made money.

Some unintentional humor that the public did not see came when we were nearly finished. The droshkies we used in the picture were converted wagons and the one Miss Bara and George took for their getaway had been worked over carelessly. When the lovers climbed in and the driver started off, the horses pulled the wagon off the runners, then broke loose, leaving the two stars stranded while the driver, still clinging to the reins, ploughed up a stretch of New Jersey real estate before someone caught the runaways.

After making *The Serpent*, Fox had not one but two big studios on his hands at Fort Lee. I went over there when the snow had melted. The streets of Moscow and St. Petersburg had returned to the Grand Plaza and *avenidas* of Seville, the original design. The hard winter had weathered the buildings and they looked more genuine. Those wheels in my mind began turning again.

In *Variety*, I read that Cecil B. De Mille was to make Bizet's *Carmen* with Geraldine Farrar. After inspecting the Fort Lee sets, I got back to Forty-Sixth Street in a hurry and found Fox and Sheehan in the office. I said, "Chief, De Mille's getting ready to shoot *Carmen* out on the Coast. We have all those *Siren* sets across the river. Why don't we beat him to it and make our own Carmen with Theda Bara? Wardrobe still has her Spanish costumes. What do you think?"

He jumped up and I thought he was going to kiss me. "You're still that damned Irisher with the Yiddisher kopf." He patted my back instead and I felt like a bird dog that had just retrieved a shot duck.

Sheehan was less demonstrative. He looked down his cigar at me. "Has De Mille started? If he has, we'd better forget it."

Fox picked up the ball. "We'll soon find out. Raoul, get on that telephone."

I asked the operator for the Fine Arts Studio in Hollywood and said I wanted to talk to Frank Woods. When he came on, he gave me the long-lost treatment: "Great to hear you. How's everything?" I asked about Griffith, then got down to business, and he said to hold the phone. When he came back, he told me that Frank Shaw, in publicity, thought De Mille would start making the picture within a week.

"A week yet?" Fox plumped down in his chair when I hung up. "We must hurry. When can you start rolling?"

I told him I had already begun and went home. That night, I sequenced the *Carmen* story on two pages. When I took them to the office next morning, Fox grunted. "Show them to Bara".

As I drove to Ninety-seventh Street, where she was living with her mother and sister, I could hear De Mille's cameras clicking in my ears. All she had to do was say no and *Carmen* would be grounded as far as Fox was concerned.

After she had read the story, she gave me that siren smile which was making her famous and nodded enthusiastically. "I like it. When do we start?"

On the way back to the office, the competition's cameras were no longer

---

(Right): When Willat's studio was first advertised for rent (as here in the Moving Picture World, *10 October 1914), his first customer was William Fox.*

(Below): Theda Bara in Raoul Walsh's production of The Serpent *(Fox, 1915) which despite Walsh's recollections had nothing to do with Rasputin, Princess Anastasia, or the storming of the Winter Palace.*

DIRECTION R. A. WALSH — WILLIAM FOX PRESENTS THEDA BARA IN THE SERPENT — Fox Film CORPORATION

---

threatening me. We had a sure-fire script, hailed on stage by the critics, and the sultriest star in America to play the title role.

I went to wardrobe and had them whip up some sketches of Spanish gypsy costumes and sent them to Miss Bara for approval. Two days later, we were at Fort Lee, making the first sequences.

Tall, dramatic Carl Harbaugh, fresh from theatrical triumphs, played Don Jose. He was dark enough to pass for a Spaniard and his patrician nose did the rest. Another stage actor who had appeared in several Paul Armstrong productions on and off Broadway was Escamillo. [Actually, Einar Linden played Don Jose, while Harbaugh played the toreador, Escamillo – ed.]

While I was shooting street scenes, I had a team of carpenters building the bull ring and I told the office I wanted some newsreel sequences of bullfights. Why, I reasoned, go to additional time and trouble shooting backgrounds when the same result could be obtained from splicing in the action as we shot it. There was a limit on what the censors would let us get away with; no *banderilleros* or killing, only cape work and perhaps the matador lining up the bull, pointing his *estoque* but not using it. It was like giving someone a piece of candy, then taking it away before they could eat it. The idea, not the real flavor, was as far as we could go.

With this in mind, I resolved on some new approaches. All the newsreels showed the matador working the bull in side shots, profiles as we called them. I would give the public something else for their money, perhaps by shooting along the bull's back, between his horns, catching the cape work and the animal's responses at the same time. That was the idea. I still had to figure how to do it.

The picture called for a gypsy encampment, so we built one on the shore of a lake four miles away. For the smugglers' boat, we used a shad fisherman's dory, which needed about four extras to row Carmen to the far side. I made the mistake of offering added pay for this bit. When I said "Action", and Miss Bara stepped into the boat, about twenty extras got in with her and the dory sank in six feet of water. She could not swim and we all ran into the lake to save her. Sopping wet, with her makeup running down her face and her hair a sodden mess, I expected her to explode and walk off the set. Instead, she gave a watery grin and said, "These things happen".

That was Theda Bara, of whom George said while playing opposite her in *The Serpent*, "She doesn't steal the show. She *is* the show." In all my directing career, I never met a more tolerant person. Today I shudder to think what a female star would have done in like circumstances. A doctor would have to examine her, after an ambulance had been called to take her to the hospital, where she would have demanded a complete physical and rest for a week. The studio would be lucky if it did not get sued and production would be held up indefinitely. Miss Bara was ready to go back to work in less than an hour. A duplicate of her costume, a toweling, a new hairdo, and fresh makeup was all she required.

We baled the boat, shot it rowing away, set up fifty yards down the shore, and shot it coming in, then packed and went back to Fort Lee.

The carpenters had finished building the bull ring, with seats for three hundred spectators. The main gate giving onto the plaza, which before had been the scene of the Russian royal family's comings and goings, was ready for the grand march of the matadors and their *cuadrillas*. Publicity had run a newspaper advertisement for a "male of Spanish descent with bullfighting experience". They got more than twenty applicants, who were handed a cape and told to do their stuff.

I finally picked a man named Valverde. He could really handle a *muleta*. I thought he was going to stab Grady with a pair of scissors while he demonstrated his skill with the *banderillas*. When casting asked him what work he was doing, after he proudly opened his shirt and displayed a long scar where he had been gored, he said he was a cook at Stanley's Restaurant. We signed him up and sent him to Fort Lee with six extras to break in for a team.

When I told Grady I would need three hundred more extras, as near to Span-

ish aristocratic types as he could manage, he got a gleam in his eye. "Do you remember those two thugs who recruited your passengers for *Regeneration*?" When I nodded, he giggled. "You won't' believe this. Their names are Levitt and Sweeney and they've gone into business. They're theatrical agents with an office on Thirty-second Street."

"Get them in here. This I've got to see."

Two very different gorillas showed up an hour later. Instead of dirty undershirts and denim trousers, they were now dressed in business suits, and one of them carried a cane. I almost laughed in their faces. They took my order and left.

Three days afterward, I shot the big bullfight scene. Valverde had taught the male lead how to use the cape and briefed the team how to march in and line up below the president and judges. They looked professional in their wardrobe suits of lights. Levitt and Sweeney showed up herding the additional extras, and I began to notice familiar faces. Slowly it dawned on me that those two fakes had brought back the same bunch of bums and pimps and whores we had hired to jump off the excursion boat. They were aristocrats, sure enough, but from Hell's Kitchen, not Spain. And it was too late to do anything about it.

The bugle blew for the grand entrance. The seats, looking like Murderers' Row, had filled up, and I sneaked a nervous glance at the bull. We had hired him and his owner, a farmer from Teaneck, with an option to renew if the first day's shooting had to be repeated. I made the farmer feed the bull bunches of alfalfa while we noosed his hind legs and tied them to a stout stake in the middle of the arena. Now he was standing quietly, munching hay and looking as though he did not have a care in the world.

While I had been filming the smuggler

Theda Bara and Einar Linden pose for a publicity shot for Carmen (1915). *Note local buildings behind the stone wall.*

A fellow came running through the gate. I walked over to him. "Did you see a bull?" His voice shook a little. "Something just went by in a shower of shit. Is that what it was?" Only God knows what was on that film in the DeBrie. When the bull was found grazing peacefully in a meadow about five miles away, the camera had vanished. Sam Kingston raised a lot of hell when he had to pay Benoit for it.

William Farnum, Theda Bara, June Caprice, Valeska Suratt and George Walsh were among the most important stars working for Fox in New Jersey, but because they constantly moved around among the various Fox studios it is difficult to know exactly where any particular films were made. During the winter some would work in California, some in Florida, and a few under the lights back east. Note how, by 1915, the reporter refers to the "Willat" and "Fox" studios interchangeably, and fails to differentiate the Éclair studio from either of them.

BILL FARNUM
A VISIT TO THE
WORK-SHOP OF A GENTLE
FIGHTING MAN

By John Ten Eyck (from *Photoplay*, October 1915, pp. 110–113)

Bill Farnum is the most unneutral chunk of masculinity I ever met. He may be an actor, but when God made him He moulded the actor from the cast of which fighting men are made.

sequences, another level of my subconscious had been mulling over the idea of a new approach to bull-ring scenes. The along-the-back-between- the-horns thing seemed like a winner if we could figure it out. Georges Benoit, Miss Bara's favorite cameraman, supplied the answer. He had a small DeBrie camera, which worked on a spring. I told him that I proposed to strap the DeBrie on the bull's rump and let the picture take itself and he said *"Magnifique!"* When the scene opened with the march in, the camera was sitting on the bull's stern about two feet forward of his tail. It could not miss the action as long as the bull's legs were fastened to the stake.

I then strapped the camera on the bull's rump, so that I could shoot through his horns. I told Valverde to show the leading man how to make a final *paso de pecho*. After the actor learned this technique, I told him to approach the bull. As he did, I turned the switch on the camera, which scared the bull. He jerked his hind feet loose and started galloping around the arena, bucking like a horse. The extra ran to a high fence, jumped over it, and we didn't see him for the rest of the day. However, the crowds of extras yelled and cheered as the bull kept up his bucking antics, trying to dislodge the camera. He finally made it over the barricades and disappeared in the general direction of Fort Lee.

Bill has the disposition of an angel, but let me say right here that there are many living today – right lusty varlets with their fists, too – who will absolutely guarantee the truth of this statement.

Not that he is a pug with a metaphorical chip on his shoulder. Not on your life; real fighters aren't that way. *Mister* Farnum is an American gentle man, as his fathers were before him.

For years before he played in studios he was a famous stage favorite, often appeared with his brother Dustin – as in *Arizona*, when the all-star revival was made in New York two seasons ago – and incidentally acquired fame as a yachtsman and as a hunter. Speaking of his stage prowess, who could have been a greater Ben-Hur?

Since applying his art to the screen, he has appeared in a number of photoplays of unusual length, the first of a long Farnum series which has been promised under Fox management.

His screen successes to date have been *The Nigger*, from Edward Sheldon's play; *A Gilded Fool*, clever screen adaptation of Nat Goodwin's old-time triumph; *The Plunderer*, and *Samson*, the last a shadowed replica of the Henri Bernstein play in which William Gillette starred at New York's Criterion theatre in 1908.

Farnum has a town house on Riverside Drive, New York, and a country place at Sag Harbor, where he spends much more of his time. Here he and Mrs. Farnum, and their little daughter, Olive Ann, are to be found every summer. There is another Olive Ann: the fastest sloop-rigged cat-boat on the north shore of Long Island. And there is a tall white flagpole from which flies an American flag from sunrise to sunset every day that the house is occupied.

Farnum has the reputation of being a hard man to interview. He won't talk about himself, and he's hard to find in any event.

But on the assignment I went forth. After much scarlet tape, interviews, conversation and telephonitis, I found myself in the subway; then upon a Hudson ferry at 128th Street, and, presently, in a big yellow car speeding along the top of the Palisades, en route to the Willat studio at Fort Lee. Here, I had been informed, Bill Farnum was sweating under the July sun, with "Bing" Thompson in command.

I entered a stone gate in the tall brick wall which apparently surrounds both the Fox and the World Film studios. Finding no one on guard save a genial old scamp in overalls, whom I bribed into friendliness with a cigarette, I marched undisputed into the studio. That was as far I got.

Thompson, with his coat off and hat on, was yelling instructions to a short, rather bewildered man with the best set of "actor's whiskers" which have ever risen above my horizon.

"What the – are *you* doing here?" he yelled

"I'm just hanging around waiting for Mr. Farnum – by appointment!" I added that as a life-saver.

"Well, you can't see him now. He's busy. I'm busy. We're all busy. Go Away. Come back in an hour."

After fifty minutes of angry consideration over a couple of steins, at the Fort Lee Hotel, I ventured to return.

Farnum   was   there.   So   was Thompson.

"Hello", I said, somewhat scared.

"Hello yourself", said Thompson, still short, but not nasty. "Sorry to have sent you away, but I can't work with anyone watching me. – if I know why."

"Artistic temperament?" I suggested, in a wave of maudlin bromidism.

"Not at all. Plain crankiness. I'm going to start up again pretty soon, and when I do, I'll have to ask you to look around the place awhile."

But before Thompson began again, he and Bill Farnum decided to negotiate a pork-chop apiece. I had been introduced. Farnum was coatless and collarless. I sat down with them at Thompson's rough but kindly invitation … .

In fact, shameful as it is to confess it, we three – a dramatic star, a director and a writer – sat around that table for an hour eating ice-cream and drinking (terribile dictu!) beer and talking of absolutely nothing but fights and fighting men.

"Of course, realism in these things in pictures as well as the stage is the great thing", I suggested, hoping to hook Thompson.

He sprang at the bait.

"The whole art of the theatre and the studio", he snapped, "is just simply this and nothing more – To do real things in an unreal way and make unreal things appear real. Think it over."

If you figure out just what the indomitable Frederick meant, you have the art and science of stage-craft in a nutshell.

"Realism", went on Thompson, "can be very easily pushed too far. In fact, it can become a ridiculous and criminal affair. Did you ever hear, Bill", he said, addressing Farnum, "of that director in Los Angeles who framed up the police against his mob?"

"No", said Farnum. "What happened?"

"Well, a certain director in California wanted a mob scene showing the police raiding the aroused citizenry, beating them up and driving them to cover. In order to achieve this, he went to a number of Los Angeles police officers, who in those days were allowed to take part in pictures when off duty, and offered each of them a five dollar bill to work in the particular scene he had in mind. When they had agreed to report at the time he indicated, he asked:

"'What would you do if you ordered a mob in the street to disperse and they wouldn't do it?'"

"In joyful accord the cops bust forth:

"'We'd beat 'em up!'"

"'Well,' said the director, 'that's what I want you to do tomorrow.'

"And they did. They clubbed those poor supers almost to death."

Thompson began to show signs of wanting to go to work again, which, of course, meant my departure.

"Mr. Farnum", I said, "I've got to leave before your brutal director harries me forth".

We shook hands.

"I'm mighty glad to have seen you", he said. "We've had a great little talk. I'm sorry this Simon Legreeful director insists on breaking up the party. We'll have another pow-wow after someone murders him, say. I wish you could come down to my place at Sag Harbor some time. I'll take you out in that sail boat you admired so much, and show you the wonderful garden Mrs. Farnum has. You know, my birthday is on the Fourth of July, and she has a wonderful patch of flowers in that garden that blossom into red, white and blue flowers every year, not on the third of July, nor on the fifth; but on the morning of the Fourth. For several years now, I've waited to see her flowers trick her; but they obey her as absolutely – well, as I do!

> By 1917 Fox was the most significant producer in the Fort Lee area, with activity going on in so many studios simultaneously that even the locals were confused. That year he made 39 films in the east, 40 per cent of his entire output.

William Farnum posing in a quarry with State Penitentiary guards during the production of Les Miserables (Fox, 1918).

THE FOX STUDIOS
A Thousand People Working In Four Studios At Fort Lee, New Jersey, Indicates The Scope Of This Company's Organization – And "The West Is Still To Be Heard From".

By Robert C. Duncan
(from *Picture Play,* February 1917, pp. 262–268)

Atmospherically the studio suggested a stock exchange. The "floor" was buzzing like "steel" on the jump. There was the rumble of shifting property, the shouted commands of the director, the undercurrent conversation of sundry employees, the clicking grind of the camera, and, above all, the melodramatic voices of the players themselves as they strutted before the lynx-eyed camera, speaking their lines.

Confusion was added to chaos in the motley jumble of sets, scattered scene decorations, and multiplied high-power lighting devices. Over all was the canopied roof of glass through which, on this particular winter day, the sunshine streamed, giving a weird radiance to the tempestuous scene of people and pillage. In this screaming scrimmage of things there was one factor that relieved the situation. Here and there in the big room were colorful maidens, sitting apart from the rehearsal where they were not needed for the moment. Gorgeously costumed and much be-rouged, they suggested huge hollyhocks or chrysanthemums, the greenhouse products of a pane-roofed studio.

Unnoticed, I slipped into this bewilderment. It might be said here, however, that I was already prepared for shocks. Arriving at Fort Lee, New Jersey, I inquired how to reach the Fox Company. I was rudely surprised to get conflicting answers. The street-car conductor was sure that if I got off at a certain street, and turned to my right, I would collide with it head-on fashion. An Italian vender of groceries directed me to bear to my left down such and such a road and then turn into a path through the woods, and I would come to it in five minutes. Other persons whom I asked had their own and very certain idea about where the company was located. The upshot was that all of them were right. The puzzle was solved when I discovered that there was not one but four studios flying the Fox banner.

The first studio to which I made my way was the Willat, the largest, best equipped, and most important. Several officials offered to show me around, but I decided to just wander about and see the plant, as an aimless tramp is supposed to see the world. It was a busy day for the imagination. Theda Bara was occupied in a set in the center of the great stage, seducing men before the all-seeing eye of the camera; while William Farnum, who was producing in the East, which was quite fortunate for me as most of his pictures are made in California, was living snatches from the life of a buxom hero in one corner. Just outside the door, looking off into a woods, June Caprice was kittenishly avoiding the arms of the famous Harry Hilliard.

I stood by the Farnum scene for a time and saw some unusually interesting things. On one of my previous visits to a Western studio I had seen an emotional actress play on her temperament with excellent results by using a victrola just outside the camera line. But Mr. Farnum did better, and he was the first man I had ever seen do it.

Sitting his bulky form in a chair, beside a table, he looked like a dressed-up mining man. His big, square shoulders and open face seemed almost out of place in a narrow inclosure of a three-sided drawing-room.

"All ready, Bill", the director called, and the smile seemed to fade from the actor's face. It was to be an emotional scene, and he was to have a battle with himself – mentally, of course – that was to be registered entirely from his features. Hardly had the director called for action, when the sorrowful strains of solemn music fell on my ears, and I looked around for their source. There, just beyond the scene, were two men, playing with as much pathos and sentiment in the refrain as possible, on a cello and violin.

Bill put his head in his hands, and the emotion began to bubble. Suddenly, while keeping the pose fixed so as not to spoil the scene, he cried: "Tell 'em to play slower – than music is getting on my nerves!"

Those standing about chuckled for a moment, but the films kept grinding, and Bill Farnum completed an exceptional bit of acting by defeating himself in the battle, emotionally speaking.

When the Farnum scene was over, I walked about the stage, watching various scenes, and discovered the interesting fact that two were being made at once for the same picture. This is quite unusual, for it is not often that two scenes are made at the same time, two entirely separate groups of players appearing at once. Even in this such was not the case, for Walter Law played in a set with Glenn White, Alice Gail, and Carey Lee, while Theda Bara posed for scenes of herself alone and "close-up". When Law finished one scene, he hurried over to Miss Bara's set and acted with her. No time was lost in waiting, for, through good fortune, Mr. Law did not have to wear different costumes in the two sets.

Such is the efficiency of the Fox plant; and Mr. Edwards, Theda Bara's director, is deserving of some praise, manipulating the scenes in order to use every minute of the players' time whenever it is possible. There was much to attract my attention, as the play was from a novel of sixteenth-century life, and it required a great deal of rehearsing to make every detail correct.

When Mr. Edwards had a minute to spare, I questioned him about something that had been bothering me for some time:

"How is it", I asked, "that Bill Farnum is in the same picture with Theda Bara? They don't seem to me to exactly harmonize in type, and, besides, I thought both were stars featured individually." He laughed a little, and then said:

"They aren't playing together. Bill has just stepped out for a second for a smoke between scenes, and the fellow you see who looks so much like him is Glenn White. They are almost doubles. Everyone speaks of the likeness."

Recalling the incident of the taking of two scenes at one time, I thought that the Fox plant must be the place where efficiency was originated, and decided to investigate the less absorbing but interesting departments where time and labor saving could be practiced.

More than passing mention should be given to the studios from the standpoint of equipment and production. They are veritable warehouses of supply when it comes to picture paraphernalia. An inventory of the stock is staggering in its completeness. Such is the importance attached to perfect working conditions that expense is not spared. An example of this is an entire street recently erected in the grounds of the company, said to have cost twenty thousand dollars. This represented the outlay for a single set. Architecturally it was a master piece, being a plaster duplicate of an ancient section of Paris, and it included the façade of the Notre Dame Cathedral.

The huge production plant is a humming factory of imagination. There are, not counting the extras that come in for a day or two and then leave, a hundred people employed there.

When a mob or battle scene is being filmed, the number often jumps to one thousand or more. Included in this small army are nearly a dozen stars who are famous in practically every corner of the world, such as Theda Bara, Bertha Kalish, June Caprice, Virginia Pearson, Valeska Suratt, Harry Hilliard, Stuart Holmes, and William Farnum, although most of the acting of the latter is done on the Pacific coast.

After looking at all the mechanical departments, I went out again to the stage. There, attracting more attention than anybody, was a little newcomer to the ranks of playerfolk. She occupied a conspicuous place in the center of the room, and gracefully submitted to the caresses and kisses that were lavished upon her. Considering her tender years, she scampered and frisked about lustily – that is, as much as the slender rope about her neck would permit. Nannie Goat was the mascot of the cast.

It happened to be pay day at the studio. The din and uproar incident to picture filming subsided when the genial paymaster began to circulate in the planetary system of movie stars and satellites. By common consent, work was suspended. Grim-visaged villains, heroic leading men, feminine luminaries, and sprightly ingénues, joined with the come-and-go element of lesser dignitaries and employees to celebrate the occasion. At all times it is a democratic, fun-loving crowd that peoples filmdom; and it needs but an excuse to unsettle its enforced dignity.

While everyone was in a happy mood, I asked many questions, and found out several things. Kenean Buel, who directs Virginia Pearson, and sometimes Theda Bara, was giving directions to stage men and property hands, pointing at plans that seemed like architectural drawings for a new mansion, but which were, in reality, designs of scenes.

When he finished talking, I got into conversation with him and found that he was "starless" for a few days or weeks, he did not know which, while he was waiting for Theda Bara to complete her picture.

"As soon as she is finished, or works on exteriors, I'll start Miss Pearson on her next film", he told me.

"Why not start now?" I asked. "Mr. Edwards is doing everything at once, it seems, and I thought Fox was a short way of saying 'save time.' There seems to be plenty of place for more sets."

"You've overcome every objection except the real one", he answered. "That is that Miss Bara never acts when Miss Pearson is playing in the studio. Probably it is due to the fact that they are both vampires, and their work might interfere or be too much alike. Each has her own little way of doing away with men, you know."

I laughed, and suggested that there was a possibility, too, that the company might run short of players if the vampires worked at the same time and put an end to all the male stars at once.

"We keep pretty busy, at that, though", Mr. Buel remarked. "We have six big directors, who are around most of the time. You've probably heard of most of them, and, if you haven't, you should, because they deserve every bit as much credit as the players. They are Jack Adolfi – John G. he is – James Vincent, Tefft Johnson, J. Gordon Edwards, Carl Harbaugh, and Miss Pearson's director. Guess who he is. William Bach does a lot of good and also hard work in the capacity of technical man. When we were taking *Her Double Life*, with Theda Bara, he broke all the records of the English army by building a big, armored car in two hours and a half, with the aid of the carpenter shops. But it wasn't quite bullet proof, because it was constructed of papier-mâché."

It was getting quite late, and I excused

Theda Bara as Esmeralda in The Darling of Paris *(Fox, 1917), based on Victor Hugo's* The Hunchback of Notre Dame. *The large glass building in the background is the Peerless studio.*

myself from Mr. Buel while I hurried across lots to catch a glimpse of the Lincoln studio – another branch of the Fox Producing plant – before going back to New York to spend the evening in the company of my typewriter. I was fortunate enough to find a play in progress with Stuart Holmes in the lead.

Owing to the fast-dimming light, it was necessary to employ a reflector device. Large mirrors held at the wide door of the studio reflected the rays of the reddening sun in spotlight glory upon the faces of the actors.

Thus they worked until the sun went down behind the Jersey hills and Director Harbaugh said the day's toil was ended. The players sauntered off to their dressing rooms, and I left, while Stuart Holmes was grumbling good-naturedly as he tried to dislodge his solemn red wig.

> *Motion Picture Classic* ran a series of features in which a reporter supposedly infiltrated one of the studios in the guise of a prospective extra. This one is typical in its ersatz "fly-on-the-wall" perspective, but useful in documenting mundane aspects of production which might otherwise have been ignored, such as the use of two studios in the production of *Camille*.

OUR *CLASSIC* EXTRA GIRL PLAYS AT THE FOX STUDIO

By Ethel Rosemon

(from *Motion Picture Classic*, August 1917, p. 39)

The Vitagraph studio had made me camera-wise, and it was like a veteran returning to the firing line that I sought my second engagement, this time with the Fox Company. And here the chief lesson I learnt, the lesson I will probably continue to engrave upon my memory during my subsequent trips into Screenland, is that an extra girl's life is one wait after another. Her patience must be limitless, her shoes painless, for good footwork is one of the main assets on the road to movie fame.

The Fox Company has no yard such as the one I graced so frequently in my attempt to make my debut on the Vitagraph screen. The studio is at Fort Lee. This means thirty cents a day carfare for the venturesome extra who goes over "on spec", as they say of a player who takes this chance of being engaged. Maybe it is to save the actor carfare, maybe it is to spare the director annoyance; anyway, a sign at the New Jersey studio notifies the applicant that all artists are engaged at the New York office on West Forty Sixth Street ...

Semi-occasionally, Mr. Kingston, the casting-director, known to every man and woman who has ever tried to enter Paradise by the extra gate, would appear in the doorway of his little office on the sixth floor of the Leavitt Building – how often have I joined the elevator chorus, "Out, six!" – and with a characteristic shake of his handsome gray head, say, "Nothing tonight, ladies and gentlemen". More frequently Mr. Foley, his assistant, would answer the numerous inquirers with "So-and-So is just finishing his picture", "So-and-So is reading his scenario", or "Director Blank has left for Florida or the Klondike".

Then one day when my face had become as familiar as the cold-cream "ads" in the subway trains Mr. Foley told me to return at 6:30 to see a director who was engaging extras. He said it with such an air of kindliness, of "Here is thy reward, good and faithful servant", that I blessed him for it. Not waiting for the final vote of Congress, I drafted all my make-up and prepared for the sea voyage to Fort Lee. On my return trip I found that I was not the only one who had been given the 6:30 call, for about ten familiar faces greeted me when I opened the door marked "Booking Office". There is still another door that leads to the inner sanctuary, closed except on special occasions to special people. But this was a special occasion and we were special people, so one by one we were permitted to pass thru the magic portal into the director's presence. The pretty applicant who entered before me returned with a happy smile which I caught as we passed in the doorway. But, alas, how short is the life of a smile!

"I've just engaged the last girl I need", the director announced as I stood before him.

"Sorry", Mr. Foley added. "I thought he needed more. Keep coming in. I'll probably have something else soon."

So I kept "coming in" and meeting some of the same girls day after day. They were typical New Yorkers – all well, many richly dressed. From their costly shoes to the latest creation of some smart milliner, they brought back the afternoon receptions that were the bane of my cub-reporter days.

"The girl in moderate circumstances has indeed a hard road to travel", I thought as I watched these pages from the fashion magazines.

"Some of them, I learnt as my acquaintance grew, had just returned from the road; others had homes in New York and were following the work for a lark or for added pin-money. With many the lark didn't last long, and as I stood in the group one afternoon after another I saw new faces take the places of the old ones who had turned elsewhere for amusement.

At last Mr. Foley told me to report at Fort Lee at 9:30 the next morning as a shopper in a Paris establishment.

"Dress as you would if you were attending a reception at Lucile's", J. Gordon Edwards, the director, added.

HERE IS A TYPICAL EASTERN STUDIO AND ITS "YARD," LOCATED IN THE MOTION-PICTURE COLONY AT FORT LEE, NEW JERSEY, PERCHED ON THE PALISADES ACROSS THE RIVER FROM NEW YORK

To me Lucile is not a name to conjure with, and the feverish excitement with which I over hauled my wardrobe in a wild endeavor to look like Paris before the war was fitting climax to my days of anxious waiting. Finally I collected an array of finery which I felt confident would make Lucile fear that a new fashion dictator was about to appear upon the horizon and started for Fort Lee at the appointed hour.

The boat that left the New York side at that hour of the morning carried a complete cargo of movie atmosphere. Several of the large Eastern studios are located at Fort Lee, and the modest ferry-boat seemed to be converted into a private yacht for directors, cameramen and player folks of all degrees. Filmland talk was everywhere, as actors hailed friends and acquaintances in hearty camaraderie. Not the least interesting were the costly limousines of the stars,

which the moment the gang-plank was in place whizzed past us and sped up the heights. The ordinary folks boarded the car that wound slowly up the hill, affording a wondrous view of the quiet Hudson and the busy metropolis beyond. For once I can truthfully say that I preferred the democratic mode of conveyance.

Arrived at the studio, I was directed to a tiny dressing-room which was occupied by two other players, one a concert singer who was breaking into pictures via the extra route, and the other a beautiful gray-haired lady who was playing a part. As we made up, the latter's gray hair became the subject of conversation.

"It literally turned white overnight", she told us. "I had a great sorrow – lost

my husband suddenly – and it took all the life out of me."

We began to sympathize.

"But I had life enough left to get another soon after", she hastened to add as she put the finishing touches to her eyebrows.

So we turned to the consideration of happier subjects.

But I was keyed up for adventure. I was anxious to get "on the set" and, above all, to see Theda Bara at close range.

Who has not read about her and who has not wondered what sort of woman would be revealed if one could extricate her from beneath the press-agent's fluent writings? She was starting *Camille* that day as a manikin in a Paris shop.

Soon my impatience became too large for my third of the tiny dressing-room, so I went out into the sunlit studio, a huge conservatory entirely enclosed in glass. Nature's lighting did away with the terrible glare of the overhead lamps, tho sidelights were being arranged judiciously here and there to heighten the artistic effect:

The call for luncheon interrupted my waiting and, tho I failed to obtain even a glimpse of "The Queen of the Vampires", I realized that in this case it was now or never, so I hastened to join the other extras at the Bungalow. Here, in exchange for the tickets supplied by Mike, a young man useful in general, and in this case in particular, around the studio, a substantial luncheon was served. It was 2 o'clock when we returned to the scene of our future flickerings.

In the meantime two professional models had arrived and had been assigned to my dressing-room. They had never been in pictures before and were at a loss how to make up. Glad of a chance to display my superior knowledge of the screen, I proceeded to decorate them. As they were two of the most beautiful girls I have ever had

the pleasure of meeting, I am sure I will be proud of my handiwork when it's screened.

Soon "On the set!" resounded thru the corridors. We all filed into the Paris fashion shop at Fort Lee, NJ, and the action began. Men and women were assigned their places in the general scheme of things, and I was stationed back in an alcove with three other women and one lone man. The director called the first manikin, and, amid admiring glances from the shoppers, the camera started to click its busy way.

Next Miss Bara appeared upon the scene, and there was no need of the warning, "All interested in the model!"

The costume the star was displaying for the customers of Madame Prudence was a black evening-dress, but one immediately became unconscious of the frock, of the whiteness of the wearer's skin, of the masses of dark hair simply arranged, as one gazed into the eyes of this woman who has done so many weird things – on the screen. One realized at a glance that her success was due to no trick of the camera, no guidance of a clever director, but to the intelligence and thought that shines from those deep gray eyes. They plainly said that Miss Bara does not take her art lightly, that she is ever reaching out for perfection. In short, the real woman behind the screen vampire has a mind that makes itself felt, that causes one to know intuitively that she would succeed in any line of work she undertook. Her voice as she talked to the director had that soft, low quality that made even the most loquacious extra stop to listen.

The fact that Mr. Edwards greeted all her suggestions with a hearty "Fine!" put the stamp of approval upon my first swift reading of Miss Bara. Evidently he knew from the past that his star had come on the set with a wealth of ideas gained from a careful study of

the script, that would prove profitable to even his wide experience.

Perhaps the Fox press-agent will not thank me for presenting his star vampire in such an unvampirish light. Probably I should picture her ranting up and down the studio and making things generally interesting. I will leave that to him and, tho not questioning his veracity or that of any man following the same calling, will simply state that I am pledged to tell the truth on the honor of an extra girl and that here you have a realistic picture of Miss Bara taken from the side-lines.

But the director says "Back to the scene!" Miss Bara is parading up and down the fashion shop, for Mr. Edwards was not satisfied to have his Camille come "out of the nowhere into the here", as she does in some of the stage versions, so he gave her a definite past in an establishment catering to the fast life of Paris. Here the Duke de Meuriac, who has come to the shop with his sister, the beautiful white-haired lady with "life enough to get another", sees in the manikin a resemblance to his lost daughter and adopts her while we all look on in wonder.

Up to this time I had been far from the camera's unlying eye, but now the field of action changed and camera-man and machine came into close range. Had they been lured hither by the hope of a "find" in the *Classic*'s extra girl? Not so. As I told you before, these are true stories.

But two of the girls who shared the alcove had confidentially remarked that they were not ordinary extras, but embryo stars there for a test. I could almost hear their hearts beating high with thoughts of future fame as the tripod was set in place for a close-up. However, their hopes were not nourished by the lone man ensconced in the alcove. In a fatherly way, in spite of his youthful appearance, he pointed out the stony path up the Moving Picture hill and did all he could to

The modiste's shop in the Theda Bara version of Camille *(Fox, 1917).*

change their rosy dream into a weird nightmare. He gazed at me as if he admired my good sense in not looking beyond the five dollars I was earning that afternoon, and I began to feel like a very superior person. I hope the camera will register that fact.

About 4 o'clock the sun began to forsake the studio and Mr. Edwards called "All thru!" There was to be a reception the next day at which the Duke would introduce his ward to his Fashionable friends.

"Would I be invited?" that was the question.

Good luck! Mr. Edwards told me to report the next morning in evening dress.

This time eight other girls and I were assigned to a room in the Éclair studio about half a block away. At least, we started with eight. An hour later two more rushed in breathlessly.

"Oh, girls, we did such an awful thing!" one of them explained. "This is our first day in pictures. We got into the wrong studio. A dressing-room door was open. The place looked cozy, so we walked in. A few minutes later a maid appeared as if by magic.

"'I guess we'll keep this dressing-room,' I smiled. 'Will you help us to make up?'

"'I'd like to but I can't,' she returned. 'You see, Miss Suratt wouldn't like it.'

"'What has she got to say about it?' Ida inquired.

"'Well, I'm her maid and this is her dressing-room and' – she hesitated – 'she doesn't like extra girls to occupy it,' she concluded, timidly.

We took the hint and quickly viewed the room from the other side of the door. Sure enough, there in letters so large that only two blind pieces of atmosphere could have failed to see it was the star's name.

"We simply fell out of that studio and here we are. Won't some one please make us up – that is, of course, if Miss Suratt won't mind?"

Half-a-dozen rushed to the aid of the newcomers, for they are a happy, helpful lot, these extra girls.

"Don't forget to take your powder-puffs with you", admonished Jackie Vaughn, who shared my popularity with Betsy and continued it all the way up the line to the directors. "You never can tell when you'll get a close-up. I had one a couple of weeks ago. My nose was greasy. If I never become a star I'll know that my shiny nose was my downfall."

"Wouldn't it be great to be a star and not have to arrive at the studio until you pleased?" a pretty blonde girl yawned. "My idea of heaven is to tumble from bed into a purple limousine and be whirled to Fort Lee."

"Wake up and run for the boat, Geraldine", her friend laughed as the girls filed out the dressing-room and made their way down the country street to the studio.

Again we were sent to the Bungalow before the scene was taken.

"You can't put anything over on Miss Bara", one of the girls at my table remarked. "Just heard the property-man throwing a fit because he had to

Fox cameraman Joe Ruttenberg with his Pathé. Ruttenberg later won four Oscars in Hollywood.

go 'way down into the heart of New Jersey to get camellias. She wouldn't wear fakes."

"She's right. Why should she?" another added.

But probably we had dawdled too long between eating and gossiping. Anyway, there was soon a frantic call for the extras to appear at the reception. Being rather uncertain about the quality, quantity and reality of the

Duke's refreshments, we hated to leave the pie, so silence reigned while peach, apple and cocoanut disappeared.

This time the scene was one befitting the residence of nobility. Expectation filled the air, for the Duke's ward was to be introduced to society. How would she take it, and how would they take it? We would soon see.

An unconscious murmur of admiration went around the room. Miss Bara was descending the stairs. The reflection from a mirror held off scene in the direct rays of the sun shone on her hair and lit up her eyes, making her look like some beautiful portrait come to life. The old Duke tottered forward and proudly escorted her thru the throng. He was sure she would create a sensation. She did. As she passed, we shrugged our shoulders and turned our backs upon her.

"Breaking into society, indeed – a shop – girl!" we murmured.

How we hated to do it! But Mr. Edwards had ordered this for all – all but the men. True to the conception prevalent among male humans, tom-cats are non-existent for this wise director.

One man was particularly fascinated by the beauty of the Duke's ward. This was Walter Law, who as Count de Varville afterwards becomes Camille's lover.

"I wonder where they'll find that cute little cottage in the country where Camille goes to live with Armand Duval after she gives up the Count and the gay life of Paris", remarked one girl who boasted that she knew the book "from cover to cover". "How do you think Miss Bara will get consumption?"

"Artistically", I answered.

"Yes, I suppose so", she assented. "Wouldn't you just love to play that part and have Albert Roscoe whisper in your ear, 'Courage, Camille; you will live till spring'?"

New Years Feature

Starting SUNDAY, Dec. 31

Big Double Program

GEORGE WALSH
Supported by
ANNA LUTHER in

'The Island of Desire'

A romantic and out of the ordinary tale of the South
Sea Isles.

and

THE SOCIAL PIRATES

The First Screamingly Funny
Foxfilm Comedy. Two Reels
of uninterrupted joy.

Miller's
Junction of Spring and Main at 9th

CHRISTMAS
SPECIAL

Week Beginning
SUNDAY, Dec. 24
FAMOUS
VALESKA SURATT
The Screen's Most Gor-
geously Gowned Actress in

"THE VICTIM"

A Magnificently Staged
William Fox Story that grips
and holds the interest from
the opening scene to the big
Dramatic climax.

Herbert Heyes and Claire
Whitney head the splendid
supporting company.

Next week you will be presented with a splendid photograph of handsome George Walsh.

"Personally, I'd rather have Mr. Edwards shout, 'Cheer up, old girl; you'll have another day's work tomorrow,'" I answered materialistically, and with a withering smile my romantic friends turned her back upon me.

"Perhaps you will", volunteered Jackie Vaughn, who had taken me under her wing. "I hear there's another scene with extras. Ask Mr. Foley about it."

"Good; more copy", I registered mentally, when at the end of the day Mr. Foley promised he would engage me for the next scene.

"I can't tell what day it will be, tho. Keep coming in", was his parting instruction.

And then old Sol began to get disagreeable. Day after day Mr. Foley informed me that the scene had been postponed on account of the weather.

(Above): For its Christmas show, Miller's Theater in Los Angeles promotes Valeska Suratt, "the screen's most gorgeously gowned actress", in The Victim *(Fox, 1916).*
(Below): Theda Bara succumbs to consumption in Camille. *Albert Roscoe as Armand.*

The weather is still with us. The *Classic* is going to press and still I "keep coming in".

At the Fox office this afternoon I heard some terrifying news.

"Did you know that Miss Bara had been thrown downstairs at the studio today?" the man who had been my companion at the Duke's reception inquired.

"Oh, what happened?" I gasped.

"Don't look so frightened", he said, soothingly. "The Count got peeved because Camille no longer loves him and took this gentle method of showing his feelings. But don't worry; Camille will live till spring."

So the ways of vampires are laid in bumpety places. Would I rather wait at the gate for a day's work as an extra or be thrown downstairs by a discarded lover? It depends upon the stairs.

While *Cleopatra* and *A Tale of Two Cities* (both 1917) were shot on the west coast, many of Theda Bara and William Farnum's most elaborate productions were still made in Fort Lee. For *Les Miserables*, Fox rebuilt much of Paris and borrowed a battalion of troops from the 71st regiment in Van Cortlandt Park to storm the barricades.

THEDA BARA ENACTS JULIET
Famous Actress Will Be Seen In An Elaborate Fox Interpretation Of The Shakesperean Tragedy

(from *Moving Picture World,* October 21, 1916, p. 418)

William Fox announces Theda Bara, the great emotional actress, in a mag-

nificent and colorful picturization of *Romeo and Juliet*, Shakespeare's tragedy. This super-production will be released as a part of the regular Fox program. It will be shown to the public for the first time at the Academy of Music.

This epochal film, which adheres precisely to the poet's masterly play, has been in work for many weeks at William Fox's studio in Fort Lee, New Jersey. Thousands of dollars were spent to insure absolute accuracy in details, as well as in essentials. From many standpoints the picture should prove one of the real triumphs recorded in the history of the silent drama.

The settings throughout are entirely worthy of the production. Among those particularly attractive are the fateful masquerade ball, the beautiful balcony scene, and the city of Verona. The story has not been sacrificed in any attempt to obtain extra film footage. It was decided that five reels would make the most effective screen version of *Romeo and Juliet* and only five reels were taken. Acting, direction, scenario, photography, film cutting – everything in connection with the picture was placed in charge of experts.

It is needless to dilate upon Miss Bara's eminent fitness for portraying before the camera the intensely tragic character of Verona's fairest maid. Miss Bara's success as an emotional artist has been recognized internationally.

Mr. Fox engaged a supporting cast which is strong and well balanced. Harry Hilliard gives a remarkable presentation of the role of Romeo.

Among the principals in the cast Glen White, Walter Law and John Webb Dillon have acted in many of William Fox's recent releases. Einar Linden will be recalled for his splendid performance as Don Jose in the Fox picturization of *Carmen*. Alice Gale has recorded a thirty years' success on the stage; for several seasons she acted the Nurse in the legitimate. Jane and Katherine Lee will not be missed from the production. These two children have the parts of pages. The name of J. Gordon Edwards, who has made most of the Bara photoplays, guarantees the excellence of the direction.

"LES MISERABLES" BEST WORK OF WILLIAM FARNUM

By Peter Pad

St. Louis Times (as reprinted in *Exhibitors Bulletin*, October 1917, pp.16–17,19)

Over in Jersey, at one of the Fox studios – Fort Lee is full of them – William Farnum is doing the biggest work of his screen career.

For the past six weeks he has lived Jean Valjean, in the new Fox production of *Les Miserables*.

When I saw him "working" under the glass top, his estate was that of Mayor, and his hair was iron gray, but Farnum said the portrayal of the character of Jean Valjean required nine different makeups, and presently his hair would turn snow-white.

"I have at last gotten rid of my beard", he added with evident satisfaction. "My director, Mr. [Frank] Lloyd, has reached the stage where he demands realism at any cost, and it took me two weeks to grow a beard that would satisfy him."

The "set" before us represented Javert's office. Fantine was about to be dragged

Authenticity of setting in Les Miserables *(Fox, 1918), one of the most elaborate films ever produced in Fort Lee.*

before the Justice by the gendarmes. Farnum was ready and waiting for the subsequent scene with the woman. (The waiting game is played by great and small in the motion pictures. Even the million-dollar star is not exempt.)

The famous actor is a man of much dignity and gentleness of manner. He speaks in measured accents, and his voice is low and well-modulated. The temperature was abnormally high, he wore a heavy coat and a heavy silk hat, and must have been thoroughly uncomfortable, but his serenity remained undisturbed.

The "acting up" of the lights caused an exasperating delay. Director Lloyd lost his patience completely, and spoke sharply to the perspiring electrician, who, high up on a ladder, struggled ineffectually to gain control of the refractory arc. The star, whatever his real feelings in the matter, wore a look of patient resignation.

Completely absorbed by part

"I hope, and believe, this will prove to be my best work", said Farnum. "No part has ever so completely absorbed me as does Jean Valjean, and surely the production is far ahead of anything in which I have appeared. Detail and historical accuracy mean much to those who know, and we have gone deeply into the matter, sparing neither time nor trouble – nor Fox's bank account.

"Take, for example, the floor of the prison at Toulon. That was made of real flagstones, with damp earth showing between the jagged edges of the stone. To show the dampness of the dungeon floor it had to be thoroughly wet every morning, and then allowed to dry out slightly while we were making the prison scenes.

"The floor you see in the set before you is of similar construction. It probably seems a small matter to you, but if you knew what a troublesome undertaking that floor was, you would realize how relentlessly Lloyd is striving for realism.

"Then there is the village of D – – , mentioned in Hugo's immortal story, and streets and corners of Paris. In producing a story laid in a period not our own, it would be fatal to 'shoot' scenes at the first convenient corner. We must build our village and our city streets. Nowadays this is a terrific undertaking. Burlap stretched on framework no longer is permissible as building material. Burlap walls are sure to shake in a high wind, and thus shake the spectator's confidence in the reality of the scenes pictured, so lumber has replaced the old standby.

"All the streets are made of cobblestones, and to preserve illusion as to time and place the location must be sufficiently secluded to insure against the untimely appearance of the anachronistic automobile or trolley.

"The scenes showing Jean Valjean as a convict were taken in an old Jersey stone quarry which is worked by convicts. The prisoners appear in the picture. This might easily have been 'faked' with 'extras,' but why should it be, when by going a little out of our way, we can get the real thing?

"The cost of the entire production? That I cannot say. I do know, however, that each little village costs $20,000 or more, and I am afraid to estimate the cost of the interiors and the thousand and one incidentals."

Fantine had just sold her glorious hair. An old character actor standing idly by – he is inevitable in the studios – volunteered the information that Lloyd was a great one to rehearse and rehearse, and take and retake until the scene was shot to his complete satisfaction.

But, according to the garrulous one, Miss Gretchen Hartmann, the Fantine, had on a $75 wig, and Lloyd not only dispensed with a rehearsal of the cutting of her hair, but brought a double shot to bear upon the operation –

two cameras working simultaneously avoided the successive shots that are taken of every scene, and made the single $75 wig do double duty.

Hose instead of sprinkler

Apparently there was a heavy rain on when Fantine was arrested, and just before she was dragged before Javert, who was none other than our old friend of "Dry Town" days, Hardee Kirkland – Miss Hartmann had turned upon her a hose instead of a sprinkling can.

The dripping, bedraggled and tattered woman was haled before the Justice and sentenced. Fantine struggled and raged. Repeated rehearsals bringing this to the point of impressiveness that satisfied the director, he declared himself ready for the "shooting" of the scene.

This was the cue for a string orchestra, stationed just outside the set, to tune up. Here was an innovation. Instead of the accompaniment of carpenters' hammers, Farnum had a 'cello and violin as an obligato to his work.

It seemed rank affectation, but Farnum is too evidently sincere to permit of the suspicion that he would simulate temperament and sensitiveness. Undoubtedly he is a believer in the charms of music.

And the ubiquitous idle actor enlarged on the virtues and the mission of the music. "Mr. Farnum always has it", said he. "In California, even when we went to Catalina on location, the string trio accompanied us. Farnum feels that it helps everyone."

But, apparently, the charm was not working perfectly in the case of Fantine. Even ten successive renditions of the "Elegie" of Massenet fail to get her through the scene.

There was a retake and another rehearsal. Fantine's arrest proved to be a complicated affair. It is a big scene and Lloyd was determined on just the right effect.

Fresh drenching for Fantine

The industrious musicians persevered. Fantine got a fresh drenching to the strains of the "Elegie", she was dragged and sentenced to the sentimental phrases, and these accompanied her pleadings and ravings.

"Farnum contends that the music establishes mood", babbled on the aged actor. "It really is a great help in giving spontaneity to the expression of emotion. Tears come readily to this music."

His words carried conviction. In fact, after the fifteenth repetition of the tune, tears were with difficulty restrained.

But Fantine's arrest was finally a feat accomplished, and there was a merciful respite from Massenet.

The next was the Farnum scene. The tune was arranged to a "Valse Triste". Fantine, still in the grasp of the gendarmes, recognizes the Mayor as he enters. She rushes at him, and hurls invectives at him until she froths at the mouth. Farnum's quiet dignity makes a fine contrast to her mad ravings.

All went well during the rehearsal of the difficult scene. Fantine's frothing was realistically accomplished through the agency of peroxide of hydrogen. A property man stood near with the bottle, ready to administer additional frothings if required.

Then, when all was in readiness for the shooting, the obstreperous arc again behaved badly. After a few ominous flickers it went out entirely.

Lloyd stormed. Farnum was the picture of amiability. He came off the set, spoke pleasantly to the lovely, newly arrived Jewel Carmen – the Cozette to be – and waited.

Eat on the Fox "lot"

My guide from the Fox offices suggested luncheon. The restaurant is on the Fox "lot", but is patronized by the players from the various studios near. A motley gathering was found there.

It seemed the melting pot of the races with a vengeance, and the foreign potentate rubbed elbows with the domestic tramp. There was no color line drawn, and blacks and whites mingled freely – only the white men all were of a yellowish hue.

The battle with the lights was still on when we returned to the studio. Mayor Farnum was discussing a sandwich, and Fantine was busy with a chocolate sundae, though the first aid to the depiction of frenzy – the bottle of peroxide – was clutched closely.

At the last the electrician expressed confidence in the pesky arc. This seemed fully warranted. The blaze was hot and steady.

But no sooner were the players well at work, and the "string orchestra" for the twentieth time had rendered the whiny, slow waltz as an obligato to the frothings of Fantine, than, with diabolical perverseness, the light went "bingo", as they have it in the studios, and ruined the scene.

Fantine's froth material was running low and Lloyd's patience was running lower. The only thing that did not seem in danger of giving out was the tolerance of the star – his patience was monumental. He waited. The players waited. The camera men waited.

After an hour of gloom, a light drizzle began. Then the director decided the waiting was over for the day and told everybody to go home.

My persevering guide suggested a third studio, and Virginia Pearson posing in interiors.

But on the way we encountered that beauty, also the victim of circumstances, making for New York in her sporty roadster. And all along the road were to be seen automobiles laden with players, and camera men, and directors, who had been driven off "location" on account of the rain.

Inanimate objects, and the elements, after all is said and done, are in control of the situation, and the director who finishes a picture on schedule time simply is playing in luck.

> At a time when hamburger was renamed "Liberty Sandwich", the motion picture industry was in the forefront of anti-German propaganda whipped up by the Creel Committee and the Office of Public Information. In Fort Lee, William Fox produced films like *Swat the Spy* with the Lee Sisters and *Miss U.S.A.* with June Caprice, but he maintained the same degree of vigilance off-screen as on.

WILLIAM FOX WILL DISMISS PRO-GERMANS

(from *Moving Picture World,* June 29, 1918, p. 1859)

In line with his energetic patriotism as shown in his successful campaigns for the Jewish War Relief Fund, the Knights of Columbus, and the Red Cross, William Fox, at the close of the fourth annual convention last week at the Hotel Biltmore of the Fox Film Corporations exchange managers and executives, took steps toward the discharge from the Fox organization of any employee who is not 100 percent American.

Mr. Fox called on all the branch managers present to submit confidential reports as to anybody whom they even suspected of not being true Americans. These reports, Mr. Fox announced, would be thoroughly investigated, and if any employee in the Fox forces should be found to be even slightly pro-German he would be dismissed.

Special effects workers at the Fox Fort Lee studio produced this elaborate miniature of an entire city around 1918. Title unknown.

While many other producers began to concentrate activity on the west coast in 1918–19, William Fox was convinced of the importance of staying in the east. He told his Hollywood production chief, Sol Wurtzel, that conventional star vehicles would continue to be made in California, while "specials" would be produced in the east, where he could supervise them directly.

MOB SCENES IN FOX'S "THE CAILLAUX CASE" ARE REAL

(from *Moving Picture World*, May 18, 1918, p. 1008)

One of the most striking features of *The Caillaux Case*, the William Fox film expose of the pro-German activities of Bolo Pasha and Joseph and Mme. Caillaux in France and America, is the thrilling realism of the mob scenes. It is declared by the Fox management that never in the history of the organization has a mob become so violent in its action and gone so completely beyond control as in the scenes where Mme. Caillaux is acquitted of the murder of Gaston Calmette and later dragged through the streets of Paris.

As a result of this mob violence several people were seriously injured. Two, a man and woman, were knocked unconscious; another man's head was badly cut by a flying missile, and Madlaine Traverse, who played the leading feminine role, was so roughly handled by the rioters that she has since been under the care of a physician. In addition, the mob wrecked part of the sets. Order was restored only when Director Richard Stanton and his assistants plunged into the fray and by sheer force compelled the extras to subside from their violent demonstration.

True to the history of the famous trial of Mme. Caillaux in Paris, Mr. Stanton had arranged for a demonstration of the populace immediately following her acquittal. He urged the crowd to be realistic. But this was before the final scene of the trial had been enacted and before the spectators had been roused to a high pitch of excitement by the closing action. Besides, many of the extras were French and had pronounced opinions on the Caillaux affair. They hardly awaited the signal to begin a wild demonstration. This demonstration, increasing with its own momentum, soon became a riot.

The courtroom became a bedlam of wild, shouting, maddened figures, completely oblivious of the fact that they were acting before a camera, and intent only on inflicting damage on the other side in a free-for-all fight. Chairs, books, court paraphernalia were hurled through the air. These missiles failing, even the court benches and pieces of the railing were used by the fiercely battling men and women. Meanwhile, the cameraman recorded on the film every detail of the violent conflict.

The same realism was evident in the street scene, where the mob finally gets in its clutches Mme. Caillaux, the assassin of the editor of *Figaro*. Remembering what had taken place in the courtroom, Director Stanton this time had warned the mob to control themselves. Miss Traverse, fearing the consequences, had tied on her clothing and had provided herself with a special bodyguard which was to protect her if the attacks became too violent. But it was all in vain. So vividly had she portrayed the heartless villainy of the ambitious adventuress that the courtroom violence was repeated in all its intensity.

The crowd seized her, pummeled her, dragged her over the stones, tore her clothing. Her pleas for mercy fell on deaf ears. Not until she was completely exhausted and had sunk to the ground pressing to her lips the Tricolor of France, did the mob leave her. Then, covered with scratches and bruises, she was able to walk to her dressing room only with the aid of Director Stanton and her maid.

TWO FOX PRODUCTIONS IN ONE

(from *Moving Picture World*, December 28, 1918, p. 1541)

Two productions made for one release is the record established by *Woman!*

William Fox.

Woman!, the William Fox Standard Picture, which Evelyn Nesbit is making at the Willett [sic] studio at Fort Lee. One of the scenes in *Woman! Woman!* shows a motion picture, *The Bride of Bushido*, being exhibited on the screen in a New York motion picture theatre.

To obtain *The Bride of Bushido*, Kenean Buel, director of *Woman! Woman!* was obliged to hire a company of players to portray Japanese roles, write a scenario that would convey a point necessary in *Woman! Woman!* and then stage *The Bride of Bushido*, just as if it were one of the William Fox releases.

As if this were not trouble enough for one director, the Japanese actors went on strike in the middle of the filming and thus tied up not only *The Bride of Bushido*, but *Woman! Woman!* An adjustment of the wage schedule, however, soon got both plays under way again.

FOX HIRES RAILROAD FOR THRILLER
Director Stanton Stages Real Train Wreck
for Henry Blossom's Melodrama "Checkers"

(from *Moving Picture World*, April 26, 1919, p. 528)

William Fox leased an entire railroad system in New Jersey, Sunday, April 13, to put a realistic train wreck into a picture. For half a mile the burning cars sped down a grade toward an open draw bridge in the Raritan River, while more than two thousand persons looked on one of the most interesting dramatic spectacles they had every seen. And when the crash came as the train tipped over the open draw into a deep channel of the river they gasped in astonishment.

Director Stanton gets realism

Richard Stanton, director of *Checkers*, a forthcoming Fox picture, which it is said, will be one of the largest spectacles of the year when released some time in the future, spent between $4,000 and $5,000 to produce this scene, which did not run more than 200 feet. It was undoubtedly one of the most costly of picture operations. But before Mr. Fox went to Europe some weeks ago, he insisted that his incident of the story should not be slighted.

Checkers a big spectacle

When Mr. Fox purchased the play, "Checkers", founded on the famous novel of that name by Henry Blossom, Jr., he determined to utilize every realistic incident of the story to make a picture which should be one of the great spectacles of the year. For that purpose he gathered a company of many first class screen actors, including Thomas J. Carrigan, Robert Elliott, Jean Acker, Ellen Cassity, Tammany Young and others. The story is one of real life, and its scenes run from vicious fights to dark and dangerous passages in an underground Chinese quarter to brilliant scenes on one of the great race tracks of the country. In fact, Director Stanton is now at the Havre de Grasse track in Maryland.

Friday, April 9, 1920 / Saturday, April 10, 1920 — diary entries.

Hal Sintzenich was a free-lance cinematographer in the silent era who documented his daily activities in an extensive series of diaries, now in the Library of Congress. He had recently moved to Englewood at the time he wrote these entries in April 1920. During the day he was working at the Fox studio in Fort Lee on the serial Bride 13. *His visit to the Paragon lab was connected with an African expedition film he had photographed earlier. The "Mr. McAvoy" he refers to is Henry McAvoy, an assistant director at Fox. As the son of an ex-mayor he was apparently able to fix speeding tickets and order the Hackensack Police Chief to open draw bridges. Already notorious for shooting a man during a riot at the Goldwyn studio, he accidentally blew himself up later that year while experimenting with motion picture pyrotechnics (see page 333).*

Fox planned to build his new eastern production center in Queens, but later decided on the west side of Manhattan. When the cornerstone of the new studio was laid in 1919, the great days of film production in Fort Lee were obviously at an end. With the war over, the coal shortages overcome, and the flu epidemic at an end, several important studios had also announced renewed interest in eastern production. Unfortunately, they were not talking about Fort Lee. The opening address at the ceremony was given by Rabbi Mayer Kepfstein of Temple Adath Israel, but Fort Lee also had a representative at the ceremonies.

FOX CORNERSTONE LAID IMPRESSIVELY

(from *Moving Picture World*, June 21, 1919, p. 1777)

... The Rev. Justin Corcoran, of the Church of the Madonna in Fort Lee, the next speaker, a motion picture enthusiast and supporter, said:

Fort Lee misses movies

"While we of Fort Lee, as a community, feel great pleasure in the progress of this corporation, we also feel lively regret at its departure from us. Personally, I have seen at Fort Lee so many battles fought in our back yards, so many boys run away, so many Huns killed, so many people married, that I will be lonesome without you.

"There is one favor that I am going to ask in behalf of the clergy before speaking my final word. Please do not make us in future pictures such 'sissies' as we have been in the past. We clergymen have hearts just as strong as any other men."

Some Fox units were already working in the Manhattan studio by February 1920 , but the laboratory facilities there would not be ready for several months. The difficulty in getting a single preview print across the Hudson during a bad winter storm suggests one reason for the abandonment of the Fort Lee studios.

NEW YORK REVIEWERS SEE AND ADMIRE "The Strongest" Despite Blizzard

(from *Moving Picture World*, February 28, 1920, p. 1508)

Despite one of the most severe snowstorms which New York City has experienced in years, William Fox, overcoming all traffic obstacles, introduced to the trade press on Thursday, February 5, the all-star super-production of Clemenceau's great and only story, *The Strongest*.

With all traffic lines blocked between the big new Fox studio building in West Fifty-fifth street, into which Fox Film Corporation recently moved, and the Fox laboratories at Fort Lee, the outlook for the trade showing of this widely heralded special looked rather dark. Mr. Fox, however, came to the aid of the projection department by turning over his private car, and in this high-powered machine the Fox messenger raced from the new building northward to the Fort Lee ferry in time to connect with one of the few boats that were kept running.

The trade paper reviewers, meanwhile, were entertained by the current issue of Fox News, a Sunshine Comedy entitled *Her Naughty Wink* and the latest Bud Fisher Animated Cartoon starring Mutt and Jeff in a timely subject called "*I'm Ringing Your Party*". With these three interesting features before them, the reviewers passed the time pleasantly.

A sensational entry

The company's messenger on his return trip raced from the Fort Lee studios to the Fifty-fifth street building through snowbanks wheel-high, testing the power of the engine to the last ounce. Finally with his engine smoking hot, and snow piled high on all exposed portions of the big machine, Mr. Fox's chauffeur swung the car onto the Fifty-sixth street ramp which leads to the second floor of the big structure, and the messenger rushed in with the film. It was a sensational introduction for the sensational film.

The production of *The Strongest* at once impressed all who saw it as distinctive and without fault as regards the detail of its French settings. Another notable feature observed was the skilful performance of the entire cast, an all-star cast including Harrison Hunter, Carlo Liten, Georgette Gauthier de Trigny, C. A. de Lima, Jean Gauthier de Trigny, Florence Malone, Renee Adoree and the young Hal Horne, a juvenile who shows great promise.

Opinions of the reviewers regarding the Fox version of the great Clemenceau's book are more than gratifying to the producer and his organization, and the effect has already been felt in the increased demand for first runs on this special.

14.
Brenon-Ideal

BRENON CORP. LEASES STUDIOS FOR FIVE YEARS
Big Plant Has All Picture Making Facilities – Will Commence
Immediately Upon "War Brides", the First Production in
Which Madame Nazimova Is to Be Starred

(from *Exhibitors Herald,* August 19, 1916, p. 14)

The Herbert Brenon Film Corporation has closed a five years' lease on the Ideal Studios and Laboratories, located on one of the most commanding sites on the Palisades, on the Hudson County boulevard at Hudson Heights, and here Mr. Brenon will begin work immediately upon his first production, *War Brides*, with Mme. Nazimova in a role in which she has scored her greatest successes.

"No perfect work of art can be created without perfect tools", says Mr. Brenon, in speaking of his plant. "Imagine Paderewski playing on a cheap piano, or Kubelik on a $5 fiddle, or Sorolla painting one of his inspiring canvases with one of those toy watercolor boxes that children play with. There has been a tendency in the motion picture business – as distinguished from the photo drama art – to be lavish with expenditures in every department except the mechanical. I have been so fortunate as to secure this studio, which was built regardless of cost by men who were determined to incorporate in it all the latest

Herbert Brenon worked for Carl Laemmle at the Manhattan IMP studio from 1912–14, occasionally filming exteriors in the Fort Lee area for films like *The Price of Sacrifice* (although his most impressive location work was done on an extensive European junket in 1913). He made one independent production in Los Angeles, *The Heart of Maryland,* but was driven back east when the constant winter rains washed out his open-air studio. He worked for William Fox at his various east coast studios in 1915, but split with Fox and formed his own company, leasing the new Ideal Studio as soon as it was completed in June 1916.

The Ideal studio in Hudson Heights, overlooking the Palisades from a spot in Hudson County just south of Cliffside Park.

ideas and equipment, from dressing rooms to laboratory. Albert Teitel, under whose supervision all the work was done, was educated in this department in France, and is conversant with all the contributions of science to the cinematograph. I am satisfied that nowhere in the world is there a studio with better facilities. There are many larger ones, but none, so far as I know, with all its refinements. I consider it a perfect tool."

Two building plant

The finishing touches on the plant were barely completed when W.I. Cherry made the lease for it for Mr. Brenon. It consists of two buildings, the stage areas being 143 by 75 and 50 by 70 feet respectively. In the larger studio there are accommodations for more than three hundred players in large, airy dressing rooms, this occupying one entire floor. Below this floor are the offices, property rooms, scene storage room, paint room, machine shop, carpenter shop, and concrete and glass tanks for taking submarine pictures. Many of these features have been installed from

original designs and are not duplicated in any other plant. Spraying systems have been devised for cooling the roofs of the studios, making it possible for the company to work in comfort in the hottest days of the summer. Visitors' galleries have been built, in order that persons interested may witness the making of pictures without interfering with the work.

All laymen who have visited large motion picture studios are aware of the general atmosphere of confusion that exists. One scene seems almost to overlap its neighbor and the unavoidable turmoil cannot but have the effect of distracting the players from their work. This has been circumvented in the new Brenon studios by a device for rotation of the scenes. It has been estimated that the finishing department has a capacity of 350,000 feet of film in ten hours, which can be increased to 600,000 feet when working at full capacity with a few unimportant additions.

Provide for laboratories

No less care has been devoted to the laboratories which were built under the direction of Mr. Teitel, the builder of the plant, and Francis Doublier, who formerly was associated with the Lumiere Company, four years laboratory superintendent of the Éclair Company, and designed the Paragon plant at Fort Lee.

In this laboratory, too, the goal has been to provide facilities for producing perfect film. The latest inventions in perforating machines, printers, filtering systems, and drying apparatus have been installed. An innovation is a new air interior drying system which insures an even temperature and prevents the settlement of dust on the celluloid. Mr. Doublier believes that the laboratory should be as much the home of the artist as the studio and he is a true alchemist of the profession. Among his chief motives for joining with Mr. Teitel in the building of the

studios which will be used by Mr. Brenon was the assurance that contracts would not be taken for a greater amount of work than could be handled in the most thorough manner.

In addition to all this equipment, there is under construction an open air studio or stage, 100 by 160 feet, to be provided with similarly complete appliances.

Brenon planned to produce his own films at Hudson Heights, while renting out unused stage space to other filmmakers working in New Jersey. But that summer he and his distributing partner, Lewis Selznick, became involved with the mysterious Iliodor Pictures Corporation, which had been organized to exploit the presence in New York of the "Mad Monk" Iliodor, said to have been advisor to the Russian court, and the closest thing available to the notorious Rasputin. The film they made was called *The Fall of the Romanoffs*, a docudrama which attempted to dramatize the events of 1917 as they were happening. Production dragged on for months, and was followed by another struggle among the partners as to who controlled the material. To add insult to injury, William Brady at World released *Rasputin, the Black Monk* just before Brenon's film was ready, resulting in a Broadway fistfight between the rival producers.

"DOWNFALL OF THE ROMANOFFS", FEATURING MONK ILIODOR, IS BEING MADE BY BRENON
Special Spiritual Advisor of Czar Nicholas Exposes Intrigues and Scandals of Royal Court in Big State Rights Drama.

(from *Exhibitors Herald,* June 9, 1917, p. 12)

The Iliodor Picture Corporation, recently chartered at Albany, has, by special arrangement with the Herbert Brenon Film Corporation and Lewis J. Selznick, obtained the services of Herbert Brenon to make a big and significant drama of the Russian revolution which will be presented in a few weeks as one of the biggest state rights attractions ever offered in films.

This drama of the overturn of a nation's rulers and the establishment of human liberty is being made under the title *The Downfall of the Romanoffs*, and Iliodor, the fugitive monk, who was the spiritual adviser of Czar Nicholas, is the featured player.

Iliodor's own story of the intrigues and scandals of the Russian court now is appearing in more than three hundred daily papers throughout the United States and this gives Herbert Brenon's picture advance national publicity of greater scope than any other state rights picture ever obtained.

Director saw court life

No director of motion pictures is so well fitted for the task of making this picture as Herbert Brenon, who, though English born, spent his boyhood days in Petrograd, where through his parents' journalistic connections he saw much of the court life and of the personalities that figure in it.

The Downfall of the Romanoffs has been under way at Mr. Brenon's New Jersey

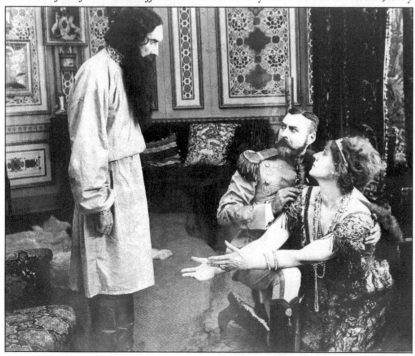

studios for the past two weeks and so well was all of the preliminary work on the production done that it will be rushed to speedy completion.

A cast of remarkable brilliancy, as yet to be announced, surrounds Iliodor, and a woman who has been the sensation of Paris and other continental capitals will have the most important feminine role.

Just as Herbert Brenon was completing *The Lone Wolf*, his latest production, the Iliodor Picture Corporation submitted its proposal to him to make this production and present it to the American public under his distinguished name and auspices.

The consent of the directors of the Herbert Brenon Film Corporation and Lewis J. Selznick was obtained after much persuasion and only because Mr. Brenon himself enthused so much over the possibilities over the story that he would have felt keen disappointment had he passed the opportunity by.

Iliodor a noted figure

Iliodor, as the featured figure in this panorama of a nation's downfall, has figured in every newspaper in America for the past six months. His last publicity was when he engaged in litigation with one of the popular monthly magazines to regain possession of his manuscripts in a series of articles exposing the intrigues of the Russian court.

At that time his interviews filled the newspapers because he charged that undue influence exerted by the Russian ambassador in Washington had succeeded in suppressing his revelations.

Immediately after effecting a settlement with the magazine a struggle

Edward Connelly as Rasputin, Alfred Hickman and Nance O'Neil as the Czar and Czarina, in Herbert Brenon's The Fall of the Romanoffs *(Iliodor Pictures Corp., 1917).*

began between two of the important Yiddish daily newspapers in New York, each claiming rights to his story. His revelations threw the East Side in New York into a ferment.

Experts handle scenario

Great attention has been paid to the scenario of the picture Herbert Brenon is making. Several noted authorities have assisted in the writing and arrangement of the story under Mr. Brenon's personal direction. Mr. Brenon lends all the weight of his skill and authority to this picture and it will be announced under his name and presentation on all of the advertising and publicity, though owned by the Iliodor Corporation.

Alexander Beyfuss is president of the Iliodor Company; E. Schay is secretary and treasurer, and John M. Zwicki and J. Deshan are directors. The offices of the company are on the fourteenth floor at 729 Seventh Avenue, New York City.

LITTLE JOURNEYS TO EASTERN STUDIOS – BRENON
How a Part of the Palisades Has Become a Setting for a Story of Russian Life – Seventh of *The Mirror's* Little Journeys Leads Across the Hudson

By Alison Smith

(from *New York Dramatic Mirror,* August 25, 1917, p. 15)

The Herbert Brenon Studio has been built around one man's knowledge of the psychology of acting. Proceeding on the assumption that the studio was made for the actors and not actors for the studio, Herbert Brenon has arranged every detail of the entire plant with a view toward creating an atmosphere that would sustain the illusion and stimulate the imagination of those

acting under the trying technical conditions of film work.

Your first impression of the studio is that it suggests a legitimate theater with an important scene continually on the stage. There is an atmosphere of eager and intense preparation throughout the entire building which is subdued, however, by the "Silence" signs out of consideration for the actors on the main stage. The keynote of the establishment is given by printed placards hanging in nearly all the rooms, which state that "The Studio Means as Much to the Artist as the Church does to the Devout Worshipper", and that "The Greatest Strength Lies in Silence, the Greatest Power in Motionlessness".

Inspiration for actor

This mental attitude of the film worker is obviously of paramount importance and nothing has been left undone to provide the actor with the inspiration that a theater performance would give, but which is too often lost in the mechanics of motion picture work. To this end, a small orchestra has its place in the studio, which plays appropriate selections especially adapted to the various pictures as they are being filmed.

The screen actor enters the studio very much as a legitimate actor takes his cue for a stage entrance, and through all the time that he is before the camera, he is made to feel the presence of the invisible audience that will greet the finished picture. A call boy, dressed in the Brenon uniform, summons the actors exactly as he would in an actual theater, and the atmosphere is so thoroughly sustained that it is hard to believe that you are not passing from the green room on to the stage of a larger theater.

A Russianized studio

At this particular time the studio had been given up entirely to the Russian setting in *The Fall of the Romanoffs.*

The corridors were crowded with Cossacks, Russian priests, burly peasants and members of the royal family, for, although the old regime was tottering it was not to fall until the following afternoon. The effort that has been made to make this important and timely theme historically accurate shows "an infinite capacity for taking pains" on the part of all concerned.

All the resources in the libraries and bookshops of New York have been used to the fullest extent in procuring historical data, and the office of George Fitch, the technical director, is piled high with files of the *Times, Pictorial Review* and other current publications dealing with the latest phase of the development in New Russia. Mr. Mandlekarn, an authority on Russian manners and customs, is specially employed to overlook every detail of the action and setting as the story is filmed. The staff includes a Russian make-up man and an interpreter for the three thousand extra people used to complete this enormous spectacle.

Equipped for a spectacle

The studio is thoroughly equipped for the production of the most elaborate spectacle. The entrance admits you to a long line of dressing rooms, now filled to capacity by the Russian hordes. A comfortable little room is occupied by George Edwards Hall, who represents whatever there is of the scenario department, although he explained that nearly all of the work on the scripts comes under the personal supervision of Mr. Brenon and that the stories are built up through the united work of a large staff.

If a member of the company begins work on a story, he is permitted to carry it through to its logical conclusion; thus the scenario writer always writes his own titles just as the camera man always does his own cutting, and so on through the various phases of the work that the continuity of a given idea many not be disturbed.

who have come in search of screen honors. Very interesting experiments in double exposure and later developments of screen art are also made here.

The large studio stretches the entire length of the building and is spacious enough to hold the entire Russian Duma with an impatient mob howling outside. It is equipped with the latest electrical devices for cooling and lighting the studio, for although the entire room is arched with glass, giving perfect daytime light, one or another of the companies is usually working at night. The spectacle of the huge building, glowing in an eerie, iridescent light is a curious sight from the other side of the Hudson and has caused considerable speculation as to its origin from the crowds on Riverside Drive.

Most of the exteriors are done in various parts of the Palisades, or further away as the script may require, but some of the smaller exterior sets are filmed on the lot surrounding the studio, which extends to the edge of the cliff and commands a view of the magnificent sweep of the river below.

(Left): Herbert Brenon at his new studio.

(Below): Publicity regarding the studio emphasized how it allowed Brenon to be personally involved in all aspects of production.

Mr. Brenon has a comfortable lounging room on the floor below, with a projection room opening into it, where he can watch the results of his strenuous work in the studio overhead in the brief interval when he is resting.

Place for small sets

A small staircase leads to the "little studio" where the sets that require relatively small space are filmed. This room is also used for the tests of the continuous line of applicants

A lake just beyond the open meadow has been surrounded by a realistic Russian village which was doomed to be destroyed by fire. A most inviting inn built on the lot seemed picturesque enough to belong to a set, but is fortunately more practical, for it provides the members of the company with their meals as well as being the Mecca of hungry automobile parties.

Brenon's spirit reflected

The spirit which Mr. Brenon has infused into his work has been communicated to the entire force that he has working with him and is noticeable in every detail of the studio's arrangement. Employees reflect the courage of the producer's convictions, which have been radical enough to inaugurate a distinct departure from the conventional method of constructing and producing films.

> Many of the studios in the Fort Lee area doubled as laboratories, processing negative and producing release prints for a range of clients. This notice regarding Brenon's solution to "the finger-print evil", which appeared in the *Moving Picture World*, is basically a free ad for his laboratory services.

FINGER PRINTS TO CORRECT CARELESS WORK

(from *Moving Picture World*, September 29, 1917, p. 1979)

George A. Rush, manager of Herbert Brenon's studio at Hudson Heights, NJ, has just applied the finger-print system to the development of negative film. Everybody "in the know" of the screen world realizes the difficulty encountered by studio managers through injury to negative films during development. Despite rules and official precautions, upon development a negative will be found to have gathered a number of finger marks. This is largely due to the lack of care of the developers. Employees have realized that there was no way to trace their carelessness.

Usually these finger prints caused slight harm, but occasionally they marred a big scene, making the cutting of the damaged part necessary. This, of course, hurt the finished product, since a re-take of the scene is then impossible. Mr. Rush has been studying the finger-print evil for some time. Recently he hit upon the idea of applying the police finger-print system to the trouble. Under the direction of Lieutenant John Simons, of the North Bergen, NJ police department, Mr. Rush has taken finger prints of various employees of the Brenon developing department. Judging from results attained with the negative of *The Fall of the Romanoffs* Mr. Rush has solved the problem. The developed negative failed to have a single finger print mark.

> Fifteen months after leasing the Ideal, Brenon felt himself able to break with Selznick and purchase the studio on his own. Notice how the stage measurements differ from those given in 1916, and what sort of buildings had since been added to the property.

BRENON BUYS STUDIO
Big Plant At Hudson Heights, NJ, Acquired From Jersey City Capitalist

(from *Moving Picture World*, November 10, 1917, p. 944)

Herbert Brenon is now the sole owner of his large studio property at Hudson Heights, NJ, a business transaction involving $250,000 having just been consummated. By this deal, Mr. Brenon becomes one of the biggest single factors in the film industry today.

Mr. Brenon recently acquired complete control of the producing corporation bearing his name, purchasing the other interests in the organization. This gave him complete control of production. The producer then turned to the actual purchase of his studio, to insure complete freedom and scope for his extensive plans. The studio property which he has been occupying was owned by William G.. Bumstead, the millionaire capitalist of Jersey City. Mr. Bumstead is an important figure in New Jersey business, being chairman of the financial committee of the New Jersey Title Guarantee and Trust Company, director of the Provident Institute of Savings, president of the Raritan River Railroad and director of the Colonial Life Insurance Bank.

Negotiations have been progressing for several weeks, being briefly held up by Mr. Brenon's operation for appendicitis. The final papers have just been signed by Mr. Brenon, who has resumed active production at his studio.

The studio property acquired by Mr. Brenon includes some two and a half acres of land, two studio buildings, laboratories, administration building, garage and carpenter shop. The studios are model ones of concrete and steel with every up-to-the-minute detail of equipment. They have a complete electrical equipment, with Cooper-Hewitts, etc. The larger studio has a floor space of 101x50 feet, while the other studio building has floor space of 50x40 feet. The construction of the studios, by means of sliding sides and balconies, permits of unusually long shots, ranging up to 125 feet. One ballroom scene in *The Fall of the Romanoffs* revealed the great depth of shot possible.

A large outdoor stage, the first in the

BRENON CORPORATION
CONTROLLED BY HERBERT BRENON
EXECUTIVE OFFICES
BRENON STUDIOS, HUDSON HEIGHTS
NEW JERSEY
DISTRIBUTION OFFICES, 509 FIFTH AVENUE, NEW YORK, N. Y.

OFFICE OF THE
PRESIDENT

January 8, 1918.

My dear Mr. Bumstead:

I am informed, although I do
not believe it, that Mr. Beyfuss and
Mr. Rush are going to be given the
studio to run within the next few days.
I ask you to note that I do not believe
this, but I think it my duty to appeal to you not to take the studio
away from me as it is in a great measure my means of earning my living,
and I shall certainly pay all my indebtedness to you.

I think you know that it is
only a matter of a week or two before
I will be busily engaged in making
pictures again. Not only I but almost
everybody in the industry is suffering
in these last few months.

I have absolute confidence in
your generosity, and most sincerely
beg you to at least trust me to pay
my indebtedness. You know my earning
capacity, so please trust me to do the
honorable thing until you have reason
to think otherwise.

If I were to show you the
condition in which my affairs have been
put by Mr. Beyfuss, you would be amazed.
You know I had absolute confidence in
him but I have been hastily awakened.

In conclusion I again respectfully beg you to take no action in regard to taking the studio from me until
the first of the month, by which time
my affairs will be settled. It only
needs the breaking of the winter for activities to begin again.

With kindest regards to Mrs.
Bumstead and yourself.
Cordially yours,

Letter from Brenon to his financial backer, William Bumstead, pleading to retain control of the studio, 8 January 1918.

East, is being constructed on the property. Aside from this, there are, atop the studios, two outdoor spaces, each 50 x 40 feet, which are utilized for exterior stuff. The two studio buildings have forty individual dressing rooms and four star dressing rooms. Adjoining the studio buildings is a restaurant capable of handling five hundred.

The office building and stucco garage have just been constructed. The administration building houses the private offices of Mr. Brenon, his general manager, secretary and departments of exploitation and accounting.

The Brenon plant, with its completely equipped laboratories, handles a motion picture from actual filming to the finished positive print. This assures Mr. Brenon of just exactly the sort of work that he desires in every department. The Brenon laboratories and factory have an unusual record for efficiency. Only recently a negative print was given the department at five o'clock in the afternoon. At nine o'clock the next morning Mr. Brenon was able to look at a finished positive print being projected in the studio exhibition room. George Rush is studio manager. The photographic department is headed by J. Roy Hunt, who has been cameraman for Mr. Brenon for four years. Mr. Hunt also supervises the film cutting department. Charles Ritchie is assistant camera man.

The technical department is headed by George Fitch, who has been associated with Mr. Brenon in every picture he has ever made. George Edwardes Hall heads the scenario department, with Joseph Echazebel as assistant. Louis Plunion supervises the property department, Fred McBann heads the electrical division, Tom Tamagne manages the carpenter department and Tom Smythe directs the scenic division. Mrs. Cashman is wardrobe mistress. The factory and laborato-

ries are in the hands of experts and the studio also has its own title man and printer. Each department has an average of from six to ten employees. The laboratories, fitted with six developing machines and four printing machines, have room provided for a staff of twenty-five girls.

The Hudson Heights studios have been occupied by Mr. Brenon since their construction was completed in June, 1916. On August 7th, Mr. Brenon started his first production there, the visualization of *War Brides*. All his subsequent productions, including the *Lone Wolf* and *The Fall of the Romanoffs* were made there. Strange as it may seem to the uninitiated, every scene of *The Fall of the Romanoffs* was "shot" on the studio property, proving the possibilities and efficiency of Mr. Brenon's studios.

After finishing with the Romanoffs, Brenon filmed *Empty Pockets* and *The Passing of the Third Floor Back* at Hudson Heights. The latter film, a mystical melodrama starring Sir Johnston Forbes-Robertson, has often been incorrectly assumed (even by the American Film Institute) to be a British production. But Brenon's plans to film Otis Skinner in *Kismet* fell apart along with his financial situation. The following interview was conducted just before Brenon heard that Bumstead was about to repossess the studio (in the letter reproduced here, Brenon blames his problems on winter conditions and his entanglement with Alexander Beyfuss, president of the Iliodor Company).

THE MELODRAMA OF SHADOWS
Showing Herbert Brenon's Foresight And Insight Into The Sentimental Possibilities Of Celluloid.

(from *Picture Play*, February 1918, pp. 183–187)

Herbert Brenon sat before a sordid tenement room constructed in one corner of his Hudson Heights, New Jersey, studios. A sliding door at the side of the studio revealed a sweep of the Jersey countryside, vivid with the browns and reds of the autumn, in strange contrast with the wretched East Side room. The scene was being filmed for Rupert Hughes' story of New York life, *Empty Pockets*. Between directorial moments Mr. Brenon outlined his ideas on the picture play.

"The motion picture camera is the greatest melodramatist of them all", he said. "The photo play may find its way to a new dramatic language – as it must shortly – through the melodrama". On the spoken stage melodrama has come to mean a form of theatrical story-telling in which the characters are developed by the situations. That is, they are puppets put through a chain of exciting incidents. The word melodrama is now defined as something 'unnatural in situation or action.' By drama we have come to mean just the reverse – situations growing out of the thoughts, moods, and feelings of the characters themselves.

"The very limitations of the theater seem to have brought about this division. The dramatist has to observe the limits of the stage. If he is starting out to tell a story of sweeping action, he has no time to work out the mental nuances which bring about this action. An act can contain so much – and no more. Again, the playwright who attempts the so-called drama must devote the limited period of his three or four acts to unfolding the mental processes of his characters. The action must largely take place off stage, to be brought out by the dialogue.

"The photo play, on the other hand, sweeps through a story with tremendous speed. If the story calls for a railroad wreck, we see the wreck before our very eyes. Then, too, we see the face of the engineer just before the accident. We know just what he is thinking. The cut-back has just carried us back to his little home. We know what causes the wreck. We see the rails spiked. We know just what the wreckers have thought.

"The photo play can carry one through a dozen big situations where the stage melodrama can achieve only one well-developed big scene. But, best of all, in the movies we see each worked up to gradually. Enemies of the screen declare that the photo play can talk only in action. Only recently Brander Matthews again presented this charge. 'He (the director) can take *Hamlet* above the violent melodrama out of which Shakespeare made it,' says Mr. Matthews. 'He can take *Macbeth*, which has a good story picturesquely set forth, and he can show the succession of incidents with the utmost splendor. But he cannot show what gives all its value to this external shell of episode. He can make visible the marching of Macduff's army and the coming of Birnan [sic] Wood, but he cannot disclose the conflict of soul of MacBeth; he cannot make us shudder at the slow and steady disintegration of a noble character under the stress of recurring temptation.'

"Mr. Matthews forgets – or does not realize the value of – the close-up, the flash-back, and the vision. These can tell the actual workings of the human mind as no living actor, going through a situation some hundred feet from an auditor, can ever do it. Again, the speaking actor must exaggerate his facial and bodily pantomime in order to put a thought over. The screen player can be human. The slightest expression is caught by the camera.

"Early photo plays were action pictures, as Vachel Lindsay truthfully calls them. The people were but types, 'swiftly moving chessmen.' 'Neither lust, love, hate, nor hunger' were in them. The new photo play is coming to tell a story of human action."

Mr. Brenon believes unwaveringly in the tremendous future of the photo play. His career has been the career of the picture drama. Straight through his list of productions from the start Mr. Brenon has revealed a steady development. *Neptune's Daughter, The Heart of Maryland, The Kreutzer Sonata, The Clemenceau Case, The Soul of Broadway, The Two Orphans, A Daughter of the Gods, War Brides, The Lone Wolf* and *The Fall of the Romanoffs* were each distinct steps ahead. These revealed a fine imaginative fantasy, a singular grasp of direct drama, and the ability – unusual to both stage and screen – of humanizing melodrama. Such versatility is rare to the celluloid drama.

"In a recent article which I read in a magazine", continued Mr. Brenon, "the author makes the statement that the movies must have their characters in blacks and whites because, to comport with an elementary logic, they must be saints or devils. 'So vanishes,' he goes on, 'from the films all nuisance [sic], all complexity, all delineation.' I might reply by asking the writer to point out the depth of character drawing to be found now in the Broadway legitimate theater. That, however, would hardly be answering the charge. I make the claim that the photo play is feeling out a new art – and a new art is not found overnight. I tried to attain human action in *The Lone Wolf*. I tried to show the human hates and desires behind this French criminal yclept the Lone Wolf. I tried to show each character with its strength and weaknesses. I am trying

Sir Johnston Forbes-Robertson in The Passing of the Third Floor Back *(Brenon-First National, 1918), the last film Brenon made in New Jersey.*

obviously not be an imitation of the stage. Neither can attain the values of the other.

"There is no doubt but that the individual charms of the photo dramatist and director's styles will be caught by the photo play of the future. Today a certain director may be famous for his handling of multitudes, another for his beauty of lighting and stage pictures, and so on. These are, of course, but tricks of the trade. These things gild the photo play. But to advance the screen drama we must keep plugging along toward a distinct technique – a technique that will not be borrowed from the artist, the dramatist, or the stage carpenter, although it may blend all these arts. *"But it will come to express life as none of these mediums express it."*

Brenon left for England after losing the studio, and became involved in another unfortunate project, a never-released British government propaganda film called *Victory and Peace.* While he stayed to direct other films in England and Italy, his old studio in Hudson Heights continued to operate as a laboratory.

WLADIMIR ALMAZOV FILM LABORATORIES OPEN IN NEW YORK
Well Known Technician Backed by American and Foreign Bankers

(from *Exhibitors Herald and Motography,* March 15, 1919, p. 35)

Under the supervision of Wladimir Almazov one of the foremost technicians in laboratory work, the Almazov

to do it again in the picture which I am now filming.

"Here is the murder mystery of a debonair millionaire, 'Merry' Perry Merithew, found dead on the dirty tin roof of an East Side tenement. There is one clew. In the dead man's hand is clutched a strand of red hair. I am attempting to invest the mystery with humanness. I am going to bring out the fancies and foibles of these characters, and the characters, I hope, will not be just black and white.

"In this story is a thrilling midnight automobile chase which dodges back and forth across the island of Manhattan, finally ending at the edge of Spuyten Duyvil Creek. This sort of thing would be impossible to the spoken stage.

"I am afraid, because the theater has found it impossible to handle big action with anything like realism, that we have come to look down upon what we term melodrama. Yet we have only to open a newspaper to realize that life is melodrama. What is the great war but the most tremendous melodrama ever enacted in the world's history? Five years ago the war, if forecast on the stage or screen, would have been pronounced preposterous melodrama.

"Vachel Lindsay and the late Hugo Munsterberg have both predicted that the supreme picture play of the future will give us things that have been but half expressed in all other mediums allied to it. The photo dramatist is a dramatist, a poet, a painter, and a sculptor in one. Possibly the future photo play will run along the border line between what we now term melodrama and drama. It will

Film Laboratories, Inc., enter the field of Eastern activities, with offices in New York City, and an extensive plant located opposite Manhattan in New Jersey.

The Almazov corporation have taken over, remodeled, and re-equipped the Ideal plant, on Boulevard Loop, Hudson Heights, New Jersey, at considerable cost, and are aggressively in the field for laboratory work.

The plant has at present a productive capacity of approximately half a million feet of film a week, but additional machinery has been ordered, which when installed will double this capacity.

It is equipped with a title printing shop, with modern presses, a convenience for the producer, enabling him to order his titles from the manuscript, where the printing of the film is done, and every other convenience that modernity affords.

The offices of the Almazov corporation are located at 1482 Broadway in the Fitzgerald Building, at 43rd Street, the heart of the film mart.

The Almazov corporation is financed by a group of American and foreign bankers and capitalists, and it is said they are planning extensive operations in the industry, which will embrace the production and other fields of the motion picture business.

Without a resident production company (and a permanent press agent), journalists found little to say about the sporadic filmmaking activities that went on at the Ideal Studio over the next two decades. Briggs Pictures, Inc. leased the studio in 1919 and made a series of Paramount-Briggs comedies under the direction of John William Kellette. More short comedies were made here by Deck Richards for Maglin (1925) and Al Joy for Ricordo Films, under the direction of Joe Basil (1926). The production of short silent comedies was almost completely centralized in Los Angeles at this time, so this activity was quite rare in the New York-New Jersey area. The studio was unused for some time after this, but was successfully revived after the introduction of sound as a second-string rental facility. During the 1930s such stars as W.C. Fields, Clark & McCullough, Bill Robinson and Moishe Oysher all worked at the Ideal, but unlike the legends that surrounded some of its larger competitors, this history was very quickly forgotten. When the studio burned in 1953 even local obituaries identified it with stars who had never worked there.

FIRE ENDS FILM SAGA
North Bergen Studios Used for Silent Movies Become Only a Memory

(from the *Newark News*, September 9, 1953)

Decades of movie-making slipped into oblivion yesterday when a general alarm fire swept the Ideal Sound Studios, at 88th Street and Boulevard East, leveling the once famous center of silent motion pictures. The old time stars who made films there included Mary Pickford and Pearl White.

The studios, idle for about 20 years, were used for film storage space and later as a warehouse for scenery and props.

Police said the fire was caused by boys playing with matches while "acting" amid the dusty, cobwebbed sets. When the smoke cleared only the memories of the silent movie heroes were left.

The boys have not been caught, police said.

Eyesore to area

The five-story wooden and stucco structure, after the movie industry moved to Hollywood, actually became an eyesore in a highly residential area. In the last few years, two major housing projects were erected near the studios but neither was threatened by yesterday's fire. The studio was on a site overlooking the Hudson River.

Damage to the studio building was estimated at $50,000. Ideal Sound Studios is a subsidiary of the National Screen Service Corp. of New York.

The fire was discovered by a watchman, Albert Hansen of 436 36th Street, Union City, who told police that he saw three small boys emerge from the basement about a half-hour before the blaze was seen. The flames spread quickly.

Nine minutes after the fire alarm at 2:45 P.M., the general alarm was tapped in. Iron girders buckled under the heat and the roof collapsed in a matter of minutes.

Flying embers started several grass fires along River Road and on some abandoned barges and sheds as far as a half-mile away, but they were extinguished by West New York fire companies. Edgewater firemen were alerted to protect that municipality's heavy industrial area from the shower of embers and sparks.

Major film companies used the structure, which, along with studios in Fort Lee, once formed the center of the silent movie industry.

15.
Paragon

Although Jules Brulatour had a hand in bankrolling almost every studio in Fort Lee, he was most heavily involved with Paragon Films, Inc. and the studio it built on John Street. Brulatour incorporated Paragon on March 31, 1915, and two months later had acquired a large property located west of the intersection of Catherine and John. His partners included Maurice Tourneur and William Brady, and their films were distributed through World. Indeed, drawing on Brulatour's resources, Paragon soon became the upscale half of World's Paragon-Peerless assembly line, leaving the smaller Peerless operation with the less interesting stars, directors, and program pictures. Maurice Tourneur, the creative partner of the new organization, made his artistic ambitions clear to the press from the very beginning.

"PHOTODRAMA IS A DISTINCT ART", DECLARES TOURNEUR

Traditions of the Speaking Stage Have no Effect on Vice-President and Director-in-Chief of Paragon, Releasing through World, in Selection of Material

(from *Motion Picture News*, 4, January 1916, p. 316)

Maurice Tourneur, until recently director at the Peerless studio in Fort Lee, New Jersey, and now vice-president, director-in-chief and general manager of the Paragon company, which is to release through the World Film Corporation, is a firm believer in the motion picture as a separate and distinct art.

He cares little for traditions of the speaking stage as applied to pictures, which statement he confirmed when he recently said:

"I do not believe in paying high prices for plays or novels that are purported to have had a successful career in their individual fields. The good picture should be written specially for the screen, and as long as it is good, the name on the leader is secondary.

"But where I do adhere to existing condition as on the speaking stage", continued Mr. Tourneur, "is in the matter of stock companies.

"The picture producer of today is crazy to get a star player, which adds to the picture's box office value but often has a deteriorating effect in respect to its artistic value. A star generally is unused to his or her support and consequently the players are not able to work in unison.

"When work starts at the Paragon studio I intend to retain a regular stock company, the members of which will by constant association with one another before the camera, be fully able to judge each other's work and become familiar with each other's peculiarities. Stars will be employed but they too will in all probability be members of the regular company."

Mr. Tourneur was asked as to the nature of the Paragon-World Film agreement and declined to go into detail.

"Paragon", he said, "is not bound by contract to produce a certain number

The newly constructed Paragon studio, 1916.

of pictures a year. We will make as many as possible, probably two or three a month. The length will be five reels."

It is generally known that Mr. Tourneur, a Frenchman by birth, was formerly connected with the French Eclair Company in a directing capacity. He has been in this country for almost two years as director at the Peerless studio, and he says heartily he likes America better than any other land.

"You, over here", he said, "have long thought foreign settings and photography much better than your own. You are wrong, for with the exception of Italy there is no country that can attain such wonderful photographic effects as this. It is merely modesty on your part, for a French producer thinks American pictures better than his in those same respects.

"As for the acting, American and English players are much easier to work with than the more temperamental Continental. Your European actor will tire after rehearsing two or three times and then fuss and fume when he is obliged to listen to the director. Americans, on the other hand, are willing to work all day on one scene if necessary.

"And as for facilities for picture producing in this country and abroad there is no comparison."

Mr. Tourneur has just finished work on a feature starring George Beban, his last with the Peerless studio. The Paragon, now practically completed, will shortly house Mr. Tourneur, Albert Capellani and Emile Chautard, the trio of French directors who have been so successful in this country.

The Paragon studio, situated in Fort Lee, NJ, only a few blocks from the Peerless, is equipped with all the latest improvements. Two revolving stages will allow for the erection of three adjacent settings while the remaining floor space is large enough to accommodate six or eight sets of average size.

PARAGON STUDIO IS WONDER-PLACE OF CONVENIENCE
Two Revolving Stages, Each with Capacity of Two Large and Two Small Sets, Constitute One of the Features – Injury to Negative from Floor Vibration is Eliminated – Steel Bridge, Capable of Traveling Entire Width of Structure, Enables Cameraman to "Shoot" Settings from Various Angles

(from *Motion Picture News*, March 1916, p. 1571)

No motion picture studio in the United States offers a more interesting study than the fine, new plant of the Paragon Films, Inc., a producing company of the World, at Fort Lee, NJ.

In capaciousness and innovations, this studio and its adjoining printing plant, make it one of the most complete of its kind in the East.

The Paragon Studio is a square building with an exterior measurement of 200 x 200 feet.

The studio floor has an area of approximately 20,000 square feet, with a wide strip partitioned off for offices and work rooms.

From the ridge of the great glass roof to the studio flooring is a drop of seventy-five feet. These figures fail to convey the immensity of the plant, which must be entered to be appreciated.

Stop floor vibration

One of the most important features connected with the studio itself is the innovation in the matter of the flooring.

Heretofore work in motion picture studios has often been marred by the effect of the vibration of the floor.

Much time is often lost through the fact that when a director is "shooting" an important scene, the work of carpenters and property men erecting other sets must be called off on account of the floor shaking under their footsteps and the shifting of large weights.

In the new Paragon studio the possibility of a vibrating floor spoiling a negative in the making is eliminated.

The flooring is nailed into a base of concrete composition to withstand shock.

In testing it, Studio Manager Henry Bayard had a cameraman take a strip of film, while from the girders above workmen dropped to the floor heavy bags of sand all around the studio.

The test film showed not the slightest "tremble". Had it been taken under similar conditions in another studio, the picture on the film would have been hopelessly jumbled together by the floor vibration.

In addition to this feature, the Paragon studio floor is unique in possessing two large revolving stages, each of which is capable of holding two large and two small sets.

With this revolving stage a director can work upon scene after scene without moving his lights or camera and thus save many hours, and as every producing company knows, studio time is the most expensive in the world.

Traveling bridge to "shoot" anywhere

Another distinctive feature is the steel bridge that travels the entire width of the studio and from which a director and his camera man may "shoot" down upon a series of settings from various angles.

It was this bridge that enabled Director Maurice Tourneur to make use of

a most remarkable setting in the picture he has just completed with House Peters as the star, entitled *The Hand of Peril*.

At one end of the studio Director Tourneur built the interior of a three-story house, showing nine rooms, with stairways connecting them.

By "shooting" from the bridge at various heights and horizontal positions, the director was able to take scenes showing action in all the rooms of the house simultaneously, as well as close-up of each individual room.

Such sets have been used occasionally on the stage but never in motion pictures.

Still another remarkable feature of the Paragon plant is the terrace, twenty feet wide, and extending entirely around the building.

The side walls have several sliding panels that can be opened, and use made of the extended floor space offered by the terrace.

Both ends of the studio can be thrown completely open with no upright supports to obstruct the vision.

Exterior and interior sets at same time

As an example of what this novel constructive idea will permit, the director can erect on the studio floor a setting showing the exterior of a house, carrying out the effect with balconies and balustrades upon the terrace.

Then he can arrange a formal garden on the studio property beyond the terrace and by placing his camera at the extreme end of the garden can "shoot" the entire vista up to and into the studio itself.

This combination of exterior and interior operation has never before been possible in motion picture studio work.

Other distinctive features of the Paragon studio are the property rooms, which are devised in two levels; one to take in material and the other to take it out; and the dressing room arrangement, which is so thoroughly planned that there

is even a private corridor and stairway for the stars and leading players, separating them from the "extra" people engaged for ensemble scenes.

The printing plant adjoining the studio is claimed to be the largest in the country, having a capacity of 2,000,000 feet a week.

Among its distinctive innovations is the spraying chamber, 150 feet long, where many reels of film can be washed at the same time through a device that travels up and down the room spraying the film with a fine water-mist.

The printing plant also includes half a dozen projecting rooms, one 75 feet long.

Cost is $750,000

A conservative estimate of the entire outlay for studio and printing plant, including the equipment, is $750,000.

Maurice Tourneur, undoubtedly one of the foremost film creators and responsible for *Trilby, The Pawn of Fate* and other World and Equitable classics, is in complete charge at the Paragon studio.

Mons. Tourneur will supervise, not alone his own Paragon-World productions, but will keep a watchful eye on such other productions as are in the making there.

Within the next few weeks, *The Closed Road* with House Peters, *The Call of Love* with Molly King and four other productions will be in the making at the Paragon studio.

The studio is now near enough completion to allow for two directors working at the same time, but within the next month four directors will be able to work at one time, and a number of the sets contemplated in the new World-Equitable policy of commercialization of film productions calls for gigantic efforts, immense floor space and unlimited room, all of which is afforded by the new Paragon studio.

> Was the motion picture an art form? Or did it debase older forms as it corrupted classical texts and dumbed down general audiences? Herbert Brenon, D.W. Griffith, and many other high-profile directors frequently issued press releases stating their (positive) opinion, while more traditional attitudes were defended by pundits like George Jean Nathan. Maurice Tourneur was heavily involved in this debate, never more so than in this curious op ed exchange with Charles Whittaker. What is most puzzling here is that Whittaker, no elitist outsider, was Tourneur's new screenwriter, responsible for his adaptations of *The Whip*, *The Undying Flame* and *The Pride of the Clan*.

MOVIES DESTROY ART

By Charles E. Whittaker

(from *Harper's Weekly*, April 29, 1916, p. 458)

In the sacred name of truth, let us abolish this new *cliche*: to speak of "the art of the movie" is to employ a vast farce of a phrase that is a contradiction in terms.

Art is the effort on the part of a human being to express life as he sees it by brush, pen, chisel, song, or stave. Art is far from the movies – not merely in absence, but in positive antithesis –

because the chief effort of the movie seems to be to present something that shall express life, not as the manufacturer sees it, but as he imagines somebody else wants to see it. This is not art but artifice.

If it be insisted that the interpreter can be an artist, such folk as think would ask what close-ups, the *piece de resistance* of the photodrama, have to do with art, whose essence is restraint. For whom, they might ask, are the close-ups of the vampire-ladies intended? A countenance six feet wide, depicting a desire for revenge, is a manifestation that, one hopes, is never encountered in public or private moments.

The appeal of the movie is based upon the fact that it presents movement and real life, neither of which is indispensable to art. Even in a mercantile way, Mr. Burton Holmes's pictures of travel fetch as much per foot of film as do the most terrifying sex-dramas that were ever issued from a Fort Lee studio. The public, insatiable in its quest for the rapid acquisition of knowledge, loves the war picture; it delights in the Gaumont and Pathé motion views of villages in Algiers, Iceland, and Hindustan. All this is real life.

One does not expect real life on the legitimate stage; and, thank goodness, one does not get it. One gets philosophy, well or ill expressed in terms of dramas. Not a living soul in the audience at the Ibsen play is disturbed if the entire wall of the room sways when Nora, making her final exit in *A Doll's House,* shuts the door; what is important is that she is leaving her husband. Yet the entire audience would be distracted beyond description if in any Egyptian scene in *Antony and Cleopatra* a cat were to appear, because the art of the drama can be smothered by reality and by the purely imitative.

The motion "picture", by reason of its lack of atmosphere and composition, design, perspective, and draftsman-

ship, has of course, nothing to do with the art of the picture. Of all the arts there are but two of which the movie is the poor relation: the drama and literature. To speak of "silent drama", as some do, is to express another contradiction. One may be gratified to think that the deaf man may enjoy the movies, but that would be no excuse for speaking of the art of the victrola, merely because it may enliven the moments of he blind. And if the words of the playwright – himself an artist – and the eloquence of the actor, are taken from the drama, what is there left of its art?

Is it as a modern exposition of the art of letters that the high-priests of the motion picture would have it judged? Mr. Maurice Tourneur, once an artist, now a director, has destroyed the possibility of that illusion. He does not believe that the author of a story, which is to be shown on the screen, should write the scenario from which the action is played. A short synopsis only of a story is what Mr. Tourneur requires. Two months after the weaver of romances has sent in his synopsis, he may see the precise effect of Mr. Tourneur's policy. His story will have been hanged, drawn, and quartered by the continuity writer, burned by the actor, and its ashes scattered to the four winds of heaven by the director.

In the Dark Ages a young prince, to whom was supernaturally revealed the fact that his father the king has been murdered by the prince's uncle – who had afterwards married the dead man's widow – entrapped a confession of the murder from the newly crowned king by reconstructing the crime in the form of a play. To obtain revenge on his nephew for this trick, the king arranged a game of fencing between the prince and a gentleman whose sister, distracted by love of the prince, had committed suicide, and it had been previously arranged that one of the foils was to be poisoned. In the intervals between the bouts, the foils changed hands, whereupon both the participants were mortally wounded. The prince, just before dying, having been apprised of the secret of the poisoned foil, killed his uncle; and the queen drank some poisoned wine, also intended for the prince, by accident, whereupon she died.

Happily, the tragedy has already been written by Shakespeare, but I invite Mr. Tourneur – should he ever produce *Hamlet* for the screen – to say whether he will work from Shakespeare's text or from my synopsis. The irreverent might tremble with unholy joy in speculating upon the close-ups of Claudius, but it is clear that Mr. Tourneur believes that the movie is purely interpretative.

As for the final test of art, its permanence, the future will decide. Shakespeare's words are still with us; but no one knows or cares what appeared in the first number of the first newspaper. Conversely, one may suppose that the permanence of the movie will rest upon the reproductions of life in the trenches and in the whaling boats, and not upon the sublimity of the story as revealed in the *Perils of Pauline*.

The movie is not art, because it is not literature; it has no persistence, save for its illustration of daily news. The life of the best of the photodramas, on the word of Mr. Daniel Frohman, is two years. That art should perish so! If it is necessary to find a definition for the movie, it would seem to be unrelated to art of which it is not even the Cinderella. Myself, I regard it as the little cutey of the crafts.

MOVIES CREATE ART

By Maurice Tourneur

(from *Harper's Weekly,* April 29, 1916, p. 459)

Movies: a quivering rift in an emerald woods, silver-shot with a summer's sun; a startled nymph beside a mirrored pool, the play of whose form is a prayer; a charnel house, grimy and shadowy, its damp marble slabs glinting green against

the moon; a baby's smile, also its tears, the one as unfeigned as t'other; a mountain ridge at night with silhouetted riders speeding by against the clouds; a jungle kraal, with a panther brood frolicking about a recumbent mother, whose eyes are lit with the maternal fire that shines not on the land nor on the sea – these motion picture miracles, the tabulation of scarce more than a single hand against an overwhelming array, many as inspiring, many more thrilling, many more enthralling alike to the artist and all others – and these are but exhibits of a craft?

Bezeul, now a confrère at the Paragon studios, several months ago stalked the woods of the Champagne section in France at the close of a battle, equipped with a movie camera, and the world has since thrilled with the chill of death as shown by war's horrors in the raw; no sheltering fiction of paint as Meissonier gives it, nor of molded mineral Rodin forms, but death real, stark, limp and fearful, carpeting an actual glade, animate only in the mute, orderly stepping from corpse to corpse to check the victim's identities by their regiment tags. Merely mechanical, to turn the crank that rolls the film upon whose solution the heroism of a nation is writ indelibly. Staging death in the mass, yet with restraint, keeping the will master of the emotions, so directing the camera that the merely gruesome shall be but an underlying terror of the whole – this, too is but craftsmanship – a cutey?

I produced the French stage version of *Alias Jimmy Valentine.* I later filmed the play for this country. Paul Armstrong's piece in its stage form needed little adapting for the films. Armstrong, as everyone knows, took the character of "Jimmy" from an O.

Maurice Tourneur working with Marguerite Clark on his most artistically ambitious production, Prunella *(FPL-Paramount, 1918).*

Henry tale and that's all he took. Scarcely more than four printed pages in length in its O. Henry form, it was the idea of a semi-polished outlaw gaily fastening himself upon the payroll of a bank that he designed subsequently to rob, that fired Armstrong. Structurally there is no more resemblance between the O. Henry fiction and the Armstrong comedy than there is between a chess board and a woman weeping. Do the learned judges of the new art deny that Armstrong created an enlivening drama? Do they deny that the mere record of Jimmy's job-taking in the bank, even without the details of its original fiction, was in essence a play? Would they deny this adaptation practice to the credentialed film director! Isn't the history of the acting drama and the printed fiction that inspires it voluminous record of interchanges? Didn't the great romances take largely from Montaigne? Doesn't Montaigne confess freely his own appropriations from multiple sources? Aren't we all creatures of just so many emotions? Isn't drama mere criss-crossed collisions of these, taking new forms with each fresh alignment? Isn't there in Shakespeare an entire gamut of masculine character, also a more or less complete feminine galaxy as it exists about us today?

Do filmdom's decriers concede the necessity for the preservation of something like a unified whole in a spoken stage piece or a mute filmed one? Do these captious weeping willows know that if a film director produced verbatim the average scenario as detailed in, say a five reel picture, the audience would consider the six-day Chinese drama a delightful tabloid in comparison? Do they know that one entire reel of one thousand feet of film may be interestingly devoted to the mere entrance of a single person into a room?

I have not seen anywhere any claim of any manufacturer of films that he considers himself an artist or even a pur-

veyor of art, or that he aspires or seeks to mold public taste in photoplays, nor do I believe he makes a practice of producing what he thinks the public thinks it wants. Considering the difficulties besetting his supply, I think the film manufacturer is doing, in the short time of his existence, a great deal more than any publisher or theatrical manager of an equally brief existence did, not even excepting the early days of the French, German and English stage and literature, which reminds me that Shakespeare shows in all his work that he would have reveled in the magical volubility of the motion camera. Not a play of his but shows his *flair* for scenic embellishment and brilliant variety. What he would have done with his filmed battle scenes – a flash here of panoply, a shift to a portentous conference, a flash of helmeted couriers, all filigrees of his main current.

The quarrel with close-ups by the present school of film decriers is without consideration. The close-up, which, by the way, is not new, is merely a director's emphasis of a phase of his play, an auxiliary he employs to insure the conveyance of a definite thought at a definite stage of the play. Reference to their abnormal size is as intelligent as the same criticism would be of the colossal bronze of Daniel Webster in Central Park, the Bartholdi Liberty Lady in New York bay, or the Sherman equestrian figure on the Plaza on Fifth Avenue, New York.

Authorities agree that the stage production methods of Max Reinhardt are art. Are film directors, who write, create, and adapt stage and camera plays less entitled to the term? Capellani, a Paragon associate director, filmed *Les Miserables*. If photoplay critics think the people – the common people – are artistically obtuse, let them scan the royalty records of the Hugo fiction in films and note the millions who came, wondered and wept with Valjean and the other unfortunates of this imperishable tale.

> *A Girl's Folly*, Maurice Tourneur's Gallic take on the illusions of the motion picture business, was a love letter to the Paragon studio and the creative energy he found there. But censors in Chicago and other jurisdictions did not always appreciate Tourneur's sense of humor. Trade papers regularly published local censor board eliminations, as with this account of the treatment of two typical World releases.

WORLD OFFERS UNIQUE COMEDY ON FILM MAKING WITH A NOTED STAR

(from *Exhibitors Herald*, January 27, 1917, p. 26)

The next Brady-made World pictureplay with Robert Warwick as its star promises to contain uncommon novelty. Its present title is *A Girl's Folly*, substituted for *A Movie Romance*, and its principal male character is a noted motion picture star.

The story is laid in the studio and "on location", and it shows everything about the manner in which a pictureplay is carried to completion, from the make-up of the star to the publication.

The dressing rooms, the setting up of scenery, the adjustment of the camera, the summoning of the players for an episode, the director's rehearsal with the players and the taking of the scenes are all reproduced with realistic but mainly comic effect.

The production is distinctly a behind-the-scenes comedy which does not even overlook the lunch room where the actors take their hurried repasts between calls to the stage … .

OFFICIAL CUT-OUTS MADE BY THE CHICAGO BOARD OF CENSORS

(from *Exhibitors Herald*, March 3, 1917, p. 26)

World, *A Girl's Folly* – Subtitle, "I'm awfully tired of her;" man unlocking door to girl's apartment; last part of scene of woman on couch in man's apartment after he kisses her hand.

World, *The Savage Instinct* – Flash eight scenes of illicit distilling; shooting of revenue officer; two scenes of tying girl's hands; entire scene in which moonshiner forcibly kisses girl.

By the end of 1916 Paragon was turning away from World and looking for another partner. Tourneur directed Mary Pickford here in *The Pride of the Clan* and *The Poor Little Rich Girl* for Artcraft. Alice Brady appeared for Select in an adaptation of *Jane Eyre* called *Woman and Wife*. Eventually the entire studio was taken over by Famous Players-Lasky, whose New York studio could no longer handle Paramount's increasing demand for product. In addition to the studio, Adolph Zukor also acquired its resident artist, Maurice Tourneur.

"BROADWAY JONES", COHAN'S INITIAL FILM PLAY, IS HELD UP AS LIGHT AFFECTS EYES OF PLAYERS
Glare of Powerful Cooper-Hewitts at Pickford Studio Temporarily Blinds Star, Who Suspends Work to Recover; Building of Sets Caused Change

(from *Exhibitors Herald*, March 3, 1917, p. 14)

Work on the initial George M. Cohan-Artcraft production, *Broadway Jones*, had to be suspended, due to the fact that practically all the principals in the cast were temporarily blinded by the powerful lights used in the big Knickerbocker Hotel lobby set. The first to become afflicted was George M. Cohan, who had to be led from the studio and journeyed to Atlantic City to join his wife and children for a short rest. He is rapidly recovering and expects to be back at the studio in a few days. Marguerite Snow, who plays opposite the star, Crawford Kent and Ida Darling were among those compelled to leave the studio, but it is expected that they will be able to resume work shortly.

The cause of the eye trouble it is thought lies in the fact that the players, who up until recently have been working at the Cohan studio, were unaccustomed to the different facilities offered them when they took up the production of *Broadway Jones* at Mary Pickford's studio in Fort Lee following her departure for Los Angeles. The building of several big sets at the Cohan studio for *Broadway Jones* prevented the players from working there and in order to lose no time the Pickford studio was taken over until such time as the New York studio was ready. It is felt however, that all the players will soon be able to resume work on the picture.

GIRL, 12, EARNS $75 A WEEK
Children Kept From School To Work In Movie Studio

(from *The New York Times*, March 10, 1917, p. 9)

The reason many children are staying away from school these days is that they can act in the movies and earn

Mary Pickford with some of the young extras needed for The Poor Little Rich Girl *(Paramount-Artcraft, 1917).*

more money than their parents can. This fact was learned yesterday in the Municipal Term Court, where the Board of Education was taking legal action against parents whose children had been staying out of school.

About a month ago truant officers of the Board of Education noticed that a large number of children were crossing the Fort Lee ferry at hours when they should have been in school. Investigation disclosed that they were acting in motion picture studios in New Jersey. The officers got about twenty-five of the children and saw their parents. In most of the cases the parents consented to make arrangements for the education of the child actors under the supervision of the District School Superintendent. Cases against these parents were not pressed in the courts.

The case of Maxine Elliott Hicks, 12 years old, of 361 West Fifty-fifth Street, however, was set for trial before Magistrate Appleton today. Maxine's mother, Margaret Hicks, explained that her daughter was busy in the filming of a new production. She admitted the charge made by Joseph L. Coppinger, Division Supervisor of Attendance, that the child had been absent from school for twenty-nine days.

Mrs. Hicks stated that Maxine was in Mary Pickford's studio, and appeared in the film play, *The Poor Little Rich Girl*.

"My daughter is getting $75 a week", she said. "She used to get $100 a week when we were out West, but salaries are smaller here in New York."

Supervisor Coppinger stated that his investigations disclosed many instances of large incomes earned by child actors. One mother, he said, was getting $30 a day for letting her six children act.

PARAGON STUDIO FOR FAMOUS PLAYERS-LASKY

(from *Moving Picture World*, March 31, 1917, p. 2126)

The Famous Players-Lasky Corporation has taken possession of the Paragon studio in Fort Lee, New Jersey, one of the largest and most completely equipped daylight studios in the world, which will henceforth be used for the production of Paramount pictures. The structure is to be renamed the Famous Players-Lasky studio, because of the fact that both the Famous Players and Lasky pictures will be produced in it.

When Madame Petrova returns from Jacksonville, where she has gone to do the exterior scenes in her first Lasky-Paramount production, she will proceed immediately to the newly acquired studio at Fort Lee, where Maurice Tourneur will complete the production. At the present time Marie Doro is finishing the Famous Players production, *Heart's Desire*, at Fort Lee, and other productions starring these two distinguished stars will be staged there from time to time.

BUTTER WITH MY BREAD

By Olga Petrova

(New York: Bobbs-Merrill, 1942, pp. 282–284)

On March seventeenth [1917] I started my first picture with Mr. Lasky, *The Undying Flame*, written by Emma Bell. The story had come into the office of Popular Plays and Players and at the time I had been very anxious to do it. Mr. Weber had turned it down for the reason that the first part was laid in Thebes under Rameses III. Mr. Weber was of the opinion that anything in the nature of a historical or "costume" play would have no chance for success, either with the exhibitors or with the public. Mr. Lasky and Mr. Tourneur, however, liked it.

More than that they were enthusiastic. So was Mr. Van der Broeck, Mr. Tourneur's cameraman.

Looking back now on the weeks spent in the filming of that picture, I see them as the oasis in the desert of my cinema experiences. The film itself, apart from any share I had in it, was one that I could view with little criticism, no embarrassment and a great deal of aesthetic pleasure. As a manager Mr. Lasky was considerate, indulgent and sensitive. Mr. Tourneur was all and more than I had expected as a director.

For the first time since I had faced a camera lens, I could relax from the tension of worry, fear and distrust, and place myself without question under the guidance of a man who, I knew, *knew*; a man who knew that he knew; a man of culture and imagination.

The story told of the death of a princess of Egypt and her shepherd lover in ancient Thebes, and of their reincarnation and reunion in modern Cairo. Scenes, situations, settings, lightings, all called for the knowledge and talent that Mr. Tourneur possessed, and while he handled the many big episodes, involving great numbers of people, with dynamic effect and with a minimum waste of time and effort, it was in the treatment of individual human emotions that he excelled.

His methods of lighting were a revelation to me. Sets, instead of being uniformly flooded with harsh blinding whiteness, were shadowed or high-lighted in spots, suggesting or emphasizing, as the case might be. This treatment of chiaroscuro created a subtler and more spiritual approach to the perception of the observer than could possibly be achieved by the older system of flat or back lighting.

When the completed film was run off in the projection room, for the first time in witnessing a picture in which I had taken part I had no feeling of

Olga Petrova in Maurice Tourneur's The Undying Flame *(Paramount-Lasky, 1917).*

ings have been hung in the salons of Paris, has given up being an intimate artist, because, as he says, he can have a greater range for his artistic expression as a motion picture director, seems to be a sufficient argument that the pictures are art. Mr. Tourneur has been called the artist who paints with human pigments. His canvas is life. His tools are elementary – a marvelous eye for proportion, an acute artistic sense and a broad understanding of human nature.

Painting with human beings

"That art is long and time is fleeting, is very true indeed", remarked the Frenchman, "if one paints in oil or water colors, even when one takes the post-impressionistic or cubistic short-cut; but when one paints with human beings, ah! then the time is even more fleeting. But achievement is very visible, and that is always a great satisfaction. Furthermore, you have art at first hand – in the flesh, so to say."

Those who have watched Mr. Tourneur at work in his studio will agree that not only is he a great artist, but a great actor as well. And that is not strange, for he studied histrionics under the Belasco of France, M. Andre Antoine. In the capacity of motion picture director he conceives each character in the photodrama and does not rest until he finds a "human pigment" to match. Then he outlines every move and expression. He selects the costume and settings. Any canvas an artist painted could not more truly be his than the thousands of feet of film after Mr. Tourneur has directed a picture.

Although he has been in this country a trifle less than four years, Mr. Tourneur has won his way to the first rank of the big directors. Among his more recent productions are the three Mary Pickford masterpieces *Less Than*

having participated in it. I saw only the smooth and beautiful unfolding of a story. And when Mr. Lasky took my hand and told me I had done well, I was more humble than proud, and very, very grateful that I had the privilege of being associated, in some manner, with what both he and Mr. Tourneur were pleased to regard as a creditable achievement.

MAURICE TOURNEUR PAINTS WITH HUMAN BEINGS
In Analysis of Film, Artist-Director Sees Splendid Artistic Future for Pictures When Dramatist Realizes Rich Field

By Charles Emerson Cook
(from *Exhibitors Herald,* June 9, 1917, p. 31)

Every now and then a heated discussion arises as to whether the "silent drama" can rightfully be classified as art. The motion picture emphatically presents it as such, and the layman is perfectly willing to accept it as such. But every now and then a member of the opposing element in the motion picture controversy comes forward with a new argument to put the films without the pale.

The fact that Maurice Tourneur, the French artist-actor-director whose paint-the Dust, *The Pride of the Clan* and *The Poor Little Rich Girl* [*Less Than the Dust* was not directed by Tourneur, but by John Emerson-ed] and *The Whip*. He now is directing Mme. Petrova in a new photoplay soon to be published.

Sees splendid artistic future

In summing up his aims and ideas in the realm of the cinema, Mr. Tourneur said:

"I submit that action does not mean melodrama, that movement does not mean speed, that there is as much drama in the glance of an eye as in the burning of a city, and that mental conflict is superior to physical. I believe that the motion picture has a splendid artistic future and that the future will be hastened just as soon as the serious American dramatist realizes that here is a field rich in material and opportunity and worthy of the highest traditions and honors."

PAULINE FREDERICK NEARLY ASPHYXIATED

(from *Moving Picture World*, June 23, 1917, p. 1919)

The most thrilling scenes which have been staged at the Famous Players-Lasky Fort Lee studios since their acquisition by that company were filmed last week under the direction of Robert G. Vignola, when the fire episodes in *The Love That Lives* were enacted before the camera.

Pauline Frederick, star of the production, is depicted as being burned to death in an office building while her son, a young fireman, rescues his fiance from the same room. These scenes provided several thrills which were not originally intended by Scudder Middleton, the author of the story. As a result of the operations Pauline Frederick was nearly asphyxiated; Pat O'Malley, who plays the fireman, was severely burned about the hands and face, and Violet Palmer,

who plays the fiance, fainted while being helped down the ladder by O'Malley.

"SEVEN KEYS TO BALDPATE", COHAN'S SECOND FILM FOR ARTCRAFT, NEARING COMPLETION
Expect Play to Be Entirely Filmed in Course of Week; Two Eastern Studios Now Being Used for Big Scenes

(from *Exhibitors Herald*, July 14, 1917, p. 34)

In order to save time in the production of George M. Cohan's second Artcraft offering, *Seven Keys to Baldpate*, adapted from his former stage success of the same name, both of the Famous Players-Lasky studios in the east are being used. A series of big scenes have already been staged at the Fifty-sixth street studio in New York, where Mr. Cohan has been appearing before the camera during the past three weeks.

At the Fort Lee studio a big exterior hotel set was recently filmed, and other scenes now are being taken while at the New York studio new sets are being built so that Mr. Cohan and his company may lose no time between scenes. In speaking of the production of this film Director [Hugh] Ford said:

"The wonderful progress we have been able to make on Mr. Cohan's new picture has indeed been most gratifying to me. The work on this film has gone ahead rapidly and without a hitch. Mr. Cohan is working day and night in an effort to get this film out as soon as possible, as a result of the demand from exhibitors for another Cohan film in the near future."

It is expected that the play will be entirely filmed in the course of another week, as far as the star is concerned, and after taking a series of other scenes in which he does not

appear the film will be ready for cutting and assembling. The publication date has not yet been announced by Artcraft.

In addition to George M. Cohan, Pauline Frederick and Olga Petrova, many other Paramount stars drifted through the Paragon studio. Douglas Fairbanks, who preferred filming in New York at this point in his career, made such films as *Wild and Woolly* and *The Man from Painted Post* here in 1917, at least those parts that did not require western landscapes. By the time the *New York Dramatic Mirror* visited the studio, it was clearly the studio of choice for Paramount's more ambitious east coast productions.

LITTLE JOURNEYS TO EASTERN STUDIOS – PARAMOUNT
The Two Studios Used for the Making of Paramount Pictures Offer Every Facility for the Best in Photoplay Production – Sixth of the *Mirror*'s Little Journey's

By Alison Smith

(from *New York Dramatic Mirror*, August 18, 1917, pp. 10–11)

Paramount has two Eastern studios, one on each side of the Hudson. Because of the infinite variety in Paramount plays, it is necessary to have them staged under varying conditions, hence the town studio, especially adapted to artificial lighting in Manhattan, and the open-air glass-domed studio on the top of the Palisades. Each serves to complete the other and if you don't see what you want in one studio you ask for it and find it in the other.

The New Jersey plant is situated just back of the cliffs behind a grove of trees which hide a view of the river. The entrance to the main floor is through the office of Albert E. Lowe, the studio manager, who has had charge of the building ever since it was built and who knows thoroughly every inch that it covers. His office commands a view of the outside lot where he can superintend the building of the various exterior sets without leaving his desk chair. The directors' rooms are in a direct line with this office, so that the entire section may be thrown open into one room when a conference of the general staff is called.

Stage under glass

The studio itself is simply a large stage completely arched by a dome of glass. It is divided into two revolving stages, making it possible for work to go on with one set while another is being built on the same section, which may be moved when ready under the same light and in the same position as the former set. Each stage has its separate lighting system which eliminates the necessity of moving and adjusting the area.

A swinging platform has been hung from the top of the glass dome from which an acrobatic cameraman may snap his overhead views with the agility and ease of a steeple-jack. This platform swings across the entire length of the building and will give a birdseye view of the stages at every possible angle.

On this particular afternoon, the studio made a vivid picture of Oriental local color, for it was filled with the interior sets for the screen presentation of *Barbary Sheep*. Maurice Tourneur, who is directing the picture, which features Elsie Ferguson, has spent several months in Algiers and is thoroughly familiar with the surrounding country where the English husband of Hitchens's story hunts his world-famed Barbary sheep. He has personally superintended every detail of the sets for this vivid drama and the result will undoubtedly be the creation

of a Far Eastern atmosphere that will surpass any picture of this type that has hitherto been shown.

Three well stocked floors

The left wing of the building comprises three floors entirely devoted to property rooms. The amount of stage properties housed in this section is valued at $300,000, for in the costly sets no attempt is ever made at substituting, and if the script calls for "an antique masterpiece" an exact copy of that masterpiece is made at great care and expense. The results of this attention to details at all cost is apparent to everyone who is familiar with the standard of excellence in Paramount settings.

In the opposite wing is the carpenter shop where a large force of workers were turning out the separate pieces that were about to be put up on the lot outside. On the balcony is a special section for molders who carve out all the designs in wood or plaster that are used in the more elaborate sets. The scenic department occupies the other half of the wing and was filled with huge canvas hung on chains which can be adjusted to any height at the convenience of the painter. Here also are the tiny models which are made of every set while its construction is still under discussion.

Like a hotel corridor

The dressing-rooms give the upstairs floor the appearance of a hotel corridor, with a special section reserved for the stars. At present Elsie Ferguson is occupying a private suite which faces on each of the lots giving a view of the Algerian village where she is working out the destiny of the imprudent but captivating heroine of *Barbary Sheep*. Miss Ferguson stopped her inspection of an Algerian costume long enough to discuss her problems in the moving picture field, which she has met with

Tourneur on the Algerian street set built for Barbary Sheep *(Paramount-Artcraft, 1917).*

the intensity and breadth of vision that characterized her work on the legitimate stage. Her point of view is absorbingly interesting and she gives one more material for thought in a five minutes' chat than could be gained in hours of research. But unfortunately all this has no direct bearing on the studio tour as such, and is, as Kipling says, "another story".

Opening out of the dressing rooms is the costume department presided over by Madame Borries. These rooms, as well as the rest of the studio, were permeated by the Oriental atmosphere and were rich in bizarre costumes of the Far East. Madame Borries has been a close student of the history of costume and is herself an expert designer. The lot that encircles the building presents a bewildering study in geography. Half of the circle is a complete Belgian village built for the screen presentation of *Arms and the Girl*, which features Billie Burke, while directly across the border is a street in Algeria as a background for the less savage moments in *Barbary*

Sheep. The Algerian scene was designed by Monsieur Ben Carré, under the supervision of Maurice Tourneur, and is one of the scenes that will give to the finished picture all the haunting charm of a Robert Hitchens novel.

Paramount has recently bought a large tract of land to add to the open space already surrounding the studio and there are indications that more and more of their exterior work will be done in Fort Lee … .

REALISTIC SCENES IN CAVALIERI FILM
Fine Atmospheric Effects for Paramount's "The Eternal Temptress"

(from *New York Dramatic Mirror*, October 13, 1917, p. 14)

The scenes of *The Eternal Temptress*, which will bring Mme. [Lina] Cavalieri to the screen, and which was written expressly for her by Mme. Fred de Gressac, and adapted by Eve Unsell, are all laid in Italy.

Besides the familiar Grand Canal of Venice, the Bridge of Sighs, and the quays of Rome, the famous church of San Marco has been reproduced at Fort Lee with startling fidelity. In several scenes the star is seen entering or leaving the doors of this picturesque old house of worship, and the populous neighborhood, with churchgoers, beggar hordes, and so on, required the use of large numbers of extra people. Not satisfied with using the ordinary types employed in "mob" scenes made up for the occasion, Director Chautard sent out a call for real Italians, and since then the studio lot has been crowded with picturesque figures, some in the very garb they wore as immigrants from their own country.

Emile Chautard is a persistent seeker for "atmosphere" in pictures, because he realizes that a large part of the charm and the convincing quality of a photoplay depends upon this elusive thing. In addition, the actors supporting Mme. Cavalieri are all splendidly equipped for their respective roles.

LION SCARING STAGE HEROES SLAIN BY HEROIC STAGE CARPENTER

(from *Moving Picture World*, May 25, 1918, p. 1160)

The last scenes in the spectacular Paramount picture starring Lina Cavalieri have been taken by Edward Jose at the Fort Lee studios of the Famous Players-Lasky Corporation, marking the completion of the biggest production thus far undertaken by this company in the east. Previously listed as *Gismonda*, it will be released under the title of *Love's Conquest*, the title symbolizing the power of love in leveling all barriers and establishing a plebeian as the consort of the Duchess of Athens.

The taking of the lion scene, in which Courtenay Foote as Almerio the huntsman, rescues the child of the Duchess from the lion's den, nearly

> The carelessness with fire and explosives seen at most Fort Lee studios was matched by the way in which lions, tigers, bears and other dangerous beasts were handled. Sometimes these animals escaped the studio premises entirely and had to be tracked through the community. A large Russian bear once fled the Solax studio and was discovered hiding under the front porch of Mayor Arthur Kerwien. For slaying this enraged lion with a fire axe, John C. Abbott, Jr. received a letter of commendation and a Liberty Bond.

resulted in a tragedy. The lion was a magnificent specimen, whose record of killing three trainers should have led to its execution, but its present owner and trainer, J.A. Cahill, believed he had controlled it sufficiently to hold its temper in check. A thrilling scene was enacted in which Foote succeeded in beating the lion off and scaling the walls with the child in his arms. The lion had become thor-

oughly enraged, and when the trainer sought to drive it back in its cage it leaped upon him and attacked him. There were five hundred persons taking part in the scene, and pandemonium reigned. The lion picked up the form of Cahill and stood at bay, undaunted by the missiles which were hurled at it and the streams from fire extinguishers striking its face and eyes. In the studio John Abbott, Jr., a carpenter, heard the cries of the mob and the roars of the lion, and snatching up a fire axe rushed to the scene. He charged upon the beast and brought the axe down upon its head. Stunned, the lion dropped the trainer, and twice more Abbott swung his weapon upon the skull of the animal, killing him. Cahill will survive.

These two interviews with Maurice Tourneur capture the moment when his reputation as the screen's most sensitive artist was at its height. Not even D.W. Griffith was considered his equal in terms of photographic effects, thematic "delicacy", and overall incorporation of symbolism, then a highly regarded artistic virtue (Griffith made *Broken Blossoms* that year in an obvious effort to recapture the crown). Tourneur discusses his most remarkable films, *The Blue Bird* and *Prunella*, attempts to bring the theater of Gordon Craig and Max Reinhardt to movie audiences. After both films failed at the box office, Tourneur never again talked about motion picture art with the same unalloyed enthusiasm.

TOURNEUR – A WEAVER OF DREAMS
A Half Hour Spent In The Workshop of a Maker of Movie Magic

By Frances Wood

(from *Picture Play,* June 1918, pp. 211–216)

A little office in the Famous Players' Fort Lee studio – the sunlight streaming in through windows looking out on a southern exposure – the smell of new pine wood. On the table, large sheets of cardboard, covered with tiny pictures of interior sets pasted in even rows – inspiration and ideas, dreams caught and empanelled. On a blackboard, more sketches of sets done in chalk.

Entered Maurice Tourneur. He walked briskly across the room, took his desk chair, fixed an abstracted pale-blue eye on a point somewhere hopelessly beyond me, and inquired: "What ees eet you weesh to know? You must ask eet me. You must ask questions." His voice had the liquid charm of his native French tongue.

He waited – still abstracted. The ticking clock on the wall seemed to say: "Hurry-hurry! He is keeping a ten thousand-dollar star waiting-waiting-waiting."

Tourneur's figure sat before me, rather good sized, his clothes built and worn with great nicety, and there was no look of impatience on his blond, thoughtful face. But it was quite plain that his thoughts were elsewhere, at work, perhaps, over some big, half-formed idea, away off in the recesses of the studio.

"About your work, " I asked. "Your characteristic creations, such as *The Blue Bird* and *Prunella* – – "

"Ah! What I am trying to do!"

Somewhere a door had opened, and Tourneur's mind entered the room for the first time.

In the presence of Tourneur's mind one feels a driving, creative force. I will not impede the telling of his ideas by attempting to reproduce his accent. Picture a big mind struggling for self-expression with the difficulties of a tongue not its own – picture a blond, French type, moist wisps of fine, straw-colored hair, a pleasant, thoughtful face – and you will have Tourneur.

"I am trying to give the idea of the author to the audience", he began rapidly. "I am trying to transmit his thought through pictures. I do this by centering the attention on the actor and on the story, and by taking it off

Lina Cavalieri with Emile Chautard, director of The Eternal Temptress *(Paramount-Famous Players, 1917).*

the set. I don't want to make pretty pictures – primarily."

I exclaimed in surprise: "But *The Blue Bird* is beautiful –the most beautiful –"

"A-a-ah, but the thought is beautiful, so that the expression of it naturally is beautiful, also", he interrupted. "Remember that it is a dream ensnared in words by a master dreamer."

"Only you lose the wonderful color effects on the screen", I observed.

"Indeed, no!" he exclaimed. "We get them by values – by light and shadow. Have you never heard an artist who works in black and white talk about the color in his drawings?

"For example. Do you remember the dance of *Fire* in *The Blue Bird*? In that I used first the leaping flames, and little by little I developed a figure growing out of the fire. For this I used real fire, with a glass between it and the human figure, so that it looked as though the figure were in the flames – a part of them. The shadow and light effects were – magnificent! And in order to strengthen the idea I showed the dance of the flames on the childrens' faces. Water was developed out of a waterfall and I produced the ripple of the stream for a similar effect on the faces and figures of the children.

"Once a big effect was the director's only goal – something stupendous, immense. Pouf! Any one can do that with a few tons of scenery and enough extras." Tourneur was gesticulating excitedly now. "I-I am trying for something else. I am creating atmosphere.

"We are doing interesting things in sets", he broke off suddenly, leaning over and picking up one of the cardboard sheets on which he pointed to a little picture.

"That's the way interiors used to be furnished – full of claptraps, knickknacks – junk, I think you call it. Now I am putting in no more than is necessary, in order to have as little as

possible to distract attention from the thought of the play.

"Take, for example. *The Doll's House,* on which I am working this morning. There is little opportunity to make the interior of the house in that play beautiful. The people living in it were poor, and the play must be consistent, always, to be convincing.

"But if I couldn't make it beautiful. I could at least make it inconspicuous; and I venture to say that no one will remember that set after they have seen the film, though the story will still be a vivid thing in their minds.

"Take *Prunella*. That's full of examples of how the set is made to convey the thought of the author and to center the attention on the actors. In one picture, a moon and a tree. That is absolutely all – beside the lovers. Again, I use cardboard houses – buildings with no depth whatsoever. Why? 'Prunella' and the 'Mummers' are cardboard persons – they cannot live in real houses, places of three dimensions. Of course it is artificial – violently artificial. But the whole thing is a phantasy." Tourneur broke off suddenly – began again as spasmodically:

"Directing is almost reflex action with me. I mean that I have certain elements to work with – actors, sets, furniture. I move them around as I need them. I am very impulsive. I speak abruptly, often impatiently. I may speak to a star as severely as I do to an electrician, or as impersonally as I push back a chair, or move a vase. Not because I do not respect the artist, but simply because he is only one of the elements with which I can get the effects. Oh, I love it – I'd do it for nothing! But don't tell Mr. Zukor that", he added hastily, with humor, rising from his chair.

We walked through a whole string of little offices, toward the set where the director's work awaited him – a day of exacting detail, difficulties big and small, but also achievement.

"But the big difficulty in making a great picture" – Tourneur stopped and shrugged his big, loose shoulders – "is that everybody wants to do the directing. No one is satisfied to confine himself to his own gift. The carpenter wants to do the interior decorating, the scenario writer wants to select the costumes, and they all want to direct the production. If you were to build a house you would, for instance, let the upholsterer install the plumbing, and the stone mason hang the curtains? Hein! You would not! A sense of fitness is a thing most desirable."

"Which means that directing, like any other art – -" I interrupted. " – -is a gift". Tourneur's mind jumps like an electric spark. "Directors are born. Travel and education count for nothing. A man who has never been outside his home village, and of small schooling, may be the great director of the future."

"Then all your education, travel, accomplishments don't enter into the directing you are doing now?" I asked, in surprise. For Tourneur, standing on the threshold of forty years, has had a most varied career. After graduating from Lycée Condorcet in Paris, where he was born, he became a painter and interior decorator at eighteen. During this early part of his career he designed textiles, stage settings, illustrated magazines, made posters and lace curtains – all with equal facility. Later, he became associated with Rodin, the famous sculptor; then Puvis de Chavannes, the great mural decorator. Three years he spent in the army. Then he became an actor, and made a world tour with Madame Rejane. All this, I thought, must have made for Tourneur the place which he holds among the foremost directors of screen art, and I expressed myself accordingly.

"Not a bit", he rejoined energetically. "We don't want to know what Spain really looks like. We want to get the

author's impression of Spain. Do you have to go to Spain to understand what I mean when I say 'Castles in Spain?' And now – ”

We had reached the set. Electricians and camera men were hurrying about. An auburn-haired girl stood knitting an army sock. “Mees Ferguson, eef you please – -”

Elsie Ferguson dropped her work and stepped into the set.

“Camera! Lights – *lights*!” The master mind was assembling the elements.

MONSIEUR TOURNEUR
Otherwise accurately called
“the poet of the screen”

By Dorothy Nutting

(from *Photoplay*, July 1918, pp. 55–57)

Monsieur Maurice Tourneur is French, there can be no mistake about that. The boom of his voice making baritone solos of perfect English phrased in the French manner, the twinkle of the poet's humor in his eyes – a twinkle most English or American men might scorn as a symptom of triviality – these symptoms bespeak his nationality. And were that not enough, one could know it by the delicacy of his touch in his picture productions that there is the soul of the Gallic troubadours somewhere in his makeup.

I shudder to think what a heavy hand would have done to such wisps of dream as *Prunella* and *The Blue Bird*. How terrible to think of some master of melodrama “putting the punch” into them! But Tourneur is a poet of the screen. Like most men who have traveled widely, and especially like most Frenchmen who have traveled, he is a true play-boy. Whenever you find a man who is interested in a great variety of things, you will find a man who can easily entertain. He has much to draw from. Monsieur Tourneur is a true citizen of the world, and that is how it is that he is such an unusual director of moving pictures.

Tourneur began life – the important part of life, that is – studying Art and spelling it with a capital A, in the Latin Quarter of Paris. He doesn't say much about his painting, though he must have been a pretty fair artist, for years later he assisted Puvis de Chavannes in

(Above): The Blue Bird (Famous Players-Lasky, 1918).
(Below): Jules Raucourt and Marguerite Clark in Prunella (FPL-Paramount, 1918), settings by Ben Carré.

decorating the grand staircase of the Boston Public Library. But it was while he was studying art that he first met the cinema. At first, it was a great sensation in Paris, and with thousands of others he rushed off to see what miracle this was, that made pictures move.

The cinema tried to beckon to him. He haunted the funny little theatres which soon sprang up, paying often as much as fifty centimes (ten cents) a ticket. This was a great extravagance for the young student at the Lycée Condorcet, and soon abandoned, for he obtained an engagement with the great tragedienne, Rejane, who was making a tour of the world, including Africa.

"One unique engagement", says M. Tourneur, "was at Dakar, on the northern edge of the Sahara in Algiers. We reached the town on a queer sort of boat, the engine of which was dying by inches. We were due at eight o'clock at night, and arrived at midnight exactly. Everyone was asleep and we would lose our evening's receipts. We were all truly dismayed! For we needed the money, so Madame Rejane, with all her adorable aplomb, merely attached bells to the necks of a few of the natives and turned them loose to announce the news of our arrival. Behold, in half an hour there we had an audience ten times larger than we would have had at eight!"

But, to come back to America and the matter in hand, the art of this poet of the screen, his views are refreshingly different from that of most of the producers. For example:

"There is an odious fallacy that a great many people still believe, in regard to the moving picture. It is almost as widespread as that the cinema is in its infancy. By that I mean the belief that we must give the public what it wants. To me, that is absurd. As absurd as if the fashion dictators should attempt to suit women's wishes in costumes. In reality the opposite is the case, is it not? The fashion dictators say: 'Next year you shall look like umbrellas, ladies – but this year you shall be as a broomstick;' and the ladies obey like lambs and even enjoy their servitude! The public does not know what it wants until it sees it – how should it? So we must try over and over again, until we have discovered what it is they really do want to see."

Another of the Tourneur antipathies is the remark that many people think must be true today because Shakespeare made it many hundred years ago, "The play's the thing". This idea M. Tourneur combats with all the force at his command.

"I know there are few to agree with me", he said "but I shall always assert that the play is *not* the thing. If it were true, one would merely read a play and the acting, the beautiful presentation, the 'ensemble' as we say, would amount to nothing. Then, if the play were the thing, the lack of these, of the acting, the good interpretation and ensemble would not spoil it. To me, neither the play, the acting, the star, the director, nor the presentation, is the thing. It takes all of them.

Of course, I believe that the play, a classic such as *The Blue Bird, A Doll's House* or *Prunella*, should not be changed. Nor should there be a dragged in illogical "happy ending" to replace the author's conclusion. But I do believe that to make a screen success of any play of this sort there must be the best acting, the best directing and the best presentation available. And with the showing of it, good music. Any one of these elements missing and your picture will not succeed.

"I enjoyed making *The Blue Bird*", he went on thoughtfully. "But if I could have had another six months to work on it, I would have enjoyed it much more. Then, too, I cannot work so well with children. They are disturbing. Work at the studio should go along smoothly like the clock – but, children, ah! they cannot be regulated! However, this I must say, that little Tula Belle and Robin MacDougall, the two child actors in *The Blue Bird* are exceptionally clever little players and will be heard of one day in the future."

Shortly before his death, Rodin expressed the belief that the motion picture was destined to become a great art form as well as a universal entertainment. "It requires", said the illustrious sculptor, "a director with

vision, imagination, a grasp of all the arts, a keen sense of symbolic values, to carry the cinema to the point where it can express the evasive values of Maeterlinck, the twilight harmonies of Debussy, the subtle evocations of Verlaine. Such a man will be the Pierre Loti of the screen."

Curiously enough, M. Tourneur was, for a time, Rodin's pupil. Is he the fulfillment of Rodin's prophecy? One can easily imagine so from his *Barbary Sheep, The Rise of Jennie Cushing, Rose of the World, Prunella, The Blue Bird*, and *A Doll's House*. This latter is a "tough nut to crack", in that Ibsen's works depend so much on symbol, upon suggestion, whispered conferences, keywords that unlock the subconscious and half said truths.

In *Barbary Sheep*, with Miss Ferguson, Mr. Tourneur achieved the haunting desert atmosphere, the lure of Saharan mystic romance to a bewitching degree. And he has found pictorial ways and means of presenting the finest shades of Maeterlinckian thought in his production of *The Blue Bird* … .

> Paramount films continued to be shot at Paragon until Zukor opened his new studio in Astoria in 1920. *Good Gracious, Annabelle* with Billie Burke and *The Dark Star,* a Marion Davies film for Hearst, were two of many. Lewis J. Selznick leased the studio in June 1920, an acquisition which gave him control of 2/3 of the stage space in Fort Lee, and held on until finally being forced out of business. But Jules Brulatour continued to occupy a corner of the building, and created Hope Hampton Productions to produce films there for his current protégé. His old partner Maurice Tourneur directed Hampton in *The Bait* (1921), but refused further offers; Brulatour then hired two of his associates, John Gilbert *(Love's Penalty)* and Clarence Brown *(The Light in the Dark)*, but they had no better luck than Tourneur. Brulatour's promotion of Hope Hampton became something of a joke, at least inside the industry, and a clear source for the Charles Foster Kane-Susan Alexander relationship in *Citizen Kane*. This surprisingly sarcastic piece in *Photoplay* is typical of the coverage Brulatour received for his troubles.

WHO AND WHAT IS HOPE HAMPTON?

By Bland Johaneson

(from *Photoplay,* November 1923, pp. 56–58)

Is She a Star?
Is She an Actress?
Has She Any Following?
Does the Public want her?
Will the Public Pay to See Her Pictures?
Why is she Featured Above Lew Cody, Nita Naldi and Conrad Nagel?

Just who and what is Hope Hampton? Is she a star? Thousands have been spent in exploitation and publicity to establish this claim. With what has it been backed up? Is she an actress? Has she ever had a following large enough to make her pictures pay?

About four years ago Hope Hampton made her picture debut as the "star" in an old-school, vamp film, labeled *A Modern Salome*. The story was frankly bunk, but it was pretentiously done, lively, intensely romantic, and curiously interesting as the gilded platter on which was served to the public a costly, dainty delectable new "star", whose obvious qualifications for her job were prettiness and youth, and who carried off her sudden situation with entirely comprehensible inexperience and rawness, while the public and the picture world awaited with tolerance and patience some hint of the "possibilities" which might have justified this elevation to "stardom" of an actress heretofore totally unknown. But was Hope Hampton even an "unknown actress?"

Questions like this obtruded themselves into the public consciousness with her prominence. As only unsatisfactory answers were coming from authoritative quarters and millions of followers of motion picture personalities, by some quaint trick of mind, expect and demand definite knowledge of the youth, training, antecedents and background of their favorites, strange legends or myths surrounding Hope Hampton came into active circulation.

Some had it that she was the daughter of a rich Texan ranch-owner and indulged by him in her whim of becoming an overnight picture pet. Others gave her the romantic O. Henry history of the Philadelphia Gimbel's bargain-basement, from which she gamboled, through the sunny pastures of the chorus "hoofers" and "ladies of the ensemble", into her screen glory and unlimited credit in any department store.

Obviously, such extravagant tales could not have gained credence in any circles not so accustomed to improbabilities and outlandish careers as that circle which follows the motion pictures. The silver screen has celebrated even stranger histories.

Still wilder and funnier stories were told. Hope Hampton's interest in letters and journalism was supposed to have led her into the writing cliques, where she made many warm friends among the clever little boys and girls who contribute to the papers and magazines. Gathering these playmates around her at luncheon, she is supposed to have entertained them with such cunning little *couvert* souvenirs as silver purses and flagons of rare perfume until their merry glee and pleasure with their pretty benefactress was communicated to all their reading public.

Feeling that no person more than Hope Hampton herself would rejoice to have all these silly delusions dispelled, the Editor of *Photoplay* asked me to see the star, form some estimate of her as an actress and a personality, and get from her, herself, if possible, her own account of her career (whether colorful or romantic, no matter, at least definite), in order to stem the flood of such questions as Who, What and Why is Hope Hampton?

My request for an interview was answered promptly by an invitation to dinner at the Ritz. Assuring Miss Hampton of my inability to accept her unusual courtesy, I suggested a later day. She placed a perfect aeon of dinner hours at my disposal, as well as an unbounded choice of smart restaurants. Finally, however, she agreed to my seeing her in her own house, which is on Park Avenue.

Arriving before her door, casement windows were opened above, and I was greeted by a cheery "yoo-hoo". Her prettiness was dazzling. Running to open the door for me, she was daintier, livelier, more animated than I ever have seen her on the screen, and of a totally different type. In a picture she is very blonde, rather limpid as to personality, slightly mature. In life she seems a fiery, redheaded little Irishman, reckless, blunt, almost tactless in the frankness with which she voices her opinions of things and people.

Expressing her surprise and relief at finding me not quite an unfriendly ogre, she led me into her drawing room and presented Mr. Jules Brulatour, the film-magnate who manages her and is credited, by rumor, with her discovery.

Miss Hampton's house is tiny, unpretentious and furnished in exquisite taste, with the almost-too-perfect touch of the interior decorator suggested in the disposal of every chair and ash-tray. Only this ultra-perfection hints of youth in Miss Hampton's luxurious wealth.

Mr. Brulatour immediately assumed command of the conversational ship, turning it into the most general, social and casual channels, prompting Miss Hampton to chatter about her dogs, her fondness for dogs, the value of her dogs, her harrowing experience of losing by theft an especially valuable and especially beloved dog, her strategy in recovering said canine, and the subsequent joy of their reunion.

I was unable, without resorting to downright rudeness, to make either the star or her manager tell me anything about her girlhood, experience, parentage, ambition, struggles, or one single anecdote which could suggest her juvenile character and environment. My own inability as an interviewer may have been entirely responsible for this.

Miss Hampton did say that she was born in Texas, raised and educated in Philadelphia, from whose public schools she came directly to the Sargeant Dramatic Academy, where she was "discovered" and selected because of her conspicuous talents to play the leading role in *A Modern Salome* as a featured star.

"Had you any previous experience in acting?"

"No. Only as an amateur with my class at the dramatic school."

"Had you ever before appeared in a picture?"

"No". (Miss Hampton later admitted that she had done a small bit, "just for fun", for which she had not been paid, in a Maurice Tourneur production which the director was making in some association with Mr. Brulatour.)

"Have you ever been on the stage?"

"Never".

"How do you account for the prevalence of the impression that you had?"

Here Mr. Brulatour answered for her: "It's because Hope makes such a wonderful 'personal appearance'. She makes a better one than any other star. Everyone thinks because of that she has had experience, but she had never been on the stage." (He refers here to the Hope Hampton exploitation stunt which was so largely responsible for landing her before the public, the practice of touring the country and appearing in picture houses to talk to the fans about picture personalities and picture-making.)

This launched the loquacious maiden into an animated recital of her experiences as a speaker in picture houses and how she never permitted the "razzers" to get her goat, although most stars were so fussed and confused before a not-quite-refined audience, the tough boys amusing themselves by throwing pennies to express their contempt.

"I give them back as good as they give me", said the Hibernian Hope, "and when they see they can't fuss me, they simply settle down".

Although it was delivered guilelessly, the pertinence of this line was not lost on me. Frankly, it is my strongest impression of Hope Hampton. She told me that she had no experience either on the stage or in the pictures, in fact, never had held any kind of job at all prior to her debut in *A Modern Salome*. She offered no explanation of the colossal piece of luck which had landed her without a single hard

knock on the top of her particular heap, told no little human story of her meeting with her first Big Opportunity.

My failure as an interviewer is especially disheartening to me in consideration of these circumstances: When Miss Hampton, after our one and only meeting, sent me a set of photographs to be submitted to this magazine, I found among them one inscribed: "To Bland, dear, lovingly Hope Hampton". I received a telephone call from Mr. Brulatour, who was anxious to tell me that I had made an awful hit with Hope, that, in fact, she really loved me and had found me the most charming, attractive and lovable creature God ever put breath into. Mr. Brulatour was not the only courier of this message. A few mutual friends of Hope's and mine betrayed the same astonishing confidence. They further instructed me to "say something nice about Hope". Why should this question be raised? Why should any one dream that things other than nice could be said about her? She is pretty, well-behaved, generous, fond of her mother, kind to dumb animals, and temperate. The Broadway phrase "a good kid" seems to fit her perfectly. But Hope Hampton, non-professional, does not concern this story.

What conspicuous ability and talent warrants her being featured above such serious and experienced actors as Lew Cody and Conrad Nagel in *Lawful Larceny*? Will the public pay for her pictures? Does the public want her? Do the pictures want her? Is Hope Hampton a star? Is she an actress?

(Above): Jules Brulatour, the powerful agent for Eastman motion picture film, had a hand in financing most of the studios in Fort Lee. Brulatour and his protégé, Hope Hampton, are photographed on their return from a European holiday in the early 1920s.

(Below): Hope Hampton and friends on the set of The Unfair Sex *(Diamant Film Co., 1926), one of the last silent features shot in Fort Lee.*

Management of the studio passed to Henri Diamant-Berger in 1925. He attracted a few independent productions, like *The Pinch Hitter* with Glenn Hunter and Constance Bennett, and also directed the last three Hope Hampton pictures. *The Unfair Sex* (1926), with Hampton and Nita Naldi, was probably the last film ever made there. Like some of the other old studios, the Paragon was turned into a theatrical warehouse and scenic shop. When it burned in 1952 it was paint and canvas, not nitrate film, that fed the flames. Fort Lee Film Storage, the borough's last remaining motion picture business, currently occupies the Sen Jacq Laboratory building, built on the lot by Jules Brulatour when he personally controlled every foot of motion picture film marketed by Eastman Kodak.

FIRE HITS OLD FILM STUDIOS IN FORT LEE
Flames Leap 100 Feet, Ruin Scenery For TV

(from the *Newark Star-Ledger*, March 24, 1952)

Fort Lee – Hundred-foot flames burned out the old Paragon Studios yesterday, turning into ashes both one of the movies' oldest landmarks and a fortune in props of the screen's newest competitor, television.

Last night only wisps of smoke moved where Lillian Russell, the Gish sisters and Eva Tanguay had emoted for some of the earliest feature films.

Scenery burns

Of more concern to Broadway, however, was the replacement of stage scenery for television shows such as the *Kraft Playhouse* and for New York theatrical productions now in the preparation stage. Fixtures for Fred Waring's show last night had been removed before the fire.

The block-square studios were used by the Kaj Velden Co. to make and store scenery. One of the owners, David Steinberg of Mt. Vernon, NY, said the loss to contents alone would reach $1,000,000.

The Paragon, which later became the Paramount Studios under Jesse Lasky and Adolph Zukor, was one of the last vestiges of Fort Lee's once-thriving film industry.

Fire companies from eight surrounding communities answered the four-alarmer, which sent smoke towering into the cloudy, flame-lit sky just after dawn.

Visible for miles

Residents of New York's Riverside Drive just across the Hudson River had a grandstand seat. The fire was visible for miles.

No one was in the studios, which were closed for the weekend. The cause of the fire was not determined immediately.

The studios consist of four two-story brick buildings, all connected. They contained a carpenter shop, paint shop, and an old studio with a 50-foot-high ceiling used mainly for storing bulky scenery.

Four firemen hurt

The fire started shortly after 6 A.M., and burned out of control for hours. Four firemen received minor injuries.

Cliffside Park firemen dragged hose 300 feet through a wooded plot to get to the fire. The studios are not far from the site of the original Biograph Studios [sic!], where the movie industry was born and Mary Pickford got her start. For some years, Fort Lee was the center for the silent picture business.

That was when Fort Lee "was in its glory", said one nostalgic policeman.

IMPERIAL SCENIC STUDIOS, Inc.
FORT LEE, NEW JERSEY
DAVID A. STEINBERG, Pres.
Call FOrt Lee 8-3269
(IN NEW YORK DIAL OPERATOR)

When the 1952 Paragon fire burned out the Kaj Velden Studios, the owners planned to reorganize as Imperial Scenic Studios. But this souvenir blotter is all that came of the project.

16

The Film Town

The "motion-picture town" described in this *Literary Digest* essay (reprinted from a New York daily) is Coytesville, the unincorporated northern sector of Fort Lee. The film company with fifteen subsidiaries to which the article refers must have been the newly organized Universal, and the local studio the Champion. The blasé attitude of the locals, and the involvement of the entire town in the filmmaking process, is a theme that would continue to mark descriptions of Fort Lee for the next decade.

A MOTION-PICTURE TOWN

(from *The Literary Digest,* November 23, 1912)

Seeing motion-pictures is just about as interesting to the people of Coytesville, a little New Jersey town on the Palisades of the Hudson, as hearing somebody tell an old anecdote they have heard before. To them battles, murders, highway robberies, and all that sort of thing thrown on the screens are a whole lot tamer than a fight between two Buff Cochin roosters in the village streets. And the reason is that they see all these thrilling dramas enacted before they are put on the films, and know all the make-believe tricks of the motion-picture people. Altho Coytesville is only one of several places where "photo-plays" are enacted, the work there is in all the essentials the same as it is everywhere else. Some of the clever tricks of the actors and camera men are described in the New York *Press*:

"When Roosevelt came out of the African jungle he did so, from a moving-picture point of view, out of the woods of Leonia, a short distance from Coytesville. Some of the residents of Leonia did not like the idea of being a part of Africa, even in moving pictures.

"But that was nothing. To show the facility with which the Jersey scenery can be adapted, the film company has recently been conducting a number of the Revolutionary battles. Ireland was freed last week several times in battles that would have put those of Hell's Kitchen to shame. Even the Boer War has not ended. Only a few days ago the "British" Lancers charged across the Jersey meadows. They did not charge sufficiently hard to suit the man behind the moving-picture camera, so they had to charge all over again, and the prompting was done through a megaphone by the manager.

"Perhaps the possibilities of the landscape of Coytesville will be better illustrated in a play, *The Toll of the Sea*. The rocks of the Palisades were not, of course, looking out over the sea, but what did that matter? The scene of the story was there nevertheless.

"A love-match that was supposed to have been in the heart of old County Kerry was really enacted in Coytesville. Another one, *The Daughter of Leah,* which was supposed to have a German setting, was very much enjoyed for its original performance in the woods around Coytesville.

"In all about fifteen subsidiary companies of the film company have the settings of their plays at Coytesville. Other companies have places in the Bronx, in Westchester County, on Long Island, Staten Island, and Jersey

Snapshot taken around 1918 looking east on Main Street from Linwood Avenue. A film crew is photographing a demonstration or parade, as a trolley car approaches in the distance. The two tall buildings at the right are still standing.

City Heights. Sometimes the scenes are enacted in the streets of Manhattan. But in none of these is the work of the community suspended while the plays are enacted.

"The other day a house was burned down in Coytesville. The people knew it was to take place in the afternoon, so at the appointed hour work came to an end and tradesmen and every one near the place were on hand for the fire.

"It was some fire, too! Jack Dalton dashed into the blazing doorway and grabbed a sleepy maiden from the flames, and smothered her torn feelings with kisses. It costs something to burn up one of the small frame houses erected especially for such occasions, but it is necessary.

"Just back of the place where the fire was held is the big barnlike structure of the film company. A trip through it will develop the fact that there is scenery inside it which can be used to make a Louis XIV drawing-room or a modern police court.

"In one of the latest plays brought out by this company a waif shown in the 'police court' was borrowed from one of the neighbors for a little while. One day the company wanted to have a Mexican scene. There was a house in Coytesville which had just the right sort of stucco front to make it appear "Mexicany". The yard and front of the house were hired for twenty minutes or half an hour, and many palms placed on the porch. It was thereby transformed into an 18-carat Mexican house. The drama was enacted and the tenant was paid for the trouble.

"Even the street-cars get into the plays sometimes. The conductors and motormen running to Coytesville have been seen throughout the country in street-car scenes. Sometimes robbers hop on the cars and the employees get in the pictures. Even a number of the residents have figured in the plays, and if any persons in San Francisco had ever lived in Coytesville they might recognize some of the citizens of the village when they walked across the screen in a moving-picture house in the Golden Gate city.

"In the summer time when campers frequent the Palisades and pitch tents on the shore front they are often stirred to the point of taking the law in their own hands when they see a villain 'chuck' a seemingly lifelike man over a high precipice. Of course the dummy doesn't get into much trouble by the drop, but the moving-picture machine gets startling results.

"In the battle of Bunker Hill, fought last week for the fifth time in recent months, the Continentals knocked the 'tar' out of the British soldiers in the encounter, and some of the small urchins of Coytesville got so excited over who had done most of the shooting that they carried the warfare into their own haunts and started a real 'mix-up'."

Practically all of the actors and 'stage hands' live in New York, and go over to Coytesville every morning. Once in a while an outsider is employed as a special performer, as in the case of a daring balloonist who ascended 500 feet above the river the other day, blew up the gas-bag with an explosive, and then descended easily with a parachute. We read on:

"The principals in the performances are recruited from regular theatrical companies. According to an official of the company which maintains its plant in Coytesville, one of their highest-paid actors gets about $300 a week, while the daily rate of pay is placed at $5 when they get someone to work by the day. While regular theatrical companies are paying only $2 and $3 a day for certain kinds of actors and actresses the "movies" companies are paying $5. Many have deserted the legitimate stage for a try at the moving-picture field because of the high rate of pay.

"Last year alone there was placed on the market in America 234,000,000 feet of films. These were shown in approximately 15,000 theaters valued at $50,000,000."

Although Fort Lee had been recognized as a popular filmmaking location since at least 1908, the construction of permanent studios made this activity much more visible. Encouraged by studio publicity departments, journalists who were invited out for a visit described not just a single business enterprise (as they would for a visit to the Biograph studio in the Bronx or the Paramount studio in Astoria), but an entire motion picture district, where a group of related businesses dominated the residential character of the town as well as its economic life. Channing Pollock, a once famous novelist, playwright, and dramatic critic, may have inadvertently helped to establish Fort Lee as the nation's original "film town" in this peculiar *Photoplay* essay.

THE DISCOVERY OF FORT LEE

By Channing Pollock
(from *Photoplay*, December 1915, pp. 63–70)

Considering its importance in the making of motion pictures, we were surprised to find that the ferry-house signs didn't star Fort Lee. In the billing on the building from which the steaming Charons take you across the Hudson, this little village, in which

For a time we feared we'd lost our road and got on Fifth Avenue.

There are only a dozen people in Fort Lee who are what they seem to be.

the drama in the world took place in Fort Lee. Persons who knew had informed us that the manifold activities of existence were concentrated in Fort Lee; that the borders of this tiny town enclosed most the mysteries of love and life and death; that here men fought and bled, and women suffered and sacrificed, and were photographed doing it. For years and years we had been interested in canned drama; now we were going to the canneries.

Our flagging spirits unfurled somewhat as we nosed into the stream. On the opposite shore tall chimneys were spouting smoke. Undoubtedly, these were the fun factories, the comedy crucibles, the melodrama mills, grinding neither slowly nor exceeding small. Letters twenty feet high told us of a "Palisade Amusement Park". Perhaps this was one of the places in which they manufactured amusement.

Romance accompanied us on the boat. There were a dozen mutable-mouthed, clean-shaven men – palpably players. I smiled at recollection of the story about an actor overboard, swimming strongly, when the searchlight found him, and, feeling himself at last in the glare of the calcium, he slipped his right hand into his coat front, bowed, and was drowned. Two cowboys, in sombreros and trousers that needed a hair cut, stood near me. Since there are no ranges nearer New York than the rifle-ranges at Coney Island, I assumed that these were riders for the camera. I was interested to observe that nobody noticed them. A director had informed me that indifference was the great advantage of Fort Lee.

"They're broken to the pictures", he said. "The moment you set-up in town crowds rise from the sidewalk like Venus from the Sea. But over there, you can fight the battle of Gettysburg without a single passer-by looking in his note book to see if it's

thousands of photoplays are filmed every year, wasn't even featured.

"Fort Lee", said the signs – just like that. And, on the other side, in the same type, "Leonia", and "Rutherford", and "Hackensack".

Later, we were to find that Fort Lee isn't temperamental, but, at the moment, this absence of distinction astonished us. We had been told that a third of all

the Fourth of July. The whole populace is a volunteer first-aid. You can borrow anything from a cow to a front parlor. A boy, walking alongside a picturesque old woman, approached me one day to inquire: "Mister; would you like to rent me mudder?"

Besides the cowboys, Charon took over three wooden cannon, a score of Belgian peasants on their way to atrocities, and a vintage automobile that seemed to have trouble keeping body and wheels together. "Bringin' it across to be wrecked", elucidated the chauffeur. We began to suspect everything in sight. There was a wagonload of pianos. "Going to wreck those, too?" I inquired.

"No."

"Sorry."

On the far side of the river, opposite One Hundred and Twenty-seventh Street, is a group of squalid, dirty, tumble-down, single-story shacks – saloons, cigar stores, quick lunch dives, garages, and accident insurance agencies.

"Fort Lee?"

The gentleman addressed shifted his quid, spat deftly upon his boot, and laconically retorted: "Sign".

There were two signs. One read, "Fort Lee"; the other, "The Road to Happiness". As both pointed the same way, we didn't discriminate, but started due North along the Hudson. On our left were occasional groups like that at the ferry – saloons, cigar stores, and thousands of Italian restaurants. The more dilapidated and ramshackle the restaurants, the grander their designations. One was called "Hudson Villa"; another, from whose porch was obtainable a fine view of a scow club, rejoiced in the name of "Buena Vista". I imagine wrestling with spaghetti must be the favorite sport of Fort Lee.

On our right loomed a subtle and illusive combination of smoke and river. When the wind blew, it was quite easy to tell which was which. In calm moments the blend impressively suggested Whistler's "Naval Engagement in the English Channel".

Fort Lee's roads were constructed by the engineer who built the Witching Waves at Coney Island, and he acknowledges indebtedness to the gentleman who invented Loop the Loop. Had we been warned, I should have nailed a double keel onto the car, or brought a stabilizer, or something. There *were* shock-absorbers, but, in the first five minutes, they absorbed all the shocks they could hold, and we got the rest. Alonzo, who isn't a sea-going chauffeur, suffered terribly from *mal de mer*, and progress was impeded further by the necessity of going back every few moments to pick up Helen. Helen weighs only a hundred pounds, and we kept losing her. Sometimes she went over the windshield, and sometimes over the sides, and once we found her hidden in the folds of our one-man-top. Finally, we pinned her to the seat. Every now and then we came to a sign remarking that the road was under repair, and that we used it at our own risk, but nothing was said of the existence of any other road. In one spot, where we had been obliged to drop into second, a board cautioned us against speeding.

Helen opined that we had missed the way to Fort Lee, and taken The Road to Happiness. "If this is The Road to happiness", I answered, "Mr. Bunyan's justly celebrated Slough of Despond should have been called The Primrose Path. Anyhow, The Road to Happiness is a play at the Shubert Theatre".

Once the car broke down, and, instantly, two little boys appeared and offered to lie under it for a dollar apiece. When we pointed out the absence of a camera they seemed chagrined. Later on, when we had struck a smooth stretch and were making up time, a farmer ran in front of us, waving both hands and calling upon us to stop. We stopped – blowing out a perfectly good tire, and ramming Helen under the rug rack so firmly that it took five minutes to pull her out again.

"I got it!" quoth the farmer.

"Got what?" said I.

"A precipice. Ain't that what you're lookin' for?"

Ten minutes later we came upon another sign. It pointed straight back, and bore the words, "Fort Lee". We must have passed the town without noticing it. A policeman hove in sight. I asked him whether, in the course of his peregrinations, he had ever come across a place called Fort Lee.

The officer stared at us blankly.

"Aren't you a policeman", I persisted.

"No", he replied, "I'm in the movies".

"Where are the movies?"

"Go back two miles, turn to your left, then to your right, run up on a car track where there isn't any road, and you'll come to Willat's, the Eclair and the Peerless."

I was about to thank the gentleman, when, somewhere on our left, rang out a succession of rifle shots. "What's that?" I asked, in alarm.

"Don't know", answered the policeman. Maybe it's a hold-up they're doing at the Solax, and maybe it's the siege of Lille."

At the turn to our right we encountered two signs. One pointed west and the other south. Both said: "Fort Lee". You've heard often enough about "a house divided against itself", but, as far as I know, Fort Lee is the only town in the world that lies in any direction you chance to be going.

We entered the zone. There was a rustic bridge "to let for pictures", there was a stable that offered, "For rent – Comedy and Heroic horses,' and there were so many women in make-up and short skirts, we feared we'd lost our road again and got on Fifth Avenue. Persons of both sexes

A villa actually did go up in smoke. Nobody paid any attention. The head of the fire department told the father of the family to "Behave!"

paraded nonchalantly in costumes of every place and period – ladies in evening dress, Roman soldiers, Servian peasantry, Russian Cossacks, gentlemen whose fur coats and cigarettes proclaimed villainy afoot, an automobile load of Egyptian slaves, a coal miner with a lamp in his cap and across his forehead a ghastly wound to which he was adding with a stick of grease paint. Movie make-ups, as you know, are the color of penny papers. The casual observer might have been pardoned for thinking himself in a colony of the jaundiced, or "up against" the Yellow Peril.

What a wonderland for Alice – fifteen minutes from Broadway! My director, however, had not exaggerated the indifference of Fort Lee. Everywhere cameras grinding out drama – to the right and left, in front and behind, burglaries and dynamite outrages and fat men rolling down hill, and nobody even turning to look at them. Along the road were pretty little cottages, and on the porches of these cottages sat nice old gentlemen, and kindly old ladies, who didn't blink an eyelid when three galloping Mexicans were shot and killed at their very door. George Cohan teaching Kaiser Wilhelm to do a highland fling wouldn't occasion comment in this village on the Hudson. Berlin may thrill, and London may quiver, but nothing terrestrial can astonish Fort Lee!

One began to doubt the genuineness of everything. Perhaps the nice old gentlemen and kindly old ladies weren't anything of the sort. Perhaps, like our bogus policeman, they merely worked for the movies. Perhaps those pretty cottages had been put up over night, to be torn down in the afternoon. Why not? A hundred yards away, in the middle of a stubbly, treeless field, stood a charming, ivy-covered wall, with a wrought-iron gate of painted wood – and nothing back of it, in front of it, or at either end of it. Just enough wall for an elopement. Still farther on, the façade of a tenement, with fire escapes, and dirty curtains at the windows, and beetle-browed foreigners thronging like flies – the front of a building without a building to back it up. And then there were stages, like the stages you see in theatres, but with no theatres around them – no roofs, no sides, only scenery and actors playing exciting little plays right out in the open. I'm as used to scenery as Fort Lee to murder and suicide, but I'm used to it decently covered and screened from the view of the passer-by. Somehow, these naked stages seemed positively obscene!

A runaway came tearing down the street – two frantic horses attached to a surrey. Nobody budged. To the end of my days I shall never know whether that runaway was impromptu, or whether the two girls screaming in the back seat of the surrey really wanted to be rescued. Neither will anybody else, but the girls and the man who took the picture – if it *was* a picture. It comforts me to reflect that by now it doesn't matter. Here and there in Fort Lee are huge iron hoops, suspended from heavy framework, a hammer hanging beside each, and these are intended for alarms of fire. But how is anyone to know when there *is* a fire in Fort Lee? Or, rather, how is anyone to know whether the fire is an honest-to-goodness, send-for-the-adjuster, goods-slightly-damaged, to-be-sold-at-cost conflagration, or a holocaust to be accompanied by an orchestral rendering of Sousa at the Strand. We saw the ruins of a stone dwelling that had been burned once by accident, and three times by design. "Condemned houses almost always are bought by the film companies", said a director, "and then used for some photoplay that requires a good blaze. Two years ago a villa in this neighborhood actually did go up in smoke. The occupants stuck their heads out of the windows and yelled for help. Nobody paid any attention, and, when the father of the family got out and telephoned for engines, the head of the fire department told him to 'Behave!'"

No wonder! As we rode along one of us observed a fine stone structure on a hill. "Beautiful", I said, "and appropriate. The man who lives there has taste. Owning property upon a crag, he has put up a real medieval castle – a building solid, and substantial, that will stand forever."

As I spoke, a gentleman in his shirt sleeves walked up to the building and pushed in one of its walls. The castle was canvas. It had been erected for a battle of the Crusaders, and, the battle being over, was doomed to immediate demolition.

After all this, was it surprising in that, coming upon a convent garden I which nuns were walking, I should have asked one of the sisters for what company she was working? Only this was a mistake. The sisters were bona fide, and just a little bit acidulous. If the wrong thing is to be done you can always count on my doing it – no matter what the handicap. There are only a dozen people in Fort Lee who are what they seem to be, but I found 'em.

Subsequently, a director informed me that this convent was the only place in town not to be rented for pictures. His voice trembled as he said it. To a director, anything that can't be used in a photoplay is a blot on the land-scape and a flaw in the utilitarian spirit of the age.

Fort Lee rents its chickens, its goats, its doorsteps, its porches, and its relatives. The summer-boarder industry is a thing of the past; the natives can do much better supplying backgrounds for the movies. Not only backgrounds, but anything else picturesque. A golden- haired child has come to be worth more than a cow. An ordinary window, even when the house is vacant and the picture people have to bring their own lace curtains, is worth two dollars any sunny morning. An old-fashioned parlor is invaluable, and a rustic bower, through which the moon can be made to shine, is worth its weight in gold. Someone pointed out to me an apple tree that had earned nearly six hundred dollars for its owner, and sheltered lovers enough – were they only "on the level" – to loft the local clergy to positions of affluence. A man who owned a stream invested two days in carting boulders, and two dollars in cement, and has lived on the pretty nook by the babbling brook ever since. Another man bought a house that had a grey stone garage. Lacking a car, he was about to tear down the garage, when wiser counsel prevailed. Within three years, that garage has netted a small fortune, masquerading as Libbey Prison, Andersonville, and the Bastile.

Before we came to Willat's, the Éclair, and the Peerless we lost our way nine times more, and once I got out in front of a brick building to ask directions. "Peerless Studio?" I inquired.

A young man sitting behind a window "gave me the once over". "Can you ride?" he queried.

"Yes."

"Drive an automobile?"

"Yes."

"Swim?"

"Yes", said I. "Look here; do you have to *swim* to Fort Lee?"

"Ain't you lookin' for a job in the movies?"

I *thought* I had recognized that contempt – the contempt only to be found in an office boy's attitude to an actor.

Willat's, the Éclair and the Peerless occupy what would be the same block, if there were any blocks in Fort Lee. The former is composed of two big brick buildings, surrounded by a high cement wall. The later are equally substantial. And yet, despite their substantiality, somehow these structures suggest mushroom growth – perhaps because they have sprung up so rapidly. Helen swore that the first time we passed the Solax there were three buildings, and that when we came back there were four. Probably, Helen exaggerated, but, at least it is true that within a half a dozen years no fewer than twenty great studios have materialized in Fort Lee.

They are all brick buildings, with plenty of glass, grouped together so that, when they don't suggest mushrooms, they do suggest the Crystal Palace, or a section of a World's Fair. Most of them are surrounded by automobiles – scores of automobiles of every grade and year – and open air stages, cluttered with modern furniture, and painted cathedrals, and Babylonian pillars. Sometimes actors are shooting at each other on these stages, and sometimes carpenters are hammering, and always masons are putting up a new studio. There are formal gardens, and tangled wildernesses, and the world's greatest mixture of beauty, and ugliness, and drama, and cement.

"Hives of industry." The bromidism fits these places. Through the windows are visible lines of girls busily reeling film. In tiny, bare, busy reception rooms one catches glimpses of ladies in waiting – waiting for the job that seems to have brought almost everybody to Fort Lee. The contemptuous office boy, and the preoccupied girl at the 'phone, are the only calm creatures on the horizon. "Phyllis!" cries a strident voice; "Phyllis, for gosh sake hurry; you're in this 'hop joint'!" Temperament, entering from the street in a fine frenzy, punches the time clock, and in a voice vibrant with emotion, demands Columbus Four One One Four. A stage hand brushes by, carrying the summit of a mountain, and another hurries out of the studio, looking for a doctor. "Somebody hit by a beam!" Following him comes one of the directors; a nervous wreck. All movie directors are nervous wrecks. If they weren't, nobody'd believe 'em, and they couldn't hold their jobs.

In the open air things are quieter. A Turkish general sits on an up-turned bucket, chewing gum and conversing with an Italian organ-grinder. A woman in low-cut bodice and hoop skirt searches an ash barrel until she brings forth a bit of film, which she holds up to the light. There is a flock of extra girls, and there are gobs of golden-haired children – invaluable for death-bed scenes and reuniting parents. Every child or two is accompanied by a mother. There is a great demand for golden-haired children.

An apple tree that had earned six hundred dollars, sheltering lovers enough—were they on the level—to lift the clergy to affluence.

In a doorway, seeking a breath of air, stands a deserted wife. We know she has been deserted because she wears a black dress, and has circles under her eyes. In the movies, as once on the dramatic stage, black dresses are the uniform of desertion and desecration. To this unfortunate creature comes a soldier in his shirt sleeves.

"Anybody seen my crutch?"

"No."

"Gee, I wish people would leave that crutch alone. I'm goin' to be wounded in a minute."

Near-by a cowboy is describing how he was killed the day before. "Crane says to me, 'You never saw a dead man fall off his horse that way.'

"'No,' I says; 'I never saw a dead man fall off his horse any way.'

"'I thought not,' says Crane, contemptuously. 'Get up and get shot over again!'"

All this was interesting, but was it Fort Lee?

"Fort Lee?" mused a Rear Admiral of the British Navy. "Keep along this road to the corner, turn to your left, and you'll see a sign."

By now we didn't believe in signs, but we followed directions. The board pointed to the right, and, sure enough, it said "Fort Lee".

At last, we were holding our own.

While we read the sign, a young girl came up and asked if we were a director. No. Well, did we know if they were taking on anybody at the Solax. Everybody in this town hopes to grow up and be a Mary Pickford. A farmer's wife, idling at her gate, watching the taking of a comedy picture, confided in us her ambition. "See that woman running?" she inquired, indicating a grotesque figure, her skirts held high, whimsically pursuing a tire that was rolling down hill. "I could run better than that. Wish't I could get a chanct in the movies."

More bad road, and more signs prognosticating Fort Lee. More mountains. Rome sat on her seven hills, but Rome had nothing on Fort Lee. Neither has any other capital of Europe. Fort Lee apparently covers more ground than London, and has more environs than Chicago. You begin to get into Chicago hours before you reach Chicago, but here we had been all morning on the very verge of Fort Lee without coming nearer than the last roadside board, which advised us that the village was "Two miles". Could it be that Fort Lee was retreating before our advance, slipping away from us into the Hudson?

No. "Fort Lee – One Mile". We were gaining. Full speed ahead, and all hands ready for action. Directly before us in the pavement was a well, or a mine pit, or something. Once more we lost time stopping to pick up Helen. "Fort Lee – One Half Mile." There was hope. Onward Christian Soldiers, and E Pluribus Unum. More rickety buildings, more saloons and cigar stores and quick lunch dives, and then – suddenly – the river and the ferry house at which we had arrived three hours before! In front of the ferry house lounged a figure strangely familiar.

"Fort Lee?"

The gentleman addressed shifted his quid, spat deftly upon his boot, and laconically retorted: "Sign".

There were two signs. One read: "Fort Lee"; the other, "The Road to Happiness".

But we hadn't come to hurdy-gurdy. Circular motion makes us sick. What we had come for was a glimpse of Fort Lee, and, apparently, there ain't no such animal. Solemnly, we drove onto the ferry, buying our ticket from one man to deliver it to another five feet away, and, resolutely, turning from the Road to Happiness, we headed back to New York.

> "Living Neighbor to the Movies" was intended to suggest the revelations of an anonymous resident of an anonymous town, but the place discussed is clearly Fort Lee. There were many such articles, most of them sharing the same fascination with how the movies had spread their tentacles across every aspect of daily life, a situation not quite so popular with the locals as some of these reports suggest.

LIVING NEIGHBOR TO THE MOVIES
They Film Your Aunt From The Country; Burglars Ask Permission To Burgle; And Your Baby Is Rented – If You Dwell Mid The Making Of Movies

Retold by Mary Dickerson Donahey

(from *Photoplay*, February 1916, pp. 63–69)

Being a neighbor to the movies! Have you ever thought what that might mean? It's an angle of the business that never entered my head, until I found myself in the heart of it.

Yards of stories have been printed in magazines and newspapers about the actors and the directors, about the making of plays, about the many strange animals that are used, the risks that are taken, the money spent, and the marvels that are accomplished.

But what the movie world is like to the ordinary, everyday folk who happen to live next door is a new point of view – one which our family is acquiring right now.

We really are very quiet people. No one in the whole family connection has ever thought of going on stage. No woman amongst us has become a politician. No man has aspired to either burglary or high finance. We haven't even produced a divorce amongst us!

My husband and I are not young people, and we dislike speed in autos or in friends. We enjoy our church and our home, and – I was about to say we enjoy life in its simple, quiet moods. But that would be wrong now. We no longer enjoy a simple, quiet life – we simply long for that brand.

Because – the movies have come upon us! The broad field across the way, which has for years been a restful and delightful stretch of open greenness, is now, much of the time, aflare with noise, aglare with color, filled with people and with things the like of which were never seen in our staid neighborhood before. When pictures are not actually being taken over there, carpenters hammer all day long, in feverish preparation for the pictures that are to come, and we stare aghast at the flimsiness of the structures that tower so frowningly, later on, when shown upon the screen.

There, in the center of that field across the way, single rooms are built. They usually lack a ceiling, and one of the four walls generally conceded necessary to a room. Most of all they lack a house to be part of! They look so lost and desolate, those stray rooms, fully furnished, gaping open to the public view.

There in that big field we see, on some days, great battles, and our ears are stunned, our eyes made weepy, our noses tickled, with the clouds of battle smoke. Again, Indians file by, or those other savages, the "Apaches" of Paris, hold forth.

At times long lines of brown robed priests file by solemnly, under gloomy cloisters of worn old stone – cloisters that were run up in a few days, and which will undoubtedly be pulled

Fort Lee cityscape: Robert Harron in The
Miser's Heart (Biograph), shot in October
1911.

down tomorrow, to make way for a palace, a slum, a circus, or the entire "Main
Street" of a village with its little stores, blacksmith's shop, Chinese laundry, and
court house, all complete – from the front. In the coming pictures, only the
parts of the buildings bordering on the street will show, so of course, why build
more? And there stands the street, every building on it ending just a few feet
back, quite open and ragged in the rear. It is the most horrible example of the
modern vice of "putting up a front", which one could well imagine!

Our porch is a wonderful place these days. I often feel as if it were in truth the
balcony of a play house, and wonder when a boy will come to hand me a
program, and how soon they'll be around to collect the money for my seat! If
the hard times strike us, we say we'll pad the porch chairs with plush, put a red
"EXIT" sign over the front gate, and play we are a theater. We think we'd have
no trouble in the selling of our seats.

For, apart from the magic, changing field across the way where the wizards
work, all day the street cars disgorge at our corner hordes of men, women and
children, suit-case laden, who go into the studios just around the corner. They
soon reappear in the weirdest of costumes, to go hurrying across to that outdoor
studio, wigs and whiskers, maybe, swinging from their hands till time to put
them on.

Sometimes auto loads of Fiji Islanders will disembark across the way, or a string
of camels will come up, laden with bales of goods and dusky veiled beauties, or
a machine that seems loaded to the brim with ruffles and frills will draw up, and
there before our eyes will leap out a bevy of "leggy" chorus girls. A real ballet
dress does look funny, in full day light, on a public street!

Famous stars and directors flash before our wondering eyes. We can study them
at close range and see them as "neighbors". Famous scenes that others pay to
see, are enacted not once, but many times, for us – for perfect films must be a
certainty.

And yet, when all is said and done, the
most interesting part of being a neighbor to the movies lies, not in what we
see other people doing, but in the
things that happen to us!

For instance, one day a dignified aunt
from the country, whose good opinion we highly valued, was sitting on
our porch when first one and then
another of us became aware that our
party was for some reason the object
of much interest to our movie friends.
First one and then another came, stole
surreptitious glances, and left, till finally the greatest of them all strode up,
stared frankly, then as openly came
forward and stated the case. Our
friend was exactly the "type" needed
for a certain picture. "Could she",
"would she", etc., etc.

Now, had our aunt been young, and
of a vain or giddy turn of mind, all that
might have been mere flattery. But she
was elderly, old fashioned, very set in
her ways, disapproved intensely of
motion pictures, and had been fighting the opening of a theater in her
vicinity for years. So the incident was
not without embarrassment to everybody concerned. And the pain was not
lessened when we observed a film being taken of our guest upon her departure.

And our scandalized aunty has not yet
recovered from the accusation of having posed for the movies, nor, need I
add, forgiven us for living next to such
ungodly neighbors!

One day, a trained mule wandered off,
went visiting, and frightened my sister
nearly out of her wits by affectionately
blowing down her neck and nipping
at her ears. And when she fled, he
thought she was in play, and followed
as far as the dining room door, taking
with him, as a halo for his wicked
head, our screen door, and braying a
bray within our humble walls that

made me quite certain that the Germans had come, and landed their first shell in our midst.

Not long ago, I was expecting the lady who laundries my hair. I had pinned myself into towels, pulled out all my hairpins, and was starting into my downstairs bedroom, when I heard a curious, unwelcome noise at the back window. Fearfully, I looked, and there, sure enough, two of the worst looking ruffians I ever saw were breaking into the house!

Quaveringly, I pounded on the door with my brush. They looked up, but they did not run away. Instead one said pleasantly, "Good morning".

My wits restored, I demanded, "What are you doing there?" The same burglar looked up at me with handsome brown eyes, and said in the tones of a Vere de Vere, "Why, pardon me Madam, but I thought we had permission to burglarize your house this morning?"

"Well, you haven't", I snapped, "I'm going to have my hair washed and dried in this very room, right away. You'll have to do your stealing somewhere else today."

"But Madam, we can't", explained the gentleman patiently, "All the other pictures have been taken around your house, you know. Couldn't you allow us to break into the parlor window now?"

"Yes", said I, "that's all right". You can burglarize any room you like except this room, and the bathroom, next door."

He thanked me, both tipped their outrageous hats, and they gathered up their tools and departed. Presently I heard sounds which told me that my living room was being burglarized in the most approved style. And not till I told the story as a grievance, did I discover that it was a joke!

I fear that nowadays honest-to-goodness burglars could come and do their worst unscathed, and that we'd let them carry off everything we own, quite secure that if they did it, we could claim every single thing at the studio round the corner at any moment.

And I want to say here that of course the firm pays us for the use of the house and grounds, and amply reimburses us for any damage done to our property. That old mule may have scared us almost into fits, but he presented us with the fine new screen door we'd been needing all summer.

The movie folk may be weird and queer and different, but they pay their way always, and they're courteous and kindly.

Another time they came to me and told me of a story they wished to put on, about a regular Peck's Bad Boy sort of person.

They wanted the young man to go into a house on horseback, and break everything inside that house. Would I let them make a copy of my lower rooms? Of course I would. And a day or two later I was astounded to be taken to their studio, and shown such a close copy of my living room and dining room – furniture, rugs, dishes, ornaments, pictures and all – that I gasped.

"Not exact, of course, but near enough", said the director briskly. "Now, may the boy ride his horse up on your porch, open your front door, and start to go in? Then the rest of the picture will be taken here."

"Oh, yes", I replied meekly. What good to say no to these people if I had wished? I felt they were magicians, capable of making my whole home fly away if they chose.

So the horse was ridden up the steps and the act made quite an impression on our porch. The marks of hoofs are still there.

Next day I was invited across the street to view the scene of interior destruction. It made me return thanks that the end of that picture was not taken in our own happy home. I know now how our possessions will appear if an earthquake or a cyclone ever strikes us.

The movies have quite surrounded us. Next door we own another house which we have rented in other times to quiet people like ourselves.

Only movie people want it now. Most of them are the pleasantest sort of neighbors. But just at first we rented it to two prize fighters and their wives. The two ladies did not agree, vocally. We heard their opinions of each other at all hours in all tones. And the two gentlemen never were able to settle the question as to which was champion of the house.

After these tempestuous ones, came a temperamental family. At least, that was what they said was the matter with them. They used to give very accurate imitations of wife beating in the small hours of the night.

"You'll murder me – you'll murder me, you brute", we would hear the lady shriek as we woke from our own quiet slumbers. The first night it happened, my husband sallied over to rescue the lady. But when he managed to quiet the racket long enough to be heard, he was informed, through locked doors, that they were merely acting a part. They explained that as they had heretofore always been "straight legit – Shakespeare you know", they could not get down to the tame and bloodless movie methods, and had to make the dialogue fit the scene, to "get the swing of it".

Maybe. But they rehearsed that scene too often to suit us, and sadly but firmly we asked these disciples of the legitimate stage to depart hence and be heard no more. Our souls being beneath art, we wanted to sleep in peace. Since then we have lived in restful comfort and friendliness with our tenants, enjoying the glimpses that the successors of the tempestuous ones bring us of the life of the movie

folk – their problems, their experiences, and their fun.

The youngest generation of our neighborhood has been deeply affected by the coming of our movie neighbors. It has made a huge difference to our babies! They have become of more importance than ever before, and more parents have had – well, differences of opinion.

For you see, babies are sometimes hard to get. Even some institutions will not rent out their defenseless, relationless infants. A pretty plump baby, who is not afraid, is worth a great deal of money "acting" and can acquire a very good job any time its parents will take it down to apply for one. And right there the trouble is apt to start.

Mother may say, "It won't hurt the dear a bit, and it will be such a good start on the fund for his college education". But father may rave and storm over the idea of exposing his offspring to the public view, or perhaps vice versa. We have found very few of our friends and neighbors who agree on this matter of the public appearance of babies, and the directors sometimes have to hunt far and wide for proper youngsters for their pictures.

Of course, from our vantage point in the heart of the movie world, we have glimpses of the employing side. If you are thinking of applying for a job, we can tell you that if you are a type that the director wants for a certain picture, it will be hard for you to escape without being accepted, and used. If not, you may be as lovely as Venus or Apollo, with clothes that would make a show girl or a Beau Brummel gasp with envy, and you'll have little chance to prove what you can do.

Hosts of untried people are taken because they are the types wanted. If they are stupid, as they generally are, the director will drill them with really wonderful patience in what they are to do, till they can do it. Then, that picture finished, there may be nothing for them to do again for weeks – maybe forever! The standbys are not stupid, and they do not need constant drilling in the work they are to do. It astounds us to see the crowds that flock out, day after day, by street car or auto, and patiently wait and wait, hoping for an opportunity to "go on". Sometimes they're pathetic, sometimes funny, sometimes just annoying.

There is too, a grim side to the activities of our neighbors. Moving picture work is dangerous. We are told that every company which amounts to anything has its own hospital, and that it is rarely empty.

Even movie fires sometimes burn, great leaps, daring rides, sensational rescues, do not always go off properly. Not nearly so much of the "thrill stuff" is faked as the doubting Thomases among the people who don't know would have you believe, and – somebody has to take the risk. But the actors look on it as just part of the day's work, and when they do get hurt, have little to say, and are always ready for the next time.

One of our best friends among the movieites had occasion, not long ago, to take the part of a negro who was tied to a tree and whipped.

He took the part – and went to bed afterward. Of course they padded him up very carefully before they tied him. The tree they had taken for the scene was in our front yard, and I looked out to make sure of that padding. But in the excitement and energy of the scene, the whipper frequently forgot the location of those padded spots on the luckless frame of the whippee, and many lashes landed in places not prepared to receive them. And that was not the worst. That tree had been inhabited by a colony of ants. They objected to having a man tied to their home and showed him that they did. But he could not get away! The little pests swarmed all over him, and caused him very real anguish before he was at last cut down.

Really, I suppose that the most odd and interesting thing that has taken place so far in the course of our neighboring with the movies, was the way in which they helped us to get money for our church.

We are a small congregation, with more hope than funds, and we very much want a new building. This fact the movie folk discovered. So they came to us with a proposition. They, in turn, wanted a congregation for a camp meeting scene. If we would furnish that congregation, ·they would give us one hundred dollars towards our new church. Well, very seldom has a thing been more thoroughly discussed than was that offer!

Some of the more conservative members objected to our doing it. They said it was making light (and movies) of religion. But most of us could not

see it that way at all. We argued that it wouldn't hurt a soul, and would bring us in a goodly and much needed sum of money to be used towards the most righteous of causes.

So we did it. We gathered at the allotted time, and found a tent all arranged in the most approved camp meeting style. I will not say there wasn't some crowding among the older members to get out of range of the camera, or that some of the younger ones weren't quite ready to step to the front. It's rather funny, the way a lot of us congratulate ourselves that we won't show in that picture. I presume, if we were "types" we undoubtedly will!

They had their own actor for clergyman, and presently he came down the aisle with a real old camp meeting character on his arm, talking to her in the most dignified, serious way, though what we heard him say, as he passed, all nervous, and on the verge of laughter as we were, was, in sepulchral tones, "Yes Madam, yes. It's a long, long way to Tipperary."

That almost upset our gravity. Then he got into the pulpit, and began to preach so earnestly! He frowned at us. He smiled slowly, gravely, sweetly, and shook his head as though in gentle rebuke for sins.

He pounded his points home upon the pulpit, leaning forward and gazing into our eyes. He got excited and gesticulated wildly, and seemed to cry out arguments at the top of his voice – seemed, I say advisedly, for all this time he said not one single word, nor made a single sound! It was extremely good acting, but it was a good big test of our powers in that line too, I can tell you! Never did I so want to giggle!

And then, at the very end, he finally said, "Now, if any of my beloved brethren have failed to understand the trend of my discourse, I will repeat it all, point by point."

"Don't laugh", yelled the director. And to the click of the picture ma-

chine, we managed to file out decorously enough.

But we certainly earned that hundred dollars!

I think the directors earn theirs too. The care they give to every detail is wonderful. Imitations of real things are used only when the real things actually are not needed. At other times, expense is not spared to get the very best. We are astounded at the beauty of the rugs that go in next door. It is hard to realize that real silk Oriental rugs are needed in the pictures, but they must be – else they would not be used. It is the same with furniture, pictures, and all kinds of furnishings. Only the best of the genuine is used.

And the gowns of the women are a never failing delight to quiet folk, who like lovely clothes well enough, but have no occasion to own them.

One day I noticed a woman I knew well by sight going into the studios, and I was very curious. She is a member of one of the best and oldest families of the state from which I come and married a man of high position in our present home city.

She has always been used to wealth, and "society". I wondered hugely what lure the movies had for her. And I found out. There have been financial reverses in her family. She was very willing to come, undoubtedly for a fee that would seem enormous to me, and give advice on the staging of society dramas. She has become a regular employee of our neighbors, and never do they produce a picture dealing with people of rank or wealth, that she is not called in as aid and critic. That is the care that these new friends of ours think necessary in their strange, engrossing work.

In the beginning, I said we longed for a chance to enjoy our old quiet life. We think we do. We talk a great deal of selling, and going far away, out to a place as retired as this one used to be not so very long ago. Sometimes we think with regret of the quiet and uneventful past, and wonder if our house itself does not feel scandalized at the wide publicity we are giving it – our pretty modest home, never built with the idea of any theatrical ventures!

And yet – and yet I wonder!

Our new neighbors have, after all, brought a great deal of wholesome interest into our lives, and they have harmed us not at all. We would miss them if they went away. It is after all, a rather interesting thing, this living neighbor to the movies!

FORT LEE ALWAYS FULL OF THRILLS, SAYS H. BELL, LOCAL TELEPHONE MAN IN TALKING OF THE MOVIES THERE
Interesting Story of How Motion Picture Studios Have Increased Telephone Business in Six Years 352 per cent – Fort Lee Full of Noted Men and Women of Stage Renown. Highly Entertaining Story of Enterprise

(from *The Palisadian*, September 23, 1916, p. 3

Although within a short distance of New York City with its teeming millions, the village of Fort Lee retained, until comparatively recently, its out-of-the-world air of rural charm. A walk along its principal thoroughfare, Main Street, conveyed the impression that the din and rattle of the city had been left hundreds of miles behind.

Of late, however, the atmosphere of the place has undergone a subtle change, an air of bustle and activity has replaced the erstwhile placidity. The reason is that Fort Lee has been chosen as the home of motion picture companies, and already some six concerns have established plants: The Peerless, Eclair, Willat, Solax, Universal, and New York Motion Pictures.

With a view to ascertaining what had led these companies to select Fort Lee as a haven, several of the various directors were interviewed. The reasons given, briefly summarized, were these: its accessibility to New York City, the compara-

tive cheapness of land, moderate taxes, wonderful variety of scenery within a radius of ten to twenty miles, purity of air, and absence of hampering municipal restrictions of one kind or another. After such a recital of desirable features, one may be pardoned for assuming that Fort Leeians generally did not realize what an El Dorado they have. Under normal conditions it is roughly estimated these companies carry on their pay rolls about two thousand people, but this number is largely augmented when plays or special scenes are being filmed.

Some idea of the work that is done by these companies will be gathered from the fact that in the case of the Universal alone, 1,500,000 feet of film are produced each week. It is interesting to know that there are 16 individual photos in each foot and it is necessary to punch 8 holes in each photo. How the statistician would revel in these figures, 284 miles of film, 24,000,000 photos, and 192,000,000 holes punched each week!

The advent of these film companies has, as can readily be imagined, brought many changes to the neighborhood, and in time will materially alter its characteristics. It will become, indeed, it is now, an industrial center of increasing importance.

House rentals have risen, new houses are being built to accommodate the film companies' employees, and various improvements of one kind or another are being effected through the borough. Everybody seems to be basking in the smiles of prosperity. People of a pessimistic frame of mind would find a visit to "Movie Town" very efficacious.

It is a liberal education to spend a day

Note the sign on the front of the Bigler Hotel advertising a public telephone in this scene from an unknown comedy, filmed c. 1918. The same sign attracted the father in D.W. Griffith's The Lonely Villa *(1909), and Griffith even shot the hotel from the same angle.*

in or about Fort Lee, or better still, if you are fortunate enough to obtain admission, at one of the studios when some play is being staged. If you happen to hit on a lucky day you may catch a glimpse of the ever youthful Lillian Russell, Mary Pickford, Clara Kimball Young, Robert Warwick, Wilton Lackaye and many other celebrities.

You can have your fill of thrills in witnessing, say an attempted suicide in a watery grave – the Hudson River – and the heroic rescue, or an attack by red Indians near the bluff of the picturesque Palisades; in fact the whole gamut of human emotions can be experienced. Sad to relate, the Fort Leeians are now so accustomed to these sights that they have become quite blasé and scarcely evince the slightest interest or curiosity, even if they see the beauteous maiden being kidnapped by the wicked "once abroad the luggar and the maiden is mine" sort of villian.

The advent of these motion picture companies has brought possibilities for telephone growth even greater in proportion than the other improvements in the town. All the film companies have P.B.X. systems and numbered among them 20 trucks, 89

stations and 5 tie lines connected with switchboards in New York offices. The telephone growth for the whole Fort Lee area has been rapid since June 1, 1910, when the Englewood local commercial office was opened, the number of telephones having risen from 97 to 440, an increase of 353 per cent.

SHARPSHOOTING AT FORT LEE

By Charles Phelps Cushing

(from *Picture Play*, December 1916, p. 187)

"Fort Lee for yours", ordered the first chief. "Remember, you're a sharpshooter, and don't fire till you see the whites of their eyes." Via the Broadway subway, I entrained to Manhattan Street, and boarded a municipal transport to Edgewater, New Jersey.

In mid-channel, an excited New Yorker on the starboard bow raised a cry that a woman was being drowned near the Jersey shore, upstream. Half a dozen citizens of Fort Lee gazed blandly in the direction indicated, and guffawed.

It was merely a movie, they explained.

I unlimbered my rapid-firer, and tried

Charles Phelps Cushing toured the Fort Lee studios in the summer of 1916. His first stop was Palisades Amusement Park, operated by future studio magnates Joseph and Nicholas Schenck at the southern end of town, where "Fatty" Arbuckle was filming *A Reckless Romeo* for Triangle (it was released a year later by Artcraft). His description of the Fox company driving down Fort Lee Road and across what is now Overpeck Park to Teaneck may be unique. Kenean Buel and Virginia Pearson were filming *The War Bride's Secret*, part of which was set in a small Scottish village. The film is said to have used the poetry of Robert Burns in its intertitles, which may explain Cushing's use of dialect here.

to get a bead on the heroine, but she was out of range. By the time our transport had docked, she and her associates had disappeared in the woods.

Having been warned to keep a sharp lookout from the moment my feet touched the Jersey shore, I cocked my piece before boarding the trolley. The car wound a tortuous course up the side of the Palisades, and, at the summit of the grade, paused for breath in front of an amusement park.

There a sudden turmoil assailed my ears. A gray-haired man and a husky youth were slugging and kicking at

View of the First National Bank, Fort Lee, N.J.

The First National Bank on the corner of Main Street and Palisade Avenue attracted so many filmmakers that Charles Cushing felt the locals would never be able to tell a real robbery from a motion picture scene.

(Left): Wilfred Lucas in The Failure
(Biograph), shot in October 1911 in front of
the First National Bank (see previous page).

(Below): Harry Hyde and Mabel Normand
in Her Awakening (Biograph), shot in
August 1911 in front of the same bank.

after juggling a boiled potato, ended the act by spearing it in mid-air with a fork.

After the meal, the company proceeded to put on various impromptu comedy stunts on the amusement devices.

I shot half a dozen rounds and hied onward in a motor car to the studio buildings in Fort Lee proper. And Fort Lee *can* be proper if it likes.

In one of the new Brady studios – a huge building with a glass roof like a hothouse – the properest sort of serious drama was being filmed under the

one another in the street. The Jerseyites looked on as blandly as they had at the "drowning", and grinned. I leaped off the car to draw a bead on the skirmish, but a brawny young man was ahead of me, pushing the fighters apart. On closer view, he proved to have make-up on his face, and any one could guess that he was a movie actor. But there was no make-up on the fighters, and their bruises were bona fide. For once, blasé Fort Lee had guessed wrong – the fight was real and earnest.

If ever a murder is committed in Fort Lee in broad daylight, or the First National Bank is plundered, the only hope of detecting the criminals will lie in the chance that some movie actors may be around to intervene. No citizen of Fort Lee would ever guess the horrible truth.

The young man with the make-up strolled across the road and joined half a dozen other actors who had just alighted from two large touring cars. Conspicuous in the group, both by his bulk and his costume, was a figure famous in filmland as "Fatty" Arbuckle. Two attractive young women marched beside him – Alice Lake and Corrine Parquet. Several young gentlemen in eccentric comedy costumes tagged along after them.

A hot trail at last! Or, perhaps, a hot *scent* would be more accurate, for Fatty and his pals, once they had passed through the turnstile into the park, made straight for a frankfurter stand. With a white bulldog and another pup of undetermined breed for a supporting company, Fatty played in pantomime there a warning to dogs to beware of the neighborhood of frankfurter stands. In the first rehearsal the bulldog appeared to be genuinely alarmed – he ducked away with his tail between his legs, and couldn't be caught for five minutes.

The aroma of boiled "hot dog" had a different sort of effect upon the humans of the comedy troupe; they adjourned to luncheon. Mr. Arbuckle was in high spirits at table. After a soup course, he slyly dipped his fingers in the tureen, a la finger bowl, made teaspoons turn back somersaults into a glass of water, and,

direction of Travers Vale. If you ever have visited a hothouse on a bright afternoon in the dog days, you can guess what the temperature was like in that studio. And the costumes the actors were wearing were Russian, with fur caps and high collars! Vronski! How those actors steamed! Doubtless they were getting well paid, but only one member of that cast could I envy. Though her lot in the play was most sad, Miss Gail Kane wore a gown which, particularly in the back, was appropriate to the temperature. I fired one round and strategically fled over the hills to the west.

Two minutes after I began my retreat from Moscow, I brought up in a walled town somewhere in Normandy. At present the population is about half a hundred, mostly carpenters and plasterers – but it is freely predicted at the headquarters of the Paragons that in a few weeks the census returns will show an amazing increase.

After a little sniping in the walled city, I doubled back, and reconnoitered the walled citadel of the Fox Film Corporation. A chariot awaited within its portals. Hailing it, I learned that an expedition was about to depart for a hut in the Scotch Highlands. Director Kenean Buel invited me in for a wee breesk wheesk. Now, let no one suppose that a wee breesk wheesk has anything to do with mountain dew. It is simply a brisk little whisk. The afternoon light was drumlie, and the highland clachan some five or six miles away. So we whisked! The chariot was gasoline propelled, and appeared to possess a great many horse powers. Through the portals we whisked around the corner, into the main street, and westward. I dimly recall glimpses of a few movies that were being filmed at Fort Lee's highways and byways as we flashed past, but I couldn't see "the whites of their eyes" through the dust.

I distinctly recall that the car dived down a steep hill on its two front wheels and that, at the bottom of the incline, it then reared up on its two hind wheels and leaped clear across the meadows to the next range of hills. Somewhere in far-away Teaneck we volplaned to earth again, and alighted.

We were in front of a weather-beaten, one-story stone cottage. Below the eaves of its all-too-modern shingle roof, a fringe of decorative straw thatch was held in place by an ingenious scaffold. If you shut off the sight of the upper half of the roof, you could swear that you were beholding a cotter's home in Argyll or Ayr. The foreground, except for the presence of a movie camera, was as good as the background. On the brae hunkered a cantie carline with a dour cock laird, and a bonny girzie beside her jo. The lassie was aye kenspeckle, but appeared to be the waur for a lack o' siller. Her claes were cotton, and her footgears auld bauchles.

But when she looked up and began powdering her nose, I ceased wasting my sympathy and sniped a snapshot of Miss Virginia Pearson.

A drumlie hour, not much light to spare; so Director Buel hurried. With a fine eye for detail, he had the roof thatch trimmed until the camera man admiringly declared: "It's as bonny now as my own mustache!" Then, with a mirror from the cottage bureau for a light reflector, the filming began. Once it was interrupted by hilarity from Miss Pearson when she tried to get into the mirror's illumination and couldn't succeed.

"*Please*, Andy", she pleaded, "let me into your halo!"

Andy stepped back too far, and got out of it himself. The whole scene, when the laughter subsided, had to be done over.

A little before sunset the clans gathered in their motor cars and sped back to Fort Lee. There Miss Pearson donned a striped blazer over her cali-cos, put on motor goggles, and rode home looking like a Newport heiress.

All the way to the ferry I passed carloads of movie actors returning from work. But they all wore goggles, and I held my fire. The first chief's orders were explicit on this point: I was not to fire until I could see the whites of their eyes.

> Famous Players-Lasky (the production arm of Paramount) was occupying the Paragon studio when Hazel Simpson Naylor visited in the summer of 1918. The facility was as valuable for its laboratory, where Paramount's release prints were made, as for its extensive back lot.

"EVERY LITTLE STUDIO HAS A TEMPER OF ITS OWN"

By Hazel Simpson Naylor
(from *Motion Picture Classic*, September 1918, p. 27–29, 80).

Temperament is a much abused word. It is used to cover up a multitude of sins, such as selfishness, egoism, bad temper, or unexplainable tempers. Underneath its shielding wing we place any little oddities of disposition that those who have registered "success" in the world's drama of art, literature or theatricals may possess.

Temperament has its uses and its abuses. In no place is there such a display of temperament as in the Motion Picture studios. Even the telephone girl and the door-man have caught the fever. With a superb air of hauteur, the telephone girl looks up and down thru her mascaroed [sic] eyelashes and demands your pedigree, or family tree, back to the time of –

Neighborhood kids and other locals visiting a set on the Paragon back lot, possibly one built for Woman *(Maurice Tourneur Productions, 1918).*

well, anyway, it takes some time and more patience to convince her of your importance so that she will even deign to submit your message to whomever you may wish to see.

However, on a recent trip to Fort Lee, NJ, the way was made easy for me at the great glass-covered studio of the Famous Players Company by a very pleasing press person, who advanced ahead of me and caroled my name and credentials. Still, the *pro tem* manager of the studio gazed at me rather blankly as he said: "I'm sure I don't know what I can show you. Maybe you'd like to see the lion that nearly killed a man the other day."

I had come in search of lions, but not the zoo variety. Nevertheless I assented and was ushered pompously down a corridor away from several very attractive-looking sets of scenery. We drew up at attention before a six-foot-high boarded-up cage.

"There", exclaimed the studio manager, "he is!"

"Oh, yes", I smiled sweetly, being all of five feet.

"Oh, you can't see him, can you? I'm so sorry. Here, let me lift you up." (Business of balancing myself, with the toe of my perfectly good new shoes thrust thru a tiny knothole in the boards while the studio manager politely bored a hole in my ribs with his tremblingly polite hands.)

"Can you see him?"

"Yes", I said, trying to be impressed; but darned if I could see a bit of difference between the shaggy, tawny brute and the ones of my circus-going days. Anyhow, I had come to see Marguerite Clark, or Ann Pennington, or all the rest of the famous Paramount stars; but the studio manager and the nice press person gathered on either side of me and told me how, when the lion was being lowered into the pit for Lina Cavalieri's picture, he broke away and attacked his keeper, nearly killing the man before an extra knocked him – that is, the lion – on the head with an iron tool and temporarily incapacitated him.

Longingly, I looked down the corridor, where I could see the Klieg lights blazing and hear the crisp tones of directors at work.

"Don't you want to see the yard?" said the studio manager. "And after that I'll take you thru the laboratories, and you can see just how the films are developed and cut and put together."

"It's awfully interesting", the nice press person assured me.

I began to feel a display of temperament coming on myself; but self-control – well, you know what it does. So, with a longing glance backward, I tripped and tumbled over the cobblestones of the street which was used in Elsie Ferguson's *The Rise of Jennie Cushing* [probably *Barbary Sheep* was intended – ed.]. Remember where the trolley-car ran round the corner. You thought it was a real street in Algiers? Oh no, my dear; just a reproduction of one in a back yard at Fort Lee. The little stucco houses were crumbling with age, and the trolley-car was rusty from the snows and rains of the past winter; but its (what do they speak in Algiers?) sign, tho weather-beaten, still hung.

A little further on we passed thru a slum alley. Somehow I expected to see the inhabitants peer out of the tumbledown red brick buildings and exchange the time of day with one another or hang out the inevitable wash of every day in the week. But no; 'twas merely make-believe. The buildings, poor dears, had no backs. 'Twas the street which housed Ann Pennington in *Nana of Sunshine Alley* [*Sunshine Nan*]. Further on, there was a Roman stadium. Here it was that the

aforementioned lion had done the dirty work.

I felt like an anthropologist. If I should dig thru the ruins, surely I would discover the bones of the dead and gone inhabitants.

"And now we shall see the laboratories."

"But", I expostulated, "I want to see them taking the pictures".

"Well, I don't really think there is to be much going on this afternoon; but I can show you the sets they will be working in."

So at last we got back to my corridor, which led to the stage floor. On tiptoe, we circled carefully away from the lighted section and down to a far corner, where we came upon the reproduction of the interior of a Western cabin.

"This is where Elsie Ferguson is working on *Hearts of the Wild* [released as *Heart of the Wilds*]."

"Oh", I exclaimed, as life assumed a rosier tint, "that's bea-u-ti-ful! I'll wait here until she comes and get an angle for my story by watching her work".

But my way to a perfectly good camp chair was barred. "Er – er – you know – Miss Ferguson – er – er – sometimes objects to having people watch her work. But – er – I might ask her." (As a matter of fact, I have watched Miss Ferguson work and obtained great pleasure thereby.)

So I said ta-ta to the inviting set, with its Navajo rugs, its open fireplace and romantic atmosphere.

It was unavoidable that on our way out we should pass the lighted set. Here Madame Cavalieri – oh, so beautiful! – with black, shiny hair and big, dark eyes, was emoting in what appeared to be the library of a Southern mansion. An actor, made up as an old negro butler, stood at attention while Cavalieri, who wore a lovely hand-embroidered frock of white handkerchief linen and a large picture hat of

palest pink, was carrying on an animated argument in French with her shirt-sleeved director.

"Oh", I said, with a sign of satisfaction, "do introduce me to Cavalieri!"

"Er – er – I don't think you really want to meet her – er – not today. Some other day – and besides, there are the laboratories still to see."

"If you don't' mind – it is so late – I think I'll save the laboratories for another day", said I and, making my exit, hotfooted it down the dusty sidewalks of Fort Lee to the World studio.

I had high hopes of finding my motive or angle here; but I found only lights blazing everywhere, heat and dust and hurrying actors. Yea, even perspiring ones.

Here another very obliging representative of the press met and ushered me – thru. Past Kitty Gordon – yes, exactly as beautiful as her pictures – who, gowned in royal purple, sat regally in a limousine, while stage-carpenters erected a platform about the limousine's hood, on which the camera was to be placed. I don't know why we circled the car, but we did, and landed in a furnished apartment – yes, a living room, bedroom and bath, all ideally laid out (no, not by an undertaker, but, like department stores often do, to inveigle people into buying their $998 sets of furniture). At a common kitchen variety of table Director Dell Henderson was poring over the script of *By Hook or Crook*. I know it was that because I leaned over his nice, plump shoulder to shake hands with him.

"Got a story for me, Mr. Henderson?" I asked.

"It's a hot day, isn't it?" he asked, mopping his brow.

"That's no story – that's the truth", the terrific glare of the lights must have been the cause for my unusual flippancy.

"Er – yes – quite so. Ben, where was I, and what's the next scene?"

(Wild business of rummaging thru the multitudinous pages of the scenario.)

Then in came Carlyle Blackwell, wearing an immaculate tuxedo.

An introduction, a handshake and the very best done matinee-idol smile were my fortunate portion.

Yes, I really watched him do a scene. Then he plumped down in a chair in the *opposite* corner for me! I was evidently as popular as a toadstool in the mushroom-bed or a mouse in a kitchen.

"You look like the end of a perfect day", I called to the dejected looking matinee idol in my bestest Sunday-go-to-meeting manner.

A smile did evanescently chase itself across his bepowdered visage, and then he rose to depart.

Desperation made me grab his fleeing coat-tails. "Won't you give me the story of your life?" I pleaded. He had such a nice face!

"Can't. Got to change. Twentieth time today. Say anything you want to." He was gone!

"Poor Mr. Blackwell gets so tired at the end of the day he really isn't able to talk", apologized the press representative. When Mr. Blackwell reappeared in pajamas and dressing-gown I decided it *was* the end of a perfect day and fled Fort Lee....

> This chilling account of a quick tour of the Fort Lee studios during the winter of 1919 seems to have been intended as a promotion – things are not so bad out here, the author insists, and all the sunshine you need can be found a day's journey south in Florida. But while the labs would hold on, the studios never recovered. The use of words here like "ruin" and "deserted" couldn't have helped.

LOOKING OVER THE FORT LEE STUDIOS
There's Work Being Done Over in the Jersey Colony – Plenty of Sunshine Found this Winter

By Samuel Spedon
(from *Moving Picture World*, February 22, 1919, p. 1025)

Just to be different we took a little hike and "pike" last week around Fort Lee and Coytesville, NJ, among the studios of that territory. The air was clear and bracing and we could not help making a comparison with rubbernecking around California. It only took an hour from Times Square to reach our destination. After dismissing our chauffeur we felt so full of ozone and "pep" we hoofed it from one point to another, up hill and down dale, and enjoyed every step of it.

This is the year the producers got fooled, going three thousand miles to the coast when they could have got all the accommodations, sunshine and everything else but the foliage forty-five minutes from Broadway. Theda Bara got the foliage twenty-four hours from New York – at Jacksonville, Fla. – and it was there for anybody who cared to use it. It is true this has been an exceptional winter in this part of the world. It has averaged as many clear days as California. There has been an ample supply of fuel, and the climate has been spring-like.

Deserted village going to ruin
At Palisade Avenue and John Street [sic] we visited the Universal plant. The studios were idle, but the laboratories were in full blast. There were the deserted streets of a deserted village still standing and going to rack and ruin. The big glass structure for indoor scenes was still and filled with valuable props to meet almost any exigency and satisfy the most fastidious director.

As there was nothing doing in the way of producing we accepted the cordial invitation of Edward F. Murphy, the general manager of the laboratories, who placed us under the guiding wing of Fred Esslinger, one of his assistants, and he took us through the plant. We were greatly impressed by its completeness and activity. It is thoroughly equipped with all the latest improvements, including several Bell and Howell printing machines and perforators. There are 250 to 300 persons employed, and the establishment is splendidly systemized and managed. Every room is cooled and heated by washed air.

Paragon for "Way Down East"
About a block away, on John Street, we visited the Paragon studios and laboratories. The same thing can be said about the Paragon as we observed at the Universal – the studios, beautiful glass buildings, were silent and the sets of the village streets were still standing and untrodden. Mr. Baudet is the manager of the laboratories, which are exclusively used for Famous Players-Lasky products, have all the up-to-date appliances, Bell and Howell machines, and a complement of 250 employees. The washed air system is used and every detail carefully handled. As we were entering the

plant we met Harley Knoles, the director, who said he had just finishing producing a [Thomas] Dixon feature about the Bolsheviks [*Bolshevism on Trial*], and W.A. Brady had engaged the Paragon studios for the production of *Way Down East*, which he expected to start very shortly [Brady soon sold the rights to *Way Down East* to D.W. Griffith]. Three or four blocks away, at Linwood Avenue and Main Street, we visited the three old New York Motion Picture Company's studios, which were afterward taken over by the Triangle company and are now being used by the Fox company. There is very little being done at these studios except an occasional indoor scene. On the day we were there Edward Dillon was taking, in one of the studios, some interiors of a sailors' boarding house or saloon in connection with a George Walsh picture. In the old Éclair studio Charles Brabin was making some interiors. The middle studio was deserted. The Fox laboratories, which are used entirely for Fox productions, are running full swing. They are located on the same property.

Adjoining the first two studios, right in the midst of the three, is the Nicholas Kessel laboratories. Mr. Kessel is a much younger man than we expected to see, and we were impressed by his keenness and business judgment. He is extremely alert on detail and efficiency. We were surprised to find a number of progressive innovations that we have not seen in other laboratories, and we have been familiar with this end of the industry for the past ten years.

Kessel laboratories large

The Kessel laboratories handle all kinds of products – industrial, independent and the standard features. They have a capacity of a million and a quarter feet of film a week and take over a great deal of the overflow work from other laboratories. On the invitation of Mr. Kessel, after going through the various other departments, we were ushered into the inspection department, where the prints are carefully examined before they are shipped, and we regret that we could not spend the afternoon and enjoy the whole show.

Around the corner from the Fox studios we ventured into the World's Peerless studio. Here we were met by E.J. Rosenthal, one of the vice-presidents of the World, and general manager of the studios. The twelve-o'clock whistle was blowing and all hands were making a bee-line for lunch. Before accepting an invitation to dine in the studio lunchroom Mr. Rosenthal took us through the plant. On entering the studio we ran into Carlyle Blackwell, who had just finished a scene under the direction of Dell Henderson. We were impressed with the system in every department of the place.

Regular Smithsonian Institution

The properties were catalogued and kept in cases with glass doors, very much like a museum or the Smithsonian Institution. It was fascinating to inspect the innumerable objects – antiques, bric-a-brac, zoological specimens, tapestry, tableware, and everything else under the sun. Every costume is numbered and tabulated with the period. There is no excuse for a player or director going astray so carefully is everything arranged. The restaurant was all right. That it was enjoyed goes without saying.

At 1:30 we were on our way to Coytesville. About a mile and a half walk and we were there. The Solax studio presented an inviting appearance. Everything about it was in excellent shape, but no evidences of life were in sight. Approaching the entrance we were greeted by an Italian caretaker, who told us the place was closed and nothing doing.

The following figures, gathered from Bergen County Board of Taxation records, suggest the impact that the mushrooming growth of the film studios (whose assessed valuation nearly tripled between 1915 and 1917) had on Borough finances. Motion picture producers were grouped together on their own page in each year's tax ledger, tacit recognition of this business as a coherent industrial unit. Assessments were published in January of each year, and were estimated at the price such property "would sell for at a fair sale by private contract on the first day of October last." While the total value of Fort Lee's motion picture properties began to decline after 1917, these still represented 10 per cent of the Borough's entire assessed worth according to the 1919 Table of Aggregates. The precipitous drop in value which followed during the 1920s and 1930s, combined with the failure to develop alternative ratables, exacerbated the effect of the depression in Fort Lee, which became one of the few jurisdictions in New Jersey to formally declare bankruptcy.

Taxable property, taxing district of Fort Lee 1915–1919. Bergen County Board of Taxation records

	Land (US$)	Personal (US$)	Improvements (US$)
1915			
Peerless Feature Producing Company	5000	5000	50,000
Éclair, now Motion Picture Property Company	4000	5000	50,000
Willat's Studios & Laboratories	8000	5000	75,000
Louisa Korbel, now Willat Studios & Lab	2000	–	2,000
Universal Film Company	10,000	–	20,000
Paragon Film Company	5000	–	–
1916			
Peerless Feature Producing Company	5000	5000	50,000
Motion Picture Property Company (Éclair)	5000	5000	50,000
Willat Studios & Lab	10,000	15,000	85,000
Triangle Film Company	–	5000	–
New York Motion Picture Company	–	5000	–
Universal Film Company	10,000	25,000	100,000
Paragon Film Company	5000	25,000	75,000
Solax	3000	10,000	50,000
1917			
Peerless Feature Producing Company	5000	5000	50,000
Éclair, now Motion Picture Property Company	7400	25,000	50,000
Willat Studio & Lab	10,000	40,000	85,000
Triangle Film Company	–	5000	–
Universal Film Company	10,000	30,000	135,000*
Paragon Film Company	5000	35,000	100,000**
Solax Company	3000	10,000	60,000
1918			
Peerless Feature Producing Company	5000	10,000	50,000
Motion Picture Property Company	7500	25,000	50,000
Willat Studio & Lab	10,000	40,000	85,000
Triangle Film Company	–	5000	–
Motion Picture Property Company	10,000	30,000	100,000
Goldwyn Film Company	–	1700	–
Paragon Film Company	5000	25,000	90,000
Solax Company	3000	10,000	60,000
1919			
Peerless Feature Producing Company	5000	10,000	50,000
Motion Picture Property Company	7500	25,000	50,000
Willat Studio & Lab	10,000	40,000	85,000
Triangle Film Company	–	5000	–
Motion Picture Realty Company	10,000	30,000	100,000
Goldwyn Film Company	–	–	–
Paragon Film Company	5000	25,000	90,000
Solax Company/U.S. Amusement Company	3000	10,000	60,000

Summary: Total Value of Real and Personal Property (Motion Picture):

1915	$246,000
1916	$533,010
1917	$670,400
1918	$624,675
1919	$622,975

Note: Total Net Valuation Taxable for taxing district of Fort Lee in 1919 was $6,247,034.

*Reduced by C.B. from 135,000 to 100,000; **Reduced by C.B. from 100,000 to 90,000

This aerial view of the approaches to the George Washington Bridge, taken around 1950, shows a few studio buildings still scattered around Fort Lee. The derelict Solax laboratory at upper left, near the high school; the peaked roof of the Peerless-Metropolitan studio to the right of the highway; and the water tower of the Universal studio at lower right, then operated by Consolidated Film Industries. Compare with map on page 11.

17.
Universal

On 8 June 1912, the most aggressive members of the "independent" filmmaking community – those operating outside the purview of the Motion Picture Patents Company – joined forces in a new umbrella organization which they called the Universal Film Manufacturing Company. Charles Baumann of the New York Motion Picture Company was elected president (his partner Adam Kessel was also a member), Pat Powers of the Powers Motion Picture Company was vice-president, Carl Laemmle of IMP the treasurer, and William Swanson of the Rex Motion Picture Company secretary. Other original members included Mark Dintenfass of Champion, David Horsley of Nestor, and Jules Brulatour, raw stock agent for George Eastman. Brulatour was quickly forced to resign by Eastman, who saw his presence here as an obvious conflict of interest; he would find other ways to involve himself in film production. Kessel and Baumann left after losing a titanic struggle with Laemmle and Powers. When the dust had settled Laemmle emerged on top, where he would remain until selling his interests in Universal in 1936.

Although the incorporators had agreed to pool all their resources as a way of funding their battle against Edison (which is how the Champion studio, for example, passed under the control of Universal), for a time the separate producing entities maintained their individual character. Universal prospered under Laemmle, and took on the distribution of additional independents, including Éclair. But as it grew larger, and began to centralize its bureaucracy, Universal realized that it needed a large new studio of its own – two studios, in fact. On 18 June 1914, ground was broken for such a studio in North Hollywood, still known today as Universal City. On 5 August, Universal purchased the estate of John Marx on Main Street in Fort Lee, and began work on what was, for a time, the largest motion picture studio under one roof in the country.

UNIVERSAL GROWING
President Carl Laemmle Talks of His Company's Big Plant at Fort Lee and of Universal City

(from *Moving Picture World,* November 21, 1914, p. 1050)

There are "goings on" at the offices of the Universal Film Manufacturing Company these days. Just before his

Carl Laemmle and Robert H. Cochrane at the groundbreaking for Universal's Fort Lee studio, 1914.

departure for the Pacific Coast on the afternoon of November 5, President Carl Laemmle outlined a few of the projects his company has in contemplation as well as under way. First of all, Universal City, the objective of Mr. Laemmle's long trip is rapidly being poured into shape – for all of the main buildings constituting that unique municipality are of concrete, reinforced. Then, again, there is the huge plant of the Universal at Leonia Heights, Fort Lee, NJ, which it is confidently predicted will be ready for the making of pictures by March or February of the coming year. As the Universal has centered all its western activities in one location – Universal City – so, too, it is preparing to combine in one comprehensive establishment, the several scattered units that in the East have been contributing to the Universal sum....

Mr. Laemmle reached across his desk and unrolled a number of blueprints. "I just want to show you what the Universal has under way in the East in the way of improvements. Here is the ground plan of our Fort Lee studio and laboratory. You will note that the plot is 300 by 600 feet." The plans, which have been executed by Edward Barnard Kinsila, provide for elaborate Italian gardens in the front of the plot, which faces the northeast. On one side is a pergola, with a pool in the center. At the left of the garden is an ornamental fountain. On the southeastern side of the plot for nearly half its length are two lakes, separated by a rustic bridge and waterfall. The studio and annex are situated just behind the Italian gardens. The studio is 151 by 80 feet. The annex is 80 by 142 by 130 by 151. At the rear of the plot is the laboratory, 145 by 65 feet. A large plaza separates the studios and the two-story laboratory. The structures are in the Tudor style of architecture, and attention has been given to the decorative as well as the utilitarian side. In the studios ten directors can work at one time. Provision has been

made completely to shut off any portion of the studio, in case a producer is putting on a "noisy" scene, so that others will not be disturbed. The studios are believed to be the largest glass-inclosed buildings in the United States. The cost of the entire improvement is expected to approximate a quarter of a million dollars. "And out on the Pacific, in Universal City, in time to come, we expect to build a studio twice as large as this one", said President Laemmle....

"On our eastern pictures we have had complaints about photography", said President Laemmle in concluding his talk. "When our Fort Lee plant is finished we intend to put into it all our eastern companies, and I think we will have no further photographic troubles. We are to spend $15,000 across the river just to get clear water. At different times we have been doing work at the plant in One Hundred and Tenth Street, where the fire occurred; at Coytesville, at Forty-Third Street, in Eleventh Avenue and at Bayonne. We intend to retain the Bayonne factory, not removing even a printer, as an insurance against emergencies. Our Fort Lee establishment will contain an equipment that is brand new throughout. We will have facilities for

staging the most elaborate productions. We have abundant room to expand if at any time it be necessary. I think you will agree with me that when our east coast and west coast plants are in full working order, as they will be in a few months, the Universal will be in a position to give its customers and the public just what they want – that is, if we can learn what that is, and I think we can."

NEW UNIVERSAL EASTERN STUDIO
Outline of the Elaborate Project Now in Course of Construction at Leonia Heights, Fort Lee, NJ.

(from *Moving Picture World*, July 31, 1915, p. 799)

Within a few months' time a new motion picture studio and laboratory will be finished at Leonia Heights, Fort Lee, NJ It will house the Eastern producing companies of the Universal Film Manufacturing Co. and will be an architectural, scientific expression of what brains and more brains, and much money can do when properly applied.

The Universal had appropriated a large sum of money for the building

Railroad passengers destined for Fort Lee would arrive at the Leonia depot and travel up the Hackensack and Fort Lee Turnpike (now Main Street) to what was commonly known as Leonia Heights (and sometimes, confusingly, Taylorville). By whatever name, the Heights were properly in Fort Lee, although Universal always referred to the facility as their "Leonia studio", as if to distinguish it from the rabble in Fort Lee. Despite Carl Laemmle's assurances, the studio was nowhere near ready by February or March of 1915. In fact, construction had ground to a halt, with Universal suing the architect, Edward Kinsila, and turning the project over to Ernest Flagg, designer of the Singer Building. Kinsila was a theater architect associated with the Shuberts, but had also designed the Peerless and Gaumont (Flushing) studios. What went wrong is still unclear, although Flagg's completed design did omit the Italian gardens, waterfall, and Tudor decoration.

of Universal City, near Los Angeles, Cal. An Eastern studio, fireproof, fool-proof, capable of providing facilities for the many busy Atlantic companies, was needed. Carl Laemmle and Robert H. Cochrane began to work over the project. What they started will be an evidence of Carl Laemmle's doctrine that the best acting, directing and management is worth the best home and advantages regardless of the cost.

Approximately four acres of ground were purchased. Then John M. Nickolaus, one of the best motion picture camera men and a technical expert, was called into consultation. Nickolaus had installed the laboratories at Universal City and now runs things at the Universal factory at Bayonne, where all the negative produced by the Eastern companies is developed and positives printed. He went out and talked laboratories and studios with everybody whom he thought might have a good idea. These ideas he brought back carefully wrapped up, forget-proof, in his memory. Some were valuable.

The preliminary plans were prepared by William Sistrom, who has had considerable experience with engineering problems with big companies. These were turned over to Ernest Flagg, an architect of considerable renown. That was in November of last year; since then the work has been progressing rapidly and the buildings are beginning to take form. Descriptions of the various buildings follow:

The laboratory building. 150 feet by 104 feet, will be a model of what a laboratory should be. The lower floor is below grade with plenty of head-room even in the developing and wash room. On this floor will be the perforating, printing, developing, washing and drying rooms. The arrangement of these rooms has been so cleverly worked out that entrances to the "dark" rooms are absolutely "light tight" and yet free from all the twists and turns of the "maze entrances" usually considered necessary. On the upper floor is the assembling, inspection and polishing rooms, a chemical room in which all of the solutions used in the developing room are prepared and delivered to the developing tanks on the floor below through a complete system of pipes, title department,

machine shop and superintendent's office. On both floors splendid arrangements for the comfort, convenience and safety of the 300 employees have been made.

Opening into, but detached from, every room in which film is handled, vaults are provided. To determine the proper design for these vaults, an extensive series of tests were conducted in conjunction with the New York Board of Fire Underwriters and the National Fire Protection Association. The plant is designed to turn out half a million feet of film a day, but will handle without trouble 800 miles a week.

The Studio Administration Building, irregular in shape, 130 x 60 feet in size, will have two floors. On the ground floor will be a general office, manager's private office, scenario department including a general office and a number of small individual offices, nine directors' rooms, two projecting rooms, still picture department, Animated Weekly department [i.e., the Universal newsreel], cutting and joining rooms, restaurant complete with kitchen, boiler room in which will be located the boilers for heating the entire plant including the laboratory, machinery rooms in which the motor generators for the stage lighting will be located.

On the ground floor of the studio section will be 24 individual men's dressing room and the same number for women. Two large waiting and dressing rooms for "extra people" will accommodate one hundred men and women respectively. There will be a wardrobe room large enough to store costumes for the present plant and for contemplated additions.

On the second floor of the Administration Building will be a carpenter shop, scene painting room, scene dock and the property department. The property department will occupy the east section and consists of a main floor with three galleries, with eleva-

Construction proceeding on the new Universal studio, Main Street west of John Street. Photo dated 26 January 1915.

tors from the main floor to the top gallery. There will also be an elevator from the ground floor to the carpenter shop, which connects with the stage floor. These departments open directly into the stage, 150 x 80 feet in size.

All buildings are constructed in accordance with the very latest fireproof standard, consisting of complete structural steel frame work with 12 inch masonry curtain walls. All interior partitions are of terra cotta block with hard Portland cement plaster finish. Because of the extremely large area it was necessary to make several of the interior partitions "fire walls". All openings in such walls being protected with double automatically closing "fire" doors. All other doors are fireproof, all window sash and door frames are of metal. In fact, as Sistrom says, unless someone gets past the gateman with a box of matches or a pencil in his pocket, there won't be any wood on the premises.

On the grounds will be a garage with sufficient accommodations for ten 7-passenger automobiles and one auto truck. There will also be a number of detached vaults for film storage, warehouses, etc.

The air conditioning plant will be of intense interest to technical experts. It is guaranteed to remove 99 percent of all foreign matter from 20,000 cubic feet of air per minute delivered into the drying room at a temperature of 70 and a relative humidity of 45 per cent. The temperature and humidity are under automatic control and are guaranteed not to vary more than 3 per cent with a variation in outside temperature from zero to 90°. On this proposition Semsch, of Flagg's organization, got in some of his best work and had the assistance of the expert engineers from the six largest concerns in the country specializing in this class of work.

The plans call for much adornment of the surrounding grounds. There will be one Italian and one Spanish garden, two lakes and a fountain. The lakes will have a surface area of 5,000 square feet, an average depth of eight feet and a capacity of 300,000 gallons of water. One lake will be higher than the other, but the lower can be raised. They may be either connected by a water fall or by a narrow stream spanned by a bridge. The water in the lake also serves as a reserve reservoir for the sprinkler system installed in the three buildings.

John M. Nickolaus, at present in charge of the Universal factory at Bayonne, will be in charge of the laboratory and will probably take many of his present staff of 250 persons with him to Fort Lee.

Julius Stern, long at the head of the Imp and Victor studios at No. 573 Eleventh Avenue, New York City, and of the Champion studio at Coytesville, will be general manager of the plant.

"The improved facilities of the new studio will provide a new order of things in the conduct of scenario department", says Raymond I. Schrock, Scenario-In-Chief of the Eastern Studios. "A system of co-operation between author, director and actor will establish perfect understanding and remove friction.

"An elaborate and comprehensive card system will be installed with which may be kept a perpetual inventory of all stories received, eliminating loss of time and material.

"The scenario staff will include William Ellery Bergh and J.E. Warren, who are admirably equipped as readers. Mr. Bergh for many years was a contributor to the *Dramatic Mirror*, and Mr. Warren sat at Sanger & Jordan's play-reading desk for five years. Foreign language scholars in the department will have the keys to the rich literature of the Old World."

Universal began production at the Leonia studio with little fanfare during the winter of 1916. Allan Holubar, who had spent several months in the Bahamas filming exteriors for *20,000 Leagues Under the Sea*, spent additional months in Leonia shooting interiors and trying to make sense of the footage, taken without a proper script, that he had brought back with him (he would then leave to shoot additional sequences in California). Gradually, the players then working in Laemmle's cramped Manhattan studios began to fill up the gigantic stage at Leonia Heights. Jane Gail was especially impressed, it seems, with Bergen County justice. Robert Duncan's description of studio operations, written for *Picture Play,* contains an especially ironic reference to fire safety, considering the fate of the valuable negatives which Universal had decided to store there.

ITEMS OF INTEREST ABOUT UNIVERSALITES
Jane Gail to Write Prison Reform Scenario

(from *Moving Picture Weekly,* April 1, 1916, p. 24)

Universal Heights has a student of prison reform. Jane Gail, who is appearing with Matt Moore in *Their Parents*, is right at home in Bergen County, NJ, wherein the studio is located, for here there is a county judge who is some little reformer himself.

"This Judge Seufert", said Jane to a

dressing room gathering yesterday, "is my idea of a man. Last week six boys were brought before him charged with setting fire to an abandoned frame building in Morsemere. The boy who actually started the fire was found to be from the Reform School at Jamesburg, where his record had been bad. The judge decided to return him there.

"But did the judge confine the weak followers of the bad boy? No, he decided that they would receive no benefit from confinement and would only be made heroes of by their schoolmates once they were freed – which is exactly what happens.

"What the judge did do, was to order the young miscreants to work every Saturday morning for some time on the streets of Palisade Park, cleaning cross-walks, picking up papers and rubbish on the roads, or cleaning up around the school buildings.

"That sort of punishment", concluded Miss Gail, "has any other form I ever heard of outclassed".

Miss Gail is writing a photoplay on the subject of prison reform.

UNIVERSAL JUNIOR – Getting on the Inside By Becoming One of the Actors in the Eastern Universal Studio.

By Robert C. Duncan

(from *Picture Play*, August 1916, pp. 39–45)

I was simply tired of writing about a studio through a tour of the place. These tours are so cut and dried. The studio press agent takes you by the arm and shows you the very same objects of interest the S.P.A. of the last studio you visited did, and spiels about 'em in the very same way:

"That is Mr. Bignoodle, there to your right, taking an underworld scene; in the set next to his, Mr. Highfalute is finishing his Mary Doughbags feature; these are the camera men's room to your left – very model, don't you think? The prison set is going up for – ."

And so the tale goes on, studio after studio. The boys don't mean to repeat, but I suppose they do it because the interesting points of moving-picture studios are all about the same. Acquit the S.P.A.!

So when the time came for me to visit the Universal Eastern studio, I decided to do it on a new tack. I crossed from New York City to Fort Lee on a ferryboat loaded with movie actors' automobiles, then trolleyed to Universal Heights. The Universal Eastern studio boasts a main entrance that would do credit to a governmental institution! But the magnificent main entrance was not for me. The seeker after work must apply to the side entrance – there are so many of said seekers that there must be a special entrance for them! I was told to ask for Mr. Adler.

Mr. Adler proved to be none other than the once celebrated – maybe still – Bert Adler, who first put punch and system into film selling and advertising. For the last three years he had been devoting himself to the studio end of the business, leaving the management of the old Jersey studio at Coytesville, when that place closed down, to become cast director and interview man at Universal Heights under Manager Julius Stern. I didn't have to wait long for him, as he seemed to possess a knack at speedily examining applicants, and he appeared to note my youth and clothes – which luckily were neatly pressed – with some degree of enthusiasm. As he spoke to me, I could tell that there was work of some sort awaiting men of my type. Finally -

"What is your experience?" was asked.

I could see that the questioner's enthusiasm took a slight drop when I

Fire sweeps the interior of the Nautilus *in* 20,000 Leagues Under the Sea, *filmed on an open-air stage at Universal's Fort Lee studio in the winter of 1916.*

admitted to no acting experience whatsoever.

"However", Mr. Adler said, "I might put you in a dress suit and place you with Director [Robert] Hill today. You look as if you could wear clothes. The scene is for this afternoon. Could you go home and get your dress suit and be back here by, say, one-thirty?"

I assured him I could, and made good on the assurance. At one-forty-five I was one of a slumming party setting out to visit the basement settlement in *Temptation and the Man*. We were calling on Sydell Dowling there. She was a wealthy girl who had founded a settlement. (Notwithstanding, I heard her admitting to Hobart Henley later that she never spent more than thirty-five cents a day for her lunch!) Hobart Henley was playing a tough who had been won back to good works by the wealthy girl – he was managing the settlement for her. With so fair a coworker as Miss Dowling, who was always smiling sweetly at him in the scene, he was to be *envied* for giving up the life of a tough. All the toughs of New York would be managing settlements if there were Miss Dowlings around to keep them company!

Well, we came automatically down the basement steps, congratulated Miss Dowling on her success with the settlement, looked sympathetically at Henley (!), and told Miss D. we were sure the poor fellow would yet die happy. Then we coddled a lot of poor children that came into the settlement. One of the poor kids was the daughter of an actor that gets three hundred and fifty dollars a week year round. Finally, having given Miss Dowling one last expression of approval, and Henley one last look of sympathy, we passed up the steps and out.

Now was my chance to examine a studio from the new angle. Lucky for me that I was rigged out in full dress, proving that I was "working". Curiosity seekers are not allowed on studio

stages – you've got to prove you're "working" – – and the full dress proved it for me. I sauntered the length of the stage floor without interference. Indeed, I covered the whole building without interference. That dress suit was my badge. I found the Universal Heights studio made up of two separate buildings. The entire producing department was in the structure where I had worked; two stories high, and I should say one hundred and thirty by one hundred and sixty feet in dimension. A full minute's walk in the rear is the laboratory building. The idea of separating the two is that in case of fire – movie fires, it appears, usually start in the laboratory – no damage will be done to the producing department, no halt caused in the producing work, be the blaze ever so fierce. Hardly any film stock is kept in Universal Heights studio overnight, and the chances of fire almost nothing. Nevertheless, the Universal heads had "fire walls" placed in the interior partitions, the openings of which are protected by automatic-shutting "fire doors". A sprinkler system covers the entire studio. Personally, I'd venture to sleep at Universal Heights studio even if there was a feller with a lighted cigarette and a tank of gasoline in the adjoining room. Perhaps the officials have been guided in their making the place so *gosh-awfully* fireproof by the fire-insurance rates. That's the only explanation I can offer. And I respectfully hold it forth because I hear that no manufacturing plant of its size *in any line* has a lower rate. You see, I fear the officials are what Colonel Roosevelt would call "practical men".

The stage on which I had been slumming is on the second floor of the structure. On the first floor, coming down from the stage, you find the dressing rooms, director's offices, scenario department, manager's office, main entrance – from which I had been shooed originally – cutting room, and restaurant, in just that or-

der. The restaurant was a model of neatness, and the one, no doubt, where the wealthy founder of the basement settlements lunched daily for thirty-five cents.

And then I was discovered! King Baggot, whom I had interviewed some time before, came out of the lunch room and straight toward me with a cheery greeting. I asked him to speak in whispers – just like a stage villain – and explained what the disguise was all about. King immediately pledged himself to secrecy and led me back to his dressing room so that we could chat without fear of – I almost wrote arrest! Getting the story from the new angle was really exciting! I began to feel like a war correspondent from London seeking for news in Berlin.

The "King of the Movies" – ask the Universal advertising department – told me he had just gotten back from Savannah, and that he had been taking some exterior scenes, that it had been very warm in Savannah, and that he had been very glad to get back to his cool dressing room at Universal Heights. Baggot's dressing room – indeed, the majority of the dressing rooms here – opened right onto a vast court. There are sixty-four dressing rooms at Universal Heights for regular members of the stock company, and four rooms of extra size for "extra people". These "extra people's" rooms have all the advantages of the stock members' rooms except privacy. When I was "made up" for the slumming scene, I was surprised what a gentlemanly lot the "extra men" working that day were – courteous and anxious to assist each other. Small wonder that the "extra" room is so often productive of movie stars. The answer is that unless an actor has great reputation, he has little chance of getting into regular movie "stock". Therefore it's "extra" work for him until appearance in a number of pictures has proven he has the necessary screen qualifications. And then, like as not, it's a small salary he gets until the girls start writing him admiring letters and the critics of the trade press admit he's great. Baggot told me he started at – well, an exact sixth of his present salary.

As I left the Baggot throne room, Ben Wilson passed by in a quandary. His room adjoins Baggot's – just as on the ladies' side Violet Mersereau's adjoins Mary Fuller's, implying that birds of a feather flock together – and he was on his way to it to puzzle out how one of his pictures, just completed, could be reduced to one reel. Baggot told me all about the Wilson trouble later. The film was entitled *The Gentle Volunteer*, and had been made in four reels. It seemed that an order went out to the directors at Universal Heights that they skip four-reel productions, because the "market" didn't want them. Ben's notice on this got mixed up somewhere, and the first he knew of the rule was when

Universal Movie Studio. - Fort Lee N. J.

(Above): Universal studio on Main Street, c. 1916.
(Below): Interior of the Universal, which claimed to be the largest glass-enclosed studio in the country.

BECAUSE SPACE IS LIMITED IN EVEN THE LARGEST STUDIO AND BECAUSE SETS TAKE UP SO MUCH ROOM THEY MUST BE DISMANTLED AS SOON AS POSSIBLE AFTER SATISFACTORY SCENES HAVE BEEN FILMED

Manager Julius Stern told him of it and gave him back *The Gentle Volunteer* to "cut". As he had started a new picture, the instructions to "cut" came at an inopportune time. But, as Benjamin Franklin Wilson is esteemed a "good cutter" in the studio, and has an assistant who is clever at the same line of work, we doubt not that he got through with his extra labors eventually. You see, movie directors don't always have pleasant out-of-town trips and nothing to do till tomorrow!

There was a Moore trouble present also. Matt had been making a comedy on the stage next to Mr. Hill's, in which Jane Gail and an expensive cast were employed – including a particular type of goat. The P.T. of goat had died – maybe it was my work in the slumming scene alongside that did it – in the middle of his scene, and Matt Moore was wild with – no, *not grief* – he was boiling angry at that goat for dying before the picture was finished. As I said above, it was a particular type of goat. Unless his double could be procured, this day and several preceding days' work would have to be thrown into the ash can. We must write "ash can" into a goat story. There was that expensive cast to consider. Matt was so excited about it that I am sure if he had known ahead the animal would die in the middle of a scene, he would for revenge have shot her first himself!

I was rather unlucky in securing work in the afternoon rather than in the morning. Most of the directors – there are ten at Universal Heights – had finished their interior sets in the a.m., and were working outside now. This was the case, for example, with Mary Fuller's director, Edna Hunter's, Edith Roberts' – but not, praises be, with Violet Mersereau's! One Universal lady star was within! There was beautiful Violet, eluding a vile-appearing Oriental in a Chinese joss-house set. The scene over, Violet dropped into an easy-chair at the side of the set and became engrossed in deep thought. What was she thinking of, this wondrous blond beauty? Of a man – a prospective husband? *Yes!* I'll tell you about it in a minute, after I have made you read about the studio lighting system, a part of my word picture that maybe *you'd "cut"* if I didn't place it before my exposure of Violet's thought!

The overhead lighting equipment here is arranged on a trolley system that enables the studio electrician to "flood" any foot of stage desired in fifty seconds after the director gives the order. That is fast work! When Director Hill wanted lights for *my* set – said like a star! – they were all overhead a "dead" set at the farthest corner of the studio where Harry Benham had been working. "Lights!" shouted Mr. Hill to Electrician Kelly, and *whiz* came those lights down the trolley and over our set.

Continuing technical, as it were, I might write that I found the carpenter shop, scenic department, and property room fronting immediately on the stage, and all of them as full of daylight as the stage itself. Speaking of

the wardrobe room, which is below the stage –

Violet Mersereau's thoughts? They were: Ought she, or oughtn't she? Sacrifice herself to the publicity gods, or nay? The company was exploiting a "Handsomest Man in America" contest, and the publicity department, to add zest to the affair, wanted to know if they could promise Violet and her salary to the winner, provided he was unmarried. There was no doubt this would improve the interest in the contest one hundred per cent, one publicity shark told her. Now, then, *would* she? Just like that!

But to Violet, who has her share of nice, admiring beaus, the question was: *Ought* she? She was sure, of course, that the press agent, *mad* about publicity as he undoubtedly was, would somehow, somewhere, some way, save her from actual marriage! The judges would mayhap be kind and pick a married man. That didn't worry sweet Violet, sitting there in Chinese garb and deep thought. *What would her beaus think? That* was the trouble! *They* would never understand publicity-depart-

ment methods, quiet business men, most of them, who knew naught of the wild ways of the modern publicity promoter.

How did I, aimless actor, know all this? Because "Billy" Garwood walked over to the reflecting girl just then. And Violet spoke to Billy – they play together now, and often exchange advice – and what Billy replied to her seemed to cheer her greatly.

And Billy, to whom I disclosed my identity for the sake of a story, gave me the entire tale going back to New York on the ferryboat that was full of movie actor's automobiles. Violet had cheered up because Billy solved the great problem by promising to run into each of the beaus and explain that publicity matter beforehand!

I met him later, about four days afterward, as he was hurrying along Broadway, and he told me that he hadn't realized what a job he had undertaken, for he had been busy ever since he had made the promise – but still had a long list of young men to see.

UNIVERSAL CONCENTRATES IN WEST
All Eastern Producing Companies Will Be Transferred To Hollywood Under General Direction of H.O. Davis.

(from *Moving Picture World*, June 10, 1916, p. 1862)

Abandoning the new half-million dollar studio in Leonia, NJ but retaining the finely equipped laboratories connected with the studio and the executive offices at 1600 Broadway, the Universal Company is preparing to move all of its producing companies to Universal City in Hollywood, Cal., where they will be under the general supervision of H.O. Davis, whose systematic organization of the great

According to an internal memorandum dated July 27, 1917, Universal had spent $280,362.79 on all the buildings at Leonia Heights, and $304,802.45 on all the buildings at Universal City (they acquired much more land in California, so those costs were $161,000 against $17,000 in Leonia). But in a surprising, and even bizarre, move, Universal announced that it would close the studio in Leonia only a few months after opening it. In a battle that would later be waged by Fox, Paramount, and other studios operating production facilities on both coasts, the Hollywood contingent had successfully cut-out its eastern rival.

western plant has eliminated unnecessary overhead expenses and made possible the production of good pictures on a sound basis. Julius Stern, for a number of years manager of the eastern studios, is no longer connected with the Universal Company. It is reported on good authority that he

will become an important factor in the L-KO organization, which makes pictures independently for release by Universal.

The glass-covered studio being vacated is one of the largest and finest in the country. Several manufacturers are negotiating for a long time lease

Director Rex Ingram with Violet Mersereau and John George (left) on the set of Broken Fetters *(Universal-Bluebird, 1916).*

with present prospects favoring the closing of a contract with William Fox.

When the shift of Universal's producing forces has been completed there will be thirty-five companies at Hollywood where the equipment is more than ample for the increased activities. Director Stuart Paton and his players have left already, and others will follow as soon as pictures started in the East are finished. Among those preparing to make their homes in the west are Mary Fuller, Violet Mersereau, Matt Moore, Edna Hunter, Jane Gail, Ben Wilson, King Baggot, Hobart Henley, Harry Benham and Edith Roberts.

This wholesale concentration of forces is explained by Universal officials as a move to do away with unnecessary expenditures that do not contribute to the betterment of the product. The practical benefits of Mr. Davis' regime at Hollywood are the result of a finely worked out system through which many of the running expenses have been greatly reduced and some of them cut in half. In the employment of extras, for example, Mr. Davis has shown how money has been needlessly expended, because the requirements of the various directors were met individually, whereas with the proper co-operation in a large studio, actors engaged by the day might be profitably utilized in more than an occasional scene. This is but one of the numerous advantages of an organization such as exists in Universal City.

An announcement sent from the Universal executive office reads in part:

"The picture business has reached a commercial stage much more rapidly than any of the old-timers imagined it would. It is now at the point where only those companies [that] would eliminate all waste and make 'everything show on screen' can hope to survive the competition. The Universal Company was the first to take any step toward the concentrating of efforts and the consequent reduction of overhead expenses, and therefore the first to reap the advantages of commercializing its business.

"About the first noticeable result of this move will be an improvement in the entire Universal program. Thousands of dollars which have hitherto been spent on overhead expenses can now be devoted to the pictures themselves, giving the Universal product a quality which others cannot hope to keep pace with unless they concentrate as the Universal has done. Thirty-five companies will eventually be operated at one place with one overhead charge.

"It has taken much longer to achieve this stage of perfection than anyone in the company anticipated. Innumerable obstacles had to be overcome one by one, but meanwhile an organization was being perfected in all its details. Expensive equipment was added at Universal City week by week, until every department had the finest and most approved 'tools' with which to do perfect work. Countless ideas have been discarded. But, after all this period of experimentation, the company has emerged with an equipment and with facilities absolutely unparalleled in the whole world of picture making."

> Regardless of H.O. Davis's assertions, the studio in Leonia proved too valuable to shut down completely, especially since the property still needed to be maintained in order to operate the laboratory and distribution facilities. Violet Mersereau was the anchor of Universal's Leonia operation, and in at least two films, *Broken Fetters* (1916) and *The Little Terror* (1917), was directed by the great Rex Ingram. Edgar Cayce also made telepathic contributions.

VIOLET MERSEREAU TO STAR IN SPIRIT FILM MADE BY UNIVERSAL

(from *Exhibitors Herald*, March 17, 1917, p. 31)

The first psychic scenario now is on the stocks at the Universal studio at Fort Lee and within a few weeks the public will be able to witness a production made from a scenario which was never written by an author, but which traveled twelve hundred miles on psychic waves to Violet Mersereau a few days ago, while the star surrounded by thirty newspaper men, was seated in Churchill's restaurant in New York.

The plot is psychological in the extreme, and the man whose powers have baffled scientists is Edgar Cayce, who, while he was physically asleep down in Selma, Ala., sent his mysterious, spiritual and uncanny "thought self" to Violet with a five-reel scenario, entitled *Through the Subliminal*.

This plot has been turned over to John Brownell of the Universal's scenario department, and he now is putting it into shape for production. He says that it offers great opportunities and that, taking into consideration the fact that the plot was delivered spiritually and that Mr. Cayce has never attempted to write a scenario in his life, the result was remarkable. Not only should it interest those who study psychology, self-suggestion, psychoanalysis and spiritualism, but it should attract scenario writers.

INGRAM FINISHES VIOLET MERSEREAU BLUEBIRD

(from *Moving Picture World*, June 23, 1917, p. 1967)

Over at Bluebird's Leonia (NJ) studio work has stopped on *La Cigale* [released as *The Little Terror*], as director Rex Ingram has completed Lotta's former starring vehicle, in which Violet Mersereau will appear among Bluebirds in August. The former stage comedy was brought down to the minute by John C. Brownell, who is now in charge of Bluebird's scenario activities in the East.

> The Goldwyn Pictures Corporation leased the Leonia studio from Universal beginning in April 1917, and on November 17 of that year Universal transferred both its Coytesville and Leonia properties to the Motion Picture Realty Company, essentially a legal maneuver. Goldwyn stayed for just over a year, and while Universal occasionally announced that it was prepared to resume production, it continued to rent out the studio whenever possible. The *Moving Picture World* reported on April 12, 1919 that Famous Players-Lasky had moved into the Universal studio and was filming *The Career of Katherine Bush* with Catherine Calvert. In August the studio was taken over by Selznick, who stayed through 1921.
>
> Inspiration Pictures, which made Richard Barthelmess features in New York, leased the Universal studio in 1923 for two elaborate productions, *The Fighting Blade*, a Cromwellian-era swashbuckler, and *The Enchanted Cottage,* Sir Arthur Wing Pinero's psychological fantasy. For a time the facility was referred to as the Inspiration Studio. But Barthelmess returned to the studios he had been using in New York, and instead George B. Seitz directed a serial for Pathé, *Into the Net* with Jack Mulhall. Then on October 24 the studio's film storage vaults exploded, causing little damage to the studio building, but destroying many of Universal's historic negatives.

TERRIFIC EXPLOSION AT UNIVERSAL PLANT ON W. MAIN ST. IN FT. LEE FOLLOWED BY A $100,000 BLAZE
Explosion Rocks Houses, Breaks Windows and Endangers Lives of Employees; All Fort Lee and Edgewater Fire Companies Fight Blaze and Save Main Buildings.

(from *The Palisadian,* October 24, 1924, p. 1)

The residents of Fort Lee were startled early in the morning by a terrific explosion at the Universal Film Company's plant on West Main Street, which rocked the houses nearby, broke windows and endangered the lives of over 100 employees working in the plant. The explosion was followed by a serious fire, which was fought by the combined Fort Lee fire companies and that of Edgewater.

The explosion and fire took place in a stone storage building, set apart from the main buildings, and is believed to have been caused by spontaneous combustion in a pile of stored films and negatives. There were two distinct detonations, employees said, one barely perceptible and the other one that almost threw them off their feet.

The fire spread instantly throughout the whole of the storage building and within a few minutes had completely gutted it. Fire companies were summoned from Coytesville, NJ to assist the Fort Lee and West Fort Lee organizations in protecting the main buildings of the large plant. The Edgewater company was also called.

Investigations are being made by the heads of the Universal Company. They would not estimate the loss until records of the stored films are checked up. It is believed, however, that it will reach somewhere in the neighborhood of $100,000. Employees did yeoman duty in keeping town folk back from the danger zone.

Among the stars in some of the films destroyed were Mary Pickford, Owen Moore, Ben Turpin, George Loane Tucker, Thomas H. Ince, J. Warren Kerri-

gan, Wallace Reid, Pearl White, Anna Pavlova, Jack Pickford, Lon Chaney, Louise Fazenda and King Baggot.

The 1924 fire had little impact on the Leonia studio's viability as a production facility. The following year Barbara LaMarr starred in two films for First National, *Heart of a Siren* and *The White Monkey,* and Universal itself produced *The Little Giant,* a Glenn Hunter comedy. Universal announced that they were so satisfied with the experience they would renew production in the east, and continued to expand and improve the property. The lot was also home to the Cello Film Corporation, a subsidiary of Universal which operated a film reclamation business, extracting the valuable silver content from worn or surplus release prints. Unfortunately, a 1927 explosion and fire which apparently started in the Cello Film operation quickly spread to Universal's own vaults, destroying what was left of their early negatives. The two unreleased features mentioned as having survived were probably still in the laboratory; if they had been stored in the vaults, they would have gone up along with the old Mary Pickford IMP negatives.

FIVE PERSONS INJURED, OVER $100,000 WORTH OF PROPERTY DESTROYED AND VALUABLE FILMS IMPERILED BY FIRE

Blaze of Unknown Origin Requires Services of Fire Departments From Five Boroughs to Master It – Thousands At Scene of Conflagration

(from *The Palisadian*, February 4, 1927, p. 1)

Five persons were badly burned and property valued at well over $100,000 was destroyed and motion picture films worth several millions were jeopardized by a disastrous fire that destroyed the film storage sheds of the Universal Film Company in Fort Lee about 9 o'clock on Wednesday morning.

The injured were:

Louise Taraburelli, 508 Ann Street, Fort Lee – burned about the right and left hand and right leg.

Terrence Mahon, Central Road, Fort Lee – burned about the right and left hands, face and neck, and taken to the Englewood Hospital.

George Herschorn, Summit Avenue, Fort Lee – cut on the right hand.

Fred Schlosser, 2038 Hafley's Lane, Fort Lee burned about the neck and ears.

Ernest Danielson, Ridgefield – burned about head and neck, and was taken to the Englewood Hospital.

The origin of the fire has not been determined. Employees differ, some saying it started in the storage room while others insist that it started in the "reclaiming" room. A muffled explosion preceded the flames and several minor explosions occurred during the blaze

The storage sheds of the Universal Company were leased to Cello Film Company, a concern engaged in reclaiming old films. They suffered the principle loss while the main buildings of the Universal plant were only scorched by flames and none of the interiors were damaged.

The fire was one of the most spectacular in the annals of this locality, the Universal plant situated on one of the highest points in Fort Lee. The flames roared skyward for hours, sometimes reaching a height of 60 to 75 feet, and the heat was intense, so much so that the metal buildings became white hot and the iron and steel supports twisted and gave way.

The homes of Messrs. Wackenhuden and George Schuthman, both of Main Street, Fort Lee, were badly scorched and dried grass fully two blocks from the burning buildings caught fire. The garages in the rear of the Wackenhuden and Schuthman homes caught fire and were damaged considerably as well as their contents including their automobiles.

Fort Lee's four fire companies responded to the first alarm and shortly an emergency call was sounded and the fire fighting equipment and men from Edgewater, Cliffside Park, Palisades Park and Leonia came to the aid of the local men. The combined forces succeeded in mastering the flames about noon after the fire had raged before a startled group of thousands of spectators for about three hours.

The two very valuable pictures that were stored at the Universal plant in Fort Lee are *Les Miserables* and *Love Me and the World is Mine* which have not yet been released and which the Universal Company recently completed. The films destroyed included many old favorites starring Mary Pickford, Douglas Fairbanks and others.

This is the second serious film laboratory fire that Fort Lee has experienced in two years. It was just about this time two years ago the Evans laboratory explosion and fire occurred, which resulted in the death of two Fort Lee firemen and injured scores of others.

Fred Hauman, proprietor of Hauman's Pharmacy in West Fort Lee supplied all the first aid materials for the victims of the fire and his store was used by the doctors in attendance. Miss Mathues, a social service nurse, who happened to be in the vicinity, worked hard and well caring for the sufferers. Joseph Setzer sent up milk, coffee and food to the firemen about noontime.

Universal never produced another film in Leonia. Business reverses forced Laemmle to borrow a great deal of money from Consolidated Film Industries, which took over the property in 1930. They operated it as a laboratory, storage facility and distribution center, adding buildings to the property over the next few years (and also acquiring most of the other laboratory facilities in Fort Lee). The original Universal building was demolished in 1963, although some of Consolidated's additions stood until 2002. Despite the claims in this obituary, neither Pearl White nor Mack Sennett ever worked there.

FORT LEE BIRTHPLACE OF MOVIES TO BE TORN DOWN FOR WAREHOUSE

By John W. Slocum

(from *The New York Times*, September 18, 1963, p. 35.

FORT LEE, NJ Sept. 17 – The birthplace of the American motion picture industry is about to be razed. It is a two-story stucco building here containing a three-gallery shooting studio in which stars of a half-century ago made movies that thrilled the nation.

The studio will be replaced with a film warehouse, continuing Fort Lee's rather tenuous connection with that industry.

The warehouse will be built on Consolidated Park, a five-acre tract with 20 buildings, that has been sold to Bonded Services division of The Norvo Industrial Corporation of Chicago.

Chester M. Ross, president of Bonded Services, which has headquarters at 630 Ninth Avenue in New York City, said the new warehouse would be the largest of its kind in the world and would be used to store movie and television films from all over the world.

Demolition soon

The demolition of the old movie studio will start soon, Mr. Ross said, and the construction of the new warehouse unit will begin in November. The new building will overlap the site of the studio and extend almost to Fort Lee Road.

The plant initially will be one story,

Despite the 1924 fire, Universal kept adding storage sheds to its Fort Lee property, apparently to accommodate more film. This 16 December 1926 permit allowed them to put up another small metal structure, and included a site plan showing the current disposition of the buildings.

with 25,000 square feet. Eventually it will be three floors high and have 75,000 square feet. When it is finished, about 150 persons will be employed in the plant.

The warehouse, Mr. Ross said, will have "refrigerated storage to protect raw color stock; air-conditioned and humidity-controlled storage for color prints, and extensive provisions for the fast growing videotape market".

"Space will also be provided for the storing of records and advertising materials", he added. He put the total cost at $1,500,000.

Only the original studio, built in 1914 by Carl Laemmle of Universal Pictures, will be demolished. The remaining buildings will be renovated for storage purposes.

The movies made here included *Polly of the Circus*, Pearl White's *Perils of Pauline* and many of the early Mack Sennett comedies.

Old hits in storage

In storage here are such silent movies as *Don Juan*, starring John Barrymore; *Peck's Bad Boy,* with Jackie Coogan, and *The Patent Leather Kid*, starring Richard Barthelmess. Also stored here is Al Jolson's *The Jazz Singer*, the first talking movie.

Universal Pictures moved to Hollywood in 1929 and Consolidated Film Libraries [i.e., Laboratories] a division of the Republic Corporation, bought the tract here in 1932 [actually January 11, 1930]. Last year Consolidated sold the plant to Metropolitan

The Universal studio in process of demolition, 1963, photographed by Tom Hanlon.

Film Storage and Service, Inc., of Fort Lee, from which Bonded Services recently acquired the property.

In World War II, the photographic division of the Marine Corps stationed a contingent of guards and technicians to edit and process secret films taken by the service cameramen during the invasions of the Pacific Islands. Later invasion strategy and tactics were based on aspects of these films. About 90 per cent of the gunnery training and instruction films made for the armed forces were also processed here.

18.
Goldwyn

WHO IS THIS GOLDWYN?

(From the *New York Times*, September 9, 1917, p. 43)

P.T. Barnum's suckers had nothing on the moving-picture companies. Any student of the movie trade journals, the dead walls, and the dramatic departments of the daily press knows that the incorporation, floating and advertising of new consumers of celluloid go on at a speed considerably above the one-minute birthrate of the humble but celebrated sucker. If he keeps his eye on the front of his favorite film theatre, he is also likely to note that the existence of a new company is just about as short as the time it takes to put out is first "release" after the flamboyant birthcards. Which – curiously enough – is a reason for, rather than against, telling a little about the

Samuel Goldfish, before he adopted the name of his company.

Samuel Goldfish was one of the original partners in the Lasky Feature Play Company, the pioneer film producer that sent Cecil B. De Mille to Hollywood. When he was forced out after Lasky merged with Famous Players in 1916, Goldfish joined with Edgar and Archibald Selwyn and formed the Goldwyn Pictures Corporation. For almost two years Goldwyn made all its films in Fort Lee, first at the Solax studio, later at Universal. The extended coverage of this new production company in the *New York Times* was unusual at the time, and seems more akin to the way "media industry" news is covered by today's newspapers.

organization and birth of a new company whose first film, *Polly of the Circus*, with Mae Marsh, makes its bow at the Strand today. For it happens that the Goldwyn Pictures Corporation came into existence just one year ago after mature deliberation, and has spent the past eight months in making the bulk of the photoplays which will be seen under its name during the coming season.

It was twelve months ago, then, that G.S.K., who used to write pieces for the *New York Tribune*, asked why the Goldwyn Corporation hadn't been called the "Selfish" instead. Which should imply to the cognoscenti of the Way that is Great as well as White that the directorate of the company is composed of equal parts of Goldfish and Selwyn – Samuel, of the first ilk, coming from the movies, and Edgar and Archibald, of the second, recruited from the drama.

To begin still nearer the beginning, Samuel Goldfish left the Lasky Corporation and its allies of the Paramount some eighteen months ago, carrying away the usual moving picture million. (It was the same Goldfish, incidentally, who rode down to work twenty years before with a loaf of bread under his arm for lunch and in his pocket ten cents for the Interborough and two cents for newspapers, whence he drew his slow but sure education.) For his re-entry into filmdom, Mr. Goldfish made careful plans. They involved alliances with what he felt to be the important and necessary elements in the dramatic, literary, and art worlds.

An alliance with the firm of Selwyn & Co. seemed most likely to achieve the larger part of this, for it involved the services of Edgar Selwyn, once an actor, frequently a playwright and a producer of quick popular discernment; his brother Archibald, business man, and other economic executives; his wife, Margaret Mayo, author of "Baby Mine", "Polly of the Circus", and "Twin Beds"; Roi Cooper Megrue, who wrote "It Pays to Advertise", as well as "Under Cover;" Adolph Klauber, former critic of *The Times* and now casting director; a long list of Broadway successes not yet screened; the archives of the American Play Company, which held many of the past successes now in stock; and it involved, further, a lien on the interest and finally the services as screen writer of one Irvin S. Cobb whose connections with the Selwyns were very intimate. Edith Ellis and Porter Emerson Browne were later added to the literary side of the venture.

Another very important addition to the staff of Goldwyn came with the enlistment of Arthur Hopkins as director general at the studio. The young manager had just made his mark as a Broadway producer and was showing evidence of an originality of method which seemed to have an immense field of application in the films. Indeed, his studio reforms proved swift and salutary. After a thorough study of current moving picture methods, as exhibited by distinguished experts employed by Goldwyn for its first pictures, Mr. Hopkins went out and hired some artists. They were Everett Shinn and Hugo Ballin. He put them in charge of settings and costumes and gave them a share in the composition and direction of the pictures. Everett Shinn, besides being an illustrator of note, had written and acted some deliciously amusing burlesque melodramas, which Mr. Hopkins once put into vaudeville. Hugo Ballin was known as a mural decorator and man of note in the world of the other sort of studios.

Mr. Shinn was given the photoplays of homely American atmosphere, with stories and localities suited to his immensely detailed and whimsical style. And so, for *Polly of the Circus*, and *Sunshine Alley,* both for the use of Mae Marsh, he made a great number of black and white sketches in his usual magazine style, which technical expert and director turned into rooms, houses and villages, peopled with odd and pungent characters.

Mr. Ballin's was more the architect's touch. He simplified his walls and his

Mae Marsh in Polly of the Circus
(Goldwyn, 1917).

decorations until all unmeaning clutter of movie drawing rooms and palaces disappeared, and something took its place which would have gone straight to the simplicity-loving heart of Gordon Craig. His work has been chiefly devoted to the second Goldwyn picture, *Baby Mine*, and to Maxine Elliott's vehicles, *The Eternal Magdalene* and *Fighting Odds,* both backgrounds for what press agents have long described as a "famous beauty;" and he is now at work on four new films including *Thais*. Another artist, William Cotton, has been employed upon a single production, *The Spreading Dawn*, by Basil King, in which Jane Cowl appears.

It was the policy of Goldwyn, laid down in the early days of organization, that with finish of productions must go a thoroughly interesting and screenwise story and adequate acting.

The last requirement was left, not without justifiable confidence, to Jane Cowl and Maxine Elliott, from the dramatic stage, Madge Kennedy from farce, Mary Garden from opera and from the movies themselves Mae Marsh, the Griffith discovery of *The Birth of a Nation* and *Intolerance*, and Mabel Normand, whose fame is linked with the comedies of Mack Sennett.

Allan Dwan and his cameraman, Rene Guissart.

In the matter of authors and stories, we come to what is perhaps the most interesting and promising angle of the Goldwyn venture. Intelligent people, patrons normally of the better sort of plays, have had a long-standing complaint against the screen, that while its drawing rooms were bad enough in their lack of good taste and appropriateness, its stories were worse in their absurd extravagance or utter banality.

The first move recommended by critics from this class and adopted by a few of the more progressive companies was to raise the price paid for scenarios from the beggarly $250 of former days to $700 or $1,000 with the avowed purpose of inducing magazine and dramatic writers to submit stories for the screen. When the results were still found unsatisfactory, some proposed royalties. The directors of Goldwyn, however, felt that something more than buying the story of a reputable and skilled author was necessary. The screen must buy his further services in the production of the tale. Where the stories of famous writers had turned out the most botched of photoplays, Goldwyn held that the fault lay both with the producer and the author. The director lacked the vital assistance of the writer in interpreting his "script", in making clear this and that effect at which he aimed; and the author needed, just as much, to be told when and why some episode of his imagining ran off the straight track of action, as dictated by the new medium, and had to be replaced by something else.

The result of such theorizing was the presence of Margaret Mayo "on the lot" at Goldwyn's Fort Lee studio during the making of both *Polly of the Circus* and *Baby Mine* and in the cutting room and the projection room up to the last minute of the assembling of both finished films. Irvin S. Cobb and

Roi Cooper Megrue gave the same character of assistance to the screening of their joint story, *Fighting Odds,* and Mr. Cobb was in constant consultation while Mae Marsh was posing for his *Fields of Honor.* Edgar Selwyn, needless to say, is even now keeping very close to the making of his comedy, *Nearly Married,* into a vehicle for Madge Kennedy, while Porter Emerson Browne does the same by his story, *Joan of Flatbush,* which is being shaped about the personality of Mabel Normand. The case of such a writer as Anatole France might seem to present difficulties. It happened, however that the star who is to introduce his *Thais* to the screen has been in France for the past three months. And that accounted for the presence of M. France and Mary Garden at the same supper table in Paris on more than one occasion recently.

GOLDWYN STARTS PRODUCTION
First Mae Marsh Picture Begun at Fort Lee – Maxine Elliott Starts Feb. 15

(from *Moving Picture World,* February 17, 1917, p. 1016)

Six weeks after its incorporation and organization, Goldwyn Pictures Corporation has begun the work of actual production in its Fort Lee studios. The first company reported for work on Monday morning, January 29th, to Director Ralph W. Ince, who was selected by the Goldwyn officers to direct the first Mae Marsh picture of the new and quickly-expanding firm of producers.

Miss Marsh, fully recovered from her recent cold and indisposition, reported at the studio early, almost hidden in furs. She was accompanied by her sister, Marguerite Marsh, who is to play the sister role opposite Mae Marsh; Mother Marsh; and at least two smaller Marsh descendants. Vernon Steele, a handsome young actor who has been chosen as Miss Marsh's

leading man, is expected to win quick popularity on the screen.

Director Ince brought with him to the Goldwyn organization his assistant director, James Dent. George Hill is the cameraman for this production; W.K. Hedwig is laboratory manager, and Herbert M. Messmore, the technical director. Goldwyn has organized and installed its own managerial staff in the Solax studio.

Maxine Elliott will begin her career as a Goldwyn screen star when she faces the camera on February 15th. Announcement is made that Miss Elliott will be directed for her debut on the screen by Allan Dwan, whose achievements in an artistic sense have made him one of the dependable factors in screen direction.

Miss Elliott's first screen play will be the work of Louis K. Anspacher, author of *The Unchastened Woman,* one of last season's dramatic successes in New York. The theme or character of Miss Elliott's first picture is not revealed.

MAXINE ELLIOTT BEGINS
Company Assembles at Goldwyn Fort Lee Studio Under Direction of Allan Dwan – Actress Gets Reception

(from *Moving Picture World*, March 3, 1917, p. 1337)

Maxine Elliott, famed throughout the world as a noted beauty, began her career before the motion picture camera on Monday, February 19, at the Goldwyn studios in Fort Lee, with Allan Dwan on the firing line as her director. Miss Elliott's first role calls for extremely big acting. The play in which she makes her first appearance, under the Goldwyn auspices, is the work of Roi Cooper Megrue, author of *Under Cover, It Pays to Advertise, Under Sentence,* and other highly successful dramatic sensations.

Miss Elliott on her arrival at the Gold-

wyn studios found nearly all of the executives of the company waiting to welcome her. Flowers in profusion and telegrams arrived ahead of her; congratulatory letters and telegrams, such as a dramatic star receives on the opening night of a play on Broadway. Each of the other Goldwyn stars had sent good wishes and flowers. Mae Marsh, who was the first star to be announced by Goldwyn at its formation in December, was working in a studio on the same floor and she at once visited Miss Elliott and together they had a long talk about screen make-up.

Miss Elliott's is the second Goldwyn company to get under way.

Goldwyn has assembled a number of well-known players to support Miss Elliott. Allan Dwan, director of several of the most successful Douglas Fairbanks pictures for Triangle, brings a skilled technical staff with him for the making of Miss Elliott's picture. Rene Guissart is the cameraman for Dwan and Mlle. Georgette Merthier will aid in the costuming. Mr. Dwan, who combines the artistic and executive capacities as few men in the industry do, also may avail himself of the fine talents of Arthur Hopkins and such units of Mr. Hopkins' brilliant producing organization as may be required.

GOLDWYN STARS' NAMES ADORN CRAFT
Hudson Ferryboats Will Have Different Appellations – No. 6 Still a Mystery

(from *New York Dramatic Mirror*, March 10, 1917, p. 23)

Perhaps the most novel idea employed by a film producing company today is that which has been put into effect by Goldwyn Pictures in giving new names to five of the sturdy ferry craft running to the Fort Lee harbor. Goldwyn wished to give significance to the entry of the firm into the life and

Mary Garden arrives for work at the Goldwyn studio in Fort Lee, 1917.

action of Fort Lee, and chose this means to that end.

Commuters from nearby Jersey towns will soon be rubbing their eyes in the morning as they gaze upon the "Leonia", now renamed Mae Marsh; the "Edgewater", henceforth will be more picturesque and interesting as the Maxine Elliott, and you may be sure that people who never thought of looking at the "City of Plainfield" will look eagerly at the Mary Garden. Who would dare to hint that Jane Cowl was not a more alluring cognomen for a ferry craft than the "Fort Lee?" The "Elberon" henceforth is to be the Madge Kennedy.

The ferry company has been asked by the Goldwyn officers to hold one ship in reserve without a change of name until a sixth Goldwyn star of great prominence is announced shortly, thereby enabling the company to have a ship for every star.

Mary Garden's last act before sailing from New York for Vigo, Spain, was to order a gold monogram plate from a Fifth Avenue firm which henceforth will occupy a frame directly under the frame of the Federal steamboat inspector's annual license to what was once the "City of Plainsfield".

GOLDWYN LEASES STUDIO
Takes Over Big Universal Plant at Fort Lee, NJ – Will Complete Twelve Subjects by September 1

(from *Moving Picture World,* April 14, 1917, p. 252)

Goldwyn Pictures Corporation, enlarging its scale of operations so rapidly that its present studios at the Solax plant are inadequate, announces that it has leased the great Universal Film Corporation studio and related plant in Fort Lee.

The big "U" Fort Lee studio is one of the finest and most complete structures on the Eastern seaboard, and its occupancy by Goldwyn will give that company one of the finest producing plants utilized by any of the larger film companies.

Goldwyn at the present time is working two companies side by side in its first Fort Lee studio, the Solax, and by dint of close crowding might operate a third company there. But the Goldwyn scheme calls for the operation of more

producing units simultaneously; hence, the taking over of the Universal equipment as a result of negotiations with Carl Laemmle and his associates.

Samuel Goldfish, Edgar and Archibald Selwyn and Arthur Hopkins are determined to make good the Goldwyn promise of twelve completed pictures by September 1 – which forms the basic condition of a sales policy unique in the history of film productions. This accounts for a more than doubling of the Goldwyn production capacities in the East.

The underlying thought in the making of so many pictures in advance of releasing any of them is the basic idea employed by the automobile manufacturers, who hold annual exhibitions of new models for dealers and the public long in advance of retail sales.

These annual shows have vastly stimulated auto sales. This policy adopted by Goldwyn now places exhibitors in the fortunate position of knowing in advance exactly what they are buying.

It is believed that Universal will make productions in its Champion studio at Coytesville, which was the first glass studio built in the East and also the first studio of any kind built in New Jersey.

Goldwyn comes into possession, through its lease, of a plant having the second largest stage in the world. The stage proper is 150 feet long by 85 feet in width. Six companies can be worked conveniently at the same time. The studio administration building, which is 130 x 160 feet in size, of irregular shape and two stories high, was designed by Ernest Flagg, who also designed the Singer building in New York and the modern group of buildings at the Naval Academy in Annapolis. In the rear of the administration building and studio are the laboratories and film vaults. The laboratories structure is 150 x 104 feet. Facilities are at hand for all of the allied departments of motion picture production, and this plant has the largest carpenter shop equipment and property department east of the Mississippi River. In the main building are sixty-four dressing rooms for principals, in addition to huge dressing rooms for supers and extras.

Not to be outclassed by Tourneur, Brenon, and other local producers who felt it important to distinguish their "artistic" films from the usual product, Goldwyn also promoted its artistic aspirations. The association with Victor Freeburg and his Columbia University class in Photoplay Writing is one of the earliest direct instances of a movie studio turning to an institution of higher learning for intellectual cover. Not much came of this, but Goldwyn's decision to place considerable creative authority in the hands of prominent artists and designers like Hugo Ballin and Everett Shinn was a major break with existing practice, and an important step in the establishment of "art direction" as a separate discipline.

TO STUDY GOLDWYN DRAMAS
Photoplay Writing Class to Visit Studios – Receives Sets of Still Photographs

(from *New York Dramatic Mirror*, July 21, 1917, p. 17)

The Photoplay Writing Class at Columbia University is the recipient of sets of still photographs, a gift of the Goldwyn Pictures Corporation, which were made during the first Maxine Elliott and Madge Kennedy productions. These examples of the cinema art are to be hung in the Photoplay Museum at the Morningside Heights' Institution and will be used to instruct the class in scenario writing, one of the most popular elective studies in the literary curriculum. This class is conducted by Professor Victor Oscar Freeburg.

The course in picture play and dramatic writing at Columbia has been inaugurated along comprehensive lines. While the potential scenario writers are enlisted under the general head of dramatic study the actual class in screen writing is apart from the stage instruction and is devoted to the study of many technicalities of both plot and mechanism that must be observed in the development of silent drama.

The theoretical instruction of the classroom will be supplemented this Fall by trips to the studios, where pictures will be seen in practical making. The first visit will be made to the big Goldwyn studios in West Fort Lee.

The Columbia University photoplay class aspires to become as nationally famous as Professor Baker's "English 47" at Harvard, whose members have contributed some of the best known plays to the American drama.

WITH ART AS HER HANDMAIDEN

By Vivian M. Moses

(from *Moving Picture World*, July 21, 1917, pp. 383–387)

The growth of any art which contains within itself the elements of utility is assured, since in the very nature of things the utilization of the art brings development. But when to this element of utility is added a characteristic of universal appeal, resulting in a popularity of a universal nature, the development becomes so rapid that the growth assumes in some of its phases the rank nature of weed growth, with the ungainly proportions characteristic of the weed nature.

That the motion picture art has enjoyed a mushroom growth is a fact too well known to need proof; and that this growth has been accompanied by certain weed-like tendencies also is no secret. It is with the first adequate measures taken toward the removal of the most serious of these defects that this article deals.

The most frequent criticisms that one hears of present-day motion pictures – and the ones that are most deserved – are indictments on the score of "bad art" and "bad taste". Whenever there is a discussion of a forward movement in motion picture making the compelling thought behind the cry for reform is the necessity for inducing into the picture theaters greater numbers of people of discriminating judgment. The mere existence of this necessity is an indictment of the shortcomings of motion pictures when measured in the true-focusing eye of art – using the word in its broader sense. And the reason for these shortcomings is not hard to find.

The motion picture industry has enlisted the services of armies of workmen of all kinds, of craftsmen, of specialists, of technicians, of artisans – but, up to the present time, of few artists; and now we are employing the term in its restricted application to the professionals of the structural and pictorial arts. And this is all the more incongruous since of all forms of entertainment the motion picture is, per se, the most pictorial! It is with an appreciation of the absurdity of this situation, and with the determination that their pictures shall not suffer from this handicap, that the producers of

Goldwyn Pictures have taken the initiative in bringing to their studios artists of established repute, and in giving them authoritative charge of the designing, construction and direction of their productions. The group of artists thus enlisted in the creation of Goldwyn Pictures embraces Mr. Hugo Ballin, Mr. Everett Shinn and Mr. William Cotton. Before reviewing their work it might be well to inform ourselves briefly concerning these three artists, in order that we may understand better their motives and purposes.

Hugo Ballin, a native of New York City, is one of America's most eminent mural artists. Although still a very young man, his mural paintings have won him many prizes and awards and brought him international recognition; his name has been a familiar one in the art journals of the world's capitals and art centers. Among his many successes may be mentioned the winning of the Thomas B. Clarke prize for the best figure composition painted in the United States by an American citizen without limitation of age; two successive Architectural League medals for decorative painting; and a medal won at the Buenos Aires International Exposition in

(Above, left): Miniature created by the Goldwyn art department for Thais *(1917).*

(Below): Jane Cowl in The Spreading Dawn *(Goldwyn, 1917).*

1910 for figure composition. Mr. Ballin's most important murals are to be found in the executive offices of the Wisconsin capital at Madison; in the home of Oliver Gould Jennings, New York; in the home of E.D. Brandegee, Boston. His paintings are to be found in many private collections, in the National Museum at Washington, the Montclair Museum and elsewhere. He is a member of the National Art Club, Rome, Italy; the Society of Arts and Letters, Paris; the Architectural League, the Society of Mural Decorators, the National Institute of Arts and Letters, an Associate in the National Academy of Design, and Artist Member of the Lotos Club.

It is significant, is it not, that a man of Mr. Ballin's standing in the world of art is devoting his entire time and effort to the cause of "better pictures?"

Everett Shinn, because of his fame as an American illustrator, probably is well known to the readers of these pages. Mr. Shinn's clever drawings have made such a place for themselves in the pages of American magazines that the "Shinn type" of illustration has become a standard. Quaintly charming in their details, his drawings are packed with human interest and peopled by figures whose richly humorous characteristics have revealed the artist as the Dickens of the pen and brush. Mr. Shinn's services are in constant demand by the art editors, and have won him a fortune. But magazine illustration is by no means the sum total of this artist's accomplishments. He is a mural painter with an established reputation and a niche all his own; he is a facile worker in pastel, and – he is an unusually successful writer of dramatic sketches.

William Cotton, whose advent at the Goldwyn Studios is more recent than that of Mr. Ballin and Mr. Shinn, is one of the most successful of the younger American artists, having already achieved an international reputation as a portrait painter, and won

distinction as well with his decorative drawings and tone studies. Mr. Cotton won success, following study in Boston and Paris, with a series of canvasses, one of the first of which to gain wide recognition was "The Princess", the painting of a little girl fresh from her bath being attended by two ladies-in-waiting. This picture won the first Hallgarten prize at the National Academy of Design, in 1907. It was followed by many portraits, notable among which were a full length figure of Chrystal Herne, the actress, a portrait of Harrison Rhodes, the author, and a study of a young girl, Madge Evans, now well known as a moving picture player. Mr. Cotton's work has won the praise of critics both here and abroad and has firmly established him as one of the forces to be reckoned with in contemporary American art.

In beginning the production of a Goldwyn Picture the first and primary service to be rendered by the particular artist in charge of it is to design the sets. Instead of being handed to a technical director or an art director or a master carpenter or any one or several of the usual train of people who look to this end of motion picture production, the Goldwyn script is turned over to Ballin, Shinn or Cotton. Actually, physically, these men design the physical settings in which the action of the photoplay takes place and this means not only scenes, but in most instances the entire minutae and details of all fixed and movable accessories, including furniture, furnishings, draperies, all species of properties, and costumes, working of course, in harmony with the star for the last named.

Mr. Ballin, imbued with the spirit of architecture, thinks in plan, and works in it. For each set he prepares a plan drawing to scale, sometimes including the larger pieces of furniture, but more often omitting them. This drawing is frequently supplemented by a flat sketch showing side walls, and

their ornamentation – or lack of it. Nothing is drawn in perspective, and figures and accessory details are omitted, these being furnished later under the verbal direction of the artist.

Mr. Shinn, as might be expected, draws in perspective; what is more, his drawings are usually a visualization of some keynote episode or situation of the photoplay the action of which takes place in the set shown. His drawings are executed with all the care and wealth of elaboration which this artist puts in a magazine illustration, and, as may be seen by the example reproduced in this article, these set drawings are illustrations in all but name. Mr. Shinn's art is impressionistic, but it suggests every detail in a room or scene; and the figures of characters are shown in correct costume and in some characteristic or actual situation. For dimensions, Mr. Shinn hands a note to his collaborators or confers with them in the production of his sets.

Mr. Cotton's method, as revealed in his work on the first of his Goldwyn Pictures – *The Spreading Dawn*, in which Jane Cowl is starred – is to make a rough plan drawing and elaborate it with sketches.

This business of designing sets, while it is the first and primary service which the artist renders his production, is by no means a perfunctory or casual matter. Many ends are served in this first fitting of a photoplay production with its physical dress. Not only is the entire atmosphere of a production created, for this is true of all sets, no matter by whom made, but in the hands of the skillful artist the actors in the photodrama are measurably assisted in getting their message "across" to the audience.

"Every known emotion", says Mr. Ballin, "can be expressed in terms of form and color. Through the physical marshaling of objects, through contour and balance (not balance of weight, mind you, but art balance), through light and shade, and their

gradations, the world's grief and the world's joy may be deftly and exactly expressed. Despair and hope, doubt and decision, hypocrisy and sincerity – these and other traits are convincingly suggested by the physical surroundings of the people who are supposed to portray them."

This is really the vital aspect of settings, when measured by the artist's standards. Do they merely provide so many scenes in which the story – and the people living it before the eye of the camera – struggle on as best they may? Or, as is not infrequently the case, do the settings positively hinder the progress of the story and the message it conveys? They may do any one of these three things.

To this end Mr. Ballin lays great stress, as do the other artists, on color, or tone values, in his scenes. Of course, the ordinary photoplay shows no color, as the layman uses the term, it being photographed and projected in black and white. But to the artist color is a relative term, and every composition registers color,

even though it be expressed in black and white. For the purpose of accurately controlling the color values of his sets Mr. Ballin has devised a chromatic scale or graded schedule of tone values. Rather he has devised a series of them. These are simply strips of board painted in sections which imperceptibly graduate from dark to light, several different colors being employed, one for each board. These scales are numbered, and the various sections are lettered. As the photographic value of every gradation in every scale has been determined, all the artist has to do to procure that precise value in any set is to call for the use of the desired number. The scene painter selects the pigment corresponding to the number given – and the result is automatic.

Inasmuch as the final object of setting is to help the actors tell a story to an audience, the one aim of the artists is to simplify. The play and the people in it are the important things, all else are mere accessories. The fact that a certain scene calls for "a rich library set" does not give the scene painter and the carpenter and the "furniture hound" license to show all that they know about what properties and what effects may be found in "rich" libraries. The artist determines, What is the province of this setting in the story? What traits of character does it expose? What emotions must it help convey or conceal? And having determined these things, the artist builds accordingly. Now the setting required may be exceedingly complex; or it may be passing plain. Which of these it is does not matter. The important fact is that the setting has been made not only to step out of the way of the story and let it proceed as it should, but actually to help the actors carry on their tale, to march with the progress of the drama. The setting, as a separate entity, has ceased to exist when it has successfully met the requirements of these tests-and in this manner simplicity has been gained.

This process, not only of eliminating every unnecessary thing, but of making every physical element in a photoplay, no matter how small or how great, no matter how costly or how cheap, place its shoulder to the wheel and help to roll the story along the main path of its progress is the process of real simplification which three eminent artists have brought to Goldwyn Pictures, and it is a new word in motion picture production.

Very interesting are the sets which Mr. Ballin designed for the first picture in which Maxine Elliott is starred – it must be nameless at this writing, as no title has been fixed upon [released as *Fighting Odds* -ed.]. Here the artist was confronted with the problem of providing settings in which the features of a woman internationally famous for her beauty would show to the greatest advantage. Also, the story recorded a conflict of open honesty with crafty vice, and of refinement with vulgarity. The picture, which will be seen very shortly, since Goldwyn productions are released in September and trade showings will antedate this by some weeks, shows the severely plain backgrounds with which Mr. Ballin furnished Miss Elliott's scenes. But plain as these settings are they yet convey a sense of beauty, of refinement, of personal elevation and strength of character, which infinitely enhance the dramatic struggle in the story; which tell, as a thousand feet of film and a thousand words of sub-title could not tell, the kind of person Miss Elliott is supposed to be in the story, and which incidentally afford at every turn a background against which Miss Elliott's strikingly beautiful profile stands out as clear-cut as a cameo.

Such settings have been utilized before in motion pictures; it remained for an artist, with that instant, intuitive perception of values which is the true artist's birthright, to bring them to the studio.

Markedly in contrast with these, but equally carrying out the artist's idea that settings should not only create an atmosphere but should actually help the players to tell their stories to the audience, is the pretty setting designed by Mr. Ballin for Zoie's bedroom in *Baby Mine*, the first of the plays in which Madge Kennedy is starred, and incidentally the third of Mr. Ballin's Goldwyn productions. Here the character which the setting is required to "plant" is that of a lovely young girl who has not penetrated far below the surface of things; of serious thought and responsibilities she knows not a whit. On the other hand, she is well reared, refined, educated, absolutely virtuous, and angelically good, despite the fact that thoughtless lies roll from her facile little tongue in an endless flood. All these things the artist bore in mind in designing his set. He surrounded Zoie with the ordinary objects to be found in the boudoir of a young bride, but he so manipulated the tone-values of his set that at every turn these physical surroundings suggest and supplement the character of the person whose choice they are supposed to be. The furnishings of the bedroom are done in a finely flowered cretonne, which conveys not only femininity, but the easy-going, surface-living Zoie herself. And every detail of the room's arrangement has some meaning in the drama of the little wife who lied to her husband about the babies she had never borne him.

"I put that mirror there", said Mr. Ballin in speaking of an unusually effective dressing-table mirror with a Chinese frame, "not just because I had to have a mirror in the room, but because in studying the story and its action as revealed in the scenario I could see many places in which the dramatic action could be heightened by the use of the mirror; it was needed, in fact, to carry on the story as I saw it. And all through the play that mirror plays a very real part.

"In designing any scene in a photoplay I have in my mind not only the general purposes for which the set will be used, but I visualize mentally the players in position in the setting, at this and another moment in the play, so that I have mental pictures of so many vital compositions of figures and backgrounds, and when I design a bench here, or a window there, or a bit of trellis there I know, before the scenery has been built, just how the actual scene in the photoplay will appear on the screen – just what the relationship between the persons and the things in the scene will be, just what effects will be produced, just what drama will flow from striking this, that, or another note in composition. And this is the reason that we can not permit the slightest departure from our plans by the artisans who carry them out in the actual production of the set. Obviously no one but the artist who has dreamed the dream – so to speak – can know just what effects, what compositions, he had in mind when he planned this or that bit of his sketch; and should these be changed by a second or third person not in on the secret, the whole drama, the whole psychology of the set would be thrown out. This may sound like taking ourselves very seriously – but it is only taking our sets seriously – which is a different thing!"

Just as Mr. Ballin is a romantic idealist in his work, so Mr. Shinn is an impressionistic realist in his. This is clearly established in the first two pictures which Mr. Shinn has designed for Goldwyn, *The Bird Doctor* [released as *Sunshine Alley* – ed.] and *Polly of the Circus*, in both of which Mae Marsh is the star. And the settings in these pictures show to a marked degree how faithfully the sketches of the artists are lived up to in the production of the actual setting on the studio stage. Reproduced with this article are sketches for scenes in the two photoplays just named – the work of Mr. Shinn before any work had been done on the sets; and paralleling these are photographs made of the actual sets as they stood on the studio stage. [The Shinn sketches have been omitted here – ed.] It will be seen that not only has the general scheme been followed in each instance, but detail for detail the artist's thought and the finished scene coincide. And this is done, not for the sake of slavishly following an artist's drawing, but for the reason that the artist, having planned scenes in which he saw, in his mind's eye, episodes of the play passing in order, is presumably better fitted to say just what are the requirements of those scenes, down to the minutest detail, than is any one else.

Mr. Shinn, however, assists his collaborators by drawing into his sketches the

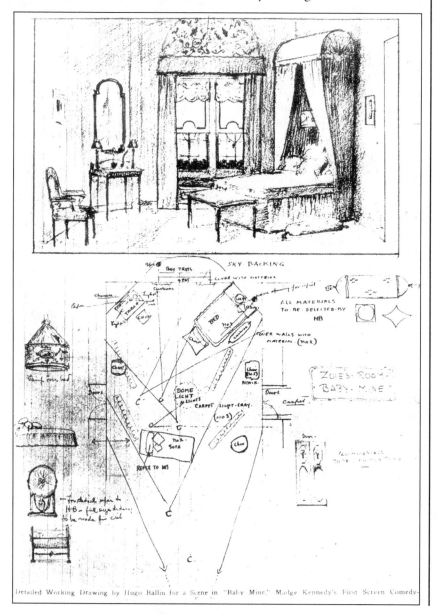

Detailed Working Drawing by Hugo Ballin for a Scene in "Baby Mine," Madge Kennedy's First Screen Comedy.

(Below, left): Hugo Ballin sketches for Baby Mine *(Goldwyn, 1917), dictating specific camera angles and lenses, as reproduced in* Moving Picture World, *July 21, 1917.*

actual figures of the actors in some episode of the play, and it is almost uncanny to see the manner in which, during the process of filming the play one scene after another duplicates the exact composition the artist has drawn, both as to the attitudes and positions of the players in relation to the settings and in relation to each other.

In all this no word has been said of the director – that august boss supreme in the land of the studio stage. How, one is tempted to ask, does this autocrat take this scheme in which such importance and authority is invested in the artist? The answer is that in the Goldwyn plan the artist and the director co-operate. This is not fancy; it is accomplished fact. Further than that, the artist and the director may act as co-directors of a production, as have Mr. Ballin and Mr. John Stewart Robinson on *Baby Mine*. And it is not without the realm of the possible, in things Goldwyn, that when the artist has become sufficiently proficient in the art of directing to stand alone.

For Art has become the handmaiden of the Movies.

One of the surprises in this visit to the Goldwyn studio is a glimpse of Marie Dressler filming *The Scrub Lady*, the first of a series of two-reel comedies she made for Goldwyn, but the only one shot in the East. Unlike the other women on the lot, Dressler was not a "Goldwyn star", but was producing the film for her own company, which explains why there was never a ferry boat named the "Marie Dressler".

LITTLE JOURNEYS TO EASTERN STUDIOS IV – GOLDWYN
The Fourth of a Series of Articles Dealing with Eastern Studios to Be Published at Intervals in The *Mirror* – This Journey Disclosed a New Era in the Development of the Film Art

By Alison Smith

(from *New York Dramatic Mirror*, August 4, 1917, p. 11)

The influence of the Goldwyn studio is noticeable miles before you reach the actual site on which it is located. The very ferry on which you cross from Manhattan to Fort Lee probably bears the name of Mae Marsh or Maxine Elliott or some other of the Goldwyn's collection of stars. On the other side of the river, you will find the little ferry station banked with automobiles which are taking the various companies, many of them in full costume, up to the Goldwyn plant or out on "locations". On the way up you are apt to pass Margaret Mayo in a runabout or Hugo Ballin meditating on color scheme in a huge limousine or other members of the large staff who dart back and forth from the city office where their ideas are formulated, to the laboratory in the woods where they are put into action.

Studio located in a grove

The road winds over the Palisades to the top of the hill where the studio is sunk in a grove so thick that a short stroll would seem to provide a set for the Black Forest. Before the door, a line of motor cars is always waiting to take the companies out to the infinite variety of exterior backgrounds offered by the diversified scenery of the Palisades.

The studio itself is a large substantial concrete building arched by a glass dome. On the ground floor are the business offices, dressing rooms and a restaurant which provides meals at all hours for the entire staff. There are a few unofficial rooms for the scenario staff, whose headquarters are nominally in New York, but who are apt to be found in odd corners of the studio at almost any time of day or night. Margaret Mayo, whom we met in one of the corridors, was perfectly frank about her inability to stay away. "I belong back in the other office", she told us, "but the place is so fascinating that I stay for just one more scene until I find the morning gone. The studio has been a revelation to me and the mechanical details, far from removing inspiration, are the greatest possible incentive in writing for the screen."

Personal pride in work

Miss Mayo's attitude is characteristic of the entire Goldwyn force. From the office boys and carpenters up to the highest officials you find this same spontaneous enjoyment in the work and same personal pride in displaying its result to visitors. You almost gain the impression that if they were not in this work as a matter of business, they might be found doing it as a fascinating and novel form of entertainment. The result is a general atmosphere of enthusiastic energy which pervades the entire plant and is soon communicated to the most casual visitor.

H.S. Messmore, the technical director, took us up to the studio floor where the stage is stretched out under its arch of glass. This wide space gives unlimited area to the sets and eliminates the necessity of putting them up in sections. When a ballroom scene is staged, for instance, it is of almost ballroom size, and the actors can go from room to room with perfect freedom of movement which sustains their illusion and makes their acting that much more spontaneous. On this particular afternoon, the stage was half covered with the interior of a stately Southern home, where Jane Cowl, looking lovely and pathetic in crinoline, was preparing to wring the hearts of her absent audience. In a less sedate corner of the room, Marie Dressler was regarding rather grimly an intricate mechanical arrangement by which she is to fall off a roof down a chute, run for several (screen) miles on a tread-mill and then crash down on the surprised occupants of the room below. The staff is provided with technical experts who can improvise on demand any variety of mechanical stage property that their scripts may demand.

Details of the studio

Connected with the studio are the carpenter shops and the property rooms which cover three tiers and look like a small department store. Here the miniature models for each of the important sets are made, and this corner is a veritable toy world which would delight the heart of a child visitor.

Long glass doors open from the studio to the surrounding lot which has unlimited scenic possibilities in its ten foot area. A few weeks ago this lot was covered by a city in Palestine but now, with a blissful disregard for historical sequence, it is the scene of a straggling New England village with a circus in the foreground. So permanent, complete and realistic is the little street that motoring parties from the city often stop at what they suppose is one of the clusters of homes that dot the banks of New Jersey.

Goldwyn's representative staff

All about the premises are the outward signs of a plant that is devoted to the art of making pictures instead of a factory for turning out films. When the company was first organized by Samuel Goldfish, it was with the purpose of building photodramas around ideas which would call into service all of the arts. To this end, he selected a staff of specialists which is representative of the best work that is being done in the United States today in the various branches of illustrative

Marie Dressler in The Scrub Lady *(Dressler Producing Corp., 1917).*

Although the first Goldwyn Picture is yet to be released in New York, their new ideals and methods have already had a material effect on the film world, for all the outward visible signs in and about the studio point to a new era in the development of moving pictures as a fine art.

While not the first film to go before the cameras, *Polly of the Circus* was the first film Goldwyn released. Very handsomely produced, *Polly* was essentially a simple circus tale with one spectacular disaster sequence. Unfortunately, it cost more to make than *The Birth of a Nation*, an example of the production inefficiencies that almost sank Goldwyn in its first year.

"POLLY OF THE CIRCUS" LAUNCHES GOLDWYN PICTURES
Story of the Photoplay Adaptation of Margaret Mayo's Famous Play in Which Mae Marsh Appears as the Star – 80,000 Feet of Film Photographed

(from *New York Dramatic Mirror*, August 11, 1917, p. 13

When the final tent stake was yanked from earth and the canvas was folded and packed away, Samuel Goldfish sighed a breath of relief. Save for the quaint Everett Shinn village that stood baking in the sun, the externals of Margaret Mayo's famous drama, *Polly of the Circus*, starring Mae Marsh,

and literary art. The scenario department, for instance, reads like a literary, "Who's Who". There is Margaret Mayo, one of our most successful later playwrights, Irvin Cobb, who is one of our most popular professional humorists, Adrien Gillspeer, author of *The Barrier*, Roi Cooper Megrue, best known for *Under Cover*, Edith Ellis, Porter Emerson Browne and other writers who have undisputedly arrived in the magazine world. The art staff includes Hugo Ballin, whose mural decorations in the Michigan State Capitol attracted attention a short time ago, and Everett Shinn, illustrator, whose drawings are primarily identified with the pages of *Vanity Fair*. The work of these specialists goes on under the direction of men like Archibald and Edgar Selwyn and Arthur Hopkins, who have established themselves as among the most able and successful producing managers in the theatrical world.

had been wiped from the face of the earth, but inside the Goldwyn studios, at Fort Lee, there were 80,000 feet of film that were to be cut, assembled and released on September 9th. With *Polly of the Circus*, by Margaret Mayo, Goldwyn Pictures Corporation makes its formal bow to the world of cinema art.

The high-water mark in elaborate and spectacular production within the metropolitan district has been reached in the staging of *Polly of the Circus*. It took ten weeks of photography, by day and night, in addition to months of preparatory effort to complete this production. In it are nine separate photo-spectacle scenes, which will make this classic of the big tops, standing out among contemporary productions, for magnitude alone. There were, in total, 1,164 scenes made with an average of five takes to each scene. From the 80,000 feet of film that have been sent to the laboratories from six to eight thousand feet will be finally elected to tell Margaret Mayo's story that made a fortune for its producers on the dramatic stage.

Living in the studios

Charles Thomas Horan and his corps of assistants who directed *Polly* lived in the Goldwyn studios during the last five weeks of its production. They slept and ate there and often worked until daybreak on the circus scenes made under the "big tops", many of which were photographed at night. Herbert Messmore and staff that supervised the art direction of the picture were at Horan's side during this long grind.

Four small New Jersey cities figured in the play. At Hohokus a race track was chartered and with a grandstand filled with "extras", a horse race with a field of seven thoroughbreds was run. In Englewood the circus parade was held and it took the greater part of two days for this circus pageant to be photographed. In Coytesville

scenes were made showing the early morning arrival of a circus in a small city as well as the departure at night.

On the lot in Fort Lee the immense canvas was spread and the circus performance proper photographed. Here also was built the village that Everett Shinn designed and which in point of size actually occupied more than two square city blocks. Marcus Loew, of New York, T.L. Tally, of Los Angeles, and other great exhibitors who visited the Goldwyn studios during the filming of the Mayo drama declared the scenic sets were of greater size than anything they hitherto had seen.

New effects in lighting

In the arrangement of lighting and artistic embellishment, George W. Hill, head cameraman, and his staff have turned out new effects, prominent among which is an episode in the story that is told entirely in photographic silhouette. Part of the plot action, which was devised by Miss Mayo, herself, calls for a fire in which the circus is burned and to accomplish the desired effect a section of the "big top" was in reality fired and the ensuing stampede of animals and spectators photographed. In this scene entire sections of occupied bleacher seats are seen to fall.

Mae Marsh, the celebrated little heroine of *The Birth of a Nation* and *Intolerance*, and now linked with Goldwyn Pictures by a long-time contract, accomplished an immense amount of work during the filming of *Polly*. For days at a stretch she worked fourteen and fifteen hours a day and to the amazement of her directors she stood the strain better than they. Director Horan and one of his assistants were blinded by the high-powered Kleigls, and others of the principals came near "cracking" under the sustained strain, but last week Miss Marsh was already preparing for her next Goldwyn picture … .

> In fact, not everything went so smoothly during the filming of *Polly of the Circus* – as this item from the local press indicates. While the art department may have been well organized, what the film really needed was an experienced production manager.

MOVING PICTURE RIOT IN FORT LEE IN WHICH WERE SEVERAL HUNDRED YOUNG CHILDREN, MANY UNDER 8

Studio Was Pulling Huge Circus Stunt Under Regulation Tent, Got Behind With Program, Failed to Give Supper As Promised – Fort Lee Talent Got Disgusted, Turned Loose, Tried to "Break Things" And Home Defense Guards Were Called Out, Claimed One Man Shot In Leg In Riot

(from *The Palisadian*, June 30, 1917, pp. 1, 3)

As a result of a moving picture stunt at the Goldwyn Studios in Fort Lee last Monday night one man was shot through the leg and is in the Englewood Hospital, and there was a hunger riot that necessitated the calling out of the Home Defense Guard to quell it.

It seems that the Goldwyn Studios near Main Street in Fort Lee was putting out a circus stunt in which a big audience, elephants, including lions and other animals, all played their respective parts.

The picture was being made under a huge, regulation sized circus tent, brilliantly illuminated, having three rings

with a typical circus performance going on in each. The scene was just like any other circus, with red lemonade boys, and peanut venders, tumblers, bare-back riding, trapeze performers, trained elephants and everything exactly as the great and only Barnum or Forepeau would hash them up.

For the audience something like 800 supes [i.e., supernumeraries, or "extras"-ed.] were required, with a large percentage of small children, many under eight years of age. The children belonged to New York families, and the "audience" was to get $1.75 or $1.85 each per session, with a midnight supper thrown in with car fare both ways. The work of perfecting the film required several days.

On Monday night things did not go just right, and the directors of the circus drama got behind, and as the story goes forgot all about the midnight supper. There were many Fort Lee boys in the scene, and when there was no hash passed, they proceeded to smash up the circus. It is even intimated that at neighboring three or four saloons the local boys had "beered up", and were thus keyed to a disturbance from over-indulgence.

When they had made a demand for supper and no spread was prepared, the disorder broke loose, and the management hastily called for the police aid, and the Home Guard Defense boys were requisitioned to quell the disturbance. The boys in Company A responded promptly, restored order, but were kept up till after 3 a.m., as were the members of the circus audience, children and all.

In the worst part of the trouble at the studio, young Mr. McAvoy, son of the ex-mayor of the name, got into an argument with a much larger Taylorville chap named Frey and when the latter made for him, McAvoy turned loose a revolver he carried, he says in the air, and got his antagonist one in the leg, necessitating an ambulance ride to Englewood Hospital. Frey's friends claim he ran into a wagon wheel and injured his knee and was not shot.

It is an open secret that the authorities have been severely criticized for allowing such an occurrence to take place in the borough. The matter of allowing young children under eight to be corralled in a performance of this character till all hours of the night, many nights in succession, is the worst feature of the movie riot. That it was an outrage on public morals is openly expressed by many of the leading citizens of the borough.

It is claimed by observers that the lights in the big tent were so intense that children and grown-ups were almost unable to see from the glare, and suffered greatly. It is alleged, also, that one of the troubles came from the elephants which refused to work on account of the excessive light glare, and this caused much delay. Also the rumor is out that one man was made blind by the light and has been unable to see since. The directors generally wore amber glasses, but the audience would have looked funnier than a circus all fussed up in auto goggles, so they had to take the light and rub their eyes. That more casualties did not occur is wondered at. Young McAvoy had arrested Frey, and this was the cause of the shooting. No bullet has as yet been located in Frey's knee. McAvoy says he fired in the air and could not have shot Frey.

Because the various state and local censorship boards (as well as the National Board of Review) each had their own sets of standards, a film might be praised in one jurisdiction and condemned in another. That may be what happened to *The Eternal Magdalene*, which was eventually released in 1919. But problems with the quality of the film – which, despite the claims here, was shot after *Fighting Odds* – may also have been an issue.

CENSORS CAUSE GOLDWYN TO HOLD "MAGDALENE" FILM

'Fighting Odds" Starring Maxine Elliott Replaces First Scheduled Feature

(from *Exhibitors Herald,* October 6, 1917, p. 22)

While the Goldwyn picture, *The Eternal Magdalene*, starring Maxine Elliott, was passed with the hearty endorsement of the National Board of Review with a special report "that the world as a motion picture audience owes Goldwyn a vote of thanks for making this sincere and beautiful production", it did not meet with the approval of the censors in Pennsylvania and in the city of Chicago.

It was therefore found necessary to rearrange the schedule and Miss Elliott's second Goldwyn picture, *Fighting Odds,* written by Roi Cooper Megrue and Irvin S. Cobb, will be presented on the date that *The Eternal Magdalene* was to have been shown.

Goldwyn was a bit premature in announcing its acquisition of director Raoul Walsh, who remained under contract to Fox for two more years. But this brief announcement does provide a glimpse of the technical facilities to be expected in one of the "world's finest" studios.

WHAT WALSH FOUND IN GOLDWYN STUDIO
Enumeration of Some of the Accessories of the Big Establishment at Fort Lee

(from *Moving Picture World*, January 5, 1918, p. 57)

Raoul A. Walsh, who is to become a member of the directorial staff of Goldwyn Pictures when his contract with another firm is fulfilled, has made an exploratory tour of the Goldwyn studio at Fort Lee, NJ, for the purpose of familiarizing himself with the equipment. Unhesitatingly he pronounces the Goldwyn plant one of the world's finest.

R.L. Lambdin's impressions of the filming of Polly of the Circus. *From* Picture Play, *October 1917.*

A Circus In Celluloid

By R. L. Lambdin

Some pen impressions of the studio-made circus at the Goldwyn plant.

Riding bareback may be easy for the circus girl who gets $18.00 per, but for a dainty star—well, its the hardest work she ever did for her several thousand a week.

"Fall!" yells the director. She does—and then repeats it eight times until the master of drama is satisfied.

An impression of the gigantic stampede scene when the big tent burns, being "shot" by the cameras in the dead of night.

A squad of happy extras—inside the big tent and being paid for their presence—imagine!

It wasn't all acted fear when "Jumbo" tore loose on a rampage, blinded by the lights.

The professional circus folk—except for the hardened clown—and the reporters, all had to wear dark glasses between scenes when the glaring lights blazed for the camera.

(Top): Arthur Hopkins directing Maxine Elliott in The Eternal Temptress (Goldwyn, 1917), held up until 1919 due to censorship problems.
(Bottom): Mary Garden in Thais.

The property room came in for a share of the director's attention. Its unusually complete equipment represents an investment of approximately $150,000 in furniture, rugs, oil paintings and other accessories of house furnishing. He was told that there were few things he could ask for that could not be at once produced from property stock. Of particular interest was the wardrobe room, where are hung costumes worth close to $50,000.

Mr. Walsh was particularly interested in the method of illuminating what is said to be the largest electric lighted motion picture stage in the world. He smiled his approval when he was told that the lighting equipment consists of fifteen wall [i.e. Wohl] broadsides, seven Kliegl broadsides, thirty-three overhead Duplex lights, thirty-five floor banks of Cooper-Hewitt mercury lights, six "gooseneck" Cooper-Hewitts, fifty overhead banks of "coops" and three six-inch and four eight-inch spotlights.

By 1918 Goldwyn began to scale back the costs of production. Mary Garden in *Thais*, another costly failure, was among the last of the studio's design-dominated films (Hugo Ballin received co-director credit). And instead of depending on legendary divas whose screen following never matched their theatrical reputations, there were more comedies with Madge Kennedy and Mabel Normand – with whom Sam Goldfish was carrying on an impossible romantic liaison.

QUEEN MARY EXTENDS HER DOMAIN
Mary Garden, While Still Holding Sway Over the Operatic World, Invades the Realm of Silence

By Ray Ralston

(from *Picture Play*, February 1918, pp. 209–211)

In perfect uniformity, a long line of dressing rooms stretches down the corridor in the Goldwyn Studio, at Fort Lee, New Jersey, unbroken save for one spot of color. It is a soft, gray-green square. It is a rug before one of the doors, the door of Mary Garden, famous the world over as *Thais* of the opera, and soon to be equally eloquent as *Thais* of the screen.

The rug is her mascot. It lay before her door at the Theatre da Monnaie in Brussels the night she created *Thais,* and it has accompanied her to all the great opera houses. She declares her success would be broken if the rug were lost or forgotten. Its presence in a building where film plays are made assumes a romantic interest second only in importance to the appearance of Mary Garden on it as she steps

across the threshold. It was thus that she was met by PICTURE PLAY MAGAZINE'S representative. "Do forgive me. It was wretched of me to keep you standing on this cold cement floor, and now I am to be bundled into a motor and taken where there are some rocks. So we can't talk, after all." Miss Garden's rapid speech, ever so slightly suggestive of her Scottish birth, is crisp and clear. "Come along", she said, with an impulsive gesture, "we can talk on the rocks", and made her way briskly down the corridor. There was no retinue attending her, no awning for the diva to pass under, only one middle-aged French-woman alert to be of service to her mistress.

"The other day I was sent dashing off

to Florida with Mr. Frank Crane, my director, and a few members of the cast. We stayed only a few hours, to do the desert scenes in *Thais;* then were raced up here again for the death of Thais in the nunnery. It's most extraordinary, and leaves me quite breathless", Miss Garden said, with a droll laugh, "but I do exactly as I'm told, and then when I see the pictures I know why!"

The voice she has nurtured all her life she knew would be exposed to dangers unknown in the great opera houses. But she was resolved to play in pictures. She had signed her contract.

Bleak enough the rocks looked, and

R.L. Lambdin sketches Mabel Normand on the set at Goldwyn's Fort Lee studio. From Picture Play, *February 1918.*

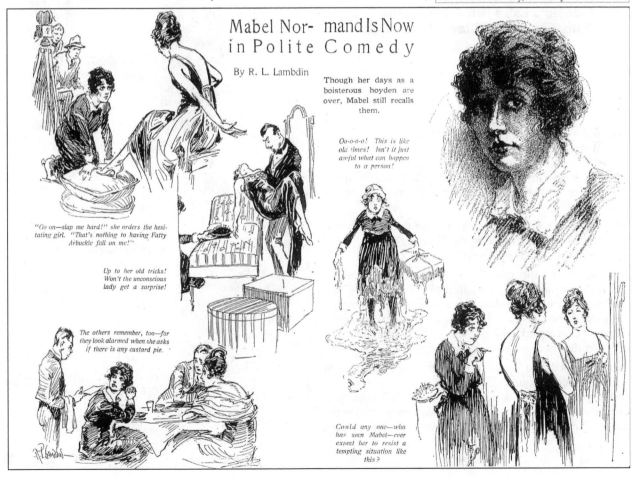

Mabel Nor- mand Is Now in Polite Comedy

By R. L. Lambdin

Though her days as a boisterous hoyden are over, Mabel still recalls them.

Oo-o-o-o! This is like old times! Isn't it just awful what can happen to a person!

"Go on—slap me hard!" she orders the hesitating girl. "That's nothing to having Fatty Arbuckle fall on me!"

Up to her old tricks! Won't the unconscious lady get a surprise!

The others remember, too—for they look alarmed when she asks if there is any custard pie.

Could any one—who has seen Mabel—ever expect her to resist a tempting situation like this?

cold, that late afternoon in December, with the damp Jersey air from the river making furs a comfort and exercise a necessity.

"Ready?" called Miss Garden, when they had gone over the scenes and the camera man had his eyes at the lens. She flung off her long fur coat, and stood there in gossamer silk, her feet in sandals, and little above the girdle around her waist. There was no tremor, no reaction from cold. Thais might have been in the crowded Metropolitan.

"Stop!" said Mr. Crane, and at that instant the fur coat once more enveloped Miss Garden. Not a fraction of a second was lost.

"Now", she volunteered, on her way to the machine", to prove to you and everybody else that I shall win in this fight against the fear others – not I – have of the eclipse of my voice, I'll tell you a secret, new today: I have agreed to sing in New York in January. A big forfeit if I do not appear. That's my answer to you, December!"

"DODGING A MILLION" WITH MABEL NORMAND
The *Classic*'s Extra Girl Answers the Phone, Sells Cigars and Stays Up All Night

By Ethel Rosemon

(excerpted from *Motion Picture Classic,* April 1918, pp. 53–56)

"Can you act?"

"Yes, indeed", I had responded, for you can all bear witness that I have been acting all over the pages of the *Classic* for the past ten months. I had visions of a chance to emote or mayhap vamp over foot after foot of celluloid. Was at last that elusive young animal, Opportunity, pecking at my shoelaces?

"Report at our Fort Lee studio at nine-thirty tomorrow morning as telephone-girl at the Ritz-Carlton in Mabel Normand's picture, *Dodging a Million*".

But what opportunity would a telephone-girl have to emote, and if she vamped when she called "1492 Columbus" the screen would not reproduce her dulcet tones? However, even telephone girls have been known to grab fate at the switch, so I accepted, with one eye on Mr. Klauber and the other on the check he was handing me.

Being engaged as a "hello girl", I naturally found myself behind the cigar counter. This happens once in a lifetime and then only on the screen. When Goldwyn's busy little carpenters gave birth to a replica of the famous hotel at the studio, they found the switchboard was one of the things

Mabel Normand.

that the movie fans would take for granted without hearing it buzz in the picture, so they naturally dispensed with it and set the operator to work behind the cigar-counter, much to the chagrin of said operator.

My dressing-room companions were a little girl who was taking her first dive into pictures, a gorgeous brown-eyed creature with the face of a vamp and the heart of an angel, and Minnie Metho of concert fame, who was playing one of the *grande dame* roles, but who, in spite of that fact, was not above being on reminiscing terms with the "extra ladies" of the dressing-room. We all gave her a prolonged vote of thanks for the stories of the days when she and Mary Garden were fellow students, first in Chicago and then in Paris. It was thrilling to hear the little, reverential touch she gave the "Mary", especially since the dear lady who made perfume famous was within earshot of the dressing-room. It was well that Minnie Metho shared our dressing-room. It was also well that she and Mary had been fellow students, for with what other stories could we have whiled away those hours so advantageously? Rome was not built in a day. The Goldwyn Ritz was, but it was night before it was finished. After we had made merry over the dinner table, not to mention the frankfurters and sauerkraut, Dan O'Brien's voice calling, "Mr. Tucker's people on the set!" resounded thru the corridors, and we made a wild scramble for the stage, as eager for work as a while before we had been for dinner. When we had been "placed", and my cigar-counter had taken the semblance of personal property, the heroine of the day, or rather the evening, made her entrance. I have read somewhere of a youth whose daily custom it was to hang upon the words of his inamorata. When I finish this story I am going to write said youth that Mabel Normand's eyelashes would be a far safer *modus suspendi* than inamorata's words, which today are and tomor-

row are as if they were not. Somewhere in far-off Egypt there may be a mummy with longer eyelashes that curl in a more alluring way than Mabel's, but then Egypt and said mummy have survived all these years without having the imprint of my petite foot upon the former or the gaze of my clear brown eyes on the latter. And speaking of eyelashes, Egypt, mummies, petite feet, etc., reminds me that every one at the studio, from extra girl to director, hails Mabel as a mighty good fellow. A player, who had just been promoted from extra to bits, confided to me his opinion of his "chief support" on the trip from the ferry to the studio.

"Why when I have scenes with her she tells me to make the most of them and never mind her", he said. "She had often turned away from the camera so that I could face it. Perhaps you haven't worked much with stars", he added, importantly. "There's only one other I know that would give away an opportunity to dominate a scene, and that one's up in the sky."

And as I watched the lady of the curly lashes, with her cheerfulness and her it's-good-to-be-aliveness, I knew that my street-car confidant had spoken wisely of the Mabel who has brought laughter to millions during her screen career.

"How's the baby?" was the first question she asked of one of the stage crew who was putting the finishing touches to the set.

"No better, no worse", he answered, with a look of gratitude.

"Are you sure you have a good doctor? Now, if you haven't, I'll send mine down to see the baby. He's splendid. Tomorrow – – -."

"Mabel, we're waiting", Mr. Tucker interrupted, and she was off to work.

But why report at second-hand when I had personal evidence of the star's thoughtfulness that very afternoon? I had stolen upstairs to the studio to

watch some scenes she was doing. It was slightly chilly. Picture companies seem to be able to produce anything from Heaven to Holland, but they couldn't bring forth an extra supply of coal that day, no matter how many times Mr. Tucker called "Camera!" and how hard Ollie Marsh, the camera-man, turned the crank. Frozen or melted, tho, I am always forced to obey Friend Editor's command "to hang around the star as much as possible". I am considered long-suffering (by some), but once or twice I gave vent to a little shiver, not so much with the cold that was slowly congealing my spinal column – the same one that had been pierced by Mr. Klauber the previous day – as with the thought of Miss Normand's attempt to play polar bear in a sheer evening-gown. She caught the shiver, I can't say whether on the first or second round, and when the scene was ended, picked up one of her sweaters that was reposing off-stage and wrapped it about my shoulders. I had already taken Mr. Marsh, the general still camera-man, into my confidence and had entrusted my faithful graflex to his tender care. He snapped the wrapper and the wrapped....

"Do your eyes hurt?" Miss Normand called after me when she saw me blinking my way down the corridor. "Come around to my room and let me give you something to help them", and she presented me with a bottle of eye-lotion just as girl to girl, not as star to extra.

"Next car three-twenty", some one maliciously announced when we had all gathered in the Goldwyn reception hall.

"Three-twenty? Oh, what will Jack say?" a married extra groaned.

"Well, why doesn't Jack send the limousine, Gwendolyn?" one of the former hotel clerks laughed. "With your combined salaries you ought to have a night and day car."

"Do you know there are moments when I don't love you?" Gwendolyn replied, haughtily.

"I smell coffee. Let's raid the lunch-room", a hungry Ritz bellboy suggested.

"Anyway, we can sit there even if we can't eat", was a *grande dame's* inspiring contribution to the general conversation.

Sure enough, the coffee was no camouflage, but as I don't indulge, it made no impression upon my tired digestive system.

"Ye gods, Columbus, where hast thou bean?" someone shouted, as one of the guests appeared in the kitchen doorway clutching a huge slice of rye bread.

With a dramatic gesture he indicated the source of supplies, and there was a general exodus in that much to be desired direction.

"What are you doing in this kitchen?" The voice came thru the doorway, as did also the form of the night watchman of the Goldwyn Pictures Corporation. The extras, like so many scampering mice, disappeared without further parley.

"Almost time for the car", emptied us from the lunch-room into the road outside the studio.

Suitcases were turned on end and weary members of the celluloid clan sat in rows with faces turned towards the road down which the car came – eventually. Cuddled up in corners of the three-forty-five we found brave adventurers who had hoped to play a joke on the river by walking thru snowdrifts to the ferry to catch an earlier boat. At five-thirty the streets of gay Brooklyn greeted my tired gaze. My poodle opened the door with:

"Glad to see you back, but why so early, old dear?"

MANY UNUSUAL SETTINGS IN "THE VENUS MODEL"

(from *Moving Picture World,* June 8, 1918 p. 1449)

In *The Venus Model*, her latest Goldwyn picture, Mabel Normand appears in a production replete with movement, interest and unusual beauty. And in the person of the sprightly star all these elements of success are concentrated, although the production in itself is unique.

Settings of unusual richness and beauty have been devised by Hugo Ballin. They range all the way from a shop window simulating a sandstrewn beach, where Mabel Normand poses in a chic bathing costume, to a restaurant where living birds are used in great numbers for decorative purposes. They are not caged, but are grouped on branches of trees set in niches in the walls. Love birds, parakeets, and Java sparrows are used, with some magnificent parrots hanging in ornamental rings. The effect is original with Mr. Ballin, and is an outstanding feature of the production.

From another standpoint the bathing suit factory is equally interesting, with its array of dummies clad in the garb of the beaches. The scenes which show the chute down which boxes are shot for shipment are highly diverting. When the star herself elects to shoot the chute and slides down head first at high speed audiences are assured the heartiest laugh of the season.

A child, a little girl named Nadia Gary, contributes almost as much as Miss Normand to *The Venus Model* with her beauty and sympathetic acting. She is the first model on whom Mabel Normand fits the bathing dress she has designed – the costume which brings the star success and love and exciting adventures.

Much of the excitement for the audience will be found in the episodes in the shop window and around it. A great crowd surrounds the place, drawn there by the promise of seeing the wonderful "Venus Model". When Mabel Normand appears clad in the already famous swimming suit she

Tom Moore and Tallulah Bankhead in Thirty a Week *(Goldwyn, 1918).*

These short notices in the trade papers might seem to be just the usual space-fillers. But complaints about heat, labor shortages, and overcrowding at the Goldwyn studio signal the inevitable move west. In November 1918 Goldwyn would lease the old Triangle studio in Culver City, California, possibly planning to return when the winter, and the influenza epidemic, were over. Instead, they purchased the studio the following June, establishing themselves on the lot that would eventually be home to M-G-M.

creates a sensation. That sensation fortunately is not confined to the shadow people on the screen, but spreads to the audience in the theater.

GOLDWYN TO TEMPER THE SUMMER'S HEAT
Installing Specially Constructed Air Cooling Device to Reduce Temperature Under Glass Roof of Studio

(from *Moving Picture World*, June 15, 1918, p. 1576)

A life-saving innovation is being inaugurated at the Goldwyn studios in Fort Lee to lower the summer temperature beneath the great glass roof when the sun begins to blaze. It takes the form of a specially constructed air-cooling device originated by Hugo Ballin, the Goldwyn art director, and involving thousands of gallons of iced water and no end of air. Through a network of pipes the water will flood the roof every hour in the hottest July and August days.

The intense heat of last summer is not yet forgotten at the big studio on the hill. It is the determination of Goldwyn that insofar as possible the conditions of last summer shall not be repeated during the months to come. Not only the stars, but every worker in the big studio, will be protected from any chance of collapse. This will be brought about by means of a plan to be put into effect within a few weeks.

At each end of the building is being built a duct about six feet in diameter. Through these openings outside air will be pumped into the studio, without, however, there being any trace of draught. A series of openings in the roof will admit more air and do away with the lack of circulation complained of in the past.

Iced water will flood the roof at hour intervals through a network of perforated pipes. In conjunction with the constant inflow of fresh air this will keep the atmosphere of the studio at a temperature considerably lower than outside. Preparations are well under way, and within the week the fifty horsepower engine necessary for the improvement will be installed.

Every Goldwyn worker is enthusiastic and the increased efficiency will, it is expected, more than justify the outlay.

COUNTRY VILLAGE AT GOLDWYN STUDIO

(from *Moving Picture World*, August 10, 1918, p. 863)

The Goldwyn studio lot adjoining the main building at Fort Lee, NJ, on which were set the big circus scenes in *Polly of the Circus*, starring Mae Marsh, and which later was the site of the artistic reproduction of the Greek-Egyptian temple of Alexandria in Mary Garden's *Thais*, has been transformed into a prosperous country village. Stores of every description, a

bank, a village hall and a large hotel, set along granitoid sidewalks, have been built for Mabel Normand's newest Goldwyn Picture, *Peck's Bad Girl*, by Tex Charwate.

A force of fifty workmen labored day and night for three weeks before the unusual and tremendous motion picture set was completed. The erection of the big hotel and the laying of sidewalks took up most of their time. The scarcity of asphalt furnished the biggest problem, delivery of it being held up owing to the shortage of labor at the asphalt works in Southern New Jersey. To hurry the work Goldwyn studio officials hired ten coal trucks to deliver the desired amount of asphalt.

GOLDWYN ADDS A STUDIO TO ITS FORT LEE "LOT"

(from *Moving Picture World*, October 12, 1918, p. 246)

With all the Goldwyn stars in the midst of production, the Fort Lee studio has become too limited to accommodate Geraldine Farrar, Madge Kennedy, Mae Marsh, Tom Moore, and Mabel Normand and maintain the schedule of releases expected by Goldwyn's exhibitor-customer.

To overcome this difficulty, what is practically a new and separate studio has been built on the "lot". Where once stood the Alexandrian street and temple created for Mary Garden's *Thais* there is now a structure of another kind. It is a frame building 100 feet square, and is in no sense an open air studio. Roofed and equipped with a full complement of lights, it offers every facility for production found in the studio proper.

Up to the present, Geraldine Farrar and her director, Reginald Barker, have had the exclusive use of this auxiliary studio, it having been planned and constructed chiefly to give full

Goldwyn's last Broadway acquisition before leaving for Culver City was Follies favorite Will Rogers. Making a silent movie star out of the laconic rope-twirler might have seemed another ill advised notion, but Rogers was a natural performer and took to the medium immediately. A success in silent films, Rogers would become the most popular star in America when talkies arrived a few years later.

play to the magnitude of the third of Geraldine Farrar's series of Goldwyn pictures.

WILL ROGERS COMING TO THE SCREEN
Roper Thrower and Wit Now Performing at Goldwyn Studio in Rex Beach's "Laughing Bill Hyde".

(from *Moving Picture World,* August 10, 1918, p. 811)

Will Rogers, the rope thrower and shrewd wit from Texas, who from the day of his debut on the stage in New York by many has been considered the biggest individual favorite of America's largest city and beloved of country-wide vaudeville audiences, has lent his talents to the screen. Rex Beach and Goldwyn Pictures Corporation have won him over and Rogers is now at work in the Goldwyn studios at Fort Lee in the name role of *Laughing Bill Hyde,* one of Rex Beach's stories, announced for release in late September.

"I felt with regard to 'Laughing Bill Hyde' ", says Rex Beach, "that there was just one actor on earth that I wanted to see the hero of my story and that actor is Will Rogers. I believe, as

Will Rogers ropes his director, Hobart Henley, on the set of his first film, Laughing Bill Hyde *(Rex Beach-Goldwyn, 1918).*

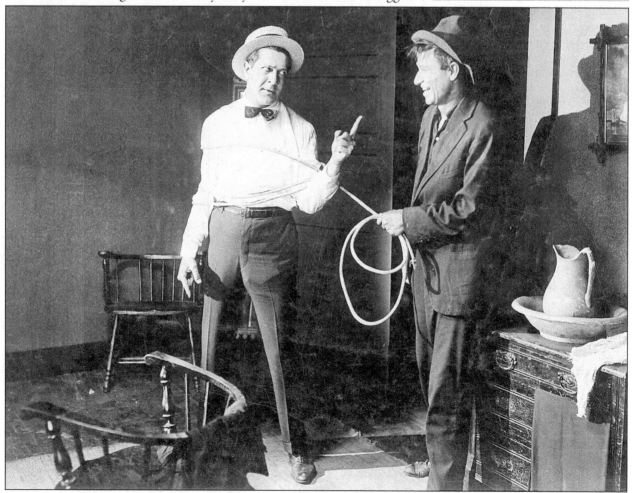

does Samuel Goldfish, that he is going to be a huge success on the screen. The role he is now playing is himself – without a change."

"I think that Rogers is the most natural and human player on the American stage today. He has the shrewdest wit and wonderful diffidence that is irresistible. And, incidentally, we are providing him with the surest-fire role that a player could have for his screen debut. Mr. Rogers didn't want to become a screen star. And of course he is not leaving the stage for a day, but is simultaneously appearing in Ziegfeld's 'Follies' and acting in *Laughing Bill Hyde*. Willard Mack has written the scenario of this story, and I feel that he has done the most brilliant scenario that has ever been made for the screen adaptation of one of my novels."

Laughing Bill Hyde is being directed by Hobart Henley. Will Rogers is in his fourth season as a featured player in Ziegfeld's "Follies" and the "Midnight Frolic" and is under contract to be starred next year in a stage play.

AN ACTOR WHO HATES CLOSE-UPS
Yes, He Really Exists, Being Will Rogers, the Oklahoma Cowboy

By Frederick James Smith

(from *Photoplay*, November 1918, pp. 56–57)

"H – l", said Will Rogers, by way of introduction, "an interview and a bunch of close-ups in one day! Take me back to the Ziegfeld Follies, where life is quiet and undisturbin'."

"You don't mean that you dislike close-ups?" we ventured.

"Dislike 'em!" growled Rogers; "I just naturally hate 'em. I ain't never going to get used to standing quiverin' all over with a camera three inches from my nose.

"You see", continued the cowboy, "I've been four weeks working in a studio now, and, naturally, I know all about the business from A to Z. Already I've decided to do away with close-ups. Don't you think it's distracting, when you see a picture, for the camera to suddenly switch from a whole scene to the hero's beaded eyelashes, magnified so that they look like Zeppelins?

"The other day we were out on location with Director Hobart Henley, and near us another company was working. They were taking long shots. So I told Henley, 'I'm going over to work for them; they've got the right idea.'"

Will Rogers used to be an Oklahoma cowboy. He drifted into the entertainment world via roping and lasso exhibitions and contests and finally reached vaudeville, where he gave demonstrations of lariat twirling accompanied by an informal sort of chatter. Rogers quickly became popular. His abashed, non-theatrical sort of style caught on strongly. Finally he became one of the principal entertainers of the Ziegfeld shows.

Rogers came to pictures by chance. Rex Beach's stories were being filmed by Goldwyn, and Mrs. Beach hit upon the idea of putting Rogers into the first one, *Laughing Bill Hyde*. Rogers accepted, more as a favor to his friend, Beach, than anything else.

"I've been trying to find out why they call it *Laughing Bill Hyde*", remarked Rogers. "So far, I've had a doleful career, with jail escapes, death of pals, funerals, and so on. I said to Henley yesterday, 'Say, Hen, when am I goin' to laugh?'"

"They sort of think I'm crazy around here. They get me blamed confused taking scenes here and there. One day I escape from prison, and three days later I'm back behind the bars doing a scene that takes place before the other one. I only hope they know how to put the darned thing together. I thought I'd kid Henley the other day, and I said to him, 'They aren't really going to release this thing, are they?' Henley looked aghast. 'Are you kidding, Will?' he demanded. 'Do I look as if I was kidding?' says I. 'Of course they're going to release it. What'd you think they'd do with it?' 'Oh, I don't know-throw it away,' I responded. 'Good Lord!' exploded Henley.

"A year ago some one suggested that I might do a picture, and I met a theatrical manager who whispered, 'Will, if you're going to try the movies, sign up for one picture, get all you can for it, and then never answer the telephone after it appears.'

"That's what I'm going to do when *Laughing Bill Hyde* comes out. Gee, I went down in the projection-room once to see the first pieces of the picture. Whew! Never again! They keep askin' me down – but I know better.

"As far as I can see, the best scene I've done is one in which I grab a man. You can see the man in the film and just see my hand appear as it seizes his shirt. That's my best piece of acting."

Just at this moment an interesting love-making scene started in an adjoining setting occupied by Tom Moore. Rogers called to Anna Lehr, who appears with him in *Laughing Bill Hyde*. "Hey, Anna", said Rogers, "let's watch this, and we'll put something like it in our picture".

"After being in the Ziegfeld Follies for two years, do you need anything like that to give you ideas?" we inquired.

"Say", said Will, "I'm as popular with those Ziegfeld queens as a Ford car.

"Lemme tell you what I'd like to do in pictures if I had my way. I'd like to burlesque a Westerner. You know what I do on the stage is to present things exactly opposite from the way an actor would. I'd like to try that on the screen. For instance, I'd play a cowboy just exactly opposite from the way he's always done. I'd make it apparent that he was always calculatin' on the camera. That would be my only chance of succeeding on the screen – and maybe then I'd flop.

"Stick around", continued Will; "I'll bet when they start the next scene that I have to change shirts. I wear two different kinds of shirts in *Laughing Bill Hyde*, and no matter what scene they take I always happen to have the wrong shirt on. I shift shirts on an average of eight times a day.

"Sometimes I wonder why they put me into pictures. Up to the time Mrs. Beach asked me, I was the only living man who hadn't an offer to go on the screen.

"Nobody's ever going wild over a poor hombre like me, but there's one man that's going to score on the screen – ."

"Fred Stone?" we interrupted, knowing Rogers' friendship for the comedian.

"You bet!" answered Will. "There's a man that has it all over Fairbanks. Doug does a stunt, and it's only a stunt. When Stone does it, that stunt has the added value of being funny. Watch that boy!"

"You taught him how to use the lariat?" we asked.

"I know Fred well, but I didn't teach him anything. He learnt by hard work."

"Mr. Rogers!" called the director.

"Yey-ah", sighed Will, gloomily.

"We're going to do some more close-ups."

Rogers leaned heavily against a bit of scenery.

"And , by the way, you've got the wrong shirt on."

"I knew it", shuddered Rogers. "Them shirts are never going to last until the end of this picture."

As investors in the Goldwyn Corporation, the Shuberts received regular updates on the profitability of Goldwyn productions. The following figures come from a memo to the executive committee of Goldwyn Pictures Corp., dated August 26, 1920 (Shubert Archives; file 2890). Although they grossed well, the first Goldwyn productions, with their elaborate settings and décor, were too expensive to be profitable; the situation improved only after budgets were slashed. Average production costs rose again after Goldwyn relocated to the west coast in the winter of 1918. Films are listed in their approximate order of production; a few titles were omitted.

THE GOLDWYN LIBRARY:
NEGATIVE COSTS AND BOOKINGS FOR FORT LEE PRODUCTIONS

Costs and Domestic Bookings as of 26 June 1920

Title	Negative cost (US$)	Estimated domestic bookings(US$)	US bookings (US$)
First Year Pictures (those made and released before September 1, 1918):			
Auction Block	68,877.71	–	148,909.33
Fields of Honor	97,132.49	–	115,307.29
Fighting Odds	95,744.07	–	151,074.99
Sunshine Alley	61,646.66	–	126,458.04
Polly of the Circus	172,748.38	–	157,752.14
Baby Mine	70,267.57	–	161,916.99
Spreading Dawn	110,707.61	–	148,483.99
Cinderella Man	90,833.98	–	129,424.69
Nearly Married	84,754.45	–	129,754.59
Joan of Plattsburg	11,830.88	–	88,287.91
Thais	140,352.37	–	122,292.19
Beloved Traitor	43,344.11	–	100,400.57
Splendid Sinner	133,676.89	–	95,073.16
Dodging a Million	79,583.49	–	113,456.59
Our Little Wife	62,895.51	–	105,671.94
Floor Below	64,947.53	–	98,131.36
Face in the Dark	64,528.78	–	91,761.93
Danger Game	45,630.39	–	92,987.41
Glorious Adventure	44,767.70	–	74,285.41
Fair Pretender	39,998.08	–	84,205.31
Venus Model	55,409.98	–	80,170.16
All Woman	37,851.17	–	81,893.66
Service Star	37,595.13	–	78,162.91
Money Mad	36,711.86	–	66,881.08
Back to the Woods	28,403.59	–	73,039.91
Friend Husband	28,899.19	–	71,141.59
Second Year Pictures (those made and released before September 1, 1919):			
Just for Tonight	22,327.14	115,000.00	90,393.69
Hidden Fires	33,475.39	90,000.00	88,201.00
Kingdom of Youth	31,304.51	115,000.00	95,455.75
Peck's Bad Girl	46,592.33	110,000.00	96,210.25
Perfect Lady	38,368.67	110,000.00	93,111.00
Bondage of Barbara	31,306.40	90,000.00	84,394.00
Perfect 36	46,979.53	110,000.00	94,964.25
Thirty a Week	21,166.89	115,000.00	90,639.92
Racing Strain	48,563.03	90,000.00	87,969.89
Laughing Bill Hyde	38,728.66	175,000.00	149,265.84
Too Fat to Fight	34,345.07	145,000.00	140,579.34
*Day Dreams**	30,694.09	100,000.00	91,116.00

*Described as "completed at Fort Lee" in *Moving Picture World*, 2 November 1918.

19.
Selznick

When Lewis J. Selznick was forced out of the World Film Corporation in 1916 he made sure that their most important star, Clara Kimball Young, went with him. He packaged her films together with those of Herbert Brenon, Norma Talmadge and various other notables, doing business as Lewis J. Selznick Enterprises. These first films were made in several different studios in Fort Lee, as well as the Biograph studio in the Bronx.

SELZNICK LEASES GREAT BIOGRAPH STUDIO
Clara Kimball Young, Norma Talmadge, Kitty Gordon and Other Stars and Directors Move to New Quarters

(from *Moving Picture World,* November 11, 1916, p. 871)

...Within the next three weeks four Selznick-Pictures companies will be producing under the Biograph roof, while other companies will continue their operations at the two studios already in use on the Palisades of the Hudson. By leasing the Biograph Studio Mr. Selznick has made possible the realization of one of his original plans, that of making use of Miss Clara Kimball Young's services in two productions simultaneously.

For the past three weeks Director General Albert Capellani of the Clara Kimball Young Film Corporation has been producing at the Solax studio in Fort Lee, NJ, the successor to *The Common Law*, now achieving tremendous success throughout the country. This, the second of the new producing company's features, is an adaptation

Lewis J. Selznick.

of Thomas Dixon's novel, *The Foolish Virgin.*

While Miss Young and her company were on a trip to the Catskills last week taking exterior scenes, Mr. Capellani's assistants, headed by studio Manager Thomas A. Persons, moved all their paraphernalia from Fort Lee to the Biograph plant and this production will be finished in the new quarter …

Herbert Brenon will continue to produce at the Ideal Studios on Hudson Heights, where he has a five-year lease.

FOUR SELZNICK COMPANIES BUSY
Four Subjects Now Completed – All For Early Release

(from *Moving Picture World,* December 16, 1916, p. 1480)

Four producing companies are at work in three studios on Selznick-Picture productions for release in December and January. The success that followed the presentation of the first Selznick-Pictures (Clara Kimball Young in *The Common Law* and Herbert Brenon's production, Nazimova in *War Brides*) has brought Selznick's new trademark to the fore.

The third Selznick-Picture will present Clara Kimball Young in an adaptation of Thomas Dixon's powerful novel, *The Foolish Virgin.* Albert Capellani, director general of the Clara Kimball Young Film Corporation, and producer of *The Common Law,* finished the final scenes of Miss Young's second picture this week. It will probably be released in seven reels and will be ready for its private exhibition soon. In the cast will be seen Conway Tearle, who made such a decided success as Miss Young's leading man in *The Common Law,* and Paul Capellani, who has been seen in powerful characterizations in a number of Miss Young's greatest pictures.

The Selznick-Pictures offering to fol-low *The Foolish Virgin* will be, according to the present plans, Joseph M. Schenck's presentation of Norma Talmadge in a film version of *Panthea,* a drama by Monckton Hoffe. Miss Talmadge has been working for several weeks on this production under the direction of Allan Dwan at one of the Willett [sic] studios, Fort Lee, NJ, and the reports indicate that the picture will be finished by next week.

Herbert Brenon is nearing the completion of his second Selznick-Pictures offering, a powerful drama of Italian life in the middle ages, entitled *Lucretia Borgia,* from Victor Hugo's famous drama, at his studio on Hudson Heights, NJ [Released as *The Eternal Sin* – ed.] Miss Florence Reed becomes a Selznick-Pictures star in this production, which for lavishness of settings as well as for its dramatic quality is said to be a worthy successor to *War Brides.* It will be ready for release in January … .

> The following year Selznick entered into a partnership with Adolph Zukor (whose participation was hidden) and reorganized as Select Pictures Corporation. Apparently, Zukor insisted on a name for the new company that did not have "Selznick" in it. One of their first moves was to poach another star from World, Alice Brady – whose father William had replaced Selznick at World. Production began at the Paragon studio in Fort Lee, which Zukor had just acquired. Selznick was making money, but found it increasingly difficult not to see his name on Broadway in electric lights. Eventually he would find a way around this.

SELECT PICTURES SIGNS ALICE BRADY
Former World Film Star to Make Eight Subjects During the Coming Year

(from *Moving Picture World,* October 6, 1917, p. 61)

Select Pictures Corporation announces that it has signed contracts with Alice Brady by which Miss Brady immediately becomes a Select Pictures star. Miss Brady will be presented during the coming year in eight pictures, which will be released under the Select Star Series system.

On the first of these eight pictures Miss Brady will begin work at once at the Paragon studio in Fort Lee. She will be directed by Edward Jose, whose work is best known to picture fans through his direction of Norma Talmadge in *Poppy* and *The Moth,* the latter being a current Select release. Miss Brady's first picture will be an adaptation of Henry J.W. Dam's successful play *The Red Mouse.* It is a story of modern life with a French flavor. The screen title of the picture has not yet been determined. [It was released as *Her Silent Sacrifice* – ed.]

Alice Brady is the daughter of William A. Brady, the celebrated theatrical manager and Director General of World Pictures … It will be the policy of Select Pictures to present Miss Brady in the very highest class productions that screen art can produce. Her stories will be selected from the greatest successes in the literary and dramatic field. Her directors will be men who have shown in their productions directing talents of the highest quality. Her company will engage the support of the best players the screen can boast. In short, Miss Brady's features will be of that quality which will mark throughout the releases under the Select Star system.

In December 1918 Selznick's twenty-year old son Myron (later an important talent agent in Hollywood), suddenly entered production as president of the Selznick Pictures Corporation. This was clearly a ploy to circumvent the agreement with Zukor intended to keep the Selznick name off the screen. Myron signed Olive Thomas and Elsie Janis and began production on the West coast, but quickly returned to New York, where a lot of studio space was suddenly available at bargain prices.

CALIFORNIA GETS ANOTHER RUDE BLOW
Myron Selznick, Back in East Permanently, Says Monopoly on Picture Production Is Undeserved

(from *Moving Picture World*, April 26, 1919, p. 521)

Once more, within the short space of a week, does sunny California get a wallop intended to jolt her off the pedestal of The One And Only Motion Picture Producing Center. P.A. Powers, of Universal, got out the mallet last week, while this time it is Myron Selznick, president of Selznick Pictures, who takes down the sledge hammer from the wall and drives gracefully therewith upon the reputation of the state which has seemed to enjoy a monopoly on the exportation of prunes and photoplay prints.

"All this stuff about California being the only place to make moving pictures is bunk", said Mr. Selznick, and with an upward motion of his hands as if to indicate that the California theory was a balloon which had just slipped its moorings and sailed off into the kingdom of the forgotten.

Entire Selznick force in east

The entire Selznick forces left the Hollywood studios last week for New York,

where they will be located permanently, proving that although the poet was right when he said that East was East and West was West, there was nothing to prevent a moving picture organization from evacuating the West and conducting a rear-guard action as it did so.

Myron Selznick, who is conducting the rear-guard word battle, went on to say to the *Moving Picture World* man:

"There is absolutely nothing in this California talk. The weather out there is just as uncertain as it is in the East, and since so great a part of the picture is devoted to interiors, a studio in New York is as good as a studio anywhere else and probably a lot better. Besides, production in New York makes possible the closest cooperation between the producing and administrative branches. What's more, you can get more and better actors in New York than you can begin to get in California .... "

In August of 1919 Selznick leased the Fort Lee Universal studio as his new Eastern production center, while still holding onto the Biograph studio in the Bronx. Katherine Anne Porter, better known later as the author of such novels as *Ship of Fools*, was making a living as a magazine journalist when she wrote this piece for *Motion Picture Times*, a Selznick house paper. Her fascination with the eerie glow of the Cooper-Hewitt mercury vapor lamps, standard lighting units of the silent era, was shared by many studio visitors.

John Noble directing Olive Thomas in Footlights and Shadows *(Selznick, 1920).*

ON THE INSIDE LOOKING AROUND

By Katherine Anne Porter

(from *Motion Picture Times*, January 1, 1920, p. 21)

We were held up at the door by a determined-looking man who asked us for our cards.

"Ah, yes, cards", we said, with false geniality. "But we do not want jobs, you know. We are visitors. This is visiting day at the Selznick Fort Lee Studios, isn't it?"

"Yes, but you must have a card of admission", he insisted politely. Four of us stood aghast, having no cards. The fifth member of our exploring party produced a crumpled slip, all over handwriting, signed with an impressive name from the Selznick Home Office, which prayed the watchman to admit Mr. So-and-So and party.

Whereat we were ushered into an anteroom, down a long concrete floored hall, past rows of somber monk-like cells each marked with a number. These were the dressing rooms. We paused to inhale the atmosphere of romance. One girl gurgled, flapped her hands feebly, and said, "Oh, look here!" The feminine eyes of the party followed her gesture toward a small brass tablet on the first door. It was inscribed simply, "Eugene O'Brien".

The guard dragged us away, up a long shallow stairway, and into a great raftered and glass-roofed acre of seething sights and sounds and colors, illuminated in spots with the greenish glimmer of the famous Cooper-Hewitts. At first glimpse, lumber, trees, furniture, coils of electric wires lying about to trip you up, and busy, shouting humans seemed inextricably tangled. But as we progressed the scene took form and order, arranging itself into gardens and drawing rooms and conservatories and boudoirs, each marked off with a blaze of incandescents, pre-

sided over by a director whose color scheme evolved into purple eyes and lips, greenish skin, and orange hair under the lights, while the stars shone, a fair-skinned and brilliantly arrayed group of beings whose make-up and general grandeur removed them far from the doings of this dusty earth.

Here we saw Eugene O'Brien himself, in the very life, engaged in one of the big scenes from *His Wife's Money*, with pretty Zena Keefe, Selznick's 1920 star, in the role of a rich and frivolous wife. She was quarreling – yes, actually – with Mr. O'Brien, while Director Ralph Ince stood by and watched approvingly. "Fancy quarreling with HIM, even in a picture", said one of the girls in our party. "I'd never take a role like that!"

In another cottage scene we came upon beautiful Seena Owen weeping helplessly while Owen Moore regarded her with a severe look. One of the boys in the exploring group wanted to tackle the brick-hearted Moore person at once in defense of beauty in distress, until some one explained that this was a scene from Moore's latest comedy, and that director Wesley Ruggles would not appreciate interference.

Around the corner we almost stumbled over Olive Thomas talking over a point of acting with her director, John Noble, and her leading man, that good-looking Alexander Onslow, who plays Jerry in *Footlights and Shadows*, Miss Thomas' latest Selznick picture. She wore a gorgeous cloak of brown chiffon over silver cloth, trimmed in fur, and is twenty times lovelier than any picture, moving or still, that was ever made of her.

"Where is Elaine Hammerstein?" asked the Chief Explorer. "I came all the way out here just to see her. Where is she?" One guide pointed out a tall, dignified girl, swathed in furs, who was leaving the studio, accompanied by her mother. Her profile was modeled clearly and beautifully against a

smart black hat pulled low over the forehead. She looked as she does in scenes from her latest picture, *Greater Than Fame*, which Alan Crosland directed.

After this we went to the scenery department, where castles and cabins, drawing rooms and hovels, gardens and balconies and office buildings are produced, literally at a moment's notice. We saw the "still room" where they make those nice pictures you see out front of the cinema theatres. We saw the art title rooms, where they draw those lovely, smoky backgrounds for the "literature" of the picture. We passed the scenario department, and rows of business offices. Every detail of the great industry is specialized to a degree we outsiders do not dream of. Art and Comerce join hands under the same roof, and get along very amiably.

> Presented as the memoir of a country girl who comes to New York to break into the motion picture business, this anonymous series in *Picture Play* (here the second of three parts) was illustrated with photos of Selznick's Universal studio, one of the few Fort Lee studios still active during the bitter winter of 1919–1920.

"DON'T DO IT, MARJORIE!"

(from *Picture Play*, February 1920, p. 54–55, 94–95.)

I took the ferry at eight the next morning, feeling most awfully professional. To me that little journey across the Hudson was as monstrous as a trip to Europe; the boat seemed to go at a snail's pace, yet as the Palisades looked bigger and bigger I almost wished it would stop; now that I was actually going to get into pictures I felt a little shakey about it.

There were other people on the boat who were going to the studio I was headed for; I heard them talking about it while we were waiting for the street car. Several of them had suit cases, as I did, and one of the men had on evening clothes under his overcoat. I didn't know what car to take, so I stood near them, thinking I'd just do what they did, and so I couldn't help overhearing them. They mentioned a lot of the pictures I'd seen at home, and told about their parts in them; I was awfully interested, and finally one of the girls turned around and spoke to me.

"I've been in pictures three years now", she said when we'd been talking a few moments. "Sure, I've had parts; doubled for a star once. But I can't count on steady work – haven't ever had a contract. How'd I get in? Registered at an agency. Say, did anybody ever tell you to try to get started by hanging around the studios waiting for a chance? Well, don't you try it – I did, and there's nothing to it! Why, out in California I did nothing else at first – many a day I've sat on that bench in the yard at the old Mutual Studio – fourteen companies working inside, and not a thing for an extra most of the time, it seemed to me. I know all the studios around Hollywood – but I think New York's a better place to break in; there's more chance to get work here in between times, you see. Los Angeles is full of women who can't do any kind of work and who want to get a job – men, too. Here you can get something – out there there aren't jobs enough in town to take care of the movie extras – 'tisn't a very big place, you know. Now I've got a job clerking in a department store, and they dock me when I take a few days off to work in a picture, but they're glad to keep me on the payroll because I'm a better saleswoman than most of their girls. That keeps me going when I can't get work at the studios."

Three years of it! I couldn't help being glad that I had that money I'd brought from home.

The studio looked as grim and forbidding as a factory, except for the glass roof that covered part of it. When we got inside, a man divided the crowds of extras;

the girls whom the director of the picture and Mr. Rowe had sent for were given a big dressing room together, and all the others were put in another room, which rather crowded them. A line of lockers ran down the middle of the room, and a mirror ran the length of either side wall, with a wide shelf below it. There were lots of electric lights, and some of the girls got out curling irons and began making elaborate preparations as we girls at home used to when we were going to a dance. They had lots of make-up; some of them had brought three or four kinds of cold cream, and powder, and they all had lip sticks and black stuff for their eyes.

One girl settled down and curled her hair all over her head in long curls – I noticed her afterwards, and she was away back in a corner where she'd never show in the picture at all. And several of the girls changed all their clothes, and fussed around as if they had been stars. Somehow, it struck me that they didn't have any good mirrors at home, maybe, and were making the best of this one – they seemed to appreciate it so. I thought of the little dressing room in my pink and white bed room back home – and then stopped remembering it as quickly as I could.

The girl who'd spoken to me when we waited for the car sat next me at the mirror, and helped me to make up; she said the powder I'd bought at one of the theatrical drug stores on Broadway was too dark, and gave me some of hers; it was very coarse and quite a deep yellow, and stood out in little grains all over my face and arms. She fixed my eyes, too; she heated a toothpick in a candle flame and rubbed it on a cake of black stuff and then along my eyelashes, making them dreadfully heavy, so that they stood way out and looked awfully exaggerated. She said

Production in one of Selznick's Fort Lee studios, c. 1920.

Director Alan Crosland and cameraman Jules Cronjager filming Worlds Apart *(Selznick, 1921).*

they'd be wonderful and make my eyes look much bigger in a picture. Janet – her name was Janet Powers – looked much nicer without her mouth made up and her eyelashes fixed, but she said that her kind of looks wouldn't get over on the screen at all without lots of make-up.

What stunned me, as I sat there all dressed and waiting till it would be time to go up to "the floor", was the number of awfully pretty girls I saw there. Every one of them was pretty – some of them were beauties. I'd never seen so many pretty girls together before, and I wondered how Mr. Rowe and Jeanne Phelps had kept from laughing at me when I urged that because I was pretty I ought to have a chance in pictures. Why, if all they had to do to make a picture successful was to get pretty girls, no director would have a worry in the world.

Some of the girls had brought wonderful evening gowns, and some of them wore the shabbiest, flimsiest little suits and hats when they came, and

got their evening clothes from the woman in charge of the wardrobe room. Janet said that was one thing that made it hard for the girl who didn't have money to get along – clothes counted so much in lots of scenes where they used extras, and if you were well dressed you were a lot more likely to get good places in a ballroom scene or anything like that, and have the director notice you. Maybe that was just her idea – she believed in it enough to have a lovely dress herself to wear that day, though she told me she'd bought it when she didn't know where her next week's room rent was coming from.

When we got up to the set, on the floor above, we were given partners from among the men who were waiting around. I got one of the men who'd come out on the ferry that morning. Janet knew him and a friend of his, and they all picked out a little table right in front of the camera for us. I forgot to say that the set was a reproduction of a famous Paris restaurant, with little tables all around, and a clear space in the middle for dancing, while the orchestra – a good one – sat on a platform at the end.

I'd rather have sat way back somewhere, but Janet and the two men said we had a dandy table.

"It's right behind the star's", she told me as we sat down. "Probably we'll all show. And lots of times in these restaurant scenes they have food for the people near the star to make it look more realistic, you know; I wish we'd get some to-day – all I had for breakfast was three graham crackers, and it's half past ten now."

The star hadn't come yet; somebody said she wouldn't be there till afternoon. They were going to take some of the restaurant stuff first – scenes showing people dancing, and the professional entertainers, and that sort of thing.

The director picked out the people who were to dance, and Janet and one of the men were chosen; so were my partner and I, but he didn't want to dance; he said they'd take those scenes over and over, and with the thermometer registering nearly a hundred under those lights he wasn't going to work as hard as all that. So we sat and drank luke warm ginger ale out of wine glasses – served by real waiters, who rushed around and pretended to take orders – and watched the others.

It was awfully funny to watch Janet and her partner try to stay in front of the camera; all the other extras were maneuvering the same way – they all wanted to "show", of course. Some of them would stay right in one spot till the director would shout at them to move on – then they'd dance off to one side, but pretty soon they'd be back again, and if they could they'd look into the camera. Next time you see a crowd dancing in the movies watch for that little trick – it's amusing, and it's rather pathetic, too, when you think of how much depends on it for these people.

Finally, after we'd been there for nearly two hours, the star appeared. She was wearing a marvelous ermine evening wrap, and thousands of dollars' worth of diamonds. I was awfully anxious to see her, of course, and she sat so near me that I had a good chance, but the blue stuff on her eyelids and below her eyes, and the yellow powder and heavy red on her lips made her look almost grotesque; it was hard to recognize her real beauty under that disguise.

Her part of the scene wasn't very long; she was supposed to be introduced to the hero, who sat at a neighboring table, and to be dreadfully overcome when she recognized him as a man she's known before, and hurry out of the restaurant. They took five shots of her coming in, and as many more of her sitting there at the table, and then when she was introduced to him and almost fainted in amazement they did it three different ways, and took it each way several times. And in between shots they waited and waited till it seemed to me I'd go stark mad. It seemed perfectly endless.

"Action, there, behind!" the director would shout at us when they began taking the star's scenes, and then Janet and the two men and I would lean over and talk and try to seem to be having a good time. Janet Powers really enjoyed it; once she said something really funny to one of the men, and the star overheard it and turned to look over her shoulder and laugh, and the director called, "Good stuff

– we'll keep that! Do it again." So they did it twice more, and Janet was so pleased that when we were finally dismissed she pinched my arm so enthusiastically that it was black and blue.

"Isn't that simply gorgeous!" she cried. "If I'm good in that bit maybe I'll get a chance in the next picture this director does." And she went on talking about it all the time we were dressing.

She and I each got three dollars and a half for that day's work; the people who'd been sent by an agent would get paid by him, so that he could deduct his commission.

I went out on location a few days after that; they were going to take a big scene calling for several hundred people, Mr. Rowe's stenographer said, when she phoned, and I was to be part of a mob – a real mob that wrecked a store and chased a man out of the little town they'd built for the set. This time I wore a dress out of the company wardrobe, a thin, slazy cotton dress, it was, and I had a brilliant yellow shawl, too – I felt exactly like a real actress. It was rather a cold day, and between waiting for the sun to shine and waiting for the carpenters to do something that everybody thought had been done the day before, we spent hours just sitting around. At noon we stood in line – such a long line! – for the little box lunches that had been provided for us. The lunches were really very good, but I don't believe I'd have cared if they hadn't been, for I was actually in the movies; I'd walked down the street right toward the camera, with nobody between me and it, I heard somebody say that that pretty little dark-haired girl – meaning me – was pretty good, and I'd learned how to put my make-up on all by myself; that was enough.

My next job was an awfully interesting one; I was maid of honor at a screen wedding, and wore a dress that was specially designed by one of the big modistes. But imagine my disappoint-

---

(Bottom): Selznick publicized its still photographer, Peter Jones, in the studio housepaper, The Brain Exchange *(2 October 1920). Except for a handful of actors, it was extremely rare for any African-American working in the silent film industry to be given this kind of attention. Jones was also involved in producing race films, both in Chicago and New Jersey.*

Introducing---

Peter Jones
of the Still Department, Selznick Fort Lee Studios

Every organization has somewhere in its personnel a man or woman who is responsible for many things, but is seldom seen or heard of outside of his or her immediate field of action.

The Selznick organization has a number of men and women who do big things, but are unknown personally to hundreds of members of the organization in the branches.

One of these shining lights is Peter Jones, the man who has charge of the still department in the Selznick Fort Lee studios. Peter's duties are many and important. He photographs the stars when a special picture is needed in a hurry, and he keeps the Home Office supplied with stills of new productions. He is a rapid worker, and his stuff is good. Therefore he should be known to every man, woman and messenger in the organization.

Mr. Jones was born in Kalama-

ment when I saw that picture and realized that in the scene at the altar the actor who played the best man had held his silk hat so that my face didn't show! However, I got ten dollars for that day's work.

Of course I hoped that Mr. Rowe would send for me again, soon; the little taste I'd had of picture-making made me more eager than ever to do more of it, but finally, after a week had gone by and I hadn't heard from him, I decided to go to the agent to whom Ted's father had given me a letter; now that I'd had experience, perhaps he could get me a small part.

To be Continued …

Selznick had bought out Zukor's half interest in Select in 1919, and that same year acquired what was left of the World Film Corporation. With Fox concentrating its East coast activities in New York by the Spring of 1920, Selznick completely dominated production in Fort Lee, untroubled by the bitter weather which had helped drive the rest of the competition away. That summer he (again) announced his abandonment of California, dropped his production activity in the Bronx, and focused entirely on Fort Lee.

SELZNICK PRODUCTION KEEPS UP; EASTERN STUDIOS SURMOUNT DIFFICULTIES OF STORM

(from *Moving Picture World,* March 6, 1920)

When the storm king who had been reigning in the East for several days,

demoralizing the commercial life of New York and its kindred cities, decided to abdicate he left a trail of upset routine from Maine to Washington.

But, according to report, the Selznick studios in Fort Lee and the Bronx surmounted the difficulties and when the sun peeped out work was progressing on current films as though California weather had prevailed all the time.

Excellent progress is reported on Elaine Hammerstein's next picture, *The Shadow of Rosalie Byrnes,* which is being made in both Eastern studios and on location in various sections of the East. Edward Langford has the leading male role opposite Miss Hammerstein in this production.

The Herbert Kaufman weeklies, from editorials written by Mr. Kaufman in the daily papers, are said to be progressing on schedule despite the weather handicap.

"The Flapper" next Olive Thomas

The next picture for Olive Thomas following the release of *Youthful Folly,* which is announced for March 8, will be *The Flapper* instead of *Jenny* as was previously reported. *Footlights and Shadows* is declared to have won further popularity for Miss Thomas as a Selznick star. Alan Crosland is named as the director who will make *The Flapper* … .

MYRON SELZNICK LEADS EXODUS OF FORCES FROM WEST COAST TO FORT LEE STUDIOS

(from *Moving Picture World,* July 10, 1920, p. 246)

Immediately upon his return from Los Angeles Myron Selznick announced in detail the arrangements he had completed during his western trip for the concentration of all production work of Selznick Pictures Corporation in the East, beginning July 1.

Olive Thomas completed her work in California on her forthcoming Selznick feature on June 27. On the same date she started for New York and all arrangements have been completed for the beginning of her next picture at the main Selznick studio in Fort Lee on July 7.

Owen Moore returned East with Mr. Selznick, and plans for his next picture were made en route. The final touches are now being made on the story which Mr. Moore will use, and work on the feature will start within the next ten days at the Paragon studio in Fort Lee, recently acquired by Selznick under a long-term contract.

Kolker's next in east

Henry Kolker will join the Selznick staff in Fort Lee immediately upon completion of the National feature *Who Am I?,* now in course of production on the West coast. Mr. Kolker's first eastern picture will be shot at the Solax studio in Fort Lee, another property that passed under control of Selznick recently.

During his stay in Los Angeles Mr. Selznick also completed negotiations in which Victor Heerman, who has been directing Owen Moore on the West Coast, will come East within a fortnight to join the Selznick directorial staff at the main Selznick studio in Fort Lee.

Another result of the trip of the president of Selznick Pictures Corporation is the addition to the scenario staff of Sarah Y. Mason. Miss Mason, who is already working at the Paragon studio in Fort Lee, has gained a reputation through her work for Douglas Fairbanks, Thomas H. Ince and Metro.

Rapf to bring technical staff

When the last Selznick star and director now working in Los Angeles has departed for New York Harry Rapf, general manager of the Selznick West Coast studios, will pack up his belongings and start for New York, bringing

Olive Thomas in The Flapper *(Selznick, 1920), directed by Alan Crosland.*

SELZNICK TAKES OVER PEERLESS STUDIO; WORK ON PLANS FOR LONG ISLAND PLANT

(from *Moving Picture World*, November 20, 1920, p. 360)

Another unit was added recently to the Selznick Fort Lee production activities when Myron Selznick, president of Selznick Pictures Corporation, took over the Peerless studio on a long term lease. The studio will in the future be known as the Selznick-Peerless studio and will be operated in conjunction with two other Selznick production units at Fort Lee, the Selznick-Universal and the Selznick-Paragon studios.

The acquisition of the Peerless studio adds a third more stage room to the working space of the Selznick organization. Three companies can work comfortably on the stages of the Peerless studios, three more are comfortably accommodated by the Paragon studio. Thus nine or ten companies can work simultaneously on Selznick productions.

Although Mr. Selznick recently signed the lease for the Peerless studio, it will not be possible for the Selznick companies to work there until after December 1. The present lease, which expires at that time, is held by the Ziegfeld Productions Company, which is producing pictures under the direction of Emile Chautard.

Four Selznick companies are now working at the Selznick-Universal and Selznick-Paragon studios. William P.S. Earle is directing Elaine Hammerstein in *Poor, Dear Margaret Kirby*, a Kathleen Norris story, at the Selznick-Universal, and Hobart Henley is directing Conway Tearle in a picture as yet unnamed. The stages at the Selznick-Paragon studios are oc-

with him a corps of technical experts who will be added to the already extensive force at the Selznick studios in Fort Lee.

With the migration to the East of Henry Kolker and Mr. Heerman, the directors working for Myron Selznick, including those now engaged in making productions in Fort Lee, will embrace Hobart Henley, Ralph Ince, Alan Crosland, William P.S. Earle, George Archainbaud, Burton George, Victor Heerman, Henry Kolker and Robert Ellis. In addition, William J. Scully and Edmund Goulding will continue making pictures for the Herbert Kaufman Weekly.

Selznick began planning a large new studio in Long Island City, not far from Zukor's new Astoria studio, as early as 1919. The new studio would probably have taken Selznick away from Fort Lee, but he quietly dropped the idea in 1921 and stayed in New Jersey. Caught off guard by the post-war economic collapse, and unable to compete with larger producers tied to national theater chains, Selznick declared bankruptcy in 1923. His sons David and Myron started over again in Hollywood, leaving the blizzards and ice storms behind.

cupied with sets for a forthcoming Owen Moore picture under the direction of Victor Heerman, *The Chicken in the Case*, and a Eugene O'Brien production under the working title of *Regret* being directed by Alan Crosland.

Owing to the fact that Zeena Keefe will shortly begin a new production, and Ralph Ince will soon start work on a Ralph Ince special for Selznick, Mr. Selznick deemed it advisable to procure more studio space. In addition to these productions arrangements are being made to film several other special productions. It is expected that within a month eight or nine companies will be in full swing at the Selznick Fort Lee studios.

Meanwhile work is progressing on the plans for the new Selznick studio in Long Island City. While no definite date has been set, it is believed the excavation for the Long Island City studios will be started early next spring.

FIERCE GALE DESTROYS SELZNICK VILLAGE SET

(from *Moving Picture World*, December 1, 1920, p. 764)

A ninety-mile gale which recently swept the Atlantic seaboard, reaching its height along the Jersey Coast, destroyed twenty location buildings, including two churches, several stores and houses, garages and out-build-

An elaborate small-town set built by Selznick just behind the Paragon studio, c. 1920.

ings, at the Selznick Pictures Corporation plant in West Fort Lee, NJ. This village was built for the Hobart Henley production, *The Sin That Was His*, starring William Faversham and written by Frank L. Packard.

In addition to this damage, about 200 panes of glass in the studio roof were blown to smithereens. The chilly drafts of one of the coldest days in the year greatly handicapped director William P.S. Earle, who was shooting a scene for the forthcoming Selznick picture, *Poor, Dear Margaret Kirby*, starring Elaine Hammerstein in a story by Kathleen Norris.

20.
Fort Lee Talks

The production of silent films in New York and New Jersey had been reduced to near zero by 1926, and even Paramount had shut down its studio in Astoria to centralize in Hollywood. But just as the local film industry finally seemed on the point of extinction, local engineers who had been working on a variety of talking film processes finally hit pay dirt. Warner Bros., teamed with AT&T, introduced the Vitaphone process that same year, while the Fox-Case Corporation followed with their own system a few months later. Talking films would have to be made in the east: first, because those engineers needed to be close at hand to work the bugs out of the new systems, and second, because the movies now needed actors who could talk, and writers who could produce scripts instead of scenarios.

Initially, it seemed that the Paragon studio, where Hope Hampton had recently made *The Unfair Sex*, would be the first of the Fort Lee studios to reopen for sound. In September, 1928, Louis Schwartz of Fotovox (one of many proprietary sound-on-disc systems) announced that he had signed George Jessel and Jack Pearl for a series of shorts to be made in what he now called the Aurora studio. But no sound films were ever made at the Paragon, which soon became a spectacular ruin.

Ideal Sound

The Ideal Studio, which had not done any real business since Herbert Brenon worked there, seemed an even less likely candidate for rehabilitation. The studio had been vacant for years when O.W. Biarmer, the current owner, announced that he was renovating it for talkies in October 1928. Smallish "sound studios" were popping up all over New York, but New Jersey was still just as hard to get to as it had been during silent days, and at first there seemed no reason to make the trip. But on December 10, 1929, a stage curtain caught fire at Pathé's studio on 134th Street in Manhattan. It was the worst studio fire in American history, killing eleven and forcing the fire marshals in New York to enforce safety regulations to the letter. Nearly all the smaller studios, and even some of the larger ones (like RCA's new Gramercy studio on 24th Street) shut down for good. When local producers looked around for viable soundstages, Biarmer was ready for them.

Photocolor, which had been working at the Gramercy Studios while awaiting the completion of their own studio in Irvington-on-Hudson, moved the production of some of their color shorts to Ideal in February, including Bradley Barker's *Ye Olde Heart Shoppe*. That same month RKO moved producer Lou Brock and director Mark Sandrich from the Gramercy to the Ideal, where they continued their "Nick and Tony" series, an Italian stereotype act featuring Nick Basil and Tony Martin (Henry Armetta replaced Martin in May). Their films included *Barnum Was Wrong* (originally to be shot in Brewster Color), *Off to Buffalo*, and *Who's Got the Body?* In May, Sandrich began directing RKO's popular Clark and McCullough series at Ideal. Another RKO

W.C. Fields in The Golf Specialist, *his first talkie, made at the Ideal studio by Radio Pictures in April 1930.*

unit was sent to the old Peerless studio in Fort Lee, now called the Metropolitan.

Today the only one of these films commonly available is not one of the series pictures, but a one-shot performance starring an old vaudevillian doing his best to break into talkies, W.C. Fields. After Paramount dropped his contract for silent films Fields had been performing his famous golf sketch at the Palace (his last appearance in vaudeville), and was eager to try the new medium. *The Golf Specialist* was shot at the Ideal studio in April 1930. As with *Animal Crackers,* filmed simultaneously by Paramount in Astoria (which sound had also forced them to reopen), the action is photographed from inside a sound-proof "ice-box" in order to shield the microphone from the noise of the camera. There are only two sets, a palpably artificial golf green, and a modest hotel lobby. Fields' first line of dialogue, "Any telegrams? Cablegrams? Radio? Television?", muttered in his trademark drawl, immediately marks him as one of those vaudevillians whose future success in talkies would far surpass anything they had achieved in silent pictures.

The reference to television was unusually topical, as several experimental stations were already on the air in New York and New Jersey when this film was shot. C. Francis Jenkins was broadcasting from Lincoln Park in Jersey City, while Hugo Gernsback, operating station W2XAL out of the Villa Richard on the Palisades, claimed to have been experimenting with television since 1928.

RKO worked on these shorts for about five months before deciding to consolidate all its production on the west coast. The loss of a major producer was a serious blow, meaning that Biarmer now had to compete for what remained of the independent business. Later in 1930 Louis Simon (who had previously been acting in George Le Maire's comedy shorts for Pathé in New York), appeared in a series of "Simple Simon" comedies at Ideal, at least one of which was directed by Morton Blumenstock. Titles included *Hot Shivers* and *Radio Madness.* A few months later the studio hosted its first feature, *Puss in Boots,* a children's operetta by Nathaniel Shilkret and Robert A. Simon. Shilkret and his Victor Salon Orchestra accompanied a cast composed almost entirely of children, many from the Elsa Greenwood Juveniles company.

In the spring of 1932 Jack Goldberg and Irving Yates formed Lincoln Pictures, Inc., and produced a pair of backstage musicals patterned on earlier Hollywood models. It was for Lincoln that Bill "Bojangles" Robinson and Eubie Blake starred in *Harlem Is Heaven* at the Ideal Studio in February, with musical numbers filmed on the stage of Brooklyn's Kenmore Theatre early in March. Lincoln followed with *Scandal,* featuring Lucky Millinder and His Orchestra, but seems to have collapsed before releasing the picture, which was generally distributed as *Gig and Saddle.*

In June and July *The Divorce Racket* was made here by Aubrey Scotto, with James Rennie and Olive Borden starring. More ambitious was *It Happened in Paris,* a musical remake of *The Two Orphans* (which had already been remade by D.W. Griffith as *Orphans of the Storm*). As with *Puss in Boots,* the film was produced and directed by M.J. Weisfeldt, with an original score by Nat Shilkret. Local band singer Ranny Weeks, who was subsequently signed by Herbert Yates for a series of B-musicals at Republic, made his screen debut. The rest of the cast was composed of the usual mix of overage silent celebrities and Broadway hopefuls. Despite the fact that the studio was reasonably well equipped and close to the midtown ferry lines, feature production shut down here by the summer of 1932. In 1935 Sidney and M.J. Kandel, who owned Ideal Pictures, left the studio business and opened Bonded Film Storage, which

Dita Parlo and Tom Moore in Edgar G. Ulmer's The Warning Shadow, *as incorporated into* Mr. Broadway *(Broadway-Hollywood Pictures, 1933).*

soon became one of the leading film warehouses in the east.

The one branch of the theatrical feature market which did continue to flourish here during the late 1930s were Yiddish films and "race movies" directed at the African-American market. Yiddish films continued to be produced in significant numbers in New York and New Jersey until the war cut off European markets. The Ideal studio was home to some of the last of these, including Max Nosseck's *Overture to Glory* (*Der Vilner Shtot Khazn*), a musical starring Moishe Oysher, which was shot here in the winter of 1939–40. Don Malkames was the cameraman. Other Yiddish films photographed by Malkames around this time, including *Kol Nidre*, said to have been made at the "Cinema Studios" in Palisades, and *Eli Eli*, reported as having been made in "Fort Lee", were probably also shot at Ideal (both were directed by Joseph Seiden). Seiden and Malkames teamed again on *Paradise in Harlem* in 1940, which producer Jack Goldberg told the *New York Times* had been shot in "Fort Lee", shorthand which in this case probably means the Ideal, but might also refer to the Metropolitan studio. Clearly influenced by such race-bending stage productions as *The Hot Mikado* and Orson Welles' voodoo *Macbeth*, this remarkable film was written by Frank Wilson, who plays a black actor yearning to quit his stereotyped roles and bring a production of *Othello* to Harlem (Paul Robeson would not bring his production to Broadway until 1942). The play is jeered by the uptown audience until the actors shift from Elizabethan idiom to contemporary street vernacular, a strategy prefiguring decades of subsequent Shakespearean stagings.

Metropolitan Sound Studios

Ultimately, it was the old Peerless studio on Lewis Street in Fort Lee that became the busiest, and most successful, of New Jersey's early talkie studios. The studio had been seized by the town for back taxes, and Phil Goldstone, a low-budget producer from the west coast, took it over with the idea of soundproofing it and making it available to other independents. Johns-Manville was installing sound proofing in October 1928 when fumes connected with the

installation process exploded, killing one man and injuring 14 others. Although the explosion was felt as far away as Edgewater, many in the vicinity at first failed to respond, confusing the blast with dynamiting already underway in connection with George Washington Bridge construction. Undeterred, Goldstone proceeded with a series of comedy shorts, including *The Honeymooners* and *The Gossips*. He was using a sound-on-disc process, first announced as Tonefilm, later as Biophone.

As was the case with the other eastern sound studios, there was an initial demand for the addition of synchronized sound tracks to films originally produced as silents, and several independent features, including Mrs. Wallace Reid's *Linda*, and Martin and Osa Johnson's travelogue *Simba*, were synchronized at Metropolitan. But Goldstone's studio was also the first in the nation to offer independent producers access to real sound stages. The first live-action feature to shoot here was *The House of Secrets*, a mystery-melodrama produced by Chesterfield, a poverty-row operation from Hollywood. In production by April 11, 1929, the film was ready for the critics six weeks later, who received it fairly well as the first all-talker from a "smaller" studio

In the summer of 1929 Rayart Pictures Corp. began to film a series of musical shorts at Metropolitan featuring Tommy Christian and His Palisades Orchestra. By September this project had grown to include a feature film, *Howdy, Broadway*, and the shorts *Cotton Pickin' Time*, *Moments of Melody* and *The Musical Sailor*. *Howdy, Broadway* is a college musical in which the hero, caught at a roadhouse, is thrown out of school and soon makes his fortune on Broadway. Unlike the equally threadbare films which Oscar Micheaux would soon be making at Metropolitan, no one involved displays any pride, interest, or imagination. *Howdy, Broadway* was not copyrighted, nor was it listed in Rayart's annual release schedule as published in the *Film Daily Yearbook of Motion Pictures*. If a copy of the film did not exist, it would be easy to conclude that it was never released, or perhaps never actually made.

The fire at the Pathé studio proved to be an even bigger blessing for the operators of the Metropolitan than it had been for Biarmer at Ideal (whether the New Jersey studios were safer to work in, or merely outside the control of New York's fire marshals, is hard to say). Pathé announced in January 1930 that they were shifting all their eastern production to Metropolitan, including retakes on *Sixteen Sweeties*, the film which was in production at the time of the fatal fire. And in addition to the work they were doing at Ideal, RKO also took space at Metropolitan, sending Lou Brock and Al Boasberg there to continue producing their Radiant comedies, including *Pullman Car, Prize Fights* and *The Speculator*.

By May, Metropolitan had upgraded its sound equipment to the tune of several hundred thousand dollars, and could boast that 30 films had been shot there in the past two months, including a Yiddish liturgical film, *Ad Mosay (The Eternal Prayer)*, and an entire opera, *Othello*, with tenor Manuel Salazar. The studio was ready for the biggest production it had seen since silent days, a religious epic financed by Mormon interests, to be called *Corianton*. Described as a spectacle in the tradition of *Ben-Hur*, *Corianton* was photographed by Dal Clawson and directed by silent film veteran Wilfred North. The six week shooting schedule (extremely long for an independent film) wrapped on January 12, 1931, with scenes of a

"bacchanalian orgy" involving "practically every available night club entertainer in New York". Only a few more scenes, featuring the Mormon Tabernacle Choir, remained to be filmed in Salt Lake City. But before *Corianton* could be released (or even completed?) producer Lester Park appears to have had a falling out with his partners, and the film simply vanished.

This "first Mormon talkie" was followed immediately by the first all-talking race movie, Oscar Micheaux's *The Exile*, and three Italian-language features shot before the end of 1931: *La Porta del Destino, Così e la Vita,* and *Cuore d'Emmigrante*. This last film (preserved today under the title *Santa Lucia Luntana*) shows the immigrant family of Don Ciccio Mauri torn apart by the corrupting influence of "American style". One daughter is infected by jazz, while the son has fallen in with gangsters. Sexual harassment forces the good daughter, Elena, out of her job. Maintaining traditional Neapolitan values in Manhattan's tenement district proves impossible. "Ah! America! A wonderful country ...rich...beautiful... but for whom????" Don Ciccio cries out (in Italian). Half the family returns to Naples, while its more acculturated members, now completely Americanized, stay behind. An unconvincing coda assures us that both groups prosper (the repentant gangster becomes a wealthy contractor!). These three Italian films appear to have been made by different companies, using different directors, but were all photographed by Frank Zucker, who may have been the staff cameraman at Metropolitan during this period. Zucker also shot *Enemies of the Law*, a gangster film starring Mary Nolan and Johnny Walker, which Sherman Krellberg produced there in April, 1931.

As if this production program was not eclectic enough, Metropolitan also hosted one of the first all-talking fea-

tures intended specifically as a children's film, Ruth Gilbert in *Alice in Wonderland*, directed by Bud Pollard. *Alice in Wonderland* opened at the Warners' Theatre on Times Square, where *The Jazz Singer* had premiered four years earlier. But the picture palace atmosphere only emphasized the distance between Pollard's modest effort and the scale of the usual Hollywood epic. "There is an earnestness about the direction and the acting that elicit sympathy", the *New York Times* wrote with its usual condescension, "for poor little Alice had to go through the ordeal of coming to shadow life in an old studio in Fort Lee, NJ, instead of enjoying the manifold advantages of her rich cousins who hop from printed pages to the screen amid the comfort of a well-equipped Hollywood studio". At a time when 16mm sound equipment was just being introduced, *Alice in Wonderland* was made available as a first run attraction in both 16 and 35mm, an effort by the distributor, Unique-Cosmos Pictures, to erase the line between the theatrical and non-theatrical markets.

As 1932 approached, with Warners laying off staff in Brooklyn and Paramount abandoning New York entirely, production was booming at Metropolitan. But this activity had very little to do with the conventional manner of producing and distributing films as practiced in Hollywood. What it did illustrate, however, was the ability of independent producers to generate business by identifying niche markets, segments of the audience not being served by Hollywood films, and finding ways of their own to offer an alternative. As the *Film Daily* put it to their industry audience in 1931, "pictures made here [in the east] have a different slant, providing needed variety on a crowded schedule".

Of course, it was possible to have too much of a "different slant", as the sorry history of Edgar G. Ulmer's *The Warning* Shadow illustrates. In February 1932 it was announced that Ulmer, "who was associated with the late F.W. Murnau as chief art director on *Sunrise*", was coming east to direct *The Warning Shadow*, "a cinema fantasy with a New York background". Ulmer began shooting on March 14 and seems to have shot the picture in two weeks, including locations outside the Waldorf-Astoria. The film starred Tom Moore, who in better days had worked in Fort Lee for Kalem and Goldwyn, and Dita Parlo, a German actress who had failed to catch on in Hollywood, and was working in the picture as a layover on her way back to Europe (she would become better known later for her work in *L'Atalante* [1934] and *La Grande Illusion* [1937]). The film appears to have been an extremely fatalistic glimpse of New York night life at the bottom of the depression, prefiguring such later works of French "poetic realism" as *Quai des Brumes* (1938) and *Le Jour se leve* (1939) – not to mention Ulmer's own *film noir* classic, *Detour* (1945). It was never released, perhaps never even completed.

That spring the full weight of the depression finally hit the American film industry, and it hit independent producers like those backing *The Warning Shadow* especially hard. "The laboratory controlled the picture", Ulmer remembered, seizing the negative when the company's financing ran dry. A new producer, Johnnie Walker, eventually took over the material and built a completely different film around Ulmer's footage. Noting the success of Walter Winchell's current novelty shorts (especially one called *Beauty on Broadway*), Walker hired columnist Ed Sullivan and retitled the picture *Mr. Broadway*. Sullivan played himself, the cameras following him around various Manhattan night spots as he gathered material for his column, greeting visiting celebrities

---

Jean Arthur in Get That Venus *(Starmark Productions, 1933).*

along the way. About two reels of Ulmer's film were interpolated into this travelogue, as a flashback narrated by Sullivan himself.

For a time, the Metropolitan studio was able to continue much as before. In March, Maurice Schwartz starred in an impressive adaptation of his Yiddish theater production, *Uncle Moses,* a critique of the material success some Jews had found in the new world. When Schwartz moved out, Bud Pollard came back to direct *The Black King* for Southland Pictures. While most white-produced race movies were content to package action, music, and comedy, *The Black King* was directly critical of African-American culture, taking plot elements from *The Emperor Jones* and grafting them onto details from the life of Marcus Garvey. Newsreel clips of Garveyesque parades and street demonstrations were cut in to illustrate the protagonist's fraudulent "United States of Africa" scheme. Although Southland used many members of Oscar Micheaux's stock company, as well as his cameraman, Lester Lang, the film failed with audiences and the lab was suing for back bills within a week of the premiere.

Dorothy Lee and Lee Moran appeared in *Mazie,* produced at Metropolitan by Plymouth Pictures, but even the name of this film's director is lost to history. *Get That Venus*, with Ernest Truex and Jean Arthur, followed in the summer of 1933. Jean Arthur had already made dozens of silent and sound films, but her screen career had never caught fire, and she had been working on Broadway, marking time between stage appearances; her triumphant return to Hollywood was still another year off. The market for low-budget independent films, always dependable during the silent era, had just about ground to a halt. Any B-movies still being made would be made in Hollywood, if not by the major producers, then at least

by producers with guaranteed access to distribution. Arthur's picture would be the last conventional B-movie shot in New Jersey, where the film industry would now be dominated by racial and ethnic production.

Micheaux Pictures

Oscar Micheaux had been producing "race films" for the African-American market at various New York and New Jersey studios since 1920, when he shot *Symbol of the Unconquered* in Fort Lee. Early in 1930 he added a dialogue sequence to his silent production *A Daughter of the Congo,* creating the sort of "part-talkie" that had also served as an introduction to the new medium for most of the mainstream studios. It is unclear where Micheaux shot this material, which allowed him to advertise the picture as "TALKING SINGING DANCING". But in January 1931 he was working at the Metropolitan studios on *The Exile,* promoted at the time as "The first all-Negro talking feature production". Rebounding from a 1928 bankruptcy, Micheaux had reorganized his operation as the Micheaux Pictures Corporation, with himself as president, and Harlem Theater owners Frank Schiffmann and Leo Brecher as vice-president and treasurer. As with any good Hollywood operation, Micheaux recognized that only direct partnership with theater interests (the equivalent of Hollywood's vertical integration of production, distribution, and exhibition), could guarantee adequate financing and access to markets.

Although clearly a low-budget film, *The Exile* was professionally produced at Metropolitan soon after the Mormon feature *Corianton* vacated the stages. Micheaux employed a union crew, and the film was photographed by Lester Lang, who would work on many subsequent Micheaux films, and Walter Strenge, president of Cinematographer's Local 644, and recently Dudley Murphy's cameraman on the Bessie Smith film, *St. Louis Blues*.

While some later critics have described *The Exile* as "a disaster", its technical quality is certainly no worse than what can be found in *Howdy, Broadway* or any other low-budget eastern production of the period. Indeed, Micheaux's sober analysis of racial distinction within and without the black community marks *The Exile* as far more ambitious, and interesting, than most other independent films of the day. Micheaux returned to the Metropolitan studio the following year, filming studio interiors for *Ten Minutes to Live* and "retakes" on *Veiled Aristocrats* in January 1932. He had shot parts of *Veiled Aristocrats* at his mother-in-law's home in Montclair, New Jersey, the previous summer. Lorenzo Tucker, whom Micheaux publicized as "the Colored Valentino", worked on all his early talkies. To historian Richard Grupenhoff, Tucker characterized Micheaux as a director who would cut every possible corner, failing to allow his actors adequate rehearsal, refusing retakes of flubbed dialogue, and often mixing professional performers with amateurs. Micheaux survived in the race movie business because, unlike the competition, he knew exactly how much he could recoup on any picture, and had contempt for rivals who wasted their resources on retakes or lighting equipment. Tucker remembered that Micheaux "rarely used electric lights", unless working in a studio. "Kodak would send a camera and crew with a couple of spots or something like that, and he might use one or two of them now and then, but mostly he used natural light."

As in the silent days, Micheaux depended on the use of reflectors to illuminate his actors, even when they were working inside homes and apartments. According to Tucker, Micheaux would direct such scenes "while lying on a couch and swallowing handfuls of raw starch from an Argo box", self-medication designed to sooth his chronic stomach aches.

Extreme examples of this use of natural lighting on interiors can be seen in *The Girl from Chicago* (which seems to have been made at or around the time Micheaux was sued for misappropriation of funds by Frank Schiffmann, his partner in the Micheaux Pictures Corp.). The first half, supposedly taking place in Mississippi, appears to have been shot in the same suburban New Jersey location as *Veiled Aristocrats*. Unusual for Micheaux, the lighting of both interiors and exteriors here seems completely unprofessional, almost like a home movie. Indeed, this is the only Micheaux talkie whose photography is credited to a non-union (non-professional?) cameraman, one Sam Orleans. The photographic style changes dramatically in the second part of the film, shot at "The Micheaux Studio", where professional equipment was available. This was probably the Metropolitan, but may have been shot in one of the rental studios in the Bronx. In any case, Micheaux still wastes no time on technical niceties. By the mid-1930s Micheaux was making most of his films in New York, but according to Lorenzo Tucker, he filmed at least part of *Temptation* in one of the Fort Lee studios in 1936.

It may or may not be appropriate to compare Micheaux's "outsider" style to that of Horace Pippin, Berthold Brecht, Alain Resnais or Grandma Moses, as some recent critics have argued. But the technical eccentricities one sees in his work do appear much less peculiar after looking at a film like *Howdy, Broadway*, or the collected works of Bud Pollard.

Grantwood revival

Pollard's films provide a good example of how the lines of demarcation which the industry had set up among conventional B-movies, ethnic and racial pictures, and exploitation films, gradually began to erode. As the effects of the depression bore down on the low end of the local film industry, no one could afford to specialize: Yiddish film producers made race pictures, B-movie directors turned to exploitation films, and exploitation producers assembled low budget compilation documentaries on the horrors of the first World War. These films were now all being made by the same group of people, in the same handful of studios, and with the same recourse to state's rights distribution (a sort of "traveling

salesman" approach which did have the benefit of circumventing the industry's own Production Code, if not the censorship statutes of the various states).

Already established in the east as a director of very low budget features like *Alice in Wonderland*, Pollard's 1932 output included one race movie, *The Black King*, one Italian language feature, *O festino a la legge* (both shot at the Metropolitan Studios), and an exploitation film called *The Horror*, made in New York. But Pollard's strangest film was certainly *Victims of Persecution*, which he made that year at his own studio on Bergen Boulevard in Grantwood (the old E.K. Lincoln studio). *Victims of Persecution* was made for William Goldberg's Yiddish film company, and was apparently the only such film ever shot in English. A politically charged indictment of racial and religious intolerance, the film parallels a story of bigotry and violence in contemporary New York (dramatic sequences combined with newsreel footage of street demonstrations), with an essay on medieval anti-semitism supplied through two reels of a silent movie spliced into the picture. Pollard continued to work the fringes of the industry until well after the second World War. His career remains almost entirely unresearched.

The Lincoln studio which Pollard took over in 1933 had been converted for sound two years earlier and renamed the Royal. RCA Photophone had wired the studio, which boasted one large 96 x 65 foot sound stage, with a smaller 64 x 36 foot stage in reserve, as well as a 35 x 46 foot swimming tank, "and an innovation is a television studio". The studio reopened on July 31, 1931 with a series of Ned Wayburn's Kid Pix, and in October Charles Bowers arrived to

Oscar Micheaux filming The Betrayal *(Astor Pictures, 1948), parts of which were made at the Metropolitan studio in Fort Lee.*

begin work on a series of eight two-reelers. Frank S. Amon was also said to have been producing cartoons there. But the Royal's most impressive tenant was Harry Langdon. In February 1932 it was announced that Langdon would also make a series of two-reelers here, a comeback attempt by a star who had fallen farther, and faster, than any silent screen favorite. The first of these, *The Show Goat*, was made that month with Ina Hayward, Maryann Lynn, Barbara Willison, and various others in support. Suddenly, *Film Daily* was reporting that "Harry Langdon's new picture...has been changed to a feature. Those who have seen the picture claim that Langdon staged such a marvelous comeback in the two-reeler it was decided to make it into a feature." The "feature" went back into production by the end of March, and that was the last anyone ever heard of it. No made-in-New Jersey Harry Langdon feature or short has ever been identified. Whatever it was Langdon made at the Royal studio immediately disappeared into the black hole of film financing, distribution difficulties, or "creative differences".

Like the other local studios, the Royal was forced to abandon traditional film production in 1932 and moved into the ethnic market. In November 1932 Yugoslavian Pictures, Inc. produced *Ljubav i Strast*, the first Croatian-language feature. Raquel Davidovitch and Ivan Plemic starred. As with many other foreign-language productions produced locally at this time, it was a romantic-drama focusing on the problems of assimilation (the title translates as *Love and Passion*, although in the English-language press it was referred to as *Born to Kiss)*. Cameraman J. Burgi Contner acquired the studio in 1935 and renamed it Producers Service Studio. Edgar G. Ulmer was listed as "production manager". Much of the work done at this time was for the burgeoning industrial-film market, although Ulmer did direct studio interiors here for the Yiddish films *Green Fields* (1937) and the expressionistic *The Light Ahead* (1939). Ulmer probably also shot the race film *Moon Over Harlem* here in 1939, although he told Peter Bogdanovich that the credited "Meteor Studio" was just "an old cigar warehouse" in New Jersey.

During the second World War there was very little film production of any kind in the east, a situation which slowly began to change by 1947. That year O.A. Peters and Thomas Taglianetti formed Gateway Productions and took over the old Metropolitan studio. They hoped to take advantage of the predicted increase in local film production, but by the time business really did pick up, Gateway was no longer around to enjoy it. In fact, the only producer known to have used the studio at all at this time was Oscar Micheaux, who seems to have filmed (or refilmed) portions of *The Betrayal* here in 1948. This three-hour epic, essentially another version of Micheaux's *The Exile* – itself filmed at the Metropolitan decades earlier – had been shot in a studio in Chicago, but apparently required extensive revisions. *The Betrayal* appears to have been the last dramatic film shot in a Fort Lee studio. The old buildings decayed, burned, or were demolished by developers. Filmmakers continued to work in Fort Lee, but just as with D.W. Griffith fifty years earlier, they were only visiting. *Kiss of Death*, for example, shot at the Academy of the Holy Angels in 1947 – a forbidden location in the old days – and film and television crews continue to come around from time to time. But despite the revival promised by the advent of talkies, the days when work at the studios drove the local economy would never return.

21.

Why Did the Studios Leave Fort Lee?

The end of the Fort Lee studios came with both a bang and a whimper. Fires and explosions in local studios and laboratories not only destroyed these buildings, but terrified many of their neighbors. Support for the "film interests" became a political football, pitting local businessmen (garage owners, restaurateurs, etc.) against residential taxpayers. Weather conditions, land and labor costs, and transportation difficulties would eventually have driven most of the film companies out of Fort Lee in any case. But at a time when the Hollywood Chamber of Commerce was actively promoting the virtues of filmmaking in Southern California, Fort Lee officials did nothing – indeed, often seemed to encourage the movie companies to go elsewhere.

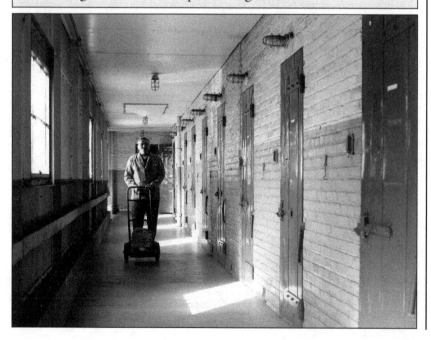

MR. KERWIEN TALKS OF HIS POSITION ON THE MOVIES

(from *The Palisadian*, September 11, 1915, p. 1)

Mayor [Arthur] Kerwien, who is the Republican candidate for mayor of the Borough of Fort Lee, was asked if he had anything to say regarding the challenge laid down in the last issue of the [Fort Lee] *Sentinel* asking where he stood upon the moving picture question. Mr. Kerwien replied:

"I don't see any sense to the question. Anybody should know where I stand on just matters relating to the borough's best interest. The effort, of course, is intended to draw me out, and I am easy to draw out on questions of this kind."

"Yes, but will you be specific on your reply?"

"Yes, as specific as necessary.

"I stand for a square deal on moving picture business exactly as I stand for a square deal on any other business in the borough that requires attention, protection or proper assessment and taxation.

"I hold to the very substantial doctrine that no institution of any kind has a right to special privileges, and I do not propose to make an exception of the moving picture interests that are now so largely congregated in Fort Lee. At the same time these people have come here to do business right and so far as I can see and judge they are not here to bamboozle anybody out of anything for any purpose. I think the people connected with the moving picture interests are entitled to the same consideration as any other business enterprise is. If their business requires special attention they ought to

Laboratories and film vaults maintained the industry's connection with Fort Lee, occasionally with disastrous results. Transporting films at Consolidated during the 1960s.

have it; if it requires special police protection they ought to pay for it.

"Just why this question was asked of me is beyond my ken. I have never faltered in my line of duty towards the people of Fort Lee, nor have I undertaken to do things that are either outlawed by custom, precedent or right. I am before the people seeking their ballots on the basis of what I represent as a man. Anybody who undertakes to interpolate into this campaign any foolish questions will have their thanks their pains [sic]. This is not a foolish business. It is a sincere effort on my part as it should be on the part of every candidate to go before the people on an issue that is square and honest. If there is any falsehood about my position, it will all come out in the wash.

"My record is behind me. I believe the people of Fort Lee will recognize that it was a proper kind of record and if they think so doubtless will back me up at the polls to the limit of their faith in me.

"I do not undertake to say that I will be elected, but I hope so because I believe the people want a clean government, and I shall not undertake to give them any other kind."

PRODUCERS TO CLOSE EASTERN PLANTS AND MOVE TO CALIFORNIA FOR WINTER
Coal Shortage Imminent – Most Big Companies With Studios in New York and Vicinity Prepared for Any Emergency

(from *Exhibitors Herald and Motography,* August 17, 1918, p. 23)

Dark days are ahead for Eastern studios as soon as the snow begins to fly. The coal shortage will necessitate it, according to reports which reached New York from Washington this week.

"You may say that I stand on the moving picture question where every honest man should stand, or any man should stand with a grain of common sense left in him."

FORT LEE GETS AFTER MOVIE CONCERNS FOR SEVERAL THINGS, SOME INSULTS, AND INJURY TO A CHILD, AMONG THEM

(from *The Palisadian*, December 4, 1915, pp. 1, 7)

The first meeting of the Council of the Borough of Fort Lee in December took place in Schlosser's Hotel on Main Street. All Councilmen were present and Mayor White called the meeting to order promptly....

After movie concerns

In a short address Mayor White stated that the borough was facing a grave problem in the handling of [text missing in original-ed.] went on to stay that he had received innumerable complaints concerning the conduct of these companies' employees. He repeated an instance of how the daughter of Mrs. Catharine Reilly had been grossly insulted upon her own premises.

Town likely to be blown up

Councilman Jennings here broke in and stated that, unless some drastic measure of licensing these companies was immediately adopted, the town stood a good chance of being blown up sometime when a big battle scene was being taken.

After considerable discussion and the hearing of complaints from Mr. Kurt, of Coytesville, and Mr. Beattie, of Main Street, who both had suffered damage to their property from transient moving picture concerns, the matter was put in the hands of Mayor White and the clerk for adjustment.

In closing the mayor stated that he had received a bill from the Englewood Hospital of $17.50 for treatment of the child which had been injured on election day by the accidental discharge of a "movie" soldier's gun and that he would take the bill up with the moving picture company responsible for the occurrence and do all in his power to see that it was paid promptly.

The meeting adjourned until December 15.

> Film production in Fort Lee was dealt a very serious blow in the winter of 1918, when a wartime coal shortage made it difficult to heat and light the studios. Not all of the local studios closed – World had stockpiled its own coal – but those producers who did operate studios on the coast had every reason to shut down their eastern operations. Most never returned.

But it will not find the big producers unprepared.

Realizing the seriousness of the fuel situation, practically every one of the larger companies, whose production centers are in New York, have quietly been making arrangements during the past few weeks so that if it becomes necessary they will be able to remove their producing staffs and studio fa-

cilities to the Pacific Coast without interference with their production schedules.

Others are now contemplating similar action, and by the time winter comes the probabilities are that not a single producing plant of any size will be in operation in the East.

Richard A. Rowland, president of

Metro, and Samuel Goldfish, head of Goldwyn, were among the first in the industry to realize the seriousness of the fuel problem which is going to confront the entire country this fall and made their plans accordingly….

Will Meet Garfield

The Fuel Conservation Committee of the Motion Picture Industry, as the new committee is called, is designed to study the problem created by the coal shortage and later make recommendations to Dr. Garfield, Federal Fuel administrator, to remedy or ameliorate conditions as far as they relate to the film industry … .

> Labor unrest was another element in the decision of most studio heads to leave New York and New Jersey behind. While the sun might not shine every day in Los Angeles, the anti-union policies of the city fathers were completely dependable. Unionization in Hollywood was about twenty years behind developments in the east, keeping labor costs far lower and encouraging producers to move everything but their executive offices to California. Major laboratory strikes hit the Fort Lee area in 1920, 1925 and 1937. The 1920 strike eventually involved 2500 workers and ran for two weeks.

MOVIE MEN ON STRIKE IN FORT LEE PLANTS

(from *The Palisadian,* July 24, 1920, p. 1)

Fort Lee is in the midst of a big strike among the movie plants. They have begun

Henry McAvoy, manager of the Hudson Fire Works Co. in Grantwood, funneling explosives in connection with a film shoot.

to get noisy, and county deputy sheriffs and local police have their hands full. The *Record* of Thursday said:

"Mrs. Charlotte Marcus, private secretary of Superintendent Murphy, was surrounded as she entered the plant and was abused in vigorous terms. Two deputy sheriffs were summoned and the strikers left.

"Superintendent Murphy, in an interview granted an *Evening Record* representative, said that the New York union is responsible for the strike in the Fort Lee plants, and hundreds of Bergen County men and women are thrown out of work as a consequence.

"'We offered an increase of 15 per cent on Monday, but the New York strikers came over here and demanded a 65 per cent increase, which would mean an increase of $200,000 a year in our payroll,' said Superintendent Murphy. 'I have 55 per cent of my people working, and thus far the strike has not inconvenienced us to any great extent.

" 'The New York men are saying that the strike is general all over the country, but this is not so.'"

A dozen deputies are assisting the Fort Lee police in the work of maintaining order.

Among the plants in Fort Lee that are closed are the Fox Film Company, Kessel, Paragon, Triangle, Famous Players-Lasky, Knickerbocker, Peerless and Capellani.

> The 1920 blast which killed studio explosives expert Henry McAvoy drew the attention of the *New York Times* not just because the victim was the son of Fort Lee's first mayor, but because police throughout the area were already on the alert for anarchist bombings.

MYSTERY IN FORT LEE EXPLOSION: 1 KILLED

Garage Blown to Pieces and Windows in Many Houses Shattered

Panic in Public School Henry A. McAvoy, Son of ex-Mayor, Dead – Had Been Experimenting with Motion Picture Explosives

(From *The New York Times*, November 5, 1920, p. 16.)

Fort Lee and neighboring towns were shaken yesterday by an explosion which caused the death of one man, shattered the windows in many houses and threw the pupils in a large public school building into a panic. The explosion is still a mystery to the police and the Hackensack Prosecutor, who are investigating it.

Henry A. McAvoy, 36 years old, son of John McAvoy, former Mayor of Fort Lee, was killed. He was in a garage next door to his father's house, Palisade Avenue and Whiteman Street, where the explosion occurred. The garage, a well-built structure, was blown into pieces. Some of the timber was hurled 100 yards, and windows were shattered within a radius of 800 feet. One heavy beam was blown completely through the roof of a three-story residence nearby.

After the explosion many persons rushed to the scene. McAvoy's body, badly mutilated, with his clothing torn to shreds, was carried out. He lived a few minutes, while Drs. C. A. Connor and C. W. Priestly worked over him. No one else was injured, although several persons were badly shaken. In the school building, about 100 yards distant, the windows were broken and several of the children were knocked from their seats by the force of the explosion.

The residence of Elmer H. Schwartz was set on fire by burning fragments, and the fire alarm brought a large crowd from miles around. The police had difficulty in keeping the throng back. Orders were given that nothing be disturbed until the cause of the explosion could be investigated.

Scattered on all sides of the destroyed building were smoke shells and motion-picture fireworks, and it was believed at first that the explosion was caused by something connected with the taking of pictures. McAvoy was employed until recently by the Fox Film Corporation, and according to information obtained at the studio, he had been experimenting with explosives. The police of Fort Lee, however, believe that the death was caused by some explosive much more powerful than any used in the film industry. Two automobiles in the garage were completely wrecked and a third standing outside was badly damaged.

McAvoy leaves his wife and three children, the youngest only a few months old.

Local residents remembered the fires and explosions at places like Éclair (1914) and Solax (1919), and may have assumed that things would quiet down after film production in Fort Lee gradually came to a halt. They failed to reckon with the continued presence of a host of laboratories, storage vaults, and even a large film reclamation business. The worst disaster was the explosion at the National-Evans lab on Linwood Avenue, the old Willat laboratory, where the final total was two dead and twenty injured.

ONE MAN IS KILLED; MANY INJURED WHEN BIG TANK EXPLODES

(from *Bergen Evening Record*, February 7, 1925, p. 1)

National Evans Film Laboratory in Fort Lee Wrecked by Fire

Flames Out and Firemen Are Clearing Up When Ammonia Tank Blows Up

Men Caught By Flying Bricks and Falling Flooring

One Dies on Way to Englewood Hospital

Others Severely Injured

Blast Shakes Whole Eastern Side of County

Less Injured Help those Badly Hurt

… Shortly after four o'clock this morning, Officer John Flynn, doing desk duty in the Fort Lee police station, received information that fire was raging in the laboratories at Linwood Avenue and Main Street.

He spread the alarm and the three pieces of motor apparatus of the borough arrived at the areas in quick time.

Fire thought out

After almost an hour's work, the flames were thought to have been subdued. Commissioner Carney, together with members of Company No. 3, started to investigate to learn the cause of the fire.

While the party was on its way through the main laboratory the other members of the volunteer department of the borough busied themselves gathering their hose and taking their ladders down from the building under the supervision of Chief George Kipp, who had directed the fighting of the blaze.

The explosion, the second during the fire, then occurred.

Bricks rained on them

A shower of bricks, falling walls and dying floors caused a deluge that caught struggling firemen unaware in the midst of their strenuous work.

Among the few of the eighty-five people employed on the night shift in the laboratory to remain in the building through the fire in an effort to aid the firemen were Salvatore Joy, the dead victim, and Superintendent John G. Van Duyne, who stuck to his task until the last.

With the one large wall of the building totally destroyed, and the floors giving way, a number of wounded firemen forgot their own injuries to aid those trapped in the building.

Citizens excited by the noise of the explosion also hurried to join in caring for the injured.

Died in Ambulance

Joy was one of the first sent to the Englewood hospital. He died in the ambulance before reaching the institution.

Private cars were also used to get the injured to the hospitals while some of those suffering slight lacerations and gashes were treated by the local physicians in the Lovell, Beatty [and] Setzer homes and the Cunz drug store located nearby.

Charles Hirliman, owner of the Hirlagraph Film Company of New York, was one of those who were blown through the wall with Commissioner Carney.

Girls much excited

The explosion aroused the entire community, some believing the world had really come to an end as predicted by the Long Island colonists.

Girls living at the Holy Angels Academy directly opposite the laboratories shrieked frantically when aroused from their slumber, and the Sisters in charge encountered great difficulty in quieting them.

The Fort Lee police who reported to the fire scene on the call of Chief of Police Thomas Aitken, sent out calls for aid to the Englewood and Hackensack hospitals, also calling every one of the local doctors to the wrecked buildings.

The National-Evans Film Laboratories advertise their services in the Film Daily Yearbook of Motion *Pictures,* 1925.

Origin a mystery

The origin of the fire remains a mystery but the Fort Lee officials said this morning they would investigate the matter thoroughly.

A special meeting of the Mayor and Council will be held this evening.

The officials of the company as well as Borough Counsel Mackay have been asked to attend the same.

The building, at least what remains of it, looks as if it may crumple up anytime and the Borough officials are contemplating an order it be razed.

Relief is planned

The Mayor and Council are also planning relief for the men who were victims of the greatest calamity in the history of the eastern Bergen hamlet.

News was received late this morning that members of the Fort Lee Board of Trade were organizing a local relief fund.

B. Duncan McClave of Cliffside Park, chairman of the Republican County Committee, has offered his services to conduct a county campaign for the benefit of the victims.

Big crowd gathers

Shortly after the echoes of the explosions had reached the far-ends of the borough, men and women were rushing to the vicinity to do what they might to render aid.

Salvage of the store rooms was started by workmen under the direction of Thomas Evans, president of the company.

Estimate conservative

When asked what he thought the damage could be estimated at, Evans replied that $2,000,000 was a conservative opinion.

He said that the actual loss could not be really announced until all the films on hand were checked up.

The wife of Frank Cavaliere, one of the four men said to be in critical condition, broke down completely upon learning of his ill fortune.

The stricken fireman is the father of a family of seven and his case is deserving of much sympathy.

Firemen William Sontag, Eugene Heft, Foreman Louis Moesig and Assistant Foreman Edward Troy, all injured, scrambled into the ruins to render aid to the less fortunate of their companions who were more severely injured in the explosion.

Sick boy exposed

The catastrophe may be responsible for the death of eight-year-old Joseph Smith, Jr., young son of parents living in a small bungalow adjacent to the laboratory.

The youngster, who has been confined to bed with pneumonia and whose condition is considered very serious, was showered with glass and brick which fell upon him as the wall of the laboratory was blown apart.

In the cold of the morning it became necessary to remove the child to the Holy Angels Academy where he was treated by the good sisters. Later his condition grew critical and the boy was ordered removed to the Englewood hospital.

FT. LEE CATASTROPHE WARMS HEART OF BOROUGH IN BEHALF OF INJURED FOR WHOM FUND WILL BE RAISED
Local Committees and All Banks Will Receive Subscriptions – Work Already Started With Liberal Response From All Classes – Sum to Be Realized Will be Considerable

(from *The Palisadian*, February 13, 1925, pp. 1, 3)

Without a doubt the most disastrous tragedy in the history of the borough of Fort Lee was the fire and explosion at the National Evans Film Laboratories on Main Street and Lemoine Avenue early last Saturday morning, which resulted in the death of two men, the injury of twenty and a property loss estimated to be $2,000,000.

Dead

Salvatore Joy, 29, of Main Street, West Fort Lee, film projector.

Fireman Frank Cavaliere, Center Road, Fort Lee.

Seriously injured

John Grant Van Duyne, 28, of 1652 Bergen Boulevard, West Fort Lee, superintendent of the laboratory.

Fireman Raymond Marcus of 157 English Street, Fort Lee.

Fireman Leonard Merkel of 530 Walnut Street, Fort Lee.

Other injured

Fireman Edward Lehman, 29, of 490 James Street, West Fort Lee.

Fireman George Muckle, 26, 1622 John Street, Fort Lee.

Those that received minor injuries were: Arthur Kerwien and Louis Hoebel, both councilmen; H. Barbieri, Dominic Joy, brother of the dead man; T. Dalton, A. Lafko, R. Duckless, R. Dittenfass and G. Beatter.

Condition of victims

Joy is believed to have been killed instantly when the walls of the building fell in upon him following the explosion.

Frank Cavaliere died on last Wednesday night in the Englewood Hospital as a result of internal injuries. He leaves a wife and several small children.

Ray Marcus is in the Englewood Hospital suffering from concussion of the brain. He will recover, it is reported.

Leonard Merkle was severely cut

about the head. He is in Englewood Hospital.

George Merkle, a brother, was in Hackensack Hospital with a deep gash over the eye.

Grant Van Dyne, superintendent of the Evans Laboratory, of Bergen Boulevard, had one ear almost completely severed with a deep cut on the face and jaw. His condition is very serious, it is said, but will recover.

John Whittaker suffered a severe gash in his right shoulder, and his wrists were slashed.

Richard Demmencurri, a watchman for the laboratory, was badly cut about the face.

Edward Lehman suffered internal injuries.

Alexander Lang, a fireman, of Washington Avenue, Coytesville is at his home with cuts about the face and internal injuries.

Girl gives alarm
Miss Florence Stillwell of Coytesville, who was working on the night shift, sent in the alarm which brought out all the fire departments from the surrounding Bergen municipalities. She told the police that she was at her work in the plant splicing film when she noticed smoke emanating from an adjoining room.

The firemen responded promptly and after working for about an hour had the flames almost extinguished. Some entered the building, while others were preparing to return to the fire house. It was at this time the big explosion occurred, causing the terrible fatality and injuring about a score.

Cause of blast
It was first reported that the cause of the blast was occasioned by the escaping fumes from an ammonia tank. This theory has been discarded, however, as the ammonia tank was seen on Monday and was said to be completely intact.

The real cause of the explosion, it is said, resulted from spontaneous combustion. A quantity of colodium [i.e., collodion-ed], guncotton and ether were said to have been stored in the basement of the plant, and the heat of the slight blaze

which had brought out the firemen was believed to have set off the highly inflammable material in storage after the actual fire had been extinguished.

Investigation on
It was only a matter of hours before a special meeting of the council was called by Mayor White to determine on a plan to aid the stricken families of the dead and injured and to probe the cause of the tragedy. An investigation will be made of all film laboratories to see that the laws concerning the storage of inflammable materials are being observed. The local authorities will have the co-operation of the prosecutor's office in making the investigation.

Organized relief
A meeting called by Mayor White was held in the borough hall on Tuesday evening last to formulate plans for immediate relief, and forty local organizations, political, social and religious, were represented. More than $1,000 was contributed at the meeting. Mayor White made the largest individual contribution, $200.

Mayor White was elected chairman of the relief fund, Charles Lebright secretary, and Edward Kaufer, Joseph Setzer and Arthur Kerwien were named as an executive committee to make an immediate survey of the needs of the families of the victims of the disaster. The cashiers of the three borough banks were named as treasurers to receive donations.

A motion picture benefit will be held tonight and next Friday night at P. Grieb's Fort Lee Theatre, and on February 24 the Palisade Sporting Club will hold a benefit boxing show at the Hirligraph studio in Fort Lee....

Although trade papers and fan magazines had been printing mournful obituaries for a decade, this depressing essay in the *New York Times* was the true kiss of death. The image of a "ghastly cemetery" where "even the ivy on the walls" was dead morphed into the "crumbled brick, warped steel and shattered glass" of a depression-era rustbelt. Fort Lee was an industrial ghost town whose stages were now occupied by "Mormons" and "a Negro producer". *The Times* even managed to find a new villain: Herbert Hoover. Not President Hoover, of course, but Hoover the World War I conservation czar, shutting down the studios by rationing power and light. It wasn't as simple as all that, of course, but by 1931 Hoover was already being blamed for every other economic failure in America, and the image of an industrial ghost town was too good to pass up.

GHOSTS IN THE CRADLE OF THE MOVIES
Fort Lee, Once The Centre Of Film Work, Is Now A Ruined Shell, Thanks To Hollywood And Herbert Hoover

By Parke F. Hanley

(from *The New York Times Magazine*, May 31, 1931, p. 15)

The cradle of the motion picture in America is now a ghastly cemetery, with monuments of scaling concrete, crumbling brick, warped steel and shattered glass to mark the early steps of an industry that presently was to take its place with manufacture, with metal, with shipping and with agriculture as a factor in the world's progress. Here at Fort Lee fame was conferred prodigally, declining careers gained rebirth and fortunes were created – and lost and stolen. Now even the ivy on the walls that housed these phenomena is dead.

Within a mile area the gigantic pier of the new Hudson River bridge stands, two towers of a radio station pierce the sky, a new road that has been blasted from solid rock traces its route direct to the Holland Tube. These manifestations of modernity throw their shadows upon buildings where the glass that once let in the essential sunlight now lies a foot deep upon the floors; pipes and wires are in twisted heaps; dressing rooms that once sheltered the screen great are dumps of broken plaster.

As if a hurricane had nursed all its demoniac tricks until it reached this spot, such is the devastation in the ten acres that once fed the world with new delights in thrills and laughter. No bonanza town ever has been laid waste with more thoroughness.

The amusement that revolutionized the habits of the two generations through which it has lived and thrived came upon Fort Lee with a tragicomic struggle between a church and a saloon.

Herbert Hoover signed the town's death warrant.

Dick Brown brought the movies to Fort Lee – Dick and his horse Jupiter. A few years ago, at the age of 97, Brown was gathered unto his fathers, but up to the hour of death his proudest boast was that his hack had delivered Mary Pickford to her first studio appointment on the Palisades. He insisted to the end that he had had a hand in her destiny and he succumbed happily in that belief. But that was after Dick gave the movies their earliest location in Fort Lee.

He drew up to Norman Coyle's saloon at William and Main Streets with a tatterdemalion hackload.

"Norman", he said, "here are some laddie-bucks who want a saloon and a church in proximity. You are fairly next to a church, so here they are."

The identity of these pioneers is lost to Coyle. All he can remember is that their manager was a man with a beard and he requisitioned the back room of the saloon as a dressing room. Then the manager wanted to know if the keys to the church could be borrowed; it is known as "Old Taylor's Church" because Taylor, who once owned the land that now is comprised in Fort Lee, Coytesville, Leonia and adjoining towns, had built it. Norman suspended his brother from his duties as bartender to seek Miss Byers, the custodian of the keys.

The ensuing proceedings were mystifying. A ragged tramp emerged from the "family entrance" while a camera was placed across the street. Within the focus the besotted creature looked toward the church; from the portals a man in clerical garb was seen to emerge. He held out merciful hands to the tramp; there was a palpable response, but at the moment of seeming surrender the face of Norman's brother appeared above the swinging doors of the saloon.

Doubt, then vacillation crept into the actions of the tramp. The man of the church and the bartender were the horns of his dilemma. Finally with a magnificent gesture of total damnation he staggered within the swinging doors.

Later Norman heard that the picture was being shown at Miner's Bowery Theatre, where it received tremendous applause from a Rabelaisian audience.

"We have had a lot of arguments", he said, when asked to fix the date. "All I

(Left and right-hand pages): Typical magazine spread on the decline of the Fort Lee film industry, from New Movie, May 1930.

On this page are three glimpses of the big William Fox studios in Fort Lee, in New Jersey, just across from New York. From these studios came the early pictures that made the name of Fox well known across the country. Here worked Theda Bara in her earliest successes. Here, too, Evelyn Nesbit made her pictures. The Virginia Pierson and Valeska Suratt productions were made here also.

know is that I have been married thirty-four years, and this happened the year before I was married."

[Within a few years] night and day the studios of Universal, Paragon, World-Peerless, Éclair, Fox, Willat, Champion and Solax were busy. The ferry boats from the foot of 125th Street were loaded to the stern and bow rails with passengers, cars were banked along the streets of the studios at all hours, saloons put on relays of bartenders, and restaurants cropped up like an alfalfa growth.

Main Street was a lane of revelry day and night. Linwood Avenue had on one side – it is there yet – the Church of the Holy Angels and on the other, so the pious said, an army of painted devils.

There had been premonitions of impending doom. For instance, the light often failed, but thousands of extras must be paid; accessories requisitioned hastily

from New York were twenty-four hours in arriving, while production costs kept mounting; extras hesitated to embark for Fort Lee for fear of being marooned by the uncertain hours of return ferries; good burghers in Leonia, Englewood and other villages, where outdoor locations had been marked, waited with shotguns for the invasion of the movie hordes, and finally the realtors of Fort Lee were up in arms … .

It was left to Herbert Hoover, however, to close up Fort Lee as a cinema centre. By virtue of appointment from President Wilson as a national conservator he decreed there should be fuelless days. Fuel was needed to heat the barn-like structure in which art was having its expression; coal was required to turn the generators which produced the light. The studios sent out men and teams to bring in wood. They left the countryside as bare as the environs of a campus bonfire. Mr. Hoover might as well have taken away their cameras.

The eyes of the producers turned toward Hollywood with its perpetual sunlight, salubrious climate, its flowers and its easy cruising distance to seashore, snow fields, deserts – and all the attributes modestly claimed by Californians. The hegira was on. Within weeks Fort Lee was totally abandoned.

Now, on the site of the old colony, Consolidated Films has savaged part of Universal for laboratory purposes and Metropolitan has taken the old World plant, where recently it produced two pictures with sound, one for the Mormons and the other for a Negro producer. Sporadic efforts have been made to recover the olden glory, but Fort Lee is a shell, an empty and battered shell.

The last major film fire in the Fort Lee area occurred in Little Ferry during the torrid summer of 1937. The films destroyed included not only the early work of the Fox Film Corporation, but materials stored for the new Museum of Modern Art Film Library and other clients.

$45,000 FIRE DRIVES FAMILIES FROM HOMES IN LITTLE FERRY
Thousands Watch Early Morning Film Fire Blamed On
Heat Wave – Film Plant, 2 Homes Are Complete Loss

(from *Bergen Evening Record*, July 9, 1937, p. 1)

Seven Little Ferry families fled their homes early today when a fire destroyed a large film storage plant at 365 Main Street. Two homes were destroyed and two others were extensively damaged by the $45,000 fire.

Three burned

Three injuries were reported. No record was kept, however, of slight burns and other minor injuries to firemen. A number of the firemen were affected momentarily by the heavy fumes given off by the fire, but none collapsed.

The injured, all members of the same family, were burned as they ran from their home. They are Mrs. Anna Greeves, treated at the Hackensack Hospital for shock and second degree burns, and her two sons, John, 12, and Charles, 13, treated for first degree burns on the back.

Mrs. Greeves received her burns when she fell in the street while carrying her daughter Patricia. The child was uninjured. The boys were burned as they ran across the street. They were taken to the Hackensack Hospital by Vincent McAvoy, 542 Chestnut Street, Teaneck.

The value of films destroyed in the building had not been determined today. The building was owned by D. J. DeTitta of North Bergen, who stored films for the Twentieth-Century Fox Corporation of New York City. DeTitta, reached at the film company office late this morning, said that there is no estimate on the damages available at present.

In addition to the loss in films, other property destroyed included the $30,000 storage plant, two dwellings, two garages and one shed, and two automobiles.

Thousands watch

The brilliance of the blaze illuminated the entire sky and was visible for many miles throughout the County. Despite the hour, several thousand persons lined the streets. Route 5, a block from the fire, was jammed with cars.

The Deserted City of FILMDOM

Once the Center of Movie Making, Fort Lee Is Now Deserted. Its Studios, Once the Center of the Industry, Are Falling in Ruins

Motion picture production has moved Westward. Apparently the move is definite. Nowhere else can directors find the wide variety of scenery and the perfect atmospheric conditions necessary to the quick making of films. In the old days, Fort Lee stopped at nothing. Cowboys rode the old Palisades with fine abandon.

Special Photographs by Arthur Pilieri

Above, the Universal studio, now used entirely as office space for the company's laboratory. It was in the old Universal studio, afterwards remodeled, that Annette Kellerman made "Neptune's Daughter" under the direction of Herbert Brenon. Barbara La Marr, Richard Barthelmess, King Baggott and dozens of other famous stars occupied its stages at various times.

Left, the wreck of the old Peerless studios, once the home of World Film pictures. Here Clara Kimball Young made her famous films. Here worked Alice Brady, Evelyn Greely, Conrad Nagel, and many other famous stars.

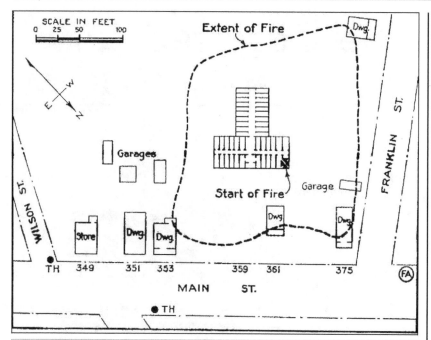

SCALE IN FEET
0   25   50   100

Extent of Fire

Garages

WILSON ST.

FRANKLIN ST.

Start of Fire

Garage

Store   Dwg   Dwg.   Dwg.   Dwg.

TH   349   351   353   359   361   375   FA

MAIN   ST.

TH

Private homes near the storage vaults were well within the zone of destruction when the Fox vault explored in Little Ferry. From 'Fox Film Storage Fire', National Fire Protection Association Quarterly, October 1937, pp. 136–142.

The flames were so bright a short time after the alarm came in that a second alarm was turned in soon after firemen left headquarters. The flames attracted firemen of neighboring towns who sent assistance without receiving any formal request from the Little Ferry Fire Department.

All six companies of the Ridgefield Park Fire Department sped to the scene to assist the two companies which comprise the Little Ferry department. In addition, firemen from two companies in neighboring South Hackensack and one from River Edge responded.

The flames were first noticed at 2:10 a.m. by Robert Davison, Abend Street, Little Ferry, who was on his way to work in a nearby market, noticing the flames shoot up from a corner of the building as he rode by.

In the meantime the intense heat and noise of the fire awakened all seven families who left their homes hurriedly. The fire soon enveloped two of the buildings and threatened the others.

The building occupied by Mr. and Mrs. Louis Bassano was the closest to the plant and was the first to go up. Bassano was caretaker of the plant. All five members of this family escaped without injury. They were awakened by Miss Ida Bassano, who was sleeping in a room facing the plant. She was awakened by the intense heat.

Julius Kosich, commander of the Corp. William E. Peterallge Post of Little Ferry, said he was awakened by the falling of a screen and breaking windows. He awakened his wife. Mr. and Mrs. Joseph Gadleski, occupants of the same building, also escaped.

Others who were forced to leave their homes were Mr. and Mrs. Louis Klather,

Mr. and Mrs. George Greeves, Mr. and Mrs. William Ross, and Mr. and Mrs. Frank Roberts.

None of those who were forced to leave their homes hurriedly was able to retrieve any clothing or personal belongings....

When firemen arrived, flames were bellowing forth from the ventilators of the plant, which was built entirely of brick and concrete. Two of the homes were already in flames, and two were smoking. The intense heat at first thwarted efforts of the firemen to play a hose on the buildings.

Seeing that little could be done to save the film plant, the firemen directed their efforts towards the dwellings. Little could be done with two of the homes, but by playing water on two other buildings the firemen saved them.

The flames momentarily died down, but then shot out with renewed vigor from the west side of the building. A bright white flame resembling an immense blow torch roared through several ventilators in the wall and reached out more than 100 feet, threatening firemen who had brought their hose to the Franklin Street side.

While the flames shot upward, they threw off hundreds of small pieces of burning film which sent the large crowds scurrying to cover. The bright flame blazed and roared steadily for 10 minutes. After that the flames died down and shot out as each compartment caught afire and burned itself out.

It was at 2:50 am that the flames started to die down, but the fire was far from under control. Tons of water from five hose lines were poured on the building steadily for two hours before firemen could enter.

Examination by firemen as they entered revealed that all of the film stored in the plant had been destroyed. The reels and tin covers, all that remained, were strewn about the inside of the building and about the premises.

The building in which the films were stored was said to be of fireproof construction. The outer walls were 12 inches thick, while the inner walls were 3 inches thick, made of brick. These inner walls were badly warped by the flames.

The building consisted of 48 separate vaults, each separated by the 3-inch wall, and a heavy steel door. The roof of the building was made with re-enforced concrete which, officials believed, prevented the fire being more serious than it was.

The building, owned by DeTitta and occupied by his caretakers, Mr. and Mrs. Bassano, was entirely destroyed. The other building entirely destroyed was the large two-family stucco dwelling at the corner of Main Street and Franklin Street, occupied by Mr. and Mrs. Kosich and Mr. and Mrs. Gadleski.

The building owned by Mr. and Mrs. Greeves, also of stucco, was saved after the framework had been burned. The building occupied by Mr. and Mrs. Frank Roberts was scorched, and every window in the building was cracked.

Two cars parked in the Bassano driveway by Joseph Aelio were also destroyed. Other property destroyed included a pigeon shed in the rear of Greeves' home, a garage in the rear of the Kosich property, and a chicken barn on the Bassano property.

The heat was so intense that the paint on a car as well as on a sign for a large distance about the building was blistered. All of the brush for a large distance about the building was burned to the ground.

The building was constructed in 1934 by William Fehrs, Little Ferry contractor. Councilman Robert B. Brown, fire commissioner at the time that the building was erected, said that the plans for the plant were taken to Chief McElligott of the New York Little Ferry Fire Department who approved them as fireproof.

The cause of the fire has not yet been determined. It is the belief of Chief Stanley A. Kuss of the Little Fire Department that it was caused by spontaneous combustion after the heat yesterday. The owner, although he said he did not believe this was the cause, could advance no other reason.

Whether an explosion preceeded the fire could not be determined. Several residents nearby said all they could recall was a puff as the flames shot out of the building.

The firemen did not leave the building until 8 a.m. today. The building was smoking in several sections, but there was no danger of another fire there.

Chief Kuss of the Little Ferry department complimented the departments of Ridgefield Park, South Hackensack, and River Edge, which assisted in fighting the flames, saying that it would have been impossible to control them without their assistance.

OLD MOVIE STUDIO BURNS IN FORT LEE

Buildings Used as Theatrical Warehouse Destroyed – Saw Many Silent Stars, Two Firemen Are Hurt, Blaze is Visible Here – 150 From 9 Towns Fight Fire for 2 1/2 Hours

By Milton Esterow

(from the *New York Times*, November 24, 1958, p. 31)

A spectacular fire witnessed by thousands destroyed the old World/Peerless movie studio here today.

The studio, which had been the setting for films with such stars as Douglas Fairbanks Sr., Mary Pickford, Norma Talmadge and William S. Hart, had been used in recent years

During the 1950s most of the remaining Fort Lee studios were destroyed by fire: the Paragon in 1952, the Ideal in 1953, and the Peerless in 1958. None of these were "film fires", in the traditional sense, because all of the inflammable nitrate had long since been removed. What destroyed these buildings was theatrical material – stored sets, paints and canvas, costumes and props. The last of these conflagrations destroyed the Peerless studio only a few weeks after J.J. Shubert had finally gotten rid of it. He had entered the movie business in Fort Lee in 1914 as a way of extending the Shubert's theatrical empire to the silver screen. It didn't work out the way he had planned, but at least the old building had been a good place to store scenery.

as a warehouse for stage and television scenery. It also had a scenery construction shop.

The studio was built in 1913 when Fort Lee became a center for moving-making [sic] in the East. It occupied about an acre of a two-and-a-half-acre plot at Lewis Street and Linwood Avenue, two blocks from the approach to the George Washington Bridge.

Several buildings, two and three stories high, had been joined into a single building. One was a huge hangar-like structure used to store tall sets.

The buildings were sold last September by J.J. Shubert, the theatrical producer, to New England Industries,

Inc., of 120 Wall St., for about $160,000.

No one in warehouse

The fire started at about 11:45 A.M. in a three-story building near Lewis Street that once housed dressing rooms. No one was in the warehouse. The cause of the fire was not determined.

One hundred fifty firemen from nine towns fought the blaze, which was brought under control by 2:15 P.M.

In addition to Fort Lee there were firemen from Palisades Park, Cliffside Park, Edgewater, Fairview, Ridgefield, Leonia, Englewood Cliffs and Englewood. .

The towns have an agreement to cooperate.

Ambulances were also sent from four towns.

Two firemen were injured. William Walker, chief of the Fort Lee Fire Department, was treated for smoke poisoning and bruises.

The fire could be seen from New York's upper West Side.

By mid-afternoon the buildings were a mass of rubble and blackened walls. Little was salvaged.

One spectator was Peter Grieb of Fort Lee. He said he had built one of the first sets used in the studio for *Man of the Hour*.

Fire destroys the World-Peerless studio on Lewis Street, 23 November 1958.

Peter Grieb, the nostalgic bystander the day of the fire, was not just a carpenter, but an ex-Councilman. Like many in Fort Lee, his own relationship to the studio was more ambivalent than this article suggests. According to coverage in *The Palisadian*, he was also at work at the Peerless the last time it exploded, in 1928. Along with a co-worker, "He was hurled to the ground some twenty feet away from where he was standing by the blast", and treated for shock. "For several hours after it occurred he was unable to discuss it", the paper reported.

* * *

Many of the world's greatest film-makers lived and worked in Fort Lee, moving on only when their careers took them in new directions. While some were just passing through, and saw little of the town beyond the walled citadels of the studios, others became part of the community, true citizens of the film town on the Palisades.

Emile Cohl, who created the first animated cartoon series at the Eclair studio, a few blocks from his home on Hoyt Avenue, felt that a reference from Mayor Arthur Kerwien was worth keeping. He kept it even after returning to France and retiring from the motion picture industry. It still remains in his family archives, a permanent record of a time and a place where Emile Cohl was not just an animator, but 'a man of good character ... respected by the community at large'.

Emile Cohl, and the rest of the men and women who worked in the local motion picture industry, had a profound effect on the development of Fort Lee. What has been harder for historians to document is the effect Fort Lee had on them.

Picture Credits

American Museum of the Moving Image: 176 (above).

American Society of Cinematographers: 99.

Lucille Bertram: 230.

Pearl Bowser: 328.

Photo by Donna Brennan: 67, 76 (below).

Ben Brewster: 171.

Pierre Courtet-Cohl: 11, 114, 343.

Fort Lee Building Department: 284.

Fort Lee Film Commission: 8, 10 (above), 14, 20, 24, 26, 34 (both), 36 (below), 38, 44 (above), 46 (above), 85, 98, 141, 142, 155, 180, 182 (above), 188 (below), 200 (below), 216, 217, 228, 238, 249, 250, 262, 263, 271, 278 (above), 285, 294, 312, 322, 323, 330, 332, 336, 342.

Silent Film Collection of the Fort Lee Public Library: 10 (below), 36 (above), 50, 60 (above), 68, 80, 88 (below), 106, 112 (above), 130, 134, 135, 144, 145, 154 (below), 156, 158, 164, 170, 172, 174 (both), 176 (below), 182 (below), 188 (above), 204, 208 (below), 212 (below), 214, 222, 234, 236, 240, 242, 287, 290, 298, 300, 302 (both), 306.

George Eastman House: 86, 88 (top and center), 104 (below), 117, 280, 308, 326.

Frances Goldwyn Hollywood Library: 226.

Richard Koszarski Collection: 12, 16, 30, 52, 64, 78, 82, 90, 115, 160, 162, 190 (below), 208 (above), 212 (above), 232, 244 (both), 274, 276, 278 (below), 292 (above), 304, 318, 324, 334.

Library of Congress, Moving Image Section: 44 (below), 61 (all), 62 (all), 63 (all), 65, 66, 70-74 (all), 258, 260 (all), 264 (all); Manuscript Division: 218.

Alison McMahon: 40, 123, 128, 136.

Museum of Modern Art, Film Stills Archive: 23, 47, 100, 118, 131, 132, 165, 220, 224 (both), 288, 314, 320; Film Study Center: 76 (above), 78 (above); Alice Guy Blache Collection: 122, 139.

Photofest: 248 (above).

Anthony Slide Collection: 124.

Teaneck Public Library: 60 (below), 126.

U.S. Department of the Interior, National Park Service, Edison Historic Site: 32.

Marc Wanamaker/Bison Archives: 28, 102, 104 (above), 112 (below), 154 (above), 173, 178 (both), 184, 190 (above), 245, 248 (below), 266, 272, 286, 316, 317, 321.

Joe Yranski: 18, 92, 138, 140, 146, 166, 202, 206, 210, 213, 282, 292 (below).

Mrs. Sydney Zanditon: 211.

Excerpts from "D.W. Griffith" and "Farewell to Biograph 1913" from BILLY BITZER, HIS STORY by G.W. Bitzer. Copyright © 1973 by Edith Bitzer.

Excerpts from "Magnifique!" and "The Censors Will Hang Us" from EACH MAN IN HIS TIME by Raoul Walsh. Copyright © 1974 by Raoul Walsh Enterprises, Inc.

Excerpts from ONE REEL A WEEK by Fred Balshofer and Arthur Miller. Copyright © 1967 by the Regents of the University of California.

Excerpts from the MEMOIRS OF ALICE GUY BLACHE reprinted with the permission of The Rowan and Littlefield Publishing group.

"One Man Killed; Many Injured When Big Tank Explodes" (February 7, 1925) and the series "Studio Town" (July 8–12, 1935) reproduced with the permission of The Record (Bergen County, NJ).

We have made every effort to locate the current rights holders of the materials reproduced here. Thank you to those mentioned above, as well as to all the other authors and publishers who helped us with this project.

(Below): Main title of Robin Hood *(Éclair, 1912), fragment of tinted nitrate film. [Courtesy of Al Dettlaff.]*

(Bottom): Three Friends *(Biograph, 1912). Filmed in Coytesville. [The Carson Collection.]*

(Right): The Raven *(Éclair, 1912). [FLFC.]*

Fort Lee and Its Films: Portfolio

(Top left): Henry Schnakenberg created a series of four murals for the Fort Lee Post Office, installed in 1941, which depicted life in Fort Lee since the time of Henry Hudson. This third mural shows a film company shooting a western on an improvised open-air platform. Photo by Donna Brennan.
(Top right): Pearl of the Army (Pathé-Astra, 1916). [The Carson Collection.]
(Left): A Girl's Folly (World-Paragon, 1917). [FLFC.]
(Below): Sheet music cover for "I've Lost You, So Why Should I Care", featuring Theda Bara (1916). [FLFC.]

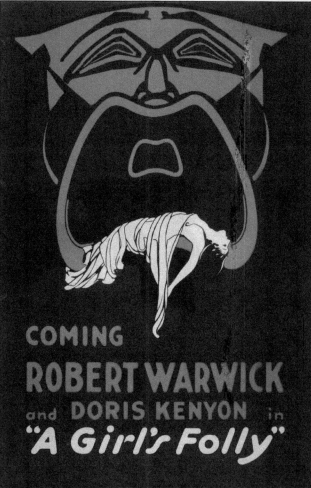

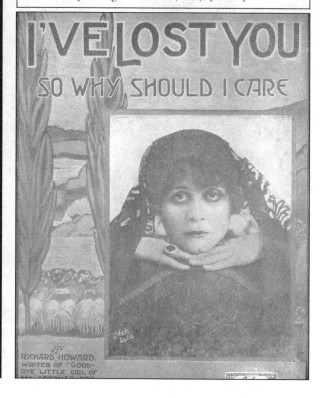

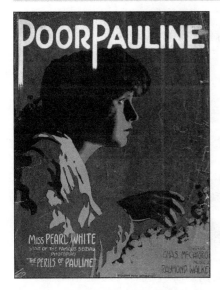

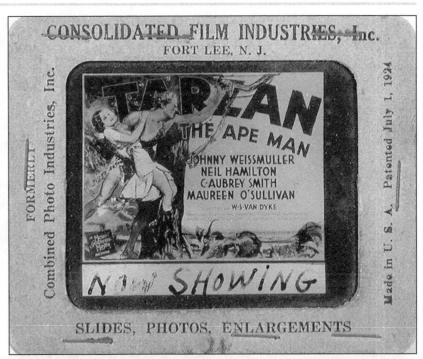

(Above): Sheet music cover for "Poor Pauline", theme song inspired by The Perils of Pauline (1914). [FLFC.]

(Below): Sheet music cover for "Universal Fox Trot" featuring Mary Fuller (1915). [FLFC.]

(Top right): Consolidated Film Industries distributed films and advertising materials from Consolidated Park in Fort Lee. Lantern slide for Tarzan the Ape Man (1932 – not made in Fort Lee). [FLFC.]

(Bottom right): Éclair's roster of stars celebrated on a souvenir stamp sheet issued by Universal, c. 1913. [FLFC.]

(Above): Barbara Tennant and Robert Frazer in Robin Hood (Éclair, 1912), tinted nitrate frame. [Courtesy of Al Dettlaff.]

(Far left): The Web of Desire (World-Peerless, 1917). [FLFC.]

(Left): 'The Moxie girl' was Muriel Ostriche, an actress at Éclair and World who became one of the first film stars identified with a commercial product. [FLFC.]

(Left): One Week of Love *(Selznick, 1922). [FLFC.]; (Centre): Promotional flier for* Saved from the Titanic *(Éclair, 1912). [FLFC.]; (Right):* Alice in Wonderland *(Pollard-Unique, 1931). [FLFC.]*

(Below): The Palisade trolley line ran north along what is now Abbott Blvd., and passed Cella's Park Hotel at the intersection of Whiteman Street. [FLFC.]

352

(Left): The Hungry Heart (World-Peerless, 1917). [FLFC.]

(Right): Love Without Question (Jans Pictures, 1920). [FLFC.]

(Lower left): Kalem's Marguerite Courtot on the cover of Photoplay, February 1915. [FLFC.]

(Lower right): Clara Kimball Young, who starred for World and Select, on the cover of Motion Picture, October, 1915). [FLFC.]

(Above): The Exile *(Micheaux Film Corp.,
1931). [The Carson Collection.]*

(Top right): Nursing a Viper *(Biograph,
1909). Filmed in Englewood. [The Carson
Collection.]*

(Right): Hearts in Exile *(World-Shubert,
1915). [The Carson Collection.]*

(Left): Betsy Ross *(World-Peerless, 1917). [The Carson Collection.]*

(Right): A Modern Salome *(Metro-Hampton, 1920). [The Carson Collection.]*

(Left): The Perils of Pauline, *episode 6 (Eclectic, 1914). [The Carson Collection.]*

(Right): Carmen *(Fox, 1915). [The Carson Collection.]*

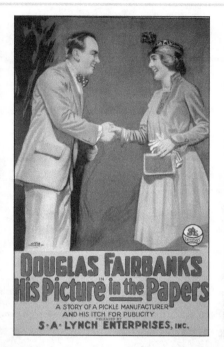

(Top left): The Girl from Chicago *(Micheaux Pictures Corp., 1932). [The Carson Collection.]*

(Top centre): His Picture in the Papers *(Triangle-Fine Arts, 1916). [The Carson Collection.]*

(Top right): The Miracle of Manhattan *(Selznick, 1921). [The Carson Collection.]*

(Left): Temptation *(Micheaux Pictures Corp., 1936). [The Carson Collection.]*

(Right): Is Life Worth Living? *(Selznick, 1921). [The Carson Collection.]*

Index

Page references appearing in **bold type** refer to illustrations appearing in the text.

CPSIA information can be obtained
at www.ICGtesting.com
Printed in the USA
BVHW01s2235160818
524590BV00039B/1/P

9 780861 966523